Peter's English Grammar

A Complete Version of English Grammar: Detail Study, Explanation & Examples

Mr. Peter

Made with ❤ on the Notion Press Platform

www.notionpress.com

Dedicated to All My beloved Students Who Want to Learn.

Writer's Academic works:

1. Study of Nouns, Pronouns, Adjectives & Articles (detail study) ISBN: 979-842-211-856-4 / 979-888-704-109-4
2. All about Verbs (Forms, Functions, Conjugation, Tense, Voice Change, Forming Questions & Negation)   ISBN: 979-840-441-149-2 / 979-888-704-411-8
3. Study of Adverbs, Prepositions, Conjunctions & Interjections ISBN: 979-840-785-010-6 / 979-888-704-532-0
4. Detail Study of Phrases, Clauses & Sentences, including Idioms & Phrasal Verbs ISBN: 979-840-881-405-3 / 979-888-704-582-5
5. Study of Subject-Verb Agreement, Narration Change, Use of Punctuation; including Analysis, Synthesis & Split-up (Study through charts, division, explanation and examples) ISBN: 979-880-723-013-3 / 979-888-704-674-7
6. **Peter's 'English Grammar, A Complete Version of English Grammar,** (detail study, explanation & examples) ISBN: 979-879-725-020-3 / 979-888-704-463-7
7. **Question Bank of English Grammar & Composition (Learn through Exercises)** ISBN: 979-883-531-890-2 / 979-888-733-132-4
8. **Rhetoric & Prosody** (A handbook of Figures of Speech, rhymes, feet of poetic lines for High School Students) ISBN: 979-840-526-645-9 / 979-888-684-952-3
9. Picture Composition; For Primary Level, Std-I to V (Development of Writing Skill from Single Sentence Formation to Paragraph Writing, incl. question patterns and answer guide) ISBN: 979-888-805-249-5 (B&W) / 979-888-783-066-7 (color print)
10. Steps to Composition (Development of Writing Skill, Part-1), includes Picture Composition, Essay & Story Writing ISBN: 979-884-408-069-2 / 979-888-805-001-9
11. Development of Writing Skill, Part-2 (includes Letter Writing- Business Letters, Application for Jobs, Letters to Editor, bank authorities, Institutional Heads & others) ISBN: 979-835-689-886-0 / 979-888-833-455-3
12. Development of Writing Skill, Part-3 (includes- E-mails, Poster Making, Notices, Processing, Dialogue, Article, Speech & Debate Writing as well as Diary entry, Summary and Reporting) ISBN: 979-836-392-249-7 / 979-888-869-544-9
13. **A Book of Advanced Writing Skill, the Complete Version** (incl Part-1, 2 & 3) ISBN: 979-836-472-826-5 / 979-888-869-835-8

Author page URL's:

https://www.amazon.com/author/mr.peter
https://www.amazon.in/~/e/B09QW2P4TY (For Indians, this and next)
https://notionpress.com/store/s?NP_Books%5Bquery%5D=Mr.+Peter
https://www.amazon.co.uk/~/e/B09QW2P4TY
https://www.amazon.de/~/e/B09QW2P4TY
https://www.amazon.fr/~/e/B09QW2P4TY
https://www.amazon.co.jp/~/e/B09QW2P4TY
https://www.amazon.es/~/e/B09QW2P4TY
https://www.amazon.it/~/e/B09QW2P4TY
https://www.amazon.com.br/kindle-dbs/entity/author?asin=B09QW2P4TY

For Readers from India and nearby, one may place order on notionpress.com for paperback. Visit notionpress.com and type 'Mr. Peter' in the search box, or copy https://notionpress.com/store/s?NP_Books%5Bquery%5D=Mr.+Peter and **avail the following discounts,** *using the* **Coupon Codes, given in the left column.** (If the coupons not work, contact to https://www.facebook.com/profile.php?id=100081822070172   or https://www.facebook.com/groups/mr.peter

Coupon Codes	Book Name	Buy for	Discount %	Rebate Prices
unique00 / bulk00	**A Book of Advanced Writing Skill, the Complete Version (incl. Part-1, 2 & 3)**	1 & more	15 & 23	~~780~~ 663 & 601
PujaDeal10 / Deal11	Development of Writing Skill, Part-3	1 & more	18 & 24	~~365~~ 300 & 278
PujaDeal9 / Deal10	Development of Writing Skill, Part-2	1 & more	18 & 24	~~365~~ 300 & 278
PujaDeal8 / Deal9	Steps to Composition (Development of Writing Skill, from Primary to Secondary Level, Part-1)	1 & more	20 & 26	~~300~~ 240 & 222
PujaDeal7 / Deal8	**Rhetoric & Prosody**	1 & more	20 & 26	~~240~~ 192 & 178
PujaDeal6 / Deal7	**Question Bank of English Grammar & Composition**	1 & more	20 & 28	~~559~~ 448 & 403
PujaDeal5 / Deal5	Study of Subject-Verb Agreement, Narration Change, Use of Punctuation; including Analysis, Synthesis & Split-up	1 & more	20 & 26	~~301~~ 241 & 223
PujaDeal4 / Deal4	Detail Study of Phrases, Clauses & Sentences, including Idioms & Phrasal Verbs	1 & more	20 & 26	~~290~~ 232 & 215
PujaDeal3 / Deal3	Study of Adverbs, Prepositions, Conjunctions & Interjections	1 & more	20 & 26	~~260~~ 208 & 193
PujaDeal2 / Deal2	All about Verbs (Forms, Functions, Conjugation, Tense, Voice Change, Forming Questions & Negation)	1 & more	18 & 26	~~420~~ 345 & 311
PujaDeal1 / Deal1	Study of Nouns, Pronouns, Adjectives & Articles (detail study)	1 & more	20 & 26	~~280~~ 224 & 208
unique01 / bulk01	**Peter's 'English Grammar' (Complete Version of English Grammar)**	1 & more	23 & 30	~~1201~~ 925 & 841

FOR COPIES MORE THAN ONE, SELECT THE 2ND COUPON, GIVEN IN EACH ROW IN THE FIRST COLUMN

Contents

Contents	Pages
Summary of The Book: xi	
1. English Alphabet (Vowels & Consonants)..................... 13	
2. Words & Syllable.. 16	
3. Parts of Speech.. 18	
Use of same words in Different parts of Speech 20	
4. Nouns: Definition and Classification............................22	
Classification of Nouns: 23	
The Number of Nouns.. 29	
The Gender of Nouns 37	
The Case vs. the Functions of Nouns 41	
Pronouns in different Cases 46	
The Functions of Nouns 47	
The Compound Nouns 50	
5. Pronouns: Definition, Classification & Functions 51	
Personal Group of Pronouns.. 52	
Definite Group of Pronouns... 57	
Indefinite Group of Pronouns 66	
The Case, & the Functions of Pronouns 68	
6. Adjectives & Its Kinds 72	
The Use of Adjectives (i.e., the functions)................................. 77	
The Formation of Adjectives 79	
The Comparison of Adjectives (i.e., Degree).............................. 82	
Arrangement of Adjectives, more than one 89	
The Adjectives need special attention...................................... 91	
7. The Determiners & Articles (a, an, the) 94	
8. The Verbs & its Classification 98	
Finite & Non-finite Verbs 101	
Principal and Auxiliaries 103	
State & Event Verbs 104	
9. Transitive & Intransitive Verbs...................................... 107	

10. Direct Object & Indirect Object 110

    Passive Voice & Retained Object...................118

11. Methods to use Intransitive verbs, Transitively...................119

    By Reflexive Objects...................120

    Using Cognate Objects 120

    By Prepositional Objects or...................121

    Using verbs in the Causative Sense...................121

12. Complement—Subjective & Objective 122

    Factitive Verb & its Complements 124

    Intransitive Verbs & Complements...................124

    Linking Verbs & Complements: 125

    Object & Complement (comparative study) 126

    Subjective & Objective Complement...................126

13. The Auxiliary Verbs and its Kinds 128

    Primary Auxiliaries ('To Be', 'To Have', 'To Do')...................129

    Modal Auxiliaries...................134

    Verb 'Need' & 'Need to' 139

    Verb 'Dare' & 'Dare to'...................143

14. Non-finite Verbs & its Branches 149

    Infinitive Verbs...................149

    Split Infinitives...................153

    The Gerund 154

    The Participle 158

    Nominative Absolute...................161

    Impersonal Absolute & Bare Participle...................165

15. The Glossary of Verbs 167

    Some more details of –Linking, Factitive, Ergative, Performative & Catenative Verbs...................170

16. The Glossary of Objects 172

    Object of Preposition, Cognate & Others...................176

17. The Conjugation of Verbs (Weak, Strong & Mixed)...................179

    The Weak Conjugation...................180

    The Strong Conjugation 183

    The Mixed Conjugation...................186

    Adjectival Past Participle 188

18. The Tense of Verb 189

    Exception in form and use: 193

The Sequence of Tense 193

Time markers: 194

The Use of Present Tense (detail study)... 194

The Use of Past Tense (detail study) 206

The Use of Future Tense (detail study) 214

19. Contraction of Verbs with Subjects and Words of Negation.................223

20. Forming Negation...225

    Negation of Ordinary Main Verb (in Simple Present & Past) 227

    Negation of 'Be Verb' 227

    Negation of 'Have Verb' 228

    Think...229

    'No' with 'don't' make a negative sense stronger.....................................230

21. Types of Questions & their Formation 230

    Direct Questions (Normal—Alternate—Tag—Rhetorical—Short)..................... 231

    Indirect questions: 234

    Formation of Questions...234

22. The Voice: Active & Passive 236

    The Use of Active & Passive Voice..242

    Passive forms of Modals & Questions 243

    Passive Voice of Verbs with Two Objects 244

    Passive Voice of Intransitive Verbs 245

    Passive Voice of Compound & Complex Sentences.................................246

    Quasi-passive or Middle Voice 246

    Use of 'Let' in Active & Passive Voice 247

    Passive of Non-Finite Verbs 247

    Verbs that have Passive Forms...248

    Objects that can be Subjects in Passive Voice 250

23. Adverbs, Kinds (16) & Their Uses..254

    Simple Adverbs (14 in numbers)... 257

    Degrees or Forms of Comparison..265

    Relative or *Wh- Adjunctive* & Interrogative Adverbs 266

    The Forms & Formation of Adverbs...270

    The Position of Adverbs.. 277

24. Prepositions, Kinds & Uses...278

    Kinds of Prepositions 280

    Prepositional Phrase...281

Functions of Preposition 284

The Place of Prepositions 292

Prepositional Object or Complement..293

Conjugation of Preposition with Other Parts of Speech 296

25. Conjunctions, Classification & Functions....................................303

Simple, Correlative & Compound Conjunctions.............................304

Coordinating & Subordinating Conjunctions 305

Special attention to the use of Some Conjunctions.........................310

26. Interjections & Examples 312

27. The Conversion of Words 315

Conversion of Words by Prefix or Suffix.......................................320

28. Words-Building (Compounds & Derivatives) 330

29. Compare: Phrase, Clause & Sentence..341

30. Detail study: Phrase & its Kinds...345

7 kinds of Phrases...345

Compare Phrasal Verbs & Idioms 348

31. The list of Phrasal Verbs 356

32. The Idioms...375

33. Detail study: Clause & its Kinds 384

How to find clauses in a sentence 384

Kinds of Clauses 385

A.   Principal Clause 385

B.   Co-ordinate Clause 385

Kinds of Co-ordinate Clauses...386

C.   Sub-ordinate Clause 387

Kinds of Sub-ordinate Clauses..388

Conditionals (if clause) -Meaning & Explanation............................393

Wish Clause 396

34. The Mood (or the manner of expression)....................................397

Verb forms in Indicative Mood 398

Verb forms in Imperative Mood 399

Verb forms in Subjunctive Mood 400

35. Classification of Sentence, based on Functions...........................402

Classification 402

Formation of Affirmative & Negative Sentences.............................406

36. Classification of Sentence, based on Structure 408

    Complex Sentence 411

    Complex Compound 414

    Compound Complex 414

37. Analysis of Simple Sentence, as Subject & Predicate 414

38. Further Analysis: Study of Subject Adjuncts, & Extension to Predicate 417

    Subjects & Adjuncts to Subject variant 420

    Extension or Adverbial Adjuncts 422

    How an object shaped 423

    Attributes or Adjuncts to Object 425

    Complement (Subjective or Objective) 426

    Infinitive & Gerundial Infinitive 428

39. Analysis of Compound & Complex Sentence 430

    Analysis of a compound sentence 430

    Analysis of a complex sentence 433

40. Synthesis, or Joining of Simple Sentences 435

    To make Single Simple Sentence 436

    To make a Compound Sentence 440

    To make a Complex Sentence 441

41. Split-up of a Sentence 443

    Split up through Analysis 445

    Split up of Complex Compound 447

    Split-up of 'Quoted Sentence', 'Parenthetic Phrase & Clause' 448

    Use of 'It' & 'There' in Split-up 450

42. Direct & Indirect Speech (Change of Narration) 452

    5 Major Rules of Narration Change 453

    Narration Change: Assertive Sentence 456

    Narration Change: Interrogative 456

    Narration Change: Imperative 457

    Use of Vocatives in Imperative: 459

    Use of 'Let' in the Narration Change 460

    Narration Change: Optative 460

    Narration Change: Exclamatory 461

    Reporting of 'One-word Replies' & 'Multiple Sentences' 462

43. The Conversion or Transformation of Sentences 463

    Conversion of Adverb 'too' 464

    Conversion of Degrees (adj. & adv.) 464

Conversion of Active & Passive 465

Conversion from Affirmative to Negative 467

Conversion of Interrogative to Assertive 468

Conversion of Exclamatory to Assertive 469

Conversion of Simple, Compound & Complex 471

Conversion of Narration 475

Conversion: From One to Thirty-Two... 475

44. The Use of Punctuations (includes 16) 476

Use of Capital Letters... 477

Brackets, Asterisk, Dot-dot-dot & Oblique 481

Parenthesis... 482

45. Subject & Verb Agreement 483

Summary of The Book:

'Peter's English Grammar' which is a Complete Version of English Grammar, is designed mainly for high school students. Almost each and every basic and important point of English grammar has been attempted to discuss here step by step, from abc to z. The topics are arranged from primary level to secondary, from words, parts of Speech to analysis of a sentence, joining and split-up, ascending as stairs to go up.

The book shows how case of Nouns define the different functions of Nouns. Without study the functions of Nouns, we hardly can identify the role of Nouns in a sentence. It is shown elaborately, how Nouns form Subjects, Objects, Phrase in apposition, Complements; and when and how they work like an adjective, and form Nominal Compounds, or Prepositional Objects, and be a part of an Adverbial phrase. Each and every topic related Nouns, like, number, gender, case, functions of nouns; role and classification of Pronouns and Adjectives have been illustrated in the book in details. It illustrates the use of Adjectives, attributively, predicatively; as pre modifiers or post modifiers, where they are same and where they are different from each other. Besides, the formation of degree, position and proper arrangement of adjectives (when more adjectives are used at a time side by side) are carefully illustrated in the book. Most of determiners have been included along with the use of articles (a, an, the) are illustrated too in the book.

The book includes fifteen major chapters merely on verbs, covering definitions, functions along with a lot of examples. It has included Finite, Non-finite, State, Event, Principal and Auxiliaries, Transitive and Intransitive, and of different objects- Direct & Indirect, Cognate, Reflexive, Retained, Prepositional Objects, Complements and also Adverbials.

As essential part of verb, verb conjugation, tense, voice-change have been discussed and shown different types of Questions, (yes-no type, wh-, alternative, tag, rhetorical, short & the indirect). Forming negative sentences with words of negation and helping verbs, detail study of **Adverbs, Prepositions, Conjunctions & Interjections** —have also been included and elaborated with examples and explanation. It shows how different Interjections express different emotions and the feelings of speakers.

The rules of Narration Change, Narration change of Assertive, Interrogative, Imperative, Optative & Exclamatory sentences have been included, besides giving a place to conversion of sentences & words, forming new words (i.e., words-building). The book deals in details of the use of Punctuations too, including the use of capital letters, use of bracket, asterisk, dot-dot-dot, oblique and parenthesis, etc. The conjugation of verb, i.e., the subject-verb agreement has also taken a part of it which is very important for any competitive examination.

The book deals in details of Phrases, Clauses and the structure of Sentences. It has shown their kinds, definitions and functions, discussed in simple and lucid language. It shows how to find out clauses from a sentence. It deals with seven kinds of phrases, three major kinds of clauses and their sub-divisions, and classification of sentences in two ways—functional and structural. The book contains also a list of some idioms & phrasal verbs in the section of phrases. The chapter of Mood shows relation of the 1st class of classification of sentences which is based on function; while different clauses form sentences, simple, compound or complex.

In the section of **'Analyses of Sentences'** Peter has dealt in details of the structural parts of a sentence, dividing a sentence first as Subject and Predicate and then identifying their adjuncts and extension. Thus, the book helps a student understanding essential parts of a sentence and other essence, like adjuncts to subjects and objects, how do they work, and how adverbial qualification or extension to predicate add meaning to the predicates, i.e., to the finite verbs and to their Complements (subjective or objective); the understanding of which helps one to form or understand a sentence better.

Besides, the book deals of synthesis or joining of sentences to make a single sentence, Simple, Complex or Compound and also about the Split-up a big sentence into many independent small simple sentences.

The book contains an illustrated table of contents, not to give you impression what it contains or has, but for your help, so that you can jump to any point of grammar and save your time.

Finally, if you feel, it made you help to get understand the topics discussed, the writer likes to pay gratitude and give lot of thanks to each and every reader; if not, he seeks forgiveness for your time and fruitless attempt.

With the above, Mr. Peter admits the deficiency of the book too. The book '***Peter's English Grammar*** ***despairingly lacks any composition in it***. However, for composition from Peter's hand, the readers may choose his **"A Book of Advanced Writing Skill"** which one is another complete version of books of writing skill, and which one is consisted of three different entities; as, **Part-1, Part-2 & Part-3.** The book takes in- Essay, Story, Paragraph, Letters, E-mails, Notices, Processing, Debate as well as Diary entry, Summary and Reporting of News for School Newsletters, Magazines and thus, many others.

In the book of writing skill, Mr. Peter has tried to include about all necessary methods of writing skill, which are suitable for students of all standard, from Primary to Higher Secondary level.

Best of luck for the current one.

Mr. Peter

1. English Alphabet (Vowels & Consonants)

Introducing Words

Grammar denotes _the rules & ways to know a particular human language (to speak, write, & understand it properly)_.

What is a 'Grammar book'?

A Grammar book is 'a book that relates those distinct rules & ways by which we come to know a particular human language'.

Why should we read an English Grammar Book?

An English Grammar book helps us to understand English Language more properly. By study a grammar book, we come to know those distinct rules and ways a language has in it already.

So, a grammar book does not produce but it presents what it has already.

1. **Read:**

A, B, C, D, E, F, G, H, I, J, K, L, M, N, O, P, Q, R, S, T, U, V, W, X, Y, Z

Read again:

a, b, c, d, e, f, g, h, i, j, k, l, m, n, o, p, q, r, s, t, u, v, w, x, y, z

There are 26 letters in English. Together they are called English alphabet. The first line of English alphabet is written in capital script; while the later ones written in small script, that means same English letters can be written in two ways—capital and small; and the same in different styles.

The English alphabet includes five vowels (a, e, i, o, u) & twenty-one consonants (b, c, d, f, g, h, j, k, l, m, n, p, q, r, s, t, v, w, x, y, z).

Vowels are those letters which _can be uttered without the help of any other letter sound_; as per dictionary, a speech sound in which the mouth is open and the tongue is not touching the top of the mouth, the teeth or lips. For example— a, e, i, o, u —the five letters are called Vowels.

And **Consonants are those English letters that** _can't be uttered without a vowel sound_; a consonant sound is made by completely _or_ partly stopping the flow of air _being breathed out through the mouth_ _and thereby our tongue touch either_ the top of the mouth, teeth or lips, etc.; as—**b** (bi), **c** (si), **f** (ef), **y**(oai), **z** (zed), etc.

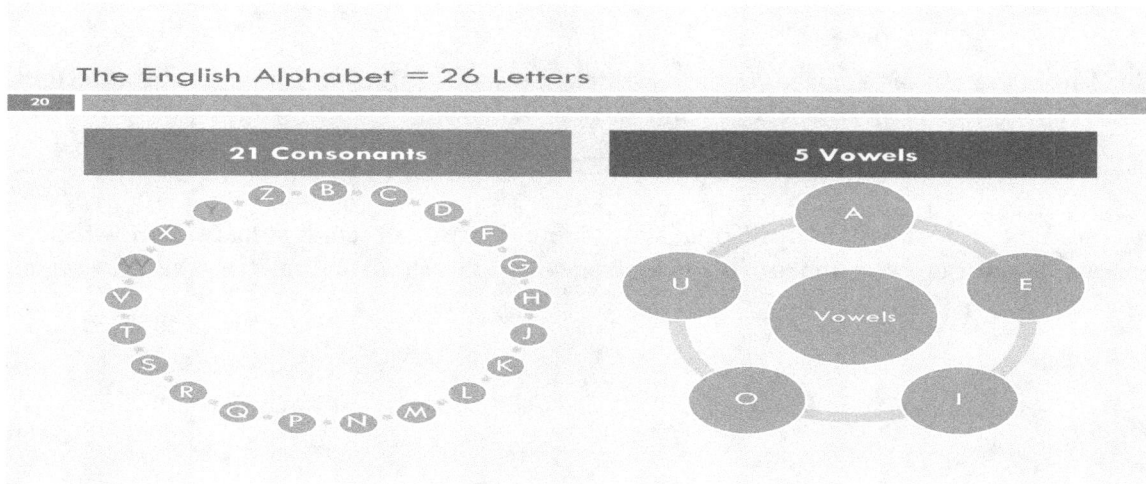

The English Alphabet = 26 Letters

21 Consonants — Z B C D F G H J K L M N P Q R S T V W X Y

5 Vowels — A, E, I, O, U — Vowels

✗ Besides the five vowels, mentioned, there are two more among the consonants. They are — **'w' & 'y', which**

are called 'Semi-Vowels, means **'half vowels.**

✗ <u>**They are called so, as they play both roles; as,**</u>
Boy— 'y' is vowel here,

You— 'y' is consonant here, [a yo yo]

Now— 'w' is vowel here,

War— 'w' is consonant here. [a/the war]

'W' & 'Y'—while used at the beginning of a word, they are consonants, but when they are used in the middle or at end of a word, they are vowels, so why these two are also called **semi-vowels.**

✗ In the following, read the English Alphabet (English Letters) and study their pronunciation. However, they may vary when used in a word.

The pronunciation of English letters

1	2	3	4	5
A = a/e/ei	B = bi	C = si	D = di	E = i
F = ef	G = gi	H = eich	I = e/i/ai	J = ja
K = kei	L = el	M = em	N = en	O = o/ou
P = pi	Q = ku	R = ur	S = es	T = ti
U = u/eu/iu/a	V = vi	W = dublu	X = eks	Y = wai/oai
Z = zed				

✗ The English alphabet or the English letters are written in two ways. One way is called **capital letters** (A, B, C, D, E, F, G, H, I, J, K, L, M, N, O, P, Q, R, S, T, U, V, W, X, Y, Z);

✗ and the other way is called **small letters** (a, b, c, d, e, f, g, h, i, j, k, l, m, n, o, p, q, r, s, t, u, v, w, x, y, z).

➢ However, they can be written in different styles, more than we can count, perhaps. We quote here only few ones popular or Peter thinks to quote for his readers. Please, go through the slides, if it helps.

English Letters in normal & cursor styles

11

- A, B, C, D, E, F, G, H, I ,J, K, L, M, N, O, P, Q, R, S, T, U, V, W, X, Y, Z
- a, b, c, d, e, f, g, h, i ,j, k, l, m, n, o, p, q, r, s, t, u, v, w, x, y, z
- A, B, C, D, E, F, G, H, I, J, K, L, M, N, O, P, Q, R, S, T, U, V, W, X, Y, Z
- a, b, c, d, e, f, g, h, i, j, k, l, m, n, o, p, q, r, s, t, u, v, w, x, y, z

English Letters in French & Kunstler

12

- A, B, C, D, E, F, G, H, I ,J, K, L, M, N, O, P, Q, R, S, T, U, V, W, X, Y, Z (Capital in French script)
- a, b, c, d, e, f, g, h, i ,j, k, l, m, n, o, p, q, r, s, t, u, v, w, x, y, z (small in French script)
- A B C D E F G H I J K L M N O P Q R S T U V W X Y Z (Kunstler)
- a b c d e f g h i j k l m n o p q r s t u v w x y z (Kunstler)

And more...

- A, B, C, D, E, F, G, H, I, J, K, L, M, N, O, P, Q, R, S, T, U, V, W, X, Y, Z *(Lucida Calligraph)*

- a, b, c, d, e, f, g, h, i, j, k, l, m, n, o, p, q, r, s, t, u, v, w, x, y, z

- A, B, C, D, E, F, G, H, I, J, K, L, M, N, O, P, Q, R, S, T, U, V, W, X, Y, Z *(Script MT Bold-capital)*

- a, b, c, d, e, f, g, h, i j, k, l, m, n, o, p, q, r, s, t, u, v, w, x, y, z *(MT Bold-small)*

2. Words & Syllable

2. **A unit of letters or simply a letter, when <u>conveys a meaning</u>, is called a 'word'.**
The following chart shows which are words, and which are not:

Words	Words Not
God	GDO
Moon	NOOM
Rose	EORS
I	AI
You	OUY
My	YM
Cat	TAC
House	USEOH

3. **About Syllable & different syllabic words:**
The <u>part of a word that can be pronounced at a time smoothly,</u> without any obstacle or break in the pronunciation, defined by a vowel sound is called a ***syllable*** (simply, a part of pronunciation of the word). In a syllable there is only one **vowel sound** (a syllable is always *'defined by one vowel sound'*, and that <u>sound may be produced due to 'a vowel' or vowel combination'</u>) with one or more consonants & thus in a word there may be one or more syllables. Study the following list:

Try to find out syllables in them...

Words	Syllables (divided by hyphen)
➢ Wind	➢ Wind
➢ Cap	➢ Cap
➢ Escape	➢ Es-cape
➢ Intizar	➢ In-ti-zar
➢ April	➢ Ap-ril
➢ Princess	➢ Prin-cess
➢ September	➢ Sep-tem-ber
➢ Jane	➢ Jane

➢ Yolen		➢ Yo-len	
➢ April		➢ Ap-ril	
➢ Henry		➢ Hen-ry	
➢ Wadsworth		➢ Wads-worth	
➢ Longfellow		➢ Long-fe-llow	
➢ Sujata		➢ Su-ja-ta	
➢ Somerset		➢ So-mer-set	
➢ Happy		➢ Hap-py	
➢ Midnight		➢ Mid-night	
➢ Siegfried		➢ Sieg-fried	

4. **Now study words and know different Syllabic Names:**

Sl.	Words & Syllables	Number	Names
1)	o Book, o shoe, o cat, o bat, o man, o pan, etc.	words of one syllable	Monosyllabic
2)	o Fa-ther, o mo-ther, o bro-ther, o sis-ter, etc.	words of two syllables	Disyllabic
3)	o Hand-ker-chief, o coun-ta-ble, o beau-ti-ful, etc.	words of three syllables	Trisyllabic
4)	o Un-coun-ta-ble, o in-di-vi-dual, o im-po-si-ble, etc.	words of four syllables	Tetra-syllabic
5)	o Te-tra-sy-lla-ble, o pen-ta-sy-lla-bic	words of five syllables	Penta-syllabic
6)	o In-com-pre-hen-si-ble, o an-te-di-lu-vi-an	words of six syllables	Hexta-syllabic
7)	o U-ti-li-ta-ri-a-nism, o a-ca-ro-do-ma-ti-a	words of seven syllables	Hepta-sylllabic
8)	o A-mi-no-a-ci-du-ri-a, o in-tel-lec-tu-a-li-za-tion,	words of eight syllables	Octa-syllabic
9)	o Ab-do-mi-no-hys-te-ro-to-my, o hy-per-cho-les-te-ro-le-mi-a,	words of nine syllables	Nobum syllabic
10)	o He-te-ro-phe-no-me-no-lo-gi-cal , o dii-o-do-hy-dro-xy-qui-no-li-ne.	words of ten syllables	Deca syllabic

3. Parts of Speech

5. **Let's get started:**

Answer these questions:
1) How many parts of speech are there?
2) Write the names of all the parts of speech with one example for each?

Stop! Don't go further, try to remember them all and one example for each.
You could? Carry on for further details.
You couldn't remember them all? Okay, no problem. Move on reading.

Whatever we speak or write **a meaningful word or sound**- is 'a part of a speech'; all the words together in a speech – are called 'the parts of speech'. Peter, he, good, play, fast, in, and, Oh! – Each one 'a part of a speech'.

6. **Definition of Parts of Speech:** When we speak something, every part of the speech together, are called the 'Parts of Speech'.

   In other words, according to the work or function, words do in a sentence; the English words are grouped into eight classes. They are together called the 'Parts of Speech'.

Read the following sentences:

My friend Charlotte speaks French fluently.
Adj.   noun   noun   verb   noun   adverb

Hurrah! We have won the match.
        Pronoun   article
Interjection   verb   noun

7. **Classification of Parts of Speech:** The Parts of Speech are eight in number. They are:
   1) Noun, 2) Pronoun, 3) Adjectives, 4) Verb,
   5) Adverb, 6) Prepositions, 7) Conjunctions & 8) Interjections.

Note: Study of Parts of Speech is very important to know the basic structure of a sentence.

Read Definitions of Different Parts of Speech & study their examples briefly:

☐ **Noun**

A noun is a word used to name persons, places, animals, things, feelings or ideas.

Note: The word 'things' used in the definition, includes actually-
   ✓ All objects that we can see, hear, taste, touch or smell; and also
   ✓ Something that we can merely think or feel of, but cannot perceive by the senses.

☐ **Read the examples carefully:**
   • **Ashoka** was a great **king**.
   • **Students** go to **school**.
   • I like **mango**. She likes **milk**.
   • **Balurghat** situated on the bank of **Atreyee**.
   • **Butterfly** flies.
   • **The sun** shines brightly.
   • The **police** reached the spot in time.
   • **A gang of robbers** robbed the white **building**.
   • **The chain is made of Gold.**

- His **courage** won him **honour**.
- Her **honesty** was praiseworthy.

□ Pronoun

□ A Pronoun is **a word used instead of a Noun**; as,
- John is absent, because *he* is ill.
- Where did you leave the books? ***Those*** are very important.
- Shilpa won everyone's attention, for *she* was excellent in her speech.
- ***Who*** are **you**? I don't know **you**.
- *It* was raining heavily. **Which** bag is yours?
- I am Peter. **They** are students of this school.
- **We** love sunshine, **we** like raining too.

Adjectives

□ An Adjective is **a word used to <u>add something to the meaning of a Noun or a Pronoun</u>, i.e., <u>describe a Noun or a Pronoun</u>.**
   o The garden is full of ***lovely*** flowers.
      ▪ *(Here, the word 'lovely' is describing the flowers. It is an adjective of quality.)*
   o Ramesh is ***tall***. He is a ***brave*** boy.
      ▪ *(Boy, Ramesh & He—refers to one person & the words—tall, brave—describing the noun 'Ramesh' or the 'boy' or 'He'.)*
   o There are ***twenty*** boys in the class.
      ▪ *('twenty' refers to the number of boys, and thus, it is an adjective of number, or so-called Numeral Adjective)*

Verb

□ A Verb is **a word used to <u>express an action or a state—being or having</u>; as,**
   o The girl ***wrote*** a letter to her cousin.
      ▪ *(The word 'wrote' refers to past action of the verb 'write' by the girl.)*
   o Balurghat ***is*** a small town.
      ▪ *('is' is a "Be Verb" form, used in present tense—refers to 'being'; here being a town of the Proper Noun 'Balurghat'.)*
   o Iron and Copper ***are*** useful metals.
      ▪ *('are' refers to being; here, being 'metals.)*
   o He ***has*** a car but I ***have*** no car.
      ▪ *('has' or 'have'—both are 'Have Verb' forms in present tense —refers to 'having' or 'not having', 'possessing' or 'not possessing' the car of the subjects.)*

Adverb

□ An Adverb is a word used to **add meaning to a Verb, or to an Adjective, or an Adverb; as,**
- He worked the sum ***quickly***.
   *(The word '**quickly**' adds meaning to the verb, 'worked'.)*
- This flower is ***very*** beautiful.
   *('**Very**' adds meaning '<u>much</u> 'to the word '<u>beautiful</u>' which is an adjective.)*
- Your eyes are ***so*** fascinating to welcome me.
   *('**So**' adds meaning 'very' or 'much' to the word 'fascinating' which is a participle adjective.)*
- She pronounced the word ***quite correctly***.
   *('**Quite**' & '**correctly**'—both are adverbs. The word 'correctly' adds meaning to the verb 'pronounced' and 'quite' adds meaning to the adverb, 'correctly'. How pronounced? —correctly. How much correctly? (Denoting the degree of adverb, the answer is '<u>quite</u>' correctly.)*

Preposition

□ A Preposition is **a word used <u>with a Noun or a Pronoun to show relation with other words</u> in the sentence; as,**
- There is a cow ***in*** the garden.
   *(By the word '**in**', it means the cow's being in the garden, denoting the location of the cow. Thus, 'in' shows a relation between 'cow' & 'garden' & 'in the garden' is an adverbial phrase, denoting place.)*
- The girl is fond ***of*** music.

*('**Of** shows '**the girl's being fond of** 'music'. Thus, the adjective 'fond' & the noun 'music' are shown related. The girl has feeling, liking or having affection for music. '**The fond of music'** is an <u>adjective phrase</u>, describing the girl's quality—the girl who loves music. The phrase 'fond of music' is <u>also a complement in the sentence</u>.)*

- A fair little girl sat **under** a tree. *('**Under**' is used before the noun 'a tree'. Thus, 'under' shows relation between 'sitting of the girl' & 'tree', and 'under a tree is an adverbial phrase, denoting 'place' or 'location'.)*

- It will be **in** the visitor's book. *('**It**' & '**visitor's book**'— are connected, not like conjunctions. So, it is better to use, they are related by the word 'in'—it's being in the visitor's book. 'in' is the preposition, used before the noun 'visitor's book' and shows its relation with 'it', a pronoun.)*

Note: Many prepositions are used as Adverb & Conjunctions. It depends on function of the word in the sentence.

□ Conjunction

□ A Conjunction is **a word used <u>to join two words, phrases, clauses or sentences</u>; as,**
- Rama **and** Hari are cousins.
  (Rama is Hari's cousin. Hari is Rama's cousin. As they are cousins to each other, so, Rama & Hari—two words cum Proper Nouns are added by the word, 'and'.)
- Tom **and** Peter are students.
  *('**Tom**' is a student. Peter is a student. As both are students, two nouns are connected by conjunction 'and'.)*
- I ran fast **but** missed the train.
- **Though** I ran fast, I missed the train.
- I ran very fast, **yet** I missed the train.
  *(In the above sentence, the words—**but, though, yet**—are simply connecting or joining two words/ two phrases or clauses. They are conjunctions.)*

□ Interjection

□ An Interjection is **a word which <u>expresses some sudden feeling or strong emotion</u>** of the speaker**; as,**
- **Hurrah!** We have won the game.
  *(**Hurrah**—is a sound expressing strong emotion of happiness or glad. Beyond this, it does not carry any other meaning. So, many say, it is not a word but a sound in the group of Parts of Speech. The sign '!' is an exclamation, one of the punctuations, generally used with an Interjection and sometimes with an Exclamatory Sentence.)*
- **Alas!** She is no more. *('**Alas**' expressing 'sadness'.)*
- **Bravo!** You have done it. *('**Bravo**' expressing 'compliment' or 'praise'.)*

Use of same words in Different parts of Speech

8. ***Note:*** Remember, words are grouped into eight classes, according to the work, they do, or as they are used in the sentences (i.e., the same word may function as different parts of speech in different sentences). So, classifying some words may seem difficult if we do not study their uses properly in the sentences. Read the examples:
- They arrived soon **after**. *(After—is an adverb here — adds meaning to another adverb, 'soon'.)*
- They arrived **after** us. *(After —is preposition here—used before 'us' pronoun and shows relation between 'they' and 'us', besides referring 'time' like an adverb. They came or arrived after we had arrived. (Most of prepositions do the function of adverbs silently, and here one may get easily confused with the uses and of their identities.)*
- They arrived **after** we had left. *(Here, the preposition 'after' do the function of a conjunction, joining the two clauses– 'They arrived' & 'we had left'. So, it is not only a preposition in the sentence, but due to its role of 'joining', it is a conjunction too.)*

- Tatum is observing a **fast** today. *(As a Noun)*
- Willow will return by a **fast** train. *(As an adjective)*
- Maria **fasts** every Thursday. *(Used as a verb)*

- Andrea does her work **fast**. (As an adverb)

❑ **But**: as a conjunction, 'but' is used to <u>introduce a clause or phrase or a word, opposite in sense or meaning,</u> i.e., the sense or meaning contrasts with what was said before; as,
- Her mother won't be there, **but** her father might.
- It isn't that he lied exactly, **but** he does tend to exaggerate.
- It was not the red one **but** the blue one.

❑ Or, it means however, despite this; as,

- I'd asked everybody **but** only two people came.
- By the end of the day, we were tired **but** happy.
- I'm sorry **but** I can't stay any longer.

❑ 'But' as a preposition, it means 'except' or 'apart from' (preposition that are used before a noun or pronoun, a gerund or a noun equivalent in other form):
- I had no choice <u>but to sign the contract</u>. (**except signing the contract**)
- We've had nothing **but trouble** with this car.
- The problem is anything **but easy**.
- Who **but Rosa** could think of something like that?
- Everyone was there **but him**.

❑ 'But' as an adverb, it means 'only':
- I don't think we'll manage it. Still, we can **but try**. (*but try = only try*)
- There are a lot of sincere teachers in this institution—K.P., Mr. P to name **but two**. (*a lot of teachers; but (only) two teachers = a lot of & two, both are numeral adjectives, 'but (or 'only') is an adverb.*)

❑ 'But' as a noun, often takes form of '**buts**' and it means '**excuses**', *'a reason that somebody gives for not doing something'* or 'not agreeing':
- Let us have no **buts (excuses),** he said firmly. You are coming'.
- With so many 'ifs and **buts' (lame excuses to say or hear),** it is easier to wait and see.

❖ 'But' is also used as **a Relative Pronoun**. 'But' is always <u>used after a negative sense & makes a forceful positive statement</u>. **As a Relative Pronoun, 'but'** means '*who not*' (*who doesn't/didn't/will not*).
  - There is none **but** will agree with me. (Who will not)
  - There is no Hindu **but** knows the story of the Ramayana. (Who does not know)
  - There is no man **but** wishes to live. (Who does not wish)

❑ <u>Try yourself-what parts of speech they are, the underlined words:</u>

1) <u>Still</u> water run deep.
2) He <u>still</u> lives in that house.
3) <u>After</u> the storm comes calm in nature.
4) The <u>after</u> effects of the drug are bad.
5) The <u>up</u> train is late.
6) He told us all <u>about</u> the battle.
7) He was only a yard <u>off</u> me.
8) Suddenly one of wheels came <u>off</u>.
9) Muslims <u>fast</u> in the month of Ramzan.
10) He kept the <u>fast</u> for a week.
11) Sit down and rest a <u>while</u>.
12) I will watch <u>while</u> you sleep.
13) They <u>while</u> away their evening with books and games.
14)

❑ Check your answers.
1) **Still** water run deep. (*Still—is adjective here— describing noun, 'water'.*)
2) He **still** lives in that house. (*Still—is adverb here— denotes time to mean 'even now'.*)
3) **After** the storm, comes calm in nature. (*After—is preposition here to show relation between 'storm' & 'calm'.*)
4) The **after** effects of the drug are bad. (*After—is adjective here—describing the noun 'effects.*)
5) The **up** train is late. (*The word 'up' is adjective here, describing the noun 'train'.*)
6) He told us all **about** the battle. (*'about' is used as preposition, shows relation between 'battle' & 'all', i.e., everything of the battle*)
7) He was only a yard **off** me. (*Used as 'preposition'.*)
8) Suddenly one of wheels came **off**. (*Used as adverb.*)
9) Muslims **fast** in the month of Ramzan. (*Fast— used as verb.*)

10) Hazel runs very *fast*. Farah runs *fast*. (Here, 'fast' in both sentences have been used as an adverb, adds meaning to verb 'runs.)
11) He kept the *fast* for a week. (*Fast — used as a noun.*)
12) Sit down and rest *a while*. They chatted for a while. (*While —as noun, to mean 'a period of time'.*)
13) I'll back in *a little while*. (*While —as noun, to mean 'in a short time or duration'.*)
14) I haven't seen him for *quite a while*. (*While —as noun, to mean 'a fairy long time'.*)
15) They walked back together talking *all the while*. (*While —as noun, to mean 'the entire period of time'.*)
16) I will watch *while* you sleep. (As a conjunction)
17) Her parents died while she was still at Primary school. (As a conjunction)
18) You can go swimming while I'm having lunch. (*While— used as conjunction to mean 'during the time that something is happening'. However, the clause is an adverbial clause in the sentence.*)
19) They *while* away their evening with books and games. (As a verb)
20) We whiled away the time reading and playing games online. (*While—used as a verb, meaning 'to spend time in a pleasant lazy way '.*)

4. Nouns: Definition and Classification

9. **Definition of a Noun:** Name of anything is called a **Noun.**
Or
A noun is a word used to name persons, places, animals, things, feelings or ideas.

Note: The word 'things' used in the definition, includes actually-
- ✓ All objects that we can see, hear, taste, touch or smell; and also
- ✓ Something that we can merely think or feel of, but cannot perceive by the senses.
- ✓ So, names of all concrete or abstract things are called Nouns.
- ✓ Name of anything, countable or uncountable, are called Nouns.
- ✓ Name of anything — person, place or things, either as common or proper, as group or individual, name of ideas or feelings, are called Nouns.

10. **The two main Nouns are actually —Common & Proper:**

The Common Nouns: A name that is applied to all, belonging to a race, class, religion, type, kind, or like this any term, sort, variety, category or breed. For examples—
→ *Cat, man, town, city, plant, chair, table, fan, river, village, park, etc. All are the examples of **Common Nouns**.*

<u>Now, read the following sentences:</u>
→ I am a man. You are a man. He is a man.
→ The man is tall. The man is short. The man is fat.

Are not these confusing, when same name is applied to all? It is difficult to understand which man is tall, who is short and who is fat. So, we require some specific names to differentiate between persons, between things even of same category; as,
→ I am *Ratan Tata*. You are *K.P. Birla*. He is *Mr. Ambani*.
→ Ratan Tata is a tall man. K.P. Birla is a fat man. Mr. Ambani is a short man.

Isn't it easy to understand, who is tall, who is fat or who is short? These specific names, like Ratan Tata, K.P. Birla or Mr. Ambani that help us to differentiate between persons of the same class or species, and facilitate to identify them particularly, are called **Proper Nouns.**

<u>Again, read the following sentences:</u>
→ I have a dog. You have a dog. She has a dog. The dog bites Shilpa.

Is not this confusing too like the before ones when particular names for each were not used? Which dog bites Shilpa?
But if we use a Proper Noun for each dog, we can overcome the confusion between Nouns.

Example No-3:

→ *Asoka* was a wise **king**.

The noun **'Asoka'** refers to a particular king, but the noun **'king'** may be applied to any other king as well as to king Asoka. We call Asoka, a **Proper Noun**, and 'king' a **Common Noun**.

Example-4:

→ A **baby** was born. His name was **Peter**. Peter grows up to a young **man**. He likes **football.** He played **World Cup 2020.** He likes **Dosa, Idli** and **Sambora.**

The word, **Peter** refers to a particular man, and thus **World Cup 2020** is a particular football game & **Dosa, Idli, Sambora** are also specific & particular names of dish of Southern India. These are **Proper Nouns.** Whereas, <u>**baby, man, football**</u> are common names, used in general to *refer any man, baby beyond Peter, and any game of football.* These are **Common Nouns**.

Similarly,

→ **'Sita'** is a Proper Noun, while **'girl'** is a Common Noun.
→ **'Paramananda'** is a Proper Noun, while **'boy'** is a Common Noun.
→ **'Kolkata'** is a Proper Noun, while **'city'** is a Common Noun.
→ **'India'** is a Proper Noun, while **'country'** is a Common Noun.
→ **'White Home'** is a Proper Noun, while **'house/home/building'** is a Common Noun.
→ **'Saidpur B.M.A. High School'** is a Proper Noun, while **'school'** is a Common Noun.

The word 'girl' is a common noun, because it is a name, common to all girls, while 'Sita' is a name of a particular girl. So, 'Sita' is a Proper Noun. **Why one is Common** and **the other, Proper**—perhaps you understood better Peter thinks for all.

Don't forget

- A Common Noun is a name given in common to every person, place or thing of the same class or kind. (**Note:** Here 'Common' means 'a name that is shared by all'.)
- It **<u>refers to a whole class, race or type</u>** of 'beings' or 'things' [not specific].
- **<u>Not bound to write in capital</u>**, if it is **not the first word** of a sentence.
- It refers to any number & **it may be <u>singular & plural in form,</u>** and thus may be followed by singular or plural verbs accordingly. [book-books; man-men, etc.]
- Articles- **a, an, the**- (as necessary) are used before a Common Noun, but generally **no article** before **<u>the name of games</u>** & <u>meals</u> of daily routine like **cricket**, **football, lunch & breakfast** [in details in the chapter of articles].

- A Proper Noun is the name of some particular person, place, animal or a thing. (**'Proper' means 'one's own; a person's, or of a place or a thing's own name, an individual name**.**)**
- Proper Nouns are always written with the Capital letter at the beginning.
- A Proper Noun is always followed by a **<u>singular verb</u>**, if not that is joined by a conjunction.
- Article - **'the'** is only used with a Proper Noun and there are some exceptions; like, The Gita, The Pacific Ocean [*which are unique & one*] and **<u>no any article before</u>** the name of God; as, 'Lord Krishna'; or a *person, place or countries* (and again exception with—the USA, the USSR, etc.)
- However, article **'a'** is sometimes also used before a Proper Noun, when a Proper Noun is used as a Common Noun; as, —
  a) Ramesh is **a Tulsidas** of our time.
  b) Kolkata is **a London** of West Bengal,
  c) Shakespeare is **a Kalidas** of Britain, etc.
  d) He was the/a Lukman (one of the wisest men) of his age.
  e) He is the/a Kalidas (one of the greatest dramatists) of our time.

11. **Words-play: *Oil, water, milk, sugar & gold*—**Identify what class of Nouns are they? Are they Material or Common Nouns? Are these countable?

Classification of Nouns:

12. There are **<u>three ways of Classification of Nouns</u>**. Look at the slide:

Classification of Nouns

10

The Nouns are naming words to name anything- concrete or abstract.	
There are two groups, Nouns of Number(countable) & Nouns of Quantity (uncountable).	Proper Noun · Common Noun · Material Noun · Collective Noun · Abstract Noun
Nouns are specific or not specific (Proper or Common).	

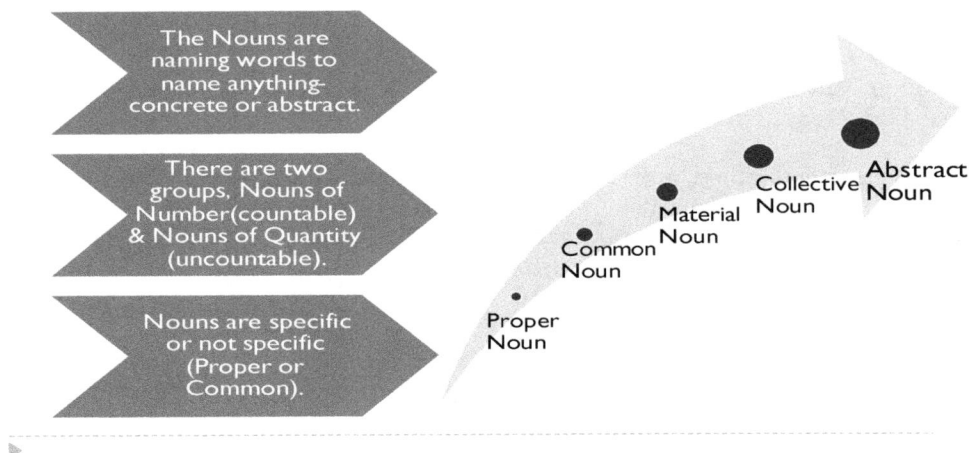

According to Wren & Martin, Common Nouns include what are called, Collective & Abstract Nouns too.

However, **I prefer the following classification of Nouns**, or is better to say, **there are 'Five' Kinds of Nouns in all**; as,

1. Proper Noun,
2. Material Noun,
3. Common Noun,
4. Collective Noun &
5. Abstract Noun

The above Nouns again fall into two groups, either in **Nouns of Number** (*Countable Nouns*) or **Nouns of Quantity** (*Uncountable Nouns*).

13. *Proper*, *Common* and *Collective* Nouns are the **Nouns of Number.** They take articles too. Let's discuss:

   a. **Proper Nouns** (the name of place, person, country & God) **does not take any article;** like, Peter, Balurghat, India & Lord Shiva;
   b. **However,** *article* **'the' is generally used in all other cases**; as, The Sun, The Ganga (which are unique or one in the universe); and
   c. **'a or the' is also used** when a Proper Noun is used as a Common Noun; as, **a Shakespeare** of our time, **a Kalidas** of his age, Kolkata is **the London** of West Bengal.
   d. **The name of place does not take any article, already we said in sl. No 1, but there are some exceptions too; as,** the USA, the USSR, The Andamans, etc.

➕ Only **Common Nouns** take articles freely,
   a. 'A' with the word, begins with consonant, except if that word does not begin with vowel sound; as, an M.A.; an FRCS.
   b. 'An' with the word, begins with a vowel, except the words pronounced like 'EU' or 'Oya'; like, a one-rupee notes, a unicorn, etc.
   c. 'The' is used to all when it refers particularly or definitely or mean the race entirely; as, the dog (*to mean a particular dog*) is barking; the cow (*denoting the race of cow*) is a domestic animal, etc.

➕ **A Collective Noun Phrase** takes **'a'** article preceding it; as, 'a pair of couple from India'; and **'the'** with one-word collective Nouns; as, the army, the police force.

14. **Material & Abstract Nouns** are generally the **Nouns of Quantity,** as neither substance (material) nor a quality, state or name of an action can be counted; they are measured broadly; as— how much/ what extent, etc., but there are also exceptions; as the followings:

Definition of Material Noun: The name of substance, a thing is made of, is called a **Material Noun**.

Read the examples:

a) The *chair* is made of **wood**.
b) The *window* is made of **steel**.
c) The *ring* is made of **gold**.
d) It is a *statue*, made of **sand-stone**.
e) The names like, ***chair, window, ring, statue***—are definitely common nouns and the substances, the things are made of, *like— wood, steel, gold, sand-stone*—are the **Material Nouns**.

Study the underline Material Nouns in the following sentences:

→ **Gold** is a precious *metal*.
→ **Wood** comes from *trees*.
→ **Steel** is a shining *object*.
→ **Sand-stone** found here, is of ten thousand years' old.

Note: All the underlined and bold are *Material Nouns*, whereas, 'metal', 'trees', 'object' are **Common Nouns**. ['Metal' means any type of solid substance which is hard and shiny; an 'object' refers to anything that can be touched or seen, but is not alive.]

15. A ***Material Noun does not take any article directly***, if that is not used to mean 'any particular amount or quantity' or 'a piece or a thing made of'. For examples: ***'a piece of gold'***, it means ***'a thing made of gold'*** & thus, ***'a gold'*** is used to mean ***'a gold coin'***, which is a Common Noun. A material turns to common. Gold is precious metal. I have many 'golds' (to mean 'gold coins').

✗ 'Gold' is Material, but 'golds' is a Common Noun to mean 'gold coins' or uncountable 'golden corns'.
✗ Silver = Material Noun, but 'silvers' (silver coins) = Common Nouns
✗ Iron = Material Noun; Irons (chains or fetters) = Common Nouns
✗ I wear a piece of gold. (That may be necklace, a ring, or anything that can be wore) = here it is Common Noun.

✗ Beside such few exceptions, a Material Noun is always without any article in general. As Material Nouns are considered uncountable, they are followed by singular verb; like,
  • 'Gold is precious metal.
  • Sugar is highly produced in the country.
  • Without water we can't live.
  • Water gives life to plants and all animals, etc.

16. A **Collective Noun** is the name of a number or collection of persons or things taken together and spoken of as one whole; as, crowd, mob, team, flock, herd, army, fleet, jury, family, nation, parliament, committee, audience, police, crew, government, or a group of…, etc.

An army of soldiers = a collection of soldiers;		A bunch of grapes
○	A choir of singers	○	A crèche of penguins
○	A crew of sailors	○	A crowd of people = a collection of people;
○	A fleet of ships = A collection of ships or vessels;	○	A flight of stairs
○	A flock of birds	○	A herd of elephants
○	A jury of judges	○	A kindle of kittens
○	A leap of leopard	○	A murder of crows
○	A muster of peacocks	○	A pack of wolves
○	A parliament of owl	○	A platoon of soldiers
○	A pride of lions	○	A scourge of mosquitoes
○	A swarm of rats	○	A swarm of bees, etc.

In sentences: The police dispersed the crowd. The Indian army celebrated its victory. The jury found the prisoner guilty. A herd of cattle is passing, etc.

Note: For more examples (to read glossary of Collective Nouns), please visit to chapter of 'Miscellaneous'.

17. **An Abstract Noun** is usually the ***name of a quality***, ***action***, or ***state*** considered apart from the object to which it belongs; as,

- <u>Quality</u>: goodness, kindness, whiteness, darkness, hardness, brightness, honesty, wisdom, bravery, etc.
- <u>Action</u>: laughter, theft, movement, judgement, hatred, etc.
- <u>State</u>: childhood, boyhood, youth, slavery, sleep, sickness, death, poverty, etc.
- **The names of the Arts & Sciences** (e.g., grammar, music, chemistry) are also Abstract Nouns.

Note: The word 'abstract' means 'drawn off' of the person or thing and the focus is on the qualities only.

❑ **Explanation regarding Abstract Nouns:**

o We can speak of a **brave** <u>soldier</u>, a **strong** <u>man</u>, a **beautiful** <u>flower</u>. But we can also think of these qualities *apart from any particular person or thing*, and speak of '***bravery, strength, beauty*** the name of qualities, which <u>*may be applied to anybody or anything beyond that soldier, man or flower*</u>.

o They sound to be common nouns, as common qualities as applied to all? But we must remember, the names of qualities fall to **Abstract Nouns**.

o So, ***bravery, strength*** or ***beauty*** — though common qualities, but we regard them as **Abstract Nouns**.

o **To be noted:**

o **As names of quality refer common qualities, as that may be shared by all or many; so why,** *if* <u>*we consider Nouns in two groups as Common and Proper*</u>, Collective, Abstract and Material Nouns fall to the group of Common Nouns, and the particular or individual names for place, person or things must be regarded as Proper Nouns. However, this classification is confusing. And, it is better to **regard Nouns as the five kinds, mentioned above.**

o *When their forms describe another noun, they become* **qualitative adjectives***; as* **brave, strong** *&* **beautiful** *(which describe some person or a thing.)*

18. **Formation of Abstract Nouns:** A lot of Abstract Nouns are formed <u>by adding suffixes lik</u>e -ship, -ment, -dom, -ness and -ity to the-

→ Common Nouns
→ Verbs
→ Adjective

<u>Like</u>

Friend + -ship = friendship;
Judge + -ment = judgement;
Firm + -ness = firmness.

Study more in the following ways and then study the charts:

➢ **From Adjectives; as,**
  ▪ ***Kindness*** from kind; (name of quality)
  ▪ ***Honesty*** from honest; (name of quality)

→ {Most abstract Nouns are formed thus.}

➢ **From Verbs; as,**
  ▪ **Obedience** from obey (name of action);
  ▪ **Growth** from grow (name of state).

➢ **From Common Nouns; as,**
  ▪ ***Childhood*** from child; (refers to the state of a child)
  ▪ ***Slavery*** from slave. (Refers to the state of being a slave)

All the above are actually different forms of certain words. Some forms are Nouns, some as verbs, and some others are adjectives in function.

19. **See the chart of Abstract Nouns which come from Adjectives**

Abstract Nouns from Adjectives

Abstract Nouns	From Adjectives	Abstract Nouns	From Adjectives	Abstract Nouns	From Adjectives
Cruelty	Cruel	Darkness	Dark	Novelty	Novel
Bravery	Brave	Depth	Deep	Quickness	Quick
Foolishness	Foolish	Width	Wide	Height	High
Length	Long	Wisdom	Wise	Poverty	Poor
Youth	Young	Goodness	Good	Justice	Just
Humbleness	Humble	Vacancy	Vacant	Vanity	Vain
Decency	Decent	Sweetness	Sweet	Sanity	Sane
Bitterness	Bitter	Humanity	Human	Honesty	Honest
Strength	Strong	Broadness	Broad	Cleanliness	Clean
Truth	True	Freedom	Free	Innocence	Innocent
Shortage	Short	Pride	Proud	Health	Healthy
Prudency	Prudent	Bravery	Brave	Happiness	Happy

20. See the chart of Abstract Nouns from Verbs:

Abstract Nouns from Verbs

Abstract Nouns	From Verbs	Abstract Nouns	From Verbs	Abstract Nouns	From Verbs
Laugher	Laugh	Starvation	Starve	Advice	Advise
Obedience	Obey	Occupation	Occupy	Punishment	Punish
Life	Live	Choice	Choose	Death	Die
Expectation	Expect	Movement	Move	Success	Succeed
Excellence	Excel	Concealment	Conceal	Freedom	Free
Knowledge	Know	Seizure	Seize	Sight	See
Stealthy	Steal	Flattery	Flatter	Judgement	Judge
Belief	Believe	Departure	Depart	Persuasion	Pursue
Service	Serve	Perseverance	Persevere	Relief	Relieve
Hatred	Hate	Defendant	Defend	Conversion	Converse
Pleasure	Please	Thought	Think	Discovery	Discover
Action	Act	Protection	Protect		

21. See the chart of Abstract Nouns from Common Nouns:

Abstract Nouns from Verbs

Abstract Nouns	From Verbs	Abstract Nouns	From Verbs	Abstract Nouns	From Verbs
Laugher	Laugh	Starvation	Starve	Advice	Advise
Obedience	Obey	Occupation	Occupy	Punishment	Punish
Life	Live	Choice	Choose	Death	Die
Expectation	Expect	Movement	Move	Success	Succeed
Excellence	Excel	Concealment	Conceal	Freedom	Free
Knowledge	Know	Seizure	Seize	Sight	See
Stealthy	Steal	Flattery	Flatter	Judgement	Judge
Belief	Believe	Departure	Depart	Persuasion	Pursue
Service	Serve	Perseverance	Persevere	Relief	Relieve
Hatred	Hate	Defendant	Defend	Conversion	Converse
Pleasure	Please	Thought	Think	Discovery	Discover
Action	Act	Protection	Protect		

22. Division of Nouns as **Concrete** & **Abstract:**

Concrete Nouns: Concrete Nouns are name of things that have a material form, what we can sense or experience through our five senses. We can see, hear, smell, taste and touch them; as,

Chair, hair, scooter, keyboard, sugar, oil and milk.

And we have already discussed of Abstract Nouns.
Abstract Nouns are names of such things that do not have material form. They refer to the name of ideas, concepts, feeling and events. We can not see, hear, smell, taste, or touch. We can only feel, think or assume of Abstract Nouns. Thus, it is only the _name of thoughts, ideas, feelings, qualities or name of events not the event itself (i.e., the name of action or state)_. **For examples:** truth, honesty, confidence, idea, justice, responsibility, hope, and childhood, etc.

23. **Note-:** Division of Nouns as **Concrete** & **Abstract**, is not needful at all, as they are neither useful in 'Subject-Verb Agreement' nor in the 'use of article'. However, we'll study them as, so we don't face difficulty to answer questions rise from that point.

24. **All five Nouns, in brief:**

❖ Actually, all Nouns or names belong to _**Common Nouns**. When some names are used for particular person, place or things, they are_ **Proper Nouns**;
❖ Some together _form a group or collection_ and thus coin a new term, **Collective Nouns**;
❖ Some refer to _substances; a thing is made of_, so **Material Nouns**;
❖ Some denote the _names of qualities, feelings, ideas, name of action or state_, they are **Abstract Nouns**.

> Don't forget
> • Nouns can be grouped in three ways— **(i)** as concrete and abstract, **(ii)** as countable and uncountable, & **(iii)** as five kinds—Proper, Common, Collective, Material and Abstract Nouns. (Excluding the classification of Nouns as Proper & Common).
> • Only countable Nouns has numbers, singular or plural. The uncountable are generally treated as the singular nouns, and mostly they follow singular verbs, except the exceptions.

Read the questions and write their answers. _Then, underline the nouns you have learnt, and classify as more as you can. Write their all names against each one._
   1. What do you like? Who is your favorite cricketer?
   2. Who is Jhilik? Do you know her? Where did you meet her first?
   3. In the last world cup who won the cup?

4. Where is situated your school? How do you go there?

25. **Words-play:** *Oil, water, milk, sugar & gold*—Identify what class of Nouns are they? Are they Material or Common Nouns? Are these countable?

➢ Let's discuss-

✓ *Proper Nouns means specific or particular names* and specific names can't be uncountable. The above are, therefore, **not Proper Nouns**.

✓ The above nouns do not hint to any *class or race* and secondly, these are uncountable Nouns. So, they are **not Common Nouns** too.

✓ The above Nouns neither the *name of a group* or *a collection* nor the *names of feelings or emotion*. So, these are **neither _Collective_ nor _Abstract_** Nouns.

✓ So, what is left to us? The above nouns are **names of substances**, things made of. So, these are **Material Nouns**.

26. **Points to remember:**

- **Nouns of Quantity** (as Material Nouns & Abstract Nouns) **do not take any article directly**; as, — gold, copper, iron, tin, water; & kindness, judgement, honesty, boyhood, etc.
- **Nouns of Number** (as Proper, Common, & Collective) **take articles, as necessary**.
- Collective Nouns sometimes are preceded by '**a**'; as, **a gang of robbers**, or '**the**'; as, **the police force, the army,** etc.
- Only **Common Noun has singular & plural forms**, *takes articles freely and takes verbs accordingly*,
- **Proper, Material, Collective & Abstract** –generally take singular verbs. *Their plurals are made either using **Conjunctions** or **considerations on facts**; as,*

▸Lila & Shilpa **are** girls. / Gold & Copper **are** metals. / The jury **are** diverse in opinions. The police **are** useless under tyrant Governments. (Here 'police' denotes the police force of different states or Govt. bodies.)

Note-1: Please visit the section of 'The Number of Nouns' for further details.

The Number of Nouns

27. **Look around your classroom and answer these questions:**
    1) How many girls are there in the classroom?
    2) How many boys are there in the classroom?
    3) How many windows are there in the classroom?
    4) How many doors does your classroom have?
    5) How many teachers are there in your school?
    6) How many teachers are there in your classroom right now?

28. **Nouns are countable & uncountable:** Countable noun has number; Uncountable has quantity. An Uncountable Noun follows a singular verb.

- **Countable Nouns:** Countable Nouns are the names of objects, people, etc., *that we can count*, e.g., book, pen, apple, boy, sister, doctor, horse. Countable Nouns have plural forms, while Uncountable Nouns do not. For Example: we say, cow- cows, but **we cannot say, 'milks' as plural of 'milk'.**

- **Uncountable Nouns:** Uncountable Nouns are the names of things *which we can't count*, e.g., milk, oil, sugar, gold, honesty. They *mainly denote substances and abstract things*.

- **Read the examples:**
   → He gave me a bunch of grapes.
   → A committee of five was appointed.
   → We saw a fleet of ships in the *harbour*.

→ Our <u>class</u> consists of twenty *pupils*.
→ I often think of the happy *days* of *childhood*.
→ The *room* is thirty *feet* in *length*.

Let's discuss:

From the above sentences, we got
→ A bunch of grapes
→ A committee of five
→ A fleet of ships &
→ Class   *-are examples of Collective Nouns.*

▶ **Remember,**

❖**Note-1:** *'bunch', 'committee', 'fleet', 'class'*—are the base/root Collective Nouns, whereas, *'a bunch of grapes', 'a committee of five', 'a fleet of ships'*—are the Collective Noun Phrases.

❖**Note-2:** *Out of the phrases, 'grapes', 'ships'*—**_cannot be treated individually as Common Nouns_**. However, harbour, pupils, days, feet—are genuine examples of **Common Nouns**.

   ❖ Childhood, length—are examples of **Abstract Nouns**.
   ❖ Five, twenty, thirty—are Number of Adjectives/Numeral Adjectives.
   ❖ 'Happy' is a Qualitative Adjective.

29. **What is number? How do they change their forms?**

Notice the change of form in the second column:

Tree	Tree**s**
Box	Box**es**
Ox	Ox**en**
Man	M**e**n

Points to be noted:

The words in the 1st column denotes 'one thing', whereas, the words in the 2nd column denotes 'more than one'.

Definitions:

❏ A Noun that denotes one person or thing, is said to be in the ***Singular Number***; as,
   ❏Man, book, pen, etc.

❏ A Noun that denotes more than one person or thing, is said to be in the ***Plural Number***; as,
   ❏Men, books, pens, etc.

❏ Thus, there are two Numbers of Nouns: 1) **Singular** & 2) **Plural.**

30. We need to study, **'How the Plurals are formed'.** Carefully study the following charts:

How it is formed		Examples	
1. By adding suffixes	i) '-s'	Desk; Chief	Desks; Chiefs
	ii) '-es'	Box; Dish	Boxes; Dishes
	iii) '-ies'	Baby	Babies
	iv) '-ves'	Half	Halves
2. By making change/adding letter(s) within the words	• -e • -en • -ren, etc.	Man Ox Child	Men Oxen Children
3. By another word	•	I He /She A Person	We They People

The Rules	Singular	Plural

Rule 1: '**-s**'suffix is added to most of nouns. (Generally, when nouns end with consonant or vowels- 'e' or 'O')	Eye; Bee; safe Ratio; dynamo Piano; photo Ant; cow; boy	Eye**s**; Bee**s**; safe**s** Ratio**s**; dynamo**s** Piano**s**; photo**s** Ant**s**; cow**s**; boy**s**
Rule 2: To make plural of **abbreviations, letters, figures** &**symbols** -'s is added.	M.A.; B.A.; P, t, etc. 5, 20 & #	M.A.'s (Faculty of 5 M.A.'s & 7 B.A.'s) There are more p's than t's on the page. Add two 5's with six 7's. There are five 20's in a hundred rupees. Underline your i' and replace them with #'s.
Rule 3: To mean 'Nationality' or 'Religion', the '**-s**'is added.	Indian; Egyptian Mussulman Brahman; Christian Abyssinian	Indian**s**; Egyptian**s** Mussulman**s** Brahman**s**; Christian**s** Abyssinian**s**
Rule 4: The suffix, '**-es**' is added with the nouns that end with- '**s, ss, sh, ch, x**'.	Gas, bus Class; kiss; Brush; dish Inch, bench, match, watch; branch Box, tax	Gases, buses Classes; kisses Brushes; dishes Inches, benches, matches, watches; branches; Boxes, taxes
Rule 5: But if '**ch**' is pronounced as-'**k**', only '**-s**' is added.	Monarch Stomach	Monarchs Stomachs
Rule 6: '**-s**'suffix is added to nouns ends with '**o' or 'y**', &**a vowel preceding** it.	Cuck**oo** Bamb**oo** Stud**io** Rad**io**, ster**eo**	Cuck**oos** Bamb**oos** Stud**ios** Rad**ios**, ster**eos**
	Play Key day	Plays Keys days
Exception-1:	Halo, solo, logo Piano, quarto, kilo, Commando, Canto, Memento, Portico	Halos, solos, logos Pianos, quartos, kilo, Commandos, Cantos, Mementos, Porticos
Rule 7: But if there is a **consonant before 'o' or 'y'**, '**-es**'/ '**ies**' suffix is added.	Her**o**, Mang**o** Buffal**o**, Potat**o** Cargo, negro Volcano, echo	Her**oes**, Ma**ngoes** **Buffaloes**, Pot**atoes** Cargoes, negroes Volcanoes, echoes
	Arm**y** **Fl**y **Ba**b**y** s**k**y	**Armies** **Flies** **Babies** skies
Rule 8: Sometimes, nouns end with '**f**'/ '**fe**'/ '**ff**', '-s' is added with them.	Roof, Proof, Chief, gulf Handkerchief Dwarf, scarf, hoof Safe Puff Cliff	Roofs, Proofs, Chiefs, gulfs, Handkerchiefs, Dwarfs, scarfs, hoofs (also-dwarves, scarves, hooves) Safes Puffs Cliffs

Rule 9: But in most cases **'f'** or **'fe'** **becomes 'v'** & <u>add '-es' with</u> them. (-ves)	Calf, Wolf, Half, loaf, elf, sheaf, Thief, Shelf Self, leaf Wife, Life, Knife	Calves, Wolves, Halves, loaves, elves, sheaves, Thieves, Shelves Selves, leaves Wives, Lives, Knives,

Plural of **Compound Noun**

Rule 10:	SINGULAR	PLURAL
In case of compound word or noun,(with hyphen) '-s' is **added with the main word** of the compound & in few cases '-s' is added with the both.	1. Commander-in-chief 2. Father-in-law 3. Son-in-law 4. Daughter-in-law 5. Maid-servant	1. Commanders-in-chief 2. Fathers-in-law 3. Sons-in-law 4. Daughters-in-law 5. Maid-servants
	1. Man-servant 2. Woman-servant	1. Men-servants 2. Women-servants
Rule 11: But **if there is no hyphen** used, '-s' **is added at the end** of the whole compound.	1. Grandfather 2. Step-son 3. step-daughter 4. Bookcase	1. Grandfathers 2. Step-sons 3. step-daughters 4. Bookcases

2. By Making Change/Adding Letter or Letters Within

Rule 12:	SINGULAR	PLURAL
There are a lot of nouns whose plural are formed **by changing or adding 'letter' within**.	1. Man 2. Woman 3. Louse 4. Mouse 5. Tooth 6. Foot 7. Child 8. Ox 9. Gentleman 10. Englishman 11. Washer man 12. Nobleman	1. Men 2. Women 3. Lice 4. Mice 5. Teeth 6. Feet 7. Children 8. Oxen 9. Gentlemen 10. Englishmen 11. Washer men 12. Noblemen

Some Nouns Are Both 'Singular' & 'Plural'

Rule 13:	SINGULAR	PLURAL
These nouns are **used as both** as necessary. They are called **'zero plural'**	1. A Beer 2. A Public was present there. 3. A Sheep 4. A swine 5. A Cannon 6. A Deer 7. A Pair 8. A Dozen 9. One Hundred 10. A Thousand 11. An Aircraft 12. A fish 13. A cod 14. A salmon 15. A score means twenty	1. Two Beer 2. Ten Public were gathering at the place. 3. Five Sheep 4. Nine swine 5. Fifty Cannon 6. Four Deer 7. Two Pair 8. Ten Dozen 9. Two Hundred 10. Ten Thousand 11. Three Aircraft 12. A lot of fish 13. Many cod, he caught 14. I got two salmon 15. Five score = a hundred

'Wh' words are both 'singular' & 'plural'

Rule 14:	SINGULAR	PLURAL
Some **relative & interrogative pronouns & adjectives** mean both—the singular & plural.	1. Who (কে?) 2. Whom (কাকে?) 3. Whose (কার?) 4. What (কি?) 5. Which (কোনটি)	1. Who (কারা?) 2. Whom (কাদেরকে ?) 3. Whose (কাদের?) 4. What (কিকি) 5. Which (কোন গুলি)
	1. Who is the man? 2. Whom did you invite? 3. Whose bag is this? 4. What does he want? 5. Which pen is yours?	1. Who are the men? 2. Whom did you invite? 3. Whose bags are these? 4. What does he want? 5. Which pens are theirs?

Number of Certain Nouns

17		SINGULAR	PLURAL
Rule 15: Some nouns have both forms but slightly different in meanings; **Rule 16:** *Some look plural in forms, but they are always singular in use.*		1. **Asset** (valuable & useful person or thing) = *He is an asset to his team.* 2. **People** (persons / a nation or race): Soon there people gathered around. (as plural) *The Japanese are a hard working people.* 3. **Means** (cause/agent/way to a goal) : *He succeeded to pass the Examination by this means.* Note: People or Peoples both follow pl verb	1. Assets (money & wealth) = *Her assets include shares in the companies and a house in New York.* 2. Peoples (only nations) : *There are different peoples in Europe.* 3. Means (riches, wealth or earnings): *His means are small but he has incurred no debt.*
		1. **Name of Subjects:** 2. **Name of Diseases** 3. **Names of some games:**	1. Mathematics, Physics, Electronics 2. Measles, mumps, rickets 3. Billiards; innings; draughts in rings

Rule 17: Some are called **'ever plural nouns';** for they always remain in the plural form & to be used accordingly, & often they can also be used as singular in the same form; as,

Ever PLURAL	
1. Name of Instruments which have two parts, forming a kind of pair; as,	Bellows = an equipment for blowing air into or through something Scissors = a tool, used to cut papers or cloths Tongs = a tool, used for picking & holding things Pincers = a tool, used to hold firmly as nails put of wood Spectacles = wear or use to see objects
2. Name of certain articles & dress; as,	1. Trousers 2. Jeans 3. Tights 4. Shorts, pajamas

3. **Some other Nouns which are always in Plural form but can be used as both; as in table no-9:**

Ever Plural Nouns	Ever Plural Nouns
Annals (*an official record of events & activities year after year*): Where is the annals of our company? Collect the annals of all companies in the state within a month. **Thanks** (*to express gratitude we use this. It is singular and plural both, like the other.*) **Proceeds** (*the earned money by selling objects or performance*): we have to run the family with these proceeds. **Tidings** (*News*): I am the bearer of good tidings. Even worse are tidings to follow after the epidemic. **Environs** (*the area surrounding a place*): Several hotels are located within the environs of the airport.	**Nuptials** (*a wedding*); I can't be there in the nuptials tomorrow. **Obsequies** (*funeral ceremonies*): Obsequies are important in Hindu religion. **Eaves** (*lower edges of a roof that stick out over walls*): The bird sat on the eaves. **Chattels** (*belongings*): Women are now regarded as equal partners, not as chattels or house keepers. **Alms** (*money, clothes or food that are given to poor*): Don't ask for alms. I see you are an able-bodied man. **Riches** (*large amount of money or possessions*); I have not those riches to build a new house.

Carefully read the following examples:
Note: Verbs-singular or plural, it depends on the sense. See the table-10:

Ever Plural	

1.	Thanks	1.	He gives her <u>thanks</u>. They expressed their gratitude by giving their <u>thanks</u>. Thanks are given. *(may regarded as both)*
2.	Spectacles	2.	Where are my <u>spectacles</u>? Or 'Their <u>spectacles have</u> been broken'. *(Verb in both cases, will be plural)*
3.	Cattle	3.	The cattle belong to me. *(Only plural)*
4.	Jeans	4.	I have bought a <u>jeans</u>. You have two <u>jeans</u>. (So, as pants, trousers & scissors)
5.	Police	5.	A <u>police man</u> died in the mob. There were two <u>police</u> on duty.
6.	News	6.	He gave me a <u>news</u>. It was sad. All the <u>news</u> were sad following that.
7.	Series	7.	I have read an <u>interesting series</u> of stories last year. All other <u>series</u> before that I had read were found so boring.
8.	Species	8.	The animal belongs to a <u>unique species</u>. Three <u>species</u> of the kind are already extinct from the earth.

Note: And thus, Trousers, Pants, Scissors, etc.

Rule 18: Many Nouns taken from foreign languages, keep their original plural forms; as,

Words	changes	Singular	Plural
a) From Latin	a> + e/'-s' um>a us>i ex>ic+ '-es'	Formul**a** Errat**um** memorand**um** Radi**us** Termin**us** Ind**ex**	Formula**e** (Formula**s**) Errat**a** memorand**a** Radi**i** Termin**i** Indi**ces** (*also* indexes)
b) From Greek	is>es on>a	Ax**is**; Cris**is** Bas**is**; Analyses Parenthes**is** Hypothes**is** Phenomen**on** Criter**ion**	Ax**es**; Cris**es** Bas**es**; Analys**es** Parenthes**es** Hypothes**es** Phenomen**a** Criteri**a**
c) From Italian	+ '-s'/ doubling of last consonant + '-i'	bandit	Bandit**s** / bandit**ti**
d) From French	a/on >es ...+-s	M**a**dame (madam) **M**o**n**s**ieur**	M**es**dames (madams) M**es**sieurs
e) From Hebrew	By adding '-s'/ '-im'	Cherub Seraph	Cherub**s**/ cherub**im** Seraph**s**/ seraph**im**

Rule-19: Most of Collective Nouns are treated as singular. But Some Collective Nouns though singular in form, follow always the plural verb.
1. These ***poultry*** are mine.
2. Whose are these ***cattle***?
3. ***Vermin*** destroy our property & carry diseases. (wild animals or birds that destroy plants or animals)
4. Who are these ***people***? (persons)
5. There are few ***gentry*** in this town. (gentlemen)

Rule-20: Material Nouns (names of substances) are uncountable nouns. So, they do not have singular or plural, but as common nouns in plural form with different meanings they follow plural verbs; as,
1. How have you collected so coppers? (copper coins)
2. Why to afraid of irons for a great cause? (fetters or chain)
3. I have no tins to carry all these. (cans, made of tin)
4. Who lives in the woods? (forest)
5. Farmers cultivate golds in this season. (corns)

6. Have you golds? (gold coins)

Rule-21: Abstract Nouns, like Material Nouns, are uncountable; like- hope, charity, love, kindness, provocation; but they also can be used specially in plural number, for rhetorical purpose or like that; like the examples:

1. I have seen ***thousand hopes*** to smash in dejection. (hope of different young men is counted)
2. ***Kindnesses of leaders*** are waters in the salty deserts. (kindness of different leaders is regarded here as to count)
3. There were found <u>instances of provocation</u>. ***The provocations*** are marked as your crime. (it denotes the number of times the person was provoked)
4. I don't need ***their charities*** at present. (charity of different persons or organizations)
5. ***Their loves*** suffocated the young man, and he committed suicide. ('love' of different members or persons—are counting)

Rule-22: Some Nouns have two forms for the plural with different Meanings; as in **table no-12**:

Singular	Plural	Meanings of plurals
1. Brother	Brothers	Sons of same parent
	Brethren	Members of a society or a community
2. Cloth	Cloths	kinds or pieces of cloths
	Clothes	garments
3. Die	Dies	Stamps for coining
	Dice	Small cubes used in games
4. Index	Indexes	Tables of contents to books
	Indices	Signs used in algebra
5. Penny	Pennies	Number of coins
	Pence	Amount in value

Rule-23: Some Nouns one meaning in singular but two in plural; as in **Table-13:**

Singular	Plural	Meanings of plurals
1. Color	Colors	Hues; The flag of a regiment
2. Custom	Customs	Habits; duties levied on imports
3. Effect	Effects	Stamps for coining; Small cubes used in games
4. Ground (earth/ reason)	Grounds	1) Enclosed land attached to a house 2) Reasons; 3) dregs/sediment found on river bed)
5. Letter	Letters	1) Letters of the alphabet 2) Epistles or graphs (written documents) 3) Literature
6. Manner	Manners	Methods; correct behavior
7. Moral	Morals	Moral lesions; conduct
8. Number	Numbers	Quantities; verses
9. Pain	Pains	Sufferings; care or exertion
10. Premise	Premises	Propositions; buildings

11. Quarter	Quarters	Fourth parts; lodgings
12 Spectacle	Spectacles	Sights; eye glasses

Rule-24: Some Nouns have two meanings in singular and one in plural; as in **table no-14**:

Singular	Double meanings in Singular	Meaning in Plural Form
1. Light	• Lamp • Radiance	Lights (lamps)
2. People	• Nation • Men & women	Peoples (Nations)
3. Powder	• A dose of medicine in fine grains like dust; • Dust	Powders (doses of medicine)
4. Practice	• Habit • Exercise of a profession	Practices (habits)

Rule-25: Some Nouns have different meanings in singular and plural; as in **table no-15**:

Singular	Meanings in Singular	Plural	Meanings in Plural
Air	Atmosphere	Airs	Affected manners
Compass	Extent; range	Compasses	An instrument for drawing circles
Force	Strength	Forces	Troops; armies
Iron	A kind of metal	Irons	Fetters or chain of iron
Physic	Medicine	Physics	Natural Sciences; a subject
Respect	Regard	Respects	Compliments
Wood	A piece of timber	Woods	Forest

> **Don't forget**
> - Nouns that can be counted are called countable nouns.
> - Nouns that cannot be counted are called uncountable nouns.
> - Article—a, an, the —are used with the countable nouns.
> - In case of uncountable nouns, generally articles are not necessary. However, where is necessary we use 'the' article.

Let us write:

- What's your favorite game. Will you tell some about this? How much do you enjoy the game? Write also about feelings. Then, point out which are countable and uncountable nouns. Circle the countable and underline uncountable.

The Gender of Nouns

31. **Let's get started:**

Complete the table with the name of relation of the members of your family and some relations you know about your relatives:

Column A	Column B
Mother	Father
Sister	Brother
Aunt	Uncle
Grandmother	Grandfather
Nieces	niece

Complete the table with the name of relation of the members at your school and also some relations you know in your locality:

Column A	Column B
Principal Madam	Principal Sir
Sister	Brother
Head mistress	Head master
Matron	Peon
Madam	Sir

Can't you also name some of animals you see and know in your locality or out of? Then try, and make a list. Show the list to your parents, elder brother or sister or to your teacher.

32. **The Definitions of Gender** (of Nouns): Gender is that sign or forms of Nouns that talks about 'sex', male, female or things.

33. **The living beings are either of 'male' or 'female' sex. And non-living things belong to neuter.**
   → A noun that denotes a male animal is said to be of the **Masculine Gender** [Gender comes from Latin 'genus', kind or sort]; as,
      o Man, boy, sultan, lion, cock-sparrow, he, bull, Rakesh, Rohan etc.
   → A noun that denotes a female animal is said to be of the **Feminine Gender**; as,
      o Woman, girl, sultana, lioness, hen-sparrow, she, cow, etc.
   → A noun that denotes one who has biological features of both sex- male or female (of the 1st or the 2nd gender), they are known as the **3rd Gender** or '**the Other**', vastly used as in the offices.
      o 'Eunuch' is such a word that denotes the third gender. In offices, it is popularly used as '**Other**'.

   → A noun that denotes either male, female or the other, is said to be **Common Gender**; as,
      o Sparrow, cat, friend, foe, teacher, student, children, etc.
   → A noun that denotes a thing (referring not living things and so why neither it is a male nor a female), is said to be of the **Neuter Gender**; as,
      o Book, pen, school, army, room, tree, etc.
   → [Neuter means 'neither', that is, neither male nor female.]

Note: So, the Gender of nouns is entirely **a matter of sex** or the **absence of sex**. And thus, we have **five kinds of Gender** in total, for examples: *Male, Female, Common, Other (3rd Gender) & Neuter.*

34. **Some Examples of Common Gender (that refer either Male or Female)**

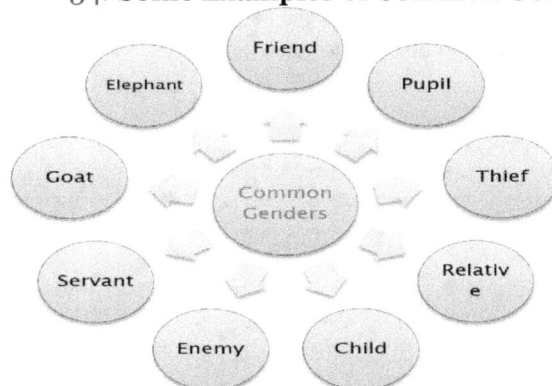

35. **Personification of Neuter Genders:**

Objects or things without life if they are personified *(qualities of persons thrown upon parts of nature, for the rhetorical purpose)*, they are often treated as living beings and to be treated as either **Male** or **Female**:

→ The masculine gender is often <u>applied to objects remarkable for strength & violence</u>; as,
  ○ The Sun, Summer, Winter, Time, Death, etc.
→ The feminine gender is often used to describe the Nature itself and rivers, countries, ships, seasons *that hold something or mean for productivity* and *to objects remarkable for beauty, gentleness, gracefulness,* etc., as,
  ○ Nature, the Moon, the earth, the Spring, the Monsoon, the Autumn, etc. India is our motherland. Her sons and daughters bravely fight for her. INS Viraat was decommissioned. She was towed out of Kochi. Mother Nature is suffering for us, and soon we will meet her wrath in forms of floods, Tsunami, or other.
→ However, the countries — Germany, Sweden, Norway, Denmark, Netherland, Estonian, and may be few others regard their land or country as father land. So, these are to be treated as the masculine gender.
  ○ Germans respect their fatherland too much and can do anything for his honour.

36. Exercises: Read the sentences and note down the gender in each:

1)	The Sun sheds his beam on rich and poor alike.	2)	The Nature laughs with her blessings.
3)	The Moon beam falls on and she twinkles to welcome the night's fairies in deep Amazon.	4)	The Mother Earth was not happy with her children and she sent COVID-19.
5)	The spring blooms and decorates her mother with her thousand colors.	6)	Liberty is that chastity, once gone never returns with her beauty.
7)	The autumn tells her sister, the Spring, "You must keep patience and not come before I return."	8)	Justice sees all with her helplessness to humane often.
9)	Mercy, Peace, Hope & Charity—are the other females who hardly keep their chastity to the end. But if can, you are the happiest man.	10)	The Moon has hidden her face behind a cloud and we heard the roar of his heavy crying.
11)	The lighting thrashed upon the houses and burnt everything in his kingdom.	12)	Peace hath her victories no less renowned than war.
13)	Spring has spread her mantle of green over the earth.	14)	The sea-God emerged from his kingdom before Rama.
15)	The ship lost all her boats in the storm.	16)	

37. Study the charts of Conversion of Gender, from <u>Masculine to Feminine</u>:

Chart-1,

RULES	Examples—column (1)	Examples—column (2)
i) By adding '**–ess**' to Masculine Nouns: **Note:** The suffix '—ess' is the commonest suffix used to form Feminine Nouns.	Poet—poetess Author—authoress Baron- baroness Heir—heiress Giant—giantess Manager-manageress Mayor- Mayoress Patron-patroness Peer-peeress Viscount- Viscountess	Host—hostess Lion—lioness Priest—priestess Prophet-prophetess God—god**d**ess Count-countess Jew-Jewess Shepherd-shepherdess Steward-stewardess

Chart-2,

RULES	Examples—column (1)	Examples—column (2)

| ii) By adding –ess after dropping vowel of last syllable | Actor—actress
Benefactor-benefactress
Conductor-conductress
Enchanter-enchantress
Founder-foundress
Traitor- traitress
Hunter—huntress
Prince—princess | Tiger—tigress
Waiter—waitress Instructor-instructress
Negro-negress
Perceptor -perceptress
Songster-songstress Seamster-seamstress Tempter- temptress |
| Variations: (by dropping more letters (vowel & consonants) & adding –ess) | Emperor—empress
Master—mistress
Sorcerer-sorceress
Abbot-abbess | Murderer—murderess
Duke-Duchess |

Chart-3,

RULES	By adding suffixes	By adding prefixes
iii) By adding others; as, '-a', '-s', '-ine', 'ina', 'trix', & 'lady', 'she', 'cow', etc.	Signor- Signor *a* Sultan—sultan*a* Mr.—Mr*s*. Hero—hero*ine* Czar-Czar*ina* Testator-testa*trix*	Inspector—*lady* inspector Goat—*she* goat Elephant—*cow*-elephant

Chart-4,

RULES	Male/Masculine	Female/Feminine
iv) By **changing the masculine part of a compound.**	Grand*father* Great *uncle* Land*lord* *Man*-servant Mil*kman* Pea*cock* Sales*man* *Father* wolf	grand*mother* great *aunt* land*lady* *maid*-servant milk-*woman* pea*hen* sales*woman* *mother* wolf
v) **By using an entirely different word; as,** Goat-she goat Gander-goose Gentleman—lady Wizard-witch	Bull/ox/bullock calf Cock Dog Drake Fox Horse/stallion Monk Nephew Buck/hart/Stag Bachelor Bachelor party Colt (a young male horse) Daddy/Pappa Earl Sheep/ram	Cow Heifer Hen bitch duck vixen mare nun niece doe/hind/deer Damsel/maid; Damsel party Filly (a young female horse); mummy/mamma; Countess Ewe/lamb

Don't forget
- Ships and countries are denoted using the feminine gender.
- India is our motherland. Her sons and daughters bravely fight for her.
- INS Viraat was decommissioned. She was towed out of Kochi.
- Nature is also commonly called 'Mother Nature' and referred to using female pronouns.
- The masculine gender is used for the country of Germany. Try remember, is there any beyond such ones?

Let us write:
- Imagine that you visited a farm. Write a short paragraph describing the animals you saw there. Include as many masculine and feminine gender forms as possible.

The Case vs. the Functions of Nouns

38. **The Case of Nouns:** How a Noun is used in the sentence, what roles they do perform, is popularly known as 'the Case of Nouns.'

    Noun has three main Cases; and based on this, there are **five major functions of Nouns**, noted in English Grammar for a sentence. Let's Discuss-

    Examine the Sentences:
    - **John** threw a stone.
    - **The horse** kicked the boy.
        - Who threw a stone?
        - Who kicked the boy?

    Do you know the answers?
    - ✖ Who threw a stone?   – **John.**
    - ✖ Who kicked the boy? – **The horse.**

    o In sentence-1, the Noun, 'John' is the Subject. It is the answer to the question, 'Who threw a stone?'
    o What did John throw? –**a stone**. 'Stone' is the object in the sentence.
    o In sentence-2, the Noun, 'The horse' is the Subject. It is the answer to the question, 'Who kicked the boy?'
    o Whom did the horse kick? –**the boy**. 'Boy' is the object in the sentence.
    o And again, in **'It is Peter's chair.'** Whose chair is this? = **Peter's.**

    Thus, **there are three main Cases of Nouns**. They are:

a. **Nominative or Subjective:** *When a Noun (or a Pronoun) is used as a subject of a verb, it is said to be in* the **Nominative Case.**
    → *Ram* is a boy. *He* is a student. The *dog* is barking.
    → *Shiva* is swimming. *We* have no car to reach home.
    → *It* is a private *building*. (In the sentence, **'It'** & **'building'**—both are in the Nominative Case, as both refer same thing. Here, 'building' is the subjective complement of verb 'Be' (is).

✦ **Note-1:** To find the Nominative, ask question to the verb with **'Who'** or **'What'**. The answer will be in Nominative Case.

b. **Accusative or Objective:** *When a Noun (or a Pronoun) is used as an object of a verb, it is said to be in* the **Objective or Accusative Case.**
    → I saw a *cinema*. You could see *me* watching so.
    → He is taller than *him*.
    → We made a *sand castle* on the beach.
    → Teacher writes on the *black-board*.

✦ **Note-2:** To find the Accusative or Objective case of Noun, ask question to verb with **'What'** or **'Whom'**. Your answers are in the Accusative or Objective Case of Nouns.

c. **Genitive or Possessive:** When a noun or a pronoun *possesses something*, i.e., *something belongs to the Noun or Pronoun*, it is said to be in the Possessive Case.
    ▪ This is *Ratan's* car. The pen is *yours*.

- The bag is *mine*. All are *theirs.*
- It is *Peter's* handwriting. *No one's* is so worse than *his*.

39. **Find out the *Nominative*, the *Accusative* or *Genitive Case* of Nouns from the following examples:**
    a) I opened Instagram on my phone. [*Who opened? What?*]
    b) Have you lost your mind? [*Who lost? What?*]
    c) I love John Keat's poems. [*Whose poems?*]
    d) It is from one of Shakespeare's dramas. [*From whose dramas?*]
    e) Do you know Zara? [*Who is to know? Whom?*]
    f) It is Shyamal's house. Is not this Zara's? [whose]
    g) Sourabh raised his hand. [*Who raised his hand? What?*'

40. **More About the Accusative case:** A Noun which comes after a preposition is also said to be in the Accusative or Objective case. An objective complement is also be in the Accusative or Objective Case in the sentence; as,
    - He gave his *son* an *advice*. (son & advice—both are objects and are in the objective case)
    - An advice was given to *his son*. (son—a prepositional object is also in the objective or accusative case.)
    - I agree with *your proposal*. She proposed to *him*.
    - The book is on the *desk*.
    - She swims in a *pond*.
    The adverbial phrases—'on the desk', 'in the pond'—are also in the objective or accusative case.)

    Note-1: All the bold & underlined nouns are said to be in the Accusative or Objective Case. Some are popularly known as **Prepositional Objects**, and some nouns like- *desk, pond* with other words in the sentence, have formed **Adverbial Phrase**.

    Note-2: Thus, we have learnt, Nouns do the following functions. They form—
    1) Subject, 2) Object, 3) Prepositional Object, & 4) An Adverbial Phrase, and **more others**.

41. **A Noun *or* an adjective *or* an infinitive *or* a gerund which completes the sense of the verb, besides the object in the sentence, is called an objective complement. An objective complement is always** in the Accusative Case like an object, Direct or Indirect. (However, a subjective complement that adds meaning to the subject is always in the Nominative Case); as,
    - He was made **captain** of our class.
    - We made Rahul, ***captain*** of our class.
    - Lucas is made **our representative** in the Lok Sabha.
    - We elected him our *leader*.

    Note-1: All the bold & underlined nouns are said to be in the Accusative Case.
    ° The nouns like- *captain, our representative, & leader*— are popularly known as **Complement** to the verb. They complete the sense of the verb, when sense is not complete even with their objects – Rahul **&** him.

42. **But, now read the following sentences carefully:**
    → He was a *student*. I am a *teacher*.
    → *A black-board* is black in color. *A sand-castle* doesn't last.

- What the bold words are doing. The words— *student* & *teacher*—of first two sentences are describing the subjects themselves. They add meanings to the subjects. These words are called subjective complements. The case of subjective complements is, as their subjects, i.e., the Nominative case.
- *And the bold words— black-board, sand-castle —*are the Nominal Compounds and subjects in the sentences, and these **are also in the Nominative case**.

- But if a compound word or a nominal compound are the parts of objects or objective complement or of an adverbial phrase, they are certainly be in the Accusative or Objective case; as,
    I wrote on a *black-board*. One cannot live in a *sand-castle*.

I offered him my **_black-board_**. I made the wood a **_black-board_**.
I saw in Rajasthan many **_sand-castles_**. He made it a **_sand-castle_**.

- All the above bold words are compounds (nominal compounds) and they are either objects, complement or part of adverbial phrases. Here, all these **are in the Objective cases**.
- So, <u>Compounds or Nouns doing the function of an Adjective or as Nouns, their case depend on their position and uses</u>; as,

→ The burglar broke the **_window_**. The **_window_** was broken.

43. **Remember: <u>Nouns have same forms</u>** for the <u>Nominative & the Accusative Case</u>, but a _Pronoun may have different for each Case_; as,
    - I—me—mine,
    - we—us—ours,
    - you—you—yours,
    - he—him—his,
    - she—her—hers,
    - they—them—theirs,
    - it—it—its,
    - who—whom—whose, etc.

44. **The position of Nominative & Accusative:** The <u>Nominative generally comes before the verb</u>, & the <u>Accusative comes after the verb</u>. Hence, in most cases, they are distinguished by the order of words, with exceptions as in the above, and the residual is left for your own sense.
    So, remember: it is said, 'generally it happens', not bound to happen always; as again in the following:
    ○ He is a **_musician_**. [Musician and he— are the same person—both are in the **_Nominative case_**, though 'musician' is placed after the verb; it is not like an action acted upon. It is in the Nominative Case.]

    ○ He listens to a **_musician_**. [Here, musician is in the **_Accusative Case_**; as his activity of 'listening' is acted to the musician.]

45. **Direct & Indirect Object:**
    ✖ Compare-
    ○ Rama gave a **_ball_**. Rama gave <u>Hari </u>a **_ball_**.

    - In each of the sentences, the noun, 'ball' is the object of verb 'gave'.
    - In the 2nd sentence, we are told that 'Hari' is that person whom the ball was given or whom Rama gave a ball.
    - The noun '**Hari**' is called the **Indirect Object**, and '**ball**' is the **Direct Object**.

    - **Definitions:** _An inanimate thing upon which an action is acted upon is said to be **Direct Object**_. We put question '**_What_** 'before a verb to get Direct Object; and,
    - _The animate person or animal becomes the **Indirect Object**_. We put question '**_Whom_**' before a verb to get the Indirect Object.
      ○ What did Rama give?
      ○ Whom did Rama give the ball?

    - **Remember:** <u>Generally, an Indirect object immediately comes after the verb and before the Direct Object</u>; as,
      ○ Please give **_me_** <u>a glass of water</u>. Will you do **_me_** <u>a favor</u>?
      ○ Rama gave **_Hari_**<u>a ball</u>. Fetch **_the boy_** <u>a book</u>.

    - In the above, the bold words are **Indirect Object** & the underlined are **Direct Object**.
    - The above <u>arrangement of words can be reversed with the help of a preposition</u>; like,
      ○ He offered <u>a glass of drink</u> to **_each guest_** present there.
      ○ She handed over <u>the book</u> to **_her teacher_**.
      ○ Ram gave <u>a ball</u> to **_Hari_**. Will you do <u>a favor</u> to **_me (for me)_**?
      ○ I bought <u>a ball</u> for **_Rama_**. Fetch <u>a book</u> for the **_boy_**.
      ○

    Note: _Perhaps, you understand, it (the position of object, before or after) depends on 'how you will use them'._

46. **More about** the **Genitive** or the **Possessive Case of Nouns:**

- ✘ **Examine the sentence:**
  - ▪ This is Rama's umbrella. (Rama's= that belongs to Rama)
  - ▪ Rama's umbrella = an umbrella that belongs to Rama.
- ✘ The form of the Noun, **Rama** *changed to* **Rama's** *to show ownership or possession*. The noun 'Rama's' is therefore said to be in the Possessive or Genitive Case.
- ✘ The Possessive answers the question, **'whose'?**
  - ▪ Whose umbrella? = Rama's
  - ▪ I saw Amitav's house. Whose house? = Amitav's
  - ▪ It was Sharukh's film. Whose film? = Sharukh's

47. **The ways to form the Possessive Case of Nouns:**
- ✘ The Possessive Case of Nouns & the Possessive Pronouns are used to show **that someone has something** or **something belongs to someone. Here, *'possessive'* means *possession*** and that shows connection with another noun. Read the sentences:
  1) Ram's shirt (a shirt which belongs to Ram or Ram who has the shirt; **use of apostrophe S with singular Nouns**);
  2) Girls' Hostel (a hostel where girls live & do study; **use of apostrophe S with plural Nouns**);
  3) Broken legs **of** the chair; (a chair whose legs are broken; **use of 'of'**)
  4) I **have** a pet dog. She has a scooter of her own. (**use of has, have**)
  5) The apartment is mine. (**Possessive Pronoun**)
  6) This is my apartment. (**Possessive Adjective**)
  7) I have to pay school fees. How do you spend Puja holiday? (**Nominal Compound**)

- ✘ **Note:** *You see, there are* **seven** *ways to form 'possessive case' or 'to show possession'.*

48. **The Uses of Possessive Case & Formation:**

- ✘ **Remember:** The Possessive case doesn't always show 'possession'. Besides 'possession', the possessive case of Nouns signifies others too –

  - → **Possession (***by using-'/'s for animate objects***) or to mean 'part of a thing'** (*using 'of' for Inanimate Objects*)**:** Raina's handkerchief (the handkerchief belongs to Raina); Patcoff's building (Patcoff is the owner of the building); Mohsin's Palace, the broken legs of the table, hands of the watch, etc.—denote definitely possessions. But beyond this one, it also denotes—
  - → **Authorship:** Shakespeare's plays = the plays written by Shakespeare; Kalidas' "Sakuntalavyam", Tagore's short-stories; Peter's "Complete English Grammar Book", etc.
  - → **Origin:** A mother's love = the love felt by a mother; A child's simplicity; her love; the book's originality, his purity; their gladness; our sadness, etc.
  - → **Kind or type:** The President's speech = the speech which is delivered by the President. Attend to the teacher's lecture; (*teacher's lecture = the lecture delivered by the teacher*)*, and thus,* the leader's speech; Lata's songs, Manoj's album, etc.
  - → **For Personified Objects:** Nature's Law; India's Heroes; Fortune's Favorite; at Duty's call; at Death's door; for Mercy's sake; to his heart's content; at his wit's end; a boat's crew, the watch's hands, etc.
  - → **Time:** A month's ritual (a ritual which lasts for one month); twenty over's game (a game of twenty over); the day's performance (the performance of the day); ten days' activity or project (a project that goes on for ten days); A week's holiday = a holiday that lasts for one week, etc.
  - → **Place:** Mr. Agarwal's house = a house where Mr. Agarwal lives. (It doesn't need or essential Mr. Agarwal be the owner of the house. He may live there on rent). And thus, Boys' Hostel; Girls' Hostel; Children's Park; etc.
  - → **Distance** or **Closeness:** Two days' walk; A month's journey. My school is not far, but at distance of a stone's throw from here. All happened at his finger's end, and he could do nothing. One hour's distance, two nights' journey, &**others.**
  - → **Space or Weight:** *Please leave a chair's space here; Move a foot's length from me, you smell disgusting!* Give a pound's weight of mustard oil, I'll pay later.

49. **The Possessive of Proper Nouns** or **some Nouns,** *denoting-* **trade, profession, relation** *have some special uses.* They are used like the following (**to short a statement**):
  - o She has gone to **baker's** (*baker's shop*).

- o Tonight, I am dining at my **uncle's** (*uncle's house*).
- o Can you tell me the way to **St. Paul's** (*St. Paul's Church or School, which is popular in that area*)?
- o Would you help me with **Peter's** (*Peter's Complete English Grammar Book*)?
- o I attend Nalanda Vidyapith but you at **B. M's** (*Badar Molla Academy*).

50. ***Avoid the Confusion:*** **Take care of the following Mistakes:**
    ✓I want the defeat of my enemy. (correct)
    ✓I want my enemy's defeat. (Incorrect)
    ✓We are proud of the victory of army. (correct)
    ✓The army's victory. (incorrect)
    ✓The victory of the army—inspired all. (correct)

Again, see the difference:
- ° The Prime Minister's reception in Delhi— it sounds as, the reception, held by the Prime Minister; but,
- ° The reception of the Prime Minister– sounds 'People welcomed him when he entered New Delhi.

Note: So, the use of 'of' & 'apostrophe 's', sometimes, may carry different meanings.

51. **Forming 'Possessive Case of Nouns & Pronouns':**

Chart-1:

How	Examples	
1. By using *apostrophe-s* ('s);	In singular	In plural
	· Om's father; · Nicky's mamma; · Man's eye/cat's paw. · The King of Bhutan's Visit; · The mouse's run to and fro in the room	· Children's Park; · Men's style; · Karim & Salim's bakery. · The Ministry of Bhutan's resignation from the Govt.
2. By using *only apostrophe* (') for words, end with hissing sounds; like— *ce/ss/sh/s.*	· For Conscience' Sake; · For Justice' Sake; · Moses' law; · Goodness' Sake; · Jesus' Sake;	· Boys' School/Gents' club; · The Prime Minister of Mauritus' Speech · The Mice' nuisance in the house, etc.
Note: –('s) or (') –is not used for inanimate objects, except with the following 1) Nouns that denote- <u>Time & Distance:</u>	° A Day's game, ° One month's leave, ° A week's job, ° One hour's distance, ° Two nights' journey,	° = a game for a day; ° = the leave for one month; ° = a job for one week; ° = the distance that takes one hour; ° = a journey that takes two nights.
2) And <u>in Personification:</u> (This happens when men's needs or attributes are thrown upon them, or the things are personified.)	· The country's rights · The Sun's light · Death's jaw	= the rights of the countrymen; = the light from the Sun; = falls to death.

A Day's game: *playing game is the human activity, but not a day's activity;*
One month's leave: leaves taken by human beings, not the month itself';
A week's job: *a job is worked on by an employee for a week; and so as 'One hour's distance', 'Two nights' journey',* ইত্যাদি।
The country's rights = rights are taken by its citizens, not the country itself.
The Sun's light = *it is unique and one; so 'The Sun' is the Proper Noun.*
Death's jaw = Death is the ultimate truth for everyone; it is really special.
   Note: So, leaving like the above examples, use **'of'** for all inanimate objects to form or to show **possession.**

How	Column -1	Column -2
3. *By using 'of' preposition for* most inanimate objects, as already we discussed.	The legs of the chair; The walls of the house; The pages of the dictionary; The charger of my mobile.	The cap of my pen; Cover of the phone; Button of her shirt; The drawer of the table.
	With ('s)/ (')	With 'of
However, for animate objects, *apostrophe-s* ('s), *only apostrophe* (') *and* '*of*'—all are *used.*	The monkey's paw; The child's simplicity; The country's call; The boys' shouting, etc.	The paw of the monkey; The simplicity of the child; The call of the country.
4. To form 'Possession' *by Possessive Pronouns;* as,	The pen is **mine.** The car is **yours.** The bi-cycle is **hers/his.**	The house is **ours.** The gifts are **yours.** These lands are **theirs.**

How	Examples	
5. By Possessive Adjective	This is *my* pen. It is *your* car. It is *her/his* bi-cycle.	This is *our* house. These are *your* gifts. All these are *their* lands.
6. By 'has or have'	I *have* a book. Have you any sense? He *has* his dictionary.	We *have* novels to read. You *have* no manners. They *have* an orchard.
7. By Nominal Compound	° I have to pay *school fees.* ° You wear a *golden chain.* ° We spent *Puja holiday* in Darjeeling. ° She is standing in *rain water.* (in rains) ° The *street dogs* are barking.	° = fees of the school ° = chain of gold/a chain, made of gold ° = holiday for Puja ° = water of rain ° = dogs of the street.

Don't forget
- Generally, possessive noun forms are only used for living beings, or for personified things (when things are considered as living beings to feel, to talk etc.)
  - → Tagore's poetry. Tina's bag, etc.
  - → Nature's cry (may be used taking the Nature as alive and feel sorrow), or 'the cry of Nature)
- However, for inanimate things, to mean a part of, we use '**of**' (not apostrophe S); as the example:
  - → The watch's strap (incorrect)
  - → The strap of the watch. (correct)

Let us write:
- Suppose, you are in the classroom. Look around what can you see. Now make a list and write some lines using the possessive nouns or to mean part of things.

Pronouns in different Cases

We know, Pronouns are words, used in place of Nouns to avoid boredom or repetition of same nouns in the sentence. Besides, pronouns are also used for other purposes in the sentences. We'll study them in the chapter of Pronouns. Here, in the following we only study the different forms of Pronouns in different cases.

Chart-2, the case of pronouns:

The Pronouns in Different Cases			
Subjective/ Nominative	Accusative/ Objective	Possessive/Genitive	
		As determiner/adjective	**As pronouns**
I/we	me/us	My/our	Mine/ours
You/thou	You/thee	Your/thy	Yours/thine
He/she/it/they	Him/her/it/them	His/her/its/their	His/hers/*/Theirs

Chart-3: The same thing, i.e., the case of pronouns in different way, separately as per Person & Number:

Persons	Singular				Plural			
	Nominative	Objective	Possessive		Nominative	Objective	Possessive	
			Pron	Adj			Pron	Adj
1st Person	I	Me	Mine	My	We	Us	Ours	Our
2nd Person	You	You	Yours	Your	You	You	Yours	Your
3rd Person	He She	Him Her	His Hers	His Her	They	Them	Theirs	Their
	It/this /that	It/this /that	*	Its	These/ those	These/ those	*	*

Note: More in the chapter of Pronouns

The Functions of Nouns

52. **The Functions of Nouns:** Through the journey of Case of Nouns or Pronouns, we have learnt the following functions of Nouns—
    1) To form Subject,
    2) To form Direct or Indirect Object,
    3) To form Prepositional Object,
    4) Be a part of An Adverbial Phrase,
    5) Sometimes, to be used as an Adjective in the sentence,
    6) To form Subjective or Objective Complement,
    7) To form a Nominal Compound, and
    8) The Noun to be used in apposition, or to form a 'Phrase in Apposition' which adds meaning to the nearest Noun.

    ➢ (ap-position means 'placing near')

53. **Study the Chart, regarding the Functions of Nouns:**

Functions	Examples
1. To form subject of verb:	**Ram** goes to school. The **cow** has for legs. **Gold** is precious. **A gang of robbers** came there. **Honesty** is the best policy.
2. To form object of verb:	I asked **Ra**m. You bought a **bicycle**.
3. To form object of preposition:	You are speaking to **Rahim.**
4. As case in apposition	P. Sarkar, **a teacher of this school**, passed away.
5. As complement to a noun or pronoun:	Lata was a famous *singer.* We elected Shree Kanta, **the President of the committee**.
6. To be a part of An Adverbial Phrase:	Ram goes to *school.* The child is playing on the *floor.* ('to school' & 'on the floor'- are examples of Adverbial Phrase)
7. To form a Nominal Compound, and	We have no *chalk-duster* in the school. (It is also an Object) They sat beside the *tea-table*. (It is also a part of the adverbial phrase- 'beside the tea-table'.
8. As an Adjective in the sentence:	I met a little *cottage* girl. He is always playing *computer* games. We are *school* teachers.

54. <u>More examples of the functions of Nouns and necessary Illustrations:</u>

1) **To form subject of a verb** [*Ask verb with 'who' or 'what' to get subject of the verb*]
   a. **Ram** goes to school.
   b. The **cow** has for legs.
   c. **Gold** is precious.
   d. **A gang of robbers** came there.
   e. **Honesty** is the best policy.
   f. **Peter** is a worse writer.
   g. **Peter** loves India and he is an Indian.
   h. **The dog** jumps over the table.

2) **To form object of a verb** [Ask the verb with '**whom**' or '**what**', '**to whom**' or '**to what**', '**for whom**' and '**for what**' to get object of the verb.]
   a. I asked **Ra**m where he had gone yesterday.
   b. You bought a **bicycle**.
   c. Rumi sang a *classical song*.
   d. The Royal Bengal Tiger hunted the *deer*.
   e. I wrote *two novels* that didn't run well.
   f. What have you given to *him*?
   g. I gave *her* a *mango pickle*.
   h. She gifted *me* with a *gift*.

3) **To form objects of a preposition** (Simply when a preposition comes between the verb and object.):
   a. You are speaking to **Rahim.** (to whom)
   b. The bicycle belongs to **Nicky.** (to whom)
   c. The hunter aimed at <u>the bird</u>. (What was aimed at?)
   d. I didn't agree with **him**. (Whom didn't you agree with?)
   e. Why did she laugh at **me**? (Whom did she laugh at?)
   f. She was honoured <u>with</u> *the prize*. (What with was she honored?)
   g. She bought a cycle <u>for</u> *her son*.
   h. She sang heartily <u>to</u> the *audience*.
   i. It was bought <u>for</u> my *uncle*.
   j. <u>For sake of</u> *country*, the soldiers stood there standstill.
   k. Everyone is not gifted <u>with</u> *intelligence*.
   l. He is praised <u>for</u> *his wisdom* in the world.
   m. She cried <u>for</u> *no reason*.
   n. We are sorry <u>for</u> *nothing*.

❖ Prepositional Object is often called an Indirect object.
❖ To get an Indirect object we ask question to the verb with '**to what/whom**' & '**for what/whom**', etc.

4) Noun to be used in apposition/ the Phrase in Apposition: (It adds meaning to the nearest Noun.):

a) P. Sarkar, **_a teacher of this school_**, passed away last week.
b) Peter, **_a grammarian_**, was always poor in English.
c) Napoleon, **_the great ruler of Greek_**, invaded India centuries ago.
d) Shakespeare, **_a great dramatist of England_**, wrote thirty-seven plays.
e) Kalidas, **_a Sanskrit man of letters_**, wrote masterpieces in his life time.
f) Akbar, **_the invader_**, was the emperor of Mughal empire.
g) Ram, **_the God_**, killed Ravana, **_the king of Sri Lanka_**.
h) Hanuman, **_a great devotee and God himself_**, jumped over the Indian Ocean to reach Sri Lanka, **_the capital of King Ravana_**.

5) As Subjective & Objective Complement: [Complement is sometimes adjective equivalent or adverbial, besides other nominal words.]

a) We elected you **_the member of parliament_**.
b) He made you **_captain_** of the class.
c) The Indian voters voted Mr. Narendra Modi to make him **_the Prime Minister of India_**.
d) We selected you **_our spokesperson_** in the coming meeting.
e) Don't hurry to make him **_your leader_**.
f) We make some foolish **_our makers,_** is the bad luck of our nation.
g) Akbar made Birbal **_his adviser_** in his court.
h) We appoint you **_our cook_** for the year.
i) We appoint you as **_a teacher_** of the school.
j) I choose you **_my father_** to act before the Principal.

55. **Study the following sentences:**

   ° _Rahul_, the _captain_ of the Indian Team, who made fifty runs, was a dependable _cricketer_.
   ° _Rahul_ is a _cricketer_. He was the _captain_ of the Indian Team.

   ✗ From the above sentence & sentences, the words— **_Rahul, captain_** & **_cricketer_**—the three words refer to the same person.

   ✗ The above three italic words are Nouns, and all <u>these Nouns are used in the **Nominative Case**</u>. So, a <u>subject</u>, <u>a noun in apposition</u> as well as a <u>subjective complement</u>—all are used in Nominative case of Nouns.

   ✗ As the **_cricketer_**, **_captain_** from the second and third sentences, refers to the same person, Rahul, as the words returns back to the subject to describe (the subject of the sentence), so why, it is said to be the **Subjective Complement**.

   ✗ **Note:** But remember, complement may also be objective, and a case in apposition may be used with an object, then they are definitely said to be in the Objective or Accusative Case. Then, what is better to say, the case of _the Complement or the Phrase in <u>Apposition, are always defined according to the nearest Noun they add meaning_</u>.

56. **So, what we learnt?**

   ⇒ A Noun in Apposition or a Complement must be in the same Case as the Noun which it explains or adds meaning.

   ⇒ **Now, note the following Examples:**

   1) Kabir, _the great reformer_, was a weaver.
   2) Yesterday I met your uncle, _the doctor_.
   3) Have you seen the artist's drawing, _Ganguli_?

   Or

   4) Have you seen Ganguli, _the artist's drawing_?

   → In sentence-1, the noun in apposition which is '_the great reformer_' –is in the **Nominative Case.**
   → In sentence-2, the noun in apposition which is '_the doctor_' –is in the **Accusative Case.**

→ In sentence-3, the noun in apposition which is *'Ganguli'* denotes the *'drawing'* which is in objective case of noun; but the word *'artist's'* in both sentences are in the **Possessive Case** in the sentence.

The Compound Nouns

57. Sometimes two or more words combining together with or without hyphen (-) form words functioning of a Noun, they are called **Compound Nouns** or **'Nominal Compounds'**.
We will discuss here, **how 'Compound Nouns' are formed,** including some **'Compound Pronouns'**.

Sl. no	Combination of-	Compound Nouns
1	Noun+Noun	Motor-cycle, steam engine, moon light, color TV, blood pressure, book binder, language teacher, founder member, fighter plane; sportsman, batsman; Children's game, lion's paw, rat's tail, etc.
2	Noun+ Verb	Bus-stop, rain fall, earth quake, etc.
3	Noun+ Gerund	Sight-seeing, boat racing,
4	Noun+Preposition	Lock up, passerby,
5	noun+noun+noun	Word formation exercise,
6	Noun+Adj.+Noun	Fire-resistant chemicals, scratch resistant glass/fiber;
7	N +Participle +N	Tea producing areas, power driven engine, etc.
8	Pronoun+ Noun	He-goat, she-goat, self-respect, self-confidence, etc.
9	Pronoun+ '-self' & Pronoun+ '-selves'	Myself, yourself, herself, himself, itself, ourselves, yourselves, themselves = (These are called Compound Pronouns, used as Reflexive & Emphatic Pronouns.)
10	Adjective+Noun	Black board, postal service, high school, etc.
11	Adj+Adj+Noun	Blue-black ink/color
12	Participle+Noun	Washing machine, dining table, flying fish, etc.
13	Adjective+Verb	Short-cut (an easy way)
14	Adjective+Adverb	Left over (cancelled things)
15	Verb+ Verb	Hearsay (a saying that is heard)
16	Verb+Adjective	Hold-all (a kind of bag)
17	Verb+Adverb	Break down, know-how (vocational knowledge);
18	Verb+Preposition	Make-up, lay out (map/design), lay-off, etc.
19	Adverb+Noun	Over load, after thought,
20	Adverb+Verb	Output, Outlet, etc.

5. Pronouns: Definition, Classification & Functions

58. Read the following two paragraphs and note which passage sound better and which seem short, a bit though. Underline the words which are replaced.

Last month, Krishna asked his mother Mrs. Gomes if *Mrs. Gomes* could buy *Krishna* a dog. *Krishna* had always a wanted a dog named Johny. *Johny* like meat. *Johny* runs fast. *Johny* barks when a stranger does pass the alley. *Johny* is a loyal animal however.

Last month, Krishna asked his mother Mrs. Gomes if **she** could buy **him** a dog. **He** had always a wanted a dog named Johny. **It** like meat. **It** runs fast. **It** barks when a stranger does pass the alley. **It** is a loyal animal however.

59. **Read the sentences:**
   - *Nihanth* is a little boy.
   - *He* reads in class-I.

   What is Subject in Sentence-1? = Nihanth
   What is subject in sentence-2? = He

Note: 'Nihanth' & 'He'— both words denote the same person. The word, 'He' is used in place of <u>Nihanth, the Noun.</u>

Read again:

   - *White Home* is a two-storied building.
   - *It* is white in color.

Which are the subjects in the above sentences? = 'White Home' & 'It'.
'It' is used instead of the Noun, 'White Home' to avoid repetition of the name.

['**Pronoun**' stands for '**for-a-noun**']

DEFINTION:

A Pronoun is a word that is used instead of a Noun.
Or
The substitute word for a noun—is called a Pronoun.

   - <u>Ritika</u> is a girl.
   - *She* reads in class V.

60. **A Pronoun acts both the subject and the object in the sentence.**
   - *She* reads in class V.
   - *I* gave *her* a book to read.

In sentence-1, there is only subject, '*She*;' but the sentence-2, has both Subject, 'I' & Object, 'her'.

Thus, a Pronoun forms both a subject & an object in a sentence.

61. **The Pronouns are grouped into the following classes:**
   1. Personal Pronoun—I, we, he, she, it, etc.
   2. Possessive Pronoun—mine, ours, yours, etc.
   3. Reflexive Pronoun—myself, yourself, itself, etc.
   4. Emphatic Pronoun—myself, yourself, itself, etc.
   5. Demonstrative Pronoun—this, that, such, so
   6. Relative Pronoun—who, which, what, that
   7. Interrogative Pronoun—who, which, what
   8. Indefinite Pronoun—one, any, some, they

9. Distributive Pronoun— each, either, neither
10. Reciprocal Pronoun—each other, one another

❖ Of the above, the first four—Personal, Possessive, Reflexive & Emphatic may be put into **Personal Group of Pronouns,**

❖ While the next three, i.e., Demonstrative, Relative, Interrogative may be put into the **Definite Group of Pronouns,** and

❖ The last three, namely Indefinite, Distributive & Reciprocal Pronouns—fall to the **Indefinite Group of Pronouns.**

Personal Group of Pronouns

62. The Personal Group of Pronouns includes-

→ Personal Pronouns,
→ Possessive Pronouns,
→ Reflexive Pronouns
&
→ Emphatic Pronouns

▪ If you carefully notice, you will see, most of these pronouns refer to persons; as name instead of persons, the possessive pronoun forms of persons that shows possession (and sometimes though as part of things), and the pronoun forms which reflex (i.e., shows mirror to Nouns or Personal Pronouns) or used to emphasis a personal pronoun to be used before in the sentence.

63. **PERSONAL PRONOUNS**

▪ The pronouns that stand for three persons;
→ The person **speaking**—1st person,
→ The person **spoken to**—2nd person,
→ The person **spoken of**—3rd person,
- are called Personal Pronouns. Besides, Personal Pronoun has **number** *(singular & plural),* **case & gender** *(he, she & it).*

▪ **I, we, me, us, you, he, she, it, they, him, her, them**, etc. are the examples of Personal Pronouns.

▪ Like Nouns, Personal Pronouns are used in the three Cases:
➢ **Nominative-** which are used as Subjects— I, we, you, he, she, it & they;
➢ **Accusative-** do the functions of an Object— me, us, you, him, her, it & them; &
➢ **Possessive-** that denote ownership or possession— mine, ours, yours, hers, his, it's, theirs.

↓ Read the Examples

Pronouns In Nominative	Pronouns in Genitive	Pronouns in Possessive
1) **I** am Bipradip.	1) Give **me** a glass of water.	1) The ball is **mine**.
2) **We** are Indians.	2) Let **us** go there.	2) Those boxes are **ours**.
3) **You** are an American.	3) What did she tell **you**?	3) That box is **yours**.
4) **He** is a pop singer.	4) Don't give **him** lecture.	4) The suitcase is **his**. (*The suitcase belongs to him. -accusative*)
5) **She** is a musician.	5) Ram gave **her** a pencil.	5) The pink bag is **hers**. (*The pink bag belongs to her. -accusative*)
6) **It** is a dog.	6) The ball hit **it** in violent force.	6) ('It'-*is not used in Possessive Case*)
7) **They** are public; they can do anything.	7) Don't ask **them** anything to do.	7) All bags & luggage are **theirs**. (*Luggage—is Uncountable Noun*)

64. Personal Pronouns are used as subject of a verb. They are doers. They are called subject pronouns.

✕ **I, we, you, he, she, it**, and **they** are the subject pronouns.
✕ Lisa likes cat. **She** has four cats.
✕ Mrs. Sharma is a good teacher. **He** is also a good player.

65. <u>Personal Pronouns are used as object of a verb. They denote to the receivers of the action. They are called object pronouns.</u>
   - ✕ **<u>Me, us, you, him, her, it, them</u>** <u>are the object pronouns.</u>
   - ✕ Lisa likes cats. She likes to feed **them**.
   - ✕ Om loves Nicky. He offered **him** his biscuits.

66. **Persons, Number & Gender of Pronouns:**

Personal Pronouns	**Subject Pronouns**		**Object Pronouns**	
	Singular Number	Plural Number	Singular	Plural
First person	I	We	Me	Us
Second person	You		You	
Third person	He	They	Him	Them
	She		Her	
	It		It	

- ✕ Personal Pronouns stand for three persons- (*1st, 2nd & 3rd*).
  - • **The person speaking**- 1st person (I, We);
  - • **The person spoken to**- 2nd person (you);
  - • **The person spoken of**- 3rd person (She, He, It & they).

- ✕ Like Nouns, Pronouns have also numbers-Singular & Plural; but ***about gender, only 3rd person singular number has three***:
  - → He-male
  - → She-female &
  - → It- neuter gender.

- ✕ **'This & that'** of Demonstrative Pronoun are treated as <u>Singular Number</u>, whereas, **these & those**—are treated as <u>Plural Number</u>.

- ✕ Others like- ***who, which, whom, what***—the Relative & Interrogative Pronouns are <u>treated as both Singular or Plural Number</u> in the sentences as situation demands.

67. **About 'It', the 'Impersonal Pronoun'**

- ✕ In old English Grammar Book, 'it' was defined as Impersonal Pronoun. *As a Pronoun, **'it'** mostly refers to or is used for impersonal; like to refer the followings-*

  - a. inanimate objects,
  - b. animals,
  - c. group nouns,
  - d. a word, phrase, clause, even a sentence,
  - e. an idea, condition, situation,
  - f. cause, effect, or
  - g. as the introductory or provisional subject or preparatory object,

  ➖So, it was called an '**Impersonal Pronoun**'.

- ✕ However, it is grouped today with the 'Personal Group of Pronouns'.

- ✕ **It' has many specific uses. Read them carefully in the following charts.**

'It' is used to refer-	Examples:
1. Inanimate Objects/Things, mostly with the 'be' verbs (**is/was/will be**— as the third person singular number) to denote-	a) Time: **It's** ten o'clock. It is Monday. b) Place: Kolkata is my birth place. It is very crowded. c) Weather: **It's** raining now. It's very cold/hot today. d) Temperature: **It's** 30 degrees Centigrade. e) Distance: **It** is ten miles to reach the station. f) Situation: **It** was horrible when the accident took place. /**It's** awful! /Isn't **it** lovely here! g) Things: Is **it** your ring? / **It** is my pen.
2. Animals	**It** is a **dog. The tiger** has bit **its** leg.
3. Baby or unknown gender	**The baby** has broken **its** doll. **It** is crying. **The cub** is crying for **its** mother.
4. Group or Collective Noun	**The Govt.** has decided **its** policy. The army fought a fight. However, **it** lost the battle.
5. For a Phrase/Clause /Sentence; sometimes to give emphasis	You, <u>reading not well </u>will regret **it**. **(For it)** <u>**If you don't read now,**</u> you'll regret **it**. <u>**You are beautiful.**</u> You are boast of **it**. **Swimming is good**, **it** is good for health. **To error is human, to forgive divine**; you should remember **it**.
6. As Introductory to 'impersonal verbs'	**It looks** very fine. **It seems** that he is mistaken. **It appears** to be quite insulting. / **It rains**.

7. As Introductory or **Dummy subjects** of **infinitive/-ing phrase/clause:**	**Infinitive:**
	Itis not easy <u>**to make friends.**</u>
	    It is good for health <u>**to exercise daily**</u>.
	Phrase with '-ing' form:
	    Itis no use <u>**telling him that**</u>.
	    It was nice <u>**seeing you again**</u>.
	Clause:
	    Itis impossible **that he will come**.
	    It does not concern me **what you think**.

8. **As a Preparatory Object**—when there is an adjective connected with the object.	I made **it** <u>clear</u> **that I disagreed**. I find **it** <u>difficult </u>**to talk to her in the meeting**.

Chart-2

9. In Cleft Sentences (cleft means divided) as Introductory to <u>**give emphasis on some part —may be**</u>	Dip bought an old car last week with one lac rupees.	**It was Dip** who bought an old car last week. **It was last week** that/when Dip bought an old car. **It was an old car** that Dip bought last week. **It was only with one lac rupees** that Dip bought an old car last week.

| a noun, pronoun, adj. or adv., phrase or to one idea of the sentence often with 'wh'/'that' subordinate clauses | 1) The wolf jumped over the wall in the evening. 2) I am struggling my best with the intention. 3) For this he failed in the exam. 4) You can't do it without this way. 5) He looks after his father. 6) You should not do like me. | 1) **Time:** It was evening when the wolf jumped over the wall. 2) **Purpose:** It is why I am struggling my best. 3) **Cause:/Effect:** It was the reason that he failed in the exam. 4) **Condition:** It is the only way that you can do it. 5) **Comparison:** It is he who looks after his father. 6) **Contrast:** It should not be done by you if you are not me. 7) **For emphasis Pronoun:** ✗ It was you who did so. ✗ It was I who am to blame. |

68. **Possessive Pronouns:** Pronouns that denote ownership or possession of persons [that stands for possessive case of nouns].
   - ✗ The Possessive Pronoun **has double functions**—the function of an adjective & a pronoun. In form they have slight difference:

Possessive Adjectives	Possessive Pronouns
My	mine
Our	ours
Your/thy	Yours/thine
His	his
Her	hers
Their	theirs
Its	* (not in use)

69. **Possessive Pronouns & Adjectives:**
   - ✗ *My, our, your, his, her, its, their*—are called **Possessive Adjectives**, as these forms of Pronouns are used with Nouns & do the function of an adjective to add meaning to the Noun. Read the examples:

Possessive Adjectives	Possessive Pronouns
This is **my** book.	The book is **mine**.
That is **our** house	The house is **ours**.
This is **your** bag.	This bag is **yours**.
It is **his/her** pen.	The pen belongs to **his/hers**. (*Pointing to the person*)
Its parts have been fallen somewhere.	(*Not in use*)
These are **their** tasks.	These tasks are **theirs**. (The tasks are for them/they will do the tasks)

70. **Compound Personal Pronouns: When** *'-self' is added to— **my, your, he, she, it**; and '-selves'; to— **our, your, them,** we get new forms of Personal Pronouns. These new forms of Pronouns are called **Compound Personal Pronouns**.

    These Compound Pronouns are *used in two ways* in the sentences, named— **Reflexive** & **Emphatic**.
    - I read a book *myself*.
    - I feed *myself*.
    - Nicky *himself* walks on.
    - Nicky hurt *himself*.

71. In **Reflexive Pronouns**, Subjects & Objects denote same person, whereas, **Emphatic Pronouns** of '-self or –selves' do not form Objects; they are used for sake of emphasis on the Subject itself.

- **Reflexive Pronouns:** When the action done by the subject, turns back (reflects upon the subject), the compounds are known as Reflexive Pronouns. The words— *myself, ourselves,* yourself, *yourselves, himself, herself, itself,* and *themselves* are the examples of Reflexive Pronouns.

    - **Examples: -**

a) My brother hurt *himself*.
b) John was looking at *himself* in the mirror.
c) We love *ourselves*. They teach *themselves.*
d) The computer destroys *itself* by its program.
e) Be careful not to cut *yourself* with that knife.
f) Our cat washes *itself* after every meal.
g) Bears like to rub *themselves* against a tree.
h) The bird washed *itself* by splashing in a puddle.
i) We exerted *ourselves*.
j) *Pray, do not inconvenience* ***yourself***.
k) The players train every day to keep *them* fit. (them is used in place of 'themselves', as adj. cum complement 'fit' is used after it.)

72. **Function of Reflexive:**

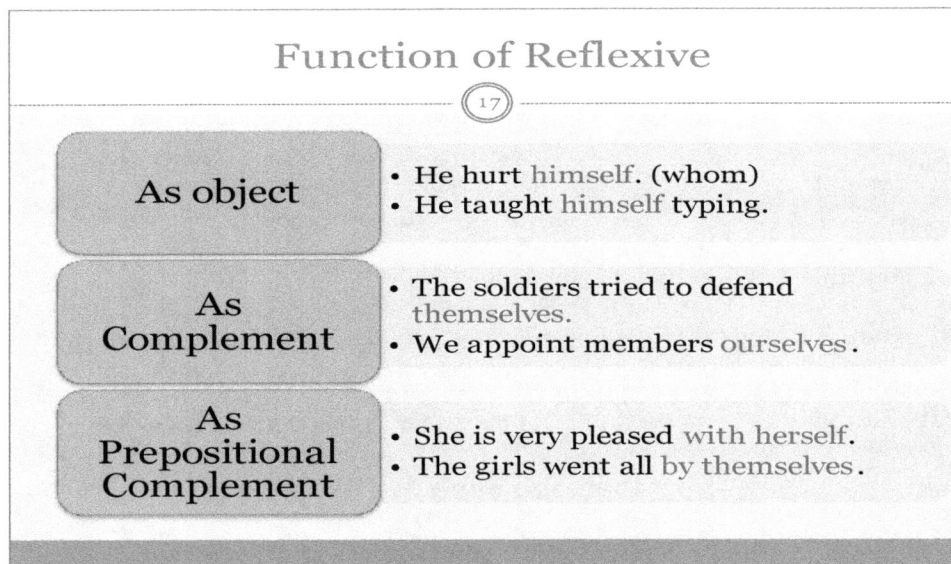

Function of Reflexive

(17)

As object	• He hurt himself. (whom) • He taught himself typing.
As Complement	• The soldiers tried to defend themselves. • We appoint members ourselves.
As Prepositional Complement	• She is very pleased with herself. • The girls went all by themselves.

73. Sometimes in poetry, a simple pronoun may be used reflexively; as,

*'Now lay **me** down to sleep,*
*And think **me** what's going on*
In her world.
*'She soothes **her** & does muse to welcome,*
More two hours, two days, O friend;
Passed two decades in desolation!'

—Peter

* The word **'self'**, with or without **'own'**, is sometimes <u>used as a Noun to refer any person, singular number, of the nearest one</u>; as,
  - → He cares for nothing but **self**. (himself)
  - → You think much of **self**. (yourself)
  - → **Self, self, self**! That's all you ever think about! (yourself)

74. **Emphatic Pronouns:** 'Emphatic Pronouns' do not make **objects**; they are used **to give emphasis** merely <u>on the subject itself</u>, so why they are called **Emphatic** *[to give emphasis]* **Pronouns**.

    * Examples.
    a) I **myself** saw the entire episode.
    b) We **ourselves** visited there.
    c) You do the work **yourself**.
    d) My brother <u>built</u> this computer **himself**.
    e) Ridhima **herself** did the project in time.
    f) They objected it **themselves**.
    g) We baked the cake by **ourselves**.
    h) Come in, everybody, and find **yourselves** a seat.
    i) The children cleaned their room all by **themselves**.

75. **Reflexive VS Emphatic:**

    * Reflexive
    1) Reflexive pronouns are *generally placed after a verb or a preposition*.
    2) Thus, it **forms an object** to the verb or preposition.
    3) It <u>completes the sense</u> of the sentence.

    * Emphatic
    1) But Emphatic pronouns *are placed after nouns or pronouns* and
    2) It **reinforces its.**
    3) It only <u>put stress on its</u> **subject or object**.

PRONOUN CHART					
		Personal Pronouns	Possessive Adjective	Possessive Pronouns	Reflexive or Emphatic
Persons		Subject Object			
1st Person	Singular	I Me	My	Mine	myself
	Plural	We Us	Our	Ours	ourselves
2nd person	Singular	You You	Your	Yours	yourself
	Plural				yourselves
3rd person	Singular	He/she/it Him/her/it	His/her/its	His/hers/*	Himself/herself/itself
	Plural	They Them	Their	Theirs	themselves

Definite Group of Pronouns

76. Definite Group of Pronoun includes-
    a) Demonstrative,
    b) Relative &
    c) Interrogative Pronouns

DEFINITE GROUP PRONOUNS

DEMONSTRATIVE	• Because they demonstrate or point out something near or far. • This, that, these, those [used as both-determiners & pronouns] & such, so etc.
RELATIVE	• The relative pronouns are those that begins /introduces relative clauses. • Who, whom, what, which, whose, that, as, but (as- who/which, who/which no), whoever, whichever, whatsoever, whosoever.
INTERROGATIVE	• For asking/making questions. (They are also called wh-pronouns for w & h used either initially or within.) • who, whom (are used only as pronouns, while) when, where, why, how (also used as adverbs) & what, which, whose (also as determiners)

77. **Demonstrative Pronouns (5): Demonstrative** pronouns, as we said, are <u>used to point out things- far or near</u>; **at hand or far**; and denoting something mentioned earlier, in the preceding clause or sentences. The words- this, that, these, those, such & so —are examples of Demonstrative Pronouns.

→ 'This' with its plural number 'these' refers to 'what is close at hand & nearest to the person or the speaker'.
→ 'That' with its plural number 'those' refers to 'what is over there, farther away & more remote.'

1) **This** is my desk. **That** is yours.
2) **This** is your house. **That** is Rahul's.
3) **These** are my books and **those** are yours.
4) **This** is a present from my uncle.
5) **These** are merely excuses.
6) *That* is the Red Fort. (In Nominative Case)
7) The ball hit *this* tree and bounced over *that* wall.
   ▪ *(Here, this and that are Demonstrative Adjectives)*
8) The ball hit *this* and bounced over *that*. (*Pointing a thing close at hand and another of far away, of at a distance- Demonstrative Pronoun in Accusative Case*)
9) The river flowed over *these* and caused ruins; you can see *those* (signs of ruins) everywhere. (these & those, both are in accusative case)

Note: This & that –are not used in possessive case.

78. **The uses of Demonstrative Pronouns:**

→ 'That' with its plural number 'those' is also *used to avoid the repetition of the preceding Noun*; as,

1) The **climate** of Belgium is like *that* of Pune. (Here, 'that' denote 'the climate')
2) The **streets** of the city are worse than *those* of Balurghat. ('those' denotes the 'streets')
3) Our **soldiers** are better than *those* of our enemies. ('those' denotes 'soldiers')
4) The **rivers** of India are longer than *those* of Sri Lanka. ('those' denotes 'the rivers')
5) Malda **mangoes** are better than *those* of Balurghat.
6) Balurghat **Local Administration** is better than *that* of Malda.
7) My **views** are quite in accordance with *those* of the University Commission.
8) There is no **period** in ancient Indian history so glorious than *that* of the Guptas. [do not write, 'as the Guptas'; that= the **glorious period**.]

→ When two things which have been already mentioned are referred to— '**this**' refers to 'the thing last mentioned'; '*that*' to the thing first mentioned'; as,

58

1) Virtue & vice offer themselves for your choice; 'this' (i.e., vice) leads to misery, that (i.e., virtue) to happiness.
2) Alcohol & tobacco are both injurious; this (tobacco) is no less than that (alcohol).
3) Lila & Sheila, both are good; but this is better than that. (or 'the latter is better than the former.') [*if we can use, 'This is my uncle, that is my aunt'—here too, we can use this & that for persons.*]

→ In a compound sentence— '**such**' refers to/is used in place of 'any name of action' (implied in the verb itself of the preceding statement) or a Noun; '**so**' denotes almost same, but reference to the preceding Noun only; as,
    1) I may have *offended*, but **such** was not my intention. [such=being offended]
    2) He was the *representative of the king*, and as **such** they honored him. (As being representative of king) (being the representative of the king)
    3) **Such** was my friend. **So** was her father. (They hint to a before statement; though they are not mentioned here.)
    4) I am a *teacher*. **So,** are you all here? ('So' denotes 'teachers')
    5) The *stranger* is welcomed as **such**. (Such- as a stranger/guest)
    6) He is the *councilor*, **so** was his father. ('so' is used in place of 'the councilor; used in Nominative Case)
    7) She is the *National Level dancer*, **so** was her mother. (so = the national level dancer, in Nominative Case)

79. **Read the sentence:** *'So,* your father is a singer.'
    ▪ Here, '**so**' is a **Conjunction**; used to introduce a comment or question; like,
        a) 'So, let's see'.
        b) 'So, what will you do now?'
        c) 'But he is poor.'
        d) 'But, will he go?' etc.
                '**So**' is also used as an Adverb; as, 'Don't look so angry.'

○**Note:**

Remember: Some adverbs like, '**here**' & '**there**' are also used to denote *'a thing of close at hand* & to mean *'a thing over there, farther away, at a distance*; as,

a) **Here is the book.** (*'Here' denotes the book is close at hand; it denotes place and position of the book; but it is not used in place of a noun. It is not the subject, though apparently looks so. Actually, the subject of the sentence is 'book' which has been used after the verb, 'is'. Remember, 'denoting place' is the function of an Adverb- The book is here.*)
b) **There is the pen.** (*'There' denotes the pen at a distance, a little far away. 'There' also denotes position & does the 'function of an Adverb- The pen is there.*)
c) **Here is the novel, you lent me to read.** (*Thus, adverbs may be used at the beginning of the sentence to give emphasis on the word.*)

      Note: *here or there denotes position of the things or persons;* **this** or **that** *denotes the things themselves.*

80. **Relative or Conjunctive Pronoun (6):**

○ Read the following sentences:

→ I met Ram. Ram had just returned.
→ I have found the pen. I lost the pen.
→ Here is the book. You lent me to read.

○ Let us now combine each of the pair of sentences into one:

→ I met Ram **who** had just returned.
→ I have found the pen **which** I lost.
→ Here is the book **that** you lent me to read.

○ Now, let's discuss what works done by the bold italic words in the sentences:

→ In sentence-1, the word, '**who**' is used in place of Ram (*which is the function of a Pronoun*) and at the same time, it has joined the two sentences (*which is the function of a Conjunction.*)

→ In the 2nd sentence, the word, **'which'** refers to the pen itself that joins the two clauses.
→ In the 3rd, the word, **'that'** points to its preceding Noun, 'book' & joins...

○Thus, they have done double works- the function of a **Pronoun** and the function of a **Conjunction**; so why, such Relative Pronouns are sometimes termed as **'Conjunctive Pronouns';** and they are called **'Relative'** as the Pronouns refers or relates some *Antecedent Nouns*; like, 'Ram', 'pen' & 'book', etc.

81. **Forms of Relative Pronouns:** Like Personal Pronouns, Relative Pronouns have three cases. Study the following chart:

Nominative	• **'Who'**-singular or plural & used in both gender- male or female. • This is the boy **who** works hard. • These are the girls **who** worked hard for the program.	**Note-1:** The Relative Pronoun *'who'* has different Forms for Accusative & Genitive Case. **'Who'** is used in both singular & plural number; *__used for persons only__* & as both, male or female.
Accusative	• **'Whom'** • This is the man **whom** everybody likes. • These are the girls **whom** you asked to come.	
Genitive	• **'Whose'** • This is the young man **whose** projects won great compliments. • Those are the boys **whose** activities defamed the Institution.	

FORMS OF RELATIVE PRONOUNS

Note-1:
➢ The Relative Pronoun **'who'** has different Forms for Accusative & Genitive Case, as shown in the chart above.
➢ **'Who'** is used in both singular & plural number; *__used for persons only__* & both as male & female.

82. **Use Of Who**
→ Blessed is he who has found his work.
→ He prayeth best who loveth best.
→ He who hesitates is lost.
→ He never fails who die in a great cause.
→ They are slaves who dare not be.

Note-2: The Relative Pronoun, **'which'** has the same form in Nominative & Accusative Case, and for Genitive, we use 'whose';

83. **Use Of Which**
➢ *'Which' is used for animals, or for things* without life.
➢ 'Which' is used in both numbers-singular & plural.
➢ Like 'it' which *may also refer to a sentence or clause going before*; as,
→ This is the house **which** belongs to my uncle.
→ The house **which** my dad-built cost him more than sixty lakhs.
→ A triangle **whose** three sides are equal is called an equilateral triangle.
→ The moment **which** is lost is lost forever.
→ The books **which** help you most are those which make you think most.
→ He said he saw me there, **which** is a lie. (Which denotes the preceding clause
→ She is here, **which** is fortunate.

84. **Defining & Non-defining Method**

❖ Relative Pronouns, when *defines more clearly the antecedent,* it is called **restrictive** or **defining method** of using Relative Pronouns; as,
   a) The <u>man</u> **who** has cheated me was arrested yesterday.
   b) The <u>book</u> **which** you see on the table cost me three thousand rupees.
   c) My <u>brother</u> **who** is a doctor has gone to America. (When defining, it means the brother who is a doctor; so, the speaker might have more brothers, is the implication.)

❖ Relative Pronouns, when *gives some additional information about the antecedent rather than define it,* it is called **continuative** or **non-defining method** of using Relative Pronoun & such clauses are separated from the main clause by commas; as,
   a) The teacher sent for the boy, **who (and he)** came at once
   b) I gave him a rupee, **which (and it)** was all I had with.
   c) My brother, **who is a doctor,** has gone to America. (Used as the case in apposition, giving information about my only brother—is the implication.)

➢ **To be noted,** this use is limited to formal English in writing only; in spoken English or informal; it is sometimes difficult to distinguish the difference.

85. **Use of Whose**

❖ The possessive form of 'who', '**whose**' is used in all genders, used in <u>speaking of persons</u>, <u>animal</u>s & <u>also things without life</u>; as,

→ The sun, whose rays give life to earth, is regarded by some persons as a god. (Non-defining method has been used, for everybody knows there is only one sun. This method has been used to give information of the sun, but not to define the Sun more clearly.)

→ This is the question whose solution has baffled philosophers of all ages. (Solution of the particular question; so, the 'defining or restrictive' method has been used.)

86. **Use Of That**

The Relative Pronoun, **'that'** is used in both, Singular & Plural and also in Nominative & Accusative Case <u>in the same form</u>, and it has no Genitive form. That is used for persons & things.
   1) Take anything **that** you like. *(It is at the same time both-singular & plural - thing or things, used in the Accusative Case.)*
   2) He **that** is content is rich. *(that= in which he, used in the Accusative Case)*
   3) They **that** touch will be defiled. *(that= whatever, singular & plural & in Accusative)* [defiled-contaminated/filthy]

   4) **That** he will go is miserable! *(In Nominative Case)*
   6) I know the house **that** he lives in.
   8) I have lost the watch **that** you gave me.

   10) All **that** I said had no effect on him.

   12) All is not gold **that** glitters.
   14) Who am I **that** I should object?
   16) The wisest man **that** ever lived made mistakes.

   5) This is the boy I told you of.

   7) Uneasy lies the head **that** wears a crown.
   9) The crowd **that** gathered cheered him to the echo of his name.
   11) He was the most eloquent speaker **that** I ever met.
   13) Man is the only animal **that** can talk.
   15) What is it **that** troubles you so much?
   17) This is the best **that** we can do.

87. **Use of What**

The Relative Pronoun '<u>What' refers to 'things' only</u>. It is used only as singular, no plural it has; and has the same form in the Nominative & Accusative Case. It does not have Genitive. 'What' without antecedent means '*that which*'/ '*the thing which*'/'*the man who*'; as,
   1) **What** has happened is not clear.
   2) I say **what** I mean. / I mean **what** I say.
   3) He failed in **what** he attempted.
   4) **What** (That which) can't be cured must be endured.
   5) **What** is done can't be undone.
   6) **What** man (the man who) has done can do it.
   7) **What** is meat for us, poison to you. This is the difference friend, between I and you.

8) Catch **what** (the thing which) I am going to throw in few seconds.
9) Give heed to **what** I say.
10) **What** I have written, I have written.
11) He found **what** he was looking for.

88. Relative Pronouns that show 'comparison' & 'contrast'.

✖ Relative Pronouns, besides joining sentences or clauses, introduces relative clauses. There are some Relative Pronouns which are used to compare or contrast. These Pronouns are —*as, such as, suchlike, the same as, as...as, & but.* Of these, *as, such as, suchlike, the same as* means '*of the same kind already mentioned or saying' / 'like';* as,

1) Tears **such as** (like) angels weep burst forth.
2) These mangoes are not **such as** (of the same kind) I bought yesterday.
3) There is no **such** thing **as** a free lunch.
4) **Such** advice **as** he was given, has proved almost worthless.
5) He is **such** a man **as** I honor. (How was he as a man?)
6) We have never had **such** a time **as** the present (has).
7) His answer was **such as** I expected him to give.
8) My trouble is the **same as** yours (is).
9) This is not the **same as** that (is).
10) I collected **as** many specimens **as** I could find.

❏ illustration:

• In sentence-1, 'such as angels weep' the clause is describing the noun, 'tears'.
• In sentence-2, 'such as I bought yesterday', the clause is describing 'these mangoes' of the principal clause.
• In sentence-3, 'as a free lunch', the clause is describing the noun phrase, 'such thing' of the principal clause.
• In sentence-4, 'as he was given' is describing the noun, 'advice'.
• In sentence-5, 'as I honor' is describing the man.
• In sentence-6, 'as the present has' is describing the 'time', a noun.
• In sentence-7, 'as I expected him' is describing 'his answer', the noun phrase.
• In sentence-8, 'as yours' is describing the noun 'trouble'.
• In sentence-9, 'as that is', describing - 'this is' in the negative sense.
• In sentence-10, 'as I could find' is describing the collection (or the number of specimens).

89. Use of 'but'

❖ 'But' is popularly known as a **Conjunction**, *used to express opposite meaning to the sense, views, opinion or thought of the preceding statement*, and joins either two words, phrases, clauses or sentences.

❖ But it is also used as **a Relative Pronoun.** 'But' is always used after a negative sense & makes a forceful positive statement. **As a Relative Pronoun, 'but'** means **'who not'** (who doesn't/didn't/will not)
1) There is none **but** will agree with me. (Who will not)
2) There is no Hindu **but** knows the story of the Ramayana. (Who does not know)
3) There is no man **but** wishes to live. (Who does not wish)
4) There is no rose **but** has some thorn. (but = which has no thorn)
5) There is scarcely a child **but** likes candy. (Who does not like)
6) There is no man **but** knows these things. (but= who does not know)

❏ The Positive Sense of the above statements are:
1) The speaker is sure that everyone will agree with him.
2) Every Hindu knows the story of Ramayana.
3) Everyman wishes to live.
4) Each & every rose has some thorn.
5) Almost every child likes candy.
6) Everyone knows these thongs.

90. Agreement of Relative Pronoun & its Antecedent

- As the Relative Pronoun refers to a Noun or a Pronoun (called its 'antecedent'), it must be of the same number & person as its antecedent.

Remember: The verb shows the number & person of the Relative Pronoun. However, the tense may vary as necessary of the sense.

1) The boy ***who*** is first in this class was awarded.
2) The girls ***who*** were active in the project were reproached unjustly.
3) I, ***who*** am your caption, will lead you in this mission.
4) I am not that person ***that*** is to blame.
5) We, ***who*** seek your protection, are strangers here.
6) They ***who*** seek only for faults see nothing else.
7) The flowers ***which*** grow in our gardens are not for sale.
8) He ***that*** is down needs fear no fall.
9) You, ***who*** are mighty, should be merciful.
10) You, ***who*** seek wisdom, should be humble.
11) They ***who*** live in glass houses should not throw stones.
12) This is the only one of his poems ***that*** is worth reading.
13) This is the only project of his may ***which*** wins fame.

All the above are in the **Nominative Case**, but ***in case of Accusative, it happens different***. So, it depends on the Case of the Pronouns; as,

- Rama is the boy ***whom*** I want.
- Rama is the boy ***whose*** pencil I have.

91. Position of the Relative Pronoun

- To prevent ambiguity, the Relative Pronoun should be placed as near as possible to its antecedent; as,

1) The boy ***who*** won the first prize in English is the son of my friend, Mr. Joshi.

- It would mean quite different if we separate the Relative Pronoun from its Antecedent and say—

→ The boy is the son my friend Mr. Joshi ***who*** won the first prize.

➢ What it seems? Who won the prize? **Mr. Joshi** or **the boy**? Again—

2) 'I have read Peter's speech ***who*** was an admirer of John Keats'—***would be improved into-***

→ 'I have read the speech of Peter ***who*** was an admirer of John Keats.

3) I with my family reside in a village near Pune ***which*** consists of my wife & three children. (***Rearrange***)

→ I reside in a village near Pune with my family ***which*** consists of my wife and three children.

Note: The sentences in ***blue color*** are in the correct arrangement of words using the Relative Pronouns, where the sentences ***in green,*** are wrongly arranged where the relative pronouns are placed far from their antecedents.

92. Compound Relative Pronouns

- Some Pronouns are made with or by adding **'–ever'**, **'-so-ever'** or **'-so'** to –***who, whom, whose, which*** & ***what***; and thus, we have:
  - Whoever, whoso, whosoever, whomsoever, whosesoever, whichever, whatever, whatsoever.

⇒ These new-formed Pronouns are called **Compound Relative Pronouns.**

- These Relatives have no antecedent expressed in the sentences as other Relative Pronouns

❑ **Whoever** (as singular & plural), **is used to mean-**

•the person (or people) who/any person who; as,

- Whoever says that is a liar.
- Send it to whoever is in charge of sales.
- Whoever comes is welcome.

•That it does not matter 'who', since the result will be the same; as,

- Come out of there, whoever you are.
- I don't want to see them, whoever they are.

˙In question form it is 'to express surprise'; as,
- Whoever heard of such a thing!

❏ **Whoso, whosoever** *mean the same as* '**whoever**'; as,

- Whoso diggeth a pit shall fall therein.
- Whosoever exalteth himself shall be abased.
- Whoever told you this/ Whoso told/ Whosoever told, told a lie.

❏ In accusative '**whomever**' & in genitive or possessive '**whosesoever**' and relating anything '**whatever**' or '**whichever**'—are used. [*The interesting fact is that in all the cases, the 'wh-' words, mostly used in the sentence are in the Assertive sense rather than in questions.*]
1) Take **whomever** (*any person whom*) you choose.
2) She was free to marry **whomever** she chooses.
3) I took it away **whosesoever** it was. (*Whomever it belonged to*)
4) Take **whichever** (*anything which*) you like.
5) Choose **whichever**(*any*) brand you prefer.
6) **Whichever** (*anything which*) of you gets here first will get the prize.
7) It takes three hours **whichever**(*any*) route you choose.
8) **Whatever** (*any or every which; anything or everything which*) he does, he does well.
9) **Whatsoever** thy hand findeth to do, do it with thy might.
10) Take **whatever**(*any/every*) action is needed.
11) Do **whatever** you like. Whatever doing, come here instant.
12) You have our support, **whatever** you decide.

❏ *Whatever* is also an adverb. As an adverb it means '**not at all**', '**not of any kind**', **nothing at all**; as,
- They received no help **whatever**. (*An adverb = Not of any kind*).
- *Pitt worked very hard but he achieved a bit* **whatever**.

93. Omission of Relative Pronouns

✘ The Relative Pronouns generally introduce a Relative Clause with its Antecedents; However, sometimes the Relative Pronouns are understood in the sentences; as,
1) A contented mind is the greatest blessing (that) a man can enjoy in the world.
2) Men must reap the things (that) they sow.
3) The meeting (that) I have to attend tomorrow has been postponed.
4) 'Tis distance (that) lends enchantment to the view.
5) The answer (which) you gave is not right.

94. Omission of Antecedent

✘ Sometimes, antecedent of a Relative Pronoun is left out in the sentence; as,
→ (He)Who works not shall not eat.
→ (Those) Whom the gods love, die young.
→ (He) Who laughs last laughs best.
→ (He) Who has lost all hope has also lost all fear.
→ Be good, sweet maid, and let (him) who will be clever.

95. Relation of Antecedent & Clause

✘ The Relative Pronouns generally *introduce a Relative Clause with its Antecedents*; without antecedents a Relative Pronouns introduce a Noun Clause.

96. Interrogative Pronouns (7)

✘ **Read the following sentences:**

- *Who* is there? *Who* are you?
- *Who* are you talking to?

- *Whom* did you give the parcel?
- *Whose* is this house? *Whosever* this house belongs to?
- *Which* do you prefer? Tea or coffee?
- *What* will all the neighbors say?

✖ It will be noticed that the ***Pronouns*** in italics are <u>similar in form to</u> ***Relative Pronouns***. But the work which they do is different. Here, they are ***<u>used to ask questions</u>***, and are, therefore, called **Interrogative Pronouns.**

✖ **more examples: -**

1) Whom do you want? Who do you want?
2) Who are you talking about?
3) About whom are you talking? Whom about are you talking?
4) Which is your house? Which is the house, you owner of?

or

5) You are the owner of which house?
6) What is the matter? What are you? What do you want?
7) Who used all my paper?
8) Who is Mom talking to?
9) Who are those people?
10) **Whose** pen is this?
11) **Whose** are these shoes?
12) **What** is your brother's name?
13) **What** does Tom want?
14) **What** is the date today?

97. **To form Indirect questions:**

✖ Interrogative Pronouns are also used to make Indirect questions; as,

1) I asked who was speaking.
2) I do not know who is there.
3) Tell me what you have done.
4) Ask what he wants.
5) Say which you would like best.

98. **Case of Interrogative Pronouns**

Like Relative & Personal Pronouns, Interrogative Pronouns are also used in different Cases; as,

✖ **Nominative:**

→ Who gave you that right?
→ Who lives there in the White Home?
→ Who is he? (About identity); What is he? (About profession)
→ What is that? Which is he? (Selection among many)

✖ **Accusative:**

→ Whom did you see? Who did you see?
→ Who were you speaking to? To whom were you speaking to?
→ What do you want? Which do you prefer?

✖ **Possessive:**

→ Whose is this book? Whose is that White Home?
→ Whose is this umbrella?

99. **Comparison between Interrogative Pronouns and Interrogative Adjective:**

COMPARE

Interrogative Pronoun	**Interrogative Adjective**
○ Whose are these shoes?	○ Which book are you reading?
○ **What** is your brother's name?	○ Which way shall we go?
○ Who are those people?	○ What books have you read?
○ Which is your house?	○ What funny games are you playing?
○ Who are you talking about?	○ What manner of man is these, that even the wind and the sea obey him.
○ What do you want?	○ Whose shoes are these?

Indefinite Group of Pronouns

100. This group includes-

Indefinite,
Distributive &
Reciprocal Pronouns.

INDEFINITE GROUP PRONOUNS

INDEFINITE	• **That does not point out particular thing or person.** • One, any, some, many, <u>you</u> audience, <u>they</u> say..., no, none etc.
DISTRIBUTIVE	• **That points out thing or person one at a time.** • Each, either, neither etc.
RECIPROCAL	• **That indicates a mutual relationship.** • Each other, one another

101. **Indefinite Pronouns (8):** An indefinite pronoun does not refer to persons or things particularly or definitely, but <u>they refer</u> to the same (the <u>person or things) in a general way.</u>

Most indefinite pronouns express the idea of number—***one, many, few***, etc., and thus it <u>may follow singular or plural verb in the sentence</u>; as,

1) I shall be glad to help ***every one*** of my boys in *their* studies.
2) ***Anybody*** can do it if ***he/she/they*** try. (In both numbers, it can be expressed the idea.)
3) ***Everybody*** is welcome at the meeting.
4) ***Many*** prefer their coffee with sugar.
5) Does ***anybody*** care for a cheese sandwich?
6) ***Few*** choose to live in the arid desert.
7) His words are in ***everyone's*** mouth.
8) ***One*** hardly knows what to do in such situation, you are the exception.

9) **One** does not like to say so, but it is only too true.

10) **One** cannot be too careful of one's (not, his) good name.

11) **One** must not be boasting of one's own success.

12) **One** must use one's best efforts if one wishes to succeed.

13) **One** must not praise one's self.

14) **One** or **other** of us will be there.

15) **None** of his poems are well-known.

16) **None** but fools have ever believed it.

17) **None** believes that/you/me.

18) What is **everybody's** business is **nobody's** business.

19) We did not see **any** of them again.

20) Behave yourself and do well to **others**.

21) **They say** (=*people in general*) he has lost heavily.

22) **They say** (*some persons*) that **one** of the local banks has stopped payment.

23) **You audience**, pay heed to me and bear few minutes only, I have **something** important to say of our leaders.

24) **All** were drowned. **No one** escaped and **all** met to deaths.

25) **All** will go heaven when the earth is a fire-ball by men.

26) **Some** are born great; **most** of us normal.

27) **Some** say he has got the job by influence.

28) **Somebody** has stolen my watch.

29) **Nobody** was there to rescue the child.

30) Did you ask **anybody** to come?

31) **Few** escaped unhurt.

32) **Many** of them were Gurkhas.

102. **Most of Indefinite Pronouns are also used as Adjectives; as,**

1) I will take you there **one day**.
2) **Any fool** can do that.
3) He is a man of **few words**.
4) **Some milk** was spilt.
5) **All passengers** were drowned.
6) **Neither** accusation is true.
7) **Each boy** took his turn.
8) At **either** end was a marble statue.

•Of the underlined the bold words are adjectives when the other is a noun.

Exercise: Find out indefinite pronouns, if has any, from the followings:

1) One never knows who might be listening.
2) Many are called but few are chosen.
3) I finished my cookie and asked for another.
4) Both were punished for the crime they committed.
5) Several applied for the job, but no one was hired.

See the chart of Indefinite Pronouns:

Indefinite Pronouns :-

All/Enough	Either	Most	Other
Another	Everybody	Neither	people
Any	Everyone	Nobody	Several
Anybody	Few/fewer	No one	Some
Anyone	Little/less	None	Somebody
both	Many/much	One	Someone

Note: Most of the above are also used as Adjectives with Nouns following.

103. **Distributive Pronouns (9):** *That points out a thing or a person, one at a time* (i.e., each, either, neither, etc.). Consider the following sentences:

• **Each/Every one** of them had their share. **Each** of them gets the prize.
• **Each/ Everybody** took it in turn.
• I bought these pine apples for forty rupees **each one /per piece**.

- ***Either*** of these roads leads to the railway station. ***Either*** of you can go.
- ***Neither*** of the accusations is true.

✘ Look at their meanings:
  → 'each'=to denote every one of a number of persons or things;
  → 'either'= the one or the other of the two, but not both;
  → 'neither'= not the one nor the other of two.

✘ The bold words refer to persons or things 'one at a time'. They are called **Distributive Pronouns.**

✘ As the Distributive Pronouns refer to single person or thing at a time, it follows always a singular verb.

104.   **Reciprocal Pronouns (10):** Some Compound Pronouns like- *each other, one another— expresses mutual relationship,* as when one is the subject the other forms the object; and when the other is the subject the one becomes the subject; as,

1) Two boys fought with ***each other.*** (Peter fought with Ananda. Ananda fought with Peter)
2) The boys fought with ***one another.***
3) The members of the family love ***one another.***
4) The two men hate ***each other***.
5) They cheated ***one another***.
6) The brothers quarreled with ***each other***.
7) They all gave evidence against ***one another***.
8) The three brothers quarreled with ***each other***. (This is also an example of **Reciprocal Pronoun**, though they denote more than 'two', for, it also shows mutual relation, 'each one quarrels with the other two'.)

Don't forget

- **Pronouns are words, used in place of Nouns**, used or understood in the sentence.
- There are ten kinds of Pronouns, based on their meaning and functions. And they are— Personal, Possessive, Reflexive, Emphatic, Demonstrative, Relative, Interrogative, Indefinite, Distributive, & Reciprocal Pronouns.
- The interesting fact is, same Pronoun form or slightly changed form of pronoun are often used as other; as, **I, My & Myself**; or **Who, which, what**—as the Relative and also as the Interrogative Pronoun. All are defined by their roles.
- Sometimes, Pronouns are used to introduce a sentence, sometimes, they can join two clauses, may relate to some nouns before them and make questions-direct or indirect. And many of them are also used as adjectives in the sentence.

Let us write:
- Look about yourself, and find things, animals or men. Make a list of them. Now try to write a paragraph of your observation. In you paragraph or note you are allowed to ask question or relate things or people or animals as far you can. Show this one to your teacher. She or He will help you for the rest.

The Case, & the Functions of Pronouns

105.   Like nouns, pronouns have three cases-
  → Nominative,
  → Accusative &
  → Possessive

✘ **The Nominative Case:** The Pronouns that forms Subjects; as,
  → ***She*** is a professor. ***It*** is a mango tree.
  → ***You***, Mokles & ***I*** are old school friends.

✘ **The Accusative Case:** The Pronouns that forms Objects; as,
  → I asked ***you*** to come. Give ***her*** a bundle. Tell ***him*** to go.
  → Request ***them*** to forgive your sins. Don't ask ***me*** to do ***it***. ('it' an infinitive object)

- **The Possessive Case:** The Pronouns that shows having, possession, or parts of something; as,
  - → It is **ours**. Which is **yours**? Is this **hers**?
  - → Definitely, this is **his**. Which is **mine**?
  - → The computers are **theirs**. (The computers belong to them.)
  - → **Your** blow broke **its** leg. (Examples of Possessive Adjective; 'it' does not have Possessive Pronoun form)

106. Study the Pronoun Charts:

	Subject Pronoun	Object Pronoun	Possessive Adjective	Possessive Pronouns	Reflexive /Emphatic Pronouns
1st Person-singular	I	Me	My	Mine	Myself
1st Person-plural	We	Us	Our	Ours	Ourselves
2nd Person-singular	You	You	Your	Yours	Yourself
2nd Person-plural	You	You	Your	Yours	Yourselves
3rd Person-singular	She /He /It	Her/him/it	Her/his/its	Hers/his/*	Herself / himself/itself
3rd Person-plural	They	Them	Their	Theirs	themselves

Chart-2

	Subject Pronoun	Object Pronoun	Possessive Adjective	Possessive Pronouns
Both in singular & plural, mainly for persons	Who **Who** are you?	Whom/who **Whom** do you like?	Whose **Whose house** do you live in?	Whose **Whose** is this book?
Both in singular & plural, for persons & things	Which The book **which** you see on the table cost me four thousand.	Which I gave him a rupee **which** was all I had.	Whose The sun, **whose rays** give life to the earth, is regarded as a god.	Whose/ of which This is the question the **solution of which** has baffled the philosophers of all ages.
Both in singular & plural, for persons & things	That A city **that** is set on a hill cannot be hid.	That Uneasy lies the head **that** wears a crown.	*	* (that has no genitive case)

107. **The Functions of Pronouns:**

- Pronouns are the words, which are used in place of Nouns.
- So, Pronouns, as substitute words of Nouns, do almost all functions of a Noun and sometimes they do more works, like joining sentences& ask questions.

  - <u>Study the uses of Noun & Pronouns in two different slides, as in the followings:</u>

Functions of Nouns	Examples
1. To form subject of verb:	· **Ram** goes to school. The **cow** has for legs. · **Gold** is precious. · **A gang of robbers** came there. · **Honesty** is the best policy.
2. To form object of verb:	I asked **Ra**m. You bought a **bicycle**.
3. To form object of preposition:	You are speaking to **Ria.**
4. As case in apposition	P. Sarkar, **a teacher of this school**, passed away.
5. As complement to a noun or pronoun:	He is a famous *singer.* We elected Shree Kanta, **the President of the committee.**
6. To be a part of An Adverbial Phrase:	Ram goes to *school*. The child is playing on the *floor*. ('to school' & 'on the floor'- are examples of Adverbial Phrase)
7. To form a Nominal Compound, and	We have no *chalk-duster* in the school. (It is also an Object) They sat beside the *tea-table*. (It is also a part of the adverbial phrase- 'beside the tea-table'.
8. As an Adjective in the sentence	I met a little *cottage* girl. He is always playing *computer* games. We are *school* teachers.

Functions of Pronouns	Examples
1. To form subject: (Nominative Case)	I am Peter. **We** are teachers. **You** are a writer. **She** is a girl. **They** are programmers.
2. To form object: (object of verb/ object of a preposition) (Objective Case)	I like **her** too much. She hurts **herself**. We should listen to *him*. He cares of *none*.
3. After 'be' verbs to mean possession. (Possessive Case)	It is **mine**. That's is **yours**. All is **hers**.
4. As an adjective before noun (Possessive adjective)	This is **my** book. That is **our** school. It is **their** city.
5. To give emphasis on its subject (noun or pronoun): (Emphatic Pronoun)	Shila *herself* has done the work. I *myself* went there.
6. To make question: (Interrogative Pron)	**Who** are you? **What** do you like?
7. To introduce relative clauses or to join clauses: (Relative Pronoun)	I know the man **who** was there. I know the place **where** he was born.
8. As case in apposition (rarely used)	° Our teacher, **she**, is afraid to go there. ° My friend, **he**, loves me very much. ° Friends, **any one**, please visit there.

108.   Beside the above functions, pronouns have other important functions to be noted, slightly different:

The following are used either as Subject or Object	In Sentences

1. As <u>determiner & impersonal subject or object</u> (of far & near) (Function of Demonstrative & Impersonal Pronoun)	**This/That** is a cat. **It** is a calf. Look at **this/that** cow. I drive **it** away. **These/Those** are not mine. I want **these** or **those**.
2. To <u>form indefinite subject or object</u>: (Indefinite Pronoun)	**Someone** has arrived. You may give the blame on **any**. **One** may call it rubbish.
3. To point out subject or object <u>separately</u>: (Distributive Pron.)	**Each** has given prize. Prizes were given to **each**.
4. To show <u>mutual relationship</u> between subject & object: (Reciprocal Pron.).	They love **each other**. (Ram loves Sita. Sita loves Ram.) You should help **one another.** (Peter should help Mr. P & Mr. P should help Peter.)

Other Functions	**In Sentences**
1. To make a complement: (Rarely used)	• A renowned doctor has made him *she* in the last year. • Nicky is a *he*, don't confuse about his gender.
2. To Form Nominal Compound: (Or to be used as an adjective)	He-goat, she-goat, self-respect, self-confidence, etc. (when self is used as pronoun; it is also used as Noun, meaning 'own'.
3. To Form Compound Pronouns:	Whoever, whatever, whichever, ourselves, myself, etc.

109. **Let's Practice,** Using...1ˢᵗ Person**. Say, which case has been used for the bold words:**
   1) **I** am a great rascal. [N/S]
   2) Do you believe **me**? [O]
   3) It is **mine**. [PP]
   4) Don't touch **my** girlfriend. [PA]
   5) **We** are all, at least, stupid, if not sinners. [N/S]
   6) Animals, don't believe **us**. [O]
   7) We demand the earth is **ours**. [PP]
   8) But in fact, **our** earth does not remain more as ours. [PA]

110. **Let's Practice,** Using...2ⁿᵈ Person**. Say, which case has been used:**
   1) **You** are a stupid, so you love me. [N/S]
   2) Actually, I don't believe **you** as myself. [O]
   3) Is the heart being **yours**? [PP]
   4) Lend me **your** soft & loving heart. [PA]
   5) **You** everyone must do the task. [N/S]
   6) I love **you**, friends. [O]
   7) All my cares are **yours**. [PP]
   8) **Your** labor should be only for **your** country. [PA]

111. **Let's Practice,** Using...3ʳᵈ Person**. Say, which case has been used.**
   1) **S/He** is the person. [Nominative/Subject]
   2) I may believe **her/him**. [Accusative/Object]
   3) The trousers is **hers/his**. [Possessive Pronoun]
   4) This is **her/his** house. [Possessive Adjective]
   5) Where are **they**? [Nominative/Subject]
   6) I need **them** now. [Accusative/Object]
   7) I have something with me which, I believe, are **theirs**. [PP]
   8) **Their** possessions are with me. [PA]

112. **Let's Practice,** Using... Impersonal 'It' & Demonstrative Pronouns**. Say, which case has been used.**

1) **It/That** is a ring, I keep with me for some special. [N/S]
2) I bought **it/that** in the market during the festival. [O]
3) These parts are **its. /Of that**. [PP]
4) <u>**Its** legs</u> are broken. / <u>The legs **of that**</u> chair are broken. [PA]
5) **These/Those** are pine apples. [N/S]
6) Do you like **these/those**? [O]
7) <u>The color **of these/those**</u> have been faded. [PP]
8) <u>**These** mangoes</u> are sweet. /<u>**Those** mangoes</u> were sour. [PA]

6. Adjectives & Its Kinds

Definition: A word that <u>adds meaning or describes a Noun or a Pronoun</u>.

113. **Read, and think about the following carefully:**
   •   Sita is a *clever* girl. (What kind of girl?)
   •   I don't like *that* boy. (Which boy?)
   •   He gave me *five* mangoes. (How many mangoes?)
   •   There is **little** time for preparation. (How much time?)
   ❑ In sentence 1, the word *'clever'* shows 'what kind of girl is Sita?' It <u>denotes the quality</u> of Sita.
   ❑ In sentence 2, the word *'that'* shows 'which boy don't like the speaker?' It <u>points out or demonstrate</u> about the boy.
   ❑ In sentence 3, the word *'five'* shows 'how many mangoes did he give me?' It <u>denotes the number</u> of mangoes.
   ❑ In sentence 4, the word *'little'* shows 'how much time is left for preparation?' It <u>denotes the quantity</u> of time.

114. **The Kinds of Adjectives ⊗ (According to Functions):** An adjective may denote the **Identity, Origin, Kind or Quality**. It may also denote **Number** (definite, indefinite or distributive), **Quantity**. It may demonstrate a Noun or a Pronoun, ask question, express surprise, show possession or **used to emphasize a noun**. It may define a thing or person particularly, or denote them in a generally, i.e., indefinitely; it may also denote a noun or a pronoun also to make question, shows emphasis & possession; and in exclamatory 'what' to mean 'very or great' of quality, etc.

   Thus, the different kinds of Adjectives are:
   1) Adjectives of Quality: —honest, poor, brave, angry;
   2) Adjectives of Origin: which have <u>mostly come from Proper Nouns</u>, so popularly known as ***Proper Adjectives*** *—Indian, British, Vedic, Islamic, etc.
   3) Adjectives of Quantity—some, little, great, few
   4) Adjectives of Number—first, two, single, few, many, any
   5) Indefinite Adjectives*— one, any, few, some, all, etc.
   6) Distributive Adjectives*—each, every, either, neither
   7) Demonstrative *—this, that, such, same etc.
   8) Interrogative Adjectives*—which, whose, what
   9) Possessive Adjectives*—my, our, your, their, its
   10) Emphatic Adjectives*—own, very
   11) Exclamatory Adjectives—**what** a man!

115. Perhaps you have noticed, <u>most of the Adjectives are actually from **Nouns** & **Pronouns**</u>. Try to remember the names-
   •   Indefinite,
   •   Distributive,
   •   Demonstrative,
   •   Interrogative,
   •   Possessive &
   •   Emphatic.
   ✗ All these names have come from Pronouns. When the Pronouns are used as Adjectives, they are called so, already examples given in the chapter of Pronouns to show the difference.
   ✗ And **Proper Adjectives**, as already said, are <u>from the</u> '**Proper Nouns**.

116. Carefully study the Charts:

Names	As Nouns or Pronouns	As Adjectives
Proper	1) I love my motherland, **India**. 2) The **Ganga** is one of the longest rivers in India. 3) This pizza is made in **China**. 4) **Shakespeare** was a great dramatist.	1) I am an **Indian**. 2) The northern plains is known as the **Gangetic** Plains. 3) Don't take **Chinese** Pizza. 4) I have read **Shakespearean** dramas.
Demonstrative	**This** is a cycle. **That** is a motor car.	**This** cycle I bought last year. **That** car is ours.
Interrogative	**Which** is your bike? **Whose** is this house?	**Which** bike is yours? **Whose** house is this?
Indefinite	1) **One** must not praise one's self. 2) **Any** may be that fool. 3) **Few** are gifted. 4) **Some** was split. 5) **All** were drowned.	• I will take you there **one** day. • **Any** fool can do that. • He is a man of **few** words. • **Some** milk was spilt. • **All** passengers were drowned.

Names	As Nouns or Pronouns	As Adjectives
Distributive	1) **Each** was given chocolates. 2) **Everybody** was excellent student. 3) **Either** of these roads leads to the railway station. 4) **Neither** of the accusations is true.	1) **Each** boy got the prize. 2) **Every** student here is excellent. 3) **Either** road here leads to the railway station. 4) **Neither** accusation was true.
Possessive	1) The shop is **yours**. 2) The company is **ours**. 3) All these chairs are **theirs**.	1) I am not going to **your** shop. 2) This is **our** company. 3) All these **their** chairs.
Emphatic	1) I **myself** went there. 2) Do your work **yourself**. 3) The man **himself** came here.	1) I went to **own** home last day. 2) Mind your **own** business. 3) The **very** man came here.

Illustrations of each kind of Adjectives:

117. Adjective Of Quality/Descriptive Adjectives (1):
These adjectives are often called as the Adjectives of Opinion. They show the kind or quality of a person or thing (they describe Nouns or Pronoun); as,
- Balurghat is a *peaceful* town.
- Dakshin Dinajpur is a *small* district in West Bengal.
- Peter is a *hard-working* person.
- The *foolish old* crow tried to sing. (quality + age)
- This is a grammar book of *English* Language. (origin/country)

118. **Adjectives of Origin** or Proper Adjectives comes from Proper Nouns. These are often classed with the Adjectives of Quality; as these adjectives denote *identity, origin* as well as *kind* or *quality* of things or persons; as, Indian (nature), British (author or cigar), American (writer), Shakespearean (drama), Gangetic (plains), Northern (region), Godly (qualities), Chinese (plate), etc.,

- ✖ Therefore, Adjectives of Quality & Adjectives of Origin or Proper Adjectives can be merged into one as '**the Adjective of Quality or Origin**'. Adjective of Quality or Origin answer the question- 'what kind'?

- ✖ **More about Proper Adjectives** or the **Adjective of Origin:** _Proper means 'Particular' or 'Exact'_ thing or person, _where they are born of, or 'come from' and thus they refer to_ (i) _citizenship' (for person)_ & (ii) producing country or place which also denote 'a quality' of the thing.

1) Study the examples:

1) I am an _Indian_ by birth & heart. (What country of?)
2) I have _American_ & _British_ friends on Twitter & Instagram.
3) _Chinese_ products are chief, but not all.
4) **What country** are you **of**?
5) **What** are **of** your friends on Twitter & Instagram? **Where are** they **from**?
6) **What kinds of products are** chief?

Note: Proper Adjectives or the Adjective of Origin answer the questions-
- ❖What kind of?
- ❖'What country or place of',
- ❖Where from?

119. **Adjective Of Quantity (2):** _The adjectives that show how much of a thing; as,_
    1) I ate **some** rice.
    2) I showed **much** patience.
    3) She has **little** intelligence.
    4) We have lost **all** our wealth.
    5) They're had sufficient rain last year.
    6) We have had **enough** exercise today.
    7) She has **no** sense. Take **great** care of my mom.
    8) Give me of its half share. The whole sum was expended.
    9) My mom had not had **any** rice before her daughter came.

    - ✖ Adjective of Quantity answer the question- **'How much'**?

120. **Adjective Of Number/Numeral Adjectives (3):** The adjectives that show how many persons or things; as,

    → Our hands have _**five**_ fingers each.
    → **Few** cats like cold water.
    → There is **no** picture in the book.
    → **All** men must die. **Some** ripe mangoes.
    → **Most** boys like games.
    → **Several** mistakes I have made in my life.
    → Saturday is the **last** day of the week.
    → There are **many/a lot** of tasks to do in the life.

    - ✖ Adjective of Number answer the question- **'How many'** or **'what position'** refers to 'the rank of person, animals or things.

121. **Adjectives of Number/Numeral Adjectives may have the following sub-divisions; as,**

    a) **Definite Numeral:** _that define definite numbers of Nouns or Pronouns; as,_

    - ❖ One, two, three = these are called cardinal; cardinal denotes '**How many?**'
    - ❖ First, second, third = these are called ordinal; ordinal denotes **the order of things** in a series, like in a race.

    - ❖ **Certain** (when to mean number, it is used to refer **'a particular person, thing or a group'**, 'a certain or fixed number, though not mentioned, as both the speaker or listener are expected to know the exact number'; as,
        - o Certain people must disagree with this. Just overlook them to run your project.

- ❖ Certain is <u>also used as the number of quantities</u> as 'some'; as,
  - ○ That's true to the certain extent.
  - ○ I felt there was a certain coldness in her manner. (Here, 'a' means 'a little')
- ❖ <u>When '**certain**' to mean '**sure**'</u>, it is the adjective of quality or an <u>example of emphatic adjective</u>; as,
  - ○ I am not certain who was there.
  - ○ Are you absolutely certain about this?

- ❖ **Study other examples of Definite Numeral:**
  - ○ We had two cars. She stands first in her class every year.
  - ○ She stood third in the race. I have one rupee.

b) **Indefinite Numeral:** <u>*The adjectives that does not point out exact Number; as,* **one, any, few, some, all, many, most, several, sundry, all & sundry,** *etc.*</u>
- ❖ '**Sundry**' to mean '**various**', it falls to Indefinite Numeral Adjective to refer 'various' which are not important enough to be named separately; a,
  - ○ A watch, a diary, and sundry other things are missing after the robbery.
- ❖ '**all & sundry**' to mean '**everyone, not just a few special people**'.
  - ○ She was known to all and sundry as Bella.
  - ○ The club is open to all and sundry.

- ❖ **Study the other examples of Indefinite Numeral**:
  - ○ One of the boys did this.
  - ○ Few students only attended the last class yesterday.
  - ○ Some of them are genius but not all.

c) **Distributive Numeral:** <u>*which refers to each one of a number; as,*</u>
- ❖ **Each** boy must take his turn. **Every** word of it was false.
- ❖ **Every** student in the class is genius. **Either** pen will do.
- ❖ Motherland expects **every** citizen to do his duty.
- ❖ On **either** side there are narrow lanes. **Neither** accusation is true.
- ❖ **Each** boy got the prize.
- ❖ **Every** student present here is excellent.
- ❖ *Either* road here leads to the nearest railway station.

122. **Some adjectives may be used as both. Study the chart:**

Same adjectives may be used in both

Adjective of Number	Adjective of Quantity
1) *Some* scholars are clever.	1) I have taken *some* rice.
2) *All* men must die.	2) He has lost *all* his wealth.
3) There are *no* picture in this book.	3) You have *no* sense.
4) Are there *any* mango trees in this garden?	4) He did not take *any* rice.
5) There are not *enough* spoons.	5) I have *enough* sugar.
Note: Answer to the question 'how many?'	**Note:** Answer to the question 'how much?'

123. **Identify the adjectives from the followings and mark as adjectives of number or quantity:**
  - → *Some* scholars are clever.
  - → *All* men must die.
  - → There is *no* picture in this book.
  - → Are there *any* mango trees in this garden?

→ There are not **enough** spoons.
→ I have taken **some** rice.
→ He has lost **all** his wealth.
→ You have **no** sense.
→ He did not take **any** rice.
→ I have **enough** sugar.

124. **Demonstrative Adjectives (4):** The adjectives that <u>point out which person or thing is meant</u>; as,
 1) **This** man is stronger than that.
 2) **That** boy is brilliant.
 3) **These** mangoes are sweet.
 4) **Those** criminals must be hanged to death.
 5) **Yonder** fort once belonged to Shivaji.
 6) **Yonder** house is ours.
 7) Don't be in **such** a hurry.
 8) I hate **such** things.

 ⌧ *Demonstrative Adjective answer the question- 'Which', used in both singular and plural.*

125. **Interrogative Adjectives (5):** What, which, whose– when <u>are used with Nouns to ask questions,</u> are called Interrogative Adjectives; as,
 1) What manner is this to ask such questions to your dad?
 2) What faults I have done, tell me at once. (Affirmative question)
 3) Which way is the best way to reach our goals?
 4) Which one is Peter? Which/ What books has he written?
 5) Whose book is this? Whose house is that white building?
 6) What books are costly? Which pen is yours?

 ⌧ **Remember:** 'What' is used in general sense; while 'which' is used in a selective sense.
 ⌧ You may compare- Interrogative Pronouns & Interrogative Adjectives, side by side.

126. **Possessive Adjectives (6):** Possessive Adjectives are nothing but the Possessive Pronoun forms which are used as Adjectives in the sentence, *to denote **having, ownership, possession** or **part of a thing***; as,

 1) This is my mobile. That is our house. It is your duty.
 2) Submit all your papers within seven days.
 3) It is her vanity bag. This is his pair of shoes.
 4) It is their faults, not ours. Blame them for their tasks.

 ⌧ **Remember:** Possessive Adjectives are basically Pronouns, used as Adjectives in the sentences.
 ⌧ You may compare- Possessive Pronouns & Possessive Adjectives, side by side.

127. **Emphasizing Adjectives (7):** In the sentence, 'own' & 'very'– are often used as Emphasizing Adjectives. They are used to give emphasize on the following Nouns, going back to the action of the subject; as,
 1) I saw it with my **own** <u>eyes</u>.
 2) The **very** <u>man</u> came here.
 3) He was beaten at his **own** <u>game</u>.
 4) Mind your **own** <u>business</u>.
 5) He is his **own** <u>master</u>.
 6) That is the **very** <u>thing</u> we want.
 7) "When all else left my cause,
      My **very** adversary took my part."

You may compare- Emphatic Pronouns & Emphatic Adjectives, side by side.

128. **Exclamatory Adjective (8):** When 'what' or 'what a' preceding a noun – are **used to express surprise, strong emotion or exclamation;** *as in the followings:*

 1) What a night it is!

2) What a weather I have never seen like this!
3) What a genius!
4) What folly has he done, falling love with a young child!
5) What an idea, Sir-ji! Welcome only to insult
6) What a blessing! A beggar from the richest man!
7) What a piece of work is woman! She is happy with none.

✠ **Remember:** Exclamatory Adjectives are vastly used in the exclamatory sentences.

The Use of Adjectives (i.e., the functions)

▪ Simply <u>to point out qualities of a Noun</u> or a Pronoun

How to use Adjectives
▪ As we discussed in the last section, Adjectives are of different kinds, but the question is, how they are used in the sentences. What their functions are. Firstly, **Adjectives are used in two ways:**
> ➢ Attributively &
> ➢ Predicatively.

✠ **Attributively Use of Adjective:** When an adjective is used with a noun as an epithet or attribute to the Noun to add meaning or information. So why it is called so, the use of Adjectives Attributively. Read the example:
  - ▪ The ***corrupted*** officer is suspended.
  - ▪ The ship sustained **heavy** damage.
  - ▪ I have called you **several** times.
  - ▪ A **live** ass is better than a **dead** lion.
  - ▪ I attended a **quite** party.
  - ▪ It was a **long** way.
  - ▪ The **infirm** minstrel was there.

✠ **Note:** *They are always followed by Nouns whose they add meaning, either that is in the part of subject or predicate.*

✠ **Predicatively Use of Adjective:** When an Adjective is used along with the verb 'to Be' and forms part of the predicate, it is called so, the use of Adjectives Predicatively; as,
  - ✓ The officer is ***corrupted***.
  - ✓ The damage of the ship was ***heavy***.
  - ✓ Say the same thing ***twice***.
  - ✓ The lion is ***dead***.
  - ✓ Neither party is ***quiet***.
  - ✓ The way was ***long***.
  - ✓ The minstrel was ***infirm***.

Note: *Simply remember, they are not followed by Nouns to which they add meaning. Compare them like the following:*

The Use of Adjectives

Attributively	Predicatively
1) The ship sustained **heavy** damage.	1) The damage of the ship was **heavy**.
2) I have called **several** times.	2) Say the same thing **twice**.
3) A **live** ass is better than a **dead** lion.	3) The lion is **dead**.
4) I attended a **quite** party.	4) Neither party is **quite**.
5) It was a **long** way.	5) The way was **long**.
6) The **infirm** minstrel was there.	6) The minstrel was **infirm**.
Note: They are always followed by Nouns whose they add meaning, either that is in the part of subject or predicate.	**Note:** Simply remember, they are not followed by Nouns whose they add meaning.

✖ However, *some adjectives are always used as Predicatively:*
   ✓ She is *afraid* of ghost.
   ✓ I am quite *well*.

129.   The Use of Adjectives as **Pre-modifiers** & **Post-modifiers:**

✖ According to the position of an Adjective in a Sentence, adjective has other two names. Remember, they are not absolutely like the use of adjectives attributively and predicatively, though some may have similarities. It is to remember here "when an adjective precedes a noun closely just before it', it is known as *'Pre-modifiers'*". "When it is used separately from its noun, it is known as the use of *'post-modifiers'*.

✖ **Pre-Modifiers:** Pre-Modifiers can be placed anywhere in the sentence (before or after 'be' or 'have' verb), but *must be before a noun or a pronoun* closely to which it adds meaning.

Adj+noun+verb/ Verb+adj+noun

✖ **Post-Modifiers:** Post-Modifiers are always placed *after the noun or separately, not closely, which it describes* or *adds meaning*. **Study the chart.**

In the Sentences: Verb to Adjectives

Verbs In the Sentences	Adjectives in the sentences
1. She **abused** her position as one of the ministry to give jobs to her relatives & friends.	1. He becomes **abusive** when he is drunk.
2. My friend Swapan, **advised** me to create a new thing in English Grammar.	2. I am one of the **Advisory** Board of Education Department of West Bengal Govt.
3. You never **cease** to amaze me.	3. His **ceaseless** questions began to annoy me.
4. **Edit** your personal details in your profile.	4. Some debates in Parliament are shown alive & are outside **editorial** control.
5. We should **enjoy** our lives.	5. Life is **enjoyable** if we can enjoy.
6. Did he **forget** everything?	6. Bhola Grandpa was a **forgetful** old man.
7. Do I need to **include** more examples?	7. The fully i**nclusive** fare for the trip is Rs. 2500 only.
8. Who **loves** not to be honest?	8. What a **lovely** idea! What a lovely surprise!
9. She **talks** too much.	9. She always remains in **talkative** mood.
10. She **trusts** none.	10. If you are too **trusting**, how one can cheat you?

c) **Adjectives to Adjectives:** The adjectives which has come from other adjectives are mostly by adding the following suffixes:

- **-al**; as: tragic-tragical;
- **-some**; as: whole- wholesome;
- **-fold;** as: two- two-fold;
- **-ish;** as: white- whitish, blue-bluish; green-greenish, red-reddish, etc.
- **-Ly;** as: large- largely; short-shortly; sick-sickly

In the Sentences: Adjectives to Adjectives

Adjectives In the Sentences	Adjectives in the sentences
1. The cover of the file is **black** in color.	1. Who put on such a **blackish** shirt in this weather?
2. I saw a **large** number of people gathering there.	2. Yours is a **largely** one, I see.
3. The lights changed to **red** before I could get across.	3. The **reddish** ship ran away from the farm.
4. He had **short** curly hair.	4. She arrived **shortly** after us.
5. His mother is very **sick**	5. She looked pale & **sickly**.
6. It would be **tragic** if her talent remained unrecognized.	6. I read the **Tragical** History of Dr. Faustus'.
7. She wanted to be more than just a **two-bit** secretary. I saw **two** men coming towards our village.	7. The problem was **twofold**.
8. I put on my favorite **white** shirt.	8. The roots are **whitish** and yellow.
9. He spent the **whole** day writing.	9. It was a clean **wholesome** (morally good) fun.
10. It is **nice** to see her long time.	10. She was a **nice-looking** girl.

✘ We can see now the formation of Adjectives at a glance, as in the following chart:

Adjective Formation- at a glance

Noun to Adjectives		Noun to Adjectives		Verbs to Adjectives	
Noun	**Adjectives**	**Noun**	**Adjectives**	**Verbs**	**Adjectives**
Boy	Boy**ish**	Storm	Storm**y**	Cease	Cease**d**
Fool	Fool**ish**	Dirt	Dirt**y**	Talk	Talk**ative**
Care	Care**ful**	Man	Man**ly**	Tire	Tire**some**
Play	Play**ful**	King	King**ly**	Move	Mov**able**
Hope	Hope**ful**	Courage	Courag**eous**	**Adjective to Adjectives**	
Shame	Shame**ful**	Glory	Glor**ious**	**Adjectives**	**Adjectives**
Venture	Venture**some**	Envy	Env**ious**	Nice	Nice-**looking**
Trouble	Trouble**some**	Outrage	Outrag**eous**	Whole	Whole**some**
Gift	Gift**ed**	Pardon	Pardon**able**	Three	Three**fold**
Silk	Silk**en**	Laugh	Laugh**able**	Black	Black**ish**
Gold	Gold**en**	Sense	Sens**ible**	White	Whit**ish**
				Sick	Sick**ly**

The Comparison of Adjectives (i.e., Degree)

132. **The term 'Degree' Means & its Classification:** Degree means *'dimension'* or *'the measurement of qualities'* or *'expansion of work'*, which is presented by some forms of adjectives or adverbs, popularly known as 'Degrees of Adjectives or Adverbs' i.e., **'the comparison of qualities or works'**. In English grammar, such a comparison is generally made between two or among many.

133. **The Three Degrees of Comparison:**

   ✗ Read the following sentences:
   1) Goutam is *tall*.
   2) Goutam is *taller* than Rabin.
   3) Ram is the *tallest* of all (in Saidpur B.M. A. High School).

In sentence-1, the adjective *'tall'* merely tells us about the height of Goutam, <u>without comparing his height with anyone</u>.

In sentence-2, the adjective *'taller'* tells us Goutam's height is higher than Rabin's. <u>The height of the two persons is compared.</u>

In sentence-3, the adjective *'tallest'* tells us Ram's height is the highest in the school. His height is more than all others'. Here, the comparison is made among all, more than two persons.

   ✗ We thus see that Adjectives changes its forms (e.g., ***tall-taller-tallest***) or add **'more'** & **'most'** before the adjective to show comparison between two or more respectively.

   ✗ These changed forms of same adjectives, due to comparison, are called **the Degrees of Comparison**.

   ✗ However, the adjective, as **'tall'** (in its simple or base form) which is used to describe the person or thing only & **no comparison is made with any one**, is said to be in the **Positive Degree; a in sentence no-1.**

✘ Study their definitions.

✱ When there is no comparison at all about the qualities, and adjective remains **in its original** (base) **form, without any change and addition**, it is known as the **'Positive Degree'**. Read the examples:

- **Tall**—taller—tallest
- **Beautiful**—more beautiful—most beautiful
- **little**—less—least

- Sonny is a **tall** boy.
- Rebeca is a **beautiful** girl.
- I was given **little** amount of sugar.

- The boy is **strong**.
- Which one is a **good** pen?
- Mango is a **sweet** fruit.

✱ When the comparison is made between two (things or animals; between two group or class), a normal adjective changes its form slightly from its base by adding a suffix **'–er/-r /-or'**, or add **'more'** / **'less'** before the base or simple form of adjective the use of adjective is known as **'Comparative Degree'**.

A comparative degree is often followed by preposition **'than'** (*or 'to' in case of some Latin comparatives*); but remember, not always; as the followings:

- Tall—**taller**—tallest
- Beautiful—**more** beautiful—most beautiful
- little—**less**—least

- Sonny is **taller than** Leon.
- Rebeca is **more beautiful than** Christina.
- I was given **less amount** of sugar **than** anyone.

- → This boy is **stronger than** that.
- → Which of these two pens is **better**?
- → Mango is **sweeter** than apple.

✱ When the comparison is made between three or more, a normal adjective changes its form slightly from its base by adding a suffix **'–est'** / **'-st'**, or add **'most'** / **'least'** before it, the use of adjective is known as the **'Superlative Degree'**.

A Superlative Degree is mostly preceded by article **'the'**, and often followed by **'of, 'in', 'out of', 'of all', 'in the', 'among all'** 'to compare qualities or ideas among many; as,

- Tall—taller—**tallest**
- Beautiful—more beautiful—**most** beautiful
- little—less—**least**

- Sonny is the **_tallest_** boy **in** his class.
- Rebeca is the **_most beautiful_** girl **in** her town.
- I was given the **_least_** amount of sugar **among all**.

- → The boy is **the strongest** in the class.
- → Which is **the best** pen of all?
- → Mango is **the sweetest** fruit of all.

✱ **Remember:** The comparison of adjectives **_mostly happens to the Adjectives of Quality_**, **_a few to the Adjectives of Number & Quantity_**, and **_some others_**.

✘ Like adjective, some adverbs also have three degrees, regarding comparisons.

134. **Let's Practice:**

❏ When two or more objects are compared with each other, 'more' & 'most' or '–er/-r' & '-est /-st' forms are to be used as normal, for comparative and superlative degree, and there, comparative is followed by 'than any other'/ 'than', and superlative is followed by 'of all', 'among' etc.; as,
   a) Iron is <u>more useful than</u> gold.
   b) Gold is <u>cheaper than</u> diamond.
   c) Diamond is <u>the hardiest</u> metal.
   d) Diamond is <u>the hardiest of all</u>.
   e) Iron is <u>more useful **than** *any other metal*</u>. (**Not**: any metal; if said, 'any metal', it meant including 'iron'; and it would mean like- 'Iron is more useful than iron.')

❏ But when two or more qualities in same person or thing—are compared, always *'more'* & *'most'* are added before the base form of adjective to form Comparative & Superlative; and article *'the'* is not used in the Superlative; as,
   a) Ananda is ***more brave*** than prudent. (*Not*: braver than prudent)
   b) Ramesh is ***more intelligent*** than wisdom.
   c) The chair is ***more heavy*** than useful. (*Not*: heavier than useful)
   d) The computer is ***more useful*** than expensive.
   e) The building is ***most living-worth***. (It hints, living worth than all other qualities of the building, like— size, worth, look, etc.)
   f) Sheila is most beautiful. (It means, out of her other qualities—e.g., intelligent, patient, etc.) [But when said-
   g) '**Sheila is the most beautiful girl**', it hints, she is compared to other girls in the class, village or in the world.]

135. **Irregular Comparisons of Adjectives**. See the chart as an example:

Irregular Comparisons of Adjectives

Positive	Comparative	Superlative
Good, Well	Better	Best
Bad, evil, ill	Worse	Worst
Few, little	Less, lesser	Least
Much, many	More	Most
Late	Later; latter	Latest; last
Old	Older, elder	Oldest, eldest
Far	Farther	Farthest
(Nigh) —*Outdated*	(nigher) —*Outdated*	(nighest)—*Outdated*, next
(Fore)	Former; further	Foremost; first
In	Inner	Inmost, Innermost
Up	Upper	Upmost, uppermost
Out	Outer	Utmost, uttermost

136. **Interchange of Degrees:**

Interchange of Degrees

- **When it is asked to change the Degree of Comparison, it does not mean to change the meanings, but to keep the original meaning almost same. Read the examples:**

In Positive Degree	In Comparative	In Superlative
No other metal is as **heavy** as lead.	Lead is heavier than all other metals.	Lead is the heaviest of all metals.
Atreyee is not so **cool** as Ganga.	The Ganga is cooler than Atreyee.	The Ganga is the coolest of all.
He is as **wise** writer as Kalidas.	Kalidas was not wiser writer than he is.	Kalidas was one of the wisest writers.
No other drama in Sanskrit is so **good** as Sakuntalavyam.	Sakuntalavyam is better than any other drama in Sanskrit.	Sakuntalavyam is the best drama in Sanskrit.
Very few Indian cities are as **peaceful** as Balurghat.	Balurghat is more peaceful than most other cities in India.	Balurghat is one of the most peaceful cities in India.

137. **Absolute Superlative (without article 'the'):**

In a sentence using Superlative Degree, we generally use the article *'the,* preceding the superlative form of the adjective, and the Superlative Degree is often followed by **'of, 'out of', 'of all', 'in the', 'among** 'to compare among many.

But, <u>often the article **'the'** is not used.</u> Know, where?

✷ When there is no idea of comparison, but <u>merely a desire to indicate the *possession of quality in a very high degree,* the **superlative is used without 'the'** (or 'the' is replaced by 'a' or 'an');</u> as,

→ This is **most unfortunate** event.
→ It was **a most eloquent** speech.
→ Truly, **a most ingenious** device!
→ Remington was an **ablest** teacher of this institution.
→ Was it **easiest to all?** All scored cent percent!
→ It is one of **ugliest creatures** and equally **most harmful** in nature.

✷ This usage of Superlative without 'the' article is known as '**Superlative of Eminence**' or the '**Absolute Superlative**'.

138. **Formation of Comparative & Superlative Degree**

1) Most Adjectives of one syllable, some of two or more syllabic Adjectives form their comparative by adding – **er** & superlative by adding –**est** to the Positive; as the following chart:

Positive	Comparative	Superlative
Sweet	Sweet**er**	Sweet**est**
Small	Small**er**	Small**est**
Tall	Tall**er**	Tall**est**
Bold	Bold**er**	Bold**est**

Cold	Cold**er**	Cold **est**
Kind	Kind**er**	Kind**est**
Young	Young**er**	Young**est**
Great	Great**er**	Great**est**
Black	Black**er**	Black**est**
High	High**er**	High**est**
Short	Short**er**	Short**est**
Weak	Weak**er**	Weak**est**
Strong	Strong**er**	Strong**est**
Hard	Hard**er**	Hard**est**
Clever	Clever**er**	Clever**est**

2) When the positive ends in **–e,** only **–r** & **-st** (instead of –er & -est) are added:

Positive	Comparative	Superlative
Brave	Brav**er**	Brav**est**
Fine	Fin**er**	Fin**est**
White	Whit**er**	Whit**est**
Large	Larg**er**	Larg**est**
Able	Abl**er**	Abl**est**
Noble	Nobl**er**	Nobl**est**
Wise	Wis**er**	Wis**est**
Pale	Pal**er**	Pal**est**
True	Tru**er**	Tru**est**

3) When the positive ends in **–y,** that will convert into **–i,** and then **–er** & **–est** are added. But if '**y**' is preceded by vowel, '**y**' _does not change into_ '**i**'; as,

Positive	Comparative	Superlative
Busy	Bus**ier**	Bus**iest**
Dry	Dr**ier**	Dr**iest**
Easy	Eas**ier**	Eas**iest**
Happy	Happ**ier**	Happ**iest**
Healthy	Health**ier**	Health**iest**
Heavy	Heav**ier**	Heav**iest**
Holy	Hol**ier**	Hol**iest**
Merry	Merr**ier**	Merr**iest**
Mighty	Might**ier**	Might**iest**

Ugly	Ugl**ier**	Ugl**iest**
Wealthy	Wealth**ier**	Wealth**iest**
Exceptions:		
Gay	Ga**yer**	Ga**yest**
grey	Gre**yer**	Gre**yest**

4) One syllabic positive word if ends with single consonant preceded by a short vowel, the *last consonant is* doubled before adding **–er** & **–est**.
   But, if the word ends with two consonants or single consonant preceded by double vowel, the consonant is not doubled:

Positive	Comparative	Superlative
Red	Redd**er**	Redd**est**
Big	Bigg**er**	Bigg**est**
Hot	Hott**er**	Hott**est**
Thin	Thinn**er**	Thinn**est**
Sad	Sadd**er**	Sadd**est**
Fat	Fatt**er**	Fatt**est**
Exceptions:		
Cool	Cool**er**	Cool**est**
Deep	Deep**er**	Deep**est**
Sick	Sick**er**	Sick**est**
Thick	Thick**er**	Thick**est**

5) Adjectives of two syllables or more ending in **–full, -less, -ing, -ed, -d, -n, -nt , -lt, -ish, -ous,** etc., take **more** or **most** before the positive form:

Positive	Comparative	Superlative
Beautiful	*More* Beautiful	*Most* Beautiful
Useful	*More* Useful	*Most* Useful
Hopeless	*More* Hopeless	*Most* Hopeless
Careless	*More* Careless	*Most* Careless
Boring	*More* Boring	*Most* Boring
Tiring	*More* Tiring	*Most* Tiring
Surprised	*More* Surprised	*Most* Surprised
Amused	*More* Amused	*Most* Amused
Stupid	*More* Stupid	*Most* Stupid

Modern	*More* Modern	*Most* Modern
Recent	*More* Recent	*Most* Recent
Certain	*More* Certain	*Most* Certain
Difficult	*More* Difficult	*Most* Difficult
Industrious	*More* Industrious	*Most* Industrious
Courageous	*More* Courageous	*Most* Courageous

6) Some other Adjectives of two or more syllables take '**more**' & '**most**' or add **-er/r & -est/st** to have Comparative & Superlative Degree. Both usages are common for them:

Positive	Comparative	Superlative
Cruel	Cruel**er** /**More** Cruel	Cruel**est**/**Most** Cruel
Common	Common**er** /**More** Common	Common**est**/ **Most** Common
Stupid	Stupid**er** /**More** Stupid	Stupid**est**/**Most** Stupid
Pleasant	Pleasant**er** /**More** Pleasant	Pleasant**est**/**Most** Pleasant
Narrow	Narrow**er** /**More** Narrow	Narrow**est**/**Most** Narrow
Simple	Simpl**er** /**More** Simple	Simpl**est**/**Most** Simple
Feeble	Feebl**er** /**More** Feeble	Feebl**est**/**Most Feeble**
Gentle	Gentl**er** /**More** Gentle	Gentl**est**/**Most** Gentle
Polite	Poli**ter** /**More** Polite	Polit**est**/**Most** Polite
Handsome	Handsom**er** /**More** Handsome	Handsom**est**/**Most Handsome**
Note:	However, '**more handsome**' & '**most handsome**' are more common in use.	

139. **The Comparative-look words which do not follow 'than':**

  ✗ *Certain English words— former, latter, upper, inner, outer, elder, utter,* etc., though looked comparative in form, have lost their comparative meaning and **these are used as Positive**. And these Adjectives forms ***are not followed by 'than' preposition; as,***
  → Santu got the ***upper*** hand. Brahmananda is my ***elder*** brother.
  → Sampa from Batun, is a member of the ***upper*** house of Parliament.
  → Ajit Master was a ***former*** teacher of this school.
  → Peter & Paramanada, I want to be the ***latter*** of the two.
  → Annanya & Ayesha, I love the ***former*** of the two.
  → To my ***utter*** amazement she agreed to come at my White Home!

  ➤ In all the above sentences, there were no any comparison made, though the adjectives have a look of comparative forms. All the adjectives are actually in the Positive Degree.

  ✗ The Use of '**that**' or '**that of**' in comparisons, with '**than**' (when comparison is made between two), and without '**than**' when there is no comparison, but merely an intension of similarity between two things; as,
  → Saint Peter's school is *better than that of* K.P. Birla.
  → This house is *better than that*.

→ My brother is *taller than that of* Ram.

→ She wants her name would be *as familiar as that of* Peter. (like Peter) [Here, comparison is not made, but has intention to bring out similarity. It is actually in the Positive Degree.]

140. **Latin Comparatives:**

✘ The Latin Comparatives are <u>only used in the Comparative Degree</u>, and <u>not in the Positive & Superlative Degree</u>. Latin comparatives end in **'–or', not '-er'.** **They are twelve in all**.

✘ **Five of them**- Interior, exterior, major, minor, & ulterior, like some English Comparatives, have <u>lost Comparative meaning</u>, and they <u>are always used in **Positive Degree**</u>; as in the following:

→ The *exterior* wall of the house is made of stone; the *interior* walls are of wood. The *interior* design of the house is great.

→ She was merely a *minor* when she achieved this medal.

→ She must have some *ulterior* (hidden or secret) motive for being nice to me. *Major* problems were solved.

✘ The remaining seven out of twelve Latin Comparatives-anterior, prior, posterior, inferior, superior, junior, & senior - <u>are followed by **'to'** (not **'than'**)</u> in the Comparative Degree [they do not have positive or superlative degree]; as,

→ His intelligence is **superior** to mine. (mine= my intelligence)

→ In the office, she is **superior** to me.

→ Her I.Q. is poor, truly speaking, **inferior** to others of her age.

→ The Ramayana and the Mahabharata are **posterior** to four Vedas.

→ This event is **anterior /prior** to that event.

→ Natasha is **senior** to Kiara Advani, and Kiara is **junior** to Asha.

→ He is **junior** to all his colleagues.

→ All his colleagues are **senior** to him.

Arrangement of Adjectives, more than one

141. **D**o **N**ot **O**bject to **S**ignificant **A**rrangement of **S**ystem.**COM** & use **Q**ualifiers (Participles) before **N**ouns. (Briefly, **DNO SASCO MQN**)

⇒ The above **bold colored letters** <u>each signify</u> 'a class of adjectives '**to be used in the order**, if each present in a sentence.

142. **The Position of Different Adjectives (Illustrations):**

✘ **Read the sentences:**
   a) A unique big antique round blue Chinese ceramic degrading plate was at our home for long days.
   b) I have bought two sturdy long old cylindrical black Japan-made wooden walking sticks yesterday from the Expo.
   c) The most expensive small new cubical white Indian silk budding stoles were sold on Amazon.

✘ <u>Steps to find out Adjectives and then to identify the order of arrangement of adjectives, used more than one</u>:
   1) **Divide the sentence according to Subject & Predicate.**
   2) **Then,** find out the <u>subject</u>, <u>verb</u>, <u>object</u> or <u>others separately</u>.
   3) Now, guess or identify where the adjectives are used.
   4) Study the order of arrangement to be used.

➢ <u>Follow the steps:</u>

   a) **A unique big antique round blue Chinese ceramic degrading plate** / was at our home for long days.
   b) **I** / have bought two sturdy long old cylindrical black Japan-made wooden walking sticks yesterday from the Expo.

c) **The most expensive small new cubical white Indian silk budding stoles** were sold on Amazon.

✗ The bold parts of the sentences are the **_Subjects_**, while the remaining parts falls to **_Predicate Group_** of sentences.

✗ What, if now we divide the sentences into **Subject, verb, object & others:**

a) **A unique big antique round blue Chinese ceramic degrading plate** / was/ at our home /for long days.
   - The bold part of the sentence is the **_Subject_**,
   - The next part— **'was'** is the verb,
   - While, **'at our home'** is an adverbial phrase, denoting *place*;
   - And **'for long days'**– is another adverbial phrase, denoting *'time'* in the sentence.

b) **I** / have bought /*two sturdy long old cylindrical black Japan-made wooden walking sticks*/ yesterday/ from the Expo.
   - The bold part of the sentence is the **_Subject_**,
   - The next part— **'have bought'** is the verb,
   - While, **'the italic words'** have formed the object of the sentence,
   - **'yesterday'**– is an adverb of time; and
   - **'From the Expo'** is an adverbial Phrase, denoting *'place'* from where it was bought.

c) **The most expensive small new cubical white Indian silk budding stoles** /was sold/ on Amazon.
   - The bold part of the sentence is the **_Subject_**,
   - **'was sold'** is the verb, and
   - **'on Amazon'** is an adverbial phrase, denoting *place, site, where budding stoles were sold.*

✗ Did you notice where the adjectives in all these sentences are? Okay, lets' check.

a) <u>**A unique big antique round blue Chinese ceramic degrading**</u> **plate** / was at <u>our</u> home for <u>long</u> days.

b) **I** / have bought <u>two sturdy long old cylindrical black Japan-made wooden walking</u> sticks yesterday from the Expo.

c) <u>**The most expensive small new cubical white Indian silk budding**</u> **stoles** were sold on Amazon.

✗ All the underlines in the above are the **_Adjectives_** *in the sentences.* Study the arrangement.

Proper Arrangement of Adjectives

Determiner	Number	Opinion	Size	Age	Shape	Color	Origin	Material	Participles	Nouns
An		unique	big	antique	round	blue	Chinese	ceramic	degrading	plate
	Two	sturdy	long	old	cylindrical	black	Japan made	wooden	walking	sticks
The		most expensive	small	new	cubical	white	Indian	silk	budding	stoles
Do	Not	Object to	Significant	Arrangemnt of	System.	C	O	M	& use Participle before	Nouns

143. **Important Notes:**

▪ **Degrees of Adjectives** are always used with the adjectives to which degree happens like – **'most expensive', 'longer' 'older'** etc. So, the degrees, if any, are put into the same box.

- ▪ **The article determiners** fall to the group of adjectives-Demonstrative (the) & Indefinite (a, an), they <u>*are used at the beginning of an adjective series*</u>, like in the chart shown.
- ▪ **Participles** do the work of **Adjective Qualifiers**; they are used just before Nouns at the end of the series of adjective arrangement.

- ▪ **Remember the line: D**o **N**ot **O**bject to **S**ignificant **A**rrangement of **S**ystem.**COM** & use **Q**ualifiers (Participles) before **N**ouns. (Briefly, **DNO SASCO MQN**).
    - ▪ The <u>Capital Bold Letters Stands for Each Kind of Adjectives</u> as they are used in a sentence.

Don't forget

- There are **eleven kinds of Adjectives** in use or functions.
- Out of which **seven kinds of adjectives** are formed from Nouns and Pronouns; as, Proper Adjective (or, so called Adjective of Origin), and
  - Indefinite,
  - Distributive,
  - Demonstrative,
  - Interrogative,
  - Possessive &
- Emphatic adjectives are derived from Pronouns.

- Though not all, but a lot of Adjectives are formed from other Adjectives, or Verbs or Nouns.
- The <u>adjective form that denotes zero comparison</u> is known as Positive Degree.
- The adjective form that denotes comparison between two, is known as Comparative Degree, &
- The adjective form that denotes comparison among three or more, is known as Superlative Degree.
- In the arrangement of adjective, more than one ina sentence, the brief note to remember is **D**o **N**ot **O**bject to **S**ignificant **A**rrangement of **S**ystem.**COM** & use **Q**ualifiers (Participles) before **N**ouns. (Briefly, **DNO SASCO MQN**).

Let us write:

- Choose any paragraph from a story, text of your syllabus, and then first identify the adjectives in the sentences. Try to find out adjective name or type.
- Try, to find out from which words have they come, if any.
- Mark out some adjectives of Quality, Number or Quantity and try for them to form other degrees.

The Adjectives need special attention

144. **Fill in the blanks with the correct words:**
   1. He had _____ money with him so he could buy the book. (some/many)
   2. How _____ papers do you need to make a file? (much/many)
   3. You need to have _____ courage to take that risk! (a lot of / all)
   4. There is nothing to worry about. Only _____ of my friends are yet to arrive. (little / a few)

   (The words you just filled with, are words showing quantity; and there are some others which show number.)

145. **The Correct Usage of—** Later, latest; latter, last; farther & further:

- ▪ **Later & Latest—refer to time**; as,
  1) He is later than I expected. (It denotes he is late more than expectation)
  2) I have not heard the latest news.
  3) What is your latest progress? (Progress of recently time)

- ▪ **Latter & Last—denote position**; as,
  4) The latter chapters lack humor & fun and so interest of the readers.
  5) The last chapter was carelessly written by the writer.
  6) Ours is the last house in the street.

- ▪ **'Farther' & 'Further'—both refer to express distance.** Besides, **'further'** denotes **'additional'**; as,

7) Balurghat is farther/further from the Sundarbans than Kolkata.
8) Further (not farther), Balurghat is a peaceful town in West Bengal.
9) He made no further remarks.

146. The Usage of— elder, eldest, older, oldest, nearest & next:

- **Elder & Eldest— are used only of persons, not of animals, or things; and now are confined to members of the same family**; as,
10) Ramananda is my elder brother.
11) Om is my elder son.
12) Brahmananda was the eldest son of Gayeshwar & Gita.

- **Older & Oldest— are used for both persons & things to mean the difference of age & time**; as,
13) This is the oldest temple in Kolkata.
14) This cow is older than that.
15) My house is older than yours.

- **'Nearest'— means the shortest distance,** While **'Next'** refers to one of **a sequence of things coming just after**; one after the other like; as,
16) Mumbai is the seaport nearest to Europe. Patiram is nearest to Hili.
17) Karim's shop is next to the Post Office. My uncle lives in the next house.
18) The next station is Shyambazar. My next step would be going there.

147. The Usage of—*some* and *any:*

- **Some, any—** are used to express both **quantity & number. 'Some'** *is used normally in affirmative or interrogative sentences; as,*
19) I will buy some mangoes. (Adj. of Number, countable)
20) There are some people left now in the hall. (number)
21) I have to buy some milk for the evening. (Adj. of quantity)
22) Will you have some ice-cream? (quantity) (expecting affirmative answer—yes)

- While **'any' denotes negative & interrogative sense; as,**
23) I will not buy any mango. (Adj. Of Number)
24) Is there any person left in the hall? (Expecting negative answer—no)
25) I didn't drink any water since last day evening. (Adj Of Quantity)
26) Is left any humanity? If not, let's go, please. (Quantity, uncountable)

- **Remember, 'any' can also be used in the affirmative sense in the conditional statements after 'if'**; as,
27) If you need any money, call me this number-000?
28) If you left any sense, just get lost from here.

148. The Usage of—Each & Every:

- **Each & every— are similar in meaning,** but **'each'** *is used when number in the group is* <u>limited & definite,</u> *like two or more as mentioned or known;* while **'every' denotes 'indefinite, 'more than two & not mentioned or known. (***But remember both these adjectives are of the group of Distributive Adjectives, which itself has come from Distributive Pronouns.***) Read the examples:*
29) Every seat was taken in the cinema hall. (Number is NOT mentioned, how many)
30) Leap year falls in every fourth year. (Every fourth year is a group, but where it ends, none knows)
31) He comes to see us every three days. (To denote such a group, must use 'every')
32) Five boys were seated on each bench. (The number 'five' is mentioned.)
33) Each of you must be punished for this action. *(How many, the speaker knows that number; the actual number is in his knowledge, though it is not mentioned in the sentence)*
34) I was away ten days and it rained each day.

149. The Usage of—Little, a little, the little:

- Little — means **'not much' (i.e., hardly any). The word has a negative meaning; as,**

35) There is little hope of his recovery. (i.e., he is not likely to recover)
36) I showed little concern for her anger from then.
37) I had little influence on my own child or children.

- **'A little'** refers to **'some though but not much'. However, it has a positive meaning; as,**
38) There is a little hope of his recovery. (i.e., he may possibly recover.)
39) A little tact would have saved the situation.
40) A little learning is a dangerous thing.

- **'The little'** means **'not much, but all there was or is'; as,**
41) The little information the Army General had was not sufficient to declare attack on the enemy.
42) The little knowledge of English Grammar I had liked to pour all over there in the book. (The knowledge is not much, but what was, was tried to pour).

150.   The Usage of—few, a few, the few:

- **Few** — means **'very small number' (i.e., almost non-existent). The word is used in the negative sense; as,**
43) Few students turned up for the extra class on a holiday. (i.e., almost no student turned up for the extra class on a holiday.)
44) Edward had few biscuits to distribute among students.
45) Sabine has few cards to give us on the auspicious occasion.

- **'A few'** refers to **'slightly more but not very much in number' (i.e., small number). However, it is used in a positive sense; as,**
46) A few students were still having their midday meal during that time. (i.e., a small number of students.)
47) A few students are enough to move the stone and pebbles from our track to the classrooms.
48) A few students performed the drama well.

- **'The few'** means **'not much in number, but all there are or were of it; as,**
49) We observed the Republic Day this year with the few students. (It means, a few students were present, and all of them observed the occasion.)
50) The few students responded well in the class. (It means there were small number of students present in the class, but who were, all responded fine in the class.).

151.   The Usage of—much, many, several, both:

- **'Much'** is used the uncountable nouns. It shows a large quantity**; as,**
51) There was much confusion over the date of examination.
52) Her recitation was frequently obstructed in much disturbance by loud speakers around of the building.

- **'Many'** is used with the countable nouns; as,
53) Many people like to go hills on summer vacation.
54) Many trees were cut down in the expansion of road and soon to experience outcome its shortcoming in the locality.

- **'Several'** is used to show a number, not very little and not very large either; as,
55) Several cars were parked in front of the building.
56) I had several bikes, but no any motorcycle.

- **'both'** is used when there are two nouns and both are being referred to; as,
57) Both Anna and Andrea performed in the school concert.
58) Both Archie and Kinsley were pop singers.

Don't forget
• Litte, a little, the little –are used with the uncountable nouns.
• Few, a few, the few – are used with the countable noun.
• Several and many are used with the countable nouns.
• Both can be used with countable as well a uncountable nouns.

Let us write:

- Suppose, you are in a grocery to buy some items. Make a list of the food or items for cook necessary at home and how much or many you need them. Ask the grocer in full sentences, using **few, little, several, one, two three**, and **both**.

.

7. The Determiners & Articles (a, an, the)

The word '**determiner**' refers to the word that comes before a Noun to show how the noun is being used (to define or decide something).

152. **Read the following lines or the passage. Note, which words are used before nouns. Circle them. Also underline the articles in the passage:**

Due to this, the Board has decided not to conduct these examinations through Haryana Board of School Education for one year. Now these examinations will be conducted at the school level itself," he said.
I want a pen. I love to be inside my house in storms. My house is on the bank of Atreyee. Must take an umbrella in rains.

(The words, circled or underlined, are either determiners or articles. They are used to define certain Nouns or Pronouns in the sentence. Thus, they are kind of adjectives. Out of which, a, an, the –are called articles. These are usually used before nouns and indicate which persons or things we are referring to in a sentence. For more, read further.)

153. **Now, read the following sentences:**

1) ***Which*** book do you want? Where is ***your*** house?
2) ***Some*** boys are playing. ***Many*** girls were singing.
3) ***This*** house is mine. That is ***our*** school.
4) Give me ***a*** pen. Give me ***an*** umbrella. ***The*** pen is red.
5) Have you ***any*** money? ***Every*** boy will get ***a*** prize.
6) ***All*** men are mortal. This is his ***third*** attempt.
7) Put a ***little*** sugar in the cup.
8) ***Neither*** of the boys went there.
9) ***Three*** persons were injured in the accident.

- In the above sentences, all the italic & bold words are the **determiners**. They are used before nouns and each determines or decides how the noun to be used. Sometimes they *hint ownership*, sometimes of *near or far*, *one or many*, etc.

154. **The following classes of words come under the term of 'Determiners':**

a) Articles— a, an, the;
b) Interrogative Adjectives— which, what, whose;
c) Possessive Adjectives— my, our, your, her, his, their, it's;
d) Demonstrative Adjectives— this, that, these, those;
e) Distributive Adjectives— each, every, both, neither, either;
f) Adjectives of Quantity & Numbers— one, two, three, etc.; first, second, third, etc.; some, many, any, few, little, several, much all, enough, great whole, etc.

- Try remember, we have already discussed most of the above, except 'Articles'. So, our current focus is on the Articles only.

Articles (a, an, & the)

155. **The Articles, actually, belong to Adjective of Number** (a, an) & **Demonstrative Adjective** ('the' to refer a particular person or a thing). But considering their importance with nouns, they are always discussed separately since the earlier time of English Grammar.

   - Among the three articles, **a** & **an**—are called the **indefinite articles**, as they denote a thing or a person generally or indefinitely.

✖ Whereas, **'the'** article is called the **definite article**, as it defines anything particularly or definitely.

156. **The Use of Indefinite articles:**

A. **The Use of 'a' article:**
   1) Before a noun that **begins with a consonant sound**; as, a boy, a mango, a guava, a hole, a woman, etc.
   2) A word that begins with a vowel but **pronounced** as, **'yu/eu/iu'** or **'oa'**; as, a university, a unicorn, a one-eyed demon, a one-rupee note, such a one, for examples:
      ▸ It is *a dog*.
      ▸ A cow is *a domestic animal*.
      ▸ He reads in *a university*.
      ▸ John is *a European*.
      ▸ I need such *a one-rupee note* to buy *a postal stamp*.
      ▸ Who saw *a unicorn* or *a one-eyed* demon?
      ▸ I like *a mango*. She like *a guava*.

B. **The Use of 'an' article:**
   1) Before a noun that **begins with a vowel**; as, an ass, an ink-pad, an orange, etc.
   2) A word that **begins with silent 'h' sound**: an hour, an honest, an heir, etc.
   3) A consonant letter **with a vowel sound** in abbreviations: M.B.B.S, M.P., S.D.O., F.B.I., L.L.B., M.A. etc.: For examples:
      ▸ She needs to study for *an hour* every day for per subject.
      ▸ Everybody likes *an honest man* but who loves to be so?
      ▸ Most of men boast of to be honest, but *an honest* hardly boasts of his honesty.
      ▸ She is *an M.B.B.S.* and she is *an M.P.*
      ▸ John tried to be *an F.B.I.* from last year.
      ▸ Now, she is *an L.L.B.* after four years of her study.
      ▸ Peter likes *an orange*.
      ▸ He is not *an honest man*.
      ▸ Who has not seen *an ass*? *An ass* has four legs.
      ▸ Study *an hour* for this subject every day.

157. **Some common Functions of A & An:**

FUNCTION of A or an	EXAMPLES
a). When the person or thing is **not definite**	I saw **a man on the road**.
b). Sometimes **to represent a whole class** as 'the' article.	**A dog** is a domestic animal.
Or, before the adjective to make it a whole class like 'the' article	**A poor** is hopeless here.
c). 'a/an' **cannot be used with adjective alone** but they are used with adjective + noun compounds, or simply before a noun.	He is **a** happy **man**. He is **a man**.
d). **Before the name of professions** or occupations often with **'be'** verb & after **'as'**	I am **a teacher**. / He is **an artist**. **As a mother** you are **a big zero**.
e). Often used in the sense of **'every/per'** <u>to relate one measuring unit to another</u>	Rice sells Rs. 50 **a** kilo. Earns Rs. 100 **a** day. The train runs 100 kms **an** hour.
f). **After exclamations with singular countable** nouns.	**What a beautiful** flower! **What a nice** fellow!

g). Before a particular **proper noun appear as common**.	He is **a Milton** of Bengal. My brother is **a Shakespeare** of our time.
h). Some expressions take a/an within the phrasal structure	**A few**, <u>a little</u>, a **headache**, <u>in a hurry</u>, **catch a cold**, <u>in a fix</u> etc.
i). In case **abstract noun is used as concrete or common noun.**	Mamtaz Mahal is **a beauty** (a beautiful monument). He is **an honesty**. (An example of honest man)
j). Sometimes, **as disguised preposition**, as short form of **'on'**.	He went **a hunting**. (On hunting)

158.   **The Uses of Definite article** (the):

USES	EXAMPLES
1. To **refer 'particular person, thing, dates & festivals.**	• The man who is in long kurta is my uncle. • Handover the book, please. • Today is the 15th August, the Independence Day in India. • The Durga Puja is the most special festival of West Bengal.
2. Before common noun **which are unique**	• The Sun give us light. • The stars twinkled at night. • The Earth revolves around the Sun. • We are inhabitant of the world • He finally reached the station. • He took service in the railways. • Leaves is **the kitchen of plants and trees.** • **He went to the toilet**, etc.
3. Before the expressions **relating our physical environment**	• **The weather** was fine on that day. • **The earth** is merely a very small part in **the Universe**. • The boys went on playing in **the sunshine.** • Who doesn't love visiting **the mountains?** • They ran through **the rain** for an hour. • **The wind** was blowing pleasant.
4. **Before the superlative degree**	• He is **the best** boy in the class. • It is **the worst** gift!
5. Before the adj—**next**, last, same, only and **cardinal number** (noun)	• Who is **the next** or **last**? • We went to **the same** school. • **The only** person whom I believe. • **The 2** is the lucky number of Ratan.
6. Before generic singular of common noun **to mean the whole class or race**	• **The dog** is a domestic animal.
7. **Before the adjective to make it a class noun**	• **The honest** must not be selfish. • **The poor** suffers lot, and anxiety lives always to **the rich.**
8. **The as an adverb with 'more' or other** comparative degree of adjective	• The more they read, the more they learn. • The sooner, the better.

9. **Before the names of 'Proper Nouns'**; a name of building, etc. (except the names of place, person, countries & God)	• The White House is in Washington. • Dell is the name of a computer. • Peter is a teacher. • India is a country in Asia. • New Delhi is the capital of India.
>Rivers, seas, ships, group of Islands, mountain ranges, deserts, forests (7)	The Ganges, The Pacific. The Titanic, The Maldives, The Alps, The Thar, The Sundarbans
>Races, famous buildings, sacred books, newspapers, musical instrument & particular proper noun, used as common noun (5)	The Indians, The French, The Bengali, The Santhals, The Hindu, The Muslim the Taj Mahal, The Gita, The Telegraph, the piano, the flute & • He is the Shakespeare of Bengal.

159. Study, where 'The' Article Is Not Used:

Where 'The' article is not used	Examples
1. The proper names of **person**, **places**, **country** does not follow 'the' article.	Dip, Balurghat, India, Canada (again exception of the USA/The USSR).
2. The common nouns of '**man', God &the name of games** & **meals** of daily routine does not follow 'the'.	• **Man** is mortal. • Where is **God**? **God** is great. • I play **cricket**/football, etc. • Every day we take our lunch & breakfast etc.
3. **The material, collective** or **abstract** nouns are not preceded by 'the' article	as '**water,** a **gang of robbers**, **honesty** etc.
4. '**The**' is not used before the name of a **language, day, month, season** or **year.**	We learn French/Bengali/ Hindi/Arabic/Chinese, etc. He came on Wednesday/in August/in Summer/in 2013.
Exception: But if the name of language is used as adjective to a noun or mean 'the nation' or 'people', 'the' is used.	• The English are conservative. • The English language is an international language. • The Bengali people are liberal.
5. '**The**' is not used before the name of a **disease.**	• The boy suffers from asthma. • The girl died in Encephalitis. • My friend died of Cholera
6. '**The**' is not used before the '**uncountable noun**'.	as '**water,** milk, **honesty** etc.
7. '**the**' is not used before the words— heaven, **hell, nature, man & God.**	Where is heaven/hell? Nature gives us life & oxygen.
8. Before the **name of single** mountain/island/country/city/village/park/street/railway station/port/airport, '**the**' is not used.	Mount Abu, Sri Lanka, India, Chakbhabani, Suresh Ranjan Park, Netaji Sarani, Balurghat Station, Haldia port, Kolkata Airport, Rammohan Street etc.

8. The Verbs & its Classification

160. **Underline the verbs in these sentences:**
  1. Salman **has** a friend, George.
  2. They **are** happy.
  3. They **play** football in the afternoon.
  4. We **bought** an umbrella.
  5. Who can **open** the lock?

Are all the verbs performing the same function?
In the first sentence, the verb **'has'** tells you that Salman possesses a friend, named George.
In the second sentence, the verb **'are'** tells us their state of being (that is, they are happy).
In the third, fourth, and fifth sentences, the verbs **'play'**, **'bought'** & **'open'** tell us about actions the subjects perform.
  (A verb is a word or a group of words that <u>tells something about a person or a thing</u> and which generally denote an action or an event, state of being, or possession.)

Again, read the followings

Carefully note the changes of underlined verbs in the sentences:

(1) Salman **_had_** a friend **_to talk_** to him, **_to play_** with him in his school days.
  I **_have_** also a friend **_to talk_** to me, **_to play_** with me in my school days.

(2) They **_are_** happy **_to see_** us.
  I **_am_** happy **_to see_** you at my home.

(3) They **_take_** exercise **_to be_** fit and healthy.
  She **_takes_** exercise regularly **_to be_** fit and healthy.

(4) We **_bought_** an umbrella **_to save_** us from rain.
  She **_buys_** an umbrella **_to save_** herself from rain

Have all the verbs changed their forms in the sentences from the first one in each pair of sentences?

There are some verbs which do not change their forms in the sentences. The verbs which do change their forms are called **Finite Verbs**, but the verbs which do not change their forms according to change of subjects and tense—are called the **Non-finite verbs**.

Actually, all the verbs, stative or event, main or helping, transitive or intransitive, regular or irregular (i.e., weak and strong), and may be thus more others by different names—are only and only and mainly, either **Finite Verbs** or **Non-finite Verbs**.

The so-called <u>Finite verbs are classified in different ways</u>, that we term as the **Classification of Verbs**.

So, all the verbs are grouped, firstly, as-
  • The Finite & the Non-finite verbs.

Then, *the Finite verbs are divided in three major ways; as,*
  • The Principal & Auxiliary Verbs;
  • State & Event Verbs; &
  • The Strong and Weak Verbs;

<u>And then, come the others, their sub-divisions or coined names for different functions or roles</u>; or due to having objects or no objects (i.e., the passing over an action to a receiver or not such a thing happen), and thus verbs may be Transitive or Intransitive; or the Linking, Factitive, Copula, etc.

• Please, study the following diagrams of **<u>Finite Verb Divisions</u>**, in which we have divided the master Finite Verbs in three major ways: as,

A. Principal & Auxiliaries
B. Regular & Irregular, &
C. State & Event verbs.

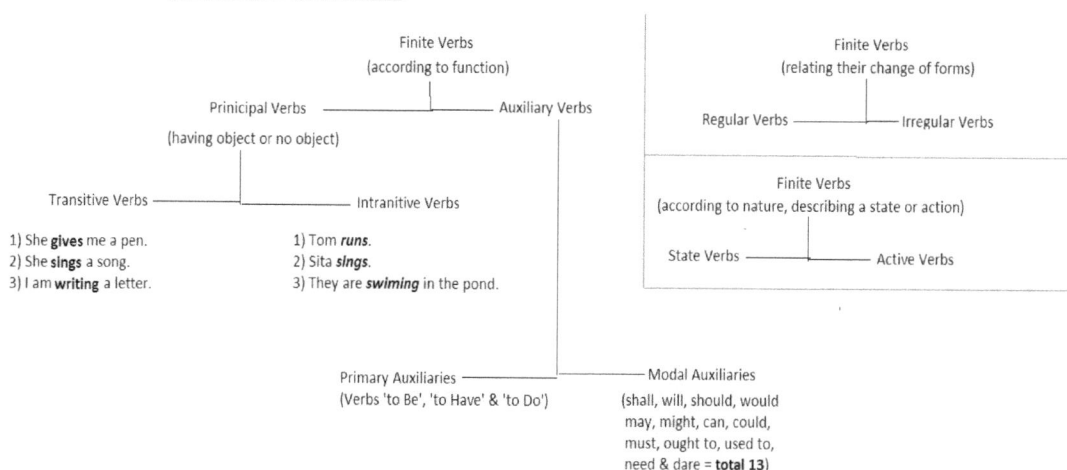

Finite Verbs
(according to function)

Prinicipal Verbs ———————————————— Auxiliary Verbs
(having object or no object)

Transitive Verbs ————————————— Intranitive Verbs

1) She **gives** me a pen.
2) She **sings** a song.
3) I am **writing** a letter.

1) Tom *runs*.
2) Sita *sings*.
3) They are *swiming* in the pond.

Finite Verbs
(relating their change of forms)

Regular Verbs ———————— Irregular Verbs

Finite Verbs
(according to nature, describing a state or action)

State Verbs ———————— Active Verbs

Primary Auxiliaries ——————————— Modal Auxiliaries
(Verbs 'to Be', 'to Have' & 'to Do')

(shall, will, should, would
may, might, can, could,
must, ought to, used to,
need & dare = **total 13**)

- And the Main or Principal Verbs again may be either Transitive or Intransitive, according to having their objects or no object to their credit.

- The Finite Verbs, also, either be 'Regular' or 'Irregular', relating their change of forms *in past & past participle in regular pattern or to be changed irregularly.*

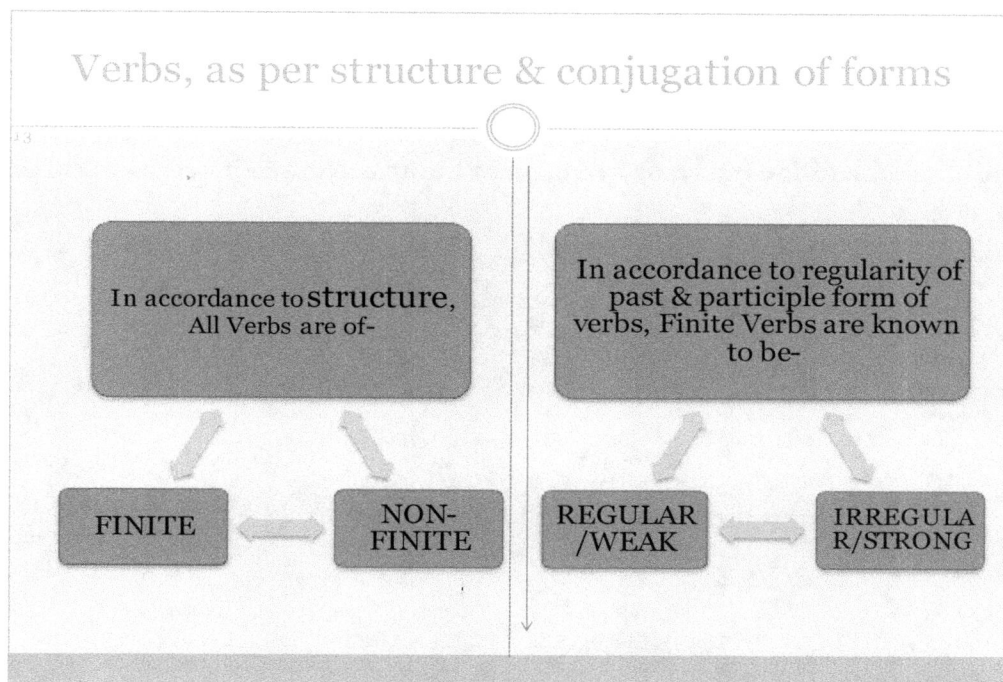

Verbs, as per structure & conjugation of forms

In accordance to **structure**, All Verbs are of-

In accordance to regularity of past & participle form of verbs, Finite Verbs are known to be-

FINITE ⟷ NON-FINITE

REGULAR /WEAK ⟷ IRREGULAR/STRONG

The interesting fact is- a verb of one group, may be the verb of other two groups too at the same time. For examples, study the following sentences:

1. Salman ***has*** a friend, George.
2. They ***are*** happy.
3. They ***play*** football in the afternoon.
4. We ***bought*** an umbrella.
5. Who can ***open*** the lock?

All the verbs, bold and italic are the examples of **Finite verbs** in the sentences. At the same time, they are **Principal verbs** too. Where, the verbs—**has & are**—are the <u>Stative</u> verbs, the verbs—**play, bought, open**—are the examples of <u>Event verbs</u>, in the sentence.

At the same time, the verbs are either in strong or weak conjugation in their forms in past and past participles. Let's see them—

> Has—had—had been
> Am, is, are—was, were—been
> Play—played—played
> Buy—bought—bought, &
> Open—opened-opened.

Did you notice, some verbs have changed their forms in past and past participle in <u>a regular rhythm or pattern</u> and their conjugation is termed as the **Weak conjugation**, whereas in other cases, the change <u>has not followed a regular pattern</u>, they are termed as the **Strong conjugation** of verbs. Thus, some verbs are called regular or weak verbs, and other as irregular or strong verbs.

In the above examples, the verbs—***play, open***—are the verbs of weak conjugation, so **weak verbs**; and the verbs—***has, am, buy***—are the verbs of strong conjugation, so they are **strong verbs**. They are named after their conjugation or unification in the change of form in past and past participle.

So, what I mean, a verb, being or falling to one group, there is no contradiction to be the others. Same verbs have different names based on their function, forms, nature & structure.

✖ <u>So, what we learnt</u>, all the verbs are either **State** <u>(i.e., Stative)</u> or **Event** <u>(i.e., Dynamic or Active)</u> verbs.

✖ And again, all the verbs are either **Finite or Non-Finite verbs** too.

✖ And at the same time, a verb always <u>either be a **helping** or a **main verb**</u> in the sentence (and if there is only one, that must be always the principal or main verb in the sentence),

✖ As well as a verb is either be <u>of **weak conjugation** or **strong conjugation** in form</u>. Though, there is a term 'mixed' has been used in the chapter of verb conjugation, it is better to consider them (verb of mixed conjugation) either to be one (however, the term 'strong conjugation' is preferred for them).

✖ **Again, see the following chart, division of Finite & Non-finite verbs in further branches:**

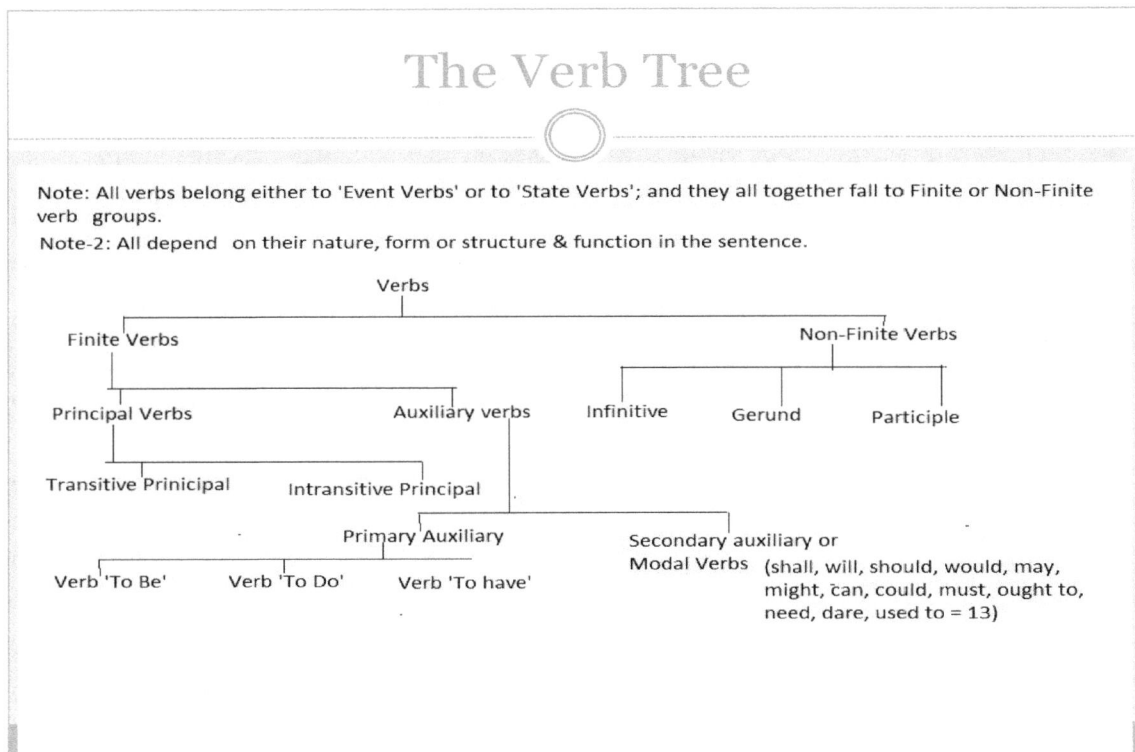

The Verb Tree

Note: All verbs belong either to 'Event Verbs' or to 'State Verbs'; and they all together fall to Finite or Non-Finite verb groups.

Note-2: All depend on their nature, form or structure & function in the sentence.

Verbs

Finite Verbs — Non-Finite Verbs

Principal Verbs — Auxiliary verbs — Infinitive — Gerund — Participle

Transitive Prinicipal — Intransitive Principal

Primary Auxiliary — Secondary auxiliary or Modal Verbs (shall, will, should, would, may, might, can, could, must, ought to, need, dare, used to = 13)

Verb 'To Be' — Verb 'To Do' — Verb 'To have'

Finite & Non-finite Verbs

161. **Read the sentences, and carefully note the changes:**
1. I <u>want</u> him <u>to paint</u> the picture.
2. She <u>wants</u> him <u>to paint</u> the picture.
3. They <u>wanted</u> him <u>to paint</u> the picture.

(Notice the underlined. Some verb forms have been changed, while some do not change their forms.)

o **Finite & Non-Finite Verbs:**

➢ To say, "All the verbs, State or Events, are also the Finite Verbs in structure.
➢ If we say, "*The Finite Verbs* are divided into *State or Event Verbs*", *I hope that will not be a blunder of Mr. Peter.*
➢ And most of Finite Verbs can also be given the form of **Non-finite** structure. You may say, it is another face of Finite verbs (<u>which do not</u> change according to the number, person of subjects & tense in the sentence).
➢ <u>Classification of verbs are, thus, based on different factors,</u> as forms, structure, meanings, use or functions and others.

✗ **Definition of Finite Verbs:** The verbs which *are changeable in forms*, according to the number, person of the subject & tense (time of action or state), are called the Finite verbs. Main verbs, Helping verbs, Transitive or Intransitive verb, all belong to the group of Finite verbs ; as,
   o We *write* essays. He *writes* an essay. They *wrote* essays.
   o Anna *thinks*. You *think* about her. They *thought* of us never.

✗ **Definition of Non-Finite Verbs:** The verbs *which do not agree, change* with number, person & tense, are called Non-finite Verbs. Infinitive, Gerund and Participle—are the examples of Non-finite Verbs.
✗ **Infinitive:** Infinitive are the base verb forms with or without 'to' preposition, non-changeable in the sentence; as,
   o We are here *to write* essays.
   o He is there *to write* an essay.
   o They are also there *to write*.
      ▪ Anna loves *to think*. You also love *to think* about her.
      ▪ They chose not *to think* about us ever.

	Finite Verb Forms	Non-Finite Verb Forms
Finite & Non-Finite VERBS Most of *Finite Verbs can be given the form or structure of Non finite*, i.e. the Finite Verbs can also be used as Non-finite (*when they are not bound to change their forms, according to number, person of the subjects & tense of the verbs*). <u>See their forms:</u>	Am, is, are, was , were	to be, being
	Has, have, had	to have, having
	Do, does, did, done	To do, doing
	Eat, eats, ate & eaten	To eat, eating
	Swim, swam, swimming	To swim, swimming
	drink., drinks, drank & drunk	To drink, drinking
	Sing, sings. Sang & sung	To sing, singing
	Fight, fights, fought, fighting	to fight, fighting

Gerund: Gerund are the -ing verb form of verbs which are mostly used as Noun in the sentence and thus form subject, object or complement; as,

- **Swimming** is a good exercise.
- Sonny like **eating** all the time.
- **Singing** is her hobby.
- I hardly like **teaching**.

Participle: Participle are also -ing verb form, or past or participle form of verbs which are used as adjectives in the sentence; as,

- Mia saw the tower **falling** on the ground.
- We saw Mia watching the **falling** tower.
- A **burnt** cow hardly goes in the sunshine.
- Andrea saw Ben **going** from the place.

  ✗ Study the following chart relating the use of verbs as Finite and Non-finite in the sentences:

Finite & Non-finite in the sentences:

Use of Finite Verbs	Use of Non-finite Verbs
1) I *am* a teacher. Teaching *is* my profession & I love it.	1) I want *to be* a teacher. She wants *to be* a teacher and many ones don't (want *to be*).
2) He *was* one of the best singers, you *were* not.	2) He wanted *to have* a bi-cycle. Shila wants *to have* a car.
3) He *had* two bi-cycles, and I *have* one.	3) I bought fish *to eat*. You buy chicken curry *to eat*.
4) I *eat* rice. Yesterday, I *ate* fish.	4) The little children went to the pond *to swim*. Rita does not know to how *to swim*.
5) The little children *swam* in the pond and got cold & fever. I *swim* in the river.	5) I took two glasses of water *to drink*. She takes one glass *to drink*.
6) We *drank* lot of last night. She *drinks*.	6) She doesn't know how *to sing*. *To sing* she reached Mumbai.
7) She *sings* nice. She *sang* a song.	7) *Singing* is her passion. I hate *singing*.
8) He *does*. He *did*. He had *done*. He is *doing*. And I am not *doing* anything.	
9) I *go*. She *goes*. He *went*, they will *go*.	

Principal and Auxiliaries

✖ Primarily, Finite Verbs are of two kinds: **main & auxiliaries**, and auxiliaries are further sub-divided into **Primary & Modals**. Study the following chart regarding division of Auxiliaries as Primary & Modals:

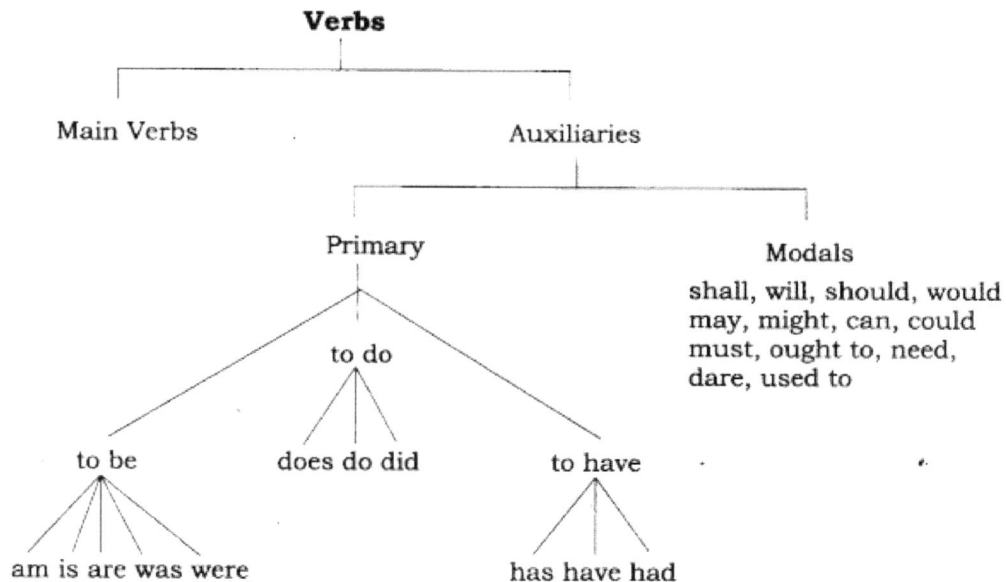

✖ The division of Finite Verbs, shown in the above diagram, is actually based on the <u>function of verbs in the sentence.</u>

✖ The diagram shows Finite Verbs to divide into two kinds, 1) Principal (main) & 2) Auxiliaries, and about further sub-divisions of Auxiliaries as primary auxiliaries (which are the verb 'to be', verb 'to have' & verb 'to do') and modal auxiliaries (**13 in number**).

o **Definitions:**

103

- ✖ **Principal verbs:** The *Verbs with definite meanings* or which are *used independently, shows action or state of being or having,* are called the **principal verbs**. These are also known as the **main verbs**.

- ✖ **Auxiliary verbs:** The Verbs which <u>assist or help</u> the main or principal verbs *to form progressive, completion of work; help to make questions, negation; to build tenses, voices* (i.e., the function of primary auxiliaries), or to express something like <u>possibility, certainty, permission, determination of an action</u> (i.e., the functions of Modals) are called the **auxiliary** or **helping verbs**.
  - → We **are** fine. You <u>can</u> **leave** us here.
  - → It **is** amazing! How <u>are</u> they **performing**?
  - → No, you <u>don't</u> **come** here. This party **is** for elders.
  - → I **stood** up. I **leaned** forward and **grabbed** his shirt collar.

- ✖ In the above sentences, the <u>bold ones are principal verbs</u>, whereas, <u>the underlines are the Auxiliary Verbs</u>.

> **Don't forget**
> - Verbs that change their form according to the number and person of the subject and the tense of the verb are called Finite Verbs.
> - Verbs that do not change their form according to the number and person of the subject and the tense of the verb is called Non-finite verb.
> - Finite verbs are further sub-divided into Main and Helping, or as Principal and Auxiliary verbs.
> - The main verbs are again two kinds regarding their passing over the action to receiver, i.e., having objects or no object to their credit at all. They are known as Transitive & Intransitive Verbs.
> - The auxiliaries are also of two kinds—Primary auxiliaries (be, do, have) and Modals (13 in number)
> - While the non-finite verbs are sub-divide into infinitives, gerund, and participle
> - Infinitive and gerunds can function as nouns in a sentence.
> - Participles do function as adjectives in a sentence.

Let us write:
- Write a short paragraph about yourself. Begins with introduction, who are you. What do you do and then about what you like or dislike, etc. After write the paragraph, try to find out verbs from the paragraph? Separate them as finite and non-finite, as main and helping, and also which are infinitive, gerund or participles.

State & Event Verbs

162.   As we said, all verbs are either Finite Verbs or Non-finite. Read the sentences:
- I **love** you, mom. You **take** so **care** of me.
- I **eat** an apple. I **read** a novel.

In nature, what do they refer, action or state? Thus, the finite verbs again may be grouped in two categories. They are either **State** or **Event** verbs. The 'State' verbs are also known as 'Stative' & 'Active' verbs are also referred to as **'Dynamic or Active verbs**.

- ✖ State verbs refer to <u>the way things 'are'</u>– liking or disliking, thoughts, feelings, perceptions & possessions; as,
- → I **think** that's a good idea. I **like** it.
- → I **love** this song! I **hate** nonsense!
- → That coffee **smells** good.
- → Do you **have** a pen?

- ✖ The Active verbs **describe actions we take or perform, i.e.,** the things we do, or things that happen; as,
- → I am not **laughing** at you.
- → Inspector Rana **put** his cup down.
- → Mrs. Saxena **is singing.**
- → She **refilled** my bowl.

163.   The Stative Verbs (More Explanation)

✖   Stative verbs describe a state *(describing mental, emotional or physical condition or existence)* rather than an action; and thus, the verbs generally are – the verbs *'to be', 'become', 'seem', 'appear',* etc. which describe the Subjects of the Verb; as,
   - Tom **is** happy. She **appears** sad. I **am** angry.
   - He **became** a politician. Radha **looks** excited.
   - She **is** beautiful. Don't **call** her fool.
   - We **made** him captain. Ayan **is** a doctor.
   - The brilliant student **became** the president of the state.
   - Dipika **looks** sad. Noah **seemed** tired.

✖   The most common state verbs in English, are the verb 'to Be', 'to Have' and the 'Modals'; as,
   - I **am** Jon. Lukas, Leon & Jon—we **are** friends.
   - I **know** Monika. Monika **is** my friend.
   - Andrey, you **are** really excellent!
   - We **should** respect our elders.
   - I **will** see this matter personally. Don't worry.
   - We **have** some land near bypass.

✖   Of State Verbs, '**To Be**' & '**To Have**'—are known as primary auxiliaries; while another primary auxiliary – '**to Do**' – *is an example of Active or Event Verb, when it is used as the main or principal verb* in the sentence.
   1. Verb 'To Be' as main or principal verb:
       - I **am** a boy. Elias **is** a doctor.
           - They **are** stupid.
   2. Verb 'To Be' as helping or auxiliary verb:
       - I **am** reading a book. He **is** operating an operation.
           - They are unpaid for last few months; yet, they **are** working very hard.

   3. Verb 'to Have' as main verb:
       - They **have** toys.
           - He **has** curly hair.
   4. Verb 'to Have' as helping verb:
       - They **have** performed well.
           - She **has** sung a song.

   5. Verb 'To Do' as helping verb:
       - **Do** you love me?
           - **Don't** go there.
   6. Verb 'To Do' as main verb:
       - She is **doing** her duty.
           - She **did** it excellent.

   7. Modal verbs as main verb:
       - He **needs** a car.
           - He d**ares**.
   8. Modal verbs as helping verb:
       - I **need** not go there.
           - He **dare** not go there.

All the verbs, bold and italic in serial nos-1, 2, 3, 4, 5, 7 & 8 – are the examples of **Stative verbs**, besides they are either Primary Auxiliaries or Modals; and those auxiliaries, sometimes, have also used as the main verbs in the above examples.

But the verbs in serial **no-6**, where verb '**To Do**' have been used as the main verbs— are the examples of **Event verbs**, besides they are another Primary auxiliary.

164.   The fields of State Verbs (State Verbs often relate to):

1) **Thoughts and opinions:** *know*, recognize, decline, deny, *believe, agree*, disagree, accept, *doubt, suspect, think,* suppose, *guess, imagine,* mean, *recognize, remember,* forget, *understand, realize, promise, satisfy, appreciate, etc.*

2) **Feelings and emotions:** astonish, *dislike,* detest, *hate, like, love, prefer, want, wish, need, dare, please, impress,* surprise, *concern, care for, adore, desire, hope, mind, value etc.*

3) **Senses and perceptions:** *look,* appear, seem, sound, verb 'to *be',* feel, hear, *smell, see, taste, touch, etc.*

4) **Possession and measurement:** - the verb 'to *have', refers belong to, own, possess, lack, consist, involve, include, contain, measure, weigh, value, cost, owe, depend, matter, etc.*

✘ The Stative Verbs **(it is better to say, 'generally, the stative verbs')** aren't usually used in the progressive *(continuous)* tenses; as,

1) *I don't **know** the answer. ~~I'm not knowing the answer.~~*
2) *She really **likes** you. ~~She's really liking you.~~*
3) *He **seems** happy at the moment. ~~He's seeming happy at the moment.~~*
4) *I **hate** this song. I **want** you to meet my parents.*
5) *I **appreciate** you helping John in time. Who **loves** me?*
6) *She **was** not a coward. She **had** cause for not coming.*
7) *The report **contains** a great deal of statistical information.*
8) *It **includes** all data of their crimes. He **seems** genius.*

✘ However, sometimes, stative verbs may also be used as the Event Verbs, considering the activities linked with or to mean the process of thinking or perception going on. **On that point, it is better to consider as an event verb (when to be used in progressing tense); as,**

1) *I **think** it's a good idea.*
   o *Wait a moment! I'm **thinking**.*

➤ The first sentence ***expresses an opinion. It is a mental state***, used in simple present tense, cannot be used in Progressive (Continuous) Tense in the same sense.
➤ In the second example, the verb is used to mean the *process of thoughts* which is going on or in progress. It refers to ***an action which is going on***. So, the Present Continuous Tense is used for the verb.

✘ **Some other examples:**

2) *'I **have** a car.'* (State verb, refers possession)
   o *'I am **having** a bath.'* – (as action verb, it refers an action to mean, 'taking bath')

3) *'I **think** she is right.* ('think', the State Verb, refers to 'mental state', the process is complete, so declared, 'she is right'.)
   o Is she right? I am thinking so. (The process is on. Thoughts going on. Still not come to the position to declare.)
   o I don't dare to say what I am **thinking**. (Here 'think' is not a State Verb, but an Active to mean 'the thoughts are in the process.)

165. **Study also some others, used as both, _Stative_ and _Event_:**

a) **have**
   → I *have* an old car. (State – possession)
   → He was *having* her meal, and the loud cry reached him outside from the jungle. (Action word – having his meal, taking food.)

b) **see**
   → Do you *see* any problems with that? (State – opinion)
   → We're *seeing* the Chairman tomorrow afternoon. (Action – we're meeting him)

c) **think**
   → 'I *think* you are cool.' (State – meaning 'in my opinion')
   → 'I am *thinking* about buying a motorbike.' (Action words as to mean– considering thoughts)

d) **be**
   → He'**s** so interesting! (State – his permanent quality)
   → He's b*eing* very unhelpful. (Action – he is temporarily going that situation)

e) **taste**
→ This coffee tastes delicious. (State – our perception of the coffee)
→ Look! The chef is tasting the soup. (Action – tasting the soup is an activity)

166. **Active** or **Dynamic Verbs**—which are also called **Event Verbs** or **Doing Words**, are <u>actually action words</u> that <u>denote any type of action</u>; as,
→ The maid has **cooked** gobi aloo & chapatis.
→ Who **told** you about Tehreek?
→ He was **shaking** his head.
→ The student had **paid** the fees.
→ Sourabh **nodded** his head.
→ You stopped me from **working** on the case.
→ The Sardar **insisted** on **kissing** his new bride.
→ She **gave** signals to calm down with her eyebrows & hands.
→ The police **shot** the convict down on the street of the town.

Note: 'working', 'kissing'-the present participles; but has the force of action, going on.

Don't forget
• Stative verbs are not used in the progressive tense, while the event verbs may be used in any.
• The state verbs and the event verbs are also together can be regarded as the Finite verbs.
• The classification of verbs as state and event verbs are actually <u>based on their meanings what they do refer or convey</u>, state or event, existence or happening, possession or creation, can be seen, touch, hear, or merely perceived in thoughts or ideas.
• So, the verbs related perceptions, thoughts, ideas, existence, possession (being or having & others) are called state verbs; and which refer an action, are called event verbs.
• He **thinks**. (Who can see it or hear, until it is expressed in action, 'he is **telling** us a story.')

Let us write:
• Write a passage or few lines on, what you thought or did on a day or in the duration of last four hours. After write it down, underline the verbs. Now contemplate what they are—stative or event verbs.

9. Transitive & Intransitive Verbs

167. Most of Dynamic (also: Active or Action) Words—generally have objects. A number of, however, do not have any object. Read the sentences.
1) Ben **gave** <u>me ten</u>.
2) Ben **runs**.
(Both sentences have a verb and a subject. But the first sentence does not make complete sense without the words following the verb, underlined; while the second sentence does, with the verb itself.)

In the above, both the verbs written in bold, are examples of **Principal Verbs** and both refer action. But one is **Transitive** and another is **Intransitive**. In the 2nd sentence, where the sense is complete with the verb itself **(as: 'run')**, the verb is known as Intransitive Verb. And in the first sentence, where the action of the verb passes over to other word or words necessarily to make the sense complete, the verb **(like: 'gave')** is known as Transitive Verb.
Again, many Stative verbs are also there, which has objects and some which do not have. Read the sentences.
• He **tastes** <u>coffee</u>. Ivy **loves** <u>me</u>.
• We **thought** <u>him</u> fool.
• Do you **know** <u>me</u>?

All the bold words are verbs, and the examples of Stative verbs and they are Transitive verbs too, as they have objects. And all the verbs belong to Finite cum Principal Verbs. And the <u>underlined words</u> are the examples of objects of the respective verbs.

Read more in the chart:

Object of a verb

Subject	Verb	Object	Others
Ember	gave	me a pen.	
Sagar	threw	the stone	to the mob.
My elder brother	hugged	me.	

In all the above sentences, the action of the verbs passes over to other; as,
- What did Ember give me? (**a pen**); Whom did Ember give the pen? (**me**)
- What did Sagar throw to the mob? (**the stone**)
- Whom did your elder brother hug? (**me**)

The answers written within brackets are the examples of Objects. Without the words, the sense of the respective verbs is incomplete, if we stop with the verb; as **Ember gave...** (what?); **Ember gave a pen...** (Whom?); **Sagar threw...** (what?); **my elder brother hugged...** (whom?) —the questions automatically rise in the listener's mind. The answer of the questions, made to the verbs, are the examples of **objects** in the sentences.

- ✗ **Transitive:** A verb (irrespective of state or event words) that denotes _an action or state which passes over_ from doer or subject or speaker to an object or receiver; as,
  - → I **gave** him a book.
  - → She **sang** a song.
  - → Mother **fed** her child.
  - → I **think** he is right.
  - → She **has** curly hair.

Transitive Verbs answer the questions with **'what'/ 'whom'** made to the verb.

But most of Stative verbs do not have any object; like in the followings:
- He**'s** so interesting!
- This coffee **tastes** delicious.
- He **appears** sad.

All the bold words are the examples of Intransitive verbs. At the same time, they are Principal verb cum Stative words by their function and nature.

Now, read through the chart:

sl. No	Subject	Verbs	Others/Complement
1.	The child	sleeps	all day.
2.	The birds	are chirping.	
3.	We	went	to the bazaar for shopping
4.	They	are	teachers.
5.	We	have	cars.

Let's question to each one of the sentences, particularly to the verbs:
- The child sleeps... (How long? [**not:** what? Or whom?])
- The birds chirping. (No question is necessary here; for the action stops with the verb.)
- We went ... (where? Why?) [**Obviously not:** what or whom?]
- They are ... (what?) [again by **'what?'**, but find out the difference.]

In the above sentences, except sentence no-2, here also we require ask question to the verb; but with other Wh-words; as, 'where', why, how, how long, in what manner, in what way, when, for what purpose, etc. (other than, by **'what'** or **'whom'**). The answer of the questions are **adverbials** or we generally mark out them, often, as **'others,'** to brief the discussion.

In examples-4 & 5, we again ask question by wh- word, **'what'** to the verb (**What are they? What do you have?**), as we did to find out an object. And here, the answers are 'teachers' and 'cars. One denotes **'profession'** and the other denotes **'possession'** of the subjects in the sentences.

However, **profession** and **possession** do not refer in the same way.

'Profession' of one person does not act upon another, [or more clearly refer to the same person who does the work; i.e., the subject of the verb; as, **'he is a teacher'**. 'he' and 'teacher' both refers same person.], **but possession refers having or ownership of something upon another;** as, 'I have a car.' Car does not refer myself, but my ownership upon the thing. [That means, my possession is acted upon then thing.] So, it is better to treat; 'car' as an object of the verb 'have'; but not as a complement. The 'state of possession' is passing over another; as, 'I love you'. My feeling is passing over you. 'You' is the object of verb 'love'. And 'have' and 'love'—both are example of Stative verbs cum Transitive verbs in the sentences.

So, in the above examples, when the word 'teachers' is a complement, the word, 'cars' is an example of object. Though, 'is' and 'have'—both are examples of stative words; 'is' is the intransitive verb, when 'have' is the example of transitive verb according to the above explanation.

So, the verbs, mentioned in 1, 2, 3 & 4 (*sleeps, are chirping, went, are,*) —are the examples of Intransitive verbs; but 'have' is an example of Transitive Verb.

- ✖ **Intransitive:** A verb (irrespective of state or event words) that denotes an action which *does not pass over to a receiver or an object (an action that stops with the word);* or the word that express 'a state', 'being' or 'perception'; is called the Intransitive Verb. Read some more examples.
  - → He **is** a school master. He **seems** sick.
  - → The water **boiled**. He **laughs** loudly.
  - → They **shouted**. We **ran** long way.

Of the above, the words— ***is, seems*** —are the state verbs, whereas, the words— ***boiled, laugh, shouted, ran*** —are the action words which stops with the action, do not pass over anything, except mention time, place or reason (adverbials), state, being or perception (complements). All they are the examples of Intransitive Verbs.

However, all the verbs, transitive or intransitive, fall to the group of Main or Principal Verbs. Therefore, it is said, **Principal Verbs are of two kinds**, which are determined by having their object or no object to their credit. In other words, whether action passes over or stops with the action.

Exercise-11

(A) Identify the verbs in each sentence and write if they are transitive or intransitive:
1. We are playing football.
2. Everyone laughed loudly at his joke.
3. The batsman hit the ball hard.
4. We went to the bazaar for shopping.
5. The first bell rings at 11:00 a.m.
6. Did you taste the delicious cake?
7. Marie sleeps soundly.
8. Angelika goes to market every Sunday.

(B) Underline the verbs in these sentences and identify them as transitive or intransitive. Then, circle the objects of the transitive verbs.
1. The guard opened the door.
2. There is very little light in this lamp.
3. Peter chose Mr. P as his pen name.
4. My mother has prepared delicious food for the occasion.
5. The lilies in the giant's garden look beautiful that enchanted the little children.
6. We had never driven that far.
7. We are moving to Mumbai soon.
8. Last year, we painted our house Asian paints.
9. We will participate in the Republic Day celebration.

10. The thief ran through the crowded street.
11. Was Shirley absent, yesterday?
12. Will you come with us in the party?

(Are there complements too, or adverbials? Try to find out them. We will discuss about them soon, in details.)

Don't forget

- Main or Principal verbs can be Transitive or Intransitive regarding passing over an action to receiver (having objects or no objects).
- A Transitive verb has object or objects. The objects may be Direct and Indirect.
- Intransitive verb does not have an object. However, it may have a complement. Complements of Intransitive Verbs always refer to subjects or they add meanings to the Subjects. And these complements are called **Subjective Complements**.
- A Transitive verb has object one or two. Sometimes, an object even is not enough to make a sense complete and clear. Then they need a Complement. These complements refer to the objects or add meanings to the Objects, so why, they are called **Objective Complement**. And the transitive verbs which need such complements, are termed as Factitive Transitive Verb in the sentence.
- The Complements are the extra word or words (generally a noun or an adjective, participle, gerund or an infinitive) which refer to the subject or object (i.e., which add meanings to the subject or object). And thus, they are either, Subjective or Objective complement.
- Study more of them in the chapter of complement.

Let us write:
- Answer the questions. Then, list the transitive and intransitive verbs used in the answer. Identify the objects of the transitive verbs and the complements of the intransitive verbs, if there are any.
  1. Have you seen '3 Idiots'?
  2. What did you like best in the movie?
  3. Do you like cricket? Watching or playing?
  4. Do you know Peter?
  5. Can you name any other movie, played by Aamir Khan?
  6. Who is your favorite actress?

10. Direct Object & Indirect Object

168. **A verb is a word or a group of words that express an action, or state or a situation**, including being, having, perceptions, ideas, thoughts, etc. about a person or a thing; as,
   a) He **runs**. (What does he do?)
   b) He **is** a musician. (What is he?) = **is** a musician.
   c) He **kicks** a ball. (What does he do with the ball?)
   d) We **call** him a fool. (What do we do?)
   e) She has a car? (What does she have?) = ... **has** a car.

➢ **What about** or **about whom** something is told, is the subject to the verbs; as,
   f) **You** are a stupid. (Who is a stupid?)
   g) **This pen** is red. (Which is red?)

➢ When **something is said about the subject** is either an object or a complement; as,
   h) He kicks **a ball**. (What does he kick?) [**a ball**—is an object.]
      i) He is **a student**. (What is he?) [**a student**= a complement, subjective].
   j) He has **an arm chair**. (What does he have?) [**an arm chair** = an object refers to the possession of something of the subject.]

Being, assume, appear — does not generally refer '**an action passing over**'; but the sense returns back to the subject. They take word or words generally adds meaning to the subjects. The words are called complement; as in 'i)' 'He is **a student**.'

➢ How a thing **happens, & when, where, why** (manner, time, place, reason or result**)** — are told by adverbs or adverbials; as,

k) Felix runs the race **very fast**. (How does Felix run the race?)
l) He walks all the way **singing**. (How does he walk?) =
m) He reads a book **in the evening**. (When does he read the book?)
n) Peter arrived home **at midnight**. (When did Peter arrive at home?)
o) He could not go there **as he is ill**. (Why couldn't he go there?)
p) We play **in the playground**. (where do you play?)
q) He was admitted **in Amri hospital** **last night** **by his uncle**. (Where was he admitted? When? By who?) ['where', 'when' ensure adverbials but 'by who' refers to actual subject of the action, who admitted him in the hospital.)

169.   Thus, a verb is the most important word in a sentence that defines a lot of things beyond the action or state (of being, having, or situation).

A question to verb helps us to define a lot of things beyond the action or verb themselves. **By ask questions to verb**, we may get *a subject*, *an object*, *a complement* and also an *adverbial* in the sentence; as,

- He kicks a ball. (Who kicks? What does he kick?)
- He is a teacher. (Who is a teacher? What is he?)

170.   *A verb tells us:*

a) What a person or a thing **does**; as,
- Shyam **laughs**. The baby **cries**.
- The clock **strikes**.
- Grandmother tells us fairy tales.

- Intransitive verbs.

b) What a person or a thing **does**, and **the action passes over to a receiver**; as,
- Grandmother **tells** us fairy tales.
- The player **hits** the ball.
- I **gave** you a pen is mine.

- Transitive verbs, and the underlined are the objects of the respective verbs.

c) What a person or a thing **is**: —
- He **is** a teacher. The table **was** broken.
- It **will be** very nice to meet her.

- Intransitive verbs. 'teacher', 'nice'—are complements.

d) What a person or a thing **possess**: —
- Christina had her own bungalow in this city. (She possessed the bungalow; so, 'have' is transitive verb, here.)
- She **has** a good character. (That means, he is a man of good character)
- 'I **have** no values in my life, no importance too to think over, except boredom, exhaustion, & an endless tiredness doing nothing at all to observe. (That means 'I am a man of no resolution and values to call.)

Note: When 'have verbs' denote qualities of a man or a thing possesses or its own, not a different entity, is the intransitive verb; as in the above. But when it is a different entity or thing, the verb is a transitive verb; as in, **'I have two torn shirts.'**

e) What a person think, perceives, senses, feels, likes appears, etc.; as,
- She **loves** me.
- I **think** you are right.
- I **like** eggs. I **hate** criticism.
- She **appears** sad.

- Transitive verbs. The underlined are the objects of the respective verbs.

Note: We have observed, having objects is the function of transitive verbs. So, all the verbs which have objects or take objects, are called Transitive verbs (irrespective of state or event word.) And all verbs, in this respect, should to be used as the main verbs in the sentence. Helping verbs cannot be treated as transitive or intransitive, if they are not used as main verbs in the sentence; as,

→ She is ***writing*** <u>a poetry</u>. She **is** a student.

→ He ***has*** <u>a black shirt</u> to wear. He has ***done*** <u>his work</u>.

In the above sentences, only the bold and italic words (**writing, has & done**) are the transitive verbs and the underlined (**a poetry, a black shirt, his work**) are their objects. Other bold word 'is' is the intransitive verb. The shaded verbs are neither transitive nor intransitive, but they are merely helping verbs in the sentences.

And all the verbs, mentioned, belong to finite verbs. Is, has—are the stative verbs and 'writing', 'done'—are the event verbs by their function, structure and nature.

✖ Same verb coins different names based on, see it from different viewpoints, based on its structure, function and nature; as, a man is a father, brother, son and a teacher.

✖ **A verb often consists of more than one word; as,**

→ The girls ***were singing***.

→ I ***have learnt*** my lesson.

→ They ***have been performing*** the dance show for last three hours.

→ My uncle ***was crying*** for help by then.

→ Rana ***had been studying*** while I reached his home.

→ Rama ***will come*** one day and he ***will free*** you.

→ She ***will be*** a singer soon.

→ We ***shall be waiting*** for our friends.

Note: the main verb has a common tendency to be used at last. The others are the helping verbs.

171. **Note:** Only Simple Present Tense & Simple Past Tense has single verb words, and they are always the main verbs. [study in detail in tense]; as,

→ Sourabh ***tapped*** his hand on his heart & ***nodded***.

→ I ***read*** a book. She ***sings*** a song. You ***speak*** too much.

→ Maizie ***has*** a skirt, green in color. Maizie ***is*** a girl of ten.

172. The Principal or the Main Verb builds the main meaning block for a sentence. Sometimes, an action is passing over from the doers to its receivers (termed as 'objects'), and sometimes, the action stops with the word, or better to say 'do not pass over; as,

• The boy ***kicks*** the football.

• Shilpa ***gave*** you a pen.

• The boy ***laughs***.

• The rose ***smells***.

Based on the above function action passes over or stops, it depends to have an object or not. **When the action passes over, we have objects and the verb is called Transitive Verb.** When the action stops with the word or says of a state, we don't have any object but a complement or adverbials, and the verb is called **Intransitive Verb**.

✖ In the first two sentences, the <u>*action passes over from doers (subjects) to their objects or receivers*</u> of the action—*football* & *pen*. The verbs—***kicks*** & ***gave***—are here **Transitive Verbs**.

✖ In the last two sentences, the action <u>*does not pass over, for action stops with the doers or subjects*</u>. They are **Intransitive Verbs** (meaning, not passing over).

✖ The verbs (state or event), including the state verbs that show possession (having) have their objects, when action is passing over to a receiver or shows possession of something; as,

→ Paul ***asked*** me a question. (**Whom** did Paul ask? **What**? = the action is passing over 'me' & 'a question')

→ Hudson ***provided*** us ample fruits in time. (**What** did Hudson provide us? **Whom** did he provide fruits?)

→ I *__have__* an iPhone. (Show possession) (**What** do you have? = 'an iPhone')
→ I *__think__* he is right.
→ We *__suspect__* her in this conspiracy. Don't judge by appearance.
→ I *__doubt__* (that) you are right.
→ Each mother *__concerns__* of her child.
→ It *__seems__*, we did mistake without doing anything for her in distress.
→ Everyone, present here, was involved in the crime. (It *__involved__* everyone)
→ It *__includes__* me. It *__contains__* three baskets, full of apples.

Did you notice, most of verbs I wrote here—are the state verbs, and they have objects too, like most of event verbs. And they all are the examples of Transitive Verbs.

✖ **The state verbs** which mean existence (being), perceptions, ideas, feelings (which describe back the subjects in most cases), and **the event verbs**, where the action do not pass over to receiver, things or person, are called the **Intransitive verbs,** and they often take complements to complete their sense; as,

→ Monika *is* intelligent. Archie *feels* tired.
→ He *dreams*. Jon *runs*.
→ The music *sounds* nice.
→ She *appears* sad. I *am* angry.
→ He *became* a politician. Radha *looks* excited.

So, to be Transitive or Intransitive, verbs are not bound to be always the event verbs or to be the action words. As state verbs equally can be both Transitive or Intransitive, like of the action words. For better understand learn to ask questions to the verb, as written above, by '**what**' and **whom**.

Note: At the same time, all the transitive and intransitive verbs are also the Principal or Main verbs. And all principal or helping, main or auxiliaries are at the same time Finite Verbs too. And the Finite verbs may either be of Strong or Weak conjugation in form.

173.   Most Transitive Verbs take a single object. But there are also some verbs that take double objects or more. Such verbs are—

⇒ *Give, ask, offer, promise, tell, etc.*

✖ **Direct Object:** The thing (animal or object) being acted on by the verb (directly), is called Direct Object. **Direct object receives the action of the verb directly; as,**
   • Jack caught **a fish**.
   • She worked **the clay** with her hands.
   • He hurts **me**.
   • I met **him** in town.
   • She gives **biscuits**.
   • The king hunted **a tiger**.
   • The teacher slapped **the student** so hard!
   • The player kicked **the ball**.
   • Please, pass **the stapler**.

✖ A noun, noun phrase or pronoun (that may refer to a person, an animal or a thing) that is directly affected by the action of a verb, is called **Direct Object**.

In the 1st sentence, the action 'caught' is directly acted upon 'fish'; so, 'fish' is the direct object. In the 2nd, the action 'worked' is acted upon 'the clay. So as, me, him, biscuits, a tiger, the student, the ball & the stapler—are the Direct Objects in the sentences.

✖ Generally, we ask question to the verb with '*what*' or '*whom*' to get the Direct Object in the sentence. It is irrespective of inanimate object or an animal.

✖ **Indirect Object:** An Indirect object denotes the nouns or pronouns which become involved in an action, acted upon the direct object. In other words, the indirect beneficiary of an action, and it *is dependent on* *direct object always. Without an indirect object, direct object can express the sense, but an indirect object can't.*

→ His father gave **him** (Indirect) a **watch** (Direct).
→ She told **me** (Indirect) a **secret** (Direct).
→ Give **me** (indirect) **the pen** (direct).

Now, if we write the sentences differently-
→ His father gave **him.**
→ She told **me.**
→ Give **me.**

Are these complete in sense, with the indirect objects merely

And again, in the following way-
→ His father gave a **watch**.
→ She told a **secret.**
→ Give **the pen**.

Are not these conveying a sense without the indirect objects, used in the sentences? Though, they miss some information about the action acted upon whom.

Therefore, it is said, <u>direct object to a far can express the sense, what the indirect objects can't,</u> without the help of direct object.

Underline the direct objects and circle the indirect objects in the followings:
• Mother beats me.
• I met her on Wednesday.
• Jenny gives biscuits to her pet dog.
• The king hunted a tiger.
• My elder brother gifted me a motor car.
• His father gave him a watch.

✘ 'A sentence, merely with a direct object is more meaningful than merely with an indirect object. So why, there is hardly any sentence with merely an indirect object. Of direct and indirect, if there is one object in a sentence, that must be the direct object. Without Direct object, an indirect object is not possible.

✘ 'His father gave a watch' — is more meaningful than the — 'His father gave him.'

✘ The first one can express itself without the other object. The direct object is the principal or main one, whereas the indirect object is dependable or helping to the main or direct object.

✘ **Object of a Preposition:** The noun, or pronoun or noun equivalent word that is followed and governed by a preceding preposition, is called the object of a Preposition.
• The fisher man fell over **the rail**.
• Cook without **salt**.
• Ava worked with **clay**.
• Ava worked the clay **with her hands**.
• Felix drove his car to **the garage**.
• Ember hits the dog with **a stick** gently to make it trained for the purpose.
• The police officer shot the accused with **his gun**.
•

Note: remember, a direct object is never in a prepositional phrase, and all the above underlined objects are examples of Objects of Preposition.

Complement: Complements are words, they either be noun, gerund, infinitive, adjective, participle or noun equivalent words, that complete the sense either of the subject or the object in a sentence. Thus, they are different from the indirect object, & from object of a preposition.

Study the following examples and spot out the *direct objects, indirect objects,* the *objects of preposition,* & the *complement, if any:*
• She told me a secret.
• My grand mom told me a story of fairy tale.

- They called me a fool.
- We elected him our president.
- He hits me.
- Felix talks to me about the solution.
- The police shot him death.
- Milo kicked the ball.
- Without any cause, she hurt me.
- Mother fed her child corn flakes.
- Ivy built Emma a fence. /Ivy built a fence for Emma.
- Catch the ball with your hand.
- She pushed the door to the wall.
- She hanged the calendar on the wall.

For your answer, follow the chart:

Direct Object	Indirect Object	Object of a preposition	Complement
Receive the action directly.	Assists or adds more information about the direct object. (Not in the way, as noun in apposition does.)	When a noun or a pronoun is governed by a preceding preposition in the sentence.	Adds meaning or complete the sense of the subject or an object in the sentence.
• She told me **a secret**. • My grand mom told me **a story of fairy tale**. • They called **me** a fool. • We elected **him** our president. • He hits **me**. • The police shot **him** death. • Milo kicked **the ball**. • Without any cause, she hurt **me**. • Mother fed her child **corn flakes**. • Ivy built Emma **a fence**.	• She told **me** a secret. • My grand mom told **me** a story of fairy tale. • Felix talks **to me** about the solution. • Mother fed **her child** corn flakes. • Ivy built **Emma** a fence. /Ivy built a fence **for Emma**. **To be Noted:** Some objects of preposition, are also regarded as the indirect object in the sentence which answer the questions with 'to whom, for whom, to what, what about' to the verb; as, In 'Felix talks to **me** about the **solution**'—both are objects of preposition and Indirect Objects	• Felix talks to me about **the solution.** • Catch the ball with **your hand**. • She pushed the door to **the wall** • She hanged the calendar on **the wall**. **To be Noted:** an object of a preposition, often does function like an adverb; as, In 'Catch the ball **with your hands**'-the underlined describes the adverb of manner, how to catch the ball; And in 3rd and 4th sentences, '**to the wall**' & '**on the wall**' denote position, 'where?' The question with '**for what**' to the verb _denotes an adverb of reason; as,_ Sonny pushed Ingrid **to make him fall.** **Why/what for/for what** did Sonny push Ingrid?	• They called me **a fool**. • We elected him **our president**. • The police shot him **death**. **To be Noted:** a complement directs or describes either to its subject or an object; as, 'fool' refers to the object 'me'; 'our president' refers to 'him', & 'death' describes the state of 'him'.

- Direct Objects answer the question of – '***what***' or '***whom***' to the verb; (when there are two objects, '**what**' ensures the direct object, and '**whom**' ensure the indirect object, mostly. If only one, it may come by either 'what' or 'whom'.)
- An Indirect Object answer the question of – '**to whom, for whom, to what, what about**' to the verb.
- An answer by the question '**for what**' to the verb, denote an **adverb of reason**; and by question '**what with**' to the verb, we get an adverb of manner, (as 'how?'). **Read the chart of comparison:**

Indirect Object (by preposition)	Simply, the Object of Preposition	Adverbial phrase

• Ivy built a fence **for Emma**. (For whom?)	• Catch the ball with **your hand**.	• Catch the ball **with your hand.** (what with to catch/how)
• Felix talks **to me** about the solution. (Whom does Felix talk to?)	• She pushed the door to **the wall.**	• She pushed the door **to the wall.** (where)
• Father gave a watch **to his son**. (Whom did father give the watch?)	• She hanged the calendar on **the wall**.	• She hanged the calendar **on the wall.** (where)
• **S**he told a secret **to me**. (Whom did she tell the secret?) [whom =to who; both in the accusative case]	**Note:** when we are telling about the object of a preposition, the preposition doesn't come to the account, but merely the noun or pronoun along with their qualifying words.	**Note:** when it is telling of an adverbial phrase, the preposition itself also come to the account along with the object.
• My grand mom told a story of fairy tale **to us**. (Whom did your grand mom tell the story of fairy tale?) **Note:** There are many Indirect objects without any preposition too.	However, the above objects do not fall to the category of Indirect Objects.	However, there are adverbials beyond this type too.

✖ The objects along with prepositions (the preposition and the object of preposition) which answer the questions with 'to whom, for whom, to what, what about' to the verb, are regarded as the Indirect Object in the sentence; as,
  • Ivy built a fence **for Emma**. (For whom?)
  • Felix talks **to me** about the solution. (Whom does Felix talk to?)
  • Father gave a watch **to his son**. (Whom did father give the watch?

✖ However, most of Objects to a preposition along with the preposition are the adverbial in nature and function, as the following:
  o Catch the ball **with your hand.** (What with to catch the ball/how do I catch the ball?)
  o She pushed the door **to the wall.** (Where did she push the door?)
  o She hanged the calendar **on the wall.** (Where did she hang the calendar?)

✖ Sometimes, the sentences with double objects (direct & Indirect) and a sentence which has a complement may arise a confusion regarding which is a complement and which one is an object. For your answer, read the following examples, and try to find out **direct**, **indirect** and **complement**:
• She told me a secret.
• They called me **a fool**.
• We elected him **our president**.
• The police shot him **death**.
• Mother fed her child corn flakes.
• Ivy built Emma a fence.

✖ Complement is a word or group of words which are related either with the subject or the object, and an object is a word, an action acted upon or involved with the action.
✖ In the above sentences, only the underlined and bold are the complements, and they are directly linked up or related with the objects, preceding them.

174.   An expert says, *"The action moves from the Subject, through the verb, to the Direct Object (that comes first) & then the Indirect Object."*

If so, let's concentrate-

  →   He tells me a story.
  →   He tells a story to me.

—which is Direct & which is Indirect?

✖ If his saying is true, then 'me' is the Direct Object & 'a story' is the Indirect Object in sentence 1; but in the 2nd sentence, that reverse, i.e., their identity or name, whatever, change. <u>To be direct or indirect object, therefore, it should be determined by the action and thing</u> (person or object) <u>it is acted upon directly, but not by position of the word merely</u>.

✖ We may check in the following:

"He tells a story" & "He tells me"—**which is more meaningful?**

> ➢ *He tells a story*—is complete in it; while
> ➢ *He tells me*—wants something more. That means it depends on 'a story'.

✖ So why, our conclusion is, '*a story*' is the **Direct Object** and '*me*' is the **Indirect Object** in the above sentences. However, in other case, it may differ; as,
   ☐ James Bond shot **him** with his **gun**. (Here, 'him' is the Direct Object ['shot' is directly acted upon him] & 'gun' is the Object of Preposition. However, **'with his gun'**, the phrase is an adverbial phrase, denotes the manner of action. [How did Bond shoot him? / What with?); &
   ☐ James Bond shot him **to death**. /James Bond shot him **death**. (Here, in both cases, **'death'** or **'to death'**—is the example of **complement**. *We get complement by question with '**What***; like we get an object. 'What did Bond do, by shoot him?'/ What happened to him when Bond shot him? [not like, where did Bond send him? For, 'to death' or 'death' is not a place but a state (or condition), from where we can't return. So, of course, it is not an adverb, like where do you live?)

Read some more examples:

1) His father gave **him** <u>**a watch**</u>.
                                        (If we write the same sentence in another way-)
   Father gave **a watch** to **his son**.

   2) She told **me** <u>**a secret**</u>.
   She told **a secret** to **me**.

   3) My grand mom told **us** <u>**a story of fairy tale**</u>.
   My grand mom told **a story of fairy tale** to **us**.

o (To who/Whom was the watch given? = the answer is same person, 'him' or 'his son'.)
o (Whom/To who did she tell the secret?) [whom =to who; both in the accusative case]
o (Whom did your grand mom tell the story?)

✖ In all the above cases, person becomes the answer— **'him/his son', 'me', 'us'**—are the answers. They all are the examples of Indirect Object. And, **'a watch', 'a secret', 'a story of fairy tale'**—are the Direct Objects.

<u>Further illustration:</u>

We have learnt, a Transitive Verb takes Objects. These Transitive Verbs, though mostly belong to the Active or Event Verbs, but verbs, related **thoughts, perceptions, feelings** (state verbs) <u>that pass upon another</u>, may equally have objects, direct or indirect; and the verbs (even being state verb) are termed as **Transitive Verbs**. <u>If a verb has only one object, it is better to regard it as the direct object, or simply 'object'</u> (irrespective of person or thing).
→ He <u>weighs</u> seven **stones**.
→ The dog <u>chewed</u> the **slippers**.
→ He is <u>playing</u> the **violin**.
→ Sana is <u>visiting</u> her **grandparents**.
→ Did you <u>complete</u> your **home tasks**?
→ Salena <u>loves</u> **him**. Salena <u>hates</u> **Peter**.
→ I <u>think</u>, **we should go now**. (What do you think? = we should go now = a noun clause, and an object to the principal verb 'think'. 'That we should go now.' 'that' is understood and comma has been used. 'think' is the state verb in the sentence, like 'weighs', love, hate & complete.)

- In each case, the underlined verb is Transitive Verb, & the bold words are the *Objects (Direct)*.
- **Love** or **hate**—are feelings, not actions like 'chew', 'play', 'visit'. They are <u>stative</u> and the <u>transitive</u> verbs;
- On the other hand, the verbs '**chew**', **play, visit**—are the <u>event verbs</u> as well as <u>transitive</u> verbs in the above sentences.

- And all they are, state, event or transitive — belong to the group of principal verbs in respect of function or use. (The principal verbs are verbs that can be used singly without any other verb, and here, they are used so) as well as they are the **Finite verbs** (as their forms are changeable according to tense, number & person in the sentence).

Passive Voice & Retained Object

175.   The term '**Retained Object**' is *related to object, Direct or Indirect which is left in a Passive Voice*. So, it is nothing but about Direct or Indirect object which is retained or left out only in the passive.

- We already know, a Transitive verb often take two objects—Direct & Indirect. <u>In the Voice-change from active to passive, one object takes the place of the Subject in the Passive Voice, while the other is retained (i.e., 'left out') as object, as it was in the Active</u> Voice, the left-out object is known as the '**Retained Object**' of the verb.
Study the examples:
  - I gave you two books. = You were given ***two books*** by me.
  - I asked him to sing. = He was asked ***to sing*** by me.
  - The host provided me the best service. = The best service was provided ***me*** by the host. / I was provided ***the best service*** by the host.
  - He offered me his car for the trip. = I was offered ***his car*** for the trip. / His car was offered ***me*** for the trip.
  - My grandmother often told me a story of fairy tale. = A story of fairy tale was often told ***me*** by my grandmother. / I was often told ***a story of fairy tale*** by my grandmother.

- Sometimes, action stops with the action itself, then it has no object, and the verb turns to be called '**Intransitive**'; as
→ He ***runs***. I ***swim***, Gita ***sings***, etc.

                                                                    And the above verbs also can be written as,

   He ***runs*** a race. I ***swam*** a swim on that day in the evening.
   Gita ***sings*** a Rabindra Sangeet at her residence.

   Thus, many of verbs can be used as both Transitively & Intransitively, and there are some which can't. <u>See the chart below:</u>

Verbs used Transitively	Verbs used Intransitively
1. He is ***playing*** football.	1. He is ***playing***.
2. The boy ***ran*** a race.	2. The boy ***runs***.
3. She ***hurried*** the children.	3. She ***hurried*** home.
4. India ***lost*** the match.	4. India ***lost***.
5. The ants ***fought*** the wasps.	5. Some ants ***fight*** very fiercely.
6. The shot ***sank*** the boat.	6. The boat ***sank*** very rapidly.
7. The priest ***rang*** the bell.	7. The bell ***rang*** loudly.
8. The driver ***stopped*** the train.	8. The train ***stop*** suddenly.
9. He ***spoke*** the truth.	9. She ***spoke*** haughtily.
10. The horse ***kicked*** the man.	10. Giraffe ***kicks*** heavily.
11. I ***feel*** severe pain in my head.	11. How do you ***feel***?
12. He ***broke*** the glass.	12. The glass ***broke.***
13. He ***burnt*** his fingers.	13. He ***burnt*** with shame.
14. ***Stop*** him from going.	14. We shall ***stop*** here for a few days.
15. ***Open*** all the windows.	15. The show ***opens*** at six O'clock.
16. Do not ***forget*** his name.	16. Don't ***forget***.
17. The Magistrate ***acquitted*** him of the charge against him.	17. He was ***acquitted***.
18. He ***enjoys*** good health.	18. They ***enjoyed*** very much.
19. His talk does not ***interest*** me.	19. It ***interests***.
20. The song ***made*** us happy.	20. The song ***made*** happy.
21. The guests ***made*** themselves merry.	21. They guest ***made*** merry.

Exercise-12

(A) **Circle the direct objects and underline the indirect objects in these sentences:**

1. The President awarded Ram Kamal the Padmashree for his contribution to games.
2. Grandmother told us a funny tale.
3. I promised my brother an ice cream this afternoon.
4. Jiten distributed sweets to his all classmates.
5. I don't show my paintings to anybody.
6. You know the reason.
7. He ordered a dozen books for the library.
8. I bought Jonathan a birthday gift.
9. The students sent the teacher an email.
10. We made him our captain.
11. She made her daughter a paper boat
12. She sang a sweet song.

(B) **Find out Direct Object, Indirect Object, or a Complement in the following sentences, if any is there:**

1) Sophia gives her brother a pen.
2) Jacob tells his friend to go there.
3) Noah asked me to hit the ball.
4) My friends gave me a bouquet.

Let's see, what if you ask these-

1) What does Sophia give her brother? Whom does she give the pen?
2) What does Jacob tell his friend? Whom does he tell to go?
3) What did Noah ask me/you to do? Whom did Noah ask to hit the ball?
4) What did your friends give you? Whom did your friends give a bouquet?

➤ Your answers by question with '**what**' to the verbs, are the Direct Objects; and your answers by question with '**whom**' to the verbs, are the Indirect Objects in the sentences. However, where there is only one object in the sentence, direct object can be obtained by ask questions, either with '**What**' or '**Whom**' (irrespective of animate or inanimate) to the verb.

➤ **To find out objects, complement or adverbials,** asking questions to the verb is very important. In the above, all the questions are related to find out merely objects (direct or indirect).

More examples for your exercise

- The teacher read a story to the class.
- The girls baked a cake for their mother.
- We gave some food to the beggar.
- The boys gifted their teacher a Kashmiri shawl.
- Little Red Riding Hood made biscuits for her grandfather.
- I bought bangles for my sister.
- We gave a map to the tourist.
- I read the newspaper to my grandmother.
- He is a *professor* of Kanpur University.
- She has a car. She had curly hair and a blunt nose.
- He possesses a large estate of his ancestors.
- We consider *her* our *head of the family*.

11. Methods to use Intransitive verbs, Transitively

176. **Most of <u>Intransitive Verbs can be used Transitively based on four factors:</u>**
  a) Either using Reflexive Objects,
  b) Using Cognate Objects,
  c) Using Prepositional Objects, or when a preposition is prefixed to the verb, coining a new word;
  d) Using the verbs in the Causative sense, and other, if any there.

By Reflexive Objects

177. Intransitive Verbs become Transitive, when they take **Reflexive Objects**; as,

Intransitive	Transitive
1. The bubble **burst**.	1. The bubble **burst** <u>itself</u>.
2. The guests **made** merry.	2. The guests **made** <u>themselves</u> merry.
3. Please **keep** quiet.	3. Please **keep** <u>yourselves</u> quiet.
4. With these words he **turned** to the door.	4. With these words he **turned** <u>himself</u> to the door.
5. The Japanese **feed** chiefly on rice.	5. The Japanese **feed** <u>themselves</u> chiefly on rice.
6. Please, don't **forget**.	6. I **forgot** <u>myself</u> after that accident.
7. He was **acquitted**.	7. **Acquit** <u>yourself</u> as innocent.
8. They **enjoyed** very much.	8. I **enjoy** <u>myself</u> sitting alone.
9. It **interests**.	9. He **interested** <u>himself</u> in his friend's welfare.
	The underline words are reflexive Objects of the verbs.
It is more usual to use the verbs as Intransitive.	Thus, verbs are used as Transitive Verbs. Actually, here Intransitive verbs are used as Transitively.

Using Cognate Objects

178. We can convert an Intransitive verb to Transitive <u>*by taking* **Cognate Object to the verb***</u> (cognate: which are akin or similar in meaning to the verb).

✖ There are *five different forms of Cognate Objects*:

A. <u>Strictly cognate, both in form and meaning:</u>
  → He <u>dreamt</u> a **dream**.
  → He <u>sang</u> a **song**.
  → He <u>lived</u> a **life**.
B. <u>Strictly Cognate in meaning, but not in form:</u>
  → He <u>went</u> a long **way**.
  → They <u>fought</u> a **battle**.

C. Partially Cognate, <u>containing a noun descriptive of the **cognate noun understood**</u>:
  → They <u>shouted</u> **applause**. (Applause= shouted a short of applause).
  → He <u>ran</u> a great **risk**. (a course of great risk)
D. Partially Cognate, when <u>an adjective qualifying the **cognate noun understood**</u>:
  → He <u>did</u> his best (**doing**).
  → He <u>breathed</u> his last (**breath**).
  → He <u>tried</u> the hardest (**trial/attempt**).
E. Partially Cognate by a **Cognate Noun** <u>expressed by '**it**'</u>:
  → We <u>must fight</u> **it** (a *fight*).
  → They <u>lorded</u> **it** (acted the *part of lord*) over us.

✖ Study more examples in the table below:

Intransitive	Transitive	
1. The soldiers **fought** bravely in the battlefield.	1. The soldiers **fought** a *fight* fiercely in the last battle.	
	2. The athlete **runs** a *race*.	

2. The athlete **runs** very fast.	3. Sita **sang** a sweet _song_.
3. Sita **sang** sweetly.	4. He **laughed** a hearty _laugh_.
4. He **laughed** heartily.	5. She **dreamt** a strange _dream_ last night.
5. She **dreamt** and woke up.	6. We **sleep** a _sleep_ every night and no work at day.
6. We **sleep** every night.	7. Let me **die** the _death_ of the righteous.
7. Let me **die**.	8. She **sighed** a deep _sigh_.
8. She **sighed** and talked to none.	9. The king **lived** a _life_ of ascetic.
9. The king lived and passed away.	10. The children shouted a shout of applause.
10. The children shouted loudly.	

By Prepositional Objects or...

179.   Some **Intransitive Verbs may become Transitive also with a Prepositional Object,** by having a preposition added to them (**when a preposition is prefixed to the verb** & that follows an object; as,

Intransitive	Transitive
1. She **laughs**.	1. All his friends **laughed at** (= _derided_) him.
2. Romesh **runs** very fast.	2. He will soon **run through** (= _consume_) his fortune.
3. He **looks** like his father. (resemble)	3. Please **look into** (= _investigate_) the matter carefully. / **Look at** (_see_) me.
4. They **talked** loudly.	4. We **talked about** (= _discussed_) the affair several times.
5. We can only **wish**.	5. I **wish for** (= _desire_) nothing more.
6. They **asked**.	6. The Police Inspector **asked for** (= _demanded_) his name.

4)   Some Intransitive Verbs (which always remain Intransitive) become Transitive **when a preposition is prefixed to the verb**; for, thereby it builds a new meaning; as,

Intransitive	Transitive
1. Shivaji **comes** to the Fort with some of his loyal men.	1. Shivaji **overcame** the enemy.
2. They **stood** there for nine hours.	2. He bravely **withstood** the attack.
3. Water **flows** in the river.	3. The river **overflows** its banks

Using verbs in the Causative Sense

Intransitive	Transitive
1. The horse **walks**.	1. He **walks** the horse. (walks the horse = _make the horse walk_)
2. The girl **ran** down the street	2. The little girl **ran** a needle into her finger. (ran a needle= _caused a needle to run_)
3. Birds **fly**.	3. The boys **fly** their kites. (i.e., _cause their kites to fly_.)
4. He **laughs**.	4. He **makes** me **laugh**.
5. He **had** punishment.	5. He **had** them **punished**.
6. Don't **move**.	6. **Move** the table.
7. Water **boils**.	7. **Boil** the water.
8. Rice **grows** here.	8. He **grows** rice in the field.

180. When Intransitive Verbs used in the causative sense, i.e., express the causative idea, intransitive verbs turn to be Transitive; as in the followings:

✖ **Note:** in such cases, the Intransitive Verbs are known also as the **'Causative Verbs** and they are used to express i) causing a thing to be done, ii) causing something to happen, or iii) cause or force someone to do something, as shown in the above table.

How the Intransitive Verbs express the causative sense or ideas:

✖ Some Intransitive Verbs have different forms to express **causative idea; as** by change of the spelling of the verbs within; as,
   → **'set'** for sit, **'fell'** for fall, **'feed'** for eat, etc. and they become Transitive Verbs; as read in the chart:

Intransitive	Transitive	
1. Many trees *fall* in the monsoon.	1. Woodmen *fell* trees in the forest. (fell = *cause to fall*)	
2. *Lie* still.	2. *Lay the* basket there. (lay = *cause to lie*)	
3. *Rise* early with the lark.	3. *Raise* your hands. (raise = *cause to rise*)	
4. *Sit* there.	4. *Set* the lamp on the table. (set = *cause to sit*)	
5. The child *eats*.	5. Mother *feeds* her child. (feed= cause to eat)	

181. Though lots of Intransitive Verbs can be used Transitively, but there are **some (verbs) which are always used Intransitively**; they cannot be used Transitively; as,
   o My uncle is *coming* from Delhi.
   o He *goes* to market every morning.
   o Fruits *fall* from the tree.
   o Every one *dies* one day.
   o Most of animals, *sleep* at night.
   o We *lay* on beds till noon.

182. **Exercise:** Some Transitive & Intransitive Verbs are thrown into the charts. Find out them from the columns:

Used Transitively	Used Intransitively
1. The boy cut his hand with a knife.	1. The sun shines brightly.
2. The policeman blew his whistle.	2. The clock stops this morning.
3. Put away your books.	3. The sun rises in the east.
4. Time changes all things.	4. An old beggar stood by the gate.
5. We eat mangoes during season.	5. The clock ticks all day long.
6. Tell the truth.	6. I looked down from my window.
7. The singer sang a folk song on the stage.	7. The man rose early.
8. My new watch does not keep good time.	8. The cat sleeps on the rug.
9. I could not spare the time.	9. Cock crows in the morning.
10. He took shelter under a tree.	10. The book lies on the table.
11. The boy easily lifted the heavy weight.	11. The fire burns dimly.
12. Bhola wrote a letter to his uncle.	12. We eat three times a day.
13. I know a funny little man.	13. The bird sings in the green trees.
14. I shall bring my camera with me.	14. You speak too loudly.
15. The dog ran after me.	15. Light rain fell last night.

12. Complement—Subjective & Objective

183. The verbs— mainly Factitive, Intransitive & Linking —take Complements (Subjective, Objective) to complete their sense.

Now, the question is **'What is called a 'Complement'?**

= Literally '*complement*' means '*to add to something*'. In grammar, however, it means '**to add something after verb** or **an object to make sense of the verb or the object more meaningful & perfect.**'

✖ A Complement is **a word** or **a phrase**, especially **an adjective** or **a noun**, and even **an infinitive, gerund** or a **participle** which are used to complete sense of a verb of Incomplete Predication like **Factitive, Intransitive & Linking** —which are mainly the State Verbs (like '*be*', '*become*', '*seem*', '*appear*', etc. which describe the Subjects of the Verb) and some Transitive verbs where verbs cannot complete its sense, in spite its object; they need extra words beyond the predicate (verb) & Object; the extra words are known as **Complements.**

> ➢ Tom is **happy**. She appears **sad**. I am **angry**.
> ➢ He became a **politician**. Radha looks **excited**.
> ➢ She is **beautiful**.
> ➢ We made him **captain**. Don't call me **fool**.

All the **bold words** in the above sentences are the examples of **Complements;** whereas the underlined verbs—*is, am appears, became, looks*—are the examples of linking cum Intransitive verbs, and the verbs—*made, call*—are the examples of Transitive cum Factitive verbs. ('Factitive' means what lacks to complete sense).

184. **Who takes a Complement?**

✖ Most of States verbs (some of which are also known as **Linking** verbs) and some of Transitive verbs of incomplete predication (which are known as **Factitive**) & **Intransitive** verbs need a complement in the sentence to complete their sense.

✖ Most of State verbs; as '**be', the verbs of perception, thoughts or ideas, etc.,** need complements to make their sense complete; as,
> ➢ Ayan **is** a *doctor*.
> ➢ Jacob **is** a *forest officer*.
> ➢ The food **was** *delicious*.
> > ➢ The underlined are the example of Subjective complement after 'be' verb.

✖ The above words (so called State Verbs) are also known as Linking Verbs. The other Linking verbs who take complements are:
> ➢ The brilliant student **became** the *president* of the state.
> ➢ Jacob **became** a forest officer.
> ➢ Dipika **looks** *sad*. Noah **seemed** *tired*.
> ➢ The food **tasted** *delicious*.

✖ The state verb '**have**', though many like to regard as the Intransitive verb, I think, it is better to consider as Transitive verb, as it answer the question with 'what'; like, 'what do you have' and the answer points to some other than the subjects. Read the following:
> o We **have** some *land* near bypass. (Land is the object, have is the transitive verb)
> o Christina had her own bungalow in this city. (She possessed the bungalow; so, 'have' is transitive verb, here too.)

The possession is applied on some land or a building; what do you possess or have? What did Chirstina have? It is not like the following:

> o I **am** a *teacher*. (What are you? Denotes a profession; and '**teacher**' & '**I**' refer same person; an example of subjective complement.); or
> o She **became** *tired*. ('**Becoming tired**' and '**she**' refer to the same person. Another example of subjective complement. And the verbs are intransitive cum linking verbs.

✖ However, when 'have' refers 'possession of a quality, not a different entity', we should regard 'have' as intransitive verb; as,
> • She **has** a good character. (*That means, he is a man of good character*)
> • 'I **have** no values in my life, no importance too to think over, except boredom, exhaustion, & an endless tiredness doing nothing at all to observe. (*That means 'I am a man of no resolution and values* to call.)

- She **has** no morality. (She is _a woman of immorality_)
- I **had** no values in life. (I was [had been] _a man of no values_).
  - Used the intransitive verbs transitively. The underlined are the complements.

Note: When 'have verbs' denote qualities of a man or a thing possesses or its own, not a different entity, is the intransitive verb; as in the above. But when it is a different entity or thing, the verb is a transitive verb; as in, 'I **have two torn shirts**.'

Factitive Verb & its Complements

185.   We have learnt, Transitive verbs have object, one or more than one. However, some of Transitive verbs, in spite of having their objects, cannot make their sense complete. These transitive verbs are known as **Factitive Verbs**. Read the examples:
- We **made** him _captain_. (The bold word is a transitive verb for, it has an object, him; and yet it cannot make its sense complete, it takes another word, captain (where '**captain**' and '**him**' refer to same person. This kind of transitive verbs are termed as the Factitive Verbs & the Complements are called Objective Complement.)
- They **regard** him _genius_. (The bold is Factitive Verb & the underlined is an Objective Complement)

Read the definition again:

The **Complements** are words, generally a Noun or a Noun Phrase, Adjective, Infinitive, Gerund or a Participle which are required after a verb (intransitive or linking) or after the object (in case of objective complement, to complete the sense of verbs (where the transitive verb is factitive).

186.   The verbs of incomplete predication (factitive transitive) are usually the words of naming, making, calling and thinking; as,
   a) I **named** her '_Rubi_'.
   b) Indians **named** Sachin _Little Master_.
   c) People **made** Gopal _king_.
   d) We **made** Romesh our _captain._
   e) They **called** John _a fool_.
   f) My loved **called** me _Peter_.
   g) We **thought** him wrong.
   h) The citizens **think** him _God of their time_.

   ✗ The above verbs or the italic words—_named, made, called, thought or think_— are the **factitive verbs** (transitive verbs of incomplete predication) and the underlined italic words—_Rubi, Little Master, king, captain, a fool, Peter, wrong, God of their time_— are the examples of **Complements (objective)**.

But this does not only happen to Transitive verbs of incomplete predication but also to Intransitive & Linking verbs. Now we will discuss which Intransitive verbs require a complement.

Intransitive Verbs & Complements.

187.   An Intransitive Verb that does not have an object. (The word or words which expresses **a state, being, having** [possession of a quality of the thing or person, not a different entity] or **an action** that stops with the word, i.e., the action does not pass over to a receiver—are generally known as the Intransitive Verbs).

✗ Like Factitive Intransitive Verbs, an Intransitive verb also sometimes needs a word or word phrase to complete its sense which we know as complements.
✗ When a Transitive Verb generally take Objective Complement; an Intransitive Verb takes only Subjective Complement (as it does not have any object); as,
   1) The sky **grew** dark.
   2) Roses **smell** sweet.
   3) Vinegar **tastes** bitter.

4) The baby **seems** <u>happy</u> (state).
5) She **appeared** <u>pleased</u>.
6) The house **is** <u>to let</u>.
7) There **is** <u>a flaw in this diamond</u>. (being)

The bold lettered words are the intransitive verbs, when the underlined are the examples of complements (subjective).

Linking Verbs & Complements:

188. **Linking Verbs or Copula:** verbs, such as— be, feel, become, grow, taste, remain, appear, act, smell, sound, stay, etc. can be used to <u>connect the subjects with its</u> A<u>djectives, Nouns or Adverbs</u> (Complement) which describe the subject itself; as,

a) <u>He</u> **is** <u>a fool</u>. ('he' & 'fool' refers to same person, the two words are linked or connected by the verb, 'is'; 'is' is the linking verb & 'a fool' is its complement)
b) <u>I</u> **am** <u>a stupid</u> that I am working on this dull project, to make 'A Complete English Grammar'! (I & stupid refers to same person [it is Peter], like the above, here it is linked or connected by the word 'am'; 'am' is the Linking verb & 'stupid' is the complement)
c) The <u>store</u> **remains** <u>open</u> the whole night. (Remains—is the Linking word, & 'open' is its complement)
d) <u>The smell of the soil</u> **is** <u>awesome</u> in the rainy season. (Awesome describes the smell of the soil, but does not refer to any action; 'is' is the Linking Verb, when 'awesome' is it's Complement).

❑ <u>All the above verbs link their subjects</u>, so called **nouns, pronouns** or **noun phrase** with **their adjectives** or **complements**. So why, they are called linking verbs; and **the most of the Linking verbs are not other than the State Verbs.**
❑ Again, all the above **Linking Verbs** or **Copula** <u>actually belong to the intransitive verbs too</u>. However, all <u>intransitive verbs are not linking verbs as well</u>; as,
   • 'He **runs**.
   • He **sings** sweetly.'
   Here the verbs are intransitive verbs, but not linking verbs, like 'be' and 'appear'.

189. **More Examples of Linking Verbs:**
   → <u>She</u> **felt** <u>tired</u>. <u>She</u> **appears** <u>dull</u> at the moment.
   → <u>She</u> **looked** <u>old</u> by her skin. <u>She</u> **was** <u>jealous</u>.
   → <u>K</u> **is** <u>jealous</u> of Peter, and P of Ruskin Bond, the famous.
   → The <u>baby</u> **grew** <u>young lady</u> after twenty years.
   → <u>He</u> **remained** <u>rich</u> even after his gigantic donation to a number of NGOs.
   → Don't **act** <u>fool</u>. <u>They</u> **are** <u>ready</u> to fight.
   → <u>I</u> **am** <u>Dr. Fernandez</u>. <u>It</u> tastes <u>sweet</u>.
   → <u>You</u> **are** <u>a fool</u>. Yet not to recognize me!

❖ **The interesting fact is, the verbs are, at the same time,**
   ✓ Finite Verbs,
   ✓ Principal Verbs,
   ✓ Intransitive &
   ✓ The State Verbs, *besides they are*
   ✓ Linking Verbs.

❖ So, the **Linking verbs** cum the **State verbs introduce, in the most cases, Subjective Complements.**

190. **The linking verbs may also be the action words; as,**
   → She **appears** in the party at the right time. (It hints her coming in the party, which is an action word) Or
   → She frequently **looked** at her fiancé in the party. (fiancé =male; fiancée= female) (her looking at her fiancé is an action word)

✖ In the above cases, the verbs are not the linking verbs (*appears, looked*). They are **neither State Verbs nor Linking Verbs any more**, for they do not introduce any complement, but object or adverbials. They are just like other normal Finite & Action Verbs. Here, they show action of the subjects and— 'in *the party', 'at the right time'*—are two adverbials, one denotes place, another denotes time; and '*her fiancé'* is an object of preposition.

Note: Introducing Complement is an important role of Linking Verbs, but not of Action words.

Object & Complement (comparative study)

191. **What is called an Object?**
= Generally, when an action is acted upon a person, animal or thing. The person, animal or the thing after the verb is called an Object. However, that may be Direct or Indirect or the Object of a Preposition.
→ She gives her brother a pen.
→ He tells him to go there.
→ They laugh at us.

192. **What is called a Complement?**
= When a verb needs more word or words to complete the sense beyond its predicate (finite verb) or object (in case of Transitive) and they are related either to the subject or object is called a complement.
→ He is a ***teacher***. ('is 'of verb 'to be' is the Principal Verb in the sentence, takes a complement, 'teacher', and which refers to the subject itself. Thus 'teacher' is subjective complement in the sentence.)
→ We made him ***captain***. ('Captain' is a complement here in the sentence. And as, it relates to the object 'him', it is objective complement.)

193. **Compare an Object & a Complement:**

Compare an Object & a Complement

Object	Complement
● **The baby wants to eat**.	● **The baby seems happy.**
➤ *The baby wants—what? Or what does the baby want? **To eat**—is the answer. The action or perception, "wants' is passing over 'to eat'. 'to eat' is an **object** of the verb, 'wants'.*	➤ *The baby seems—how does the baby seem to be? **happy**—is the answer which describes or relates the baby itself. In the sentence, 'happy' is the Complement and as it relates to the subject, the Complement is Subjective Complement.*
● **My friend gifted me a pen**.	● **My friends made me a hero.**
➤ *Here, **me** & **pen**—are objects, Indirect and Direct. Are they describing the subject or the object? No, the action is acted upon 'me' and 'pen' which was gifted. Gifting 'me', 'a pen'.*	➤ *'**made**' here is the Transitive verb and it has an object— '**me**'; and yet, look, it can't make complete the sense. My friends made me, what? **A hero**—is the answer and it returns back to 'me' to the object to describe 'me'; hero, who? 'me'. Thus, it is Objective Complement in the sentence.*

Subjective & Objective Complement

194. **Subjective & Objective Complement:**
Both *Transitive* and *Intransitive* verbs, as we discussed already, take complement; where the **Linking** & **Intransitive** verbs take Subjective Complement, the Transitive verbs (which are Factitive) take Objective Complement to make sense complete.

✖ So, complement is of two types—
- **Subjective Complement** (in case of Intransitive (which are also Linking Verbs); &
- **Objective Complement** (in case of Transitive Verbs of Incomplete Predication (which are known as Factitive); a factitive verb may have both type of complements to its credit.)

✖ Now read the following sentences:
- The baby **sleeps**. (Action word but Intransitive)

- The baby **seems** (to be) *happy*. (State Verb & Intransitive cum Linking verb; 'happy' is its complement.)

✗ **Note:** So, all <u>Intransitives</u> **are not bound to have** a 'Complement'. It may have or not.
✗ Similarly, **all Transitive are not factitive** and they do not bound to have a Complement.
✗ Remember, a Complement may be a word, or a phrase, and also may be a clause. Generally, it is a noun, noun phrase, an adjective, an infinitive, gerund, or a participle.

195. **Study the Complements Comparatively in the following chart:**

The Complements

Subjective	Objective
1. The earth is round.	1. The boys made Rama Captain.
2. John became a soldier.	2. His parents named him Peter.
3. Joe seems tired.	3. Joy Biden called him a liar.
4. You look happy.	4. God called the light day & lack of light night.
5. The car is to let/sell.	5. We thought him a rascal.
6. She appears pleased after the nano meeting.	6. They choose him their leader.
7. The report proved false.	7. The jury found him guilty.
8. The wind was cold.	8. Exercise made his muscle strong.
9. The results are out.	9. Do you consider me trustworthy?
10. The child fell asleep.	10. He makes me laugh.
11. The rumor seems true.	11. They elected him president.
12. The poor woman went mad.	12. We found her weeping.
13. The sky looks threatening.	13. She made herself wounded.

Exercise-13

(A) **Circle the verbs in these sentences. Then, pick out the complement and identify them a subject complements or object complements:**
   1. The quiz master was funny.
   2. The farmers looked tired.
   3. The principal selected Rajnish to be the class captain.
   4. We should be kind towards animals.
   5. We should respect our elders, parent and teacher.
   6. The class performed well in their examination.
   7. We named our son, Bipradip, and his younger brother a Nick.
   8. Nick loves abbreviation.
   9. He left the parcel untouched.
   10. Rahul's success in the examination earned him a reward.
   11. A long walk up the hill made us tired.
   12. The music sounds quite good.
   13. The class considers him intelligent.
   14. Will you do me a favor?
   15. John is a good athlete.
   16. The teacher handed us the answer sheets.

13. The Auxiliary Verbs and its Kinds

AUXILIARIES ARE OF TWO KINDS:

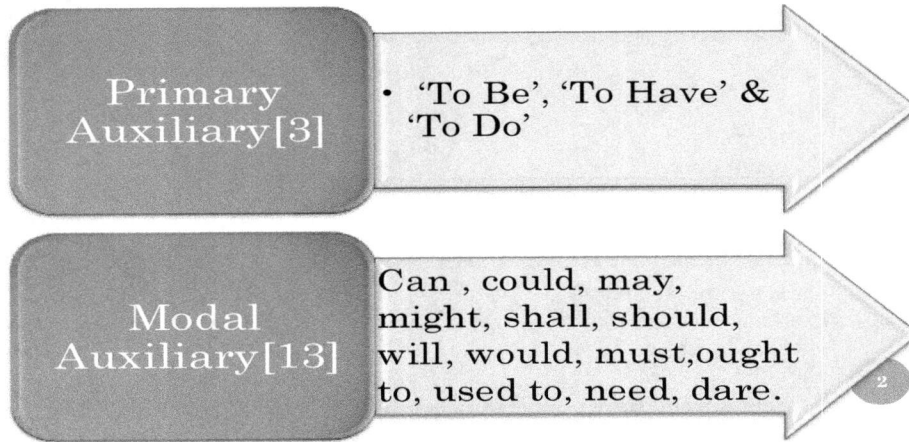

| Primary Auxiliary[3] | • 'To Be', 'To Have' & 'To Do' |

| Modal Auxiliary[13] | Can , could, may, might, shall, should, will, would, must,ought to, used to, need, dare. |

DUAL FUNCTION OF PRIMARY AUXILIARY VERBS

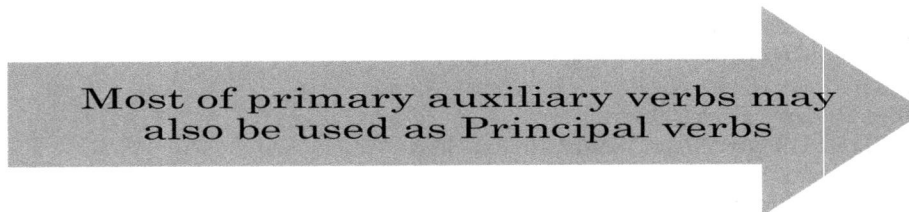

Most of primary auxiliary verbs may also be used as Principal verbs

STUDY THE SENTENCES

As Principal Verbs	As Auxiliary Verbs
1) I **am** a teacher.	1) I **am** <u>taught</u> English.
2) She **has** a wrist watch.	2) She **has** <u>bought</u> a wrist watch.
3) Rita **did** her job.	3) Rita **did** not <u>do</u> her job.
4) I **shall be** there.	4) I **shall be** <u>going</u> there.
5) It **was** my past.	5) It **was** <u>happened</u> in my past.
6) How **dare** you!	6) I **dare** not <u>say</u> who is wrong.
7) She **needs** me.	7) **Need** she <u>write</u> him?
	Note- The <u>underlined are main verbs</u>.

✘ Though, Primary auxiliaries—Be, Have, Do— are, often, used as the main verbs in sentences, modals are mostly used merely as the helping verbs, except 'need' & 'dare', as shown in first column of the above chart. In the first column the verbs (written in bold and single ones) have been used as the main verbs.

✘ But the same verbs in the second column (written in bold) have been used only as helping verbs, along with the main or principal verb which are underlined.

Primary Auxiliaries ('To Be', 'To Have', 'To Do')

196.   Primary Auxiliaries:

Definition: When the verbs 'To Be', 'To Have', & 'To Do', are used with ordinary verbs to make tenses, passive voice, questions & negatives, they are called **Primary Auxiliaries**.

The Auxiliaries are also known as Helping Verbs in English Grammar.

The Forms of verb 'To Be':
➢ Am, is, are, was, were, shall be, will be, be, being & been. ('shall be' & 'will be' are the compound forms of modal 'shall & will' with verb 'be') [10 in total]

The Forms of verb 'To Have':
➢ Has, have, had, having; and the compound have verb forms are— <u>shall have</u>, <u>will have</u>, <u>has been</u>, <u>have been</u>, <u>has been being</u>, <u>have been being</u>, <u>had been</u>, <u>had been being</u>, <u>shall have been</u>, <u>will have been</u>. (4+10 = 14 in total)

The Forms of verb 'To Do':
➢ Do, does, did, done and doing and the compound forms are– shall do, will do. [7 in total.]

✘ If we count all the primary auxiliaries and modals together, there are 31+ 13= 44 auxiliaries (verb-forms) in total (including all simple and compound verb-forms).

197.   The use of 'Be' Verbs in Tense & Passive Voice:
a) The Primary auxiliary *'Be verb forms'* (am, is are, was, were) are often used as the main verbs in Simple Present & Past tense.
→ He ***is*** an engineer.
→ I don't know the field where he ***is***.
→ It ***was*** you who did it.

b) The Primary auxiliary *'Be verb forms'* (am, is, are, was, were, shall be, will be, being) is <u>used in the formation of progressive or continuous tense; as,</u>

1) Shankar *is reading* a book. I *am writing* a letter.
2) You *are watching* alive show on the television.
3) Shankar *was singing* a Rabindra Sangeet on his harmonium. You *were playing* a guitar.
4) You *were dancing* cute on the stage in the function.
5) I *was swimming* in the river Atreyee and I saw the animal six yards far from me!
6) I *shall be eating* my lunch by then.
7) You *will be fighting*, everyone's attention must be drawn, and we will enter then through the main entrance.
8) Shankar *will be entertaining* everyone by his all means and tricks to attract everyone's attention on the main stage; will be the right time for our action.

c) The Primary auxiliary *'Be verb form'* **'been'** is used in perfect tenses of the passive voice, combined with **'have'** verb always, and in all <u>perfect continuous tenses,</u> in the active voice; & in passive voices along with another be verb form **'being'**; as,

1) The work *has been done* by me. (I have done my work.)
2) The prestigious rank *has been hit and won* by her. (She has hit the prestigious rank.)
3) She *has been singing* a song.
4) A song *has been being sung* by her.
5) I *have been reading* the book since morning.
6) The patient *had been fighting* patiently and the doctors were busy over their fresh demands.

d) The Primary auxiliary *'Be verb forms'* (am, is, are, was, were, be, been, being) is compulsorily used in the formation of the passive voice <u>(without 'be verb' there is no passive verb forms); as,</u>

1) A song *is sung* by him. (He sings a song.)
2) A rat *was killed* by a cat. (A cat killed a rat.)
3) The national anthem *will be sung* by them together. (They will sing the national anthem together).
4) The drama *has been being performed* by them. (They have been performing the drama.)

Use of 'be' verb with infinitive

e) 'Be' followed by an Infinitive is used-
✘ <u>To indicate a plan, arrangement, or agreement to be held in near future; as,</u>
  o *I am to see him tomorrow. (I am going to see him…)*
  o *We are to be married next month. (We are going to be married/ going to get married/ going to marry…)*
✘ <u>To denote a command; as,</u>
    o *You are to write your name at the top of each sheet of paper.*
    o *Mother says you are to go to market at once.*
✘ <u>With 'let', 'be' is used to denote allow or give permission; as,</u>
    o *Let him to be a doctor. Let him be our leader in the mission.*

f) **Verb 'To Be' is also used in past tense with perfect infinitive** <u>to indicate an arrangement that was made but not carried out; as,</u>
    o *They were to have been married last month but had to postpone due to the lockdown.*

The use of 'be' with Modals & 'let'

g) <u>**We have noticed the use of 'shall be' & 'will be',**</u> are actually are the compound use of 'modal 'shall' & 'will' followed by 'be'. They are used in the formation of future continuous tense & to form passive voice of simple future tense; as,
    o *I shall be reading a book by then.*
    o *You will be going along the street during that time.*
    o *It will be done by me. (I will do it.)*

h) Remember, **'be' is also used with other modal verbs**, in active or passive voice; as,
  - *You must be present in the meeting. It can be done by anyone.*
  - *You should be modest in your manner.*
  - *I would be glad if you come.*

i) **'be' is used with let causative verb in passive; as,**
  - *Let it **be** done. (Cause it to be done.)*
  - *Let him be flourished in his business.*

Use of 'Being' as Present Participle

j) **We have already seen, 'being' is used in all continuous tenses in passive voice** to refer the continuity of the action, when the principal verb turns to past participle form.
  - *A drama was being performed by them. (They were performing a drama.)*
  - *A drama had been being performed by them. (They had been performing a drama.)*
k) Remember, 'Being' is also used as present participle to join sentences.
  - *He was an honest man. He did not refuse to return. = Being an honest man, he did not refuse to return.*
  - *I am a teacher. How can I receive that? = Being a teacher, how can I receive that?*

198. **The use of Have Verbs:** Have verb has the following forms:
  - *Has, have, had, having;*

  - Compound have verb forms are— *shall have, will have, has been, have been, has been being, have been being, had been, had been being, shall have been, will have been.* (14 in number)

a) **Has, have** — as the principal verb, denotes possession, having or occupying something (physical or abstract) and treated as **Simple Present Tense** and **'had'** to form **Simple Past Tense**; as,
  - She has curly hair. I have an idea.
  - He had his house in the town. She had ill manners.

✖ **In the negation:**
  - They don't have any idea relating this. We had no building to call ours.
  - She has no manners. I have no idea. I have not any such a book.

  Note: There are more than two explanations about doing negation of 'have' verb when it is used as Main or Principal Verb in the sentence. Please, see the chapter of 'Forming Negation & Questions' for details.

b) **Has, have, had, shall have, will have**— as auxiliary, are **used to form Perfect Tenses)**; as,
  - *We have passed in the examination. We had paid the fees in due time.*
  - *We shall have been given examination by that month.*
  - *We shall have done the project by that time.*
  - *The project will have been done by us by that time.*

199. The Use of **'have had** & **had had':**
  - have had
  - had had

  ✖ Our topic to discuss:

  - have had to
  - had had to

  ✖ And also, about

✖ These are both **perfect constructions**. And the construction of a perfect tense is as the following:

→ Subject+ **_has/have_** +**_past participle form of verb_** + object (if any) + complements & others (adverbials).
→ Subject+ **_had+3rd form of main verb_**+ object or others (in past tense)

✖ 'Has', 'have' or 'had 'are primary auxiliary verb forms of verb **'to Have'** is followed by the past participle form of lexical (main or principal) verb.

So, we have already 'has or have' as helping verb in such a sentence. Now if the principal verb is itself another **'have'** meaning **possession** of something, **take** breakfast, dinner or meal or simply **eat**, what would be its past participle form? What is the pat participle form of main verb 'have'? Is not **'had'**?

If yes, you have got your answer. However, read the examples.

✖ 'Let's start with something very common what you and I fully understand and make understand. If I give you a chocolate **to eat**, you may write or say -

→ I **eat** a chocolate.

✖ *But then, in good English we practice*

→ I **have** a chocolate. ('have' means 'eat')

Note: (In good English 'have' means 'eat'; 'have' also refers to <u>all things or items that we eat</u>, like, breakfast, meal etc.)

✖ In modern English, we'll not use **'eat'**. Instead, we'll use **'have'**:

• I **eat** breakfast = I **have** breakfast.

• I **eat** my meal at 10 O'clock. = I **have** my meal at 10 O'clock.

✖ Writing that again:

• I **have** breakfast.

➢ Here, 'have' is used as a **main verb**. Is not it? And, we are talking about the **present** situation i.e., present indefinite tense.

➢ **NOW**, what if this present tense gets a *little* old matter? In other words, little time **has passed** and you want to tell that a bit later.

➢ You know that it is called 'present perfect tense,' because here we connect the present thing with the recent past.

➢ When you have breakfast at 8 am, and that you reveal at 10 am **or a time later**, what do you say with our old traditional writing?

➢ *I have eaten breakfast.*

✖ *The sentence is now in **present perfect tense**. You see that **'eat'** here became **'eaten'** the past participle form of 'eat'. And still 'eaten' is the main verb and preceding 'have' which is an auxiliary verb to form present perfect (to make recent past or denoting an action, a little older than simple present.)*

But as we discussed, we don't use 'eat'. We have our **'have'** *in place of 'eat'*. So, if we use the <u>past participle of **'have'** which in this case is **'had'**.</u>

Tell me then, what will be the sentence?

➢ *I have had breakfast. (In place of: '<u>I had eaten breakfast</u>')*

✖ I think it'd be now easy for you to understand the use of 'have had', 'had had' or 'have had to' & 'had had to' (when 'have to' = must).

200. Use of 'have' & 'had' with Infinitive 'to':

✖ 'have' is used with the Infinitive 'to', **'have to'** to indicate <u>obligation in present time;</u> & **'had to'** to express <u>obligation in the past time; as,</u>

• *I **have to be** there by five O'clock.* (The obligation refers to in present time, still to carry on.)

• He **has to move** the furniture himself.

• I **had to be** there by five O'clock. (The obligation is already past, already is late, now nothing to carry on, only to be informed.)

• He **had to move** the furniture himself.

✖ In *negatives and questions*, **'have to'** & **'had to'** are <u>used with **'do', 'does', 'did'**</u> as with another ordinary main verb; as,

• They **have to go**. > They **don't have to go. Do they have to go**?

132

- He **has to go**. > He **doesn't have to go. Does he have to go**?
- I **had to do** that work. > I **didn't have to do** that work. **Did I have to do** the work?

✘ But in Future obligation, do, does, did—does not need to add; as,
  - They **will have to go**. > They **will not have to go. Will they have to go**?

201. **More Examples:**

Now read the sentences carefully:

- I **had** ~~eaten~~ **had** breakfast. (The example is in **past perfect**)
- I **must** go. = I **have to** go. (**must** = **have to**)
- I **have had to** go. (To express obligation in recent past. The sentence is in present perfect tense; I have already gone under obligation.)
- I **had had to** go. (To express obligation in the past. The sentence is in past perfect tense. The first 'had' is an auxiliary verb, when the next 'had to' is the past participle form of 'have to' which is 'must'; nothing to carry on, it is already past or the speaker is already too late.)
- I **have eaten** my lunch. = I **have had** my lunch.
- She will have ~~taken~~ **had** her dinner by the evening.
- I **have had to** explain the perfect construction. (To express obligation in 'recent past'; the action is done in 'recent past'. The sentence is in present perfect tense)
- Two minutes ago, I wrote that I **had had to** explain the perfect construction. (The sentence is in past perfect tense; the action is already done or nothing is to carry on, for it is already past, said only to be informed.)

202. **The Use of 'Having' in Perfect Participle:**

✘ **Having**—is **used to form perfect participle**, generally to join sentences as 'being' (the present participle);
as,
  ➢ *They had waked up early. They started their journey by 8 a.m. = **Having woken up** early, they started their journey by 8 a.m.*

✘ **As perfect participle absolute, 'having' is also used; as,**
  ➢ The sun rose up. The army began their march. = The sun having risen up; the army began their march.

✘ **Note:** When there is time gap between two actions, use '*having*'; if the time gap is minimum, or hardly has any, use the present participle '*being*' for joining such sentences.

203. **The use of Verb 'to do':**

✘ **The following are the verb, 'To Do' Forms':**
  ➢ *Do, does, did, done* and *doing* and compound forms– *shall do, will do.*

a) **'Do'** verb is used both as **Principal** and **Helping** verb. As Principal verb it means **'doing something'** or
'doing a work'.

b) When it is used as Primary Auxiliary, it helps to form '**negation**' & '**questions**' in Simple Present &Simple Past Tense; as,
  ➢ We *did* our work.
  ➢ *Did* you *do* yours? *Don't* you?
  ➢ He *didn't do* his work.

✓In the above sentences, the underlined *did*, *do* & *do*– are Principal Verbs, when the bold **did, don't** and **didn't**—are the helping verbs.

c) The auxiliary 'do' is used to form the negation & questions of other verbs too; as
  ➢ He *doesn't* work. He *didn't* work.
  ➢ *Does* he work? *Did* he work?
  ➢ *Didn't* she go there? Why *didn't* he sing?

d) <u>Verb 'To Do' is also used to avoid repetition of a previous ordinary verb; as,</u>
> ➤ Do you know him? Yes, I **do**. (*Here, 'do' means 'know'; 'yes, I know him.'*)
➤ 'She sings well' or 'Does she sing well?' Yes, she **does**. (*Here, 'does' refers to 'she sings well'.*)
➤ You met him, **didn't** you? (*'didn't meet' / 'not met him.'*)
➤ She eats fish and so **do** you. (*So, you eat...*)

e) **'Do'** is also <u>**used to emphasize the affirmative nature of a statement**</u> (*not said of Negative & Questions*); as,
> ➤ You **do** look pale. (*Looking pale is emphasized by using 'do' before the ordinary verb*)
> ➤ I told him not to go, but he **did** go.

f) <u>**In the imperative, 'do' makes a request or invitation more persuasive**</u>; as,
> ➤ **Do** be quiet. (***Please** be quiet.*)
> ➤ Oh, **do** come! It's going to be such fun. (*Please come.*)

❖ In such cases, 'do' is strongly stressed.

Modal Auxiliaries

➤ There are 13 modals. All are used as auxiliaries, except need & dare. Besides to be used as helping or auxiliary, 'need' & 'dare' are also used as ordinary or main verbs in the sentence.

204. **Modal Auxiliaries** or simply **'Modals'**:
   o We use modal verbs to give more information about <u>obligation</u>, <u>ability</u>, <u>capability</u>, <u>willingness</u>, <u>possibility</u>, <u>permission</u>, <u>intention</u>, <u>logical conclusions</u>, etc. of a work.
      o Thus, Modals, more or less using before ordinary (main) verbs, describe the verbs (main) & define them or their functions (*like an adverb*); as,

   'We go'– a normal statement; but if we say,
   'We should go', it refers our 'moral obligation' to go; and thus define/modifying the verb 'go'.

   • All modals do the same functions—they do assist the main verbs to form particular meaning or mode of expression; as the followings:
      o <u>Sure,</u> you will go there. = You **_must_** go there.
      o <u>Politely</u> I am asking you to come. =<u>Please</u> you come. = You **_should_** come.
   • The above bold underlined and italic words are modals do almost same functions as of the other underlined words (not italic and bold), which are adverbs—**sure, politely**, and **please**.
   • Modals are basically used only as auxiliary or helping verb, except 'need' & 'dare'. Need & Dare are also used as the main verb; as,
      o How **dare** you!
      o She **needs** me.

205. There are thirteen (13) Modals. They are— *can, could, may, might, will, would, shall, should, must, ought to, used to, need & dare.*

206. **Points to remember:**
   • What 'Case' do for the Nouns or Pronouns, 'Modals' do the same for the Verbs, add meaning and give them a 'particular way', a new significance in the sentence.
   • The idea expressed by modals, more or less, is always different from ordinary statements. Using Modals, modality occurs in the expression, it changes and leads to particular way of expression.
   • *Modal Auxiliaries directly affect 'the way of expression'*, while the *Primary Auxiliaries are used to assist to form tense, question or negation of the sentence*. Where some of Primary Auxiliaries are also used as main or principal verb, of the modals only 'need' & 'dare' are often used as the main verb. Read the examples-
      ❑ I want to come.
      ❑ **May** I come in sir? (same thing that 'I want to come'; but it seeks permission and express politeness of the speaker.)
      ❑ I do the work.
      ❑ I **can** do the work. (express ability and strength to do the work.)
      ❑ She **needs** me. (here, 'needs' is used as the main verb to mean necessity of the speaker to her.)

- He **need** not go. He **dare not** do it. (here, in both cases, the modals are used as the helping or auxiliary verbs to assist the main verbs—go & do. One adds meaning 'necessity of his going', while another qualifies him, express his 'lack of courage' to do the work.)
- Pass me the salt.
- **Could** you pass me the salt? (express politeness in referring the same thing, 'pass me the salt.')

207. Compare-

Primary Auxiliaries	Modal Auxiliaries
Primary auxiliaries—can also be used as ordinary or principal verbs; as, a) I am a stupid, and so you are. b) Do your duty, I will do mine. c) Have you any car?	Modals are always auxiliaries, except need & dare; as, a) I can't go. I must do it before the end of the year. b) You may go on your choice. c) May I come in, sir? d) He needs me there. e) Even if none stands beside me. I dare be there.
1. Primary auxiliaries like <u>'Be' & 'Have' help to form tenses</u> (continuous and perfect) &<u>'Do' verb helps to form questions</u> & <u>negations</u> in simple present & past tenses; as, a) I am going to market. b) Have you done your homework? c) Do you like me? d) Don't go there. e) Do you have any objection?	2. <u>Modal auxiliaries</u> form moods of expression, <u>give 'particular way of expression'</u>; such as (they express) abilities, permission, possibilities, certainty & necessities, etc.; as, a) I can do this. b) Can I borrow your pen? c) May it rain. d) You must do it for me. e) Would you be mine? But alas!

208. **Modals as 'Defective Verbs':**

- <u>*Modals*</u> belong to **State Verbs** and they <u>*do not have **progressive ('-ing') forms***</u> *(though some State verbs can be used in Progressive and used as Event Verbs).* Unlike other State or Event Verbs, Modals <u>***do not have '-ed'***</u> *(the 3rd or* past participle) <u>*form*</u> too.
- Modals do not add ***'-s'/*** or ***'-es' to the third person singular number*** in Simple Present Tense *(**except**, 'need' & 'dare' & only in affirmative sense', not in negative or in questions).* So why many an expert of Grammar, defines them as '***Defective Verbs***'*(as some features of other auxiliaries & main verbs do lack in them; as already discussed).*
- However, modals have 'distinctive qualities', as we said to <u>*give main verbs a particular way to expression*</u>. Follow their uses or functions.

209. **Can, Could, May & Might:**

1) <u>'Can' usually expresses ability or capacity; as</u>
   a) I can swim across the river.
   b) He can work this sum.
   c) Can you lift this box?

2) <u>'May' is used to express 'a wish'; as,</u>
   d) May God bless you.
   e) May you live long & happily.
   f) May success attend you.

3) <u>Can & May are used to express permission or request. However, may is rather formal. It refers more politeness.</u>
   g) You can/may go now.
   h) Can/may I borrow your umbrella?

4) <u>'Could' & 'might' are also used to express permission or request as the versions of 'can' and 'may'; as</u>
   - i) Might/could I borrow your bicycle? (A different way of saying 'May/Can I...')
   - j) Could you pass me the salt? (polite request)

5) <u>May is used to express possibility in affirmative sentences. Can is used in corresponding interrogative & negative sentences; as</u>
   - k) It may rain tomorrow. (express possibility)
   - l) He may be at home. (express possibility)
   - m) Can this be true? (First, it is a question, asked corresponding to an earlier statement and at the same time express doubt, as, 'This cannot be true.' (It is the second part.)

   Note-1: Remember, either one part can be omitted or be kept silent, but it has the sense same. For Example, if the speaker says the 2nd part only, 'This cannot be true'; then too, it means well that the speaker has the question in his mind—negative statement is the result.

   Note-2: If we compare '**It cannot be true**' with '**It may not be true**'; '**Cannot**' denotes impossibility, while '**may not**' denotes improbability. Thus, they are different to express meaning.

6) <u>'Could and might are used as the past equivalents of can & may'; as,</u>
   - n) I **could** swim across the river, when I was young. (past ability)
   - o) He said I **might/could** go. (past possibility & ability)
   - p) I thought he **might** be at home. (past possibility)
   - q) She wondered whether it **could** be true. (possibility)

   Note: Could as in the first example, expresses only ability to do the act, but not the performance of an act. We can replace the words with 'was/were able to' for '**could**' & 'was/were possible to' for '**might**', but this may carry different meaning somewhere; as,
   When the boat was upset, we were able to (or, managed to) swim to the bank. (**not**: 'we could swim to the bank' for we swam and be saved. We did or performed the act, not only thought to do.)

   Note: In negative statements, however, either '**could**' or '**was /were able to**' may be used.

   I **couldn't** (or: **was not able to**) solve the puzzle. It was *too difficult*.

7) In <u>present-time contexts 'could' & 'might' are used as fewer positive versions of 'can' and 'may'; as</u>
   - r) I could attend the party. (Less positive and more hesitant than 'I can attend the party.)
   - s) Might/could I borrow your bicycle? (a different way of saying, 'May/Can I...')
   - t) It might rain today. (Less positive than 'it may rain...')
   - u) Could you pass me the salt? (polite request)

8) <u>'Might' is also used to express a degree of dissatisfaction or reproach; as,</u>
   - v) You might pay a little more attention to your appearance.
   - w) You might do some better result than this.
   - x) You might be present here on due time.

9) Note the use of can, could, may & might *with the Perfect Infinitive*:
   - y) He is not there. Where **can he have gone**? (= Where is it possible that he has gone? '**Can**' <u>expresses annoyance.</u>)
   - z) You could have accepted the offer. (Why didn't' accept the offer?)
   - aa) Fatima may/might have gone with Saroja. (Possibly Fatima has gone with Saroja.)
   - bb) Why did you drive so carelessly? You might have run into the lamp post. (It is fortunate that you didn't run into the lamp post.)

210.   **Shall, Should, Will & Would:**

1) **Shall & will**– are *used to build future tense*. 'Shall' is used in the 1st person, singular & plural; whereas, 'will' is used in all persons, both in singular & plural to express pure future; as,
   - a) I shall/will be thirty-five on next birthday.
   - b) We will need the money on 15th.
   - c) When shall we see you again?

d) Tomorrow will be Sunday.

e) You will see that I am right.

- ✱ With this, remember, use of 'I shall/we shall' is less common than 'I will/we will', and thus, <u>there is a growing tendency to use only '**will**' in all persons, both in singular or plural to express future.</u>
- ✱ However, *besides to express future, 'shall & will' are used to convey different goals:*

2) **Questions with 'shall I/we' is used to ask the will of the person addressed;** as,

f) Shall I open the door? (i.e., 'Do you want me to open it?')

g) Which pen shall I buy? (i.e., 'What is your advice?')

h) Where shall we go? (i.e., 'What is your suggestion?')

3) **'Will' is used to express:**

➢ Volition (free will); as,

i) I will (= am willing to) carry your books.

j) I will (= promise to) try to do better next time.

k) I will (= am determined to) succeed or die in the attempt.

➢ Characteristic habit; as,

l) He will talk about nothing but films.

m) She will sit for hours listening to the wireless.

➢ Assumption or probability; as,

n) This will be the book you want; I suppose.

o) That will be the postman, I think.

4) **Will you?** −indicates <u>an invitation</u> or <u>a request</u>; as,

p) Will you have tea?

q) Will you lend me your scooter?

5) **'should' & 'would'** are used <u>as the past equivalents of **'shall' & 'will'**; as,</u>

r) I expected that I ***should*** (more often: would) get a first class.

s) He said that he ***would*** be twenty-five on his next birthday.

t) She said she ***would*** carry my books.

u) She ***would*** sit for hours listening to the wireless. ***(past habit)***

   Note: She ***used to*** sit for hours listening to music in his boyhood days. ***(Discontinued past habit.)***

6) **'should/would'** is used to express more **politeness; as,**

v) I **should** (also would) like you to help her. **(should/would like—**<u>is the polite form of</u> **'want')**

w) **Would** you lend me your scooter, please? **('Would you?'** <u>is more polite than</u> **'will you?')**

x) **Would** you help me to solve the sum? **(Definitely more polite than 'will you?')**

7) **'Should'** is used in all persons to express **'duty or obligation'** & **'probability'** & **'should + perfect infinitive'** is used to indicate **past obligation; as,**

y) We **should** obey the law. (duty & obligation)

z) You **should** keep your promise. (duty & obligation)

aa) Children **should** obey their parents. (duty)

bb) She **should** be in the library now. (probability)

cc) You **should have been** more careful. (Past obligation)

8) <u>**'Would'** after **'wish'** expresses</u> **strong desire.**

dd) I <u>wish</u> you ***would*** not chatter so much.

ee) I <u>wish</u> she **would** be cure soon.

ff) Priya <u>wished</u> I **would** be her husband and liked to cut me into pieces through years before my salvation at her hand.

211. 'Must' & 'Have to':

1) **Must= have to** > is used <u>to express necessity or obligation of</u> present or near future.

2) **Had to** > refers to past necessity or obligation

   Note: ('must' does not have any past form directly; we use 'had to' to mean 'the past obligation or past necessity' and also as the past form of 'must'. And besides, remember 'have to' though similar in meaning with 'must', they may be used differently. Must see the following chart to find their different uses).

   Read the examples:

a. You must improve` your hand writing.
b. You must get up early in the morning.
c. Yesterday, I had to get up after midnight to shut the windows in the storm.
d. I had to break up the relation, sorry madam.
e. I had to shut up when she just began.

Compare

Must	Have to
• **'Must' is used when the obligation comes from the speaker.**	• **When the obligation comes from somewhere else, 'have to' is often used.**
1) I must be on a diet. (It is my own idea.)	1) I have to be on a diet. (The doctor has told me to be on a diet.)
2) You must be present there.	2) 'I have to go', as you wish.
3) He must go.	3) 'I have to be honest or I'll be in danger', people say.
• **Note:** In all cases, the obligation has come from the speaker, 'I'. I am telling about myself, telling 'you', and 'him' (command) respectively.	• **Note:** In sentence 2, the obligation comes from you (you wish); and in sentence 3, the obligation has come from 'people'.

3) 'Must' express **necessity & obligation**. Besides, **'must'** express **'logical certainty'.** *Something you are or the speaker is sure about to be or to happen relating situation or time, or any other thing, related.* Read the Examples:
  ✓ Living in such crowded conditions, must be difficult. (I am sure it is difficult, judging on facilities, difficulties, etc., of the place)
  ✓ She must have left already. (I am sure she has left already, as time is enough to leave for her.)

➤ **So, 'must' express**

  • 'Necessity or obligation' &
  • Logical certainty (something the speaker is sure about to be or happen)

212.   'Must' & 'Ought to':

▶ **Must** is used to express '**necessity or obligation**'; as,
  → You must do the sum & submit in due time.
  → I had to help her. (Had to = past of 'must'/ 'have to')
▶ & '**logical certainty**'; as,
  → Living in such pollution must be to live in hell.
  → Doing nothing in life must be like having no organs at all.

▶ **'Ought to'** is used to express '**moral obligation**' in past or present; as,
  → I ought to help her, being she was <u>an orphan/my neighbour/my countryman</u>.
  → She ought to give money to the old man, he is like her father.

▶ & '**probability**' (the probability is stronger than 'may'); as,
  → This ought to be helpful.
                      → That ought to be dangerous.

Compare-

Must	Ought to
• Must express *necessity or obligation*. • *Has the tone of command or order; more forceful.* • You must sing the song for me. • Shila must come on that day. • **Must express 'logical certainty'.** • Reading in such noises must be difficult. (I am sure it is difficult.) • She must have reached the station. *(I am sure she has reached.)* • Prices must have hiked during the lock down.	• 'Ought to' express *moral obligation' or 'desirability.* • It is *more about wish, or want or desire of the speaker; less forceful.* • We ought to love our neighbour. (our moral duty, like should, to live happily.) • You ought to know better. *(I wish you know better.)* • 'ought to' express **probability'** • Prices ought to come down after everything will be okay. (based on 'idea' but stronger than 'may'; if 'may' refers probability 50, 'ought to' refers 70) • This book ought to be helpful.

213. **'Used to'**

The Modal Verb '**used to**' is used to say –

1) '*a discontinued past habit*' (used to = *doing something often in the past. /did often*); as,
   - ➤ I used to swim in the pond. (Often, I did so)
   - ➤ I used to live there in my holidays. (lived there often)
   - ➤ We used to go sailing on the lake in summer.
   - ➤ My sister used to read till late night and she fell ill often. (She often did & often fell ill)

2) '*Something that happened or existing continuously*'; *as,*
   - ➤ There used to be a house long years ago. (There was a house for a time being)
   - ➤ I used to live there when I was mere a boy. (I was living there for a time being)
   - ➤ I used to be her best partner in her all visits to London when we were quite young. (This also does not mean only 'a habit frequently happened but for a time being when we were young, for a long time, but that happened when she made the visits)

3) The modal auxiliary '**used to**', is also *often used with '**did**' in questions* to mean '*happened often*' & *in negative to mean '**always or never**'; as,
   - ➤ Did you used to swim in the river? (Swim often)
   - ➤ He did not used to visit her house. (Either he visited regularly or never, but not visited often)

   - ➤ **Remember:** 'used to' has only one form and is used only in the past tense; as in the above examples:

Verb 'Need' & 'Need to'

214. **The use of 'Need'-as a Principal Verb:**

i) When '**need**' means 'require something or somebody which or who is very essential or very important to be with, to do, or to have, they are Principal or main Verb in the sentence.

ii) **Remember:** Only in *assertive affirmative* 'need' & 'dare', as principal verb, take '**-s**', '**-ed**' forms; as,
   - → I need him beside me in this situation. (His being [to be] with me is very necessary in this situation.)
   - → We need plans to become success. (Plans or planning is very important to become success.)
   - → He needs a pen for writing his papers. (Pen is essential for writing)
   - → When you needed me, I was not there. (When you required me, I was not there.)

iii) The **principal verb 'need'** can be conjugated with or without 'do', generally in the negative & interrogative sentences & in affirmative only for emphasis; as,

→ Do you need any help?
→ Don't go, I might need you doing this one.
→ What do you need your own computer for? You can use ours.
→ I don't need your comments. Thank you. I needed you in my need.

iv) and the principal **'need'** do not follow any **'to'** preposition and not any other verb but an object, like a transitive verb, gives answer to the question of 'what' & 'whom' to the verb; as,

→ It's here, if you need it. *(What do you need? =it)* I don't need you. *(Whom? =you)*
→ They badly needed a change. *(What did they need very much? = a change)*
→ Food aid is urgently needed. *(What is urgently needed? = food aid.)*

v) As Principal verb **'need'** may be conjugated with or without **'do'** ('do', 'does' & 'did'); & it has usual form of **'needs'** (in 3rd person singular number, *but only in assertive sentence, not in negative & questions*) & **'needed'** in the past tense**; as,**

→ I need a pen. /I do need a pen.
→ Need I a pen? /Do I need a pen?
→ I need not a pen. /I do not need a pen.
→ She **needs** a saree. (assertive & affirmative)
→ **Does she need** a saree?
→ She **doesn't need** a saree.
→ She **need** not a saree. (**Not:** *needs*)
→ You **needed** my bicycle & I lent you then.
→ Didn't I let you my bicycle **when you needed it**?
→ I didn't let you my bicycle **when you needed it**.
→ You **needed** an auto-rickshaw on that night but there was none.
→ **Needed** you an auto-rickshaw...? (As you are a good walker.)
→ **Did** you **need** an auto-rickshaw for that distance? (It is too short distance to go on an auto.)
→ You **needed not**... / You **didn't need** an auto-rickshaw on that night.

215. **'Need' or 'Need to'-as Modal Auxiliary:**

1) Auxiliary **'need'** is often followed by **'to'**. It is actually of **'need to'**.
2) **Need** or **need to**– both can be used as auxiliary. We can say, 'need' may be used with or without 'to' in the sentence. The same thing happens to 'dare & dare to'; but not with 'ought to' & 'used to' (for 'ought to', 'used to' cannot be used without preposition 'to'.).

3) **Need:** 'Need' as a Modal Auxiliary assists the main verb to mean 'doing, going, being, having or whatever the action or state is meant by the main verb, is **very necessary'**; as,

→ He need to go. (**Do not use:** 'needs' when 'need' is an auxiliary). [It means, his going is very urgent.]

4) However, when auxiliary 'need' is used in **negative** & **question**; or with the phrase **'all you need'** in affirmative sentence, it means '**something which is not necessary**' or 'that only **very little**', as,

→ All you need *bring* some white sheets for project work. (Affirmative, but the action to bring the sheets is less important)
→ You need not bother of my safety. (It is actually not necessary to bother of my safety.)
→ Need I write him? / Need she write him? (**correct**) (**Do not use:** 'needs' when 'need' is an auxiliary).
→ Do I need write to him? / Does she need to write to him? (**correct**)

5) As a modal auxiliary verb, **'need'** or **'need to'** –either may be used in affirmative, but in negative & interrogative sentences, only 'need' is used; however, it can follow 'to' and can be used as **'need to'**, if they conjugated with **'do'** in the negative & interrogative sentence; as,

→ I **need to buy** the medicine by the evening. (Affirmative, so 'need to')
→ You need not buy any medicine. Need I go there anymore? (Need is used without 'to')
→ You **do not need to buy** any medicine. **Do I need to go** there anymore? (as 'need' is conjugated with 'do', so 'need to')

6) The auxiliary 'need' or 'need to' does not take **'-s' or '-ed' forms** and is always followed by a Main Verb, like all auxiliaries ('-s' or –ed forms are used only in assertive affirmative by the principal 'need').

→ He **need** not go. **Need** he go there? He **need to go** there. (**Not**: needs, as 'need' is used here as auxiliary verb, followed by main verb 'go' in each sentence. **All are *correct***)

→ He need**s** not go. He need**s** not **to** go. Needs he go there? He needs to go there. (All are ***incorrect here***.),

7) Like the principal 'need', the auxiliary 'need' or 'need to' can be conjugated with 'do' 'does', & 'did'. **When conjugated with 'do', 'does' & 'did',** 'need' may follow its preposition **to,** and to be used as **'need to'** even in the negative and interrogative sentence.; *as,*

→ He *does* not **need** to go. (**Correct**).

→ (Does, need—both are auxiliary verbs; does is primary & need is modal auxiliary)

→ Need I write him? / Need she write him? (***correct***) (without 'do' & 'to')

→ Do I need write to him? / Does she need to write to him? (***correct***)

→ You **need** not **bother** of my safety. ('to' is not used, as negative is the sense, and another auxiliary 'do' is absent.)

→ All you **need bring** some white sheets for project work. (Affirmative, but the action to bring the sheets is less important)

→ *You **need** not **have worried**.* It all turned fine. (In perfect it means, "it was not necessary for you to worry, but you did.")

216. **'Need' do function both, as verb & adverb:**

✖ The auxiliary ***'need' or 'need to',*** which denotes **'necessity' or 'obligation to an action',** is used like 'must' or 'have to'; as,

○ He need to go.

⇒ **Note:** It is like, 'he is to go' or 'he has to go' or 'he must go'. The main verb is 'go'; the auxiliary **'need'** denoting 'the necessity of his going', like an adverb, adds meaning to the verb, 'go'. Thus, a 'modal' has uniqueness to describe the lexical or main verb in the sentence, when it is a verb itself (modal auxiliary). Need & other Modals, except 'dare' all are adverbial in nature.

⇒ 'Dare' is mostly used in the sense of qualifying the subject to describe his courage 'to be brave enough to do something'.

➢ **So, what we learnt:** 'need' is used as principal & also as a helping verb, like another 'dare', out of total 13 modals.

✓ 'Need' or 'need to'—is an auxiliary verb used in affirmative assertive sentence.
✓ When the sentence is negative and interrogative, only 'need' is used.
✓ 'Need to'—can be used in negative & interrogative, when it is conjugated with 'do', 'does', 'did'.

217. In the **semi-negative sentence**, principal ***'need'*** & auxiliary ***'need to'*** when they are used with semi-negative words like **'scarcely', 'hardly', 'rarely',** etc., they do not follow '-s' or '-es' forms, but may use past or past participle form **'needed'** as the principal verb in the sentence; as,
✓ Scarcely she need us. (**Not**: **needs**, as the sense is negative; the verb 'need' is principal)
✓ She needs us. (**correct**) ['needs' is principal, and sense is positive, not negative or semi-negative]
✓ Hardly she *need* us. (**Not**: needs) [Here, 'need' is used as principal verb.]
✓ Hardly has she needed us. (**Needed**: past participle form of main verb) [used as principal]
✓ Hardly need we go there. ('need' an auxiliary verb)
✓ Rarely need she do it by herself. (As auxiliary)

218. **Study the uses of 'Need'** in Assertive, Questions, Negative & in Semi-Negative Sentences in **chart-1,** and in **chart 2,** study the comparison of uses of 'Need' in Simple Tenses and in the Perfect Tenses

Use of 'Need' in Sentences

In Assertive & Semi Negative	In Questions & Negative
• I do need it. Scarcely I need it. (**as principal**) • He needs it. Hardly he need it. (**as principal**) • You needed it. Rarely you needed it. (**as principal**) • I need (to) take his help. I need hardly take his help. (**as auxiliary**) • Hardly I need meet him. (**as auxiliary**) **Note:** hardly, scarcely—are negative in sense, so don't use 'need to' or '-s/-es' form, but only 'need'.	• Do I need it? I do not need it. • Does he need it? He doesn't need it. • Did you need it? You didn't need it. • Need I take his help? Do I need to take his help? I need not take his help. I do not need to take his help. • Need you go now? Do you need to go now? You need not go now. You don't need to go now. • Need I meet him? Do I need to meet him? I need not meet him. I do not need to meet him.

Compare, the use of Need

In Simple Past & Present	In Perfect Tense
• I didn't need to buy it. *Note: It was not necessary for me to buy it & I didn't buy it.* • I didn't need to go, so I sent a letter. *Note: It was not necessary for me to go & I didn't go, so I sent a letter.* • I don't need to sell my house. *Note: It is not necessary for me to sell my house & I don't sell.*	• I needn't have bought it. *Note: It was not necessary for me to buy it, but I bought it.* • I needn't have gone, and I asked him about his health. *Note: It was not necessary for me to go, but I went and asked him about his health.* • I needn't have sold my house. *Note: It was not necessary for me to sell my house, but I have sold.*

219. The word **'Need'-** is also used as **a Noun,** 'to describe a situation (**'very necessary something'**) or **'a strong feeling that we want'**. The noun 'need' often form a phrase with a preposition preceding and following it; as, **'need of', 'in need of', 'need for',** etc.

> ➤ However, with **'no'** preceding 'need', it means the opposite, to mean **'not necessary at all'**; as,
> ➤ There is an urgent **need** for qualified teachers. (It describes *the situation of lack of teachers* in the institution; the word 'need' is used as a Noun.)
> ➤ The house is **in need of** a thorough clean.
> ➤ There is **no need** for you to get up early tomorrow.

> ➤ I had **no need** to open the letter.
> ➤ There is **no need** to cry. (Stop crying)
> ➤ She felt **the need** to talk to someone.
> ➤ I am **in need of** some fresh air. (Want of; very necessary to take in)
> ➤ She had no more **need** of me. (She had not that strong feeling; used as an adjective and noun)

Note: As a noun, 'need' always takes a complement like a gerund. Read the above examples.

Verb 'Dare' & 'Dare to'

220.   **Modal Auxiliary- 'Dare' & 'Dare to':**

✖ **The State Verbs-** are not (usually) used in the progressive tenses. So as to need & dare, and also with other modals. [All modals belong to the State Verbs.]

'Dare' as the Main Verb in the sentence:

221.   **The main verb 'dare' does not take 'to' following it, nor directly follow any other verb.** The main verb 'dare' is *'Qualitative' in nature, and describes a noun (here a person')*; as,
> → She said it as loudly as she *dared*. (Was brave enough)
> → Go on! Take it! **I dare you.** (I persuade you).

> ➤ **The main verb 'dare' means the following in the sentences:**
>   • 'Persuade somebody';
>   • 'To defy or challenge someone;
>   • 'Be brave enough'; or 'brave very much'; as,

> → Go on! Take it! **I dare you.** (*I persuade you.*)
> → **She dares you**, kiss her & see the result. (*She challenges you, ...*)
> → **Will you dare death**; then accept his challenge. (*Will you defy death; ...*)
> → Will you *dare death* to reach your goal? (*Will you defy death to reach your goal?*) [here: 'to reach' is an infinitive, not a part of 'dare to', nor attached.]
> → She said it as loudly <u>as she *dared*</u>. (... as she was brave enough.)

Note: The main verb '**dare**' with '**-s' and without '-s'** following third person singular number (of subject) in the simple present tense—both are correct usage in assertive affirmative sentence. However, in negative and interrogative, it **does not used with '-s' form ever**. And the main verb '**dare**' may also take its past form '**dared**'.

> ➤ As main verb phrase, '**I dare say**', simply means '**I believe**' or '**most probably**':
> → I *dare say* he must come tomorrow. (*I believe, he is coming tomorrow*)
> → I *dare say*, he may/will visit tomorrow. (*Most probably, he is coming.*)

The use of 'Dare' & 'Dare to'- both as the helping or auxiliary verb in the sentence.

222.   The *auxiliary* '*dare*' or '*dare to*' takes the journey through the person to his work, '***brave enough to do an action***', it is ***Adverbial*** *in nature* like 'need' & other Modals; as,
> → She dare not breathe a word of it to anybody.
> → *Jayden dare to* do it.
> → *Peter dare not do* it.
> → Peter asked Mr. P if he dare go there.

✖ **'Dare' & 'dare to' as the modal auxiliary help the main verb to mean:**
  a) 'Persuade somebody for doing something';
  b) 'To defy or challenge someone to do something;

143

c) 'Be brave enough to do something'; as,
- o I *dare to say* who is right & who is wrong.
- o I *dare not say* who is wrong.
- o I don't *dare to say* what I am thinking.
- o *Dare* Routella *ask* for money?
- o *Does* Routella *dare to ask* for money?

✖ ***The** auxiliary **'Dare'** does not take **'-s'** or **'-ed' forms**. However, **'s' or 'ed' forms** may be used with verb* **'do'** *as* **'does'** *in simple present tense.*

✖ 'Dare' can be conjugated ***with*** or ***without 'do'***. When conjugated with **'do'**, it is followed by **'to'**.

✖ Auxiliary **'Dare to' is only used in assertive affirmative.**

✖ **In negative & interrogative it may use 'to' when it is conjugated with verb 'do'.** *But if negative word comes between auxiliary* **'dare'** *and the main verb,* **'to'** *is not used.* Read the examples and study them carefully, only once, and compare, the same thing happened to modal verb 'need'.

→ He *takes* the step. He *took* the step. ('take' is the main verb.)
→ He **does** dare *to* **take** the step. He **did** dare *to* **take** the step.

❏ ('dare to' is an auxiliary; even with 3rd person singular number of the subject 'he' in simple present tense, **the auxiliary 'dare'** does not take **'-s'** or **'-ed' forms in either assertive affirmative, or in negative or in the interrogative sentence.**)

❏ Only the main verb 'dare' like 'need' takes the '-s' or '-ed' forms and only in the assertive affirmative sentence, *not in negative and interrogative.*

❏ And main verb 'dare' never uses 'to' along with it in the sentence.

→ He *dare not take* the step. / He *doesn't dare to take* the step.
→ He *did dare not take* the step. / He *did not dare to take* the step.

→ He *dare not take* such a step. (**correct**)
→ He *dares not to take* such a step. (**incorrect**),
→ He **does not dare** take such a step.
→ He **does not dare** to take such a step. (**Both are correct with or without 'to'**).
→ *How dare you contradict* me?
→ *How **do you dare to** contradict* me? (Both are **correct**)
→ How *dare* you *to* contradict me? (*incorrect*)
→ He dare not do it. (**Correct**).
→ He dare**s** not *to* do it. (*Incorrect*).
→ He doesn't *dare/dare to* do it. (**Both correct**)

223.   **Use of 'dare' & 'dare to'—Examples with Meanings. And try to find out which ones are used as the main verb and which ones as the helping verbs in the sentences:**

•	I do it.	• *To mean 'simply doing'. 'Do', an action word & the main verb.*
•	I *dare to* do it.	• *'I am brave enough to do (the action)'*
•	*Dare to* be different!	• *Be brave enough to be different*
•	*Dare you* go there?	• *(Are you brave enough to go there?)*
•	No, he *dare not*.	• *(He is not as brave/brave enough)*
•	Yes, *he dare*. / Yes, *he dares*.	• *(Yes, he is brave enough)*
•	*Did* he *dare to* do it?	• *(Was he brave enough...?)*
•	He *did not dare to* do it.	• *(was not brave enough ...)*
•	Yes, he *dared* to do it.	• *(Yes, he was brave enough ...)*
•	I would not *dare argue* with my boss.	• *(Would, dare—are modals, argue is the main verb)*
•	*Did* you *dare to* accept my proposal then?	• *(Were you brave enough) (Had you that guts to accept my proposal then?)*

224.   **The word 'dare' is also used as a noun**; as in the followings:

'Dare' *as a Noun, it* **means** 'an adventure', 'a risk', defiance' 'challenge'—; as,

→ He climbed onto the roof for **a dare**. *(An adventure).*

→ She learned to fly on **a dare**. *(risk)*

→ She is so modest in her behaviour; she has not that **dare** to say like that. *(defiance)*

→ Don't indulge in anybody's **dare** to you, my dear friend, think that as a trap. A noble man fell and found its salvation with millions' death. *(challenge)*

225. **Study the use of 'need' & 'dare' in the chart:**

Need & Dare without 'Do'	Need & Dare with 'Do'

• Dare you <u>do</u> this?
        - (Are you brave enough to do this?)
• Dare he not <u>do</u> this?
    - (**Don't use 'dares'**: is he not brave enough to do this?)
• I dare not <u>do</u> this.
      - (I am not brave enough to do this?)
• Need you <u>go</u> there?
        - (Is it necessary to go there?)
• He need not <u>love</u> you.
    - (**Don't use 'needs'**; he does not feel the need to love you.)
• How much **need** she the job?
      - ('need' here is the principal verb)
• **Note:** all the underlined are actually the principal verbs, and 'dare' & 'need' are used as auxiliary to mean 'brave enough to do' or to mean 'necessity'. However, 'need' in bold, of the last sentence is used as principal verb.
	• Do you dare to <u>do</u> this?
	• Does he not dare to <u>do</u> this?
	• Doesn't he dare to <u>do</u> this?
	• I don't dare to <u>do</u> this.
	• Do you need to <u>go</u> there?
	• He doesn't need to <u>love</u> you.
	• How much **does she** <u>**need**</u> the job?
	• **Note:** all the underlined are the principal verbs; with 'dare'/dare to' & 'need/need to' as their auxiliaries. 'Need' in the last sentence is also a main verb.

226. **'need' & 'dare'** with **'to'**

✗ Modal auxiliary **'need to'** & **'dare to'** do not follow **'to'** in negative & interrogative sentences; however, they follow 'to' when they are conjugated with 'do'; as,

- We need not **go** today.
- You need not **do** it.
- We do not need **to go** today.
- You don't need **to do** it.
- Need we **go** today?
- Need you **do** it?
- Do we need **to go** today?
- Do you need **to do** it?

227. **Study also the other verbs with 'to', besides 'dare to' and 'need to' :**

1) **Is to:**
❑ He is to give a public statement in the evening today.
       ❑ (**Express:** *is going to.*)

2) **Have to:**
❑ We have to reach in time or we will miss the train.
       ❑ (**Express:** *necessity & obligation, like 'must' & 'need'.*)

3) **Used to:**
❑ They used to live in Kashmir till 1987.
       ❑ (**Express:** *past habit or occurrence something often.*)

4) **Ought to:**
❑ We ought to help the poor. We ought to go.
       ❑ (**Express:** *moral obligation, like 'should' to express 'duty'.*)

5) **Need to:**
❑ He need to go. He need to do.
       ❑ (**Express:** *necessity & obligation. However, less forceful than 'must' or 'have to'.*)

6) **Dare to:**
- ❑ Finally, he did dare to say. (past)/ Finally, he dare say. (present)
    - ❑ (***Express:*** *brave enough to say.*)
- ❑ "How dare you", he said.
- ❑ She dare not express her love.
    - ❑ (***Express:*** *brave enough to express.*)

228. **Revised Lesson of the Use of Modal Verbs,** (briefly and in assembling way, what Modals generally express):

A. **Ability:** by > (can, could, be able to); as,
- → **Can** you swim? **Can** you sing?
- → I **could** swim, even when I was five.
- → I **couldn't** find my car's keys where did you leave it?
- → I **am able to** do finish the project.
- → Will people **be able to** live on the moon one day, do you think?

B. **Possibility:** by > (may, might, could); as,
- → He **may/might/could** be ill, I'll phone her.
- → **Could/Might** you have lost it on the way home?
- → I **may/might** have left my purse in the shop I went to.
- → You **may/might** know the answer, but you didn't give.
- → She **could** have finished the work by that duration.

C. **Permission:** by > (can, could, may); as,
- → **Can** we come in?
- → **Could** we possibly stay at your flat?
- → Staff **may** take their break between 12 & 2. (As by written permission)
- → **May** I sit here? May I come in, Sir?

D. **Prohibition:** by > (must not, may not, cannot); as,
- → You **mustn't** tell her anything.
- → Crockery **may not** be taken out of the canteen.
- → You **must not** begin until I tell you.
- → You **can't** get up until you're better.

E. **Obligation:** by > (have(get) to, must); as,
- → **Do** I **have to** sign on the papers?
- → Peter **had to** throw the used & inkless pen into the dustbin.
- → You **will have to** wait; the Dr. is on round of the Hospital.
- → All visitors **must** report to the reception on their arrival.
- → All poling personnel **must** report to DC in due time of their arrival.

F. **No necessity:** by > (don't have to, shouldn't have, didn't need to, needn't have); as,
- → You **don't have to** pick us up, we can book a cab.
- → They **didn't have to** go through customs; they are special for the Government.
- → We **shouldn't have** bother bothered about lunch; she must arrange something for us.
- → He **didn't need to** have any fillings at the dentist's.
- → They **needn't have** waited; the bus came at the right time.

G. **Advice & Criticism:** by > (ought to, should); as,
- → **Ought** we **to/should** we write and thank him?
- → She **ought to/should** go out more often. (It may be criticism)
- → You **ought to/should have** gone to bed earlier.
- → You **shouldn't** take car on loan. You are already in huge debt.
- → I become fatty; I **ought to/should** go on a diet.
- → I **ought to/should have** asked her first for her consent.

H. **Assumption & Deductions:** by > (will, should, must, can't); as,
- → That **will** be Peter, he gets up early.
- → The book **should** be interesting.

→ There **must** be a leak. You **must have** dialed the wrong number.

→ She **can't** have finished yet! She **can't** handle that, give it somebody.

I. **Requests:** by > (can, could, will, would); as,

→ **Can** you pass me the book?

→ **Could** you help me with my translation?

→ **Will** you buy me an ice cream?

→ **Would** you type this letter for me, please?

J. **Offers & Suggestions:** by > (will, shall); as,

→ **Shall** I do this for you?

→ **Shall** we go now? Will you help me please?

→ I'**ll** take you to the airport.

→ Don't worry; he **will** help you to reach you to the airport.

229.   Practice, using of proper Modals. **Set-1**

✖ **Choose the correct alternative:**
1) I don't think I (**shall, should, can**) be able to go.
2) He (**shall, will, dare**) not pay unless he is compelled.
3) You (**should, would, ought**) be punctual.
4) I wish you (**should, would, must**) tell me earlier.
5) (**Shall, Will, Would)** I assist you?
6) (**Shall, Should, Would**) you please help me with this?
7) You (**ought, should, must**) to pay your debts.
8) He said I (**can, might, should**) use his telephone at any time.
9) If you (**shall, should, would**) see him, give him my regards.
10) He (**need, dare, would**) not ask for a rise, for fear of losing his job.
11) I (**needn't to see, needn't have seen, didn't need to see**) him, so I sent a letter.
12) (**Shall, Might, Could**) you show me the way to the station?
13) To save my life, I ran fast, and (**would, could, was able to**) reach safely.
14) I (**would, used, ought**) to be an atheist but now I believe in God.
15) You (**needn't, mustn't, won't**) light a match; the room is full of gas.
16) The Prime Minister (**would, need, is to**) make a statement tomorrow.
17) You (**couldn't wait, didn't need to wait, needn't have waited**) for me; I could have found the way all right.
18) I was afraid that if I asked him again, he (**can, may, might**) refuse.
19) She (**shall, will, dare**) sit outside her garden gate for hours at a time, looking at the passing traffic.
20) (**Should, Would, Shall**) you like another cup of coffee?
21) I wish he (**should, will, would**) not play his wireless so loudly.
22) I (**am to leave, would leave, was to have left**) on Thursday. But on Thursday I had a terrible cold.
23) He (**used, is used, was used**) to play cricket before his marriage.
24) (**Shall, Will, Would**) I carry the box into the house for you?
25) He (**will, can, might**) come, but I should be surprised.

Answer to the Exercise A:

Choose the correct alternative:
1) I don't think I **shall** be able to go.
2) He **will** not pay unless he is compelled.
3) You **should** be punctual.
4) I wish you **would** tell me earlier.
5) **Would** I assist you?
6) **Would** you please help me with this?
7) You **ought** to pay your debts.
8) He said I **might** use his telephone at any time.
9) If you **would** see him, give him my regards.
10) He **dare** not ask for a rise, for fear of losing his job.
11) I **didn't need to see** him, so I sent a letter.

12) **Could** you show me the way to the station?
13) To save my life, I ran fast, and **could** reach safely.
14) I **ought** to be an atheist but now I believe in God.
15) You **mustn't** light a match; the room is full of gas.
16) The Prime Minister **is to** make a statement tomorrow.
17) You **needn't have waited** for me; I could have found the way all right.
18) I was afraid that if I asked him again, he **might** refuse.
19) She **will** sit outside her garden gate for hours at a time, looking at the passing traffic.
20) **Would** you like another cup of coffee?
21) I wish he **would** not play his wireless so loudly.
22) I **would leave** on Thursday. But on Thursday I had a terrible cold.
23) He **used to** play cricket before his marriage.
24) **Would** I carry the box into the house for you?
25) He **might** come, but I should be surprised.

Set-2

✘ **Rewrite each of these sentences, using a modal verb (if there is already a modal, use another):**
1) **Possibly** she isn't Anil's sister.
2) **Perhaps** we will go to Shimla next month.
3) My sister **was able to** read the alphabet when she was 18 months old.
4) **It is necessary** that you <u>do not wash </u>the car. (The <u>paint is still wet</u>.)
5) It is **not necessary** for you <u>to wash </u>the car. (<u>It is clean</u>.)
6) I am **certain** that they have left already.
7) **Do you allow** me to use your phone?
8) I **was in the habit of** going to the beach every day <u>when I was </u>in Chennai.
9) He will **probably** pass his driving test easily.
10) **Perhaps** he forgot about the meeting.
11) I **suggest** visiting Qutab Minar.
12) Nobody has answered the phone; **perhaps** they have gone out.
13) I am **sure** she is over seventy.
14) I was **_not necessary_** <u>for me to meet </u>him **_but_** <u>I met him</u>.
15) It was **_not necessary_** <u>for me to meet </u>him (**_and I didn't_** <u>meet </u>him).

Answer to the Exercise-**B**

1) **Possibly** she is**n't** Anil's sister. = She **may not** be Anil's sister.
2) **Perhaps** we **will** go to Shimla next month. = We **may** go to Shimla next month.
3) My sister **was able to** read the alphabet when she was 18 months old. = My sister **could** read the alphabet when she was 18-month-old.
4) **It is necessary** that you <u>do not wash </u>the car. (The <u>paint is still wet</u>.) = You **must not** wash the car. (*Logical certainty*)
5) It is **not necessary** for you <u>to wash </u>the car. (<u>It is clean</u>.) = You **need not** to wash the car. ('need not' refers to 'not necessary; doesn't hint 'certainty' like 'must'.)
6) I am **certain** that they have left already. = They **must** have left already. (must = certainty)
7) **Do you allow** me to use your phone? = **Would** you allow/let me to use your phone?
8) I **was in the habit of** going to the beach every day <u>when I was </u>in Chennai. = I **used to** go to the beach every day when I was in Chennai.
9) He will **probably** pass his driving test easily. = He **may** pass his driving test easily.
10) **Perhaps** he forgot about the meeting. = He **might** forget about his meeting.
11) I **suggest** visiting Qutab Minar. = **Would** you (like to) visit Qutab Minar?
12) Nobody has answered the phone; **perhaps** they have gone out. = Nobody has answered the phone; they **may** have gone out.
13) I am **sure** she is over seventy. = She **must** be over seventy.
14) I was **_not necessary_** <u>for me to meet </u>him **_but_** <u>I met him</u>. = I **needn't have met** him.
15) It was **_not necessary_** <u>for me to meet </u>him (**_and I didn't_** <u>meet </u>him). = I **didn't need** to meet him.

Don't forget

• The primary auxiliaries (Be, Have, & Do) can also be used as the main verbs in the sentences.

- But the modals are merely helping verbs or auxiliaries, except 'need' and 'dare'.
- Need and dare—the modals can be used as both; as helping and as the main verbs.
- **Need** and **Dare**—as the <u>helping verbs often take **'to'**</u> following it immediately, <u>like **'used to'**, **'ought to'**</u>; but when used as principal, they **never take 'to' preposition directly after them**; though a separate infinitive verb may be used afterward.
- **Only main verbs- Need & Dare—take '-s' forms** (as 'needs' /'dares') following the third person singular number of the subject in the simple present tense only, and only in the assertive affirmative sentence.
- In the past tense, it also takes '-ed' forms (as 'needed'/'dared'), and never to be used in the progressive forms (i.e., the '-ing forms') in sentences.

Let us write:
- Work in small groups. Choose a place for each group, like hospital, school assembly hall, computer lab or park. Then, write the rules that one should follow at these places using the modals and primary auxiliaries.

14. Non-finite Verbs & its Branches

230. Non-finite verbs are those which don't take other forms in terms of tense (of verb), number & person of the subject.
   ✘ The Branches of Non-Finite Verbs-

          a. Infinitive,
          b. Gerund, &
          c. Participle.

INFINITIVE, GYRUND, PARTICIPLE

INFINITIVE
- The base form of verb, with or without 'to' preceding, being a non-finite remains, unchanged in tenses and according to the number or person of the subject in the sentences.
- She is excellent ***to act*** her role.

GERUND/ VERBAL NOUN
- **The '-ing' form of verb**, being non-finite remains, used as a noun in the sentence, is called a Gerund; as,
- *The rising view of sun* over sea-shore is very refreshing itself.
- ***Sun rising*** is a good view. ***Swimming*** is a good exercise.

PARTICIPLE
- The '-ing', 2nd & 3rd form of verbs (The **progressive, past & past participle form of verb**), being non-finite remains, often used as determiner/adjective in the sentence.
- ***Boring*** teachers often make ***bored*** students.

Infinitive Verbs

231. The ***base form of verb, with or without 'to' preceding***, being non-finite remains, unchanged in tenses and according to the number or person of the subject in the sentences, which has the force of both of a Noun and a Verb, is called an Infinitive.

- She is excellent ***to act*** her role.
- They were excellent ***to act*** their roles.
- Mr. P hardly knew ***to act*** a role.

❖ **Study more sentences-**

- Teach me how ***to swim.***
- ***To give*** is better than ***to receive.***
- ***To see*** is ***to believe***.
- Stop ***to play***; I want ***to go*** very now.
- I like ***to read*** poetry now, though I like ***to read*** novels.
- He contemplated ***to marry*** his cousin.
- Children love ***to make*** mud castles.
- What I most detest is ***to smoke***.
- They tried ***to find*** fault with us.

❖ In all the above sentences the *verbs with 'to' preposition preceding them*—are the example of **Infinitives** or **Infinitive Verbs.**

❖ **Read again-**

1. ***To error*** is human.
2. Birds love ***to sing***.
3. ***To respect*** our parents is our duty.
4. He refused ***to obey*** the orders.
5. Many men desire ***to make*** money quickly.

→ In sentence ***1***, *the infinitive*, like a noun, *is the Subject* of the verb ***'is'***.

→ In sentence ***2***, *the infinitive*, like a noun, *is the Object* of the verb ***'love'***.

→ In sentence ***3***, *the infinitive*, like a noun, is the Subject of the verb ***'is'***, but, like a verb, it *also takes an Object* ***'our parents'***

→ In sentence ***4***, *the infinitive*, like a noun, is the Object of the verb ***'refused'***, but, like a verb, it also *takes an Object* ***'the orders'***

→ In sentence ***5***, *the infinitive*, like a noun, is the Object of the verb ***'desire'***, but, like a verb, it also *takes an Object* ***'money'*** & is modified by an Adverb ***'quickly'***.

✖ It is seen that an Infinitive, though a form of verb, it does function like a Noun (forming Subject, Object, etc.), and as, it is a verb (though Non-finite) keeps certain features of the verb like, take an object, and also can be modified by an Adverb.

✖ An infinitive verb precedes by 'to' preposition, expressed or understood.

232. **The Use of Infinitive Verbs**

▶ The infinitives are used in two ways:

o **Like a Noun;**
- As the subject,
- As the object of verb & preposition,
- As the complement (subjective & objective), etc.

➢ When infinitive is used in this way, it is known as ***Simple*** or ***Gerundial Infinitive***.

➢ (Gerundial means ***'pertaining to or behaving like a Gerund'***; when 'Gerund' itself does the work of a Noun, we can say, it means 'belonging to or be part of a Noun'/relating to Noun/applying like a Noun.)

o **Like an Adjective or an Adverb;**
- To qualify a Noun,
- To qualify a Verb,
- To qualify an Adverb,
- To qualify a Clause or a Sentence (use of Infinitive Absolutely or parenthetically)

> ➤ This kind of use of Infinitives is popularly known as *'Qualifying Infinitive'*.

233. The Use of **Simple** or **Gerundial Infinitive.** Study the following Charts:

The Use of *Simple* or *Gerundial Infinitive*

Functions	Examples
i) As a subject	*To smoke* is dangerous. *To error* is to human. *To walk* is good for health. *To find* fault is easy.
ii) As an object	He likes *to swim*. He likes *to play* chess. I taught him *to read*.
iii) As subjective complement	He seems *to be* rich. He is *to die*. (he is dying) Her greatest pleasure is *to sing*. His custom is *to ride* daily.
iv) As Objective Complement	I saw him *go*. I ordered him *to be* punished.
v) As the object of a preposition	He had no choice but (= except) *to obey*. The speaker is about *to begin*. Daniel was about *to die*.

234. The Use of **Qualifying Infinitive:**

The Use of *Qualifying Infinitive*

Functions	Examples
i) As an adjective (*to qualify a Noun*)	a) The person *to consult* was Dr. Sen. (qualifying the noun, person) So as: We had no water *to drink*. b) I saw the man *to run*. They had examination *to pass*.
ii) As an adverb (*to qualify an Adjective*)	a) Cherries are good *to eat*. b) This medicine is pleasant *to take*. c) The boys are anxious *to learn*. d) He is too weak *to do* the work.
iii) As an adverb (*to qualify a Verb*)	a) She has come *to stay*. (purpose/reason) b) We eat *to live*. (purpose) c) We came *to buy* some books. (purpose) d) We wept *to see* the desolation caused by the flood .(cause)
iv) Absolutely or Parenthetically (*to qualify a clause or sentence*)	*a) To tell* the truth, I quite forgot my promise. b) He was petrified, so *to speak*. c) He tries to make the function a great success, which is *to be held* tomorrow. (they are separated by 'commas'.)

235. In Case of **Double Infinitive:**

In Case of Double Infinitive	
When two infinitive structures are joined by— 'and', 'or', 'except', 'but' conjunctions, <u>denoting same subject</u>, the <u>second one is used often without 'to'</u> preposition.	1. I'd like **to lie** down <u>and</u> **go** to sleep.
	2. I'd like **to be** a doctor <u>and</u> **treat** patients free at cost.
	3. Do you want **to go** now <u>or</u> **wait** for some time?
	4. Do you want **to do** it <u>or</u> **leave** it for someone?
	5. You are asked **to do** anything <u>except</u> **sing**.
	6. You are permitted **to do** here anything <u>except</u> **make** a noise.
	7. I am ready **to do** anything <u>but</u> **work** here.
	8. I am eager **to do** anything for men <u>but</u> **do** that not free at cost.

236.   Bare Infinitive

✗ There are **certain verbs** <u>which do not follow</u> **infinitive verbs** *with 'to'.* Such infinitives without 'to' are called **Bare Infinitives.**

✗ <u>And the **certain verbs** which take bare Infinitives, are</u> the *causative verbs; as,* **'make', 'let', 'bid', 'have'**; *& the state verbs; as,* **'see', 'hear' 'appear', 'seem', 'feel'**; *&the modal verbs;* **'need' & 'dare'**;
— We <u>use infinitives</u> after them without **'to'**; as,

→ Make him **stand**. I made him **run**.

→ Let him **sit** here. I will not let you **go**.

→ Bid (tell) him **go** there. I bade (told) him **go**. They had him **have** fun.

→ I saw him **do** it. See her **do** the work. I heard him **cry**. Who heard you **cry**?

→ The rate of interest appears **fall** from the last year. Peter seems **laugh** at us.

→ We need not **go** today. You need not **do** it. You dare not **do** it. How dare you **do** it.

✗ The bold lettered words in the above sentences are called **Bare Infinitives** (infinitives without 'to') in English Grammar.

✗ In all the above cases the verbs form a group, <u>they do mean by joining only</u> what the speaker means to convey, and in that case the former always do the function of helping verb or half main verb, as in case of 'need' and 'dare'.

237.   Bare Infinitives, hardly to be used in the Passive Voice:

✗ The **certain verbs** which generally take Bare Infinitives (infinitive used without 'to'), are not used so (being without 'to') in the Passive Voice; as,

	In Active Voice	*In Passive Voice*
See	We saw her **come**.	He was seen **to come**.
Hear	He heard Ram **say** that.	Ram was heard **to say** that.
Make	They made me **sit** down.	I was made **to sit** down.
Let	Let him **go**.	He was let **to go**.
Ask	She asked me (to) **sing** a song for her.	I was asked **to sing** a song for her.
Feel	I felt you touch my shoulder & I jumped.	You were felt **to touch**...

238.   **The use of Infinitive in Active & Passive Voice:**

✖   The infinitives can be used in both active & passive voice. However, in Active Voice whereas Infinitive has all forms of _Simple_, _Progressive_, _Perfect_ & _Perfect Continuous_; in Passive, it has only simple & perfect forms. See the table:

Tense	Active	Passive Voice
Indefinite/Simple	To love	To be loved
Progressive/Continuous	To be loving	(_Not in use_)
Perfect	To have loved	To have been loved
Perfect Continuous	To have been loving	(_Not in use_)

Split Infinitives

239.   **Split Infinitives:** 'Split Infinitive' is the name, given to an Infinitive form where an infinitive (**to + base form of verb**) is split up by another word, generally an Adjective or an Adverb, that comes between them. It happens in emotion or for the emphasis to the verb; as,
- Police schools have been started **to** better **train** rural constables.
- I request you **to** kindly **help** me.
- I request you **to** quickly **do** this.

240.   Exercise-1: **State how the Infinitive is used in the Sentences:**

1) There was nothing for it to fight.
2) Let us pray.
3) The mango is fit to eat.
4) The mango is to eat.
5) I heard her sing.
6) I have come to see you.
7) The order to advance was given.
8) Men must work and women must weep.
9) I am sorry to hear this.
10) He is slow to forgive.
11) A man severe he was and stern to view.
12) And fools who came to scoff remained to pray.
13) Thus, to relieve the wretched was his pride.
14) Full many a flower is born to blush unseen.
15) Music hath charms to soothe the savage beast.
16) Never seek to tell thy love.
17) To retreat was difficult; to advance was impossible.
18) Everybody wishes to enjoy life.
19) My desire is to see you again.
20) There was not a moment to be lost.
21) The counsel rose to address the court.
22) My right there is none to dispute.
23) The ability to laugh is peculiar to mankind.
24) He has the power to concentrate his thoughts.
25) He was quick to see the point.
26) I am not afraid to speak the truth.
27) Better dwell in the midst of alarms than reign in this horrible place.
28) Can you hope to count the stars?
29) To toil is the lot of mankind.
30) It is delightful to hear the sound of the sea.
31) It is a penal offence to bribe a public servant.
32)

241.   **Answers of the above:**

•   **State how the Infinitive is used in the Sentences:**
1) There was nothing for it to fight. (_adjective; qualifying the pronoun 'nothing'; nothing what? nothing to fight_)
2) Let us pray. (_bare infinitive/object of verb 'let'_)
3) The mango is fit to eat. (_as adverb, qualifying the adjective 'fit'_)
4) The mango is to eat. (_complement of verb 'is'_)
5) I heard her sing. (_bare infinitive/Objective complement_)
6) I have come to see you. (_adverbial/ show purpose_)
7) The order to advance was given. (_Adjective, qualify the noun 'the order'_)

8) Men must work and women must weep. *(here: work & weep—both are principal verbs; so **no infinitive in the sentence**; Modals & Primary Auxiliary, generally do not take Infinitives, except- need to, dare to, used to, ought to, is to & have to)*
9) I am sorry to hear this. *(adverbial/reason, qualifying 'sorry')*
10) He is slow to forgive. *(adverbial, qualifying the adjective cum complement 'slow'.)*
11) A man severe he was and stern to view. *(adverbial, qualifying adjective 'stern')*

12) And fools who came to scoff remained to pray. *(adverbial, show reason, qualifying the verb 'remained'; remained for what? =to pray)*
13) Thus to relieve the wretched was his pride. *(Subjective Complement; worked as a Noun; his pride was 'to relieve' the wretched; 'the wretched'—is the object of the Infinitive 'to relieve" relieve whom? =the wretched)*
14) Full many a flower is born to blush unseen. *(adverbial, modifying the verb 'born'; 'unseen' is the complement to the verb 'born')*
15) Music hath charms to soothe the savage beast. *(as adjective, describing noun 'charms')*
16) Never seek to tell thy love. *(never seek for what? To tell thy love. Adverbial)*
17) To retreat was difficult; to advance was impossible. *(both as subject)*
18) Everybody wishes to enjoy life. *(object of the verb 'wish')*
19) My desire is to see you again. *(formed complement of the verb 'is')*
20) There was not a moment to be lost. *(as adjective, describing the noun 'moment')*
21) The counsel rose to address the court. *(adverb, show 'why'; qualifying 'rose')*

22) My right there is none to dispute. *(as adjective to describe 'none', a pronoun)*
23) The ability to laugh is peculiar to mankind. *(as adjective to describe 'ability, the noun)*
24) He has the power to concentrate his thoughts. *(as adjective to describe 'power' the noun)*
25) He was quick to see the point. *(as adverb to modify 'quick', the adjective)*
26) I am not afraid to speak the truth. *(as adverb to modify 'afraid' the adjective)*
27) Better dwell in the midst of alarms than reign in this horrible place. *(the main verb is 'is' which is understood; as 'It is better to dwell/ to dwell is better...'; here the two bare infinitives '(to) dwell' & '(to) reign' are used as subjects of the two clauses which are compared)*
28) Can you hope to count the stars? *(as Object of the verb 'hope')*
29) To toil is the lot of mankind. *(As subject)*
30) It is delightful to hear the sound of the sea. *(as an adverb to modify the adjective 'delightful')*
31) It is a penal offence to bribe a public servant. *(as an adjective to describe 'offence', a noun)*

The Gerund

242. **Definition: The '-ing' form of verb**, being non-finite remains that <u>does the work of a Noun, like forming subject, object</u>, etc. (i.e., has the force of both of a noun and a verb). It is, therefore, a Verb-noun and often is called a **Verbal Noun**, or simply **Gerund**.

→ **Reading** is his favourite pastime.

➤ The word *'reading'* has come from the verb, **'read'** by adding **'-ing'** to its base form, and the word has been used here as the subject in the sentence. And thus, it does the work of a Noun. It is, therefore, a Verb-Noun, or the so-called **Gerund**.

✖ **Study more examples:**
- *The rising view of sun* over sea-shore is very refreshing itself.
- *Sun rising* is a good view.
- *Swimming* is a good exercise.

243. **Read the illustrations of the following sentences about Gerund:**
1) **Playing** cards is not allowed here.
2) I like **reading** poetry.
3) He is fond of **hoarding** money.

In sentence 1, the Gerund, like a Noun, is the subject of a verb, but like a Verb, it also takes an object, 'cards'; thus, clearly showing that it has also the force of a verb.
In sentence 2, the Gerund, like a Noun, is the object of a verb, but like a Verb, it also takes an object, 'poetry'; thus,

clearly showing that it has also the force of a verb.

In sentence 3, the Gerund, like a Noun, is governed by a preposition, 'of', but like a Verb, it also takes an object, 'money'.

✓A Gerund acts both of a Noun & a Verb.

244. **Gerund & Infinitive (comparative study):**

✘ *It will be noticed that the Infinitive and the Gerund are <u>alike in being used as Nouns,</u> <u>while still retaining the power that a verb has</u>.*

✓ **Definition of a Gerund:** A Gerund is that form of a verb which ends in '-ing', and has the force of a Noun and a Verb.

✓ **Definition of an Infinitive:** The base form of a verb, often preceded by 'to', which has the force of both of a Noun and a Verb.

▪ When the infinitive acts like a noun, it is **Simple or Gerundial**; when it acts like an Adjective, Adverb or other, it is **Qualifying Infinitive**.

✘ They both have similar functions, almost:

They both have similar functions, almost:	
Gerund	**Infinitive**
1. Teach me **_swimming_**.	1. Teach me **_to swim_**.
2. **_Giving_** is better than **_receiving_**.	2. **_To give_** is better than **_to receive_**.
3. **_Seeing_** is **_believing_**.	3. **_To see_** is **_to believe_**.
4. Stop **_playing_**.	4. Stop **_to play_**.
5. I like **_reading_** poetry.	5. I like **_to read_** poetry.
6. He contemplated **_marrying_** his cousin.	6. He contemplated **_to marry_** his cousin.
7. Children love **_making_** mud castles.	7. Children love **_to make_** mud castles.
8. What I most detest is **_smoking_**.	8. What I most detest is **_to smoke_**.

✘ However, the use of Gerund is preferred in the following:

In case, object of a preposition; as,

a) I am tired of **_waiting_**. (**Not**: to wait) And thus-
b) He is fond of **_swimming._** (**Not**: to swim)
c) He was punished for **_telling_** a lie. (**Not**: to tell)
d) We were prevented from **_seeing_** the prisoner.
e) I have an aversion to **_fishing_**. (**Not**: to fish, etc.)

245. **Kinds of Gerund:**

✘ Whatever we discussed till now, they are examples of **Simple Gerund**; there is another kind of Gerund, and it is called '**Compound Gerund**'. They are formed of '**having**' or '**being**' (gerund of 'have' or 'be' verb) with **Past Participle**.

See the examples:

a) I heard of his *having gained* a prize.
b) We were fatigued on account of *having walked* so far.
c) They were charged with *having sheltered* terrorists.
d) Everyone is desirous of *being praised*.

Note: They look like Perfect Participle or Present Participle, passive in form, but they do work of a Noun and a Verb.

✘ So, we got gerund of two kinds:

a) Simple Gerund, &

b) Compound Gerund

246. Like other normal or ordinary verbs **Gerund has also Active & Passive forms. Read the chart.**

Gerund, Active	Gerund, Passive
• Loving (simple gerund)	• Being loved (simple gerund)
• Being loved (compound Gerund)	• Being been loved (comp. Gerund)
• Having loved (compound Gerund)	• Having been loved (comp. Gerund)
1) I heard of his *having gained* a prize.	1) His *having been gained* a prize was heard (by me).
2) We were fatigued on account of *having walked* so far.	2) *Having been walked* so far made him only too tired.
3) They were charged with *having sheltered* terrorists.	3) *Having given sheltered* terrorists is also a terrorist activity, the court said.
4) Everyone is desirous of *being praised*.	4) *Being been praised* by all or everybody made him only more crazy for it.

Gerund has Active & Passive forms

247. Carefully note the difference between Gerund & Participle in the following two charts:

Gerund	Participle
Loving (simple gerund) **Being loved** (compound Gerund) **Having loved** (compound Gerund)	**Loving** (present participle) **Loved** (past participle) **Having loved.** (perfect participle)
1) I heard of his *winning* the prize. 2) *Winning* prizes is now natural to P. 3) *Being praised* by all who doesn't want? 4) Everyone is desirous of *being praised*. 5) *Having won* prizes get celebration every time by Tom. 6) I heard of his *having gained* a prize. 7) We were fatigued on account of *having walked* so far. 8) They were charged with *having sheltered* terrorists. 9) He is fond of ***playing*** cricket. 10) The old man was tried of ***walking***. 11) We were prevented from ***seeing*** the prisoner. 12) ***Seeing*** is ***believing***.	1) *Loving* the baby, the mother left the cottage for earning her bread. 2) *Laughing*, he went away silently without a word for us. 3) *Winning* the first prize he returned home. 4) We saw him *lost* in the midst of troubles. 5) Police reached and found animals *burnt* under the shade. 6) *Having won* the match, the players made an arrangement for celebration. 7) *Having walked* a long distance finally they reached home. 8) *Having sheltered* terrorists, they fell in fresh trouble. 9) ***Playing*** cricket, he gained health. 10) ***Walking*** along the road, he noticed a dead cobra. 11) ***Seeing*** the prisoner, we intended to return from there. 12) ***Seeing***, he believed.
➢ The Gerund has the force of a Noun and a Verb; so, it is **Verbal Noun**.	➢ Simple Participle (Present & Past) has the force of an Adjective and a Verb; so, it is **Verbal Adjective**.
13) I hope you will excuse ***my leaving*** early. 14) We rejoiced at ***his leaving*** early. 15) I insist on ***your being*** present. 16) Do you mind ***my sitting*** here?	13) I hope you will excuse ***me leaving*** early. 14) We rejoiced at ***him being*** promoted. 15) I insist on ***you being*** present. 16) Do you mind ***me sitting*** here?

17) All depends on ***Karim's passing*** the exam. 18) I disliked the ***manager's asking*** me personal questions. 19) The accident was due to the ***engine-driver's disregarding*** the signals.	17) All depends on ***Karim passing*** the exam. 18) I disliked the ***manager asking*** me personal questions. 19) The accident was due to the ***engine-driver disregarding*** the signals.
✓ The words preceding the Gerund, in each case, are in Possessive Case (Possessive Adjectives) and they are describing the ***succeeding*** Gerunds.	✓ The Participles, in each case, are describing the ***preceding*** Nouns or Pronouns in Objective case.

248. **The use of Gerund:** A Gerund being a verb-noun may be used as—

1) Subject of a verb:
   → ***Seeing*** is believing.
   → ***Hunting*** deer is not allowed in the country.
2) Object of a Transitive Verb:
   → Stop ***playing.***
   → I like ***reading*** novels.
3) Object of a Preposition:
   → I am tired of ***waiting***.
   → Yamuna was fond of ***swimming***.
4) Complement of a verb:
   → Seeing is ***believing***.
   → What I most detest is ***smoking***.
5) Absolutely (as free-standing unit):
   → ***Playing*** cards being his aversion, we did not play bridge.
   → ***Seeing*** porns being his addiction, his parents has cut the net connection with his computer.
   ⌘ *('being' is the present participle here in the above sentences)*
6) *To form Compound-Nouns*; as,
   → *Walking* stick; *frying* pan; *fencing* stick;
   → *hunting* whip; writing table; *looking* glass (a mirror)

Note: Other may consider them as Present Participle, but they are not so, as the '–ing' forms here are not describing the words come after them; as,

- '**Walking stick'** refers to the stick which is used to walk', (**not like this, - *a stick which walks***).
- *When we say 'a frying pan' it means a kind of,* which one is used to fry something in the cooking; and so as 'a whip used in hunting'; a table for writing'. They are more Nouns than Adjective. They are not as, 'running dog'= a dog which runs 'sleeping cat' = a cat which is in sleep, etc.)

7) *To form Gerundial Phrase*: when a Gerund takes '**the**' preceding it, and **'of'** after it:
   → ***The*** indiscriminate ***reading of*** science-fiction is injurious to mental health.
   → ***The making of*** the plan is in his hand.
   → The time of ***the singing of the*** birds has come.
   → Adam consented to ***the eating of*** the fruit.
   → The middle station of life seems to be the most advantageous for ***the gaining of*** wisdom.

249. Exercise-1: **Point out Participle** or **Gerund**. In the case of the Participle, name the Noun or Pronoun which it qualifies. In the case of Gerund, state whether it is subject, object, complement, or used after preposition:

1) He was found fighting desperately for his life.
2) He has ruined his sight by reading small print.
3) Hearing the noise, he ran to the window.
4) He saw a clown standing on his head.
5) Asking questions is easier than answering them.
6) Waving their hats and handkerchiefs, the people cheered the batsman.
7) Walking on the grass is forbidden.
8) Jumping over the fence, the thief escaped.
9) The miser spends his time in hoarding money.
10) Much depends on Rama's returning before noon.
11) Amassing wealth often ruins health.
12) I was surprised at Hari's being absent.
13) We spent the afternoon in playing cards.
14) The miser hated spending money.

15) She was angry at Saroja trying to lie to her.

16) Praising all alike is praising none.

17) Are you afraid of hearing you?

18) I determined to increase my salary by managing a little farm.

19) Success is not merely winning applause.

20) The year was spent in visiting our rich neighbours.

21) Singing to herself was her chief delight.

22) He preferred playing football to studying his lessons.

23) I thank thee, Jew, for teaching me that word.

24) I cannot go on doing nothing.

250. **Answer to the Exercise-1**

1) *He* was found ***fighting*** desperately for his life. (participle describing 'he')
2) He has *ruined* his sight by ***reading*** small print. (gerund, as Ind. object after prep. to mean instrument or agent, as the reply of 'by what?')
3) ***Hearing*** the noise, *he* ran to the window. (participle describing 'he', who heard the noise)
4) He saw a *clown* ***standing*** on his head. (participle describing 'clown', who was standing)
5) ***Asking*** q*uestions is* easier than ***answering*** them. (gerund, as subject & Ind. object after prep. 'than')
6) ***Waving*** their hats and handkerchiefs, *the people* cheered the batsman. (participle describing 'people' who were waiving...)
7) ***Walking*** on the grass is forbidden. (gerund phrase, as subject of the verb, 'is'.)
8) ***Jumping*** over the fence, *the thief* escaped. (participle describing 'the thief' who jumped)
9) The miser spends his time in ***hoarding*** money. (gerund, as object of prep. 'what in does he spend his time?')
10) Much depends on Rama's ***returning*** before noon. (gerund, depends on what?)
11) ***Amassing*** wealth often ruins health. (participle describing 'wealth')
12) I was surprised at Hari's ***being*** absent. (gerund, surprised at what?)
13) We spent the afternoon in ***playing*** cards. (gerund, spent in what?)
14) The miser hated ***spending*** money. (gerund, what did the miser hate?)
15) She was angry at Saroja ***trying*** to lie to her. (participle describing 'Saroja', a noun)
16) ***Praising*** all alike is ***praising*** none. (gerund, as subject & complement)
17) Are you afraid of ***hearing*** you? (gerund, object of a preposition)
18) I determined to increase my salary by ***managing*** a little farm. (gerund, by what manner or how?)
19) Success is not merely ***winning*** applause. (complement)
20) The year was spent in ***visiting*** our rich neighbours. (gerund, spends in what?)
21) ***Singing*** to herself was her chief delight. (gerund, as subject)
22) He preferred ***playing*** football to ***studying*** his lessons. (gerund, as Object, preferred what / to what?)
23) I thank thee, Jew, for ***teaching*** me that word. (gerund, thank for what?)
24) I cannot go on ***doing*** nothing. (participle describing 'I')

The Participle

251.   The '**-ing**', **2ⁿᵈ & 3ʳᵈ form** of verbs (The progressive, past & past participle form of verb), being non-finite remains, often used as determiner/adjective in the sentence. study the following definition.

Definition: A participle is **that form of the verb that takes the nature** *of* <u>both of a verb</u>, (having a subject, or object) **and of an adjective** (describing a noun or a pronoun).

✗ <u>Read the sentence:</u>

Hearing the noise, the boy woke up.

- The word '**hearing**' which is formed from the verb '**hear**' <u>governs on object (the noise) like a verb does</u> in a sentence (*as, the boy heard the noise and he woke up*); <u>and qualifies the noun 'boy'</u> (*which boy woke up?* = *who heard the noise*) as an adjective.
- '**heard**', the Finite verb has turned into Non-finite present participle, '**hearing**.'
- The same form' hearing' can also be used as Gerund, like the following:
   ✓ His **hearing** is poor. (Here, 'hearing' is the Gerund.)
   ✓ He is **hearing-impaired**. ('hearing-impaired' is a Compound participle, forms a complement that completes the sense of the verb 'is', and describes the pronoun 'he', like an adjective does; as, **He is a teacher**. [in the sentence, 'a teacher' is a complement of verb 'is', but here the word 'teacher' is a noun. However, it adds information about his profession.])

✗ **Study more examples**
- *Boring* teachers often make *bored* students.
- *Boring* actors make *bored* audience.
- *Boring* lectures always make *bored* (dull) spectators.

'**Boring**' and '**bored**' —both are the participles, non-finite remains, remained unchanged according to number, person of the subject; and tense of the verb. And in each they describe either a noun or a pronoun.

252. **The Participle & its Kinds:** The participles are of three kinds:
   A. **Present Participle** *(the '-ing' form of verb that represents an action which is going on or incomplete.)*
   B. **Past Participle** *(that represents a complete action or a state, generally '-d', '-ed', 't', 'n' or 'en' forms of verbs)* &
   C. **Perfect Participle** *(with 'having' followed by the 'past participle' form of verb, to refer an action completed sometime earlier than another in past.)*

Examples:

➢ We saw a man ***running*** towards us.
➢ ***Burnt*** dogs seldom bite.
➢ ***Having infected*** by COVID-19, the old man died last year.

253. **Present Participle**

⇒ We met a girl ***carrying*** *a basket of flowers*. *(We met **a girl** who was carrying a basket...)*
⇒ Loudly ***knocking*** *at the gate*, he demanded admission. (***Knocking he*** *demanded his admission—here, 'knocking' qualifies the pronoun, 'he'*).
⇒ The child ***thinking*** *all was safe*, attempted to cross the road. (*a child who thinks...*)

Note:
All the above bold letters are doing the function of an adjective. They are usually called the **Present Participle,** which ends in '**–ing form**' and represents an action, incomplete or imperfect, as going on by '**carrying**', '**knocking**', & '**thinking**'.

254. **Past & Perfect Participle**

✗ Besides **Present participle**, there are other two participles—Past Participle and Perfect Participle.
✗ **Past Participle** represents a completed action or state of the thing spoken of.
✗ **Perfect Participle** that represents an action as completed at some time earlier in past than the other past event or action.
✗ Generally, *both, Past & Perfect Participles have same form, only Perfect Participle is used with* '**having**' ('have+ing' form) *before the Past Participle.*

255. **Examples & Explanation of Past Participle:**

1) ***Blinded*** by dust storm, they fell into disorder.
   ▪ *Explanation: As they got blind by dust storm, they fell into disorder.* (***Two past events, as happened simultaneous***. *The sub-ordinate adverbial clause, 'As they got blind by dust storm' has been turned into the participle phrase, 'Blinded by dust storm' and described the pronoun, 'they' who got blind; and thus, the word, 'Blinded' did the both function of a verb and of an adjective.*)

2) ***Deceived*** by his friends, he lost all hope.
   ▪ *Explanation: Two past events 'deceived' & 'lost' are simultaneous. 'Deceived by his friends' described the pronoun, 'he' who was deceived, and thus the participle has done dual function, both of a verb and of an adjective.*

3) Time ***misspent*** is time lost.
   ▪ *Explanation :(If time is misspent, it is time lost. 'Misspent is a participle as it describes the noun, 'time'.)*

4) ***Driven*** by hunger, he stole a piece of bread.
   ▪ *Explanation :(How was he? He was 'driven by hunger'. The above underlined particle phrase describes the pronoun, 'he'. So, 'driven' is the participle here.)*

5) We saw a few trees *laden* with fruits.
   - *Explanation: (How were* the trees? The trees were 'laden with fruits.)

6) *Burnt* dogs seldom bite. *Explanation:* (what kinds of dog? 'Burnt' describes the noun, 'dog'.)

7) He had them *punished*. (Punished- past participle described the pronoun, 'them'.)

Note: It is noticed Past participle usually ends in **–ed, -d, -t, -en**, or **–n**. (However, it depends on the nature of the verb, regular or irregular.)

256. **Perfect Participle**

Note: Perfect Participles are not other than the form of Past Participle, only it has **'Having'** before it. However, note the difference.

1) *Having rested*, we continued our journey.
   - *Explanation: Here two incidents are mentioned.* 'After we had taken our rest, we continued our journey.' There is a gap between the two incidents or actions; they are not simultaneous, or incomplete or continuous. And the adverbial clause has been turned into a participle phrase.

2) *Having the sun set*, we started for our home.
   Explanation: There is a gap of time being between the two incidents— 'setting of the sun' and of our 'starting for home'; as, 'The sun has set. We started for our home.'

3) *Having burnt*, he died painfully after three months. (There is a time gap between the incident and his death.)

4) *Having passed* the examination in 2014, Rakesh joined the service in 2021 under West Bengal Government. (There is seven years' gap between the two incidents 'giving examination' and 'the recruitment'.)

5) *Having infected* by Corona Virus, he died last year. (The man didn't die immediately after he was infected.) The sense is like that: 'The man had been infected by Corona Virus. He died last year.'

6) *Having born the prince*, the king had no worry of his successor. (Having born the prince, the king had the cause not to worry throughout his life. So, there is sufficient gap between the two incidents.)

257. **The use of Participles:**

   ✗ **Read the Examples carefully:**
   1) A *rolling* stone gathers no moss.
   2) We had a drink of the *sparkling* water.
   3) His *tattered* coat needs mending.

   ✗ In the above sentences, the Present & Past Participles, like- *rolling, sparkling, tattered*- are often called the **Participle Adjectives** or **Simple Participles.** They are called so, as they are used as simple qualifying adjectives, used before a noun.

   ✗ **More example of using Participle as Adjectives:**
   4) The *creaking* door awakened the dog.
   5) A *lying* witness ought to be punished.
   6) He played a *losing* game.
   7) A *burnt* cow dreads the fire.
   8) His *finished* manners produced a very favourable impression.
   9) He wears a *worried* look.
   10) He was a *tensed* person.

258. <u>The Use of Participles in Nominative Absolute:</u>

First know, what is <u>Nominative Absolute</u> or <u>Absolute Phrase</u>.

To define, '**A Nominative Absolute**' is *<u>a free-standing part of a sentence</u>* that describes the main subject & verb.

- ✖ A <u>nominative absolute consists of a noun or a pronoun</u> in the nominative case (i.e., the case of a subject) <u>and a participle form</u> (either present, past or perfect), as the non-finite verb remains.
    1) *<u>**The sun having set**</u>*, we returned our homes.

- ✖ In the above sentence, '*the sun having set*' is an example of **Nominative Absolute**, which consist of a noun 'the sun' and the perfect participle which is here 'having set'. The phrase is used as a free-standing part, separated by a comma (,) from the main part of the sentence, and describes the subject & verb of the main part of the sentence, that is 'we returned'. For better understanding, read more examples.
    2) *<u>The dragon **slain**</u>*; the Knight took his rest.
    3) *<u>The truck finally **loaded**</u>*, they said goodbye to their neighbours & drove off.
    4) We sat side by side, *<u>our legs **touching**</u>*, comfortable in the warm silence, our two bodies did create.
    5) *<u>The play **done**</u>*; the audience left the room. (After the play had been acted, the audience left the room.)

- ✖ **Note:** Remember, the <u>Nominative absolute may be used at the beginning</u>, <u>in the middle</u> or <u>at the end</u> of the sentence.
- ✖ An Absolute Phrase, i.e., the Nominative Absolute can easily be turned into a sub-ordinate clause & vice-versa; as in the followings:
    1) Spring advancing, the swallows appear.
        → *When spring advances, the swallows appear.*
    2) The sea being calm, we went for a sail.
        → *Because the sea was calm, we went for a sail.*
    3) God willing, we shall meet again.
        → *If God is willing, we shall meet again.*

259. **Participle (like an adjective) admits of Degrees of Comparison too:**
- Education is <u>the most **pressing** need</u> of our nation.
- He was reputed to be <u>the most **learned** man</u> of his time.
- He was <u>the best fast **racing** driver</u>.
- He is <u>the best **living** actor</u> of our time.
- It was <u>the most **acquired** success</u> in his life.
- It was <u>the worst **achieving** attempt</u> of the man.

260. Carefully note, **the Active & Passive forms of Participles** and their uses in the sentences, given in the chart and thereafter:

In Active Voice	In Passive Voice
Present Participle: Setting /hearing/loving ° The sun <u>setting</u> in the east, we returned. ° <u>Hearing</u> his cry for help, I ran forward to the direction only to see him lying in blood. ° <u>Loving</u> her child, she set for work. **Perfect Participle:** Having set/ having heard/ having loved	**Present Participle**: Being set /being heard/being loved ° <u>Being set</u> in the new environment his company shifted him again for a new place. ° <u>Being heard</u> her cry what you did for her? ° <u>Being loved</u> by her so many years, how you asked me to break up? **Perfect Participle:** Having been set / having been heard/having been loved ° <u>Having been set</u> here, what the fuck you did for us these long years! ° <u>Having been heard</u> yet, you never thought to visit me in these days, and you say, you loved me very much!

° The sun <u>having set</u>, the army marched for the battlefield. ° <u>Having heard</u> her cry for help, men gathered but it was too late! ° <u>Having loved</u> for years she broke up leaving me in tears.	° <u>Having been loved</u> by mom, I feel gratitude, like all other millions, life-long. **Past Participle:** set/ heard/loved ° <u>Set</u> at the new place, he began his work. ° <u>Heard</u> of him, I thought to visit him this weekend. ° <u>Loved</u>, I am your lover since this evening.

261.　The <u>Past Participle is Passive in meaning</u>, so why it has no active form; as,

→ 'a burnt dog' = a dog which is burnt.

✖ <u>Read more examples</u>:

→ When I reached there, I saw a **spent** *swimmer.* (*a swimmer who is tired out*)
→ A **burnt** *child* is under his care. (*a child who is burnt*)
→ I bought two **painted** *dolls* in the fair. (*Dolls which were painted*)
→ I saw her **loved** by her lover on my bed at midnight. (Who was being loved by her lover)

262.　**While Present & Perfect Participles are in active voice, they can be turned into passive forms.; as,**

→ There is nothing smoother than a **rolling** *stone* (*a stone which rolls.*) *[in active]* = ... *a stone being rolled.*
→ = There is nothing smoother than a stone **being rolled**.
→ Who is faster than a **running** *cheetah?* (*a cheetah who is running/who is on run.*) [in active] = ... than a cheetah being run?
→ = Who is faster than a cheetah **being run**?
→ Who doesn't like **loving** guys?
→ = The guys who are **being loved** are liked by all.
→ **Having loved** her, I am almost ruined in my savings.
→ = She **having been loved**; I am almost ruined in my savings.

263.　**Let's check, what we have learnt:**

❖ A participle is a **verbal adjective.** It is a verb as well as an adjective in function or in use.
→ <u>Like a verb it may govern on a noun or a pronoun</u>, i.e., takes a subject or an object; as '*Hearing the noise...*' (*The noun 'noise' is governed by 'hearing'; 'noise' is the object of 'hearing' participle*).

→ <u>Like a verb, it may be modified by an adverb</u>; as in '*Loudly knocking...*' (*'Knocking' is modified by 'loudly', an adverb*)

→ <u>Like an adjective it may qualify a noun or a pronoun</u>; as '*Having rested, the man continued his journey.*' ('Having rested' the participle phrase is qualifying the noun, man.)

→ <u>Like an adjective, it may be compared</u>; as '*Education is the most pressing need of our country.*' ('Most pressing' refers to the superlative degree, which is a quality of an Adjective.)

264.　**Study the Common Uses of Participle:**

Functions	Examples
i) Present Participle is used <u>to</u> form Continuous Tense with 'be verb':	I am **writing.** He was **going.** They will be **waiting** for us there.
ii) Past Participle is used <u>to</u> form Perfect Tense with 'have verb' before it:	He has **gone.** They had **done.** We shall have **reached** there by the time.
iii) Past Participle is used <u>to</u> form passive voice of the verb with be verb:	It was **done** in due time. He was **suspended.** I am **honoured** with this reward.

iv) Present and Past participle are used *as* <u>an adjective to describe a noun</u> or a pronoun:	**<u>They may be used attributively</u>**<u>; as,</u> Look at the ***falling*** leaves. The girl is collecting ***fallen*** leaves. A ***rolling*** stone gather no moss. His ***tattered*** coat needs mending. A ***lost*** opportunity never returns. **<u>Or predicatively</u>**<u>; as,</u> The story is ***exciting***. The man seems ***worried***. (Modifying the subject) He kept me ***waiting***. (Modifying the object) **<u>Absolutely with a noun or a pronoun going before; as,</u>** <u>The weather being fine, I went out.</u> <u>Many having arrived, we were freed from anxiety.</u> <u>God willing, we shall have another good Monsoon.</u>
v) *As participle* or *adjective phrases*	1. It was a table ***<u>covered with papers</u>***. 2. Anyone ***<u>touching that wire</u>*** will get a shock. 3. ***<u>Being ill</u>*** he could not attend the meeting.
vi) *As an adverb*	1. It is **freezing** cold. 2. ***<u>Loudly knocking at the door</u>***, he demanded admission.

265. As we already said, a Participle partakes the nature of both of a verb (takes subject & object) and an adjective (qualifying a Noun), read the following: **how a Participle takes an object**

In the following, a participle like a verb (transitive) <u>takes an object</u> and also <u>modified by an adverb</u>; as,
1) We met a girl **carrying** <u>a basket of flowers</u>.   *(Carrying what? = a basket of flowers.)*
2) **Seeing** <u>him</u> excellent, she agreed to marry him.   *(Seeing whom? = him.)*
3) <u>Loudly</u> **knocking** at the gate, he demanded admission.   *(Knocking how? = Loudly).*
4) <u>Loudly</u> **shouting** at her, he demanded her arrest.   *(Shouting how? = Loudly)*

✼ In sentences-1 & 2, the participles- '***carrying***', '***seeing***' have taken objects- '<u>*basket of flowers*</u>' & '<u>*him*</u>'.
✼ In sentences-3 & 4, the participles- '***knocking***', '***shouting***'- have been modified by an Adverb '<u>*loudly*</u>'.

266. We have studied <u>three main types of participles</u>, and also <u>its uses in</u> **Nominative Absolut**e. Now carefully note down some other features (difference in their uses), if any, in the following comparison of participles:

Compare-

Present Participle	Nominative Absolute
• **Being occupied** with important matters, he had no leisure to see us.	• **The boss being occupied**, we escaped our tasks.
• **Being fine**, I joined my work.	• **The weather being fine**, I went out.
• **Being permitted**, we did the task.	• **Weather permitting**, we will go there.
• **Being willed**, she agreed to marry.	• **God willing**, we will meet soon.
• **Advancing**, the year came to end.	• **Spring advancing**, the swallows appear.

Compare-

Perfect Participle	Nominative Absolute
1. **Having burnt**, he died painfully after three months.	1. **The corns having burnt**, the farmer fell in financial difficulties.
2. **Having passed** the examination in 2014, Rakesh joined the service in 2021 under West Bengal Government.	2. **His son having passed the I.C.S,** the father felt proud for his son.
3. **Having infected**, he died last year.	3. **The patient having infected with Corona new trend,** no staff came forward for help.

✖ Have you noticed any difference through the examples?

✖ The participles (present, past or perfect) when they are used in joining two clauses or sentences, generally they take **same** subject (noun or pronoun) which they describe; <u>whereas,</u> in nominative absolutes (the free-standing part of a sentence) they <u>take **different** subjects</u> (nouns or pronouns before it) and these are used as a whole and finally it modifies the action of the main subject, like an adverb, in the sentence; as,

→ *<u>Having burnt</u>*, he died painfully after three months.

→ *<u>The corns **having burnt**</u>*, the farmer fell in financial difficulties.

➢ In sentence-1, the subject of the participle '*having burnt*' is the same which <u>*it describes*</u> which is '*he*' here.

➢ In sentence-2, <u>the subject of</u> the participle 'having burnt' is 'the **corns**', and joining together the <u>absolute phrase describes the **action** or **state** of another subject</u> (action of the main subject of the sentence) i.e., 'the farmer's falling in financial difficulties.

267. **Errors in the use of participles / Transferred epithet:**

Errors in the use of participles / Transferred epithet:	
Since the **participle** is a verb-adjective, it <u>must be attached to some noun or a pronoun</u>; in other words, it <u>must have a proper 'subject of reference'</u>. Note: the use of participles in the sentences are wrong as participles are left here without proper agreement with its subject of reference:	1. **Standing at the gate,** a scorpion stung him.*(Doesn't it read as, the scorpion was standing at the gate? So, it is wrong. When it was 'he' who was standing at the gate and got stung by the scorpion.)* 2. **Going up the hill,** an old temple was seen.*(Here, the old temple, of course, did not go up but 'the tourists who went up to see the temple.)* 3. **Entering the room,** the light was quite dazzling.(who entered the room? It was I or you or (s)he but of course, not the light.)

268. **Proper use of participles:**
❑ The *'transferred epithet'* is often happen in using participle too; and the grammarians are divided about its use in participles too. However, we like to put here, the proper agreement of participles of those where these errors happen, though with few examples only, to make you understand the fact.
❑ <u>The proper agreement of participles with their 'subjects' reference' will be as the following</u>:
   → <u>Standing at the gate</u>, **he** was stung by a scorpion. (While he was standing at the gate, a scorpion stung him.)
   → <u>Going up the hill</u>, **we** saw an old temple. (When we went up the hill, we saw an old temple.)
   → <u>Entering the room</u>, **I** found the light was quite dazzling. (When I entered the room, I found the light quite dazzling.)

Impersonal Absolute & Bare Participle

269. **Impersonal Absolute:**

Though participles should be used with their proper agreement with the subject of reference, but sometimes **participles are left out from their proper subject of reference**:

❑ *Taking everything into consideration*, the Magistrate was perfectly justified in issuing those orders. (Who justified the magistrate taking everything into consideration about his issuing or passing orders? Of course, it is not the Magistrate himself but some other men in position. But as they are uncertain, who they are, it can be used like this one. You may take these as exceptions.)
❑ *Considering his abilities*, he should have done better. (It is 'we', the other men than 'he' who consider his abilities, not he himself.)
❑ *Roughly speaking*, the distance from here to the nearest station is two kilometres. (If one speaks roughly; this one is uncertain. So, it is another exception about proper agreement of participles with the subject of reference.)

Note: such uses of participles are known as **Impersonal Absolute.**

270. **Bare Participle** or **Zero Participle**
❑ Sometimes, Participles are understood (i.e., they are omitted) from the sentences. Read the examples:
   → Sword (being) in hand, he rushed to the jailor.

→ Breakfast (having been) over, we went out for a walk.

❑ Can these be termed as '**Bare Participle**' or '**Zero Participle**' as 'Bare Infinitive' or 'Zero Infinitive'? Then they are, and thus are abound in English Language.

Exercise-15

✖ **Pick out the Participle and tell which kind of they are:**
1) Generally speaking, we receive what we deserve.
2) Having gained truth, keep truth to end.
3) I saw the storm approaching.
4) Hearing a noise, turned around.
5) Considering the facts, he received scant justice. (Scant: hardly any; not very much and not as much as there should be)
6) The enemy, beaten at every point, fled from the field.
7) Being dissatisfied, he resigned his position.
8) The rain came pouring down in torrents.
9) Having elected him President, the people gave him their loyal support.
10) The traveller, being weary, sat by the Woodside to rest.
11) The fat of the body is fuel laid away for use.
12) Being occupied with important matters, he had no leisure to see us.
13) The children coming home from school look in at the open door.
14) Dr. Mishra, bereaved of his daughter Lucy, died of a broken heart.
15) Books read in childhood seem like old friends.
16) Lessons learned easily are soon forgotten.
17) Seeing the sunshine, I threw open the window.
18) Overcome by remorse, he determined to atone for his crime.

<u>Answers to the exercise-A:</u>

✖ **Pick out the Participle and tell which kind of they are:**

1. Generally **speaking**, we receive what we deserve. (Present Participle)
2. **Having gained** truth, keep truth to end. (Perfect Participle)
3. I saw the storm **approaching**. (Present Participle)
4. **Hearing** a noise, turned around. (Present Participle)
5. **Considering** the facts, he received scant justice. (scant: hardly any; not very much and not as much as that should be) (Present Participle & Impersonal Absolute)
6. The enemy, **beaten** <u>at every point</u>, fled from the field. (Past Participle in apposition)
7. **Being** dissatisfied, he resigned his position. (Present Participle)
8. The rain came **pouring down** in torrents. (Present Participle)
9. **Having elected** him President, the people gave him their loyal support. (Perfect Participle)
10. The traveller, **being** weary, sat by the Woodside to rest. (Present Participle in apposition)
11. The fat of the body is fuel **laid away** for use. (Past Participle)
12. **Being occupied** with important matters, he had no leisure to see us. (Present Participle in Passive Voice)
13. The children **coming** <u>home from school</u> look in at the open door. (*Phrase of Present Participle, used in apposition without comma before or after it*)
14. Dr. Mishra, **bereaved** <u>of his daughter Lucy</u>, died of a broken heart. (*Past Participle, used in apposition to describe Dr. Mishra*)
15. Books **read** <u>in childhood</u> seem like old friends. (Past Participle, describing books)
16. Lessons **learned** easily are soon forgotten. (Past Participle)
17. **Seeing** the sunshine, I threw open the window. (Present Participle)
18. **Overcome** by remorse, he determined to atone for his crime. (Past Participle)

✖ **How to change Participle into Finite Verb:**

1) Quitting the forest, we advanced into the open plain.
2) Driven out of his country, he sought asylum in a foreign land.
3) Going up the stairs, the boy fell down.

4) Having lost my passport, I applied for a new one.
5) I once saw a man walking on a rope.
6) Walking on the roof, he slipped and fell.
7) Having no guide with us, we lost our way.
8) The stable door being open, the horse was stolen.
9) Being paralytic, he could not walk.
10) Hearing the noise, I woke up.
11) Caesar being murdered, the dictatorship came to an end.
12) Working all day, I was fatigued.
13) We met an old Sadhu walking to Varanasi.
14) Having failed in the first attempt, he made no further attempt.
15) Walking up to the front door, I rang the bell.
16) Enchanted by the scene, I lingered on my voyage.
17) Mounting his horse, the bandit rode off.
18) Not knowing my way, I asked a nearby policeman about the route.

<u>Answers to exercise-C.:</u>

✘ **How to change Participle into Finite Verb:**

1)	Quitting the forest, we advanced into the open plain.	➤	We quitted the forest and advanced into the open plain.
2)	Driven out of his country, he sought asylum in a foreign land.	➤	As he was driven out of his country, he sought asylum in a foreign land.
3)	Going up the stairs, the boy fell down.	➤	When the boy was going up the stairs, he fell down.
4)	Having lost my passport, I applied for a new one.	➤	Because I had lost my passport, I applied for a new one.
5)	I once saw a man walking on a rope.	➤	I once saw man who was walking on a rope.
6)	Walking on the roof, he slipped and fell.	➤	While he was walking on the roof, he slipped and fell.
7)	Having no guide with us, we lost our way.	➤	As we had no guide with us, we lost our way.
8)	The stable door being open, the horse was stolen.	➤	As the stable door was open, the horse was stolen.
9)	Being paralytic, he could not walk.	➤	He could not walk as he was a paralytic.
10)	Hearing the noise, I woke up.		= I heard the noise and I woke up.
11)	Caesar being murdered, the dictatorship came to an end.		➤After Caesar was murdered, the dictatorship came to an end.
12)	Working all day, I was fatigued.		➤As I worked all day, I was fatigued.
13)	We met an old Sadhu walking to Varanasi.		➤I met an old Sadhu who was walking to Varanasi.
14)	Having failed in the first attempt, he made no further attempt.		➤After he had failed in the first attempt, he made no further attempt.
15)	Walking up to the front door, I rang the bell.		➤I walked up to the front door and I rang the bell.
16)	Enchanted by the scene, I lingered on my voyage.		➤As I was enchanted by the scene, I lingered on my voyage.
17)	Mounting his horse, the bandit rode off.		➤The bandit mounted his horse and he rode off.
18)	Not knowing my way, I asked a nearby policeman about the route.		➤As I did not know my way, I asked a nearby policeman about the route.

15. The Glossary of Verbs

271.   <u>**Verbs have more than twenty names:**</u>

✘ There are more than twenty (20) names of Verbs. It does not mean there are twenty kinds of verbs, but one verb has different names as it is used and viewed from different corners; as,
   ➤ Peter is a father. The father loves his child. He is a good husband. The husband buys a bunch of flowers for his wife on every weekend.
✘ In the above, <u>Peter</u>, <u>father</u>, <u>husband</u> —all refer to same person. The same thing happens to verbs. A verb plays different roles and thus it has different names. Carefully study the chart of verbs with their different names. Most of we have already gone through:

Verbs	Functions/Definition	Examples

1. State Verb	Verb that **relates to a state of being, having, existence, etc. but not an action**. They are not generally used in continuous tenses & in imperative structures.	• He **_is_** a student. • I **_have_** a pen. • She **_seems_** weak. • I **_feel_** drowsy. • She **_looks_** like her mother.
2. Event Verb	**that denotes an action**, can be used in continuous tense.	**Do, go buy, play** & many more.
3. Finite Verb	**Changeable with person-number of subject and tense of the verb.**	• I **_go_** to school. • He **_goes_** to school. • They **_went_** to school.
4. Non-finite	**Not changeable with number, person of subject and tense**, formed by adding **'to'** before and **'-ing'** after verb or past participle form.	• **_Going_** to school he learns. • **_Going_** to school they learnt. • I saw the animal **_burnt._** • He went there **_to meet_** our uncle.
5. Regular/Weak	Past and Participle are formed by **adding- '-d', '-ed', '-t', '-n' or '-en'.**	**_Work—worked,_** **_Live—lived_** **_Burn-burned-burnt_**
6. Irregular/Strong	Have their **own past** and **participle forms**	**_Write—wrote—written,_** **_Go—went—gone_**
7. Principal/Main	**Can be used alone in the sentence.**	**Go, read take etc.** • He **goes** to school every day. • I **took** the novel from there.
8. Auxiliary/Helping	The verbs which **help principal verbs to form negative question, tense** & to define **mood of expression.**	**Verbs 'to Be', 'to Do', 'to Have' & the 13 modal verbs.** • I **am** reading a book. • **Has** he passed the exam.? • She **does not go** there. • He **could** do it. • **May** I come in sir?
9. Primary Auxiliary (Be, have & do verbs)	**Can be used alone** as well as **to assist main** verbs.	• I **am reading** a book. • I **am** a boy. • He **had** a car. • He **had done** his work. • He **does**. • **Do** you **work**?
10. Modal Auxiliary (Can, may, shall, will, must, could, might, should, would, ought to, used to, need, dare.)	They are used only as helping verbs except **'need' and 'dare'.** • Need & dare are often used as the main verbs. • 'need' denotes 'to want or necessity; • 'dare' denotes 'brave enough' or 'defy a challenge'.	• You **_must_** do it. • He **_may_** pass. • We **_can_** run. • You **_should_** listen to your teacher. • How **_dare_** he go? • He **_dare_** not say that. • He d**_ares_** to fight. • We **_need_** enough teaching staff to run the institution. • What **_need_** he care for me?
11. Transitive	the verbs which are followed by an object or needs an object to complete its meaning.	• Rita **_reads_** a book. • I **_bought_** a pencil. • She **_cooked_** delicious food.

12. Intransitive	The verbs do not require any object.	• They **run** fast. • She **sleeps** sound. • I am **swimming**. • She is **standing** there.
13. Factitive (Transitive verbs of incomplete prediction)	A transitive verb that requires a word or words (Complements) beyond its object to complete the sense. (Usually naming, making, and thinking verbs)	• I **called** John a <u>fool</u>. • We **made** him our <u>captain</u>. • I **thought** you <u>wrong</u>. • They **proclaimed** him <u>king</u>. • I **appoint** you, my <u>secretary</u>. • We **elected** you our <u>M.L.A.</u> • We **choose** him our <u>boss</u>.
14. Causative (When an Intransitive verb used transitively)	A verb that **denotes causing something to happen.** (Besides 'make, 'have' there are some, having different forms as '<u>set' for sit</u>, '<u>fell' for fall</u>, '<u>feed' for eat</u>)	• He **had** them punished. • She **makes** me laugh. • They **set** me to see the movie. • Mother **fed** her child. • The banana peel **fells** me on the floor.
15. Prepositional Phrase Verbs	It is a combination of a <u>verb and two prepositions</u>, the first one act an adverb, when second as the preposition.	• **Put up with** your hands, or I'll shoot you down on the lane. • **Look down upon** the trees, they are covered with white snow, like a mountain in the lake.
16. Quasi Passive	**Verbs which are active in form but passive in sense.** (Read details in chapter of 'Voice Change'.)	• Honey **tastes** sweet. • The house **is building.**
17. Catenative	**When Finite & Non-finite verbs together form a chain like structure** (i.e., the main verb is used with participle, gerund or infinitive after it).	• He **keeps singing**. • She **got hurt**. • It **began raining**. • I **like swimming**.
18. Ergative	The verbs which are <u>able to be used in both a Transitive & Intransitive way with the same meaning,</u> where the object of the transitive becomes subject of Intransitive.	• She **opened** the door. • = The door **opened.** • She **grew** flowers in her garden. • = Flowers **grew** in her garden.
19. Performative	Some verbs <u>clearly state the kind of speech,</u> **or** the <u>act being performed</u>.	*apologize, forbid, inform, promise, request, thanks, etc.*
20. Copula or Linking	A verb **that joins a subject to its complement.**	• I feel drowsy. • She became mad. • Raina got hurt.
21. Factive Verbs:	The verbs talking about something **as true fact; as,**	o I **know** the reason why he refused. o I **know** why she has not come. o I **understand** your problem. o Yea, we have **realized** it well.
22. Non-factive Verbs:	The Verbs, talking about something **may or may not be true fact;** as,	o I **believe** he will return in time. (<u>He may or may not</u>) o I **believe** he must return in time. (<u>There is some sureness about his return</u>) o We **doubt** he has died. We doubt his death. (<u>The fact may not be true</u>)

23. Contrafactive Verbs:	The Verbs talking **about something that is not true**; as,	o He **pretends to be** a good listener in the seminar. (When the truth is, 'he is not listening') o I **wish** you bet me in the race. Best of Luck. (When the reality is, 'you can't beat me'.)

Some more details of –Linking, Factitive, Ergative, Performative & Catenative Verbs

272. **Linking Verbs** or **Copula:** a verb, such as— *be, feel, become, grow, taste, remain, appear, act, smell, sound, stay,* etc. can be <u>used to connect the subjects with its Adjectives</u>, <u>Nouns or Adverbs (Complement)</u> which describe the subject itself, is known to be the **Linking Verbs** or **Copula**; as,

→ <u>He **is** a fool</u>. ('he' & 'fool' refer to same person, the two words are linked or connected by the verb, 'is'. 'Is' is a linking verb.)

→ <u>I **am** a <u>stupid</u> that I am working on this dull project! (I & stupid refer to same person, like the above, and they are linked or connected by 'am'.)

→ The <u>store</u> **remains** <u>open</u> the whole night. ('The store' & it's being 'open' are connected by the verb 'remains'.)

→ The <u>smell of the soil</u> **is** <u>awesome</u> in the rainy season. (Awesome describes the smell of the soil, but does not refer to any action; so why most of the linking verbs are the State Verbs as well.)

✗ More Examples of Linking Verbs

→ She **felt** <u>tired</u>. She **appears** <u>dull</u> at the moment.
→ She **looked** <u>old</u> by her skin. She **was** <u>jealous</u>.
→ The <u>baby</u> **grew** a <u>young lady</u> after twenty years.
→ He **remained** <u>rich</u> after his gigantic donation even.
→ Don't **act** <u>fool</u>. They **are** <u>ready</u> to fight.
→ I **am** <u>Dr. Fernandez</u>. It tastes <u>sweet</u>.

✗ All the above verbs link between their subjects, so called nouns, pronouns or Phrase with their adjective or complements. So why, they are called linking verbs. These verbs are, at the same time,
  ✓ *Finite Verbs,*
  ✓ *Principal Verbs,*
  ✓ *Intransitive &*
  ✓ *The State Verbs.*

✗ The words after the verbs which refer or describe the subjects themselves are the *Complements* in the sentences. So, the **Linking verbs** cum the **State verbs introduce,** in the most cases, **Complements.** [Though there are lots of state verbs which take objects, and they are transitive verbs too.]

✗ When the Linking verbs are no more Linking words, but Finite or Action Verbs:
✗ The linking verbs may also be used as the action words; as,
  → She **appears** in the party at the right time. *(It hints her coming in the party, which is an action) Or*
  → She frequently **looked at** her fiancé in the party. *(fiancé =male; fiancée= female) (her looking at her fiancé is an action)*

✗ In the above cases, the words (**appear, disappears, look**, etc.) are **no more linking** or **state verbs**; for <u>they do not introduce any complement, but object</u> or <u>adverbials</u>. They are just like other normal Finite & Action Verbs. Here, they show action of the subjects.
✗ **Remember, introducing Complement is an important role of Linking Verbs.**

273. **Factitive Verbs**

✗ When a transitive verb can't complete its sense even with its object after it, the verb is called **Factitive Verb**, and its object is called the **Factitive Object**. *A factitive object follows a complement* in the sentence. Let's discuss with an example:
  → They **proclaimed** him <u>king</u> of their country.

➢ In the sentence above, '**proclaimed**' is the verb, factitive. It is a transitive verb too, for it has an object, '**him**'. But the object does not complete the sense. To complete the sense, we need more words and here it is, '**king**'. The word, 'king' is the complement in the sentence.

➢ That means a factitive verb has both an Object & a Complement, not like the Linking Verbs (having complements) or the other Transitive Verbs (having objects).

➢ A Factitive verb *describes a situation (of an action)* where there is a *result or answer in the Complement.*

✖ **More Explanation**

→ I *painted* it red. (Here the situation of the action is "painting it", its result or answer lies in the complement, 'red'; painting which color?)

→ They *made* her captain. (Making her – is the situation; while its answer lies in its complement, 'captain'; she was made 'captain'.)

✓'**painted**' and '**made**' –both are Factitive Verbs. Thus, *elect, appoint, make, choose, deem, assign, name, select, judge, designate, proclaim*— are some other examples of Factitive Verbs.

✓Remember, **Complements describes either the subjects or Objects**. In case of Linking Verbs, they describe the Subjects; but in case of <u>Factitive Verbs, they mostly and generally, describe the Objects.</u>

More Examples of Factitive Verbs:
a) People *elected* him the Member of the Parliament.
b) The boss has *appointed* me his personal secretary.
c) The teacher *made* Peter the captain of the class,
d) *Choose* him your partner, it is your last option.
e) The evening was *seemed* a great success.
f) I *deem* it an honor to be invited. She *deemed* it prudent not to say anything.
g) The tour was *judged* a great success. They *judge* it wise to say nothing.
h) The floor has been *designated* a no smoking area. She d*esignated* him her deputy.
i) They *named* him 'the Rebel Poet'.
j) We *select* you, our chairman. They *call* us fool.
k) The teacher *assigned* each of the children a different task.

274. Ergative or Inchoative or Labile Verbs:

✖ The Ergative Verb is also known as '**Labile Verb**' or the '**Inchoative**' Verbs. The verbs which are able to be used in both ways—transitively and intransitively without changing their meaning. In Ergative, *the object of the Transitive is used as the Subject of an Intransitive Verb*; as,
  o She <u>grew</u> flowers in her garden. = The flowers *grew* in her garden.
  o I <u>ring</u> the bell. = The bell *rings*.
  o He <u>broke</u> the glass. = The glass *broke*.
  o He <u>burnt</u> his fingers. = His fingers *burnt*.
  o <u>Stop</u> him from going. = He *stops*.
  o <u>Open</u> all the windows. = All the windows *open*.
  o They <u>began</u> the show at six O'clock. = The show *opens*/begins/ starts at six O'clock.
  o The priest of the temple <u>opened</u> the door. = The door of the temple *opened*.

Note: If carefully note, you will see, the doers have become understood in the 2nd case of sentences.

Substitute Definition of Ergative Verb: The verb that expresses <u>a change of 'state' (position) that seems the</u> <u>object happens on its own.</u>

275. Performative Verbs:

✖ The Verbs that <u>state the kind of speech or act itself</u>. **All of them are state verbs, but have objects or adverbials to the sense; as,**

→ I *promise* I must go there tomorrow evening. (What do you promise? = that I mut go there.)

→ The Principal *promised* to look into the matter.

→ I **apologize** for the mistake. (Why should you apologize?)
→ He **forbade** them from mentioning the subject again. (Whom?)
→ She **requested** that no one be told of her decision until the next meeting. (What?)
→ I must write & **thank** Mary for the present. (Thank, whom?)
→ Please, **inform** us of any change of address. (Inform, whom?)
→ Uncle **advised** me to go home at once. (Advised, whom and what?)
→ The General **ordered** the soldiers to march on. (Whom and what?
→ I **begged** him to excuse me. (Whom and what?)

276.   **Catenative** or **Serial Verb Construction**:

✖ **Catenative Verbs:** It *denotes a verb that governs a non-finite form of another verb (that may be a gerund, infinitive or participle).* These verbs are called 'Catenative', because their ability to form a chain of verbs in the same clause of the sentence; as,

→ I **like** swimming.

    Note: In the sentence, Finite verb 'like' governs the non-finite verb form 'swimming', and forms a serial verb construction, known as **Catenative**.

✖ It is noted, here the verb 'like' is simultaneously—
       a.   a **State Verb**,
       b.   a **Finite**,
       c.   the **Principal or Main Verb**,
       d.   a **Transitive** &
       e.   a **Catenative** Verb form, along with 'swimming'..

➤ At the same time, the verb in the sentence, i.e., 'I **like** swimming' is in **Simple Present Tense** & in the **Active Voice** and such many more, everything based on see it from different perspectives; as *Peter, a father, a husband,* and *a teacher*—may refer to same person. Merely roles are different of a single man.

➤ Thus, a verb may perform multi roles, may have different identities or names.

→ He is **going** to market to buy a shirt.

    ▪   Here, the verb **Going** governs on an Infinitive **'to buy'**.)
    ▪   **'Going'** is an **Active** or **Event Verb** as well as a **Finite**, a **Principal**, an **Intransitive** & a **Catenative Verb** to call.

        ✖   **Some More Examples of Catenative Verbs:**

→ He **deserves to win** the cup.
→ You **are forbidden to smoke** here.
→ We **need to go** to the tennis court to help Jim to get some practice before the final game.
→ He **agreed to work** on Saturday.
→ He **admitted taking** money.
→ It **began to rain**.
→ It **began raining**.

✖ **Note:** The use of infinitive or gerund following the main verb, though sometimes bears same meaning, like the above, but not always; as,
    → I forgot to go to the shopping center. (I wanted to go, but then forgot to go, means, 'I did not go'.)
    → I forgot going to the shopping center. (I can't remember the experience of going to the shopping center.)

✖ The whole construction following Catenative Verb is often called as **'Serial Verb Construction'** or **'Compound Verb'**.

16. The Glossary of Objects

277. **What is called an Object?**

✖ Generally, when <u>an action is acted upon</u> a person, animal or thing. The person, animal or the thing after the verb is called an Object.

➢ She gives her ***brother a pen***.
➢ He tells ***him to go*** there.
➢ They laugh at ***us***. The bubble <u>bursts</u> ***itself***.
➢ Please *look into (investigate)* ***the matter*** carefully.
➢ He will soon run through (consume) his ***fortune***.
➢ *Don't look at* ***me*** like that. It's irritating!
➢ He <u>fell</u> a great ***fall***. Mother feeds ***her child***.

278. There are **more than twelve kinds of Objects** and all the objects are not objects of Finite cum Transitive verbs only, but some object are also of the Non-finite verbs (like of gerund, participle and infinitive verbs), and some others, are named after the words which govern the respective objects in the sentence; as,

a) Maradona <u>hits</u> ***the ball***.
b) I went to market <u>to buy</u> ***a book***.
c) <u>Playing</u> ***football*** is a good exercise.
d) <u>Hearing</u> ***the siren***, they got alarmed.

➢ In sentence a, '*the ball*' is a direct object of the transitive verb '*hits*. (It is a Transitive Direct Object.)

⬚ In sentence b, '*a book*' is an object of the infinitive verb '*to buy*'. (It is an Object to the Infinitive Verb.)

⬚ In sentence c, '*football*' is an object to the gerund '*playing*'. (It is known as a Gerundial Object.)

⬚ In sentence d, '*the siren*' is an object to the participle verb '*hearing*'. (It is known as Participial Object)

279. **Go through the List of Objects:**

1) Direct Objects
2) Indirect Objects
3) Retained Object
4) Object of a Preposition
5) Cognate Object or Cognate Accusative:
6) Object of Causative Verb
7) Reflexive Object
8) Object of Gerund
9) Object of Participle
10) Object of Infinitive Verb
11) Adverbial Object
12) Object of Complement

❑ Of the above, the two most familiar objects are **Direct** & **Indirect** Objects of Transitive Verbs, and the two often also raise confusion among teachers, experts, grammarians and learners about their nature and roles. So, we must begin with these two along and with a bit more illustrations.

280. **Direct Objects**

✖ Generally, a Transitive Verb takes Objects—Direct & Indirect Object.

✖ **Direct Object:** A noun, noun phrase or pronoun (that may refer to a person, animal or thing) that is directly affected by the action of a verb, is called Direct Object.

➢ I met ***him*** in town.
➢ She gives ***biscuits***.
➢ The king hunted ***a tiger***.
➢ The teacher slapped ***the student*** so hard!
➢ The player kicked ***the ball***.
➢ Please, pass ***the stapler***.

In the 1st sentence, the action 'meeting' is directly acted upon 'him'; so, 'him' is the direct object. In the 2nd, the action 'giving' is acted upon 'biscuits. So as, a tiger, the student, the ball & the stapler—are the Direct Objects in the sentences.

Note: Experts of Grammar in decades ago, ascertained, "The Direct Object refers to an object, while the Indirect Object usually refers to a person or an animal" and that we had so in the earlier grammar books or in books which are not updated till date. Now, the concept is made a bit changed. A Direct Object may refer to a person, an animal and even a thing. It is only based upon what or whom the action is acted upon directly.

281. <u>**What is the relation between Direct Objects & Active Verbs?**</u>

✖ **Note-1:** We have learnt, a Transitive Verb takes Objects. These Transitive Verbs are mostly belonging to the Active or Event Verbs; as, if there is no action, nothing is to be acted upon. But there are also a lot of state verbs which take objects—direct and indirect; as,
- We *considered* <u>him</u> as a good man. (**Whom** did you consider as a good man?)
- I *thought* <u>you are right</u>, but I was wrong. (**What** did you think of me?)

✖ The above verbs in bold, are state verbs and they are transitive verbs too, as <u>they have objects</u> in their credits, <u>underlined</u>.

✖ So, having objects or being transitive, does not bind to be merely event or active verbs. Study more examples:
- He *weighs* seven <u>stones</u>.
- The dog *chewed* the <u>slippers</u>.
- He is *playing* the <u>violin</u>.
- Sana is *visiting* <u>her grandparents</u>.
- Did you *complete* your <u>home tasks</u>?
- Whom do you **love**? (When the answer is like: 'I *love* <u>you</u>.')

✖ In each case, the bold word is a verb, transitive (**irrespective of state or event**) & the underlined words are the **Objects (Direct).**

✖ **Note-2:** Sometimes, **action stops with the action itself**, then it has no object, and the verb turns to be called '**Intransitive**'; as
- He *runs*.
- I *swim*,
- Gita *sings*, etc.

✖ **Note-3:** Generally, State verb does not have an object, but may have too and in most cases, they take a Complement; as,
- He <u>is</u> a ***professor*** of Kanpur University.
- We <u>regarded</u> him as a ***good man***.
- We <u>consider</u> our mom as ***head of the family***.

✖ The underlined words are the State Verbs, whereas, the Italic bold words are the Complements of the Verbs. '**Our mom**' is the object of verb '**consider**' & '**him**' is the object of the verb '**regard**'. So, they are Transitive verbs in the sentences.

✖ So, to be Transitive, it does not depend on to be State or Event; only we regard, Transitive verbs are mostly Event Verbs; whereas, the State & Linking Verbs are mostly Intransitive (they may have Complements), but not all.

282.   **Indirect Objects**

Indirect Object: *When an action is done to or for* a noun, noun phrase or pronoun (that may be a person, animal or thing), is linked or connected with a Direct Object closely, is called an Indirect Object. Without a Direct object, there cannot be (or not should be) an Indirect Object in the sentence.
- His father gave **him** <u>a *watch*</u>. ('what is giving' is more important than 'to whom the thing is given' in this case; therefore, '**a watch**' is the Direct Object, when '**him**' is the Indirect Object)
- She told **me**, *a secret*. ('**a secret**' is Direct Object, while '**me**' is the Indirect object.)
- My grand mom told **me** <u>*a story of fairy tale*</u>. (<u>a story of fairy tale</u>', the phrase is the Direct Object, while '<u>me</u>' is the Indirect)

➢ And this may reverse; as,
  ➢ He hit **me** with a ball.
  ➢ Police shot **him** dead.

> In both cases, the bold words are examples of Direct Objects (not Indirect).

Direct Objects answer the questions of – *'what'* or *'whom'* to the verb; while,
An Indirect Object answer the question of – *'to what'*, *'what about'*, *'whom'*, *'to whom'* or *'for whom'*.

> The question with **'for what'** <u>to the verb</u> <u>*denotes an adverb of reason; as,*</u>
> Sonny pushed Ingrid **to make him fall**.

Why/what for/for what did Sonny push Ingrid? = to make him fall.

283.   Let's argue with the following two sentences, to understand Direct and Indirect, better-
  → He tells me a story.
  → He tells a story to me.

- Which is Direct & which is Indirect in the above two?
- One expert says, *"The action moves from the Subject, through the verb, to the Direct Object (that comes first) & then the Indirect Object."*

- If he is true, then 'me' is the Direct Object & 'a story' is the Indirect Object in sentence 1; but in the 2nd sentence, that reverse, i.e., their identity or importance, whatever, change. Is not ridiculous!

- <u>Okay, discuss:</u>
1) "He tells a story" & "He tells me"

→ Which is more meaningful & complete by itself?

→ *He tells a story*—is complete in itself; while
→ *He tells me*—wants something more. That means it depends on 'a story'.

- So why, our conclusion is, *'a story'* is the **Direct Object** and *'me'* is the **Indirect Object** in this sentence. However, in other case, it may differ; as,
2) James Bond shot *him* with his *gun*.
→ (Here, 'him' is the Direct Object & 'gun' is an Object of the Preposition. However, **'with his gun',** the phrase is an adverbial phrase, denotes the manner of action. [How did Bond shoot him? / 'shot', what with?)

284.   **For more illustrations, study the following Sentences:**
  ✠ 'Give me the money.' / 'Give him the money.'
  → Which is the subject in the sentence? = 'You', which is understood in an Imperative Sentence.
  → Which are objects in the sentences? = 'me' & 'the money'
  → Which is the Direct & which is Indirect Object in the sentence?

⇒ Let's discuss:
  → 'Give him.' Has it any sense? = It is incomplete and you can't tell it even a sentence.
  → 'Give the money.' Despite being a part, it has a sense.

- So, **'what is giving'** is more important than **'to whom the thing is given'** in the above pair of sentences.
- <u>And sometimes,</u> **whom the action is directly acted upon,** is more important than **by what or what about. Direct object depends on importance upon what or whom the action or feeling is acted or thrust upon (as, 'I love you, my son).**
- <u>Which is more important and carry more sense than the other between two or three,</u> is the **Direct Object** in case of Transitive Verbs; if they have more than one. If there is single one, that might me Direct, or call merely as 'an Object'.

285.   **Find out Direct & Indirect Objects:**
  1) Sophia gives her brother a pen.
  2) Jacob tells his friend to go there.
  3) Noah asked me to hit the ball.
  4) My friends gave me a bouquet.

⇒ *Let's see, what if you ask these-*

1) What does Sophia give her brother? Whom does she give the pen?
2) What does Jacob tell his friend? Whom does he tell to go?
3) What did Noah ask me/you? Whom did Noah ask to hit the ball?
4) What did your friends give you? Whom did your friends give the bouquet?

⇒ And more to find out D & I Objects:

5) The teacher read a story to the class.
6) The girls baked a cake for their mother.
7) We gave some food to the beggar.
8) The boys gifted their teacher a Kashmiri shawl.
9) Little Red Riding Hood made biscuits for her grandfather.
10) I bought bangles for my sister.
11) We gave a map to the tourist.
12) I read the newspaper to my grandmother.

286. The Retained Object:

✗ **Retained Object:** Having two objects of Transitive Verbs, if one object takes the place of the Subject in the Passive Voice, the other is retained as object as it was in the Active Voice, which is left in the passive, is known as '**Retained Object**' of the verb.
- I gave you ***two books***. = You were given *two books* by me.
- I asked him ***to sing***. = He was asked *to sing* by me.
- The host provided me **the best service**. = The best service was provided *me* by the host. / I was provided *the best service* by the host.
- He offered **me** his car for the trip. = I was offered *his car* for the trip. / His car was offered *me* for the trip.
- My grandmother often told **me** a story of fairy tale. = A story of fairy tale was often told *me* by my grandmother. / I was often told *a story of fairy tale* by my grandmother.

Object of Preposition, Cognate & Others

287. The Object of a Preposition:

✗ **Object of a Preposition:** When an Intransitive Verb becomes Transitive (takes an object) by having a preposition added to them (intransitive verb), the object is known as '*the Object of a Preposition*'.
- All his friends *laughed at* (= *derided*) **him**. (Whom did they laugh at?)
- Please *look into* (= *investigate*) **the matter** carefully. (What to look into?)
- He will soon *run through* (consume) his **fortune**. (What will he run through soon?)
- I *talked about* (discussed) the **affair** several times. (What did you talk about?)
- I *wish for* **nothing** more than your love. (What do you wish for?)
- *Don't look at* (*see*) **me** like that. It's irritating! (What not to look at? What's irritating?)
- The police officer *asked for* his **name**. (What did he ask for?)

Exception: - When the preposition is prefixed to the verb, they become normal Transitive Verbs with their new & different meanings, and their objects are either Direct Object or Indirect Object; as,
- ➤ Shivaji **overcame** the *enemy*. (What did Shivaji overcome?)
- ➤ He bravely **withstood** the *attack*. (What did he withstand?)
- ➤ The river **overflows** its *banks*. (What does the river overflow?)

✗ In the above sentences, the bold words are ***Transitive Verbs***, and the underlined words are *__Direct Objects__*.

288. Cognate Object or Cognate Accusative:

✗ **Cognate Object or Cognate Accusative** (*from Latin, 'cognatus', akin*)**:** When an Intransitive Verb takes an object (after them) that is akin or similar in meaning to the verb, and thus the Intransitive verb turns to be Transitive. Such Object is known as ***Cognate Object or Cognate Accusative;*** as,
- ➤ They fought a good ***fight***. He fell a great ***fall***.
- ➤ The athlete runs a ***race***. Michael ran a ***race***.
- ➤ Elizabeth sang a sweet ***song***.
- ➤ Emily sighed a deep ***sigh***.
- ➤ He laughed a hearty ***laugh***.

➤ Let me die the **death** of a martyr.
➤ She *dreamt* a strange **dream** last night.
➤ She slept a sound **sleep** last night.
➤ Aurangzeb lived *a* **life** of an ascetic.

289. The Object of a Causative Verb:

✖ **Object of Causative Verb:** When an intransitive verb is used transitively in the sense of causing a thing to be done (that denotes causing something to happen), the object is known as the **Object of a Causative Verb**.

➤ He walks **the horse**. (Walks the horse = *makes the horse walk*)
➤ The little girl ran*a* **needle** into her finger. (Ran a needle= *caused a needle to run*)
➤ The boys fly **their kites**. (i.e., *cause their kites to fly*.)

✖ Some Intransitive Verbs are made ***causative*** by change the spelling of the verbs; as '**set**' for sit, '**fell**' for fall, '**feed**' for eat, etc., and they become Transitive Verbs. These also take object; as,

➤ Woodmen fell **trees** in the forest. (fell = *cause to fall*)
➤ Lay **the basket** there. (lay = *cause to lie*)
➤ Raise your **hands**. (raise = *cause to rise*)
➤ Set **the lamp** on the table. (set = *cause to sit*)
➤ Mother **feeds** her child. (feeds = makes eat)

290. The Reflexive Object

✖ **Reflexive Object:** When an intransitive verb is used reflexively, they become transitive, and the reflexive pronouns become their objects. They are known as reflexive objects; as,

➤ The bubble bursts ***itself***. (*When we could also write*, 'The bubble bursts.')
➤ The guests made ***themselves*** merry. (The guests made merry.)
➤ Please keep ***yourselves*** quiet. (Please keep quiet.)
➤ With these words he turned ***himself*** to the door. (...turned to the door.)
➤ The Japanese *feed* ***themselves*** chiefly on rice. (Feed chiefly on rice.)

✖ The underline words are actually intransitive verbs, which are used reflexively and we have reflexive Objects of the verbs, and thus, verbs are made Transitive.

The Object of a Gerund

291. **Object of a Gerund (8):** The '-ing form of verb' that does the work both of a noun (*to form subject or object, etc.*) and a verb (*having subject & object*), It is, therefore, a Verb-Noun and is called a Gerund.

→ Playing **cards** is not allowed here.
→ I like reading **poetry**.
→ He is fond of hoarding **money**.

▪ In sentence 1, the Gerund 'playing' like a Noun, is the subject of a verb 'is', and like a Verb it also takes an object, 'cards'; thus, the gerund 'playing' has the force of a verb and same time it does the work of a noun. '**Cards**' is the object of Gerund here.
▪ In sentence 2, the Gerund 'reading', like a Noun is the object of a verb 'like and like a Verb, it also takes an object, 'poetry'. '**Poetry**' is the object of Gerund 'reading'.
▪ In sentence 3, the Gerund, like a Noun, is governed by a preposition 'fond of'; and like a Verb, it also takes an object, '**money**'.

292. **The Object of a Participle:** A participle is a *verb form, ending in '-ing' or '-ed', '-t', '-en', etc.* (present, past & perfect participle form) *that partakes of the nature* (that takes the nature of/take part in the activity of) both of a verb, (having subject & object) and of an adjective (describing a noun or a pronoun).

(1) *Hearing* the **noise**, the boy woke up.

➤ The italic word '**hearing**' is the participle form of verb '**hear**' and it governs on its succeeding word or words; '**the noise**' which is the object of the participle. The action 'hearing' is acted upon 'the noise'. 'Hearing' what? = the noise. 'Noise' is the object of 'hear' verb. *Who woke up? = The boy who heard the noise woke up. The sentence is thus,* 'the boy heard the noise and he woke up/ the boy who heard the noise woke up.'

*Thus, a clause (principal or sub-ordinate of a compound or complex respectively) has turned into a phrase in the above sentence, using a present participle **'hearing'.***

(2) We met a girl **carrying** a basket of flowers. *(Carrying what? = a basket of flowers. Whom did you meet? = The girl who was carrying a basket of flowers. Thus, 'carrying', the verb form acts both roles of a verb and an adjective.)*

(3) ***Judging*** him handsome, she agreed to marry him. *(Judging whom? = him. What? = handsome. Who agreed to marry him? = She who judged him handsome.)*

➢ **Note:** In the above three sentences, the words, ***'the noise'***, ***'a basket of flowers'***, ***'him'***—are the Objects of Participles respectively.

293. Object of the Infinitive Verb:
  ✗ **Object of Infinitive Verb:** *The basic form of verb, being non-finite remains, which is generally preceded by marker 'to', and which remains unchanged in tense of the verb and the person, number of the subject, is called an Infinitive.*

  ✗ An infinitive, being a form of verb, like a Participle & a Gerund, takes sometimes an object after it in the sentence that is we call an ***Object of an Infinitive***.
  → I am ready to do **anything.**
  → To love **you** is my passion.
  → Noah asked me to hit **the ball**. She asked me to sing **a song**.
  → To hate **everyone** was his fatal characteristic fault.
  → He has gone to market to buy **some articles** for his coming project.

294. The Adverbial Objects
  ✗ **Adverbial Object (11):** *When a noun is used adverbially to modify a verb, an adjective, or an adverb denoting time, place, distance, weight, value etc., is called an **Adverbial Object** or **Adverbial Accusative**.*
      o Adverbial Objects are often known as 'Others' or simply 'Adverbials' by many Grammar experts, while discussing them in Tense.

1) He held the post ten **years**. (How long did he hold the post? = ten years. 'Ten' is the numeral adjective, used with the noun 'years. The noun phrase, 'ten years' has done the work of an adverb, modifying the verb, 'held' how long.)
2) I can't wait a **moment** longer. (How long? = a moment longer; here 'a' is an article, 'moment' is a noun and 'longer' an adjective in comparative degree, the noun phrase, 'a moment longer' has done the work of an adverb.)
3) He went **home**. (Where? /Where did he go? = home—is a noun, but actually has done the work of an adverb. So, it is also an adverbial object.)
4) He swam a **mile**. (How far? A mile, denoting 'distance' —is also an Adverbial Object like others.)
5) He weighs seven **stone**. (How much or many? Seven stone—similarly is an adverbial Object.)
6) The watch cost nine hundred **rupees**. (How much? 'Nine hundred rupees' is an adverbial accusative.)

295. Object of Complement:
  ✗ **Object of a Complement (12):** *A complement is a word or a phrase, especially an adjective or a noun, and even an adverb, that is used with a verb of Incomplete Predication (like Transitive [factitive verb] or Intransitive) and mostly after a Linking Verb (which are mainly the State Verbs like 'be' [am, is, are, was, were—to be used as principal verbs], 'become', 'seem', 'appear', etc. which describes the Subjects of the Verb. In case of Transitive, [factitive verb] they are used to complete the sense of the object. And thus, there are two types of Complements -subjective & objective.*
  ✗ *A complement has the force of a verb & sometimes it takes an object, though not always; as,*
      a) I am happy **to see** you here.
      b) I am angry **with my girlfriend**.
      c) She appears sad **seeing** the rascal there.
      d) It is so beautiful **to look at**.
      e) We made him captain **of our team**.

f)   The club needs <u>players</u> ***to play*** for them.
g)   Finally, he became a <u>professor</u> ***to guide*** Ph.D. scholars.
h)   Radha looks <u>excited</u> ***seeing*** her result.
i)   Javed was almost <u>ready</u> ***to come.***
j)   He became a <u>leader</u> ***of the National party.***
k)   Don't call me <u>fool</u> ***judging*** my activities apparent.

✖   All the bold Italic words are the objects of complement, and the underlined are the examples of complements.

17. The Conjugation of Verbs (Weak, Strong & Mixed)

The *Conjugation* of *Verbs* is 'to show the chief parts (read: forms) of verbs; and every verb (main) has three chief forms—the *Present*, the *Past*, the *Past Participle & then comes the others.*

296.   Study the Different Forms of Verbs:

Verbs	Present	Past	Past Participle	Future	Progressive /Continuous
Be	Am, Is, Are	Was, Were	Been	Shall be, Will be	Being
Have	Has, have	Had	Had	Shall have, Will have	Having
Do	Do, does	Did	Done	Shall do, Will do	Doing
Think *(as State Verb)*	Think, Thinks	Thought	Thought	Shall think. Will think	*(Not In Progressive Form)*
Think *(as Active Verb)*	Think, Thinks	Thought	Thought	Shall think, Will think	Thinking
Write	Write, Writes	Wrote	Written	Shall write, Will write	Writing
Modals	Can, May, Shall, Will, Must, have to, Need, Dare, Etc	Could, Might, Should, Would, Had To, Needed, Durst/Dared, etc.	*(Not Available)*	*(Not Available)*	*(Not Available)*

What is Conjugation?

297.   ***To conjugate a verb is to show its chief parts*** (*read: forms*). In a wider sense, it means all the forms to denote ***Mood, Tense, Voice, Number, & Person***. But all those are profoundly depend, directly or indirectly, on the verb's three chief parts, namely- the Present, the Past, & the Past Participle forms.
■   So, in this chapter, let's come to discuss about merely on the chief (three) forms of verbs which are very important to form any tense, simple or progressive, active or passive.

■   Regarding the <u>uniformity of change of forms of verbs,</u> the verbs are grouped into two main divisions.
          a)   Weak Verbs &
          b)   Strong Verbs

Definition: Weak Verbs
■   **Weak Verbs:** The verbs that have its past & past participle forms *by adding '-ed', '-d', or '-t' to the base form of verb, with or without a change of the inside vowel –* all they are called Weak Verbs.

- **Note-1:** *Where there is 'y', the semi vowel at the end of the base verb, sometimes, that changed into 'i' before adding '-d' or '-ed'.*
- **Note-2:** **'-ed'** – is the commonest suffix in the conjugation of Weak Verbs. (Formerly known as Regular Verbs, for their uniformity or regularity of the change of forms).
    - add-added-added; call-called-called;
    - Arrive-arrived-arrived; say-said-said;
    - Creep-crept-crept; sweep-swept-swept;

Definition: Strong Verbs

Strong Verbs: the verbs 1) that have *same forms* in past & past participle; or have their different forms either 2) *by changing their inside vowels* (mainly) & consonant (occasionally) or 3) *having new forms*, (some of these verbs may end with or without **'-n', '-en'** and **'-ne';** and they are not regarded as regular suffixes as we have them only in the third form [past participle]; it is better to regard the verb with them as a new form, and thus 'three forms are different) —all they are called Strong Verbs (formerly known as Irregular Verbs, for less uniformity or regularity but more arbitrary in them, regarding change of form).

- Come-came-come; go-went-gone; am/is/are-was/were-been
- arise-arose-arisen; break-broke-broken

Note: The ***decisive mark of Strong verb conjugation*** is **'the absence of the suffix'** *'-ed', '-d', or '-t';* for the 'change of inside vowels also happen to Weak Verbs.

298.   There are Three Categories of Verbs (of Weak &Strong) which distinguish the conjugation pattern and that define which 'Weak' are and which are 'Strong'.

Note: 'Conjugation' means-showing chief forms of verbs.

A. **Category-1:** Verbs in which ***three forms are same*** (They are grouped into Strong Verbs); as,
    ➢ *put-put-put; cut-cut-cut*, etc.
B. **Category-2:** Verbs in which ***two of the three forms are the same*** (applicable to both Strong & Weak Verbs; both have such forms in abundance); as,
    ➢ *say-said-said*; *come-came-come*, etc.
C. **Category-3:** Verbs in which ***all the three forms are different*** (only in case of Strong Verbs); as,
    ➢ *Go-went-gone; see-saw-seen*, etc.

✖   Judging the three categories, the verbs with two forms, one for present, & the other form is for both, past & past participle—only are defined as the Weak Conjugation of Verbs; as, *keep-kept-kept;* while the remains fall to the Strong Conjugation.

✖ For debate, the first category with three forms same of the verb, they can be grouped into Weak Conjugation, but Peter doesn't dare to challenge the custom.

The Weak Conjugation

299.   The Weak Conjugation of Verbs:

The Weak Conjugation

- ***As per definition, Weak Verbs are formed by adding suffixes:***
1. By adding **'-ed'**; as,
   ask-asked-asked; add-added-added;
2. By adding **'-d'** where the base verb ends with '-e'; as,
   arrange-arranged-arranged, etc.
3. By adding **'-t'**; as,
   build-built-built; feel-felt-felt,

- ***Weak verbs generally have two forms***, one is for present, when the other form is used for both, past & past participle.
- ***The '-ed' is the most common used suffix to the conjugation of Verbs*** (known as 'Weak Conjugation').

✖ Study the following charts for the Weak Conjugation of Verbs (fall in category-2). Also read the following instructions before go to tables:

(1) by adding **'-ed'**;(two forms are same)
(2) by adding **'-ed'** (in case, verb ends with **'y'** and that is preceding by a consonant, it turns into **'i'** before adding '-ed';)
(3) by adding **'-d'**; two forms are same; semi vowel **'y'** changed to **'i'** befor add 'd';
(4) by adding **'-t'**; (two forms are same);
(5) by adding **'-t'** &- **'ed'**, both are available (two forms are same);
(6) when the verb ends in –c, the simple past is formed by adding -**ked**).

Base/Present form	Past form	Past Participle	Base/Present form	Past form	Past Participle
Ask	Asked	Asked	Borrow	Borrowed	Borrowed
Add	Added	Added	Call	Called	Called
Attack	Attacked	Attacked	Clean	Cleaned	Cleaned
Abolish	Abolished	Abolished	Destroy	Destroyed	Destroyed
Accept	Accepted	Accepted	Enjoy	Enjoyed	Enjoyed
Abandon	Abandoned	Abandoned	Fail	Failed	Failed
Adopt	Adopted	Adopted	Fix	Fixed	Fixed
Afford	Afforded	Afforded	Help	Helped	Helped
Act	Acted	Acted	Look	Looked	Looked
Allow	Allowed	Allowed	Pull	Pulled	Pulled
Appear	Appeared	Appeared	Pass	Passed	Passed

Alight	Alighted	Alighted	Publish	Published	Published
Base/Present form	Past form	Past Participle	Base/Present form	Past form	Past Participle
Roar	Roared	Roared	Beg	Begged	Begged
Stay	Stayed	Stayed	Fan	Fanned	Fanned
Thank	Thanked	Thanked	Drop	Dropped	Dropped
Wish	Wished	Wished	Control	Controlled	Controlled
Walk	Walked	Walked	Compel	Compelled	Compelled
Want	Wanted	Wanted	Stop	Stopped	Stopped
Cry	Cried	Cried	Plan	Planned	Planned
Carry	Carried	Carried	Travel	Travelled	Travelled
Apply	Applied	Applied	Annoy	Annoyed	Annoyed
Bury	Buried	Buried	Betray	Betrayed	Betrayed
Copy	Copied	Copied	Convey	Conveyed	Conveyed
Decry	Decried	Decried	Decay	Decayed	Decayed
Base/Present form	Past form	Past Participle	Base/Present form	Past form	Past Participle
Arrange	Arranged	Arranged	Overhear	Overheard	Overheard
Arrive	Arrived	Arrived	Owe	Owed	Owed
Advise	Advised	Advised	Rehear	Reheard	Reheard
Clothe	Clothed	Clothed	Mishear	Misheard	Misheard
Change	Changed	Changed			
Close	Closed	Closed	Lay	Laid	Laid
Dance	Danced	Danced	Mislay	Mislaid	Mislaid
Hear	Heard	Heard	Overlay	Overlaid	Overlaid
Hope	Hoped	Hoped	Overpay	Overpaid	Overpaid
Like	Liked	Liked	Pay	Paid	Paid
Live	Lived	Lived	Say	Said	Said
Base/Present form	Past form	Past Participle	Base/Present form	Past form	Past Participle
Burn	Burnt	Burnt	Mean	Meant	Meant
Creep	Crept	Crept	Sleep	Slept	Slept
Deal	Dealt	Dealt	Spell	Spelt	Spelt

Dream	Dreamt	Dreamt	Spoil	Spoilt	Spoilt
Dwell	Dwelt	Dwelt	Sweep	Swept	Swept
Feel	Felt	Felt	Weep	Wept	Wept
Keep	Kept	Kept	Learn	Learnt	Learnt
Kneel	Knelt	Knelt			

Present/ Base form	Past form	Past Participle	Present/ Base form	Past form	Past Participle
Burn	Burnt/burned	Burnt/burned	Smell	Smelt /Smelled	Smelt /Smelled
Dream	Dreamt /Dreamed	Dreamt /Dreamed	Spell	Spelt /Spelled	Spelt /Spelled
Lean	Leaned/ leant	Leaned/ leant	Spill	Spilt/spilled	Spilt/spilled
Learn	Learnt/learned	Learnt/learned	Spoil	Spoilt /Spoiled	Spoilt /Spoiled
Leap	Leapt/leaped	Leapt/leaped	Misspell	Misspelt /Misspelled	Misspelt /Misspelled
Picnic	Picnicked	Picnicked			

The Strong Conjugation

300.   The Strong Conjugation of Verbs:

As per definition, **Strong Verbs** have the following three ways to have their forms. They get forms-
1) By without change (where three forms are same); as,
   - burst-burst-burst;
   - Put-put-put;
   - cut-cut-cut,
2) By changing inside vowels (mostly) or consonant (occasionally->*from d/k/ch to t; or k changed into d*) [where two forms are same]; as,
   - come-came-come;
   - Sit-sat-sat;
   - Make-made-made ('k' changed into 'd'.)
3) By changing inside vowels or having an entirely new form (where three forms are different); as,
   - Ring-rang-rung;
   - Begin-began-begun

Note: The present form of the verb is also known as 'the base or root form' of the verb.

   ✶   Read the following charts of Strong Conjugation of Verbs:

Base/Present form	Past form	Past Participle	Base/Present form	Past form	Past Participle
Bet	Bet	Bet	Read	Read	Read
Burst	Burst	Burst	Rid	Rid	Rid
Cast	Cast	Cast	Set	Set	Set
Cost	Cost	Cost	Shed	Shed	Shed

Cut	Cut	Cut	Shut	Shut	Shut
Hit	Hit	Hit	Spit	Spit	Spit
Hurt	Hurt	Hurt	Split	Split	Split
Let	Let	Let	Spread	Spread	Spread
Put	Put	Put	Sweat	Sweat	Sweat
Quit	Quit	Quit	Thrust	Thrust	Thrust

Base/Present form	Past form	Past Participle	Base/Present form	Past form	Past Participle
Awake	Awoke	Awoke	Fling	Flung	Flung
Abide	Abode	Abode	Get	Got	Got
Become	Became	Become	Grind	Ground	Ground
Behold	Beheld	Beheld/beholden	Hang	Hung/hanged	Hung/hanged
Bleed	Bled	Bled	Have	Had	Had
Breed	Bred	Bred	Hold	Held	Held
Cling	Clung	Clung	Lead	Led	Led
Come	Came	Come	Light	Lit	Lit
Dig	Dug	Dug	Make	Made	Made *
Feed	Fed	Fed	Meet	Met	Met
Fight	Fought	Fought	Run	Ran	Run
Find	Found	Found	Shine	Shone	Shone
Shoot	Shot	Shot	Sting	Stung	Stung
Sit	Sat	Sat	Strike	Struck	Struck
Sling	Slung	Slung	Swing	Swung	Swung
Slink	Slunk	Slunk	Teach	Taught	Taught
Speed	Sped	Sped	Tell	Told	Told
Spin	Spun	Spun	Think	Thought	Thought
Spit	Spat	Spat	Understand	Understood	Understood
Spring	Sprang/sprung	Sprung	Win	Won	Won
Stand	Stood	Stood	Wind	Wound	Wound
Stave	Stove/staved	Stove/staved	Bind	Bound	Bound
Stick	Stuck	Stuck			
Base/Present form	Past form	Past Participle	Base/Present form	Past form	Past Participle

Bend	Bent	Bent	Sell	Sold	Sold
Bring	Brought	Brought	Send	Sent	Sent
Build	Built	Built	Spend	Spent	Spent
Buy	Bought	Bought	Teach	Taught	Taught
Catch	Caught	Caught	Tell	Told	Told
Leave	Left	Left	Think	Thought	Thought
Lend	Lent	Lent	Seek	Sought	Sought
Light	Lit	Lit	Gild	Gilt/gilded	Gilt/gilded
Lose	Lost	Lost	Rend	Rent	Rent
Make	Made	Made	Beseech	Besought	Besought

Base/Present form	Past form	Past Participle	Base/Present form	Past form	Past Participle
Be	Was, were,	Been	Fly	Flew	Flown
Begin	Began	Begun	Forbid	Forbade	Forbidden
Bite	Bit	Bitten	Forget	Forgot	Forgotten
Blow	Blew	Blown	Forgive	Forgave	Forgiven
Break	Broke	Broken	Freeze	Froze	Frozen
Choose	Chose	Chosen	Give	Gave	Given
Do	Did	Done	Go	Went	Gone
Draw	Drew	Drawn	Grow	Grew	Grown
Drink	Drank	Drunk /Drunken	Hide	Hid	Hidden
Drive	Drove	Driven	Know	Knew	Known
Eat	Ate	Eaten	Lie	Lay	Lain
Fall	Fell	Fallen	Mistake	Mistook	Mistaken
Ride	Rode	Ridden	Steal	Stole	Stolen
Ring	Rang	Rung	Stink	Stank	Stunk
Rise	Rose	Risen	Swear	Swore	Sworn
See	Saw	Seen	Swim	Swam	Swum
Sew	Sewed	Sewed/sewn	Take	Took	taken
Shake	Shook	Shaken	Tear	Tore	Torn
Show	Showed	Showed/shown	Throw	Threw	Thrown
Shrink	Shrank	Shrunk	Wake	Woke	Woken

Sing	Sang	Sung	Wear	Wore	Worn
Sink	Sank	Sunk	Write	Wrote	Written
Speak	Spoke	Spoken	Spring	Sprang	Sprung

The Mixed Conjugation

301.   **Some Verbs have double identities**. Some may group them into Strong, while some like to treat them as Weak. They have strong conjugation in the Past form, while in Past Participle, they are (like other Weak Verbs) formed by adding a Suffix, **'-n', '-en' or '-ne'**. *Though a many simply said, the verbs end with '-n', '-en' or '-ne', and thus gets different form in past participle, so more they can be regarded as Strong Verb conjugation. But they do not seem different from other suffixes (like **'-ed', '-d', & '-t'**), as happen to the Conjugation of Weak Verbs.*

✘   However, judging them based on have three different forms in Present, Past & Past Participle & irregularity in Pat & Past participle, or having the forms only by changing vowel in them, it is better to treat all these verbs of mixed character to the group of **Strong Verbs**.

✘   These mixed verbs are formed *by adding suffixes* to the base or past, and sometimes also to the past participle to have another past participle (known as **Adjectival Participle**); or simply say their **Past Participle forms end with-**

- **'-n'**; as, *arise-arose-arisen; choose-chose-chosen;*
  - **'-en'**; as, *fall-fell-fallen; forget-forgot-forgotten;*
    - **'-ne'**; as, forbear-*forbore-forborne; bear-bore-borne.*

Base/Present form	Past form	Past Participle	Base/Present form	Past form	Past Participle
Arise	Arose	Arise**n**	Choose	Chose	Chose**n**
Bear (produce)	Bore	Born	Draw	Drew	Drawn
Bear (carry)	Bore	Bor**ne**	Drink	Drank	Drunk/Drunken
Beat	Beat	Beat**en**	Drive	Drove	Driven
Beget	Begat/Begot	Begot/Begotten	Eat	Ate	Eaten
Bid	Bit	Bit/bitten	Fall	Fell	Fallen
Do	Did	Done	Fly	Flew	Flown
Blow	Blew	Blown	Forbear	Forbore	Forbor**ne**
Break	Broke	Broken	Forget	Forgot	Forgotten
Chide	Chid	Chid/Chidden	Forsake	Forsook	Forsaken
Freeze	Froze	Frozen	See	Saw	Seen
Get	Got	Got/gotten	Shake	Shook	Shaken
Give	Gave	Given	Shrink	Shrank	Shrunk
Go	Went	Gone	Sink	Sank	Sunk/Sunken
Grow	Grew	Grown	Slide	Slid	Slid/Slidden

Hide	Hid	Hid/Hidden	Slay	Slew	Slain
Know	Knew	Known	Smite	Smote	Smit/Smitten
Lie	Lay	lain	Speak	Spoke	Spoken
Ride	Rode	ridden	Steal	Stole	Stolen
Rise	Rose	Risen	Stride	Strode	Stridden
Crow	Crowed/Crew	Crowed/Crown	Mow	Mowed	Mowed/mown
Grave	Graved	Graved/graven	Shear	Sheared	Sheared/Shorn
Melt	Melted	Melted/molten	Show	Showed	Shown
Prove	Proved	Proved/proven	Sow	Sowed	Sown
Rot	rotten	rotten	Swell	Swelled	Swollen
Rive	Rived	Rived/Riven	Strike	Struck	Struck/Stricken
Saw	Sawed	Sawn	Strive	Strove	Striven
Sew	Sewed	sewn	Strew	Strewed	Strewn
Shave	Shaved	Shaved/shaven	Swear	Swore	Sworn
Take	Took	Taken	Weave	Wove/weaved	Woven/weaved
Tear	Tore	Torn	Wear	Wore	Worn
Thrive	Throve/thrived	Thriven/Thrived	Write	Wrote	Written
Throw	Threw	Thrown	Writhe	Writhed	Writhed/Writhen
Tread	Trod	Trod/Trodden	Prove	Proved	Proved/Proven
Sew	Sewed	Sewed/Sewn	Sow	Sowed	Sowed/Sown
Strew	Strewed	Strewed/Strewn	Strive	Strove/Strived	Striven/Strived
Swell	Swelled	Swelled/Swollen			
Base/Present form	*Past form*	*Past Participle*	*Base/Present form*	*Past form*	*Past Participle*
Abide	Abode/ Abided	Abode/ Abided	Hang	Hung/ hanged	Hung/ hanged
Beseech	Beseeched /Besought	Beseeched /Besought	Heave	Hove/ heaved	Hove/ heaved
Bust	Bust/busted	Bust/busted	Input	Input/inputted	Input/inputted
Cleave	Cleft/clove/ cleaved	Cleft/clove/ cleaved	Narrowcast	Narrowcast/ narrow casted	Narrowcast/ narrow casted

Dive	Dived/dove	Dived	Plead	Pleaded /Plead	Pleaded /Plead
Dwell	Dwelt/ dwelled	Dwelt/ dwelled	Spill	Spilled /Spilt	Spilled /Spilt
Fit	Fit/fitted	Fit/fitted	Spoil	Spoilt/ spoiled	Spoilt/ spoiled
Forecast	Forecast/ forecasted	Forecast/ forecasted	Stave	Staved /Stove	Staved /Stove
Speed	Speeded /Sped	Speeded /Sped	Wed	Wedded /Wed	Wedded /Wed
Spell	Spelt/ spelled	Spelt/ spelled	Wet	Wet/wetted	Wet/wetted

Adjectival Past Participle

302. *There are **a quite number past participle forms** (both of Strong & Weak Verbs) which are **mainly used as Adjective than to be used as a Verb**,* they are known as **Adjectival Participle**; *as,*

- I met a ***drunken*** man on the road.
- ***Molten*** ice fell into the streams and caused floods in Uttaranchal.
- She saw his clean-***shaven*** face and got quite impressed at the first glance.
- Her ***shorn*** voice startled all of us present there in the hall.
- We consoled the grief-***stricken*** woman with our promise to help.
- It is a ***proven*** fact that leaders hardly help without any reason.

And thus, *molten iron, shorn sheep, shrunken head, sunken ship, grief-stricken widow* and many more.

✘ The adjectival Participles have often two forms in Past participles. Study the chart with their examples in the sentences:

Base form	Past form	Usual Past Participle	Adjectival Past Participle	Phrase with participle
Drink	Drank	Drunk	Drunken	A drunken soldier
Melt	Melted	Melted	Molten	Molten gold
Prove	Proved	Proved	Proven	Proven fact
Shave	Shaved	Shaved	Shaven	Clean-shaven face
Shear	Sheared	Sheared	Shorn	Shorn hair
Shrink	Shrank	Shrunk	Shrunken	A shrunken head/skin
Sink	Sank	Sunk	Sunken	A sunken ship
Strike	Struck	Struck	Stricken	Grief-stricken man; A stricken deer
Forget	Forgot	Forgot	Forgotten	Forgotten hero
Sew	Sewed	Sewed	Sewn	Sewn design
Forbid	Forbade	Forbidden	Forbidden	Forbidden zone
Break	Broke	Broken	Broken	Broken leg
Base form	*Past form*	*Usual Past Participle*	*Adjectival Past Participle*	*Phrase with Participle*

Steal	Stole	Stolen	Stolen	Stolen watch
Throw	Threw	Thrown	Thrown	Thrown stone
Write	Wrote	Written	Written	Written documents
Learn	Learned	Learned	Learnt	Learnt lesion
Lean	Leaned/lent	Leaned/lent	lent	Lent wall
Burn	Burned/burnt	Burned/burnt	Burnt	Burnt organs
Spoil	Spoiled/spoilt	Spoiled/spoilt	Spoilt	Spoilt child
Bind	Bound	Bound	Bounden	Our bounden duty
Get	Got	Got	Gotten	Ill-gotten wealth
Hide	Hid	Hid	Hidden	The hidden meaning

303.   There are also some verbs similar in past and participle forms that raise confusion among readers and learners, but they have always different meanings. Study the table:

Base/Present form	Past form	Past Participle	Base/Present form	Past form	Past Participle
Bear (produce)	Bore	Born	Bear (carry)	Bore	Borne
Beat	Beat	Beaten	Bite	Bit	Bit/bitten
Feel	Felt	Felt	Fill	Filled	Filled
Fall	Fell	Fallen			
Lie (to be in flat position)	Lay	Lain	Lie (to say something, not true)	Lied	Lied
Lay (to keep something in flat position)	Laid			Laid	
Leave	Left	Left	Live	Lived	Lived
Loose	Loosed	Loosed	Lose	Lost	Lost
Raise	Raised	Raised	Rise	Rose	Risen
Show	Showed	Shown	Sow	Sowed	Sown
Sew	Sewed	Sewn	Saw	Sawed	Sawn
Arise	Arose	Arisen	Arouse	Aroused	Aroused

18. The Tense of Verb

✗   The Conjugation of Verb means 'to show its chief parts', i.e., the Present, Past & Past Participle forms of the verb which we have already discussed in the last chapter. In this chapter, we will discuss of some other parts (forms), about the Tense of a verb.

Let's get started:

304. **Read the following sentences:**
  1. I **write** this letter to invite you.
  2. I **wrote** the letter in his very presence.
  3. I **shall write** a novel soon.

(In the first sentence, the verb 'write' shows present time.
In the second sentence the verb 'wrote' shows the past time.
In the third sentence the verb 'shall write' tells us about the future time of the action.)

✕ **Thus, a verb may refer to**
  i. Present time,
  ii. Past time, &
  iii. Future time.

✕ The form of verb that shows 'the time of an action or situation (situation means 'existence of being or having'), is called **Tense**.

✕ Thus, there are three main tenses of verb, based on 'time':
  (1) Present Tense,
  (2) Past Tense, &
  (3) Future Tense.

Note: The word, **'tense'** comes from Latin **'tempus'**, meaning **'time'**.

305. **Definitions of Three Main Tenses & Meaning of their sub-divisions:**

  1) A verb that refers to *'present'* time, is said to be in the **Present Tense**; as,
    I write.   *I play.*
  2) A verb that refers to *'past'* time, is said to be in the **Past Tense**; as,
    I wrote.   *I played.*
  3) A verb that refers to *'future'* time, is said to be in the **Future Tense**; as,
    I shall write.   *I shall play.*

✕ And each of them has four different states of that particular time.
  1) Simple or Indefinite,
  2) Progressive or Continuous,
  3) Perfect, &
  4) Perfect Continuous.

Their meanings:
1) **Simple or Indefinite:** (an action, neither complete nor incomplete),
2) **Progressive or Continuous Tense:** (an action which is incomplete, but on continuous or in progress.),
3) **Perfect Tense:** (an action which is complete or perfect (finished) &
4) **Perfect Continuous:** (an action that has been started and is going on at the time of speaking or reporting).

  ✕ Thus, there are total twelve tenses in English grammar.

306. The following are of the Present Tense only. Read them carefully:
  → I *write.*   - (Simple Present)
  → I *am writing*.   - (Present Continuous)
  → I *have written*.   - (Present Perfect)
  → I *have been writing*. - (Present Perfect Continuous)

✕ The Verbs in all these sentences refer to the *present* time, and are therefore said to be in the present tense. But they are different from each other too.

In sentence 1, the Verb shows the action which is *mentioned simply,* without anything being said about the completeness or incompleteness of the action.

In sentence 2, the Verb shows that the action, mentioned, **is incomplete & continuous,** *that is still going on.*

In sentence 3, the Verb shows that the action mentioned is **finished, complete, or perfect,** *at the* *time of speaking (perfect means 'complete).*

In **sentence 4**, the Verb shows that the *action has been* **started but not finished yet** *and it is going on at the present time, at the time of speaking.*

> ✖ Thus, the Tense of a verb shows not only <u>the time of an action</u> or situation, but also <u>the state (status) of an action referred to.</u>

307. **Four divisions of Past Tense:** Just as the Present Tense, Past Tense has four forms, denoting *four states of the Past Time.* <u>For conversion from Present to Past; we have done only little changes.</u> The strikethrough words were used in the present tense, whereas the bold lettered words are used in place of them and the underlined are the full-form of the tense.

<u>Now, read the sentences carefully:</u>

- → I ~~write~~ **wrote**.   - (Simple Past)
- → I ~~am~~ **was** *writing*.   - (Past Continuous)
- → I ~~have~~ **had** *written*.   - (Past Perfect)
- → I ~~have~~ **had** *been writing*.   - (Past Perfect Continuous)

Noted that <u>only one verb form has been changed</u> from the present to past, when the remaining of each sentence is almost same. The strikethrough ones we used in the present tense & the bold lettered words are the new changed forms of verbs to refer *past* time, and the underlined stands for the full verb forms, used in the past tense.

In **sentence 1**, the Verb shows ***simply a past event***, already happened or over.

In **sentence 2**, the Verb shows that the action mentioned was as ***incomplete or progressive (continuous)*** *by then, it was going on, not completed then.*

In **sentence 3**, the Verb shows that the action mentioned was as ***finished, complete, or perfect***, at the *time of speaking in the past.*

In **sentence 4**, the Verb shows that the *action had been* **started but not finished** *then in the past time.*

And thus, the Future Tense has also four forms.

308. **Four divisions of Future Time:** <u>Read the sentences carefully & find out the differences or the inclusion:</u>

- → I ~~write/wrote~~/**shall** *write*.   - (Simple Future)
- → I ~~am/was~~/**shall be** *writing*.   - (Future Continuous)
- → I ~~have/had~~/**shall have** *written*.   - (Future Perfect)
- → I ~~have/had~~ **shall** *have* *been writing*.   - (Future Perfect Continuous)

Noted that ***shall*** or ***will*** has been included in all tenses compulsorily; more as ***'be'*** has come after shall or will in Continuous and ***'have'*** has been added in both Perfect & Perfect Continuous Tenses, in comparison of Present & Past tenses. These changes in form of verbs or inclusion have been done in the sentences to refer the *Future* time, and so they are, therefore, said to be in the Future Tense.

In **sentence 1**, the Verb shows *an action to happen in future* **simply, like a plan.**

In **sentence 2**, the Verb shows that the action mentioned will be go on as ***incomplete or continuous***.

In **sentence 3**, the Verb shows that the action mentioned will be as ***finished, complete, or perfect*** in *Future.*

In **sentence 4**, the Verb shows that the *action will have been* **started and will go on** *in the future time.*

Now, must study the charts attentively to follow the changes and understand tenses and their different states better.

1)   The Chart of Present Tense

Tense	Types	Function/Definition	Examples

Tense	Types	Function/Definition	Examples
Present Tense	Indefinite	Habit and general action	I write. He writes.
	Continuous	Action going on	I am writing. He is writing.
	Perfect	Just completed action (whose time is not given)	I have written. He has written.
	Perfect Continuous	Started in the past and still going on	I have been writing. He has been writing.

2) The Chart of Past Tense

Tense	Types	Function/Definition	Examples
Past Tense	Indefinite	Action completed in the past	I wrote. He wrote.
	Continuous	Action continuing in the past	I was writing. He was writing.
	Perfect	Action done earlier than another action	I had written. He had written.
	Perfect Continuous	Action continued for some time in the past	I had been writing. He had been writing.

3) The Chart of Future Tense

Tense	Types	Function/Definition	Examples
Future Tense	Indefinite	Action to happen in the future	I shall write. He will write.
	Continuous	Action to continue in the future	I shall be writing. He will be writing
	Perfect	Action will be complete before a particular time in the future	I shall have written. He will have written.
	Perfect Continuous	Action to continue for some time in the future and also end in the future.	I shall have been writing. He will have been writing.

The Chart of Twelve Tenses of Verbs
(v1=present form; v2=past form; v3=past participle form)

Twelve Tenses of Verbs	Their Structures	
1. Present Indefinite/ Simple Present	Subject + **Verb-1** + Object & Others	
2. Present Continuous	Subject + **am/is/are** + **Verb-ing** + Object & Others	
3. Present Perfect	Subject + **has/have** + **Verb-3** + Object & Others	
4. Present Perfect Continuous	Subject + **has/have** + **been** + **Verb-ing** + Ob. & Others.	
5. Past Indefinite/ Simple Past	Subject + **Verb-2** + Object & Others	

6. Past Continuous	Subject + **was/were+ Verb-ing** + Object & Others
7. Past Perfect	Subject + **had+ Verb-3** + Object & Others
8. Past Perfect Continuous	Subject + **had + been + Verb-ing** + Obj. & Others.
9. Future Indefinite/ Simple Future	Subject + shall/**will+ Verb-1** + Object & Others
10. Future Continuous	Subject +**shall be/will be+ Verb-ing** + Obj & Others.
11. Future Perfect	Subject + **shall have/will have+ Verb-3** + Ob & Others.
12. Future Perfect Continuous	Sub. +**shall /will +have + been +Verb-ing** + Ob. & Others.

Exception in form and use:

309.   Sometimes, a ***past tense*** in form may refer to '***present time'*** in sense, and *present tense* may express '*future time*'; as,

  1) I wish I ***knew*** the answer. = I am sorry I ***don't know*** the answer.

Note-1: In the sentence the verb, *'knew'*, though is in the past form, actually expresses '*present*' time of the state, '*I **don't know**' the answer. Another conditional clause, 'If I knew the answer' bears the same expression of present time.*

Similarly,

  2) Let's wait till he **comes**. [We will wait till he will come.]

Note-2: Actually, both clauses in the sentence express *'future time'—his coming and of our waiting till the time; as,* 'He will come, till then we will wait for him.

Practice yourself:

→ I wish I could see it. I wish I had been there. I wish she would go there. If I knew to fly over through the high sky, I could see her, my love in an hour.

→ Let's take the classes till the final result comes out in June. I am going to Kashmir on next month. Modi is to go to attend the next summit in Mosco.

The Sequence of Tense

310.   **The Sequence of Tense:** Sequence of tense occurs in sentences with clauses. It tells about the rules that the tense in the main clause should govern the tense in the sub-clauses. Study the rules' as,

  Rule-1: If the ***main clause is in the present or future tense*** the verb in the sub-clause may be in any tense.

  • He ***says*** that he ***went*** to school.

  Rule-2: But if the ***main clause is in the past tense,*** the verb in the sub-clause must be in the past tense.

  Exception: if the sub-clause expresses a universal truth that never becomes old, the sub-clause will remain as it was.

  He ***said*** that he ***went*** to school.

  • Teacher ***said*** that the earth ***moves*** round the sun.

• All the above mainly happens in case of narration change or reporting a statement, where there is more than one clause in a sentence. Study the table:

Main clause	Sub-clause
He <u>says</u>	that he goes to school. (Present Tense) that he went to school. (Past Tense) that he will go to school. (Future Tense)

She <u>will say</u>	that she goes to school. (Present Tense) that she went to school. (Past Tense) that she will go to school. (Future Tense)	
He <u>said</u>	that he was ill. that he was going to school. that he had gone to school.	

Time markers:

311.   Some words in a sentence help us to understand the time of happening, being or having. These are called, '<u>time markers</u>.

1) **Main time markers** in a sentence **are the verbs themselves** in their tense forms.
   - He **went** to Kolkata.
   - They **are reading** books.
   - We **will visit** the zoo.

2) 2) However, we have lots of **time adverbials** that denote *present, past* or *future time* of an action or situation.

- Today, this week, this month, this year, this fortnight, this decade, in this century, for/since (to refer a period of time), never, ever, so far, till now, yet, already recently, etc. are used mainly <u>for **Present Tense**</u>;

- Yesterday, last night, last week, last month, last year, last decade, a week ago, long ago, in 1977, etc. are time-marker adverbials <u>for **Past tense**</u>, &

- Tomorrow, next week, next month, next year, etc. are used <u>for **Future Tense**</u>.

312.   **How verbs change its forms in Tense:**

- The auxiliary as well as main verbs change their forms according to different tenses of Verbs; as,
  - I am doing > I have done. > I have been doing. > I was doing > I had done. > I had been doing. > I shall do.>I shall be doing, etc.
- In Simple Present & Simple Past, as there is only one verb and that is the main verb, this change only happen to the main verb; as,
  - I/We/You/They **_do_** the work. > He/She/It/Ram **_does_** the work.
  - I/We/You/They/He/She/It/Ram **_did_** the work.
  - I **_am_** a boy. > I **_was_** a boy. / He **_has_**> He **_had_**, etc.

Don't forget
- Verbs can show actions in the present, past or future time.
- It also shows time of a situation and possession.
- The verb **'be'** used as main verbs, tells you of a situation or existence of something. There are also other stative verbs which tell you about a situation, and its time by their different tense form,
- The verb **'has' or 'have'** used a main verb, tells us of 'having or possession of something'.
- The two modals mainly −**shall** and **will** are used to form future tense.

Let us write:
- Today, we read books that are printed on paper. We also read book in digital format, or eBooks. What are the things you like about printed books? What do you think books in the future will be like? Write a short paragraph on the books of today and of the future. Use the various tense correctly.

The Use of Present Tense (detail study)

Let's get started:

Identify the verbs in these sentences:

1.   I read story books at night.

2. We are planning a vacation.
3. They have completed their homework.
4. I have been working on this project since last year.
   (Are the verbs or the unit of verbs denote same state of the actions, complete, incomplete or any other?)

313. The use of Present Tense includes-
     1) The use of Present Indefinite,
     2) The use of Present Continuous,
     3) The use of Present Perfect,
     4) The use of Present Perfect Continuous.

314. **How looks a <u>Present Indefinite</u> or <u>Simple Present Tense:</u>**

✖ A sentence with a <u>verb in simple present tense looks like</u> the following:

<u>Subject</u>+ <u>base form of the verb</u> + <u>object</u> or <u>others</u>.

(While, base or root form of verb refers to the 'present form of the verb; object refers to Direct, Indirect or Prepositional Objects; and '**others**' refers to adverbial or complement (the complements are mainly adjective or adjective equivalent words; may be formed by a noun, noun phrases, an adjective, infinitive, participle or a gerund); as,

→ I work. We work. You work. They work.
→ I am a boy. I am a teacher.
→ They visit Taj Mahal every year. Tina visits Darjeeling.
→ They have three house-boats. We have none.

✖ **Note:** <u>If subject is 3rd person singular number, '–s' or '-es' is to be added</u> with the base form of the verb; as,
→ He **works**. She **works**. It **works**.
→ She **watches**. He **studies**.

✖ <u>To form negative or question</u>, **do/does** (or 'did' in Simple Past Tense) and often '**modals**' may be used with '**no/not** or <u>any other words of adverbial negation</u>; as,
→ I **do not** work. We **do not** work. You **can't** do this work. You **cannot** go. You **may not** be allowed.
→ You **do not** work. They **do not** work.
→ I **have not** my own car. I **am not** a doctor.
→ He **neither** goes nor comes. He is a permanent resident of this place. He **never** comes. She ever goes.
→ Do you want to go? Do I? May we come in, sir?
→ They **should not** do this. Should they?
→ **Don't** they work? How do they earn?

The Use of Simple Present Tense

315. **The Use of Simple Present Tense**

✖ **Simple Present Tense is used:**

1) To talk about <u>things that happen regularly</u> (or to express <u>habitual action</u> that we generally do every day); as,
→ She **leaves** for school at 8 O'clock.
→ He **drinks** tea every morning.
→ School **closes** at 4.30 p.m.
→ I **get up** early in the morning.
→ What time do you **catch** the bus?
→ Sara **works** 5 days a week.
→ My watch **keeps** good time.
→ Bob **watches** TV every night.

2) To talk about <u>a permanent situation</u> or something that is always <u>true or universal</u>; as,
→ She **lives** in Spain.
→ Peter **lives** in India, West Bengal.

→ Water *is* important to live.
→ The sun *sets* in the west.
→ We *can see* Moon at night.
→ Fortunes *favours* the brave.
→ The sky *is* blue. Honey *is* sweet. The bird *chirps*.

3) To give introduction; as,
→ *Meet* my friend, Apurba, he *is* an Assistant Teacher of Saidpur B.M. A. High School.
→ She *is* Priya, Tom met her last week and promised to help her with books.
→ She *is* my girlfriend. The tall boy *is* my brother.

4) As substitute of Simple Past to give vivid narrative of past or historical events; as,
→ Sohrab *rushes* forward and *deals* a heavy blow to Rustam.
→ Immediately the king *hurries* to his capital.
→ Ashoka *wins* victory in the battle of Kalinga.

5) To express a future event that is a part of fixed time-table or fixed programme; as
→ The train *is about to leave* the station.
→ Mr. Prime Minister *is to visit* Japan next week.
→ The next flight *is at* 7.00 tomorrow morning.
→ The match *starts at* 9 O'clock.
→ The train *leaves at* 22.30 O'clock.
→ When *does* your coffee-house *reopen*?
→ My plane *leaves at* 8:30. The show starts at 9 p.m.

6) **To introduce an Exclamatory sentence** with '**here**' or '**there**' *(even to mean 'an event' taking place in the present, we use simple present instead of continuous)*; as,
  • Here *comes* the bus! (The bus's coming here is surprising)
  • There she *goes*! (Her going there is wonderful)
  • Here *comes* the President! (Unbelievable event to visit Balurghat, a small town)

  Note: Introducing such exclamatory sentence, with here & there, can also be used in Simple Past tense; like,
  • Here *came* the P.M.! Here you *came*! When?
  • There it *happened*! There *reached* her mom!

7) Simple Present Tense is also used in **the clauses of time** or **condition** of a complex sentence, *along with the future tense in the principal clause; as,*
  • I shall wait till you *finish* your lunch.
  • If it *rains*, we shall get wet.

8) **In broadcast commentaries in the sports** *(the Simple Present Tense is used instead of the Present Continuous to describe happening in the progress); as,*
  • Sourav *hits* the ball and he *gets* his hundredth century in ODI.
  • He *runs*; let's see what to happen, if Messi *can goal*.
  • Oh, no! He *misses* his second chance in this season.

9) **To introduce a quotation.** *(Simple past or simple future can also be used); as,*
  • Keats says, "A thing of beauty is a joy forever."
                                          • 'There is no short-cut to earn fame or a name', Peter said once.

10) Simple Present Tense is also used for the State or Linking verbs (in place of Continuous or Progressive Tense). Such verbs are-
  ➢ **Verbs of Perceptions:** (see, hear, smell, notice, recognise ;)
  ➢ **Verbs of appearing:** (appear, look, seem ;)
  ➢ **Verbs of emotion:** (want, wish, desire, feel, like, love, hate, hope, refuse, prefer, etc.) &
  ➢ **Verbs of thinking:** (think, suppose, believe, agree, consider, trust, remember, forget, know, understand, imagine, mean, mind, etc.)
  ➢ **Have (to mean possess or own, part of):** (the verbs are— own, possess, belong to, contain, consist of, include, comprise of, etc.)

➢ **Verb 'To Be' & 'Modals':** (am, is, are, & can, may, etc.)

✗ **Study the examples, used in following sentences-**

❖ **Verbs of Perceptions**

11) The verbs (which do not take progressive forms) are used either in **Simple** or **Perfect Tenses**; as,

→ I _hear_ the train coming. We _have heard_ of the woman crying.

→ I _smell_ smoke. It _smelt_ very bad!

→ I _see_ you looking gorgeous. Who has _seen_ God? I will _see_ you later.

→ The soldier notices everything from the tower. /They _noticed_ her coming to their camp.

→ Dr. D. Souza _recognised_ her to be her lost daughter. Who _recognise_ you, here?

❖ **Verbs of Appearing in simple or Perfect**

12) Verbs of appearing: (appear, look, seem); as,

• The little child _looks_ so beautiful! A bud in Heaven!!

• She _appeared_ as an angel in time of his misery.

• He _seemed_ a genius to the experts; and they continued to measure his depth.

• She _looks_ like her mother.

• It _seems_ to me that she is a doctor. What do you _think_ about her?

❖ **Verbs of Emotion in Simple Tenses (Present or Past)**

13) Verbs of emotion: (want, wish, desire, feel, like, love, hate, hope, refuse, prefer); as

• I _want_ to be a doctor.

• She _wished_ him to be her husband.

• Who _wished_ you at the gate?

• Who _desires_ not to be great ones?

• I _feel_ the warmth of the sun.

• She _likes_ to be a nurse.

• I _hate/love_ you. I _hope_; you will be fine.

• Who _refuses_ to be a volunteer in this great mission?

• They _prefer_ experts and we are not either one of them, Peter or Mr. P

❖ **Verbs of Thinking (as State Verbs), not to be used, generally, in Progressive Tenses**

14) Verbs of thinking: (think, suppose, believe, agree, consider, trust, remember, forget, know, understand, imagine, mean, mind); as,

• I _think_, he is a genius, a fraud & a cheater.

• _Wish_ you have great success in your life.

• _Suppose_, we met them by chance; what would happen then?

• She _believes_ me, and I am cheating with her.

• I _believe_ you; you carry on, my boy.

• You'll do, I believe you.

• He finally _agrees_ with the project.

• Don't _consider_ me I can't do that task for you.

• _Trust_ me, I have not done that.

• _Remember_, we didn't ask you to come.

• _Forget_ that all things. I _know_ him.

• I _understand_ your situation but you have to.

• Do you _understand_ mine? If we can't submit it on time, they'll cancel.

• _Imagine_, you are a king, what would you do?

• = I'd like to give Peter a huge land to produce stupidity like him.

• You _meant_ me? Then I must give you a dozen.

• Don't _mind_, but it's not a joke. Hmm...

❖ **The Verbs Of 'Possession Which Refer To 'Own' Are Also Used in Simple or Perfect Tenses:**

15) Verbs of possession or own: (have, own, possess, belong to, contain, consist of, include, comprise of, etc.) –are used also in Simple or Perfect Tenses merely; as,

• He _owns_ a gold ring, and his wife _possesses_ a necklace of diamond.

• They _have_ lot of wealth in their motherland, but they _belong to_ none.

• Whose does this _belong to_? It _belongs to_ Shyamal, my brother-in-law who _lives in_ New Jersey.

• It _contains_ only three chambers under the ground.

- Each chamber *comprises of* three tables and five arms.
- It *consists of* twelve. I *have* no house to call own. White House *belongs to* none.
- She *has* five brothers, and her mother *had* none to take her care.

❖ Verb **'To Be'** & **'To have'** when used as Main Verbs, they are used in Simple Tenses.

16) Verb **'To Be'** (am, is. are, was, were, be) & verb **'To Have** (has, have, had) when they are used as main verb, they take simple tenses (Simple Present, Simple Past & Simple Future); as,
→ *Are* you hungry? I *am* not a coward like you.
→ She *is* a famous singer. And her boyfriend *is* a renowned writer, Shelley, her sister call.
→ John *is* loose in character; everybody *knows* that.
→ He *was* my boss. They *were* unknown about it, and they misbehaved. Why men *judge* on dress?
→ I shall *be* a leader one day, and everyone will *know* my name & I will *become* famous in my land.

316. **Exercise-1:** Fill in the blanks, **choosing the correct form of the following verbs within brackets:**

[open(s) - speak(s) - take(s) - do(es) - cause(s) - live(s) - play(s) - close(s)]
a) Ann _____ hand ball very well.
b) The swimming pool _____ at 7:00 in the morning.
c) It _____ at 9:00 in the evening.
d) Bad driving _____ many accidents.
e) My parents _____ in a very small flat.
f) The Olympic Games _____ place every four years.
g) They are good students. They always _____ their homework.
h) My students _____ a little English.

Match your Answers with the following.
a) Ann **plays** hand ball very well.
b) The swimming pool **opens** at 7:00 in the morning.
c) It **closes** at 9:00 in the evening.
d) Bad driving **causes** many accidents.
e) My parents **live** in a very small flat.
f) The Olympic Games **take** place every four years.
g) They are good students. They always **do** their homework.
h) My students **speak** a little English.

The Use of Present Continuous

317. Study the following structure:

Subject Pronouns	Affirmative	Negative	Question
I	I am playing.	I am not playing.	Am I playing?
he, she, it	He is playing.	He is not playing.	Is he playing?
you, we, they	You are playing.	You are not playing.	Are you playing?

318. Study the following chart too, how verbs given 'Continuous Forms':

How Verbs can be given 'continuous forms'		
1. Simply **by adding** '-ing' with the base form of verbs; as,	Add—adding Fly—flying	Do—doing Eat—eating

2. By **omitting** 'e' from the end of verbs, preceding a consonant, before **adding** '-ing'; as,	Give—giving Write—writing Come—coming	Drive—driving Double—doubling Manage—managing
3. By **doubling the single** last consonant of verb, preceding a vowel, before **adding '-ing' when stress falls on the last syllable of the word.**	Set—setting Hit—hitting Admit—admitting Forget—forgetting Quarrel—quarrelling	Refer—referring Run—running Occur—occurring Omit—omitting Travel—travelling
But if stress does not fall on the last syllable, doubling does not happen.	Listen—listening Remember—remembering	Visit—visiting Say—saying
4. By **replacing** 'ie' **with** 'y' at the end of verbs before **adding** '-ing'.	Tie—tying Lie—lying	Die—dying Fly—flying

319. **A Present Continuous Form or Tense is used:**

1) For **an action going on** at the time of speaking (now).
   - → He *is playing football*. She *is singing*.
   - → The boys *are playing* hockey.
- ✖ **Explanation:** The **action is going on (now).** Signal words like **now**, **at the moment** are often used to emphasize that the action is taking place at the moment of speaking. Signal words are not always really necessary to express the continuation of the action.

✖ **More Examples**

   - → We are having breakfast.
   - → What are you reading?
   - → She's not listening to me.
   - → They are getting late for the cinema hall.
   - → They are performing superb! I saw their performance last five years back.
   - → What are they asking for?
   - → They are not listening to their authorities.
   - → What actually are they doing?

2) **Actions taking place around now** (not at the moment of speaking though).

   - → I'*m studying* for my exams.

✖ **Explanation:**

➢ This action takes place around now; not exactly at the moment though.
➢ We don't have to use signal words here, but we often find signal words in such sentences, e.g., **now, at the moment, these days, etc.**
   - → I *am reading* Macbeth. (may not at the moment, but in present time)

✖ **Thus-**

   - → Jim *is helping* in his brother's firm this week.

✖ **Explanation:**
➢ Jim does not usually work in the firm; he is helping his brother temporarily and his action is not completed yet.
➢ **This week/month/ year, in the present decade, this decade**, etc. are the signal words may be used in Present Continuous. And thus, **in the decade of 1990's, in the last decade**, etc. are used in Past Continuous.

✖ **More Examples:**

→ I'm learning Italian.
→ She's writing a novel.
→ They're spending a year in Spain.
→ We are progressing in the project, and soon to declare our launch date.
→ They are working and soon to complete the building.
→ Peter is working on his third book.
→ Om is developing his knowledge on coding with his Whitehat Jr. coaching classes online.
→ The population of China *is rising* very fast.

3) **Arrangements for the near future:** (for an action going to happen in near future; actually, in place of Future Indefinite)

→ *I'm going to* the theatre tonight.

✗ **Explanation:**
➢ In the example you can see that the tickets are already bought, and it is a part of near future plan. It is like, "Tonight, I'll see a movie." "Tonight, I'll go to theatre."
➢ Such continuous takes signal words like **tonight, tomorrow, next Friday, at noon, soon, etc.** Read more:
→ My uncle is arriving tomorrow. (It is decided & to mean future time; present continuous in form, but simple future in meaning)
→ My uncle will come tomorrow. (a future event; practically I don't find any difference)

✗ **More Examples**
→ He is flying to Japan in August.
→ What are you doing this evening?
→ I'm not starting my new job till next Monday.
→ I am going to join City Police next year.

➢ *(be + going+ infinitive)*

→ The book is going to be published on Monday.
→ He is about to leave. *(be+ about+ infinitive)*
→ He is to join the post by tomorrow.

➢ *(be+ infinitive)*

4) With **always, constantly, continually**, to **talk about something that happens often, and that we find annoying** (*to refer an obstinate habit that persists* in spite of attempt for correction by advice or warning).
→ He *is always coming* late to class.

✗ **More Examples**
→ He's always disobeying his parents.
→ He's always asking silly questions.
→ They are repeatedly coming round here to borrow something.
→ Constantly they are playing music in high volume.
→ He's continually doing the same mistake of forgetting the switch off.
→ She's always round of me with her silly excuses.

✗ **Thus-**

→ He *is constantly talking*. I wish he would shut up.

→ I don't like them because they *are always complaining.*

5) The State & Linking Verbs do not have progressive forms; as,
   → I need some new shoes.
   → He wants to go home.
   → Do you know Tania Smith?
   → They love Japanese food.
   → She hates her job.

✘ **But when State Verbs are used as event verbs, the Progressive Tense can be used for them; as,**
   → I am thinking, what should I do now?
   → She is intending to kiss me. (Talking about her actions taken by her to kiss the man, like going forward, leaning towards, etc., but not merely of her intension)

Read more in the following chart:

Compare-

As State Verbs	As Event Verbs
▢ The soup tastes salty. (express a state)	▢ He's tasting the soup. (defining the activities of drinking, eating, etc.)
▢ She's a difficult child. (states the condition of the child)	▢ She's being difficult again. (hints to her activities or actions)
▢ Do you think I should leave? (asking for his thoughts)	▢ What are you thinking about? (hints to his mental process of thinking, his taking decisions)
▢ They have a car. (implying possession of the thing)	▢ They are having their lunch. (having=eating)

320.   **Exercise-2:** Using the words in parentheses (within brackets), complete the text below with the appropriate present continuous tense.
   1) Shhhhh! Be quiet! John (sleep) _____.
   2) Don't forget to take your umbrella. It (rain) _____.
   3) I hate living in Seattle because it (rain, always) _____.
   4) I'm sorry I can't hear what you (say)_____ because everybody (talk)_____ so loudly.
   5) Justin _____ (write, currently) a book about his adventures in Tibet. I hope he can find a good publisher when he is finished.
   6) Jim: Do you want to come over for dinner tonight?
      Denise: Oh, I'm sorry, I can't. I (go) _____ to a movie tonight with some friends.

✘ **Answers**
   1) Shhhhh! Be quiet! John (sleep) **_is sleeping_** .
   2) Don't forget to take your umbrella. It (rain) **_is raining_** .
   3) I hate living in Seattle because it (rain, always) __ is **_always raining_** .
   4) I'm sorry I can't hear what you (say) **_are saying_** because everybody (talk) **_is talking_** so loudly.
   5) Justin **_is currently writing_** (write, currently) a book about his adventures in Tibet. I hope he can find a good publisher when the book is finished.

6) Jim: Do you want to come over for dinner tonight?
Denise: Oh, I'm sorry, I can't. I (go) **_am going_** to a movie tonight with some friends.

The Use of Present Perfect Tense

321. Read the sentences:
  - He **_has gone_** out.
  - We **_have given_** the annual examination.

✘ **The verbs of the above sentences indicate:**
  a) 'Completed activities in recent past 'as the verb in the 1st sentence; or,
  b) 'Activities or actions in the past but they retain (continue to hold or have something) more of their effect mere than complete by itself'; as the verb in 2nd sentence.

The verb in the 1st sentence indicates the **action is complete but in the recent time.**

The verb in 2nd sentence indicates, *examination has been given, but yet to come out the result*. Outcome of the action is not yet complete.

322. **Present Perfect Tense is used:**

1) To indicate **_'completed activities in recent past'_**; as,
  - He has (just) done the task.
  - Have you visited there?
  - I have not arrived in time.
  - It has just struck ten.
  - Have you read Gulliver's Travels?
  - I have never known her to be cool.
  - She has been in Kolkata for her treatment. (perfect)

✘ **Note:** *Adverbs of time, like-* **now, just, already,** *may or may not be used in Present Perfect Tense.*

2) To refer '*activities or* **_actions in the past but they retain_** (continue to hold or have something) **_more of their effect_** *mere than complete by itself*; as,
  - Gopi has not eaten any biscuits (i.e., *all are available for you*).
  - I have eaten all mangoes. (i.e., *nothing is left for you*).
  - We have given examinations for the recruitment three years ago. (A past event, but *the recruitment has not done yet.*)
  - We have arranged everything for the programme.
  - Subject teachers have given a lot of tasks for the vacation.
  - They have organised a meeting with the workers, now to see what happens.
  - We have built up the farm, but the machines have not arrived till now.

3) Present Perfect is also **used for the verbs which are thought to be Present Perfect Continuous in sense**, but as the verbs (the State Verbs) have no continuous forms, they are used in Present Perfect Tense'; as,
→ I have known him for a long time.
    = It is continuous in sense, for still I know the man after I have come to know him long time ago first. The action 'to know' has started long time back and still I know the man, here, 'him'. But as 'know' verb does not have Progressive or continuous form, it is used in present perfect tense.

✘ **Read more:**
→ He has been ill since last week.
    (*He has fallen ill a week's back and still he is ill. It is* **perfect continuous in sense,** *but used in perfect tense*).

→ We have not seen Padma for several months.
    (So as, '*see' verb has no continuous form*)

→ We have ~~been living~~ lived here for ten years.
    ('**have been living**' *is an incorrect usage*)

→ Subject teachers have given a lot of tasks for the vacation.

→ They have organised a meeting with the workers, now to see what happens.
→ We have built up the farm, but the machines have not arrived till now.

Remember some other factors about Present Perfect Tense

323. Present Perfect Tense **can easily be replaced with the Simple Past**, with or without time marker; as–yesterday, the day before, etc.

Present Perfect Tense	Simple Past Tense
a) He has *already* packed his suitcase.	a) *Yesterday by this time*, he packed his suitcase.
b) They have *just* finished their meal.	b) They finished their meal & went to sleep.
c) Haven't you finished *yet*?	c) Didn't you finish it?
d) He has *just* gone out.	d) He went out *at ten*.
e) It has *just* struck ten.	e) It struck ten *then*.

324. **The use of 'before' & 'after' as connectors in the Perfect Tense:**

✗ **In case of double clauses in a sentence (like in complex sentences),** *'before' is used with the clause referring an action happened later*, or *simply say with the indefinite or simple tense*; & **'after' is used with the clause referring an action happened earlier**, or *simply say with the perfect tense*:

a) We have closed the door <u>before</u> we get (go) to bed.
b) We had closed the door <u>before</u> we went to bed.
c) We shall have closed the door <u>before</u> we go to bed.
Or
a) We get to bed <u>after</u> we have closed the door.
b) We went to bed <u>after</u> we had closed the door.
c) We go to bed <u>after</u> we shall have closed the door.

✗ **More Examples**

a) We have reached the station <u>before</u> the train leaves/takes off/runs off/departs.
b) They had left the place <u>before</u> the confusion started.
c) I shall have arrived my home <u>before</u> it starts raining.
Or
a) The train takes off <u>after</u> we have reached the station.
b) The confusion started <u>after</u> they had left the place.
c) It starts raining <u>after</u> I shall have arrived my home.

The use of **'as soon as', 'no sooner…than'**

325. **'Soon'** is an adverb. The phrase of soon, **'as soon as'** & **'no sooner than'** are two conjunctions (subordinate). Definitely they join clauses to make a complex sentence.
✗ We use **'as soon as'** to show that ***something happens immediately***, i.e., *after the end of another* or *at the very moment after another;* or to refer ***two actions to happen almost simultaneously but after the end of another'***. So, generally, simple tenses are used; as,
• Call him <u>as soon as</u> you can.
• I'll call you <u>as soon as</u> I arrive.
• Please send it <u>as soon as</u> possible.

✗ When the clause begins with **'as soon as'** we use **'comma' (,)** after end of the clause: as,
• <u>As soon as he finished his work</u>, he went out.
• <u>As soon as the bus arrived</u>, the passengers rushed to board it.
• <u>As soon as the child saw his mother</u>, he embraced her.
• <u>As soon as the bell rang</u>, the students ran out of the class.

✗ **'No sooner than'** is used to say ***that something happens on the neck of another's end*** *(immediately after another, not even finished),* **at the last point of first action, even not before the end of** *first action completely; (here <u>the time gap seems too minimum</u> between the two actions); but practically the two terms or phrases—__as soon as__ and __no sooner than__—have hardly any differences.*

> ✘ *Not before the end of another.*
> Or
> ✘ *'The 1st event happens not too before than the 2nd event'.*

- She had no sooner spoken of him than he entered the room.
- She had no sooner spoken than the telephone rang. (*The telephone rang immediately after she spoke*)
- No sooner had she said it than she burst into tears. (*She burst into tears immediately after she said it.*)
- No sooner had she finished her speech than the lights went out.
- No sooner did I walk through the door than the phone rang.
- No sooner had I shut the door than the phone rang.
- No sooner did I start to walk than my cell phone rang.
- No sooner had I spoken about him than he appeared.

✘ *If __as soon as__ has five second's gaps, __no sooner than__ has gap of no second—is the difference between them.*

✘ *Now it depends how a reader will use the terms. The clause begins with '__no sooner__' and ends with '__than__' is a <u>sub-ordinate clause</u> of a **Complex sentence.***

The Use of Present Perfect Continuous Tense

326. **Study the sentence:**
- James <u>has been teaching</u> at the university since 2012.

> ✘ **Explanation**

- **To refer 'duration from the past till now',** we use the <u>Present Perfect Continuous Tense</u> to show that something started in the past and is still continuing or going on.
- For, since, from; & for five years, for two weeks, since Tuesday, from Monday, from June, etc. *are the signal words or time markers* of Present Perfect Continuous Tense.

> ■ **Study the following table:**

Subjects PRONOUNS	AFFIRMATIVE	NEGATIVE	QUESTION
I	I have been playing.	I have not been playing.	Have I been playing?
he, she, it	He has been playing.	He has not been playing.	Has he been playing?
you, we, they	You have been playing.	You have not been playing.	Have you been playing?

> ✘ **More Examples**

a) What <u>have</u> you <u>been doing</u> for the last 30 minutes?
b) She has been working at that company for 3 years?
c) He has been sleeping for five hours.
   (He has fallen asleep five hours ago and he is still sleeping. = present perfect + present continuous)
d) I have been watering the garden. (*In answer of: 'why are your clothes so wet?*)
e) Peter has been working on the project since last year.
f) I have been typing for last seven hours.
g) She has been working since eight O'clock.
h) I've been learning English for several years.

327. <u>The use of **'when', 'because'** as connector</u> in the Perfect Continuous Tense:

✘ **In case of double clauses in a sentence, 'When' is used with the clause referring an action that happens later** than the other which has already begun or started, <u>or simply to say</u> '**when**' <u>is used with the clause of simple tense</u> (past, present or future) & '**because**' in the **progressive** or **perfect continuous tense**:
  a) I have been reading the novel ***when*** <u>she visits</u> my home. (Present Perfect Continuous)
  b) I had been reading the novel ***when*** my <u>friend visited</u> my house. (Past Perfect Continuous)
  c) We shall have been discussing the matter ***when*** <u>you arrive</u> there (before you arrive there).

&

  d) My hands are dirty ***because*** <u>I've been gardening</u>.
  e) I can't go ***because*** <u>I am now studying</u>.
  f) They can't join us ***because*** <u>they have been working</u> on a project, very urgent.

328. The use of '**since**' & '**from**' in Perfect Continuous

SINCE (point of time)	**FROM** (specific time)
1) I have been walking since dawn.	1) I have been walking from 4 a.m.
2) You had been doing the work since last summer.	2) You had been doing the work from last April.
3) She has been suffering from this disease since her childhood.	3) She has been suffering from this disease from 2004.

329. The use of '**since**' & '**for**' in Perfect Continuous

SINCE (point of time)	**FOR** (period of time)
1) I have been walking since dawn.	1) I have been walking for three hours.
2) You had been doing the work since last summer.	2) You had been doing the work for last three months.
3) She has been suffering from this disease since her childhood.	3) She has been suffering from this disease for last fifteen years.

330. The Use of '**Lately**' & '**recently**':

✘ **Lately** to mean '**recently**' & '**recently**' to mean '**in the recent past**'—can be used in all states of a Tense; as,

✘ **In Simple Tense:**
  • *Recently* he dies, leaving his three sons and two daughters.
  • We received a letter from him *lately*/*recently*.

✘ **In Continuous:**
  • *Recently* they are living in New York.
  • *Until recently* they were living in New York.

✘ **In Perfect:**
  • Have you seen her *lately*? Have you used it *recently*? (In the recent past)
  • I have not seen them *recently*. (It is sometime since I saw them)
  • It's only *lately* that she has been well enough to go out.
  • She has *lately* returned from London.

In Perfect Continuous:
  • I haven't been sleeping well just lately.
  • Recently, Sophia <u>has been working on a tiring project.</u>

✘ *We can use a tense, <u>with or without a signal word or marker</u>* like "**for two weeks**", 'lately', 'recently', etc. in the Present Perfect Continuous to denote time of duration, and <u>one marker can easily be replaced with the other</u>.
  a. *Lately*, he <u>has been studying</u> with his geography. = He <u>has been studying geography</u> *for last two hours*.
  b. She <u>has been watching</u> television *lately*. =*Till 5 p.m.* she has been watching television.
  c. Have you been exercising *lately*? = Have you been exercising *for last three hours*?
    d. Sophia has been feeling vomiting *lately.* = Sophia <u>has been feeling</u> vomiting *for last three minutes*.

(Here: 'feel' is treated as event verb, but not as State verb that it means, she is doing wak, wak to vomit.)

Note: and '*lately*' means '*recently*' or '*in the recent past*' or '*till the recent past time*'.

331. **Exercise-3: Fill in the blanks, using Present Perfect Tense of the verbs-**
   - I'm exhausted. I_____(study) in the library all day.
   - It_____ (snow) a lot this week.
   - Your brother and sister have been getting along?
   - How long _____ (you/teach) German?
   - We _____ (watch) TV for 3 hours.
   - You _____ (work) too hard today.

Answers

   - I'm exhausted. I have been studying (study) in the library all day.
   - It has been snowing (snow) a lot this week.
   - Have (you /get) brother and sister been getting along?
   - How long have you been teaching (you/teach) German?
   - We have been watching (watch) TV for 3 hours.
   - She has been working (work) too hard today.

Don't forget
• The present tense of the verb indicates a state or an action that happens now, or at the time speaking.   • Present Indefinite Tense denotes a universal truth, habitual fact, or etc.   • Continuous means an action going on at the time speaking of, not completed.   • Perfect means a complete action at the time of speaking.   • Perfect continuous means an action has started but still going on at the time of speaking. It is both complete and incomplete.

Let us write:
- Imagine that you are on a jungle safari. Write a short composition mentioning your experiences. Try to use all forms of the present tense. You can use the following verbs.

See, drive, arrive, show, tell, drag, leave, travel, spot, graze, roam, spot, enter, watch

The Use of Past Tense (detail study)

Let's get started:
Identify the verbs in these sentences:
1. I played a video game in the afternoon.
2. We went to Manali last year.
3. I was washing my clothes when she arrived home.
4. They had done before we reached.
5. We had been waiting for hours before the minister came.

(What time of actions or the state of actions denoted by the verbs you identified?)

The use of Past tense includes-
   1) The use of Past Indefinite,
   2) The use of Past Continuous,
   3) The use of Past Perfect,
   4) The use of Past Perfect Continuous.

The form of Simple Past/ Past Indefinite Tense

332. A sentence with a verb in simple past tense looks like the following:

Subject+ past form of the verb (i.e., '-ed' form) + object or others

→ I *worked*. We *worked*. You *worked*. They *worked*.

Note-1: '-ed' or any other past form, it depends on the nature of the verb, regular or irregular. The following are the examples of irregular verbs.

→ I *ate* food. He *swam* in the river. They *sang* a bhajan. You *hit* the ball.

Note-2: To form negative or question, **'did'** helping verb is used in the Simple Past Tense; as,
→ I *did not* work. We *did not* work. You *did not* work. They *did not* work.
→ *Did* I/we/you/they work?
→ *Did I not* work? *Did you not* work? *Did they not* work?
→ *Didn't she* work? What *did* we work?

The Use of Simple Past Tense

333.   **Simple Past Tense is used:**

1) To talk about *an action that took place in the past* (it may also include the historical events):
→ He *got up*, *paid* the bill & *left* the bar.
→ I *didn't read* the letter.
→ Akbar *invaded* Kashmir. Ashoka *won* Kalinga.
→ I just *gave* it to Lee. What *did you s*ay? *Did you go* there?

2) To talk about *an action or state or relation that continued for some time in the past, but now complete and finished* (time of adverb may or may not be used); as,
→ Lee *went* to school in Scotland.
→ *Did she really work* there for ten years?
→ The building, White Home, *completed* last year.
→ I *got* my Master degree from the Kanpur University.
→ Moklesur *was* my class-mate from school to university level. (Classmate-relation is now over, now we are good friends.)

3) to talk about *an action that happened regularly in the past* (it may include the *past habits*) [adverb of frequency— often, always, never, ever, & modal verb 'used to' may be used for the sense]; as,
→ He *studied* many hours every day.
→ I often *played* tennis with her. She always *won*.
→ She always *carried* an umbrella. Sara *worked* 5 days a week.
→ They never *went* to the cinema when they *lived* in the country.
→ Bob *watched* TV every night.
→ I *used to* play chess with my dad in the evening.

4) *To mean 'accustomed to something* or to do something occasionally, continually or frequently' or '*to do the something habitually*', **'used to'** is used in the Simple Past Tense only (to refer a '*past occasional habit*'); as,
→ She *used to* show her anger to her husband. [Now everything is over. He is either dead or she behaves human.] (Occasional or frequent past habit of the woman is past now.)
→ He *used to* grumble. No one felt comfortable with him.
→ He used to bargain with the shop-keepers. (Now, that is past)
→ The woman *used to* quarrel with her husband & neighbours, and one day she died in heart-attack!
→ My mother-in-law *used to* say, "Clap is not made by one hand."
→ We *used to* organise debate competition in our school.
→ I *used to* be undecided in difficult situations, and then she took my all decisions.
→ I *used to* sit under a peeple tree and wondered how men are made with love and hate together!

5) To introduce a quotation; as,
→ "The sun rises in the east", the teacher *said*.
→ 'You should pay respect to your teacher', father *used to say*.

334.   **Compare -**

Present Perfect	**Simple Past Tense**
○ This tense is used to indicate '*completed action, recently past*'. However, all are not recent. Many past events are also written to make them alive.	○ This tense is used to indicate '*an action completed in the past*', including past habit or what happened earlier.

207

o The Adverbs like— since, for, <u>never, ever, so far, till now,</u> yet, already, today, this week, this month or year — are used.	o Adverb of time; like, *yesterday, last day, last week, last month or year,* <u>never, ever, so far, till date, etc.,</u> —are used.
1) We have sailed in the lake. It is refreshing.	1) We used to go sailing on the lake in summer. (Now, we don't go.)
2) I have overcome with her. There was drug in her eyes, my love and her shrug.	2) I didn't use to like him when we were at school.
3) We have lived here for ten years.	3) They watched a movie yesterday.
4) He has never seen a movie in his college life.	4) Last year we lost the match to them. This year, the same will not happen.
5) They have been there since 1990's.	5) Sheila used to visit her uncle in Hyderabad during all summer vacations.
6) Yet, you have not done the task.	
7) So far/till now, we have completed only half of the project.	6) I used to take bath in the river in my boyhood.
8) Have you been ever in the city?	7) I used to <u>ride</u> horses even when I was mere a boy.
9) This week, they have given only thirteen.	8) Last year, he gifted me with a Taj Mahal.
10) Finally, today, you have come to me.	9) You never visited my house till date.
11) I have eaten thirteen eggs.	

335. **Exercise-1: Use the correct form of the following verbs using simple past:**

a) I _____ to the mall after school. (go)
b) My brother _____ a bear an hour ago. (see   )
c) _____Mike visits his grandmother last night? (do)
d) Alex did not _____ last weekend.   (work   )
e) _____Judy and Liz at last month's meeting? (is)
f) We _____ not happy after the sad ending. (are)
g) _____you see Jody's new dog yesterday? (are)
h) Sorry, I _____ hear you at the door. (do)
i) I _____ English for two years.   (study)
j) What _____ you eat for lunch yesterday? (do)

Answers

a) I _went___ to the mall after school. (go)
b) My brother _saw___ a bear an hour ago. (see)
c) ___Did__ Mike visit his grandmother last night? (do)
d) Alex did not _work_ last weekend. (work   )
e) Were___ Judy and Liz at last month's meeting? (is)
f) We _were_ not happy after the sad ending. (are)
g) _Did__ you see Jody's new dog yesterday? (do)
h) Sorry, I _didn't hear you at the door.   (don't)
i) I _studied____ English for two years. (study)
j) What ___did___ you eat for lunch yesterday? (do)

The Use of Past Continuous Tense

336. Study the structures:

Subject Pronouns	Affirmative	Negative	Question
I, he, she, it	I was playing.	I was not playing.	Was I playing?
you, we, they	You were playing.	You were not playing.	Were you playing?

337. **The Past Continuous Tense is used-**

1) To talk about **an action that was in progress in the past**.

John **was playing** football.

✶ Explanation

208

➢ The speaker is speaking of an <u>action that was going on at some time in the past.</u> Signal words like then, at that moment may often be used to emphasize that the action was taking place at that moment, but truly, not necessary at all.

➢ **<u>Signal words are not really necessary to express the continuation of an action or time</u>**, when the <u>form of verb itself express that quite well.</u>

✶ **More Examples**

· What *were you doing* in the lock-down of 2020 & 2021?
· I *was writing* a novel. *Were you reading* any book?
· *Was it raining*? They were absent in the meeting. (1st is in Continuous, but the second is in Simple past)
· How *were they doing* their task with little men-power?
· They *were singing* together. They sang the best of them.
· We *were performing* our best at that time.
· I *was asking* for help, but no one came.
· *Was it raining*, when you left for home?

✘ If you study carefully, you will find there is tend to mention two actions in the progressive or perfect tenses, though not always happen.

2) While an action was going on, other took place:
· While I *was having* breakfast, the clock struck half past seven.
· While I <u>was studying</u>, the phone suddenly rang.

· When you called her, she *was writing* a letter.
· While we *were having* the picnic, it started to rain.

✘ **Use of 'While' or 'When' in Past Progressive tense**

✘ Examples:
· I *was studying* **when she called.**
· **While I <u>was studying</u>**, she called.
· The doorbell rang while they **were having** their breakfast.

✶ Explanation

✘ Clauses are groups of words which have meanings and a sense, complete or incomplete. As the term defines, they are not complete sentences, but parts of. <u>Some clauses begin with</u> the word **"when"** such as *"when she called", "when it bit me".* Other clauses begin with **"while"** such as *"While she was sleeping"* and *"while he was surfing".*

✘ When you talk about things in the past, "*when"* <u>is most often followed by the verb tense</u> ***Simple Past***, <u>whereas **"while"** is usually followed by Past Continuous.</u> **"While"** expresses the idea of **"during the time"**, **"when"** denotes '**a time**'.

✶ More Examples
· We *were listening* to the radio all the evening.
· It was getting darker **when** <u>we reached our home.</u>
· What were you doing in the summer of 1999?
· Was it raining **when** <u>you left home?</u>
· The doorbell rang **while** <u>they were having breakfast.</u>
· ***While*** <u>she *was preparing dinner, he was washing the dishes.*</u>
· The light went out **while** <u>I was reading.</u>
· **When** <u>I saw him</u>, he was playing chess.

✘ **Note:** In a complex or compound sentence where there is more than one clause are present; we may use more than one tense, like the above sentences.

3) Two progressive actions may happen at the same time.
   · While she _was preparing_ dinner, he _was washing_ the dishes.

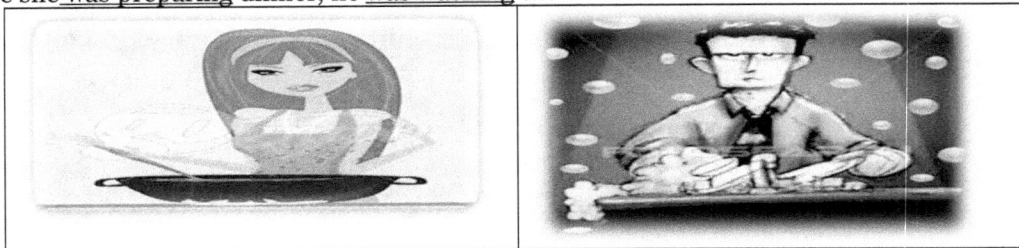

As both actions are in progressive, there is no problem using progressive tense for both.

4) With **'always'**, **'constantly'**, to talk about something that happened often, and that you found **'annoying'**. And the same to be used in Present Continuous Tense as well as in Past Continuous:
   · He _was always coming_ late to class.
   · He'_s always asking_ silly questions. (is/was)
   · They'_re always coming_ round here to borrow something. (are/were)
   · He _is always coming_ late in the class.
   · _Constantly, you are disobeying_ your parents or teachers.
   · _Constantly they were bargaining_ on the issue.

✗ **Note:** "always" or **constantly, repeatedly, continuously,** etc. may be used between **"be"** and **"-ing"** form of verb, or at the beginning of the sentence, as in the above & following, and can be used in progressive of both in present & past condition:

   · He _was constantly talking_. I wished he would shut up, but he didn't. I went up from there.
   · I didn't like them because they _were always complaining_ about their boss.
   · He _was always grumbling_ with anybody else, known or unknown. He is responsible for his present condition.
   · He _was always bargaining_ with the shop-keepers. He is not any more allowed in the shopping mall.
   · The woman _was always quarrelling_ with her neighbours.

✗ **Note:** Like in Present Progressive tense, the State Verbs cannot be used in the Past Continuous; instead, they can be used in Simple Past; like,
   · The fresh bread ~~was smelling~~ **smelled** wonderful. (**Not:** was smelling)
   · It ~~was tasting~~ **tasted** spicy. (Not: was tasting)
   · She ~~was looking~~ **looked** very beautiful. (Not: was looking)

5) To narrate an 'atmosphere of a place' of past time being in the present:

   · When I walked into the office, several people _were busily typing_, some _were talking on_ the phone, the boss _was yelling_ on some, and customers _were waiting_ to be helped.
                              ✗ Explanation

✗ In English, or in any other language, we often use a series of parallel actions to describe 'the atmosphere of a place' at a particular time in the present or past.

   Note: Time of Adverbs, **'yesterday'**, **'last night'**, etc., may or may not be used in Simple Past Tense a well as in the Past Continuous; as Tense itself (the form of verb) is a great time-marker:
   · Last night at 6 pm, I _was eating_ dinner.
   · I was eating dinner at 6 p.m.
   · Yesterday at this time, I _was sitting_ at my desk at work.
   · I was sitting at my desk.

338.   **Active** & **Passive Forms** of Past Continuous:

active	passive

1. I *was studying* when she *called*. 2. While I *was studying*, she *called*. 3. They *were playing* football when their parents reached to the stadium.	1. I <u>was being studied</u> when she called. (When I was called by her) • When I was called (by her), I was being studied. 2. While I was being studied, she called. • She called while I was being studied. 3. Football was being played by them, when their parents were reached the playground.

Note: In case of Compound or Complex sentence, though as per grammar rule, each clause can be converted to passive voice, it is not necessary at all. To do always. The sense is important, and thus some clauses may be kept unchanged.

339. **Exercises:** Fill in the blanks using the past continuous tense:
   a) My brother and sister _____ (play) tennis at 11am yesterday.
   b) _____(be)you still working at 7pm last night?
   c) At 8.30am today I _____ (drive) to work.
   d) We _____(be)sleeping at 11pm.
   e) Why _____(be) he having lunch at 4pm?
   f) I met John in town yesterday. He_____ (shop).
   g) Mary_____ (wait) for me when I arrived.

Answers

   a) My brother and sister <u>were playing</u> (play) tennis at 11am yesterday.
   b) <u>Were</u> (be) you still working at 7pm last night?
   c) At 8.30am today I <u>was driving</u> (drive) to work.
   d) We <u>weren't</u> (be /not) sleeping at 11pm.
   e) Why <u>was</u> (be) he having lunch at 4pm?
   f) I met John in town yesterday. He was <u>shopping</u> (shop).
   g) Mary <u>was waiting</u> (wait) for me when I arrived.

The Use of Past Perfect Tense

340. **The Past Perfect** is used

1) **'To talk about something that <u>happened before another</u> action in the past'**; *as,*
   → When I got to the station, the train **had left**. (I missed the train. It had left the station)
   → When I reached the station, the train **had started** to leave. (Too risky to get into or get down from a running train. However, I missed this train for seconds.)
   → I **had done** my exercise when Tom came to see me.
   → I **had written** the letter before he arrived.
   → I **had already met** him at New Delhi before he came to my White Home.

   Note: *Between two actions in the past, for the earlier one, we use Past Perfect Tense and Simple Past is used for the latter. Sometimes, it may also be possible that the two actions are mentioned not in a single sentence, then must be in the succeeding lines or be understood; as,*
   → I <u>could not meet</u> him at New Delhi last year. I <u>had seen</u> him last five years back at somewhere, I can't remember, 'where'.
   → We <u>did</u> it together. Last, we <u>had done</u> the same task together ten years back.
   → I <u>had passed</u> my master degree before you <u>were born</u>. (The last clause is in passive of simple past, as it is always used in passive)
   → We <u>had done</u>. ('**They** <u>did not</u>/**you did not'**— the second sentence, may not be used. We may keep it understood or to be unused, but the sense is implied.)

   ✖ In Present Perfect & Past Perfect, we do almost the same thing, for earlier action we use the Perfect Tense and for the latter action we use Simple Tense; as,

      • I *had already met* the minister before he *came* with his complaint. (Past tense)
      • I *have already met* the minister before he *comes* with his complaint.

✖ But in case of Future Perfect Tense, when we use Perfect for the earlier, for the later, we use Simple Present Tense in place of Simple Future; as,
  • She *will have arrived* the station before the train *leaves*. (Not: will leave)
  • She *will have got* the recruitment before I *die* in my old age.

The Use of Past Perfect Continuous

341. **Study The table:**

Pronouns	Affirmative	Negative	Question
I	I had been playing.	I had not been playing.	Had I been playing?
he, she, it	He had been playing.	He had not been playing.	Had he been playing?
you, we, they	You had been playing.	You had not been playing.	Had you not been playing?

342. **The Past Perfect Continuous Tense is used –**

   i. To mean '***duration before another thing happened*** in the past'.

a) They *had been talking* for over an hour before Tony arrived.

✖ We use the Past Perfect Continuous to show that *something started in the past and continued up until another action in the past*. "**Since**", "**for**", "**from**" as well as "**For five days**" and "**for two weeks**" –such are the markers to mean the durations which can be used in Past Perfect Continuous Tense.

b) How long *had* you *been waiting* to get on the bus?

c) I *had been waiting* there for more than two hours when she finally arrived.

d) Jason was tired because *he had been riding a horse.*

   ii. To denote cause of something in the past'. The cause of other past will be in the Past Perfect Continuous Tense.

e) My hands were dirty because I **had been gardening**.
f) Rwitika failed, because she **had not been attending** her classes.

g) She was exhausted, as she **had been working** on her project since morning that day.

h) He was died, he **had been suffering** from lung cancer.
i) She missed the shot at Final Olympic, as she **had been making** plan for some other thing.
j) Sam gained weight because _he had been overeating_ since last year.
k) Betty failed the final test because she _had not been attending_ class.

343. **Past Continuous vs. Past Perfect Continuous**

✖ If you do not include a duration marker such as _"for five days"_, _"for two weeks"_ or _"since Friday"_, _etc._ You may use the Past Continuous rather than the Past Perfect Continuous. However, this can change the meaning of the sentence too.

✖ Past Continuous emphasizes interrupted actions, whereas Past Perfect Continuous emphasizes a duration of time before other action in the past.

✖ Study the slide to understand the difference.

Past Continuous	Past Perfect Continuous
He was tired because he **was exercising** so hard.	He was tired because he **had been exercising** so hard.
• This sentence emphasizes that he was tired because he was **exercising at that exact moment in the past**. When he was exercising, he was tired or he felt tired.	• This sentence emphasizes that he was tired because he had been **exercising over a period of time in the past**. It is possible that he did not do exercise anymore or that he had just finished.

Adverb Placement in Past Perfect Continuous:

344. The examples below show the placement of adverbs (**always, only, never, ever, still, just**, etc.) in the tense; as:
a) You had **only** been waiting there _for a few minutes_ when she arrived.
b) Had you **only** been waiting there _for a few minutes_ when she arrived?
c) He had been **always** gambling and he lost his everything.
d) She had **never** been there in her life time. (Past perfect)
e) She had **ever** been working and she got the call from heaven.
f) She had **still** been working on her project, and she got chance from UNESCO.
g) She had **just** finished her task; a call came from her boss. (Past perfect)
h) She had **just** been starting, it was declared to postpone everything.

345. The Passive forms of the Past Perfect Continuous are not common like in Future Perfect Continuous tense. However, we may study the constructions as follows:

active	passive
• Chef Jones **had been preparing** the restaurant's fantastic dinners for two years before he moved to Paris.	• The restaurant's fantastic dinners **had been being prepared** by Chef Jones for two years before he moved to Paris.
• Sophia **hadn't been guiding** Mark in his guitar lesson.	• Mark **had been being guided** in his guitar lesson by Sophia.
• I **had been watering** plants in my garden.	• Plants in the garden **had been being watered**.
• They **had been waiting** for one hour.	• They **had been being waited** for one hour.

346. **Exercise:** Use the Past Perfect Continuous Form in the sentences:
a) They _____ (shout) for a few hours before their parents arrived.
b) They _____ (eat) noisily for a few minutes before they were called out.
c) They _____ (play) music at full volume for long time before we reached there.
d) They _____ (jump) on the beds for a short period before their teacher arrived.
e) They _____ (try) on Mary's clothes before Mary herself arrived at the spot.

Answers
a) They *had been shouting* (shout) for a few hours before their parents arrived.
b) They *had been eating* (eat) noisily for a few minutes before they were called out.
c) They *had been playing* (play) music at full volume for long time before we reached there.
d) They _had been jumping_ (jump) on the beds for a short period before their teacher arrived.
e) They _had been trying_ (try) on Mary's clothes before Mary herself arrived at the spot.

Don't forget
- The past tense of the verb is used to show action that happened before the time of speaking.
- Simple past tense talks about an action that happened regularly in the past.
- Past Continuous Tense talks about an action that was in progress in the past.
- Past Perfect Tense is used to talk about something that happened before another action in the past.
- Past Perfect Continuous Tense is used to mean 'duration before another thing happened in the past'.

The Use of Future Tense (detail study)

Let's get started:
Identify the verbs in these sentences:
1. I will watch the film in a cinema hall.
2. We are planning a vacation.
3. She will finish reading this book next week.
4. They will have completed their syllabus by next month.
5. I will have been working on this project for one year by next month.

(What time or state of the actions denoted by the verbs you identified?)

347. The use of Future Tense includes-
    - The use of Future Indefinite,
    - The use of Future Continuous,
    - The use of Future Perfect,
    - The use of Future Perfect Continuous.

348. **Shall & will—** the two modals must be used to form Future Tense. Shall & will as modal auxiliary, are generally used between the subject & the main verb; as,

    I *shall order* the carriage. We *shall visit* soon.
    You *will become* a great singer. He *will do* it himself.
    They *will pay* you what you want. It *will be* a great chance for us.

✘ **Note:** The above usage is of general or Traditional tendency to use two modals to form future tense, **but not of USA or recent British;** the recent British & Americans, nowadays, tend not to use "shall" at all to form the <u>future tense</u>; as,

    I *will arrive* on Tuesday.
    He *will arrive* on Tuesday too.

✘ **However, 'shall' is still used in English of most of other countries, including India.** We will follow the traditional track; <u>it is your choice whether you like to use 'will' for each person & number</u>. (**We will, you will, she will**; or as, **I shall, we shall, you will, he will**, etc.) ['We will' means 'we must', denotes 'determination' also in the traditional usage of Modals.)

349. Future Tense & Use of 'Shall'

1) 'Shall' is used with **'I'** & **'We'** for talking about the future tense; as,
    Next week, *I shall be* in Scotland.
    We shall be there in time.

2) Also used in questions with **'I'** & **'We'** for making <u>offers</u>, <u>suggestions</u> or <u>asking advice</u>; as,
    Shall I send you the book?

· What *shall we* do this weekend?

3) Used **to show determination** (strong belief), **duty** or **obligation**, or to **give order** & **instruction** in the Second- & Third-Person Singular & Plural Number; as,

· *You shall go* to the hostel next week. (Determination of the speaker to send him ['you'] to the hostel; as a father is determined to send his son to hostel.)

· *Citizens shall provide* proof of identity to the authority on demand. (An official instruction, must be followed)

· *Candidates shall remain* in their seats until all the papers have been collected.

350.   Future Tense & Use of '**Will**'

1) 'Will' is used with '**You**' & '**He**', '**She**', '**It**', '**They**', etc. for talking about the future tense; as,

· *You will be* responsible for the outcome.

· Soon, *she will perform* her dance on the stage.

· *It will be* wonderful, if you win.

· *They will have* their own house in the town.

2) Also used in questions with '**You**' & '**He**', '**She**', '**It**', '**They**', etc. for asking something; as,

· *Will you go* there finally? Though I don't believe you will.

· What *will he do* this weekend? He could come with us.

· *Won't they admit* it finally? Then it would be fine.

3) However, **to show determination** (strong belief), **duty** or **obligation**, or **to give order** & **instruction** 'Will' is swapped with 'Shall' ('will' is used in place of 'shall') in the First-Person Singular & Plural Number; as,

· *I will do* it, even they refuse all.

· *We will not surrender*—should be our motto and we will meet our deaths like heroes.

· *I /we will have to go* there in time, or *we will be sacked of* our posts by the boss.

The Use of Simple Future Tense

351.   The structure of a sentence with a <u>verb in simple future tense</u> looks like the following:

Subject + shall/will + base form of the verb+ object or others (if any)

· I shall work. We shall work.
· You will work. They will work.

✗   To form negative, the adverb '**not**' <u>comes between shall/will & the base verb</u>; and **to form question, 'shall/will'** comes first in the sentence or before the subject; as,

· I/We shall not work. Shall we work?
· Will you go there? You will not do the job.
· Shall I be old too? Will he die? You will not do this with me?

✗   Simple Future Tense is used:

❑   **To express a** *future event* **or** *state*, **as part of intention, plan decision;** or **beyond the mentioned** (it includes that too that you know, think, believe, hope, expect, wish or want to happen); as,

1) I *shall be* a doctor. *(a dream of being).*
2) I *shall have* a car by next year, *(a plan of having, not instant)*
3) I *shall go* to Delhi tomorrow. *(Generally, an instant plan, though not practically)*
4) I *shall be* twenty next month. Her mother *will be* ninety next week.
   a.   *(Future happening, we have no control over)*
5) It *will be* Diwali in a week. *(Schedule occasion)*
6) The result *will be* published in May. *(We hope, or as a part of fixed programme)*
7) I think England *will win* the Cup.
8) I am sure, you *will score* the highest mark.
9) Will he pass the exam, do you think? This job won't take long.
10) She believes I *will not cheat* her ever. *(To mean her strong belief)*
11) Probably, *you will reach* in time.

12) <u>He expects</u> I **will fulfil** his goal. His failure is to throw upon his child! (Strong belief, 'I must fulfil his goal')
13) It is raining. I **will take** an umbrella. (I have to take, or sure to get wet in rains)
14) It's cold here, ok, **I'll close** the window. (You might not have to worry about whether to use "shall" or "will" in the <u>contractions</u>, for both it has one form.)
15) **I'll have** the salad, please.
16) "Mr. Sinha is very busy at the moment." All right, we **will wait**.

352. How, Present Indefinite & Present Continuous — are used to express Simple Future:
1) **Simple Present Tense** is used <u>to express official time table</u> or <u>program in the future</u>; as,
   · We **leave** Dehradun at 10 a.m. and **arrive** at 4 p.m. at New Delhi.
   · School **starts** on 9ᵗʰ September.

2) **Simple Present** tense is also used **along with the Simple Future tense** and also with the **Future Perfect tenses**, generally after '<u>when</u>', '<u>as soon as</u>', '<u>before</u>', '<u>until</u>', etc., (but not always) <u>in a complex sentence; as,</u>
   · I'll look after Joe **until** you get back.
   · You will recognize the street **when** you see it.
   · I'll return **before** you complete your home task.
   · You will ring me **as soon as** she returns.
   · Ring me **as soon as** you'll hear of her news.

3) 'Present Progressive' is moreover used **_to express future plans where time is mentioned_**; as,
   · He **is flying** to Japan in August.
   · What **are you doing** this evening?
   · **I'm not starting** my new job till next Monday.

353. The Use of '**be** + <u>going to</u> + **base verb**' /

/ '**be** + <u>about to</u> + **base verb**' /&
/ '**be** + <u>infinitive...</u>

1) '**Be** + <u>going to</u> + **base verb**' - is used '_to talk about what you intend to do in the future_' _(may also be used in past; thus, **'he was going to confess and stopped'**)_; as,
   · I **am going to phone** Michael tonight.
   · What **are** you **going to do** when you leave school?
   · Have you decided what to do? = Yes, I **am going to resign** the job.
   · I **am going to submit** the papers with the CBI.
   · Why do you want to sell your motor-bike? = For, I **am going to buy** a car.

2) '**Be** + <u>about to</u> + **base verb**' - is used '_to talk about very near future' of the moment_ (present or past); as,
   · Go and ask him quickly to bring that, that of some vegetables, fruits and etc. on his return.
   · He**'s about to go out** for his office. (**'Present** or **Past indefinite--both** can be used.)**
   · She **is about to speak** of her condition to her father and stops, thinking, it is not the suitable time.

3) '**Be** (am/is/are) + **infinitive**' - is used '_to talk about something as part of an official program, time-table or obligation_; as,
   · Mr. Modi **is to attend** the Summit in November.
   · You **are to go** now from here. I have some urgent tasks to do.
   · I **am to visit** my uncle on next Monday. He is very sick for few days.
   · '**I am about to reach Delhi**' (supposed, while you are entering the capital=which is going to happen, here to mean 'near of the destination'.)

4) **Sometimes only base form of verbs**- is used '_to mean the future sense_'; as,
   · '**Go and ask** him politely, if you can officer. Why did he do that with my daughter?' the old man said and backed to his silent world.
   · '**Go and ask** him that I have called.'

354. Compare Between **Simple Future** & Use Of '**be** + <u>**Going to**</u> + **the Base form of Verb**'. Many of those have similarities and dissimilarities, as both are used in future tenses. Note the distinctions, if any:

Shall/will + base verb	'be+ going to + base verb'
○ **To express a *future event, activity* or *future state* of being or having** (not as a part of instant planning); as, a) I shall be a doctor. (*a dream of being in the future; it is not a part of plan; planning has not made yet, but simply express a 'desire' of the speaker to be*). b) I shall have a car by next year, (*a plan of having, not made instant*) c) I shall go to Delhi tomorrow. 　　　✖ **It's better: 'I am going to Delhi tomorrow'**, as part of plan of near future, preparation is ready. **Note;** Actually, most of things depend on you, how you will use different verbs to make your sentences. Others are only guide-lines not to follow like a blind.	○ If action is **already decided upon and preparation have been made to do** before talking about; as, a) I am going to buy a car. b) I am going to resign the job. ○ It is also used **to talk about what seems likely or certain to happen**; as, a) It is going to rain, Look at the dark clouds. b) The boat is full of water. It is going to sink. c) She is going to have a baby. ○ **To express an action this is on the point of action** or **to happen**. Such one, for 'for the immediate future', we also use '**be about to**; as, a) Let's get into the train. It's going to leave = It's (It is) about to leave. b) Be aware! There is fire. The cracker is going to explode. c) Don't go out now. We are about to have lunch.

355. The Use of Shall & Will beyond to express Simple Future

❑ **We know modals- "shall" & "will" are used to express future tenses. But beyond this, they are used to express 'request, promises, offers** & also assumptions'; as,

　　a) *Will you buy* some bread on your way home?
　　b) *We'll be back* early, don't worry.
　　c) *I'll help* you with your homework.
　　d) *Shall I do* the washing-up?
　　e) *Shall we go* now?
　　f) *I'll take* you to the airport.
　　g) *Will you buy* me an ice cream, please?
　　h) *That will be* James—he's early riser.

356. Exercise-1: Using the words in parentheses, complete the text below with the appropriate tenses.

1. A: Why are you holding a piece of paper?
　B: I (write) _____ a letter to my friends back home in Texas.

2. A: I'm about to fall asleep. I need to wake up!
　B: I (get) _____ you a cup of coffee. That will wake you up.

3. A: I can't hear the television!
　B: I (turn) _____it up so you can hear it.

4. We are so excited about our trip next month to France. We (visit) _____ Paris, Nice and Grenoble.

5. Sarah (come) _____to the party. Oliver (e) _____there as well.

6. Ted: It is so hot in here!
Sarah: I (turn)_____ the air-conditioning on.

Answers

1. A: Why are you holding a piece of paper?
　B: I (write) **am going to write** a letter to my friends back home in Texas.

2. A: I'm about to fall asleep. I need to wake up!
　B: I (get) **will get** you a cup of coffee. That will wake you up.

3. A: I can't hear the television!
   B: I (turn) **will turn** it up so you can hear it.

4. We are so excited about our trip next month to France. We (visit) **are going to visit** Paris, Nice and Grenoble.

5. Sarah (come) **will come** to the party. Oliver (be) **will be** there as well.

6. Ted: It is so hot in here!
   Sarah: I (turn) **will turn** the air-conditioning on.

Note: It is noted, "will" suits here to form the sense more explicit and clearer with the subjects 'I' or 'we'. 'Will' is preferred also for referring 'strong wish' of the speaker.

The Use of Future Continuous Tense

357. **Study the structure:**

Subject Pronouns	Affirmative	Negative	Question
I, he, she, it	I shall be playing.	I shall not be playing.	Shall I be playing?
you, we, they	You will be playing.	You will not be playing.	Will you be playing?

Positive	Negative	Question
• I **will be** waiting. • You **will be** waiting. • We **will be** waiting. • They **will be** waiting. • He **will be** waiting. • She **will be** waiting. • It **will be** waiting.	• I **will not be** waiting. • You **will not be** waiting. • We **will not be** waiting. • They **will not be** waiting. • He **will not be** waiting. • She **will not be** waiting. • It **will not be** waiting.	• **Will** I **be** waiting? • **Will** you **be** waiting? • **Will** we **be** waiting? • **Will** they **be** waiting? • **Will** he **be** waiting? • **Will** she **be** waiting? • **Will** it **be** waiting?

Using "Be Going To"

Positive	Negative	Question
• I **am going to be** waiting. • You **are going to be** waiting. • We **are going to be** waiting. • They **are going to be** waiting. • He **is going to be** waiting. • She **is going to be** waiting. • It **is going to be** waiting.	• I **am not going to be** waiting. • You **are not going to be** waiting. • We **are not going to be** waiting. • They **are not going to be** waiting. • He **is not going to be** waiting. • She **is not going to be** waiting. • It **is not going to be** waiting.	• **Am** I **going to be** waiting? • **Are** you **going to be** waiting? • **Are** we **going to be** waiting? • **Are** they **going to be** waiting? • **Is** he **going to be** waiting? • **Is** she **going to be** waiting? • **Is** it **going to be** waiting?

358. The Future Continuous Tense is used-
   1) To talk about an action (part of plans or intentions or beyond) that will continue for a period of time in the future
      a) Tonight at 6 pm, we *are going to be having a* dinner. (Future Continuous)
      b) Tonight at 6 p.m., we are going to have a dinner. (Simple Future)
      c) At midnight tonight, we *shall still be driving* through the desert.

d) I *shall be waiting* for you in the park.
e) He *will be meeting* us next week.

= He is going to meet us next week (is better).

f) The meeting *will be going* on for an hour.
g) The post man *will be coming* soon to deliver the letter.

= The post man is coming soon to deliver the letter (is better).

h) How many nights *will you be staying* with us?
i) I *shall be staying* here till Sunday.

✠ **Note: A**s Future Continuous tense conveys the meaning of "duration" as well as "continuation" of an action well, many a grammarian do not find any utility to use Future Perfect Continuous Tense. However, we'll study the form with examples as well.

2) To express Interrupted Action in the Future.

a) I *shall be watching* TV when she arrives.

Explanation

✠ The interrupted action may be both in Simple Present Tense or in the Simple Future Tense (depends on sense), when the **action which will be going on for a duration** (the time of duration, may or may not be mentioned) **will be in the Future Continuous Tense.** Study more examples:

b) I *shall be reading* when you come.
c) She *will be performing* when we'll reach (or: reach) the station.
d) I *shall be waiting* for you when your bus arrives.
e) I *am going to be staying at* the Madison hotel, if anything happens you must will contact me.

3) Parallel continuous Actions may also take place in the Future time, like in other progressive tenses.

a) I *am going to be studying* and he *is going to be making* dinner.

Explanation

✠ **Two progressive actions in the same sentence** are known as Parallel Continuous Actions (may be found in Present & Past too, we had discussed already). See more examples:

b) I *shall be going* on writing, while she will enter asking of her Tiffin.
c) She *will be watching* TV, while her only son *will be studying* his lesson sitting beside her mom.
d) Tonight, they will have great fun, as they are going to be having dinner together, and discussing their future plans.
e) While Ellen is talking, Tim *will be listening* to her.

4) To narrate Atmosphere of a place in the future, as part of a plan.

✠ In English, we often use a series of parallel actions to describe the atmosphere of a place at a specific point in the future.

a) When I likely to arrive at the party, everybody **is going to be celebrating.** Some **will be dancing**. Others **are going to be talking**. A few people **will be eating** pizza, and several people **are going to be drinking** beer. They always do the same thing.

b) I *shall be waiting* near the ticket office.
c) *I'll be wearing* a green hat.
d) This time next week *you'll be relaxing* in the sun! *(Expressing hope)*
e) This time tomorrow I *shall be sitting* on the beach in Goa. *(Hope to happen or expectation about the fact)*
f) I suppose it *will be raining* when we start. *(supposition)*
g) *Will you be flying* back or going by train? *(Asking about intensions or plan)*
h) How many nights *will you be staying* with us? *(Asking about plans or intentions)*
i) "Can I see you at 5 O'clock?" = Please, don't come then. I *shall be watching* the football match on the TV. *(a future plan)*

359. **Voice Change in Future Continuous Tense:**

active	passive
a) At 8:00 p.m. tonight, John ***will be washing*** the dishes.	a) At 8:00 p.m. tonight, the dishes ***will be being washed*** by John.
b) He ***will be teaching*** us.	b) We ***will be being taught*** by him.
c) They ***will be dancing*** on the floor.	c) They ***will be being danced*** on the floor.
d) Cats ***will be mewing*** for long time.	d) Cats ***will be being mewed*** for long time.
e) The players ***will be performing*** their drama on the stage.	e) The drama ***will be being performed*** by the players on the stage.

Note: (Practically, passive voice of Future continuous and Future perfect continuous do not happen).

360.   Exercise:

✗ **Fill in the blanks in future continuous tense:**
1. He _____ (wait) for quite some time.
2. Tomorrow at this time I _____ (dance) at a party.
3. Next week at this time I _____ (sunbathe) at the beach.
4. At 5 o'clock you _____ (help) your brother.
5. This evening at 8 o'clock, she _____ (watch) a movie with her friends.
6. At three o'clock tomorrow, I_____ (work) in my office.
7. Tonight they _____ (talk), _____(dance) and _____ (have) a good time.
8. It_____ (rain) tonight.

✗ **Answers**

1. He **will be waiting** (wait) for quite some time.
2. Tomorrow at this time I **shall be dancing** (dance) at a party.
3. Next week at this time I **shall be sunbathing (**sunbathe) at the beach.
4. At 5 o'clock you **will be helping** (help) your brother.
5. This evening at 8 o'clock, she **will be watching** (watch) a movie with her friends.
6. At three o'clock tomorrow, I **shall be working (**work) in my office.
7. Tonight they **will be talking** (talk), **dancing** (dance) and **having** (have) a good time.
8. It **will be raining** (rain) tonight.

The Use of Future Perfect Tense

361.   Study the structure:

Subject Pronouns	Affirmative	Negative	Question
I, he, she, it	I shall have done.	I shall not have done.	Shall I have done?
you, we, they	You will have done.	You will not have done.	Will you have done?

362. **The Future Perfect Tense is used** to talk about something that will be completed by a certain future time; *as,*
   a) I *shall have completed* my novel *by then.*
   b) *By the end of this month*, I *shall have worked* here *for twenty years.*
   c) They*'ll have lived here for four years* in next May, 2022.
   d) She'll *have been working here for five years* in this October, 2021.

   ✖ **Note:** Between two actions in the future, for the earlier one-use Future perfect tense, and for the other, use Simple Present Tense in place of Simple Future; as,
   e) He *will have left before* you go to see him.
   f) Our teacher *will have left us before* we reach there.
   g) She *will have performed her dance before* we arrive there.

   h) The construction *will have been completed by that time.*
   i) The project *will have been done by next three months* when it will be published on Amazon.
   j) I *shall have finished* my three works *by 2023.*
   k) We *shall have reached the station by next two hours.*
   l) You *will have performed before* we come.
   m) They *will have done* the entire task *before* some more join them.
   n) The task *will have been done* by them *by that time.*
   o) You *will have been* a grown-up man *before* I return.

The Use of Future Perfect Continuous Tense

363.   Study the following charts-(1) & (2):

PRONOUNS	AFFIRMATIVE	NEGATIVE	QUESTION
I	I shall have been playing.	I shall not have been playing.	Shall I have been playing?
he, she, it	He will have been playing.	He will not have been playing.	Will he have been playing?
you, we, they	You will have been playing.	You will not have been playing.	Will you have been playing?
PRONOUNS	AFFIRMATIVE	NEGATIVE	QUESTION
I	I am going to have been playing.	I am not going to have been playing.	Am I going to have been playing?
he, she, it	He is not going to have been playing.	He is not going to have been playing.	Is he going to have been playing?
you, we, they	You are going to have been playing.	You are not going to have been playing.	Are you going to have been playing?

364.   The Future Perfect Continuous Tense is used

1) *For an action that will be going on being started at a point of certain future time.*
   Or
2) To show that **something that WILL CONTINUE up UNTIL a particular event or time in the future.**

Many a grammarian or experts in language believe that generally we don't use sentences in *Future Perfect or Future Perfect Continuous* Tense and it has no passive forms or that is not in use in the practical sense. They may be right to a distance but there should be no problem knowing its structures and how may be their passive forms too, if sentences such are available in future by some renowned writer.

   a) They *will have been talking* for over an hour by the time Monica will arrive.

- Time of duration or **duration of time**—whatever it may be—<u>is very important in any perfect continuous</u> <u>tense</u>, either it is Present Perfect Continuous or Past Perfect Continuous or the Future Perfect Continuous.

- <u>Anyway</u>, which is the right term? 'time of duration' or 'the duration of time? 'the chair of legs' or 'the legs of chair'? (**Find out yourself**)

- "**For five minutes**", "**since Friday** "and "**for two weeks**" are the durations which can be used and thus many in the Future Perfect Continuous Tense.
  b) She *is going to have been working* at that company for three years when it finally closes.
  c) How long *will you have been studying* when you graduate?

- Using the Future Perfect Continuous before another action in the Future is a good way to show cause and effect; as,

  d) Nick will be tired **when** he gets home **because** he *will have been jogging* for over an hour.

  - **Note: In** Future perfect tense, for the earlier action we have used the future perfect tense and for the latter, we have used Simple Present Tense; but in case Future Perfect Continuous Tense, for the latter we generally use Simple Future Tense (not simple present).
  - **All the more, '_when_'** is used with the clause of simple tenses, and '**_because_**' is used with the progressive clauses.

Future Continuous vs. Future Perfect Continuous

365. If you do not include duration implying words such as **"for five minutes," "for two weeks"** or **"since Friday,"** it is better to use Future Continuous rather than the Future Perfect Continuous tense for the verb.

However, be careful it may also change the meaning of the sentence too. Future Continuous emphasizes interrupted actions, whereas Future Perfect Continuous emphasizes duration of time before something in the future. Study the next slide to understand the difference.

Future Continuous	*Future Perfect Continuous*
• He will be tired because he **will be exercising** so hard, then you can defeat him easily.	• He will be tired because he **will have been exercising** so hard and then we can defeat him easily.
➤ This sentence emphasizes that he will be tired because he **will be exercising at that exact moment** in the future.	➤ This sentence emphasizes that he will be tired because he **will have been exercising for a period of time**. It is possible that he will still be exercising at that moment or that he will just have finished.

366. The Active & Passive Voice of Future Perfect Continuous:

Active	*Passive*
• The famous artist **will have been painting** the mural for over six months by the time it will be finished.	• The mural **will have been being painted** by the famous artist for over six months by the time it will be finished.
• The famous artist **is going to have been painting** the mural for over six months by the time it will be finished.	• The mural **is going to have been being painted** by the famous artist for over six months by the time it will be finished.

367. **Exercise:**

Fill in the Blanks with Future Perfect Continuous tense of Verb:
1. By midnight, you_____ (dance) for 4 hours.
2. By dinner, she_____ (cook) the whole afternoon.
3. He _____ (work) there for 10 years by 2015.
4. By next year, I _____(study) English for 7 years.
5. By next week, we _____(renovate) for over a month.
6. In 2012, they _____ (live) here for 4 years.

7. Before December, Barbara _____ (teach) for a year.
8. By this time tomorrow, I _____ (do) this exercise for a long time.
9. Jessica _____ (help) them for 12 months.
10. Bob and Sarah _____ (cook) for 2 hours at 8 o'clock.

Answers

1. By midnight, you **will have been dancing** (dance) for 4 hours.
2. By dinner, she **will have been cooking** (cook) the whole afternoon.
3. He **will have been working** (work) there for 10 years by 2015.
4. By next year, I **shall have been studying** (study) English for 7 years.
5. By next week, we **shall have been renovating** (renovate) for over a month.
6. In 2012, they **will have been living** (live) here for 4 years.
7. Before December, Barbara **will have been teaching** (teach) for a year.
8. By this time tomorrow, I **shall have been doing** (do) this exercise for a long time.
9. Jessica **will have been helping** (help) them for 12 months.
10. Bob and Sarah **will have been cooking** (cook) for 2 hours at 8 o'clock.

Don't forget
- The future tense of the verb is used to denote actions that will happen in the future.
- Future time can also be denoted by using the **be + going to** structure, and others
- **'when'** follows clause of simple structure, while **'because'** follows progressive structures in the sentences.

Let us write:
- Imagine it is a world beyond your earth and the universe. Life in solar system is past billions of years ago. How would be that world, and the inhabitants. Write a short paragraph describing life during then.
- Imagine it is 2150. What will your school be like? How will your classroom look? Write a short paragraph describing your future school and classrooms in 2150.
    You can use the following points.

Students may come in flying cars or no a school building at all; only a computer for registration— Electronic pen and pencils — Computer -operator classrooms — Interactive study sessions — Robots as teachers.

19. Contraction of Verbs with Subjects and Words of Negation

368.   Follow the charts of Verb Contractions –subjects with their helping verbs (in case of Positive or affirmative sentences) as well as the contraction of verbs with negative words, (i.e., verbs with the adverbs of Negations); as,

1. Verb- 'to Be'	2. Verb- 'to Have'	4. Modal Verbs'
Positive:	*Positive:*	*Positive:*
I am—I'm	I have—I've	I shall/will—I'll
We are/were—We're	We have—We've	We will—We'll
You are/were—You're	You have—You've	You will—You'll
He is/was—He's	He has—He's	S/He will– S/He'll
She is/was—she's	She has—She's	Who will—Who'll?
It is/was—it's	It has—It's	It will– It'll
They are/were—They're	I had—I'd	They will—They'll
Besides _____	We had—We'd	I would—I'd
That is—That's	You had—You'd	We would—We'd
What is—What's	He/she had—S/he'd	You would—You'd
Who is—Who's?	They had—They'd	He/she would—S/he'd
Where is—Where's	Besides _____	They would—They'd
Here is—Here's	That has—That's	

There is—There's What has—What's

369. **Contraction of verbs with words of negation -**

1. Verb- 'to Be'	2. Verb- 'to Have'	3. Verb- 'to Do'	4. Modal Verbs'
Negative:	*Negative:*	*Negative:*	*Negative:*
I am not—I'm not Is not—isn't Are not—aren't Was not—wasn't Were not—weren't	Has not—hasn't Have not—haven't Had not—hadn't	Do not—don't Does not—doesn't Did not—didn't	Shall not– shan't Will not—won't Would not—wouldn't Cannot—can't Could not—couldn't Should not—shouldn't Must not– mustn't

370. Study the Contractions of '**Be**' verbs with their subjects, and with adverb of negation:

Full forms	Short Forms	Negative Short Forms
Verb 'to Be' (present tense)		
I am	I'm	I'm not
He is	He's	He's not / he isn't
She is	She's	She's not / she isn't
It is	It's	It's not / it isn't
We are	We're	We're not / we aren't
You are	You're	You're not / you aren't
They are	They're	They're not / they aren't
Verb 'to Be' (past tense)		
I was	*	I wasn't
He was	*	He wasn't
She was	*	She wasn't
It was	*	It wasn't
We were	*	We weren't
You were	*(as hardly they are used)	You weren't
They were		They weren't

371. Study the Contractions of '**Have**' verbs with their subjects, and with words of negation 'not':

Full forms	Short Forms	Negative Short Forms
Verb 'to Have' (present tense)		
I have	I've	I've not / I haven't
We have	We've	We've not /we haven't
You have	You've	You've not / you haven't
They have	They've	They've not / they haven't
He has	He's	He's not / He hasn't
She has	She's	She's not / she hasn't
It has	It's	It's not / it hasn't

Verb 'to Have' (past tense)		
I had	I'd	I'd not / I hadn't
We had	We'd	We'd not / we hadn't
You had	You'd	You'd not / you hadn't
She had	She'd	She'd not / she hadn't
They had	They'd	They'd not / they hadn't

372.   Study the Contractions of '**Do' & 'Modal'** verbs with their subjects and Adverbs of negation:

Full forms	Short Forms	Negative Short Forms
Verb 'to Do' (present tense)		
I/we/you/they do He/she/it does	* (does not have positive short forms)	I/we/you/they don't He/she/It doesn't
Verb 'to Do' (past tense)		
I/We/you/he/they did	* (does not have positive short forms)	I/We/you/he/they didn't
Modals		
I / We shall	I'll / we'll	I'll/we'll not; I/we shan't;
You/he/they will	You'll / He'll, etc.	You'll not / You won't
You would	You'd	You'd not / you wouldn't
She can	*	She can't
You could	*	You couldn't
They should	*	They shouldn't
I must	*	I mustn't

20. Forming Negation

✖   Mainly by the help of Auxiliaries (**Do/Be/Have** & **Modals**) along with Adverbs that refer to Negation.

373.   **The Words that refer Negation & Affirmation:**

The Words that refer Negation & Affirmation
(2)

Words of **Negation**	Words of **Affirmation**
No, Not, Never, No longer, No more, Nothing, Not a bit, Nobody/None/ No one,	One, any, all, some, ever, always, anybody, somebody,
Nowhere, Nothing but, Scarcely, Hardly, Rarely= *15*	Everyone, someone, something, anything somewhere, anywhere = (14)

374. Forming Negation, (as per Tense)

Assertive Affirmative	Assertive Negative
1. You write. She writes. • I am a teacher. I have an idea. • I have a shirt. I love mango.	1. You *do not* write. She *does not* write. • I *am not* a teacher. I *have no* idea about this. • I *have not any* shirt. I *don't have* love for mango.
2. You are writing.	2. You are *not* writing.
3. You have written.	3. You have *not* written. *Hardly* have you written anything.
4. You have been writing.	4. You have *not* been writing
5. You wrote.	5. You *did not* write
6. You were writing.	6. You were *not* writing.
7. You had written.	7. You had *not* written.
8. You had been writing.	8. You had *not* been writing.
9. You will write.	9. You will *not* write.
10. You will be writing.	10. You will *not* be writing.
11. You will have written.	11. You will *not* have written.
12. You will have been writing.	12. You will *not* have been writing.

✖ What did we notice in the sentences above to form negation? What changes (addition or subtraction) are found there from **Assertive to Negative**?

✖ In each case, there is addition of words denoting negation in the formation of Negative Sentences. Besides, we have used verb **'To Do' (do/does)** in Simple Present & **'did'** in Simple Past Tense only.

✖ We already know there are twelve tenses in English grammar. And out of these twelve, there are **only two tenses** (Simple Present & Simple Past) **where we do use single verbs**. And that single verb may be-
  1)   Any normal or ordinary main verb; like, **'take', 'eat', 'write', 'sing'**, etc.

226

a) She **sang** a song. Tamalika **wrote** a poem.
b) You **took** photos of the madam. I **eat** cherry.
c) Tamalika **love**s to sing. John **fights** well.

2) The verb 'To Be' **(am, is, are, was or were)**, the primary auxiliaries, when they are used as the Main or Principal verb in the sentence; as,

d) I **am** Peter. She **is** Sayoni, my girlfriend.
e) You **are** a rascal. They **were** brilliant players.
f) He **was** my friend. We **were** classmates then.

3) The verb 'To Have' **(has, have, had)**, the primary auxiliaries to be used as Principal or Main verb; as,

g) Olivia **had** long hair. We **have** our own houses.
h) I **have no** hair style. She **has** her own.
i) You **have no** car; we know that well.

Note: Presently our focus is centered only with those two tenses, how to express negative sense by the sentences in Simple Present & Past.

Negation of Ordinary Main Verb
(in Simple Present & Past)

375.   The **negation of any normal main verb** in Simple Present & Past is possible by-
1) **Directly adding 'no'**, succeeding the main verb, and preceding a noun in the sentence (so, '**no**' is used as an adjective in the sentence); as,

a) I **took** *no* <u>photos</u> of the madam. (Affirmative: I took photos of the madam.)
b) I **eat** *no* <u>cherry</u>. (Affirmative: I eat cherry.)
c) She **sang** *no* <u>song</u> on that day.
d) Tamalika wrote *no* <u>poem</u>.

The underlined are the nouns in the sentences.

2) By the help of '**Do verb**' (*do, does, did*) + *not,* preceding the main verb; as,

e) I **didn't** take **any** photos. I **do not** eat cherry.
f) She **did not** sing. Tamalika **did not** write any poem.

'**No**', '**any**'—the words are not adverbs, but adjectives, used before a noun in the sentence.

3) By help of **other** *Adverbs (besides 'not')* or **by other Words of Negation** (that may be adverb, adjective or pronouns); as,

g) He ate **nothing**. He ate **not a bit** since the morning.
h) Tamalika **never** wrote a poem.
i) **No longer** have I eaten cherry. I eat cherry **no more**.
j) I love fruits, **nothing but** mangoes.
k) **Hardly** have I eaten mango. **Rarely** did she write poems. **Scarcely** had she sung a song in the party.
l) You went **nowhere**.
m) **None** came. **No body** entered the room. (Many a people entered the room)

Negation of 'Be Verb'

376.   When the primary **auxiliary 'Be Verb'** is used as **main verb** in Simple Present & Past, *its negation is possible* by the following-
1) Directly adding '**no**', succeeding the 'Be verb' in the sentence; as,

a) You are **no** my friend from this moment, understand? (Here; 'no' means 'no more'.)
b) They are **no** players, but audiences.

2) Or by adding '**not**', succeeding the 'Be verb' in the sentence; as,

c) Sorry, I am **not** Peter; that would be some other.
d) She is **not** my Shyamali. Shyamali is quite black pretty.
e) You are **not** a teacher, but a co-worker of the institution.

f) He is **not** a gentleman to be called at all. I am **not** a member of the club now.

3) By the help of other **Words of Negation** (that may be adjective, adverb or pronouns); as,
   g) He is **nothing**, his brother is the boss. I was **nothing but** servant of my brother.
   h) I am important to them? **Not a bit** at all. **No longer** are you in the project.
   i) I am **no more** in the project. You are **no more** a member of our club.
   j) He is **no more** with us. She is interested in **none of** them. **No one** is in the meeting.
   k) **Hardly** am I interested. **Rarely** is she present. **Scarcely,** they were on time.
   l) You are now of **nowhere**. **None** is here around, only you & me, face to face.
   m) **Nobody** was there; we two lovers made love under the sky.

Negation of 'Have Verb'

377. When the primary auxiliary '**Have Verb**' is used as **main verb** in Simple Present & Past, its negation is possible by the following-
1) Directly adding '**no'/'not'**, succeeding the 'Have verb' in the sentence; as,
   a) I had **no** photos then to send to your WhatsApp. She has **no** cherries to eat.
   b) I have **no** qualities; you have a lot of. Tamalika has **no** a poem to call her own.
   c) I have **no** car. I have **not any** car. You have **no** friends to call yours, I have lot of.
   d) You have **no** qualities to be my friend. You have **not** those qualities what my friend should have.
   e) The club had **no** players, to play for them. We had **no** house to call ours. Olivia had **not** short hair.

('**no**', '**any**' are used as an adjective in the sentences, and the underlined are the nouns.)

2) By the help of 'Do verb' (**do, does, did**) + **not,** preceding the verb '**to have**'; as,
   f) I **do not** have cherries to eat. She **doesn't** have **any** car.
   g) I **didn't** have **any** photos to give you.

3) By the help of other **Words of Negation** (that may be adjective, adverb or pronouns). Also notice the changes or addition of other words, if any; as,
   h) He had **nothing** to eat; now he is the richest man of our town.
   i) He has **not a bit** quality to call of a gentleman.
   j) I have fruits, **nothing but** mangoes.
   k) **No longer** have I had riches to donate you.
   l) No more I had cherries to supply to your shop.
   m) **Hardly** have I any mango.
   n) **Rarely** did she have poems to call her.
   o) **Scarcely** had she have voice to sing, but she was a singer.
   p) **Nowhere** had she have place to hide from his wrath indomitable, and happened what awaited for her fate!
   q) It has **nothing** to worry of us.
   r) **None** came. (Negation of: someone came).
   s) **Nobody** entered the room. (Many a people entered the room)

378. **What we learnt:**
* **That negation (of Simple Present Tense & Simple Past Tense) is possible by three ways:**
  1) by using '**no**' & '**not**', used after the main verbs;
  2) By using '**To Do**' helping verbs, proceeding, along with '**not**', applied to all main verbs (except- verb '**To Be**'. For, in case of verb 'To Be' which are used as Main verb, there we do not use '**To do**' verbs as helping.)
  3) By help of '**Words of Negation**' which can be used at anywhere in the sentence, at the beginning, center or at end.

* And also, we learnt that there are three kinds of verbs in Simple Present & Past which are all used as the Main or Principal verb. And they are:
  a) **Ordinary main** verbs (that may be state or event, & including 'need' & 'dare');
  b) **Be** verbs, to be used as Main, &

c) **Have** Verbs, to be used as Main.

Think

379.   Some confusions regarding using **'no'** or **'not'** with the main **'Have'** verbs are popular. Let's check what they think:

✗ **'no/not'**—is to be used at specific occasion or situation to mean negation; as, '**I have no car/I have not any car**' to mean '<u>he has no car for the moment of speaking</u>' (<u>actually he has but now he may have left it at home or with the garage, etc.</u>) &

✗ **'don't have'**—to be used with 'general, recurrent, habitual act'; as, '**I don't have any car**' to mean the <u>speaker does not possess any car at all</u>'.

These are highly confusing, for neither **'Do verb'** nor **'No/Not'** have that responsibility to bear that meaning (inherent) of the speaker, though we may use that for the same meaning, but its difference does not provide warranty for all. That means, its uses like that, if had, is now out-of-date.

➤   Remember, **'Do'** is an ordinary verb. It is also <u>a primary auxiliary</u> which are <u>used to help the main verb</u> ***mainly to form negation & question***; and sometimes, it is used before the main verb ***to emphasis a statement***. ***'I do go there myself.'***

➤ However, as **'Have' means 'to own, hold or possess something**' and that may be 'physical or abstract'.

• <u>To mean negation of qualities, attitudes or desires</u>, like 'he has no character or moral' or 'he has no high personality'— **'has or have no' can be used**; and

• <u>to mean 'physical negation'</u> like 'I don't have any car'—**don't have' can be used**. But in meaning, there is no lexical difference, both the uses mean only 'negation'.

❏ Examples
○ He has no character = He has not any character (to call him a gentleman) = He doesn't have any character.→There is no semantic difference, like the next;
○ The boss had no right to fire me. He had not any right to fire me. The boss didn't have any right to fire me.
                                     ➤   Is there any difference, if any, find out?

➤ However, we may choose, **'no'** for negation of quality, like 'character', attitudes, desires; and **'not'/ 'don't have'** for the negation of physical thing, like, car.
○ She has no moral in relationship. It has no quality. She has no patience.
○ The girl has not any money. Has he not any car?
○ I have no courage. I have not any book. I don't have any shirt.

❏ **'I don't have any book'** & **'I hardly have any book'**—both are same in meaning, can be used for some long term of the situation; and **'I have no book'** & **'I have not any book'**, we <u>may use for a time being, for the moment</u>; but, as we said, this does not secure place for all, as all negation finally bear same meaning— **'having not'** the character or thing. Finally, all are judged based on, how the words are able to bear the meaning (carry the message of the speakers) to the listeners.
○ I have no book sir; I have forgotten it at home.
○ I have not any book, I didn't buy.
○ I don't have any book; I don't need them at all.
                    —are better to use to avoid confusion, if there is any in the speaker him or herself.

380.   There is another popular illusion of using **singular nouns after 'no'**, the negative word. The fact is *both nouns, singular and plural — can be used after **'no'** adjective. Only it depends on sense.* **Remember, 'no' is also an Adverb**. It depends on the use of the word.

Note-1: * = <u>The word of negation 'no' (an adjective) can be used with both singular & plural nouns following it</u>. '*Interjection has **almost no** Phrases*'; it *means it has 'few'* or '*some phrases though*'. It does not hint 'zero'.
Note-2: 'no' is also an adverb of negation. No need to get confused it always to be 'an adjective'. For, often, it may not describe a noun or a pronoun, like an adjective does; but it is also an adverb adds meaning to the

verb 'have' or 'possess' or 'be'; having or possessing (or being at somewhere) 'nothing' or 'few'. [**Almost no = few; but not 'zero'.**]

❏ **Read the Examples**

a) They run. = They **do not** run.
b) He reads a book. = He **does not** read a book.
c) She talked. = She **did not** talk.
d) I am giving = I **am not** giving exam this year.
e) He is going. = He **is not** going there.
f) We are going. = We **are not** going.
g) Keats was a poet. = He **was not** an essayist.
h) They were sailors. = They **were not** sailors.
i) There is **no end** to our sufferings.
j) I have a bi-cycle. = I have **no bi-cycle**.
k) We shall visit. = We shall **not visit**.
l) You can do it now. = You **cannot do** it now.

'No' with 'don't' make a negative sense stronger.

381.   In answers (with **'No' & 'don't**) to any question, the negative sense is made some stronger; like,

→ Do you sing? = _No, I don't_ sing.
→ Do you have any car? = _No, I don't_ have.
→ Do you love me? = _No, I don't_ love you.
→ Do you like bear? = _No, I don't_ like.
→ Did you take my book? = _No, I didn't_.
→ Do they hurt you? = _No, they don't_. They are my friends.

➢ And the same like are—

➢ Is she your sister? =_No_, she _is not_. (_She is my girl-friend_)

382.   **Forming Negation by opposite words:**
✗ Sometimes, to keep intact of the meaning of the sentence, we use **negative words + opposite of verbs, adverbs, adjectives or pronouns**, and also sometimes by breaking the meaning of a phrase (_no people/no one=none_); as,

(_Generally, in simple present, past or perfect tenses_)

(1) I **always** remember you. = I **never** forget you.
(2) I want **everything**. = I decline **nothing**.
(3) There were no people. = There was **none**.
(4) It will be distributed to **no one**. = **none**.
(5) God is **everywhere**. = **No one** can say God is **nowhere**. /**None** can say God is **not anywhere**.
(6) I like my friend **very much**. = I **hardly** dislike my friend.
(7) He **no longer** writes to me. = He **never** writes _after that_.
(8) I am **no more** interested in politics. I have **hardly any** interest in politics **any far**.
(9) He _lives **no more**_. = He **ceases to exist**. / He **expires**.

21. Types of Questions & their Formation

383.   Questions are mainly two types- **Direct** & **Indirect**.

✗ **Direct Questions** are again two kinds- **Yes-no Type** & **Wh-Type**; and they together (the Direct Questions) include the following variations:

a) Normal Yes-no type & Wh- type Questions,
b) Alternative Questions,
c) Tag Questions,
d) Rhetorical Questions &
e) Short Questions.

✗ **Now, study in detail the division of Questions:**

Direct Questions (Normal—Alternate—Tag—Rhetorical—Short)

✗ Study the following chart:

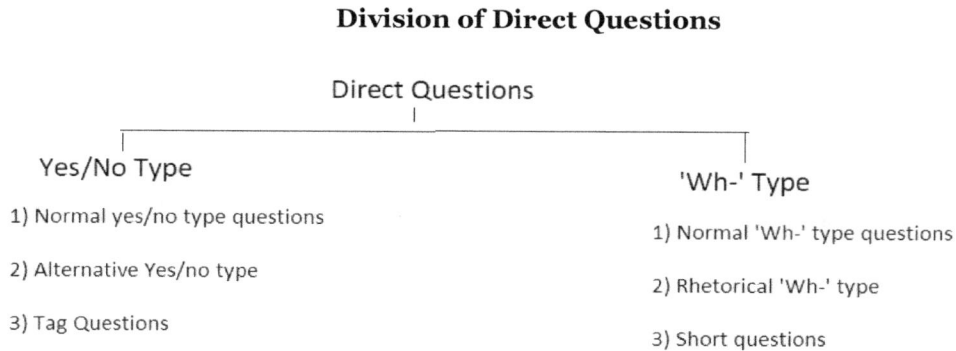

Division of Direct Questions

```
                    Direct Questions
        ┌──────────────────┴──────────────────┐
   Yes/No Type                             'Wh-' Type
```

Yes/No Type

1) Normal yes/no type questions

2) Alternative Yes/no type

3) Tag Questions

'Wh-' Type

1) Normal 'Wh-' type questions

2) Rhetorical 'Wh-' type

3) Short questions

➢ The division of Direct Questions (**Yes-No type** and **Wh- type**) has three more sub-divisions, each; and they are like:
→ **Normal yes-no type**, **Alternative** & **Tag** (division of Yes-no type Questions);
→ **Normal Wh- type**, **Rhetorical** & **Short** Questions (division of Wh- type questions, as shown in the above chart).

1) **Yes-no type questions:**

Yes-no type questions

Normal yes-no type question	• Do you like tea? • Is he your brother? Are you a student? • Have you a car?
Alternative question, using 'or'	• Is this a pen or a pencil? • Do you like it or not? • Have you eaten or not?
Tag Questions, at the end of a statement	• Neil didn't do his work, did he? • You have a bike, haven't you? • She is not there, is she?

- **Do** you care me?
- **Does** she sing folk-songs?
- **Did** I feel anything possessive for her?
- **Did** he stand up seeing his teacher come?
- **Am** I a stupid? Are you a fool? Are they men?
- **Had** Zara love for me?
- **Haven't** you any common sense to ask such questions before the public?
- **Can** you do this work? **May** I help you?
- **Will** you go there? **Should** we do this?

Note: Answers of all above questions come with '**yes**' or '**no**'; so why, they are called so; as,

- **Do you love me? = No, I don't love you**. Instead, I hate you, as you are too beautiful, intelligent and score better marks always than me. (I feel jealousy of you.)
- **Do you like coffee? =Yes, sometimes** I like to have that. However, I like cold tea.

2) **Alternative question**, using **'or'**:
- Were they common public **or** criminals? **(No,** they were not common public; they were criminals**.)**
- Do you love me **or** hate? **(Yes,** I love you. / **No,** I don't hate you. I love you more than me.)
- Have you any bicycle **or** not?
- Have you a bike **or** a motor car?
- Am I a man **or** superman?
- Is he a hero **or** a zero?
- Can you do this **or** not?
- Will we study **or** recite this poem of our favorite Keats?
- Is Shakespeare **or** Kalidas superior?
- Is Peter **or** Paramananda author of this book?

3) **Tag Questions:** the questions that set at the end of a statement; as,
- I saw their conversions, *did I*?
- They were dating, *were they*?
- You have started avoiding me, *haven't you*?
- Your father will disown you, *will he*?
- I will do the work, *will I*?
- You will do the project, *will you*?
- My mother said something, *did she*?
- You met her last night at her bedroom, *didn't you*?
- Yu brought a Kashmiri shawl, *didn't you*?

Note: All the above type of questions (**alternative** or **tag**) are the variations rather than division of **Yes-no type Questions**, and thus also happen to others in the group of **Wh- Questions**. Study them in utmost attention. Actually, hardly there is any major difference.

4) **'Wh' questions:**

'Wh' questions

Normal 'Wh' questions
- Who are you? Whom do you love?
- Whose pen is this? What does he want?
- Which is your book? Why did he go there? When will he return?
- Where are you coming from? How is your health?

Rhetorical questions
- Some forceful statements, since they are in question form, they are called rhetorical questions.
- Who can predict the future? (No one can)
- Who will do this heinous act? (No one will)

Short Questions
- To draw attention of the listeners/learners or to know more or to give focus on the part of preceding statement, short questions are made.
- The boy is reading a novel to know the story. Who? Why? What?

✗ How 'Wh-' words are used:

Wh words	Pronouns	Adjectives	Adverbs	Applied to/ to know
1) Who	✓ Yes			Person only

2) Whom	Yes			Persons only
3) Whose	Yes	Yes		Person & things
4) What	Yes	Yes		Things & profession
5) Which	Yes	Yes		Person & things
6) Why			Yes	For what reason
7) When			Yes	At what time
8) Where			Yes	To what place/position or direction
9) How			Yes	In what way

✗ More examples of 'Wh- Questions'-Normal:
- Who is Peter? What is he?
- What did your father say about the book, 'Peter's Complete English Grammar'?
- Who is the white man in white dress in the corner?
- Whose house is this, White Home in West Bengal?
- Why did she go there? What was the reason?
- Where did she go in the last evening?
- Why will I stop? What is she singing?
- When will you stop this Zara business?
- What can I do for you?
- When do you take bath in the morning?

5) **More examples of Rhetorical Questions (wh):**
- Who can say that she will cheat like this? (None can)
- Who will do this heinous murder? (None will)
- Who will give you these all at free of cost? (None)
- Who will give you such a large amount of loan without security or bond? (No company or bank)
- Who will believe you to go on with your proposal?
- Who will be your father to face the tough Principal?
- Who will be your partner in such your heinous plan?
- Who want to be your friend to get disgrace at every moment?
- What the cause may be to do this heinous act?
- What the foremost cause may be behind his going there that he couldn't wait for us?

6) **More examples of Short Questions (wh):**

Short Questions are made using generally **by one** or **two words**.

a) The boy is reading the novel to know the story.
- Someone is reading the novel ...., **who**?
- The boy is reading..., **what**?
- The boy is reading the novel ..., **why**?

b) He has bought a dictionary book at book fair to know meanings.
- Someone has bought a dictionary...., **who**?
- He has bought..., **what**?
- He has bought a book, **which one**?
- He has bought a dictionary..., **why**?
- He has bought a dictionary..., **when**?
- He has bought a dictionary..., **where**?

Indirect questions:

7) Indirect questions:

When 'Wh-' questions are asked indirectly, they are called as **Indirect Questions**.

▪ It is a type of <u>question made **without any question mark (?)**</u> in the sentence.

▪ Indirect questions do not need **'do'**, **'does'** or **'did'**; as,

→ He stopped there and thought **what my name is**.

→ **What my name is**, he thought and stopped.

→ **Who I am**, he went on thinking... and there reached a white bear.

→ **What you want**, you didn't tell me then nor now.

→ **What I want**, I can't find out and float in the aimless current unending.

→ **Why he did**, he did not know, but he carried on counting one after one.

→ **Where the treasure was**, none knew but jumped in the mission to dig the whole land out.

→ None knew, **how to solve** and they began fighting over the trifling matter.

✘ **The normal 'Yes-no type' & 'Wh- type Questions'** are normally asked questions made by people, while others (the variations) are used on special purposes & in needs in communication or in learning. So why, they are **special** in kind or uses, and occasional.

Formation of Questions

384. **Forming Questions (normal) as per Tense:**

Assertive	Interrogative
1. You write. She writes. I am a teacher. I have an idea. I have a shirt. I love mango.	1. ***Do you*** write? ***Does she*** write? ***Are you*** a teacher? ***Have you*** any idea? ***Have you*** any shirt? ***Do you*** like mango?
2. You are writing.	2. *Are you* writing?
3. You have written.	3. *Have you* written?
4. You have been writing.	4. *Have you* been writing?
5. You wrote.	5. ***Did you*** write?
6. You were writing.	6. *Were you* writing?
7. You had written.	7. *Had you* written?
8. You had been writing.	8. *Had you been* writing?
9. You will write.	9. *Will you* write?
10. You will be writing.	10. Will you *be* writing?
11. You will have written.	11. *Will you have* written?
12. You will have been writing.	12. *Will you have been* writing?

✘ *What **did you** notice in the sentences to form questions?*

✘ *What changes are found there from **Assertive** to **Interrogative** sentences?*

1) Use of *'do/does'*– at the beginning of sentence, before the subject of the verb in Simple Present Tense, where there is only main verb (single-verb tense);

2) Use of only *'did'*– at the beginning of sentence, i.e., before the subject of the verb in Simple Past Tense (single-verb tense);

3) And for the remaining ten Tenses, ***there is only*** <u>conversion of position of the first auxiliary verb</u> **& <u>the subject</u>**. The 1st auxiliary is used at the beginning of the sentence, and then comes the subject.

✘ ***And this happens with most of the verbs*** in forming Normal Questions-Yes-no type & Wh-type. **In 'Wh-'** the wh-word comes at the beginning of the sentence as an extra word, and then to use 'do/does' & 'did' as per tense, simple present or simple past.

385. **Forming Negation of Questions:**

Interrogative Affirmative	*Interrogative Negative*
1. *Do* you write? *Does* she write? *Are* you a teacher? *Have* you any idea? *Has* she an extra shirt?	1. ***Do*** you ***not*** write? ***Does*** she ***not*** write? ***Aren't*** you a teacher? ***Haven't*** you any idea? ***Has*** she ***not*** an extra shirt?
2. Are you writing?	2. Are you ***not*** writing?
3. Have you written?	3. Have you ***not*** written?
4. Have you been writing?	4. Have you ***not*** been writing?
5. *Did* you write?	5. ***Did*** you ***not*** write?
6. Were you writing?	6. Were you ***not*** writing?
7. Had you written?	7. Had you ***not*** written?
8. Had you been writing?	8. Had you ***not*** been writing?
9. Will you write?	9. Will you ***not*** write?
10. Will you be writing?	10. Will you ***not*** be writing?
11. Will you have written?	11. Will you ***not*** have written?
12. Will you have been writing?	12. Will you ***not*** have been writing?

- *What did we notice in the sentences to form negative questions?*
- *What changes are found there from **Interrogative affirmative** to **Interrogative negative**?*

➢ From the first to last there is only one change and that is the ***use of 'not' after the '1st auxiliary** & **subject***. And thus, it's structure is like the following:

1) 1st auxiliary verb+ subject+ **'not'** & others as they are in the sentences.

Or

2) Contraction of ***1st auxiliary & 'not'***+ subject+ & others as they are in the sentences.

386. Read now the **questions in contraction** in the following chart:

Normal Negation of Questions	Contraction of Negation
1. ***Do*** you ***not*** write? ***Does*** she ***not*** write?	1. ***Don't*** you write? ***Doesn't*** she write?
2. Are you *not* writing?	2. *Aren't* you writing?
3. Have you *not* written?	3. *Haven't* you written?
4. Have you *not* been writing?	4. *Haven't* you been writing?
5. *Did* you *not* write?	5. *Didn't* you write?
6. Were you *not* writing?	6. *Weren't* you writing?
7. Had you *not* written?	7. *Hadn't* you written?
8. Had you *not* been writing?	8. *Hadn't* you been writing?
9. Will you *not* write?	9. *Won't* you write?
10. Will you *not* be writing?	10. *Won't* you be writing?
11. Will you *not* have written?	11. *Won't* you have written?
12. Will you *not* have been writing?	12. *Won't* you have been writing?

387. Study the **contraction forms**:

Verbs + Adverb of Negation	Negative Contraction
Do not /does not/did not	don't /doesn't/ didn't

Am not	* (not available)
Is not	Isn't
Are not	Aren't
Has not	Hasn't
Have not	Haven't
Was not	Wasn't
Were not	Weren't
Had not	Hadn't
Will not/shall not	Won't / shan't

388. '***How to form Questions***', already we discussed. However, study the following chart as a revision:

1) By use of 'Do' verb: (Do/Does/Did+ Sub.+ Main Verb+ Obj.+ Others)	Rita sang a sweet song. = **Did** Rita sing a song? He reads a novel. = **Does** he read any? I apologize to you. = **Do** you apologize?
2) By use of other Primary & Modal Auxiliaries: (P. Aux./Modals+ Sub.+ Main Verb+ Obj.+ Others)	I am reading a book. = **Are** you reading? She has done her task. =**Has** she done her task? You will be there? = **Will** you be? You may come in.= **May** I come in, sir? I can do the work. =**Can** you do the work?
3) In case of 'Wh' questions: ('Wh' word+ Aux. +Sub.+ Main Verb+ Obj.+ Others) Note: Use the 'wh' word before the 1st auxiliary.	I went to Kolkata. = **Where did** you go? I am eating rice. = **What are** you eating? I have a car. = **What do** you have? He had gone there to meet her. = **Why had** he gone there?

22. The Voice: Active & Passive

(To show *'subject'*, *active* or *passive* by the forms of Verbs)

389.   What is 'Voice'?

Voice literally means '***type to speak or to express your opinion***', showing subject prominently (**active voice**); *or* show it inactive or understood in the sentence, when action or receiver becomes 'prominent' (**passive voice**).

390.   The chapter of 'Voice' is about the study of forms of verbs to show subject '**Active**' (when 'doer' does something) or '**Passive**' (when 'doer' becomes inactive, & action becomes prominent with the receiver ones).

Thus, the Voice of the verbs are of two kinds:
1.   **Active Voice:** when subject does an action.
2.   **Passive Voice:** when subject receives the action.

Compare:

• Sheila **sings** a song.
• A song **is sung** by Sheila.

Both the sentences express same meaning.

✗   But, in sentence-1, the verb-form '**sings** 'shows **the doer** who does **the action** as the subject of the

236

sentence. In the sentence **the subject** (which is 'Sheila') **is prominent** and is **set before the verb-form; &**

✶ In sentence 2, the verb form **'is sung'** shows the thing (the thing **acted upon** [or the person, to whom something happens]) **which, here it is, 'a song'** active & is used at the place of a subject (before a finite verb), and the actual subject, which is **'Sheila'** becomes 'inactive' or 'passive', not prominent in the sentence and is used after the passive verb form and a preposition.

In passive voice, subject & object change their position or place in the sentence. An object, generally, comes before the verb, and the actual subject is used after the finite verb and a preposition.

However, when there is no object in the active voice, subject retains its position, to be used at the beginning, as it is in the active voice.

In passive, *the receiver of an action* as well as *the action itself becomes prominent* by the verb form, when the 'doer', subject of Active Voice becomes inactive, and often omitted.
Read the examples:

Liton hits. Liton knocks down. Liton kills.

In each, Liton is the doer; he does all the actions, mentioned above. He is active in all the sentences. Now, **if we turn the 'doer' into 'receiver' of actions, and we write:**

Liton is hit. Liton is knocked down. Liton is killed.

In each, Liton is the receiver but not the doer; he receives all the actions, done upon him (by someone) it means. So why, change of the position of the subject is very necessary in the passive voice along with passive verb forms, if the meaning is to kept intact. **Where there is no object, generally, the verbs are not used in passive forms**. The verbs having objects (Transitive Verbs) are used in passive forms, but the verbs, not having any object (Intransitive verbs) are not used in the passive verb forms.

In the above all sentences (**of second line**), Liton turns to a victim of all the actions, acted upon him by someone. He does not moreover remain the doers, as he was in the series of first line sentences.

But if we write the sentences again in the following way:

Liton hits the ball. Liton knocks down Kamal. Liton kills a mosquito.
And if we turn them into Passive:
The ball is hit by Liton. Kamal is knocked down by Liton. A mosquito is killed by Liton.

The subject 'Liton' remains same, as the doer of all actions, only its position has been changed, and the action comes prominent, and the inactive doers comes at last, to be used after a preposition.
In the succeeding two series, the meaning of the sentences remains intact and same.

The purpose of the 'Voice Change' is never to change the meaning of a sentence, but to show 'subject' active or 'passive' by the verb forms.

391.   Rules of Voice Change from Active to Passive:

Rule No-1:
1) **The object of the Transitive Verb** in the Active Voice **takes the place of the subject** (not becomes the subject) in the passive voice; the inactive subject is used after the verb and a preposition (generally after 'by' or 'to'; and often after 'at', 'with', etc); as,
→ The boy hit a ball.
→ A ball was hit by the boy.
→ Peter teaches us grammar.
→ We are taught grammar by Peter.

- **To keep the meaning of the sentence intact, exchange of the place or position of subject & object (doer & receiver) in the passive voice is very important.** In Passive, **'receiver'** comes first (generally) before the verb [as it seems to be the subject] and **'doer'** is set after the verb preceding a preposition [as it seems to be the object to the verb].
  - If we don't do that, the **following difference of meaning** will happen.

a) **I kill a rat.** ('I' is the subject, the doer of the action, and here 'I' is the 'killer who kills, here 'rat'; and 'a rat' is an object who receives the action and 'a victim' of the action in the sentence.) Now, read the next:

b) **I am killed by a rat.** (Here, the 'rat' becomes killer; and 'I' becomes a victim. The meaning has been changed from the earlier. But this is **not the goal** of doing Passive of the verb.)

Note: We do give passive form of the verb to make the action prominent along with its object, not to change the meaning.

So, the proper passive form of the verb will be like in the following conjugation of verb with the object; & subject to be used after the verb and a preposition:

a) **I kill a rat.**

b) **A rat is killed by me.** (by exchange place of the subject and object in the sentence.)

- **Thus we see, exchange of the position of subject & object (doer & receiver) in the passive voice is very important** along with <u>**the passive form of the verb**</u>.

- As Object is very necessary, and it takes an important role in the passive voice, **voice change only happens to a Transitive Verb**, not with an Intransitive; however, there are <u>**few exceptions;**</u> we'll discuss soon.

Rule No-2:

2) <u>At least one 'To Be' verb form is must to be added</u> in the Passive Voice. (Along with already it had a 'To Be' verb form in the Active Voice); as,

- **'am', 'is'** & **'are'**– either one is to be used in Simple Present Tense, according to the subject-verb agreement, [where the object takes place of the subject in passive form];
- **was, were** – either one is to be added in Simple Past Tense;
- **'be'** along with modal verbs **'shall'** or **'will'** (like **'shall be'** or **'will be'**)-- either one is to be used in Simple Future Tense;
- **'being'**–the Be Verb form is to be used in all Progressive tenses along with other verbs which already it had in the active voice; &
- **'been'**— the Be Verb form is to be used in all Perfect Tenses in the passive voice—along with other helping verbs it had from the Active Voice.

Rule No-3:

3) 3rd form, i.e., <u>past participle form of the main verb must to be used</u> in all passive voices after the 'Be' verb form; as,

He was **made** our captain. (We **make** him our captain.)

RuleNo-4:

4) Prepositions — **by, at, with** or **to,** etc. <u>either one is to be used according to the sense before the passive or inactive subject</u> in the Passive Voice.

- **'by'** is used with both animal or thing, ('by whom' or 'what' a thing or an action happens); but when there are two agents, one is animal & another is thing, we use **'by'** with the animate agent, and for instrument we use **'with'** before the inactive or passive subject; as,
  - → A cruel boy hit the dog.
  - → The dog was hit **by** a cruel boy.
- But **when it is an instrument**, we use **'with'**; as, the passive forms are: -
  - → 'A cruel boy hit the dog with a stick.',
  - → The dog was hit **with** a stick.
  - → The dog was hit by a cruel boy **with** a stick.

- Thus, other prepositions are also used with or without 'by' in the passive, based on sense of the verb; as,
  - → We listen to the professor in the seminar.
  - → The professor is being listened **to** in the seminar.

→ His own friends laugh at him.
→ He is laughed *at* by his own friends.

392. For Voice-Change another thing is very important that is the **tense of verbs**. In the following charts, you will study the 'Structure' of different tenses. Study them carefully. Except knowledge of tense, voice-change is hardly possible.

(Here: v1=present form; v2=past form; v3=past participle form of the verb)

Twelve Tenses of Verbs	Their Structures
1. Present Indefinite/ Simple Present	Subject + **Verb-1** + Object & Others
2. Present Continuous	Subject + **am/is/are+ Verb-ing** + Object & Others
3. Present Perfect	Subject + **has/have+ Verb-3** + Object & Others
4. Present Perfect Continuous	Subject +**has/have + been + Verb-ing** + Ob. & Others.
5. Past Indefinite/ Simple Past	Subject + Verb-2 + Object & Others
6. Past Continuous	Subject + was/were+ Verb-ing + Object & Others
7. Past Perfect	Subject + had+ Verb-3 + Object & Others
8. Past Perfect Continuous	Subject + had + been + Verb-ing + Obj. & Others.
9. Future Indefinite/ Simple Future	Subject + shall/**will+ Verb-1** + Object & Others
10. Future Continuous	Subject +**shall be/will be+ Verb-ing** + Obj & Others.
11. Future Perfect	Subject + **shall have/will have+ Verb-3** + Ob & Others
12. Future Perfect Continuous	Sub. + **shall /will + have + been +Verb-ing** + Obj. & Others.

✗ **Now, study the passive forms of the above tenses comparatively:**

1. Passive Forms of Verbs- Indefinite

Tense & Voice of Verbs	Rules
1. Simple Present	Subject + Verb-1 + Object & Others
Passive form	Object becomes Subject + is/am/are+ verb-3+ prep (by)+ subject becomes object+ others.
Example:	I read a novel = The novel is read by me.
5. Simple Past	Subject + Verb-2 + Object & Others
Passive form	Object becomes Subject + was/were+ verb-3+ prep (by)+ subject becomes object+ others.
Example:	I read a novel = The novel was read by me.
9. Simple Future	Subject + shall/will+ Verb-1 + Object & Others
Passive form	Object becomes Subject + shall/will + be + verb-3+ prep (by)+ subject becomes object+ others.

Example:	I shall read a novel = The novel will be read by me.

2. Passive Forms of Continuous Tenses

Tense & Voice of Verbs	Rules	
2. Present Continuous	Subject + is/am/are+ Verb-ing + Object & Others	
Passive form	Object becomes Subject + is/am/are+ <u>being</u> +verb-3+ prep (by)+ subject becomes object+ others.	
Example:	I am reading a novel = The novel is being read by me.	
6. Past Continuous	Subject + was/were+ Verb-ing + Object & Others	
Passive form	Object becomes Subject + was/were+ <u>being</u> + verb-3+ prep (by)+ subject becomes object+ others.	
Example:	I was reading a novel = The novel was being read by me.	
10. Future Continuous	Subject +shall be/will be+ Verb-ing + Obj & Others.	
Passive form	Object becomes Subject + shall be /will be+ <u>being</u> + verb-3+ prep (by)+ subject becomes object+ others.	
Example:	I shall be reading a novel = The novel will be being read by me.	

3. Passive Forms of Perfect Tenses

Tense & Voice of Verbs	Rules	
3. Present Perfect	Subject + has/have+ Verb-3 + Object & Others	
Passive form	Object becomes Subject + has/have+ <u>been</u> +verb-3+ prep (by)+ subject becomes object+ others.	
Example:	I have a read a novel = The novel has been read by me.	
7. Past Perfect	Subject + had+ Verb-3 + Object & Others	
Passive form	Object becomes Subject + had+ <u>been</u> + verb-3+ prep (by)+ subject becomes object+ others.	
Example:	I had read a novel = The novel had been read by me.	
11. Future Perfect	Subject + shall have/will have+ Verb-3 + Ob & Others	
Passive form	Object becomes Subject + shall have/will have + <u>been</u>+ verb-3+ prep (by)+ subject becomes object+ others.	
Example:	I shall have read a novel = The novel will have been read by me.	

4. Passive Forms of Perfect Continuous

Tense & Voice of Verbs	Rules	
4. Present Perfect Continuous	Subject +has/have + been + Verb-ing + Ob. & Oth.	

Passive form	Object becomes Subject + has/have+ <u>been + being</u> +verb-3+ prep (by)+ subject becomes object+ others.
Example:	I have been reading a novel = The novel has been being read by me.
8. Past Perfect Continuous	Subject + had + been + Verb-ing + Obj. & Others.
Passive form	Object becomes Subject + had+ <u>been + being</u> + verb-3+ prep (by)+ subject becomes object+ others.
Example:	I had been reading a novel = The novel had been being read by me.
12. Future Perfect Continuous	Sub + shall have/will have + been +Verb-ing + Ob. & Oth.
Passive form	Object becomes Subject + shall have/will have + <u>been + being</u> + verb-3+ prep (by)+ subject becomes object+ others.
Example:	I shall have been reading a novel = The novel will have been being read by me.

464.   Carefully study the **addition** in Passive Voices, as per three main Tenses.

A.   First, the addition in **Present Tenses**:

Tense		Active	Passive
Present Tense	Indefinite	Write/writes	***Am/is/are*** written
	Continuous	Am/is/are writing	Is/are ***being*** written
	Perfect	Has/have written	Has/have ***been*** written
	Perfect Continuous	Has/have been written	Has/have been ***being*** written

B.   Second, the addition in **Past Tenses**:

Tense		Active	Passive
Past Tense	Indefinite	Wrote	***Was/were*** written
	Continuous	Was/were writing	Was/were ***being*** written
	Perfect	Had written	Had ***been*** written
	Perfect Continuous	Had been written	had been ***being*** written

C.   Third, the addition in **Future Tenses**:

Tense		Active	Passive
Future Tense	Indefinite	Shall/will write	Shall/will ***be*** written
	Continuous	Shall/will be writing	Shall/will be ***being*** written
	Perfect	Shall/will have written	Shall/will have ***been*** written

	Perfect Continuous	Shall/will have been written	Shall/will have been **being** written

Notes

- Though, the passive form of 'Future Perfect Continuous Tenses' are discussed or shown in the last table, practically **passive of Perfect Continuous** does not really happen or we **hardly use** them.
  - Moreover, it doesn't need actually to convert every sentence or tense into passive.

- **Active & Passive has some distinct uses.** Some verbs are best to be expressed in Active; & some only in Passive.
- We can change the form, but we need to know **'their uses'** too, which is very important.

The Use of Active & Passive Voice

393.   The Active Voice is used **when the agent** *(doer of an action, i.e., subject of the verb) is to be made prominent*; as,

a)   **I am reading** the book loudly.

1)   The Passive Voice is used **when the receiver** *of an action is made prominent* rather than the doer or subject of the verb; as,
   a)   **Everyone is asked to present** at the meeting hall. (**Who** gives the order or asks everyone to present— has been omitted; as it is regarded not so important to mention, but important is 'everyone's presence' in the meeting hall; if you feel it is important, add— 'by the president/boss/chairman', etc.)

2)   The **passive voice is preferred where the subject is indefinite,** or **is made of vogue pronouns like,** someone, everyone, one, some, they, people, we, etc. i.e., when we **don't know or need not to know** of the subject; but the action or receiver of the action; or when **doer is clear enough**; no need to mention at all; as,
   b)   **My pen has been stolen.** ('**Somebody** has stolen my pen.') [who stole—is not important; might be 'Somebody' or 'One' or 'A thief']

   c)   **I was asked my name.** (**They** asked me my name.) [who asked—was not necessary to mention; and thus-]

   d)   **I have been invited to the party.** [here, 'someone' is the 'host' of the party is known to all, so, no need to mention at all. (**Someone** has invited me to the party.)]

   e)   **All orders will be executed promptly.** (**We** will execute all orders promptly.)

- In all the above cases, **the doers** or **subjects were less important** to mention than the action or receivers of the actions, so sometimes they are kept understood in the sentences.

3)   The passive voice is used in **situations of Social** or **Historical Significance,** where the event, discovery, or the matter is more important than the agent; as,
   f)   English **is spoken** all over the world. (People speak English all over the world.)
   g)   America **was discovered** by Columbus.
   h)   The caste system **is carried** on by the Indians till today.
   i)   Devi Durga **is worshipped** as the destroyer of all ill powers in the Universe.

4)   In **Invitations, requests** and **announcements,** the passive voice is used; as,
   j)   Passengers **are requested** not to smoke in the bus.
   k)   Trespassers **are prohibited**.
   l)   Bachelors **are not allowed** in the party.

5)   The *passive voice is also used to describe the mechanical* or *mathematical process, in giving scientific descriptions* & in *explanation* or *giving definition*; as,
   m)   In an internal-combustion engine the mixture of air & petrol **is compressed** in the cylinder by a piston.
   n)   Two and two **are made** four.

o) The lion **is called** the king of beast.

6) In _reporting a statement_ or **in newspaper report,** the passive voice is widely used; as,
p) Mumbai **was lashed** by a thunder shower last night.
q) Ten people, including two women **were died** in the accident.
r) The injured **were taken** to the hospital.

Passive forms of Modals & Questions

394. **Study the chart of passive verb forms with Modals.** [**Passive form:** Modal + be + Past Participle of Main Verb.]

Active	Passive
He **can do** the work.	The work **can be done** by him.
We **may help** her.	She **may be helped** by us.
You **must take** this medicine in due time.	This medicine **must be taken** in due time.
The boy **should read** the book.	The book **should be read** by the boy.
He **might take** your help.	Your help **might be taken** by him.
We **should guide** our children properly.	Our children **should be guided** properly.
They **could do** it by themselves.	It **could be done** by them themselves.
Would you **help** me?	**Would** I **be helped** by you?

The passive forms of Questions

395. **Study the chart of passive verb forms in Interrogative.** [Note the changes or addition of 'Be verb' forms along with past participle form of the main verb.]

Active	Passive
Do you know him?	**Is** he **known to** you?
Does he want this?	**Is** this **wanted** by him?
Did he take tea?	**Was** tea **taken** by him?
Was he reading the book?	**Was** the book **being read** by him?
Have you done the task?	**Has** the task **been done** by you?
Where did you see him?	Where **was** he **seen** (by you)?
Who will do the work?	By whom **will** the work **be done**?
What will they do?	What **will be done** by them?
Why have you bought this?	Why **has** this **been bought** (by you)?

✘ **Now, read the instructions carefully.** If, it is a question, 'yes/no' type or 'wh-' type, simply follow the steps:

Step—1: Convert the question into assertive (take out 'wh-' or any helping verb, like— 'do/does/did, if any);
Step—2: Change the sentence now into passive;
Step—3: Now, convert the passive assertive sentence again into a new Question with the 'wh.' word and a helping

verb after it; as, **'do/does/did'**, or any other. Study the examples:

- <u>**Do you know him?**</u> > You **know** him. > He **is known** to you. > <u>**Is he known to you?**</u>
- <u>**Why did she love you?**</u> > She **loved** you. > You **were loved** by her. >Were you loved by her? ><u>**Why were you loved by her?**</u>
- <u>**Is she singing a song?**</u> >She **is singing** a song. > A song **is being sung** by her. > **Is a song being sung by her?**

This is only for the benefits of the beginners. You can skip the steps anytime when you get the mastery over voice change and tense.

<u>The use of Preposition 'by' & other than 'by'</u>

396.   Inactive or Passive Subject in the Passive Voice generally takes preposition **'by'** before it, but sometimes, it takes others too, like **'at'**, **'with'**, **'to'** etc., while verb with a preposition forms a **phrasal verb**. Study the chart:

Active	Passive	
His conduct _annoyed_ me.	I **was _annoyed at_** his conduct.	
This news will _please_ you.	You **will be _pleased with_** the news.	
His behavior _charmed_ us.	We **are _charmed at_** his behavior.	
Smoke _filled_ the room.	The room **is _filled in_**/with smoke.	
I _know_ him.	He **is _known to_** me.	
His result _surprised_ me.	I **am _surprised at_** his result.	
He _promised_ me a present.	I **was _promised to_** have a present.	
Her manners _displeased_ me.	I **was _displeased with_** her manners.	

✘   In the voice change of the **group verbs** (the verbs with a preposition, used at its end) retains in the passive voice (in the passive verb forms) with or without preposition 'by'. Study the examples:

Active	Passive	
They _laugh at_ us.	We **are _laughed at_ by** them.	
He _dispensed with_ my services.	My services **were _dispensed with_ by** him.	
He _agrees with_ me.	I **am _agreed with_** him.	
The audience _cheered up_ the players.	The players **were _cheered up_ by** the audience.	
The storm _blew down_ the house.	The house **was _blown down_**.	
He _overcame with_ difficulties.	Difficulties **were _overcome with_ by** him.	
The dog _jumped over_ the fence.	The fence **was _jumped over_ by** the dog.	

Passive Voice of Verbs with Two Objects

397.   There are lots Transitive Verbs which take double objects and often more than two. The object(s) between two or more, which is or are left (which retain{s}) in the Passive Voice, is called **'Retained Object'**. (R.O. is either D.O. or I.O. by its role or importance in the active voice). Study the following chart:

Active	Passive

He gave <u>me a book</u>.	○ I was given *a book* by him. ○ A book was given *me* by him.
The institution refused him, to say <u>his admission</u>.	○ He was refused *admission* in the Institution.
Peter sir teaches <u>us, English Grammar</u>.	○ We are taught *English Grammar* by Peter sir. ○ English Grammar is taught *us* by Peter sir.
My elder brother gifted <u>me, a wrist watch</u>.	○ A wrist watch was gifted *me* by my elder brother. ○ I was gifted *a wrist watch* by my elder brother.
Who taught <u>you French</u>?	○ By who were you taught *French*? ○

Passive Voice of Intransitive Verbs

398.   Generally, an Intransitive verb does not take any object<u>, but when it is used transitively</u> by the way taking a **Cognate Object** (*that is akin or similar in meaning to the verb*), and when an Intransitive verb <u>causes a thing to be done</u> (*that denotes causing something to happen*, producing **Objects to the Causative Verbs**) the Intransitive Verb plays the role of Transitive and their passive forms are possible. Read the following chart.

Note: However, reflexive pronouns that become objects to the Intransitive Verbs (i.e., **Reflexive Objects) are not made as Subjects** or take the place of acting subject in the Passive form.

Active	Passive
They fought the ***battle*** at this place.	<u>The battle was fought</u> at this place.
Yesterday they ran a ***race***.	<u>The race you speak of was run</u> yesterday.
The people of Kalinga fought a good ***fight*** against Ashoka, the king Maurya.	<u>A good fight against Ashoka</u>, the king of Maurya <u>was fought</u> by the people of Kalinga.
She sleeps a deep ***sleep*** in the night.	<u>A deep sleep is slept</u> by her in the night.
They lived a happy ***life*** after that incident.	<u>A happy life</u> after that incident <u>was lived</u> by them.
He dreamt a ***dream***.	<u>A dream was dreamed</u> (by him).
We sang a ***song***.	<u>A song was sung</u> by us.
He went a long ***way***.	<u>A long way was gone</u> by him.

399.   **Some expressions look like Passive, but they are not actually in Passive Forms:**

<u>Read the expressions:</u>
- He is gone. (*Some may use this form as passive of '**He goes.**'*)
- He is come. (*Some may use this form as passive of '**He comes.**'*)

✖ The above expressions are not passive, since '**go**' & '**come**' are the <u>Intransitive Verbs</u>, and cannot be used in the passive voice. However, they <u>can be treated as the alternative forms</u> of '***He has gone***' & '***He has come***', but of course not as passive of 'he goes' or 'He comes'.

✖ And here also, the expressions are a bit different from 'he has gone' or 'he has come'; for, in '**He has gone**' *emphasis is laid on the time of action*, the action is complete (the rule of perfect tense) but '**he is gone**' *refers to 'the state of the agent*', i.e., 'his absence' or 'he is no more'. Here 'gone' is a participle adjective describing the pronoun 'He'. The same thing happens to the second sentence 'He is come', *refers to 'the state of the agent*', i.e., about 'his presence'. '**He is come**' meaning '<u>he is present</u>'.

✖ **Note:** So, we should remember, **Intransitive Verbs cannot be used in Passive Voice**, <u>except</u> with that

'Cognate Objects' and 'Objects to the Causative Verbs'.

Passive Voice of Compound & Complex Sentences

400.   Double Passive should be avoided in a single clause: However, double, triple passive is possible in succeeding different clauses of a Compound or a Complex Sentence:

Incorrect Passive Forms	Correct Passive Forms
The spy was ordered (by him) to be shot.	• We *are ordered to shoot* the spy. • He ordered the spy *to be shot*. • We are ordered that the spy *should be shot*.
The evil was sought to be corrected.	• They sought the evil *to be corrected*. • The evil *was sought to correct*. • The evil *was sought* and it *should be corrected*.
A meeting was proposed to be held.	• They proposed a meeting *to be held*. • It *was proposed to hold* a meeting. • It *was proposed that* a meeting *should be held*.

✖   In case of Complex & Compound Sentences, Principal & Co-ordinate, Principal & Sub-ordinate—both the clauses should be changed into Passive Voice; as the third sentence each of the above, and more in the following:

Compound or Complex in Active Voice	Their Passive Forms
I know that he did the work.	• It *is known* to me that the work *was done* by him. • That the work *was done* by him *is known* to me.
• Everybody says that they knew it. • It is said that they knew it.	It *is said* that it *was known* to everybody /them/people.
We must endure what we cannot cure.	What **cannot be cured** must be endured.
I thought that you did it	It *was thought* that it *was done* by you.
It is expected that he will win the prize.	It *is expected* that the prize *will be won* by him.
I shall help you if it is done in time.	If it *is done* in time, you *will be helped* (by me).

Quasi-passive or Middle Voice

401.   Some Transitive Verbs are active in form but passive in sense, they are called **Quasi-passive Verbs** or Verbs of Middle Voice; as,

1)   The book *reads* well. (Here, the verb is in active form 'reads', passive in sense, 'the books reads well when it is read by readers = 'sounds to or affects a reader well when it is read.)
2)   Honey *tastes* sweet. (Honey cannot taste itself = It tastes sweet when it is tasted by someone.)
3)   This book *is printing*. (= is being printed. The book cannot be printed itself; but it is being printed when it is operated by an operator, a living being. And thus, the followings too...)
4)   The cows *are milking*. (= are being milked.)
5)   The rose *smells* sweet. (= is sweet when it is smelt.)
6)   The house *is building*. (= is being built.)
7)   The floor *feels* smooth. (= is smooth when it is felt.)
8)   The cakes *eat* short & crisp (i.e., are short & crisp when they are eaten).

Use of 'Let' in Active & Passive Voice

402.   If the active verb is in the imperative mood, the word *'let' is usually placed at the beginning in the passive voice*.

The structure is like–

'Let + subject+ be + past participle form of verb (3ʳᵈ form)
/or/
Subject + should+ be+ 3ʳᵈ form of verb (past participle form of *verb*.)

- Do it. Let's do it. = Let it be done. It should be done.
- Finish the game. = Let the game be finished. The game should be finished.

✖ If 'Let; is already present in active voice, no problem, it can be changed into passive like the above.

✖ Remember: 'Let' generally comes with Imperative Sentence.

In active voice	In passive voice
1. Let's do it. / Do it.	1. Let it be done. It should be done. / You **are suggested** (ordered or commanded) **to do** it.
2. Tell him to go.	2. Let him be told to go. He **should be told** to go.
3. Finish the game.	3. Let the game be finished. / The game **should be finished**.
4. Keep your word.	4. Word **should be kept**.
5. Please keep off the grass.	5. You **are requested to keep off** the grass.
6. Enter by this door.	6. The visitors **are requested /asked to enter** by this door.
7. Help the poor. /We should help the poor.	7. The poor **should be helped**.
8. Take the medicine regularly.	8. You **are advised to take** the medicine regularly.

Passive of Non-Finite Verbs

403.   Study the Passive Forms of Non-finite Verbs (Infinitive, Gerund, Participle):

Tense	In Active	In Passive
Passive Of Infinitive Verbs		
Present Tense	To love	To be loved
Perfect Tense	To have loved	To have been loved
Progressive	To be loving	*(Does not have passive form)*
Perfect Progressive	To have been loving	*(Does not have passive form)*
Passive Of Gerund		
Present Tense	Loving	Being loved
Perfect Tense	Having loved	Having been loved
Passive Of Participle		
Present Tense	Loving	Being loved
Perfect Tense	Having loved	Having been loved
Past Tense	*(Does not have active form)*	Loved

✗ Study the Passive Forms of Non-finite Verbs (Infinitive, Gerund, Participle) through the sentences:

1) It is time _to do_ the work.
   - ✓ It is time that the work **should be done**.
   - ✓ It is time for the work **to be done**.
2) We saw him _watering_ the plants.
   - ✓ He was seen watering the plants.
   - ✓ We saw the plants **to be watered** by him
3) We insist on _playing_ the music late at night.
   - ✓ We insist that we must **be allowed to play** music late at night.
   - ✓ We insist the music **to be played** on late at night.
4) There are many stories _to read_.
   - ✓ There are many stories **to be read**.
5) There is no time _to waste_.
   - ✓ There is no time **to be wasted**.

Verbs that have Passive Forms

404. **Let's check, which Verbs can be used in the Passive forms & which are not:**

Name of Verb	Active Voice	Passive Voice	Y/N
1. State Verb	• He *is* a student. • I *have* a pen. • She *seems* weak. • I *feel* drowsy. • She *looks* like her mother.	❖ Literally not possible; as, ✓ **'Drowsy'** is not an object of verb 'feel', but a complement, like 'student'; so, have no passive form. ✓ 'Have verb' used as main verb to denote possession, does not have any passive verb form; and **'like her mother'**—is the adverbial describing 'how does she look?'	N
2. Event Verb	• They *did* it. • I *bought* a book. • We *played* cricket. • They *went* to school.	❖ Some event verbs are Transitive & some Intransitive ✓ It was done by them. ✓ A book was bought by me. ✓ Cricket was played (by us). ✓ However, verb 'went' is an Intransitive verb and it does not have any passive verb form.	Y/N
3. Finite Verb	I *bought* a book. He *goes* to school.	❖ Finite are both Transitive & Intransitive; so, some have, and some do not have; as, ✓ A book was bought by me. ✓ ('goes' does not have passive verb form.)	Y/N
4. Non-finite	○ To love = to be loved, ○ to have loved=to have been loved, ○ to be loving=to be being loved; ○ Loving=being loved, ○ having loved=having been loved	❖ Non-finite Infinitive, Gerund & Participle have both active & passive forms.	Y
5. Regular/Weak	○ We are working on a project. ○ We used to live here years ago. ○ The fire burned the house to ashes.	✓ (Intransitive) ✓ (intransitive) ✓ The house was burned to ashes (by the fire).	Y/N

6. Irregular/Strong	o I wrote two novels before it. o They went to Shimla last week.	✓ Two novels were written before it. ✓ (intransitive)		Y/N
7. Principal/Main	o He goes to school every day. o I took the novel from library.	✓ (intransitive) ✓ The novel was taken from library.		Y/N
8. Primary Auxiliaries (be, have& do) **when used as main**.	o I am a teacher. o We are friends. o She is a singer. o He has a car. o He does her work. =Her work is done by him. o Rita did her work in time. = The work was done by Rita in time.	❖ Auxiliary **be** or **have**, even to be used as main verb, they do not have passive forms; but main verb 'do' has; as the examples.		Y/N
9. Primary Auxiliary (Be, have & do) when **used ass helping verb**	o I am reading a book. o He had done the work. o Do you like tea?	❖ When primary auxiliary **be, do, have** are used with main verbs, the verbs have passive forms along with main verbs; as, ✓ A book is being read by me. ✓ The work had been done by him. ✓ Is tea liked by you?		Y
10. Modal Auxiliary (Can, could, may, might, etc.)	o You must do it. o He may pass the examination. o We can run. o You should listen to your teacher.	❖ Like primary auxiliaries, modal auxiliaries too assist the main verbs, and they have passive forms along with the Main Verbs only; as, ✓ It must be done (by you). ✓ The examination may be passed by him. ✓ (Run is intransitive) ✓ Teacher should be listened to (by us).		Y
11. Transitive	o Rita reads a book. o I bought a pencil. o She cooked delicious food.	✓ A book is read by Rita. ✓ A pencil was bought by me. ✓ Delicious food was cooked by her.		Y
12. Intransitive	o They run fast. o She sleeps sound. o I am swimming. o She is standing there. o We ran a race yesterday during this time.	❖ Intransitive Verbs do not have Passive forms, if they are not used as causative or do not take any cognate object; as, ✓ A race was run by us.		N
13. Factive (Transitive verbs of incomplete prediction)	o I called John a fool. o We made him captain. o I think you wrong. (name/make/call/think—the factitive verbs required Complements)	✓ John was called a fool. ✓ He was made captain (by us). ✓ You are thought to be wrong.		Y
14. Causative (When Intransitive verbs used transitively, they become Transitive)	o He had them punished. o She makes me laugh. o They set me to see the movie. o Mother fed her child. o The banana peel fell me on the floor.	✓ They had been punished by him. ✓ I am caused to laugh (by her). ✓ I was set (by them) to see the movie. ✓ The child was fed (made eat) by his /her mother. ✓ I was fallen on the floor by a banana peel.		Y

15. Prepositional Phrase Verbs	o Finally, the couple **put up with** each other after long fight for years. o She **looks down on** people who haven't been to college. o She **looks for** her ex boy-friend still now.	❖ (Object is not clear in mutual relationship, so not passive form) ✓ People who haven't been to college are looked down on by her. (However, bad English) ✓ Her ex boy-friend is looked for still now (by her). (Bad English)	Y/N
16. Quasi Passive Verbs	o Honey tastes sweet. o The house is building	❖ The Quasi-Passive Verbs are active in form but passive in sense. They do not have extra passive forms.	N
17. Catenative	o Niketan keeps singing Rabindra Sangeet. o She got hurt. o It began raining. o I like swimming. o I was jumping to see the movie.	✓ Rabindra Sangeet is kept singing. (Bad English) ✓ (Linking verb 'got' takes a complement 'hurt' and thus, it is Intransitive) ✓ (linking & Intransitive) ✓ Swimming is liked by me. (Bad English) ✓ **Note:** So better to say 'no passive forms of verb **catenative.**	N
18. Ergative	o She <u>opened</u> the door. (<u>Normal transitive</u>) o = The door **opened**. **Ergative**) o She <u>grew</u> flowers in her garden. (Normal transitive) o = Flowers **grew** in her garden. (**ergative**)	✓ The door was opened by her. ❖ (Ergative verb does not have Passive form.) ✓ Flowers were grown in her garden. ❖ (Ergative verb does not have Passive form.)	N
19. Performative	apologize, forbid, inform, promise, request, thanks, etc.	❖ When they take objects, Passive forms are possible; otherwise not.	Y
20. Copula or Linking	o I feel drowsy. o She became mad. o Raina got hurt.	❖ In true sense, linking verbs do not have objects, so do not have passive forms.	N

Objects that can be Subjects in Passive Voice

405.   **Let's check <u>which *objects*</u> can be used as Subjects & which not in the Passive**

Name of Object	Active Voice	Passive Voice		Y/N
1. Direct	o I met *him* in the town. o She gives *biscuits*. o The king hunted *a tiger*.	✓ He was met in the town. ✓ Biscuits are given by her. ✓ A tiger was hunted by the king.		Y
2. Indirect	o She told *me* a secret. o His father gave *him* a watch. o Mom told *me* a story of fairy tale.	✓ I was told a secret. ✓ He was given a watch by his father. ✓ I was told a story of fairy tale by mom.		Y
3. Retained	o I gave you *two books*. o I asked him *to sing*.	✓ You were given **two books** by me. ✓ He was asked **to sing** (by me).		Y

4. Object of Preposition	o His friends laughed at **him**. o Please look into **matter**. o The police officer asked for his **name**.	✓ He was laughed at by his friends. ✓ You are requested to look into the matter. ✓ He was asked for his name by the police officer.	Y
5. Cognate	o They fought a good **fight**. o He fell a great **fall**. o She sings a **song**.	✓ A good fight was fought by them. ✓ A great fall was fallen by him. ✓ A song is sung by her.	Y
6. Object of Causative verb	o He walks the **horse**. o Mother fed her **child**. o Wood men fell **trees** in the forest.	✓ The horse is made to walk. ✓ Child is made to eat by mother. ✓ Trees were caused to fall (cut to fall) by woodmen.	Y
7. Reflexive	o The bubble bursts *itself*. o Keep *yourself* quiet. o He killed *himself*.	✓ The bubble is burst by itself. ✓ Let you be quiet yourself. ✓ He was killed by himself.	N
8. Object of Gerund	o Playing **cards** is not allowed here. o I like reading **poetry**.	✓ Cards is being played is not allowed here. (complex) ✓ I like poetry being read. (simple)	Y
9. Object of Participle	o Seeing **him** handsome, she agreed to marry. o We met a girl carrying **a basket** of flowers. o I saw a burnt cow. o The fire having burnt **the house**, we became hopeless.	✓ He was being seen handsome, she agreed to marry. (Though became complex by turning participle into a finite verb) ❖ (When participle is with object of main verb, object of the participle is hardly been possible to form direct subject, but may be used with other; as,) ✓ A basket of flowers being carried by a girl was met by us. ✓ A cow which was burnt was seen. ✓ The house having been burnt by the fire; we became homeless.	Y
10. Object of Infinitive	o To love **you** is my passion. o All the time I am ready to do **anything**. o To hate everyone is not good at all. o I am to buy **a book**. (I am here to buy a book)	✓ You *to be loved* is my passion. ✓ I am ready for *anything to be done*. / *Anything to be done* I am ready all the time. ✓ *Everyone to be hated* (by you) is not good at all. ✓ *A book is to be bought* by me.	Y
11. Object of Complement	o I am happy *to see* you. o I am angry *with my girlfriend*. o We made him captain *of our team*.	❖ A complement & the object of Complement— (here: 'happy to see', 'angry with my girl-friend', 'captain of our team')— cannot be made subjects in the passive voice.	N
12. Factitive Object (Secretary, king— are the complements to the objects)	o They proclaimed **him** king. o I have appointed **you**, my secretary.	✓ He was proclaimed king by the people. (Here: they=people) ✓ You have been appointed my secretary.	Y
13. Adverbial objects	o He held the post *ten years*. (How long?) o The watch cost *nine hundred rupees*. (How much?)	❖ (Adv. Objects cannot be used ever as subjects in the sentence) ❖ However, it happens for others: ✓ The post was held by him for ten years.	N

o He worked *an hour*. (For how long?)	✓ Nine hundred rupees was paid as cost for the watch. ✓ He was worked for an hour (by some other agent) **Note:** The last sentence, actually not in the passive form, but the case of causative verb; he was made the work. 'Worked' is an Intransitive, and Intransitive does not have Passive forms.)

Exercise-20

406.   **Exercise-1:** <u>Identify Active or Passive of the following verbs in the sentences:</u>
1) Masked thieves stole a valuable painting from the museum last night.
2) He handed over a cheque to his needy friend.
3) The director told the staff the news this morning.
4) They saw the storm approaching.
5) I've sold my bicycle.
6) The town was destroyed by an earthquake.
7) By whom was this broken?
8) A valuable painting was stolen from the museum last night.
9) The building is damaged by the fire.
10) The letter has just been posted.
11) He was taken to the hospital by his friends.

407.   **Exercise-2:** <u>Study the Changes from Active to Passive& vice versa: -</u>

Active	**Passive**
They use video for teaching the students.	Video is used for teaching the students.
I saw him opening the box.	He was seen opening the box.
One should keep one's promise.	Promise should be kept.
His subordinates accused him of various offences.	He was accused of various offences by his subordinates.
When will you return the book?	When will the book be returned by you?
He told me to leave the room.	I was told to leave the room.
Someone has picked my pocket.	My pocket has been picked.
One may accomplish many things by efforts.	Many things may be accomplished by efforts.
Circumstances obliged me to go.	I was obliged to go.
Manners reveals character	Character is revealed by manners.
We must listen to his words.	His words must be listened to.
An earthquake destroyed the town.	The town was destroyed by an earthquake.
Who broke this?	By whom was this broken?
The fire damages the building.	The building is damaged by the fire.
Someone stole a valuable painting from the museum last night.	A valuable painting was stolen from the museum last night.

He handed over a cheque to his needy friend.	A cheque was handed over to his needy friend.
The director told the news to the staff this morning.	The staff were told the news by director this morning.
His friends took him to the hospital.	He was taken to the hospital by his friends.
The police will question every staff on duty.	Every staff on duty will be questioned by the police.
We compelled the enemy to surrender.	The enemy was compelled to surrender.
I have just posted the letter.	The letter has just been posted.
The sudden noise frightened the horse.	The horse was frightened by the sudden noise.
He promised me (to give) a present.	I was promised to have a present.
The police arrested him.	He was arrested by the police.
The boy is climbing the cliff.	The cliff is being climbed by the boy.
He kept me waiting.	I was kept waiting.
I am watching you carefully.	You are carefully being watched by me.
A policeman caught the thief.	The thief was caught by a policeman.
The boy's work pleased the teacher.	The teacher was pleased with the boy's work.
Your behavior vexes me.	I am vexed with your behavior.
Passive	**Active** (by mentally supplied a suitable subject, where necessary)
It is said he will come.	They say he will come.
He is expected soon.	We expect him soon.
My book has been lost.	I have lost my book.
The lion is called the king of beast.	People call the lion the king of beast.
The shed was burnt to ashes.	Fire burnt the shed to ashes.
The injured were taken to a hospital.	They/The local people/The rescue team took the injured to a hospital.
The painting is valued at 10 million rupees. Ten million rupees is valued for the painting.	The customer values the painting at 10 million rupees. The customer values 10 million rupees for the painting.
The lock had been broken and the cameras had been switched off before the dacoity in C-Block.	The thieves/robbers had broken the lock & switched off the cameras before the dacoity in the C-Block.
The security of the block is to be improved.	The authority should improve the security of the block.
The liquid is boiled at 100 degree.	We boil water at 100 degree.
The theft is being investigated by the police.	The police are investigating the theft.
The drawing is drawn by a student.	A student draws the drawing.
The news was told to the staff by the director this morning.	The director told the staff the news this morning.

253

The thief was caught.	Police caught the thief.
The captive was bound to a tree.	The people bound the captive to the tree.
The exhibition was opened by the Governor.	The Governor opened the exhibition.
His command was promptly obeyed.	We obeyed his command promptly.
Nothing will be gained by hurry.	We'll gain nothing by hurry.
Passive	**Active**
A very remarkable discovery was made by him.	He made a very remarkable discovery.
Smoking is prohibited here.	No one will smoke here.
He is loved by all/everyone.	Everyone loves him.
Their admission is refused.	The college authority refuses their admission.
Good new are expected.	We expect good news.
A doll was bought for the baby.	I bought the baby a doll.
The light has been put out.	Somebody has put out the light.
He was found guilty of murder.	The court found him guilty of murder.
TVs are sold here.	They sell TVs here.
My bicycle has been sold.	I've sold my bicycle.
It will be forgotten soon.	People will soon forget it.
The ocean cannot be pumped to dry.	You cannot pump the ocean to dry.
The theatre was opened only in the last month.	They opened the theatre only last month.

23. Adverbs, Kinds (16) & Their Uses

408.　　There are more than **'16' kinds of adverbs** present in English grammar which are grouped in '3' main classes. **However**, we will discuss this chapter under the following heads:

        A.　Definition & Classification,
        B.　Illustration of Simple Adverbs (14 in numbers),
        C.　Relative Adverbs &
        D.　Interrogative Adverbs;
        E.　Degree & Comparison,
        F.　Forms & Formation of Adverbs &
        G.　The Position of Adverbs in the sentence.

Definition & Classification of Adverb

409.　　Study the following sentences.
        1)　Peter **runs**.

2) He runs *fast*.
3) He runs *very* fast.
4) It is a **mango**.
5) It is a **sweet** mango.
6) The mango is *very* sweet.
7) I have read *all* through this book.
8) *Unfortunately*, no one was present there.
9) This is the reason *why* I left her.
10) *When* did he come?

Explanation

➤ In sentence-1, '**runs**' is a verb which shows an activity of Peter. It tells us, what Peter does.

➤ In sentence-2, '*fast*' adds meaning to the verb 'runs. How does he run? = *fast*.

➤ In sentence-3, the word '**very**' adds meaning to the word 'fast'. How fast does he run? = *very* fast.

➤ The sentence-4 is a statement which tells us a name of a fruit, = **a mango**. The 'mango' is a noun. (However, here the word 'mango' is a complement to the verb 'is').

➤ In sentence-5, the word '**sweet**' describes the noun, so it is an Adjective, but

➤ In sentence-6, the word '**very**' adds meaning to the adjective 'sweet'. How sweet is the mango? = *very*.

➤ In sentence-7, the word '**all**' adds meaning to the phrase 'through this book'. How much have you read? = **all** through this book, refers 'degree of quantity'.

➤ In sentence-8, the word '**unfortunately**' adds meaning to whole sentence following it 'no one was present there'. 'Unfortunately,' is an adverb, modifying the verb 'being present'.

➤ In sentence-9, the word '**why**' joins the two clauses, besides, modifying the clause, 'I left her' or to the verb sense 'leaving her'. 'Why' is a relative adverb.

➤ In sentence-10, the word '**when**' is used to ask question, and its answers are always simple adverbs. Here: 'when did he come?' = *yesterday at 9 p.m./in the morning/ in the evening/ at night*, etc. are the examples of adverbial phrases, denoting 'time' & '**when**' is an Interrogative Adverb. **All the italic & bold** words are the examples of adverbs in the sentences.

✖ **The Definition:** An adverb is a word that generally modifies or adds meaning to a *verb*, or an *adjective*, or an *adverb*, *and often **a phrase** or **a sentence** using at the beginning of them (clause or sentence)*. Besides, an adverb is also used to ***join clauses*** & to ***ask questions*** like in the above sentences.

Note: The above definition itself reflects different roles of an adverb in the sentence. It has mainly three parts—

1) modifying a verb, an adjective or an adverb (which are single words;

2) it may modify also a phrase or a sentence too;

3) Besides modifying words, phrase or sentence, it also joins clauses (the function of Relative Adverbs like a Relative Pronoun), and asks questions (the function of Interrogative Adverb) to find other adverbs from the sentence.

➤ A **Relative adverb** joins two clauses, refers **place, reason, time**, etc, doing the function of an adverb, *but introduce always a relative or adjective clause in the sentence*. Study examples.

➤ *Answers to Interrogative adverb are always the simple adverbs*. The answers may be an **adverb of time, place, reason, cause, purpose** or any other.

410. **Study the examples:**

1) The engineer worked **carefully** on the engine.
   - How did he work? =carefully, refers 'manner'.
2) Ruby is a **very** good student.
   - How good? =very good, refers the degree.
3) He left the place **quite** suddenly.
   - How did he leave the place? = suddenly, refers the 'degree' of manner)

Read also others:

4) She was sitting ***close*** beside him. (Where, refers place)
5) She lives ***far*** of us. (Where, refers distance of place)
6) At what hours is the sun ***right*** above us? (Where, refers the point of position; 'at what hours?'--the answer of the question will be the adverb of time; as, = at 12 pm.)
7) The tiger was ***just*** behind us howling. (Where, refers the point of position.)
8) The building was ***in the right*** of the Post Office. (Where, in which side, refers the direction.)
9) Have you read ***all*** through this book? (How much have you read this book? = all through this book, refers degree of quantity.)

10) She was dressed ***all*** <u>in pink</u>. ('in pink' itself is the phrase of adjective refers the color, and the phrase is modified by the adverb 'all'. How much pink? = all, refers the degree of color.)

11) He paid his debts ***down*** <u>to the last penny</u>. (The bold word refers manner, while the phrase, 'to the last penny' refers the degree.)

12) He *slowly* sipped his wine ***all*** <u>to the bottom</u>. (The phrase, 'to the bottom' refers quantity, while the bold word 'all' refers the degree of that quantity, and slowly refers the manner of sipping' his wine in the sentence.)

➤ All the above underlined are the examples of phrases, modified by the bold adverbs in the sentences.
➤ **Adverbs also modify a Sentence** or **a Clause** using before them; as in the above by **'all'**, **'down'**, etc.
➤ <u>Adverbs standing at the beginning of sentences sometimes modify the whole sentences</u>, rather than any particular word; as,

13) **Probably** <u>he is mistaken</u>. (The state or the condition is 'he is mistaken', and by the word 'probably' the condition is modified, which is a sentence. Thus, the sense is 'It is that he is mistaken to be a doctor., when he may not be so.)

14) **Possible** <u>it is as you said</u>. (It is possible what you said to be true or not be true.)

15) **Certainly,** <u>you are wrong</u>. (It is certain that you are wrong.)

16) **Evidently** <u>the figures are incorrect</u>. (It is evident that the figures are incorrect.)

17) **Unfortunately,** <u>no one was present there</u>. (No one was present there & it was unfortunate.)

18) **Luckily,** <u>he escaped unhurt</u>. (He was lucky that he escaped unhurt.)

➤ All the above underlined are the examples of clauses or sentence, modified by the bold adverbs, used in the beginning of the sentences, being themselves parts of the sentences or clauses.

Classification of Adverbs

411.   The following is the chart of the division of adverbs, which are put into three main classes. <u>Together they are sixteen in number</u>. Study the chart carefully:

Kinds of Adverbs		
Simple adverbs	*Relative or Wh-Adjunctive Adverbs*	*Interrogative adverbs*
The simple adverbs are used to modify meanings of a verb, or an adjective, or an adverb, or a phrase, clause or sentence. **They are fourteen in number.**	Where adverbs besides modifying, relate or refer back to their antecedents & thereby do join clauses. These are also some 'wh' words; as, why, when, where, how, in what manner, how long, how much, how often, etc. **Read the examples:**	Where adverbs are used to ask questions with 'wh' words-why, when, where, how, in what manner, how long, how much, how often, etc., and their answers are mostly simple adverbs (denoting **time. place, reason, result**, or other); as,
1) Time, 2) Frequency, 3) Place, 4) Movement or direction, 5) Manner, 6) Affirmation, 7) Negation, 8) Reason or Cause, 9) Purpose & Result, 10) Conditions, 11) Concession or Compromise 12) Certainty, 13) Focusing, 14) Degree or Quantity;	1) Tell them the reason *why* I came. 2) I know the street *where* the bank is. 3) This was the reason *why* I left her. 4) I remember the house *where* I was born. 5) Tell us the time *when* you will come. 6) Tell her *how much* you love her. If can't, just shut-up before us.	1) Where is your Ram? 2) Why are you late? 3) How did you do it? 4) How much work can you do in a day? 5) How high is the Kutub Minar? 6) When will he arrive tomorrow? 7) How often did she come? 8) How much she loved you. 9) In what manner you did it.

➤ **Note:** The relative adverbs & the interrogative adverbs are mostly same in form. They are both are the 'wh' words. The difference lies in their uses only. The relative adverbs are used to join clauses, and they, like relative adjectives or pronouns, relate or refer back to their antecedents to show 'relation' and introduce always 'Relative Clauses'. Whereas, the interrogative adverbs are used to ask questions to find Simple Adverbs.

Simple Adverbs (14 in numbers)

➤ *In use, adverbs may group into 3 major classes; however, in meaning, they are '16' or more in number (kinds). Study them now one by one.*

1. <u>Adverb of Time</u>

➤ **Adverbs of Time:** the adverbs or adverb phrases which show '<u>when</u>'; <u>when an action is being done/takes place/happens.</u>

1) We have seen the film **before**.
2) I have heard this **before**.
3) We shall **now** begin to work.
4) I had a letter from him **lately**.
5) I have spoken to him **already**.
6) Mr. Gupta **formerly** lived here.
7) That day he arrived **late**.
8) The end came **soon**.
9) A year **hence** (after a length of time in the future), it will be forgotten by everybody here present.
10) Wasted time **never** returns.
11) The train has **already** left the station.
12) We moved into our new house **last week**.
13) Our favorite T.V. program starts **at 6'o clock**.
14) I'm going to join my new school **tomorrow**.
15) He once met me in Cairo; I have not seen him **since**.
16) He went away two hours *ago*.
17) I will do it *soon*.
18) The boy arrived *late* in class.
19) He has *already* arrived.

➤ Adverb of Time answer the questions, '**when'/at what time?**

2. <u>Adverb of Frequency</u>

➤ **Adverb of Frequency:** The adverb or adverb phrases which answer to the questions, '<u>how often</u>' or '<u>how many times</u>' an action is done:

1) I have told you *twice*.
2) I have not seen him *once* since then.
3) He *often* makes mistakes.
4) He *seldom* comes here.
5) The postman called *again*.
6) He *always* tries to do his best.
7) He *frequently* comes unprepared.
8) Our children **always** go to school on the bus.
9) I'll **never** make that mistake **again**.
10) I clean my bedroom **every day**.
11) Dad polishes his shoes **twice a week**.
12) He *often* makes mistakes.
13) I used to watch movies *twice* a week.
14) She *seldom* writes me.
15) I *always* wake up <u>early in the morning</u>.
16) *Firstly,* mangoes are bought from market.
17) *Sometimes* an ignorant also works <u>excellent</u>.
18) He comes here *daily*.
19) He *occasionally* visits the place.
20) She began to call *daily*.

➤ Adverb of Frequency answers to the question, '**how often'/how many times?**

3. **Adverb of Place or Position**

➤ **Adverb of Place:** the adverb or adverb phrases that show *'where'*/ *'at what place'* an action happens or takes place.
  1) The boys are playing **upstairs**.
  2) The dog is **in the garden**.
  3) We're going **to New York City** on our school trip.
  4) It's very sunny but cold **outside**.
  5) Stand **here**. Go **there**. Walk **backward**.
  6) The little lamb follows Mary **everywhere**.
  7) He looked **up**. My brother is **out**.
  8) Is Mr. Das is **within**? Come **in**.
  9) The horse galloped **away**.
  10) Stop **here**. Go **there**. Come **in**.
  11) The teacher is **out**. The doctor is **in.**
  12) He fell **down**. The rust is **everywhere**.
  13) Go **inside**. Get **out**. The bird flies **upward**.
  14) He gets **into the train**. He works **at an office**, etc.

  ➤ Adverb of Place answer the questions- '**Where?**'

4. **Adverb of Movement or Direction**

➤ The adverbs or adverb phrases that show 'direction'/ 'movement of an action' are called the **adverb of Movement** or **Direction**. *The Adverb of Movement or Direction may be included in the class of Adverb of Place, for they also denote location.*
  ➤ It answers to the questions '**where to**', '**what along**', **to which direction or place**' or *'from where'*; as
1) They are running **towards the city**. (Where are they running to?)
2) They are walking along **the road/along the sea beach**. (What along are they walking?)
3) We moved **forward.** They moved **northward.** (To which direction did they move?)
4) These were falling **from the top.** (From where were these falling?)
5) He is coming **hither** (to this place). (Where is he coming to?)
6) **Hither** he is coming, everyone be alert.
7) **Thither** (to/towards that place) she is going, keep watch on her. (Where to is she going?)
8) People began rushing **hither & thither**. (Also, hither & yon) (where to did they begin to rush?)

Whither = where/ to which place; used to ask what is likely to happen to something in the future.

9) **Whither** should they go? They did not know **whither** *(what place)* to go.
10) **Whither** modern architecture will go after this decade?
11) **Whither** modern technology do, let us know in the seminar.
12) Get thee **hence** *(from here, from this place)*, Satan! (Where to go for Satan?)
13) I am going **hence** *(going from here?)* to my own land.
14) They made their way from Spain to France & **thence** *(from that place)* to England. (Where to go from France?)
15) He was promoted to manager, **thence** *(from that position or situation)* to a partnership in the farm.
16) The aliens returned **whence** *(from where)* they had come. (Where did they return to?)

5. **Adverb of Manner or Means**

➤ **Adverb of Manner/Means:** It shows *'how'* or *'in what way or manner' something happens or is done*; as,
  1) Soumya reads **clearly**.
  2) The letter is **well** written.
  3) This story reads **well**.

4) The plane flied **smoothly**.
5) The child slept **soundly**.
6) Slowly and **sadly,** we laid him down.
7) You should not do **so**.
8) The Sikhs fought **bravely**.
9) The boy works **hard**.
10) I was **agreeably** disappointed. Is that **so**?
11) **Thus** only, will you succeed?
12) The girls answered all the questions **correctly**.
13) He was driving **carelessly**.

14) Ramu plays guitar **skillfully**.
15) He spoke **confidently**.
16) Mampi sits **silently** besides me.
17) The bus runs **soundly** on the road.
18) The train runs **slowly**.
19) The leader said all that **wisely**.
20) Nick spoke something, I could not hear **clearly**.
21) They did the task **rapidly**.
22) He fell down **suddenly** and died **in this way** giving us no time to take him to the nearby hospital **even**. Thus sometimes, one's end comes **by chance**, and we **hardly** get time to think over **even** on the eternal truths of life.
    However, here the mentioned adverb '**hardly**' is an **adverb of negation**' and '**by chance**' is often termed as '**time**' rather than be an adverb of manner.

6. Adverb of Affirmation &
7. Adverb of Negation

➢ The adverbs that say—yes, certainly, definitely, surely, etc. which denote _affirmation or certainty of something to happen_, _refer acceptance_, etc. are called the **Adverbs of Affirmation**, and the adverbs that says— no, not, never, none, perhaps, probably, etc., _which denote negation or no to something to do,_ or _refer denying_, etc., are called the **Adverbs of Negation**.

The Words that refer Negation & Affirmation
(Remember, all are not Adverbs)
(24)

Words of **Negation**	Words of **Affirmation**
No, Not, Never, No longer, No more, Nothing, Not a bit, Nobody/None/ No one,	Yes, of course, certainly, definitely, surely, only, any, all, some, ever, always,
Nowhere, Nothing but, Scarcely, Hardly, Rarely= *15*	something, anything somewhere, anywhere = (15)

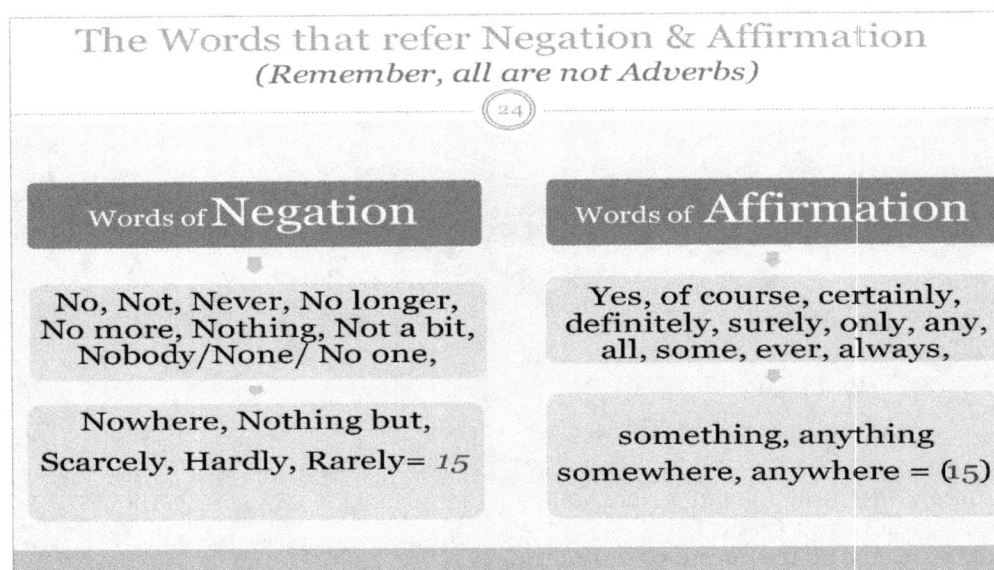

➢ Ways, how Adverb of Affirmation or Negation comes out as answer to the questions with 'Verb 'To Be', 'To Have', 'To Do' or by any other helping verb, like 'modals':
  → Are you a man? =**Of course**, why not?
  → Is she your girlfriend? =**No**, she is not.
  → Have you seen the film? = **Yes**, I have.
  → Have you written her? = **No**, I haven't.
  → Do you know him? = **Yes**.
  → Do you want this? = **No**, thanks.
  → Will you go there? = **Certainly**, I will.
  → Should I go? =**Definitely** not. / **Sure**.

➢ The adverbs **which affirm** or say **'yes'** to some action; as,
  1) Have you got it? = **Yes.** I have got it.
  2) **Surely** you are mistaken.
  3) He **certainly** went there.
  4) **Yes**, **of course**, you **must** do it. ('must' is a modal. The modals are mostly used like an adverb, add meaning to the verb. For details, read the chapter of Modals.)
  5) **Certainly,** they did it.
  6) **Surely** go there & tell him to flee.
  7) I drink **all** to the bottom.
  8) He **ever** asks me of my name.
  9) Go **anywhere**. **Only** do*n't* ask me *again* this matter.
  10) **Somewhere** it was lost, and **somewhere** it was found.

➢ The adverbs which say **'no'** or **'not'** to certain action; 'denies something' or introduce negation in the sense;
as,
  1) Have you done it? = **No.** I have **not** done it. Is he busy? = **No**, he is **not**.
  2) I do **not** know him.
  3) Things are **no** better at present.
  4) **No longer** has he lived. **No longer** does she live.
  5) **Never** come here.
  6) I have **not** any car.
  7) He remained of **nowhere**.
  8) **Scarcely** had they liked us.
  9) **Scarcely** had she love for me. (**Here:** had is used as main verb, and 'love' is a noun)
  10) **Hardly** had we listened to her shout for help last night. **Hardly** did we hear her.
  11) **Rarely** there was a sit for us. *All* were *merely* booked.

Note: *No longer, scarcely, hardly*—**generally are used in perfect tenses** and *has, have, had* or *any other* *helping verb* (if not perfect tense) follow the words as in the above sentences.

8. Adverbs of reason or cause

✘ **The adverb which tells about a reason or cause** of an action done or to happen is called the adverb of Reason or Cause. They are introduced <u>by the following sub-ordinate conjunctions</u>; as, —*because, as, since, hence, etc.*, and <u>answer to the question</u> '**why'**?

1) He cannot come, ***because*** he is ill. (Why can't he come?)
2) ***As*** he is ill, he cannot come.
3) ***Since*** you are ill, you need not come. (Why need I not come?)
4) I am sorry ***that*** you said this. (Why do you feel sorry?)
5) I am going hence (from here), ***because*** you have insulted me. (Why are you going?)
6) ***As*** he did the offence, he is unable to refute the charge. (Why is he unable to refute the charge?)

9. Adverb of Purpose & Result

✘ **Adverb of Purpose:** The adverb of purpose are <u>introduced by the following sub-ordinate conjunctions</u>, like that of Result; as, —*that, in order that, so that, lest*, etc.
1) We read ***that*** *(for the purpose that/in the result of)* we may learn.
2) He works hard ***in order that /so that*** he may succeed.
3) Walk slowly and carefully ***lest*** *(in order somebody not)* you fall in the ditch.
4) She studied hard ***so that*** he would pass in the examination.

✘ The relative pronouns— ***who, which*** —make relative or adjective clauses in the sentences but they may refer both cause or purpose. Read the chart.

Relative clause but refer Cause	Relative clause but referring Purpose
• My brother ***who*** *(because he) is ill* cannot come.	• I shall send my brother ***who*** *(that he may)* will do the work.
• The picture ***which*** *(because it) was spoiled*, has been thrown away.	• I have bought a dog ***which*** *(in order that it)* would guard my house at night.
Note: In the above sentences, the sub-ordinate clauses — 'who is ill' & 'which was spoilt'—both are the relative clauses; they have described their antecedent nouns— 'brother' & 'picture' respectively; but the words 'who' meaning = *because he/she*; & 'which' meaning = *because it*— are the adverbs, denoting cause'.	*Note:* In the above sentences, the sub-ordinate clauses — 'who will do the work' & 'which would guard my house at night'—both are the sub-ordinate relative clauses; they have described their antecedent nouns— 'brother' & 'dog' respectively; but the words 'who' meaning = *that he may*; & 'which' meaning = *in order that it* are the adverbs, denoting 'purpose'.

Adverb of Result

✘ **The adverb of result** often may be treated as differently from the adverb of purpose. In that case, one number might be added to fourteen to be fifteen Simple Adverbs. *The Adverb of Result is that refers to result or outcome of an action*.
✘ The adverbs of result are introduced by the following sub-ordinate conjunctions; as, —***that, so that, such that, therefore, hence***, etc.

1) I am so tired ***that*** (in the result of) I can't walk.
2) *What have I done **that*** (in the result of) *you desert me?*
3) *He is* <u>such</u> *a fool **that*** (as a result of) *I can't depend on him.*
4) He did the offence; ***hence*** (for this reason/as a result of) he is unable to refute the charge. (What is the result of his doing offence?)

5) He was ill treated by all for his caste. He ***therefore*** left the school. (What happened that he was ill-treated in the school?)

6) I wanted to buy a book; ***therefore,*** I had gone there. (What did you do to buy a book?)

   ✻ Sometimes, 'that' is understood (omitted); and in place of 'that' we use comma (,) like in the following sentences:

7) He is so weak, he can't walk.

8) You were so late; I could not wait.

10. Adverb of Condition or Supposition

✻ The adverbs that refer to condition (supposition, provision or situation) for an action to happen, is called the adverb of ***Condition or Supposition.***

✻ They are introduced by the following sub-ordinate conjunctions; as, – *if, unless, in case, whether, on condition, provided (that), supposing that,* etc.

   1) ***If*** I succeed, I shall help you.
   2) I shall not go ***unless*** you come.
   3) I may come in; ***in case*** I have time.
   4) He will come ***provided*** he gets leave.
   5) I shall try, ***whether*** I succeed or not.
   6) ***Had I been*** (If I had been) rich, I would help you.
        7) ***Were I*** (If I were) present there, I would oppose to that proposal.

   ✻ Compare: Adverbs of Reason, Result & Condition

Adv. Of Reason	Adv. Of Result	Adv. Of Condition
• ***Because of*** I doubtlessly believe her, I gave her the attorney power. • ***Because*** she played the day long, she didn't stand first in her Examination. • ***As*** he failed to catch the train, he was late in the meeting. • ***As*** I worked very hard, good was my result.	• She was always lazy; ***consequently,*** she didn't get any job in her life time. • She is not studying well, ***so*** she'll not stand 1st position in the Exam. • He failed the train, ***hence/therefore*** *(for the reason, as a result)* he was late. • I worked very hard, ***accordingly*** good was my result in all exams.	• ***Even if*** none loves you, you should not hate them. • ***Even*** I had insulted you, you offered your help. • ***Unless*** you start now, you will miss the train. • ***If*** I didn't work very hard, I missed my position at any time.

11. Adverbs of Concession or Compromise

✻ The adverbs of Condition & the adverbs of Concession are honestly to say are same and not different.

   ✻ The adverb that refers to *concession* or *compromise* which *often refers to contrast* situation of an action, is called the **Adverb of Concession or Compromise** (popularly known as **Negative Condition** for happening of an action).

   ✻ They are introduced by the following sub-ordinate conjunctions; as, – *though, although, even, even if,* etc.

   1) ***Though*** he is poor, he is honest.
   2) ***Even if*** I fail, I shall not give up hope.
   3) ***Although*** they were present, they were for nothing, they said nothing.
   4) ***Even*** I had insulted you, you offered your help.
   5) ***Even if*** none loves you, you should not hate them.

Note: Carefully note, *the adverb of Concession and the Adverb of Condition, have hardly any difference, or they are closely related.*

   ✻ Adverbial clause of concession

✻ Sometimes, adverbial clause of concession is introduced by *pronouns with an adverb 'ever'*; as, ***whomever,***

whatever, ***however***, etc.

1) ***However*** very strong you may be, I am not afraid of you.
2) ***Whatever*** you may say, I don't believe you.
3) ***Whoever*** he may be, he can't be allowed.
4) ***Whoever*** you may be, I am not scared of you.
5) ***Whatever*** you do, you'll sure fail in this examination.
6) ***However,*** I helped her so many times, she admitted that never.
7) ***However***, I loved her, she merely hated through her life.

- *The adverb of Concession is almost like the adverb of Condition, already mentioned. However, carefully note down the minute difference in them.*

Adverb of Condition or Supposition	Adverb of Concession or Compromise
1) ***If*** I succeed, I shall help you.	1) ***Though*** he is poor, he is honest.
2) I shall not go, ***unless*** you come.	2) ***Even if*** I fail, I shall not give up hope.
3) I may come in, ***in case*** I have time.	3) ***Although*** they were present, they were for nothing, they said nothing.
4) He will come, ***provided*** he gets leave.	4) ***However*** very strong you may be, I am not afraid of you.
5) I shall try, ***whether*** I succeed or not.	5) ***Whatever*** you may say, I don't believe you.

Points to remember: The minute difference lies in the fact that the adverb of condition, all do not express contrast but positive condition for an action, though contrast is it's a part. In case of concession or compromise, all express the contrast situation of an action.

12. Adverb of Certainty

- The Adverbs of Certainty mostly like the Adverbs of Affirmation & Negation and they easily can be merged in. It tells us of *'certainty* of an action' or *'the probability'*.

- The words that assure certainty or probability of an action are: ***definitely, certainly, probably, perhaps***, etc.

1) **Certainly,** they will visit by tomorrow evening.
2) **Definitely** she will do or where will she go?
3) It will **probably** rain today by the evening.
4) **Perhaps** the train is late. It is half past ten, still no announce of its arrival at the station.

To be Noted: There are a group of adverbs we have, almost same in meaning & uses, or they are closely related, like-Time & Frequency, Place & Movement, Affirmation & Negation with Certainty & Focusing, Condition with the Compromise, Degree with the Manner, Time & Distance.

- Ways, how Adverb of Certainty Modify Verbs. Follow the chart:

Ways Adverb-Certainty Modify Verbs

(41)

What of certainty
- She will **definitely** <u>pass</u> the exam.
- I am **sure** he'll come. ('sure' about his coming)

What of probability
- The patient will **probably** <u>die</u>.
- **Perhaps** she <u>loves</u> me.

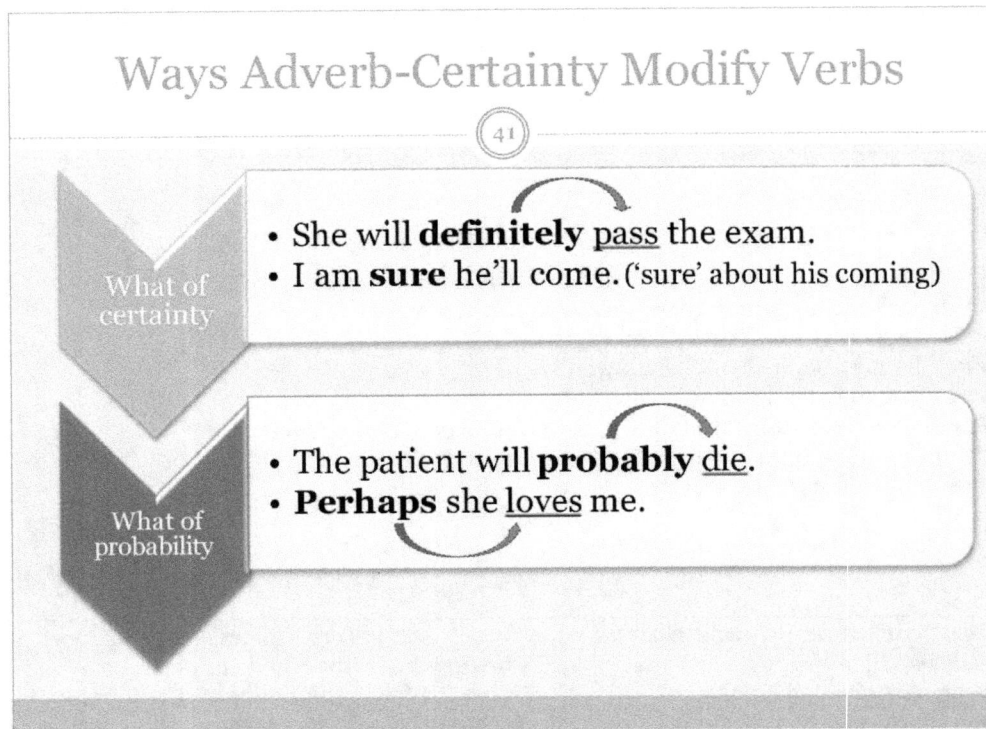

13. Focusing Adverb

✖ The adverbs <u>that point to</u> *one part of a clause/sentence*, i.e.
   1) He has **even** gone to his enemy.
   2) We are **only** going for two days.
   3) The people present there were **mainly** politicians.

✖ This class of Adverb is used only to ***give focus on some particular part of a clause or sentence.***
✖ Like in the above, <u>in the</u> *first sentence the adverb* **'even'** *gives focus to the part of the sentence* ***'gone to his enemy',*** and adds meaning to the verb 'gone'.
✖ In the 2nd sentence *the focus is centered on the duration of time*, '**only going for two days**.
✖ In the third sentence, the word '**mainly**' points to the <u>present number of people</u> who were 'politicians.

14. Adverb of Degree or Quantity

✖ **Adverb of Degree or Quantity:** The adverb or Adverb-phrases which show (answer to the questions) **'how much', 'in what degree',** or **'to what extent'** something happens; as,
   1) These mangoes are **<u>almost</u>** ripe. (Adds meaning to the adjective 'ripe'; <u>and thus, the following too</u>)
   2) He was ***too*** careless.
   3) The sea is ***very*** stormy.
   4) I am ***rather*** busy.
   5) I am ***fully*** prepared.
   6) He is good ***enough***.
   7) I am ***so*** glad to see you again.
   8) You are ***altogether*** mistaken.
   9) Things are ***no*** better at present.
   10) You are ***quite*** wrong.
   11) She sings ***pretty*** well. (Adds meaning to another adverb)
   12) He went/came ***nearer/further***. (How far or near?)
   13) I am ***partly*** right. He is **as** tall as Tom. (How much?)
   14) I love her **little**. (How much?)
   15) She believes me **enough**. (How much?)

16) We have done **a part of the project**. (To what extent?)
17) **Still,** we could not complete it. (To what extent?)
18) He is a genius **enormous**. (In what degree?)
19) I am **rather** a fool. (In what degree?)

Degrees or Forms of Comparison

412.   Some adverbs, like adjectives, **have three degrees (or forms) of comparison:** <u>where the comparison is made with none or nothing</u> (zero comparison), namely '**Positive Degree**'; when it is <u>between two</u>, namely '**Comparative Degree**', & <u>among</u> more than two, namely the '**Superlative Degree**'; as,

o   He runs **_fast_**. (Here: 'fast', the adverb form only modifying the verb 'run'; no comparison is made with anybody)
o   He runs **_faster than_ you**. (Here: 'faster', besides modifying the verb 'run' hints the comparison which is made between 'he' & 'you'.)
o   He runs **_fastest of all_** in the race. (That means among all)

Note: In superlative, the article '**the**' is not essential like in the superlative degree of adjective ('the fastest runner').

❑   Mostly the Adverb of **Degree, Manner, Time & Position** has their <u>Forms of Comparison</u>; as, (far-further-furthest; near-nearer-nearest, etc.)

413.   **How to form Degrees or Forms of Comparison:**

✖   <u>If the adverb is of one syllable</u>, we form the comparative by adding '**-er**' & the superlative by '**-est**' to the positive degree or form; as,
▪   Fast—faster—fastest,
▪   Hard—harder—hardest,
▪   Long—longer—longest
▪   Soon—sooner—soonest

✖   <u>If the adverb ends in '**ly**'</u>, then add '**more**' & '**most**' before the adverb respectively in comparative & superlative Degree; as,
▪   Skillfully—more skillfully—most skillfully
▪   Swiftly—more swiftly—most swiftly
Except some; like,
▪   'Early'—earlier—earliest.

❑   It is noticed that mostly, though not only, the **Adverbs of Manner, Degree, Time & Position** admit of comparison; and many Adverbs, from their nature, cannot be compared; as, **now, then, where, there, once**—do not admit any comparison.

<u>Study examples in the sentences:</u>

a) Bhima shot his arrow *skillfully*.
o   Yudhishthira shot his arrow **_more skillfully_** than Bhima.
o   But, Arjuna shot his arrow **_most skillfully_** of all.

b) I did the job *swiftly*.
o   You did the job **_more swiftly_**.
o   But, she did hers **_most swiftly_** of all of us there.

c) I came *early* this morning.
o   You came **_earlier_**.
o   But, Shyamal came **_earliest_** of all.

d) Rama writes *well.*
o   Arjun writes **_better_** than Rama.

- o Narayan writes **best** of all.
  e) Do you work *much*?
     - o I work **more than** you do.
     - o She works **most** of three of us. She is our mother.

❑ **To be noted:** Article 'the' is **not essential to be used with superlative adverb** in the sentence, though that is with the superlative adjective in the sentence; as,
  → He is the best student in the class. ('**best**' is the superlative adjective, preceding 'the' article.)
  → He runs worst of all. ('**worst**' is the superlative adverb, does not precede 'the' article in the sentence.)

✗ **Study the 'Degrees' or 'Forms of Comparisons' of Some Adverbs:**

Positive	Comparative	Superlative
Ill, badly	Worse	worst
Well	Better	Best
Much	More	Most
Little	Less	Least
(nigh) Near	Nearer	Nearest
Far	Farther/further	Farthest/furthest
Late	Later	Latest
Loud	Louder	Loudest
Wisely	More wisely	Most wisely
Patiently	More patiently	Most patiently

414. **Compare the Degree of Adverbs & the Degree of Adjectives**

Degree of Adverbs	Degree of Adjectives
1. He <u>runs</u> **faster**.	1. He is a *fast* <u>runner</u>.
2. The work is **badly** <u>done</u>.	2. You are a **bad** <u>boy</u>.
3. It <u>worked</u> **worst**!	3. He was one of the **worst** <u>boys</u> in the class.
4. The leader <u>spoke</u> **loudly**.	4. Don't use **loud** <u>speaker</u> here.
5. It <u>worked</u> **better**.	5. He is a **better** <u>boy</u>.
6. **Wisely** they <u>performed</u> their tasks.	6. <u>They</u> were *wise* in their task.
7. They <u>went</u> **nearer** to the beach.	7. <u>You</u> are **nearer** to me.

Note: the above bold words are the superlative forms, while the underlined are the words they add meaning or qualify. In the first column they add meaning to the verb underlined. In the second column they bold words qualify the nouns or pronouns underlined.

Relative or *Wh- Adjunctive* & Interrogative Adverbs

15. Relative Adverbs

✗ The adverbs ('wh' words) which like relative pronouns, *relates or refers back to its antecedents & modifies as usual an adverb does* to some words like verb, an adjective or another adverb or a phrase or a clause, are called the **Relative Adverbs**.

✗ Relative adverbs like relative pronouns <u>join two parts of a sentence</u> or <u>two clauses</u>, and introduce Relative or

Adjective clause in the sentence. Study the examples carefully:

1) Tell them the reason **why** you came.

   [You came for some purpose or for a reason. You tell them the reason.] After joining the independent sentences, the first one has turned to be '***why you came***', which is a relative clause, introduced by Relative Adverb '***why***'. 'why' denotes the reason.

2) I know the street **where** the bank is.

   [The bank is located somewhere at Gayeshwar Street. I know the street.] After joining the independent sentences, the first one has turned to be '***where the bank is***' which is a relative or adjective clause, introduced by Relative Adverb '***where***', which denotes 'place'.

3) Show me the house **where** (=in which) he was assaulted.

   [He was assaulted in a house. You know the house. You show me the house.] After joining the independent sentences, the first two sentences have turned to be one clause '***where (= in which) he was assaulted***' which is a relative clause, introduced by Relative Adverb '***where***', denotes 'place'.

4) This is the reason **why** I left her.

   [There was a reason. [May be, she boasts of too much. This is the reason.] For which I left her.] After joining the independent sentences, the first one, two or three sentences have turned to a condensed clause '***why I left her***' (*where one sentence is understood or implied*) and the clause is a relative clause, introduced by Relative Adverb '***why***', which denotes reason.

5) Do you know the time **when** Gour Express comes?

   [Gour Express comes at a certain time. I don't know the time. Do you know the time?] After joining the independent sentences, the first two sentences have turned to a condensed clause '***when Gour Express comes***' where one sense 'I don't know the time' remains understood or implied, and the clause is a relative clause, introduced by Relative Adverb '***when***', denoting time.

6) I remember the house **where** I was born.

   [I was born in a house. I remember the house.] After joining the independent sentences, the first one has turned to be '***where I was born***' which is a relative clause, introduced by Relative Adverb '***where***', denotes 'place'.

7) Tell me the direction, please; **where** is the Post Office?

   [I don't know the way to the Post Office. Tell me the direction, please.] After joining the independent sentences, the first one has turned to be '***where is the post office***' which relates back to its antecedent noun 'direction'; so, the clause is a relative clause, introduced by a Relative Adverb '***where***'.

8) Tell me at least a reason **why** should I believe you?

   [You want I should believe you. Tell me at least one reason.] After joining the independent sentences, the first one has turned to a clause '***why should I believe you***' which is a relative clause, introduced by Relative Adverb '***why***'.

9) Confess your crime **how** you committed.

   [You committed a crime. In what way you did that. You must confess. /In what way you committed the crime. You must confess.] After joining the independent sentences, the first one or ones have turned to be '***how you committed***' which is a relative clause, relates back to its antecedent noun 'crime'. The clause is introduced by Relative Adverb '***how***'.

✠ **To be remembered:** The **type of a clause depends upon the work done by it**, but not on linking words solely. Based on its work, role or function, a clause may be a **Noun, Adjective or Adverbial clause**.

Read the chart. (For details, visit to the chapter of Clause.):

A sentence in different clauses:

The **type of a clause depends upon the work done by it**, but not on linking words. That's why a clause may be **a Noun/ Adjective /Adverbia**l clause.	I know *where he lives*.	**Noun clause**, (object of 'know' by question —what do you know?)
	I know the place *where he lives*.	**Adjective clause**, (qualifying or describing the 'place' by question—which place?)
	I shall go *where he lives*.	**Adverbial clause**, (add meaning to the verb 'shall go'-by question —where? Where will you go?)

To be Noted: The **wh- relative adverbs**—where, why, when, how—when preceding antecedent noun or pronoun, are often termed as 'Relative Pronouns' by some grammarians, like 'Who', What' & 'Which'; but it is confusing, for **they [where, why, when & how]** hardly used in place of any noun or a pronoun, like 'who', 'what', 'which' do.

To avoid this confusion, Peter suggests, you may put blame solely on him, to term these as 'Wh- Adjunctive Adverbs' rather than to say as **'Relative Adverbs'** or as **'Relative Pronouns'**, as they do not only introduce relative or adjective clauses, but also Noun, or an Adverbial clause too, by their function or role in the sentence, like in the above chart. For the rest, however, you may try with written above.

16. Interrogative Adverb:

✘ When adverbs ('wh.' words) are used *in asking question*, they are called **Interrogative Adverbs**. The interesting thing is their answers are always other Simple Adverbs; as,
  - o When, how, why, how many, how far, where etc. are the *wh. words which are used to ask questions to get Simple Adverbs*. Study the examples and read their answers what roles they do in the sentences.
  1) **Where** is your Ram? (The answer is 'adv. of place' = in Heaven / at Ajodhya, etc.)
  2) **When** will He come to save you from your difficulties? (The answer is adv. of time = after my salvation / when time will come, etc.)
  3) **Why** are you late? (The answer is adv. of reason = Because I was with her in her bed / Because my spouse had not me fed / Because I woke up late, etc.)
  4) **How** did you do it? (The answer is adv. of manner = patiently/in patience)
  5) **How** much work can he do in a day? (The answer is adv. of degree = seven tones in a day, etc.)
  6) **How** high is Kutub Minar? (The answer is adv. of degree, adds meaning to an adj. = 73 meters long. [Long/tall—are adjectives. 73 metre are adv. Of degree.])

✘ In the above sentences, the bold **'wh' words** are the interrogative adverbs but their answers are the simple adverbs, either they are in single words or in phrases.

✘ Compare-**Relative Adverb** & **Interrogative Adverb** in the following chart:

Relative Adverb	Interrogative Adverb
1) Tell her the reason <u>why</u> I love her.	1) <u>Why</u> do I love her?
2) I know the place <u>where</u> she lives.	2) <u>Where</u> does she live?
3) Tell me the time <u>when</u> you'll come, my love.	3) <u>When</u> will you come?
4) Tell the way <u>how</u> you succeeded.	4) <u>How</u> did you succeed?

- Exercise-1: In the following sentences, **(1) pick out the Adverbs & tell what each modifies; (2) tell whether the modified word is a Verb, an Adjective, or an Adverb, a phrase or a clause; & (3) classify the Adverb** (denote their class, as Adverb of Time, Place, Manner, Degree or other).

1. Try again. He is too shy.
2. We rose very early. I am so glad to hear it.
3. Cut it lengthwise. Too many cooks spoil the broth.
4. Are you quite sure? This is well said.
5. Once or twice, we have met alone.
6. The railway station is far off.
7. I have heard this before.
8. Father is somewhat better.
9. I am much relieved to hear it.
10. The walk was rather long.
11. The patient is much worse today.
12. Ambition urges me forward.
13. She was dressed all in black.
14. We were very kindly received.
15. Her son is out in India.
16. I surely expect him tomorrow.
17. He could not speak; he was so angry.
18. You are far too hasty.
19. The secret is out.
20. He is old enough to know better.
21. I would much rather not go.
22. You need not roar.
23. He went off on Monday.
24. Wisdom is too high for a fool.
25. There is a screw loose somewhere.
26. I see things differently now.
27. Rome was not built in a day.
28. The door burst open and in they came.
29. Do not crowd your work so closely together.
30. Do not walk so fast.
31. Order the carriage round.
32. He has been shamefully treated.
33. I wonder you never told me.
34. The snake stealthily vanished from our sight.

- ## Fill in the blanks with suitable Adverbs

1) Tortoise walks _____ (Manner).
2) We will have our Semester exams on _____(Time).
3) The accident happened near the _____(Place).
4) At least _____ a week I used to go for Temple (Frequency).
5) We all go for a picnic just for _____ (Purpose).
6) The sea is very _____ (Degree /Quantity).
7) _____you are mistaken (Affirmation/Negation).

Answers

1) Tortoise walks slowly (Manner).
2) We will have our Semester exams on <u>April 1st week</u> (Time).
3) The accident happened near the <u>Highway</u> (Place).
4) At least twice a week I used to go for Temple (Frequency).
5) We all go for a picnic just for <u>enjoyment</u> (Purpose).
6) The sea is very <u>stormy</u> (Degree /Quantity).
7) <u>Surely</u> you are mistaken (Affirmation/Negation).

- **Try this exercise with the adverbs supplied below:**
    1) His face was dirty and he was dressed ---------------------. (manner)
    2) Have you---------------- ---------------------- been in a plane? (frequency)
    3) She was so ill that she missed school ------------------------. (duration)
    4) I did some homework last night and finished it--------------------. (time)
    5) We went------------------------------- to play. (place)
    6) Dad takes the dog for a walk -----------------------------. (frequency)
    7) Sally left her pencil case--------------------------------. (Place)
    8) Speak ---------------------------so everyone can hear you. (manner)
    9) It was a fine day and the children played in the garden ------. (duration)
    10) "Go and do your homework." "I've-----------------------done it." (time)
        (Outside – this morning – ever – on the bus – clearly –all day –in old clothes– for a week– already–
        every day)

Answers:
1. His face was dirty and he was dressed ***in old clothes***. (manner)
2. Have you ***ever*** been in a plane? (frequency)
3. She was so ill that she missed school ***for a week*** (duration)
4. I did some homework last night and finished it ***this morning***. (time)
5. We went ***outside*** to play. (place)

6. Dad takes the dog for a walk **every day**. (frequency)
7. Sally left her pencil case **in the bus.** (place)
8. Speak **clearly** so everyone can hear you. (manner)
9. It was a fine day and the children played in the garden **all day**. (duration)
10. "Go and do your homework." "I've **already** done it." (time)

The Forms & Formation of Adverbs

When we are reading of forms of adverbs, it means, how adverbs look. Like any part of Speech, Adverbs too have multi forms. However, there are also a lot of which can be formed from others. Study the following points, regarding the forms and formation of Adverbs:

A. Different parts of speech, generally, take different forms. However, *some may have also corresponding forms but their uses & meanings are different; as,*
   o It is so **yesterday** fashion! (As an Adjective)
   o They arrived **yesterday**. (As an Adverb)

   B. Some adverbs end in '**-ly**' but there are others which **do not have 'ly' ending**; as,
   o **Kindly** do the favor. (Adverb ends in '-ly')
   o Come **here**. (Adverb without '-ly' ending)

✖ The best way to identify a part of speech is to study the functions of certain part of speech and to know its difference from others. However, understanding of forms and formation help a learner quite a far.

✖ **Adverbs**, **Prepositions**, **Adjectives** as well as **Nouns** have lots of corresponding forms, but their uses, as said, are always different.

   C. Corresponding forms of **Adjectives** & **Adverbs**. Study them carefully:
1. He spoke in a **loud** voice. (In the underlined phrase, '**loud**' is an adjective, as it describes its following noun 'voice'; but the entire phrase '**in a loud voice**' is an adverbial phrase, modifying the manner of the verb 'spoke'; how did he speak? = in a loud voice.)

2. He talks so **loud**. (He talks so **loudly**) (here in 'loud' & 'loudly'—both are adverbs, adds meaning to the verb, 'talk')

Note: Thus, identity or classification of words vastly depend on their uses in the sentence, but not merely on forms.

Study more in the following chart:

Used as Adjectives	Used as Adverbs
1. Roshan is our **fast** bowler.	1. Roshan can bowl **fast**.
2. He lives in the **next** house.	2. When I **next** see him, I shall speak to him.
3. He went to the **back** entrance.	3. Go **back**.
4. Every **little** difficulty ruffles his temper.	4. He is **little** known outside India.
5. This is a **hard** sum.	5. He works **hard** all day.
6. It's an **ill** wind that blows nobody good.	6. I can **ill** afford to lose him.
7. He is the **best** boy in the class.	7. He behaves **best**.
8. He is **quick** to take offence.	8. Run **quick**.
9. Are you an **early** riser?	9. We started **early**.
10. The teacher has a **high** opinion of that boy.	10. Always aim **high**.
11. He is the **only** child of his parent.	11. You can **only** guess.
12. We have food **enough** to last a week.	12. She sings well **enough**.
13. He is no **better** than a fool.	13. He knows me **better** than you.

14. There is **much** truth in what he says.   14. The patient is **much** better.

D. **Adverbs with double forms:** There are some adverbs which have two forms, one <u>ends in 'ly'</u> & other <u>without 'ly'</u>. They may have same meaning; like, '**he sings very loud**' & '**he sings very loudly**'—both have same meanings.

         ✖   However, *most of adverb with double forms have different meanings*; as,

a) William works **hard** (=diligently).
b) I could **hardly** (scarcely) recognize him.

c) Stand **near** (opposed to distant).
d) They two are **nearly** (closely) related.

e) We arrived **late** (opposed to early).
f) I have not seen him **lately** (recently).

g) I am **pretty** (quite; fairly) sure of the fact.
h) She is **prettily** (neatly, elegantly) dressed.

E. The use of '**Adverbial Accusative**': Nouns or Adjectives denoting **adverbial** relations of time, place, distance, weight, measurement, value, degree or the like, are often used as adverbs — are known as '**Adverbial Accusative.**
[However, the term '**accusative**' refers to nouns, adjective or the forms of pronouns used in the direct object or connected with the direct object.]

Study in the following of adverbial accusative.

1) The program lasted <u>a *week*</u>. ('week' is a noun, refers 'the name of seven days' as a unit, but 'a week' is used in the sentence as **an adverbial phrase** <u>*to denote 'time of adverb'*</u>; as it adds meaning to the verb 'lasted'. 'How long did the program last for?')
2) He went **home**. ('home' denoting 'place of adverb', adds meaning to the verb 'went'. Where did he go? When 'home' comes from a noun.)
3) The load weighs <u>four *tones*</u>. (refers 'weight')
4) The cloth measures <u>three *meters*</u>. (Refers measurement of 'length')
5) The wound was **skin-deep**. (refers 'degree')
6) This will last me <u>a *month*</u>.
7) We walked <u>five *miles*</u>.
8) It measures <u>five *feet*</u>.
9) The watch is only <u>fifty *rupees*</u>.
      (Refers 'value', the price of the watch, 'how much did you pay? /How much you paid?' Here, it may raise a confusion regarding 'The watch is costly'. 'Costly' is an adjective describing the noun, 'watch'; but 'The watch is only fifty rupees', 'fifty rupees' neither refers to the watch itself nor describing it as 'costly', but refers its value, its price, 'how much one pay for the watch. So, it is an adverb.)
      The nouns used so, are known as '**Adverbial Accusative**'.

         ❑   However, there are some adverbs also <u>may be used as</u> **Nouns & Adjectives**:

✖   Some Adverbs are used as Nouns used after preposition; as,
     ▪ He lives far from **here** (this place).
     ▪ He comes from **there** (that place).
     ▪ I have heard that before **now** (this time).
     ▪ By **then** (that time) the police arrived on the scene.
     ▪ Since **when** (what time) have you taken to smoking?
     ▪ The rain comes from **above** (the sky).

✖   Certain <u>Adverbs can be used also as Adjectives</u>, when some participle is understood in the sentence; as,

- The **then** king = the king then reigning.
- A **down** train = a down-going train.
- An **up** train = an up-going train.
- The **above** statement = the statement made above.

Formation of Adverbs

A. Adverbs of Manner are mostly formed from Adjectives by adding '-**ly**'; as,
  - ➤Beautiful—beautifully; clever—cleverly; wise—wisely;
  - ➤foolish—foolishly; kind—kindly; quick—quickly;
  - ➤Sad—sadly; sweet—sweetly; wonderful—wonderfully;

  B. When adjective ends in '**y**' preceded by a consonant, *change '**y**' into '**i**', and then add '-**ly**'*; as,
  - ➤Happy—happily; heavy—heavily; ready-readily;

C. When the adjective ends in '**le**', simply *change '**e**' into '**y**' to form adverb*; as,
  - ➤Double—**doubly;** single—**singly,** etc.

    - o I am living here **singly**. No problem till now with the locals.
    - o They did it **doubly** but the credit goes to the boss only.

❏ **Study the differences in Forms & Uses:**

Used as an Adjective	Used as an Adverb
1. John is a **kind** man.	1. John spoke to him **kindly**.
2. They were **happy** couple.	2. After that they lived **happily**.
3. It is a **beautiful** garden.	3. It was decorated **beautifully**.
4. The load was **heavy**.	4. He bounced **heavily** to crack it down.
5. She spent **single** life.	5. She lived life **singly**.
6. He led a **double** life.	6. **Doubly** we are incomparable.
7. It is so **yesterday** fashion.	7. They arrived **yesterday**.
8. The baby was sound **asleep** (*sleeping deeply, describing the baby. It's an adjective).*	8. He replied **asleep**. *(Adverb of manner; replied while he was sleeping)*

Note: '-ly' ending words are not only the adverbs:

✗ The words *friendly, lively, kindly,* and *lonely* are usually adjectives. Study them in the following sentences:
  - o He is **friendly.**
  - o He is **lively.**
  - o He is **kindly.**
  - o He is **lonely.** (He feels lonely)

✗ In each sentence **the '—ly' words** are qualifying a person, 'he'. However, it may also describe things; as,
  - o She was wearing a **lovely** dress.
  - o It was a very **lively** party.

✗ Though we have adverbs with '**ly**' ending, there are larger than that number have adverbs without '-**ly**'; as,

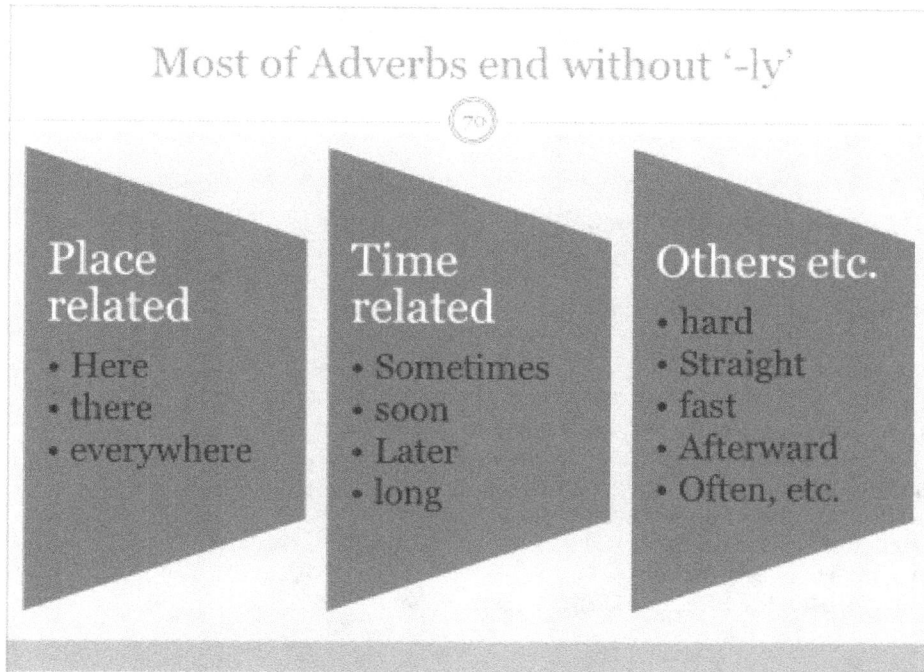

Most of Adverbs end without '-ly'

Place related
- Here
- there
- everywhere

Time related
- Sometimes
- soon
- Later
- long

Others etc.
- hard
- Straight
- fast
- Afterward
- Often, etc.

D. Some Adverbs are made up of a **Noun** & **qualifying Adjective**; as,

➢*Meantime, meanwhile, midway, otherwise, sometime, yesterday;*
1) I was thinking to go. **In the meantime**, he arrived.
2) I'll contact them soon. **Meantime** don't tell them I'm back.
3) The doctor will see you again next week. **Meanwhile**, you much rest as much as possible.
➢*Meantime = meanwhile= while something else is happening in the period of between two times or events)*
4) The hotel is situated **midway** between two stations.
5) The goal was scored **midway** through the first half.

➢*Midway= in the middle of a period of time; between two places.*
6) Shut the window, **otherwise** it'll get too cold in here.
7) My parents lent me the money. **Otherwise**, I couldn't have afforded the trip.

➢*Otherwise = used to state what the result would be, if sometimes did not happen or if the situation were different.*
8) **Sometimes**, I go by car. (=*occasionally rather than all the time*)
9) She **sometimes** writes to me. I like to be on my own sometimes.
10) Where were you **yesterday morning**? They arrived **yesterday**.

E. Some adverbs are compounds of a **preposition** like 'a' (weakened form of 'on') or 'be' (from middle English 'bi' ['by']), 'to', 'over' & a **noun**; as,
   ➢Abed (on bed), aboard (on board), afoot (on foot), ahead (on head), asleep (on sleep), away (on way); besides (by + sides), betimes, overboard, to-day, to-morrow (also: today & tomorrow), etc.
1) He was lying ***abed*** and cursing us for our deaths. What a man!
2) We went ***aboard***. He was already ***aboard*** the plane.
3) The plane crashed, killing all 157 passengers ***aboard***.

➢Aboard = on or onto a ship, plane, bus or train.
➢ Afoot = being planned, happening; on foot

4) There are blue prints ***afoot*** to increase taxation.
5) Sometimes they come ***afoot*** (on foot).

➢Ahead = further forward in space or time; in front.

6) I'll run ***ahead*** and warn them. The road ***ahead*** was blocked.
7) We've got a lot of hard work ***ahead***.

8) He replied **asleep**. (Adverb of manner; replied while he was sleeping)
9) The baby was sound asleep (sleeping deeply, describing the baby. It's an adjective).
10) The beach is a mile **away**. (= to or at a distance from somebody or something)
11) Christmas is still a month's **away**.
12) I don't really want to go. **Besides,** it's **too** late now.
➤ Besides = used for making an extra comment that adds to what you have just said.
➤ Betimes =in a good season of time; early, especially in the morning. / In a short time or soon)
13) I'll try my best to finish it **betimes**.

F.   Some are compounds of a **preposition**& an **adjective**; as, (along, aloud, anew, behind, below, beyond, etc.)
1)   I was **just** walking **along** singing myself
2)   We're going for a swim. Why don't you come **along**?
3)   The book is coming **along nicely**.
4)   Along= forward with somebody, towards a better state or position, etc.
5)   Aloud= in a voice that other people can hear/ in a loud voice
6)   He read the letter **aloud** to us. She cried **aloud** in protest.
7)   What am I going to do? She wondered **aloud**.
8)   Anew = to do something in a different way.
9)   They started a life **anew** in Canada.
10) Sit **beside** me. He is **behind** us.
11) The rabbit is **under** the tree. It is **beyond** our reach.

G.   Many a preposition are used to form adverbial phrase; as, (In, out, on, up, above, below, over, within, without, before, beneath, etc.) Now study them in the sentences to understand the difference better.
1)   He is shouting **_from the top_**.
2)   We are learning **_in class-room_**.
3)   She is sitting **_under a tree_**.
4)   Two other guards stood **_behind him_**.
5)   We were walking **_along the road_**.
6)   They were walking **_on the treadmill_**.
7)   All of us sat **_in awkward silence for a few seconds_**.
8)   The maid skipped her work **_two days in a row_**.
9)   Who were grazing **_in the field_**?
10) Stand you all **_in a line_**.

H.   Study the chart of adverb which are said to come from pronouns—the(that), he (here), who ('wh'):

Pronouns	Place	Motion to	Motion from	Time	Manner
That	There (that place)	Thither (to or towards that place)	Thence (from that place)	Then (that time)	Thus (that way)
this	Here (this place)	Hither (to this place)	Hence (from here/from this place; after a length of time in the future; for this reason)	--	--
wh	Where (what place)	Whither (where or to which place; what is likely to happen to something in the future)	Whence (from where)	When (at what time)	How (in what manner)

How to use them in the sentences

1)   He is coming **hither** (to this place).
2)   **Hither** he is coming, everyone be alert.
3)   **Thither** (to/towards that place) she is going, keep watch on her.
4)   People began rushing **hither & thither**. (Also, hither & yon)

274

5) *Whither* = where/ to which place; used to ask what is likely to happen to something in the future.
6) ***Whither*** should they go? They did not know ***whither*** they should go.
7) ***Whither*** modern architecture after this decade?
8) ***Whither*** modern technology, let us know in the seminar.
9) We have belief in his abilities. ***Hence*** (for this reason), we must motivate the child.
10) We suspect she is hiding something; ***hence*** it needs an impartial enquiry.
11) They made their way from Spain to France &***thence*** (from that place) to England.
12) He was promoted to manager, ***thence*** to a partnership in the farm.
13) The aliens returned ***whence*** (from where) they had come.
14) Many scholars have argued ***thus*** (in this way/like this).
15) The university has expanded colleges, ***thus*** allowing more students the chance of higher education. Don't come ***here*** (this place) so frequently. Don't go ***there*** (that place) ***ever***.
16) ***Where*** (what place) have you been ***yesterday***?

I.   Many adverbs are compounded with Prepositions (i.e., they are formed by 'adverb+ preposition'); as,
* **'here' + prep** = Hereabouts, hereafter, hereby, herein, hereof, hereto, heretofore, hereupon, herewith,
* **'there' + prep** = Thereabouts, thereafter, thereby, therefore, therefrom, therein, thereof, thereon, thereto, thereunder, thereupon, therewith,
* **'hither'/ 'hence'/ 'thence' + prep** = hitherto, henceforth, henceforward, thenceforth, thenceforward, etc.
* **'where' + prep** = whereabouts, whereby, wherever, wherefore, wherein, whereon, whereupon, etc.
* Besides using as adverb, some of the above, and others as _whereas_, _whereof_, are used as Conjunctions.

Using them in the sentences

1) There aren't many houses ***hereabouts*** (also: hereabout, near this place).
2) Here is not found your name on this page & ***hereafter*** (in the rest of the document).
3) ***Hereafter*** (also: 'hereinafter', from this time) you are not my friend.
4) ***Hereby*** it is admitted, most sorrowfully, she is no more with us.
5) ***Hereby***, it is declared we have no objection with Mr. Sarkar if he gets a better chance. (Legally declared something/as a result of this statement)
6) He is not ***herein*** (in this place) since the last year.
7) ***Herein*** (in the document/statement) I have not found any discrepancy.
8) Neither party is willing to compromise and ***herein*** lies the problem.
9) I'll not take a part ***hereof*** (of this), as I donated her all.
10) Please see the policy ***hereto*** (to this) appended.
11) She never behaved so ***heretofore*** (before this time).
12) She insulted me. I haven't visited ***hereupon*** (after this, as a direct result of this situation). She didn't come ***hereupon*** as I have insulted her once.
13) I enclose ***herewith*** (with this letter, book or document) a copy of my Aadhar card for verification.
14) Please, enclose ***herewith*** a copy of your policy.

15) Peter is from Balurghat or ***thereabouts*** in Wet Bengal. (Near the place mentioned)
16) They paid ten million rupees or ***thereabouts*** for the piece of land. (Near about the particular number, quantity, time or age, mentioned, which is not exact)
17) She must be 18 or ***thereabouts*** by then.
18) She married at 17 & gave birth to her first child shortly ***thereafter*** (after the time or event), swallowed her career and dream!
19) Regular exercise strengthens the heart, ***thereby*** (as the result of an action or situation, mentioned) reducing the risk of heart attack.
20) He is only 17 and ***therefore*** (due to that reason, logical) not eligible to cast vote.
21) There is still much to discuss. We shall, ***therefore***, return to this topic at our next meeting.
22) The committee will examine the agreement & any problem arising ***therefrom*** (from the thing mentioned).
23) The insurance policy covers the building and any fixture contained ***therein*** (in the document, place or object, mentioned).
24) In court she denied any knowledge of the article and the allegations made ***therein***.
25) Is the property or any part ***thereof*** (of the thing mentioned) used for commercial activity?
26) A meeting to discuss the annual accounts & the auditor's report ***thereon*** (on the thing, mentioned).
27) The lease entitles the holder to use the buildings and any land attached ***thereto*** (to the thing mentioned).

28) This savings plan is only available under the Finance Act 1990 & any regulations made **thereunder** (under the thing, mentioned).
29) The audience **thereupon** (immediately after the situation) rose cheering to their feet.
30) A large notice with black letters printed **thereupon**.
31) **Therewith** (with the thing already mentioned /soon after) I like to give 'thanks' for all you have done for me.
32) Friday, 31 July 1925 **henceforth** (also: 'henceforward', from this particular time and all the times in the future) became known as Red Friday.
33) Thursday, 25 Dec. 2019 **henceforward** became known as 'Covid Day'.
34) **Thenceforth** (starting from that time) he became known as the lord of protector.
35) Her life **hitherto** (until now, until the particular time) had been devoid of adventure.
36) In my last visit to Sundarbans, I discovered a **hitherto** unknown species of moth.
37) **Whereabouts** did you find it? (Used to ask general area where somebody, something is)
38) They have introduced a new system **whereby** all employees must undergo regular trainings.
39) **Wherever** (where) can he have gone to? (Used to ask expressing surprise to mean 'where')
40) **Wherefore**, art thou Romeo? (What for/why/because of what)
41) It is an organization **wherein** (in which place, situation, condition or thing) each employee I valued & respected.
42) **Wherein** lies the difference between Feminism & Monism?
43) I love the ground **whereon** (on which/on what/where) he stands.
44) He told her, she was a liar, **whereupon** (as a result of this) she walked out.

J. Sometimes, two adverbs go together, joined by conjunction 'and'; as,

a. **Again & again** = more than once, repeatedly;
b. **By and by** = before long; presently; after a time;
c. **Far & away** = decidedly; beyond all comparisons; by a great deal;
d. **Far & near** = in all directions;
e. **Far & wide** = comprehensively;
f. **First & foremost** = first of all;
g. **Now & again** = at intervals; sometimes; occasionally;
h. **Now & then** = from time to time; occasionally;
i. **Off & on** = not regularly; not intermittently;
j. **Once & again** = on more than one occasion; repeatedly;
k. **Out & away** = beyond comparison; by far;
l. **Out & out** = decidedly; beyond all comparison;
m. **Over & above** = in addition to; besides; as well as;
n. **Over & over** = many times; frequently; repeatedly;
o. **Through & through** = thoroughly & completely;
p. **Thus & thus** = in such & such a way;
q. **To & fro** = backwards & forwards; up & down

Using them in the sentences

1) Good book should be read _again and again_.
2) I warned him _again & again_ not do that.
3) _By and by_ the tumult will subside.
4) _By and by_ he became a renowned writer.
5) Her fame has spread _far & near_.
6) As a statesman he saw _far & wide_.
7) This is _far and away_ the best course.
8) He is _far and away_ the best bowler in our eleven.
9) He _now and then_ writes on fiscal questions.
10) I write to him _now and then_.
11) He worked five years, _off & on_, on 'Peter's Complete English Grammar'
12) I have told you _once and again_ that you must not read such trash.
13) This is _out and away_ the work on philosophy.
14) He gained _over and above_ this, the goodwill of all people.
15) _Over & above_ being hard-working he is thoroughly honest.
16) He reads all the novels of Paul _over & over_.
17) I believe he is _out and out_ the best Indian batsman.
18) He has read Milton _through & through_.
19) _Thus, and thus_ only we shall succeed.

20) He walked *to & fro*, meditating. He walked *to & fro* doing nothing.

The Position of Adverbs

o   The place or position of an adverb in a sentence can be defined in the following ways:

A.   Adverb of **Manner**, adverb or adverbial phrase of **Place, Time**—are generally placed after the verb or an object, if any, & if there is only one adverb; as,
   1)   It is raining **heavily**.
   2)   The ship is going **slowly**.
   3)   She speaks English **well**.
   4)   He does his work **carefully**.
   5)   He will come **here**.
   6)   I looked **everywhere**.
   7)   Hang the picture **there**.
   8)   I met him **yesterday**.
   9)   They are to be married **next week**.

B.   When there are two or more adverbs and they are to be used after verb or an object, the normal order of adverbs is: adverb of **Manner** > **Place** & >**Time**; as,
   1)   She sang *well **in the concert*** in *last year*.
   2)   We should go *there **tomorrow evening***.
   3)   He spoke *earnestly **at the meeting*** *last night*.
   4)   All of us sat ***in awkward silence*** *in the meeting hall* ***for a few seconds***.
   5)   Inspector Rana ***awkwardly*** put his cup ***down on the table***.

C.   When an adverb modifies a verb, an adjective, another adverb, a phrase or a clause, it is usually used before it. This happens to Adverb of Frequency & other adverbs; as,
   1)   I am **never** *late* for my school.
   2)   He is **always** *at home* on Sundays.
   3)   We are **just** *off*. He is a **rather** *lazy* boy
   4)   I worked **only** *two* sums. She has slept **only** *three* hours.
   5)   The dog was **quite** *dead*.
   6)   The book is **very** *interesting*.
   7)   Do not speak **so** *fast*.
   8)   I have read **all** *through the book*.
   9)   **Suddenly**, *he arrived there*.
   10) His wife **never** *cooks*.
   11) He has **never** *seen* a tiger.
   12) I have **often** *told* him to write neatly.
   13) We **usually** *have breakfast* at eight.
   14) My uncle has **just** *gone out*.
   15) I **quite** *agree with* you.
   16) He was **almost** *dead*. **Hardly** *has he done his work in time*.
   17) He reached the party before **nearly** *three hours*.

D.   When **the adverbs are stressed**, generally in replies, the adverbs may be **used just after the subjects** (adverbs shift to be used between subject & the verbs), **but not before the word it modifies; as,**
   1)   Amal has come late again. Yes, he **always** does come *late*.
   2)   When will you write the essay? But I **already** have *written* it.
   3)   Will you be free on Sundays? I **usually** am *free* on Sundays.
   4)   Do you eat meat? Yes, I **sometimes** do. (do = eat meat)
   5)   I **often** have to *go* to college on foot.
   6)   He **always** used to *agree* with me.
   7)   I **only** worked *two* sums.
   8)   He has **only** slept *three* hours.

E.   However, some like 'enough' comes after the word it modifies; as,
   1)   Is the box **enough**? (here 'enough' modifies the number of box or its' size, understood; i.e., modifying

the adjective, not the noun 'box')
2) He has *rash* **enough** to interrupt.
3) He spoke *loud* **enough** to be heard.
4) Amal has *come* **late**.

✘ **Note:** we noticed that though adverbs generally used before the words it modifies, but they are also used after verb and object in the examples of Manner, Place & Time.
✘ When they are stressed, adverbs are shifted, and with certain adverbs like 'enough' adverb is used after the 'word' it modifies.
✘ Thus, *adverbs, based on its nature, may be used at anywhere in the sentences, at the beginning, center (like between subject & verb) and also at the end.*

o **Exercise-1: Insert** the adverbs (or adverb phrases) in their normal position:
1) He invited me to visit him (often).
2) I am determined to yield this point (never).
3) I know the answer (already).
4) We have seen her (just, in the squire).
5) I have to reach the office (by 9.30, usually)
6) Will he be (there, still)?
7) I shall meet you (this evening, in the park).
8) The train has left (just).
9) Can you park your car near the shop? Yes, I can (usually).
10) You have to check your oil before starting (always).
11) He is in time for meals (never).
12) We should come (here, one morning).
13) He has recovered from his illness (quite).
14) He goes to the cinema (seldom).
15) That is not good (enough).
16) You must say such a thing (never, again).
17) Suresh arrives (always, at 9 o'clock, at the office).
18) He played the violin (last night, brilliantly, in the concert).

24. Prepositions, Kinds & Uses

o The chapter includes-
  ❑ Definition,
  ❑ Kinds of Prepositions,
    ▪ Prepositional phrase,
  ❑ The Functions of Prepositions,
    ▪ Special attention to some prepositions,
  ❑ The Place of Prepositions,
    ▪ When they are used at the end.
  ❑ Prepositional Objects or Complement.
  ❑ Conjugation of Preposition with Nouns, Adjectives or Participle & Verbs (i.e., Certain Nouns, Adjective or Participle & Verbs take some particular Prepositions).
o **Read:**
  → There is a cow **in** the field.
  → He is fond **of** tea.
  → The cat jumped **off** the chair.

▪ **In sentence 1,** the word '*in*' is placed before '*the field*' (mainly 'field'; 'the' is an article to define 'field') & *shows relation between two words, '**cow**' & '**field**' (both are Nouns).*

▪ **In sentence 2,** the word '*of*' is placed before '*tea*' & *shows relation between two words, '**fond**' & '**tea**' (Adj.& Noun).*

- **_In sentence 3,_** the word '_off_' is placed before '_the chair_' (mainly 'chair') & thus _shows relation between the two words, 'jumped' & 'chair' (Verb & Noun)._

- **Note:** Thus, **Prepositions generally used before Nouns** and they <u>**show relation with**</u> other words that may be <u>**another Noun, an Adjective or a Verb,**</u> like the above.
    - Here, the words— **_in, of, off_** —are the examples of Prepositions.

o **Definition: -<u>Preposition is a word</u>**, which is <u>**generally used before a noun, noun phrase or a pronoun**</u>, connecting it with another word in the sentence [that may be <u>**another Noun, an Adjective or a Verb**</u>] that shows relation between them.

Study the following examples.

➤He is swimming **_in_** the evening. ('in' is used before 'evening', and shows its relation with 'swimming', a _noun with a verb_. Here 'in' is the preposition. However, the phrase '**in the evening**' is an adverbial phrase, _denoting_ '**time**' of the action 'swimming'.)

➤We were looking **_towards_** the sky. ('looking' & 'sky', the verb and the noun— are shown related by the word 'towards' which is a preposition. However, the phrase 'towards the sky' denotes the adverb of movement.)

o **When Prepositions, used with Adjectives:**
❏ Prepositions are often used with some adjectives, preceding them. The adjectives in these examples are underlined**.**
- → Dad was angry **_with_** us.
- → We were afraid **_of_** the big dog.
- → She's not very interested **_in_** sports.
- → John is very good **_at_** drawing.
- → Mr. Lee is pleased **_with_** our work.
- → The teachers are always kind **_to_** us.
- → What's wrong **_with_** the computer?

o **When Prepositions, used with Verbs:**
❏ Prepositions more frequently follow the verbs; like the followings _(The verbs in these examples are underlined and in color):_
- → I'm looking **_for_** my pencil. Have you seen it?
- → Can you think **_of_** another word for 'pleased'?
- → Does this book belong **_to_** you?
- → We're listening **_to_** CDs.
- → I agree **_with_** you, regarding this issue.
- → Tell me **_about_** the show you saw.
- → Cut the cake **_into_** five pieces.
- → They borrowed money **_from_** the bank.
- → The girl boasts **_of_** her out beauty.
- → They laughed **_at_** us & we bore the humiliation.
- → The principal sends **_for_** Kakuli madam for our help. (Ask somebody to come)

o **When Prepositions, used with Nouns:**
❏ Prepositions are also used with nouns, preceding them like verbs & adjectives in the previous examples. The nouns in these examples are written in color and underlined.
- → What's the answer **_to_** this question?
- → Is there a reason **_for_** this delay?
- → What's the matter **_with_** you?
- → Here's an example **_of_** good behavior.
- → Congratulations **_on_** winning the competition!
- → Traffic can cause damage **_to_** the environment.

o **Exercise-1: Fill** _in the blanks with suitable prepositions that denote **'the functions of adverbs',** written within the bracket:_
- a) A cat was sitting _____the roof of my car. (place)
- b) Some people were talking ____the movie. (time)

c) A man was coming_____ us on his bike. (direction)
d) The party starts_____ six o'clock. (time)
e) She put the book _____her bag. (place)
f) We walked_____ the street to the park. (place)
g) She keeps her slippers_____ her bed. (place)
h) We always wash our hands _____meals. (time)
i) She ran _____the house because she was frightened.   (direction)

o **Exercise-2:** *Find out the relation the preposition made between:*

a) He kept the **pen in** the **bag**. (pen & bag, by preposition 'in'; shows 'place'.)
b) She wants money to become one of the rich **in** her town. (rich & town, between two Nouns)
c) I *listened* **to** you attentively. (listened & you, verb-pronoun)
d) The patient *wants* to be cure **before** her board examination. (between 'cure' & 'board examination')
e) We had *started* **by** then. (started & then, verb &adverb)
f) He was *surprised* **at** her saying this. (Between verb & -ing clause)
g) He was *surprised* **at what he said**. (verb & wh- clause)
h) He *wants* to go **in** the cinema hall. (go & cinema hall, verb & noun.)
i) Give *alms* **to** beggar. (Between two nouns)

Kinds of Prepositions

o <u>According to form or structure</u>, Prepositions may be arranged in six types or classes—
  (1) Simple,
  (2) Double,
  (3) Compound,
  (4) Prepositional Phrase,
  (5) Participial Prepositions &
  (6) Disguised Prepositions.

  ➢ **Read them now in details-**

(1) **Simple Prepositions:** Prepositions which consist of only one word. They are mostly of single syllable & some of two; as, *at, by, for, from, in, on, of, off, out, round, through, till, to, under, up, with,* etc.
  1) I place my book **on** the table.
  2) I saw a girl **in** the garden.
  3) The dry leaves fall **from** the trees.
  4) The boys are sitting **under** a tree
  5) Girl is sitting **on** the table.
  6) We shall have a Transparency Integrity seminar **in August** (*time*)
  7) The visitors are walking **round** the school(*direction*)
  8) Our principal will travel **by** train(*method*)
  9) Tima is walking **towards** the borehole.
  10) The boy was seen going **through** the fence.
  11) There is a cow **in** the field.
  12) He is fond **of** tea.
  13) The cat jumped **off** the chair.

(2) **Double Prepositions:** The Prepositions which are formed <u>by adding two simple prepositions, joined together or placed side by side</u>. Such prepositions are used when a single preposition does not express the sense properly; as, *away from, from among, from under, from within, into, onto, out of, throughout, unto, upon, within, without,* etc.
  1) The mouse ran **into** the room.
  2) Grace threw the ball **into** the bucket.
  3) She overturned the burning candle **onto** the table.
  4) One should be chosen **from among** the rest of candidates.
  5) The mouse peeps **from under** the table.
  6) A man in ragged cloths comes **from within** the house.

(3) **Compound Prepositions:** The Prepositions which are generally formed by prefixing *a shortened form of a simple preposition* (*like* **'a'** *in place of* **'on'**, **'be/b'** *in place of* **'by'**, or '<u>to any changed form</u>' of a simple preposition) with a *Noun*, *Adjective*, or an *Adverb*; as,

1) *about (on + bout),*	11) *behind (by+hind),*
2) *ab<u>ove</u> (on+**by**+**up**),*	12) *below (by+low),*
3) *across (on + cross),*	13) *beneath (by+neath),*
4) *again**st** (on + gain)*	14) *beside (by+side),*
5) *along (on+long),*	15) *between (by+twain),*
6) *amidst (on+ middle),*	16) *beyond (by+yonder),*
7) *among (on+**gemong**, meaning 'mingling'),*	17) ***but** (by+**out**, meaning except),*
8) *among**st**,*	18) *inside (in+side),*
9) *around (on+round),*	19) *outside (out+side),*
10) *before (by+fore),*	20) *underneath (under+neath),* etc.

1) Jeremy is **behind** the chair.
2) Who is lying **underneath** the tree?
3) **Beyond** there you can see daffodils thousands in number.

Note: Practically, we don't need study these forms (how do they form) but study their uses; however, study of formation always helps to understand its meaning hidden.

Prepositional Phrase

(4) **Complex or Phrase Prepositions:** The Prepositions which are <u>formed by two or more words</u>, with the force of a single preposition at the end; as, *according to, as for, because of, due to, owing to,* etc. and their meanings need to study differently other than the meaning of a simple preposition; as,

1) Act **according to** my instructions.
2) Why don't you come **along with** us?
3) **Agreeably to** the terms of the settlement, I herewith enclose a demand draft for Rs. 20000.
4) He could not attend the classes **because of** his illness.
5) **By reason of** his perverse attitude, he estranged his best friends.
6) **In consequence of** his illness, he could not finish the work in time.
7) **In event of** his dying heirless, his nephew would inherit the whole property.
8) There is an open field **in front of** our house.
9) Tom was standing **in front of her** house five hours.
10) You have come **from outside**.
11) He got the flat **in lieu of** all his sundry.
12) I took Arts **in place of** science.
13) **In spite of** hard labor, he could not succeed.
14) Mrs. Gosh joined the meeting **instead of** her husband.
15) He went there **instead of** me.
16) **Owing to** excessive rain, the flood occurs this year.
17) Rs 75,000 **in full settlement of** all your claims is up-to-date.
18) Whatever he does, he does **with an eye to** the main chance.

✗ **Exception:** Some phrases do not take any simple preposition at end; as, '*on this side*', '*on board*', etc.
   ○ **On this side** yo<u>u</u> can see the stretched green land.
   ○ **On board**, she recalled her boyfriend & rushed towards the door.

To be noted: On this side—is better to call an adverbial phrase, and '**on board**'—is an adjective phrase, used as participle to qualify a noun or a pronoun, here a pronoun 'she'. However, remember: most of prepositional phrases or prepositions have an adverbial sense in their uses, besides they show relation between words. And some are used as participial too (as an adjective), to describe a noun or a pronoun.

✗ Here is **the list of Complex Preposition** or **Prepositional Phrase**. Study them carefully:

Prepositional Phrases	Meaning...	Examples

At home in	Familiar with/skilled in	He is <u>quite at home in</u> Mathematics.
At the top of	Highest point	The man began to cry at the top of his cry.
Because of	Due to reason	She could not sing because of cough & cold.
By dint of	With help	By dint of hard work, he succeeded.
By force of	By power of	Even a difficult thing is made easy by force of habit.
By means of	Way of/virtue of	He won the honor by means of selfless service.
By the side of	Beside	A small river flows by the side of the small village.
By virtue of	With help	She stood first by virtue of hard labor.
For the sake of	For/cause	Netaji sacrificed his life for the sake of his country.
For want of	Due to lack of	The drought occurs for want of rain.
In accordance with	accordingly,	Your action is not in accordance with your word.
In connection with	Relating	In connection with your query, I am writing this letter.
In case of	If happen (something)	In case of his death his son will get the benefit.
In common with	Agree with	You should also be favored with the others.
In course of	During the time	In course of conversation, he also mentioned it.
In consideration of	Considering	In consideration of his hard work, he may succeed.
In defense of	In support of	The pleader made a good proceeding in defense of his client.
In favor of	In support of	The students spoke in support of their teacher.
In front of	Before/at front	They saw a hut in front of the palace.
In keeping with	Accordance with	His interest in religion is in keeping with his age.
In lieu of	Instead of/in place of	Please take my subscription in lieu of her.
In opposition to	On contrary of	Your view is in opposition to mine.
In order to	For/ due to	In order to get a good result, he studied very hard.
In quest of	For seek of	He went to the town in quest of any job.
In regard to	Regarding/about	I have nothing to say in regard to this matter.
In reply/response to	Giving reply	In response to your advertisement, I am writing this one.
In respect of	Regarding	In respect of service, he is senior to me.
In spite of	Even of	In spite of his poverty, he refused help.
In support of	In support of	The students spoke in support of their teacher.
In the teeth of	Against	In the teeth of strong opposition, the bill was passed.

In view of	On considering	In view of the importance, I'll take prime carefulness.
On account of	Because of/due to	On account of his illness, he failed in the Exam.
On behalf of	For (somebody)	On behalf of me kindly give it to my wife.
On the brink of	At the point of	Bengal was on the brink of a terrible famine in 1942.
On the eve of	At the moment of	He made a great confusion on the eve of the occasion.
On the point of	At the moment of	She was on the point of bursting into tears.
With a view to	For purpose of	He went to Delhi with a view to taking part...
With reference to	Referring/mentioning	With reference to your letter, I have the honor to inform you.

✗ **Some words with different prepositions used in different situations.**

1st uses	Referring	2nd uses	Referring	3rd uses	Referring
Agree with	a person	Agree on	(a point)	Agree to	(a proposal)
Apply to	a person	Apply for	(the post)		
Angry with	a person	Angry for	something	Angry at	(conduct)
Appeal to	a person	Appeal for	something	Appeal against	(a wrong)
Blind in	(one eye)	Blind to	(a fault)		
Die of	(a disease)	Die from	(an effect)	Die for	(a cause)
Heir of	a person	Heir to	a property		
Live on	(food)	Live by	(a way)		
Pleased with	a person	Pleased at	something		
Quarrel with	a person	Quarrel for/ over/about	something		
Think of/ about	a person	Think over	something		

(5) **Participial Prepositions:** When a participle (present or past) is being used as a preposition in a sentence, & show relation with the subject or main verb of the main clause, it is distinguished as Participial Preposition; as, during, notwithstanding, preventing, being, except (being excepted), past (which is passed), having, considering, regarding, owing, etc.

  1) ***Barring (= except, apart from)*** accident, the mail will arrive tomorrow.
  2) ***Concerning (=about)*** yesterday's fire, there are many rumors in the bazaar.
  3) ***Considering (=on consideration)*** your age, you have done a great thing.
  4) Fresh fruit is available ***during (=through the time of)*** the winter.
  5) All the boys passed ***except (=but)*** one. There was lot of ***but*** none.
  6) ***Notwithstanding (=in spite of)*** his frown, his son went for an adventure to the jungle. I started reading at the hour ***past (=after)*** sunset.
  7) ***Pending (=until)*** further orders, Mr. Ghosh will act as Headmaster.
  8) I know nothing more ***regarding (=in regard of / about)*** this matter.
  9) ***Respecting*** the plan you mention, I shall write to you hereafter.
  10) ***Touching (=with regard to)*** this matter, I have not as yet made up my mind.

(6) **Disguised Prepositions:** These Prepositions are so called as outwardly they do not look like Prepositions, but actually they are derived from some Prepositions; as, *'a'* from **'on'**; *'o'* from **'of'**; *'be'* from **'by'**. (**Compare:** Compound Prepositions). Read the examples:

1) The journey costs at three miles *a* rupee.
2) The garbage carrier van visits the locality once *a* week.
3) The ship came *a*shore.
4) It's five *o*' clock now.

Functions of Preposition

o Functions of Prepositions
   A. Prepositions are ***mostly adverb in nature***. In many cases they form adverbial phrases with nouns; as,
      o 'In the evening' (adv. of time),
      o 'Towards the sky' (adv. of direction),
      o 'In the class-room', etc. (adverb of place)

   B. Preposition 'to' is ***used to form Infinitive Verb***; as,
      o He is thinking ***to*** go there.
      o He went market ***to*** buy a book.
      o I took Peter's English Grammar to read.

   C. A lot of prepositions are ***used to form phrasal verbs***; as,
      o He ***laughs at*** us. He ***sends for*** Bhima.
      o He is ***searching for*** the note.
      o He ***aims at*** to be a doctor.
      o He ***boasted of*** his accomplishments.

   D. Preposition ***'of'*** is used to ***show possession or parts of*** & ***'by'*** is used to ***show the agent of an action***; as,
      o We were charmed ***by*** the beauty ***of*** nature.
      o The book is designed by Mr. Peter and who is also Mr. P.

The Adverbial Functions of Prepositions

o There are a lot of prepositions which have adverbial functions, i.e., they are used to form Adverbs. They do functions of an adverb in the sentences. Carefully study the examples. Before so, study the following chart:

Place, Position	Time	Movement	Direction	Agent/Instrument, Manner	Cause / Reason	Contrast/Concession, etc.
At, about	At, In	Through	To	By	For	Of
Above, under, up	On, By	Across	Towards	With	From	About
On, In	before	Along	From	For	Of	Without
By, over, below	After, till/until	Up, down, onto, into,	Into	In	With	Out of
Between	During	Downward	At	From	Because of,	
Among	For, past	Off	In	Without	Due to	
After	From	Away from	around	Throughout	As for	
Beside	Since	Upward				
Down	Within	up to				

1. Prepositions, denoting *Place*:
   Preposition often with Nouns or adjective form a phrase which denote place of adverb, where something happens or exits; as,
   a) Saini was sitting ***under*** a tree.
   b) Lay ***under*** the table.
   c) I leaned ***against*** the wall.
   d) Don't sit ***beside*** me.
   e) There's a wooden floor ***underneath*** the carpet.
   f) He fell ***among*** the thieves and lost his all.

g) Some geese flew **_over_** their house.

h) She lies **_upon_** bed.

i) They quarreled **_among_** themselves.

j) John and Sarah were hiding **_inside_** the wardrobe.

k) He was **_at_** death's door. The cliff hangs **_over_** the sea.

l) There was a tree **_beside_** the river.

m) Balurghat is **_on_** Atreyee.

n) Sit **_on_** deck. Stood **_before_** the door.

o) We live **_within_** the house.

p) She hides **_behind_** the curtain.

q) It was **_below_** the surface.

r) I have a friend who lives **_in_** America.

Prepositions *of Place*

(23)

	Pointing	Examples
At	Less known village/ town/ a small region	We live at Balurghat.
In	Large town/district/country/a large region	We are residing in West Bengal.
On	Position touching surface/supported by/attached to	The book is on the table.
By	Nearness	I always sit by my window.
Between	In the middle of two things or objects	It fell between the two houses.
Among	In the centre of more than two objects	The plane crashed among the trees.
Above	Very up in the sky without touching surface	The sun shines above our head.
Over	Up in the sky without touching the surface.	The shirt is hanging over the table.

2. Prepositions, denoting *Time*:

❑ Some prepositions with other parts of speech form phrase that show when something happens. They are known as adverbial phrase, denoting time.

❑ Examples: -

➢ School starts **_at_** nine o'clock.

➢ **_At_** 3 pm is your online class.

➢ We're going to the zoo **_on_** Saturday.

➢ **_In_** the morning everyday she does exercise.

➢ It's **_past_** your bedtime already.

➢ I visited my grandparents **_during_** the summer.

➢ You must finish the work **_by_** Friday.

➢ I'll do my homework **_before_** dinner.

❑ Prepositions *of Time*

Prepositions *of Time*

	Pointing	Examples	
In/on	In to mean a duration; on to mean specific day	It happened in the month of June. In Summer season, the building completed. In 1977 I was born. In August of 1977 I was born. On 16ʰ August, 1977 I was born in West Bengal.	
At	Specific point of time	He wakes up 3 o'clock everyday.	
By	Before the time	By noon I'll finish this task.	
During	To mean season or period of time	During morning walk I met her hundred times. During school days she was my best friend.	
For	For a period of time, in all tense.	He was sleeping for ten hours. I am working here for last twenty years.	
From	Starting from particular time	From seventeen she was in love with me, and we didn't get married. Marriage is not last word in love.	
Since	Mainly to use in perfect tense	He has been working in this project since last year. Since Monday she is in ill.	
Within	Before the specific time	We'll reach within two hours Within five days you must complete this work.	

3. Preposition that indicates 'Movement' or 'Motion', i.e., form the adverb of Movement; as,

3. Preposition that indicates 'Movement' or 'Motion'

Prepositions	Examples	
Through	We are walking through the jungle and not know theend.	
Across	He ran across the road & slightly saved from the accident.	
Along	Peter walked along the beach road and enjoyed scenic beauty.	
Past	The car went **past** me.	
Above	The kite is flying **above** the tress.	
Over	The dog jumps over the table.	
To , Into	The dog fell into the ditch. The boy goes to school.	
About	The sailor went about the world.	
Towards	We travelled towards Nasik after this.	
Up	The thief climbed up the ladder & stole into the room.	
Down	I came (got) down from the running bus.	

4. Prepositions of **Direction**:
Some prepositions show where something is going. They are adverb in nature or form Adverb of Direction: as,
- The boys chased **_after_** each other.
- The football rolled **_down_** the hill.
- A man was walking his dog **_along_** the riverbank.
- The freeway goes **_right_** through the city.
- We were travelling **_towards_** Miami.

❑ Prepositions that show 'Direction'

Prepositions	Prepositions that show 'Direction', almost similar to 'motion', but have difference. Study them carefully.
To	Turn to him and say whatever you have concern or grievance.
Towards	Nicky turned towards north & started hi journey again.
From	Don't let your attention to divert from this point.
Into	He entered the room. He came into the room.
At	He looked at me & said nothing.
In	He went in the east of the country. (In east part) He went to the east. (Merely direction, towards east) He went at the east of the country. (At last point)

5. Preposition that indicates '**Agent/Instrument /Manner**' (including measure, standard, rate, value, etc.)

	Examples
By	Send the parcel by post. It was destroyed by fire. I was stunned by the sudden blow.
With	Cut the cake with a knife.
Through	I heard of this news through one of my friends.
At	Sell good s at auction. (It means agency more than a place) The bank charges interest at eight percent. Stories like these must be taken at what they are worth.
	Prepositions that show Manner:
By	The patient was dying by inches since last August. Cloth is sold by the yard. I am taller than you by two inches. It was one by the tower clock.
With	The soldiers fought with courage. They won the battle with ease. They worked on it with earnestness.

6. Prepositions that show **Cause, Reason** or **Purpose'**

	Examples
For	o Everyone should labour for the good of humanity. o It is a place for a picnic. He took medicine for cold.
From	o She has been suffering from gout. o No one died from fatigue. However, it is a popular illusion.
Of	o Shyam, my friend died of fever.
With	o She shivers with fever.
Pending	o She was held in custody **pending** trial.
In	o My father died in accident. o Many died in cholera in the last famine.
Through	o The soldier retreated through fear of an ambush. (Due to the cause of his fear; don't confuse it with manner; and thus:) o You have lost your purse through negligence. (For the cause of). o He concealed his talent through shame. Lockdown gave him a chance.

7. Contrast & Concession
- o After (in spite of, notwithstanding) every effort, one may fail.
- o For (in place of) one enemy he has a hundred friends.
- o For (in spite of) all his wealth he is not content.
- o With (in spite of) all his faults I admire him.

8. Inference, motive, source, or origin
- o **From** what I know of him, I hesitate to trust him.
- o The knights were brave **from** gallantry of spirit.
- o He did it **from** gratitude.
- o Light emanates **from** the sun.
- o From labor health, **from** health contentment springs.
- o This is a quotation **from** Milton.
- o His skill comes **from** practice.
- o He comes **of** a good family.
- o It was good **of** you to help me.
- o He has come **from** a royal family.

- o **Exercise-1:** Identify the Functions of Prepositions in the following sentences:
  - o There is a cow **in the field.** (It denotes 'place of adverb', denoting the position of the cow.)
  - o He is fond **of tea**. (It has formed the complement of adjective, 'fond'.)
  - o The cat jumped **off the chair**. (Denotes adverb of movement, adds meaning to the word, 'jumped')
  - o *We* shall have a Transparency Integrity seminar **in** August (time)
  - o The boys are sitting **under** a tree
  - o Girl is sitting **on** the table
  - o The visitors are walking **round** the school(direction)
  - o Our principal will travel **by** train(method)
  - o Rubi was <u>behind</u> the tree.
  - o I was standing in front of the tree.
  - o Tima is walking **towards** *t*he borehole.
  - o Grace threw the ball **into** the bucket.
  - o The boy was seen going **through** the fence.
  - o She was standing in front of the tree.
  - o Tima is walking **towards** *t*he borehole.
  - o Grace threw the ball **into** the bucket.
  - o The boy was seen going **through** the fence.

o **Some prepositions need special attention:**

1) **Usage of 'at':** *(for exact location, near at small place, at exact time, & many others)*; *as,*
   - o We started at eight o'clock. At any time, I am ready to go.
   - o He woke up at dawn. At day time we do our work. (**Also:** in the dawn, in the day time, during day time)
   - o Why to sing so loudly at bed-time? Eat this one at a time.
   - o They are at work. The boys are at play now.
   - o He is now at home/at school/at his office.
   - o He was at the door, when he heard her cry for help.
   - o We were at dinner, then my aunt visited us.
   - o Suddenly I fell at sea. Feel at home, we are like your own.
   - o He ran at full speed, and yet was beat by others on the track. He was standing at a distance when I saw him. He is at the meeting.
   - o He studied at this university. Everyone is asked to present at the meeting at a short notice. The professor shouted at the boys.
   - o I did not expect such treatment at your hands (from you)
   - o Look at me. He is very good at cricket. He is seen at all places.
   - o We will hear at the latest by Saturday. At any moment he may come.
   - o This can be found at all places. At age of sixty he married again.

2) **Usage of 'by':** *(when we talk about* **'means of transport'** *to mean* **'an agent of an action that may be person or thing'** *& to mean* **'manner of doing an action'** *we use 'by' before the noun & preceding a*

verb.)

- We travelled by train. (Not: by the or by a train); and thus, travelling by boat, ship, plane or by air & by car, etc.;
- By day time I don't go sleep, but only at night.
- What is your routine in the day and in the night?
- The machine was driven by steam (by electricity or by petrol).
- It was destroyed by fire, not by earthquake.
- Send him the message by telegram.
- I know him by sight everyday morning while I myself go out.
- Students like teaching by suitable examples by teacher.
- By next Sunday we will reach there.
- She is indomitable by word of mouth.
- He studied his lessen by heart. Send this letter by post for me.
- By chance they met and fell in love to each other.
- Sell things by kilogram or meter, keep the calculation in hand always.
- He died by poison (by accident). She is older by five months.
- Eggs are sold by dozen. Sit by me. I did this work all by myself.
- It is 10-30 by my watch. Pay the amount by NEFT please.
- Everyone was struck by sudden lighting.
- This room is ten by fifteen feet. We live by the river.

3) **Usage of in:** *(before a **big town, region, country, state, district**, etc.; and as time of preposition, it is used before **year**, **month**, etc.); as,*
- I was born in 1986. In last holiday we went there.
- They lived in Canada. It was written in ink.
- It was happened in last February.
- The town is in ruins now. In every afternoon they walk along.
- His party is n power how. I sat in arm chair.
- You were in haste to buy the scooter.
- Be careful to fall in danger. She was in pain, I saved her.
- I was in difficulty; he helped me to out from there.
- The people are in arms against the king.
- She threw dust in my eyes, none realized this.
- Wait, I am coming back in five minutes.
- He came in time. Fill in the forms. Fill in the blanks.

4) **Usage of 'on':** (**on particular date**, **occasion**, **place** or **upper surface**, **on banks of river**, **hanging on something**, and to mean '**specific transport**'). **Note:** We already said for transport we use **'by'**; but, when we mean walking or cycling or any '**specific transport**', we use **'on'** or **'in'** in place of 'by'. Carefully study the examples:

- I travelled two kilometers on horseback & three kilometers on a bicycle on rent.
- We reached the peak climbing on rough hills.
- He goes to office on foot. I went there on bicycle.
- Suresh went there on my bike.
- We travelled in Mr. Joshi's car. They came in a taxi.
- I'll go on the 7.30 bus in the morning.
- On Wednesday my child was born.
- On 16th August, he joined his job.
- He was lying on bed. Write an essay on the topic/subject.
- The house was on fire. On oath I say, I didn't take yours.
- He is on the way to office. He was on time always.
- He is sitting on the sofa. The train is running on time.
- My uncle came on holiday. It was on left.
- Kolkata is on the Hooghly.
- He lectured on a common topic
- We live on rice. We live on our small income.
- He is playing on a musical instrument.
- He is on that committee. (Not: in)
- Our house is on the main road. It is on the Bhanumati Road.
- There is hanging a picture on the wall.

- o I had a ring on my finger. Now I am listening news on TV.
- o Balurghat is on the north of India. It was done on request/on demand.
- o No animal on land, on sea or in air is as large as a blue whale.
- o The car is on hire. He was on trial. I met him on the road.
- o We walk on foot. It is nice to look a fruit on the tree. I am on duty.

5) **Usage of 'Of'** (*to show related something, parts of or possession*):
- o Our modules are full *of* real-life examples.
- o I ate a plate *of* rice and a quarter *of* milk.
- o Would you like a glass *of* lemon juice?
- o I need three pieces *of* paper.
- o Most *of* the children in my class like Education.
- o There are several ways *of* cooking Upma.
- o The Museum *of* Balurghat was not visited by me ever.
- o My father was a man *of* means, and he gathered money not more than penny.
- o Do not lose sight *of* the fact.
- o I had cured *of* illness finally.

6) **Usage of 'for'**: (*mainly to show cause, reason, allotted for or availability*); as,
- o I made this bookmark ***for*** Mom.
- o She was crying out *for* fear.
- o Is there room ***for*** me on this seat? (To mean 'availability')
- o This house is *for* sale.
- o I'd like a new computer ***for*** Christmas. (To mean 'on the occasion of' rather than cause')
- o It is time *for* going out.
- o We're going down town ***for*** a meeting.
- o We bought a white Hyundai car *for* Rupees seven lakhs.
- o I made this gift *for* my mother.
- o You are unfit *for* the post.
- o Is there place *for* me on this seat?
- o I am getting ready *for* school.
- o I'd like a new Laptop ***for*** Next year.
- o Why has he got the draft *for* Rupees ten lakhs?

7) **Usage of 'Than'**: 'than' is *often regarded as preposition when it is used before a noun or pronoun* and *show relation with other; used in comparative degree* and *also to mean 'except'; as,*
- o My backpack is bigger ***than*** John's.
- o Dad is taller ***than*** all of us.
- o This painting is more beautiful ***than*** that one.
- o The neighborhood streets are less busy ***than*** downtown streets.
- o A stone is heavy, and sand is weighty; but a fool's wrath is heavier than them both.
- o The shop keeper refused to accept less than ten rupees for the soap.
- o No one other than a graduate need/can apply. (except)
- o She did nothing else than cry. (than = except)

8) **Usage of 'with'**: (*to show essential parts of or the instrument for an action with, mix something with other, accompany with, etc.*); as,

- o He pounds nails ***with*** a hammer.
- o Mix the flour ***with*** water.
- o She painted the picture ***with*** her new paints.
- o Would you like to come ***with*** us to the cinema? (Give company)
- o I can do difficult problems ***with*** help from Mom.
- o Who is the man ***with*** the beard?
- o The boy ***with*** red hair I met last Sunday at temple.

9) **Usage of 'in', 'at'** (when they denote place, '**in**' is used for larger or bigger region, '**at**' for small region):
- o Mr. Peter lives in West Bengal.
- o I live at Balurghat.

Note: We use 'in' with the names of streets and 'at' when we give the house-number:
- o He lives in Park Street.

    o   He lives at 26B, Gayeshwar Sarani Lane.

10) **In, at, to, into** (‘in’ or ‘at’ are used to denote rest position; while ‘**to**’, ‘**into**’ for motion):
- The snake is in the hole. He is in his room.
- Where do you live at? He is at the door.
- The snake scrawls into the hole. He goes into the room.
- The boy goes to school.

11) **On, upon** (‘**on**’ is used to mean something is at rest on the upper surface; while ‘**upon**’ for both upon surface at rest or in motion):
- The baby sits on/upon the mother's lap. (Rest position but on upper surface)
- The cat jumped upon the table. (‘motion’ position)

12) **With, by:** ‘with’ is used for the thing (instrument) with which something is done; while ‘by’ for the person or animal (agent) who does the thing; as,
- He killed the snake with an iron rod.
- The snake was killed by the peasant.

13) **In, on, within, after:**

    a) ‘In time’ denotes ‘not late, early enough’;

    b) ‘On time’ denotes ‘at the appointed time’; meaning at the close of;

    c) ‘within’ refers to ‘before the close of time’&

    d) ‘after’ refers to ‘over the period of time’; as,
- She will return in twenty-four hours. (Early enough before twenty-four hours) /she will return in time.
- She will return on a day. (At the appointed time; not late & not early)
- She will return within a week's time. (Before the close of week)
- She will return after a week's time. (After the week)

14) **Between, among:** between is used in case of two persons; while among is used in case of more than two persons; as,
- The two thieves shared the booty between themselves.
- The four thieves sat in a cave to distribute the booty among them.

15) **Before, for:** ‘before’ to mean ‘earlier of a point of time’; while ‘for’ is used to mean \'for a space of time’; as,
- He will be here before six o'clock.
- He will not be here for an hour.

16) **Since, from:** both are used to denote ‘a point of time’, while ‘since’ is used in the perfect tenses, ‘from’ is used in any tense (though not so rigid in present days); as,
- She will begin to learn Sanskrit from to-morrow.
- She has been suffering from fever since Monday last.

17) **By, since, before:** ‘by’ to mean ‘near about the point of time’, ‘since’ from point of time’ & ‘before’ is used to denote earlier than the point of time; as,
- She wants to come back **by** seven o'clock in the evening.
- She has been here **since** four o'clock in afternoon.
- She could not come back **before** ten o'clock at night.

18) **‘But’,** as a preposition is used to mean ‘**except**’; ‘**instead of**’ is used to mean ‘in place of’ something; as,
- I like all kinds of food **except** Upma. (But Upma)
- Everyone likes chocolate **except** Tom. (But Tom)
- We go to school every day **except** Saturday and Sunday. (Leaving Saturday & Sunday)
- You should eat fruit **instead of** candy. (In place of)
- Dad is coming to the theater with us **instead of** Mom.
- We could watch TV **instead of** reading our books.
- All the girls in class-X passed **but** (except) one.

19) **Beside, besides:** ‘beside’ denotes ‘at or by the side of’ or ‘**outside of**’; ‘besides’ denotes ‘**in addition to**’; as,

- o   She came & sat beside me. (By my side)
- o   Beside the village, there flows a small stream. (By the side of/ outside of)
- o   Your answer is beside the question. (Outside of/irrelevant to)
- o   Besides his friends, his neighbors also came to his help. (In addition to)

20) The preposition **'a'** as the shortened form of **'on'** & **'o'** as the shortened form of **'of'** is used like the following:
- o   I wake up 3 ***o'***clock (3 of the clock).
- o   The tutor comes here twice ***a*** week (twice on a week).

21) The word **'like'** is used as a preposition to mean **'as**. Study the examples:
- o   Kathleen looks ***like*** her dad.
- o   Andrew smiles ***like*** his mother.
- o   Peter sings ***like*** a professional singer and his son Om ***as*** a pop.
- o   Are these shoes the same ***as*** those on the rack?
- o   Sue is nearly as tall ***as*** the teacher.
- o   He is stupid ***as*** his brother.

- o   Exercise-2: ***Mark out the function of prepositions:***

- O   He works **in an office**. (As adverbials)
- O   The boy **with a blue shirt** came here. (As post modifier)
- O   I congratulate you **on your success**. (As verb complement)
- O   I am good **at counting**. (As adjective complement)

The Place of Prepositions

- o   Like adverb, preposition has no such definite place to be used; rather, they can be used at anywhere. However, <u>generally it is used before a noun or a pronoun or a noun equivalent word</u> and <u>shows a *relation of that noun*</u> or pronoun *<u>with any other noun, verb or adjective</u>*. <u>Sometimes, with a noun it forms adverbial phrase or adverb</u>, and <u>using with a verb it forms phrasal verbs</u>; and thus, it is sometimes used at the end of a sentence. Study the following for further understanding.

1)   A Prepositions is ***<u>used before its object</u>*** that may be a Noun, Pronoun, Adverbial Phrase or a Clause; as,
- →   My younger brother is reading ***in*** <u>class vii.</u>
- →   The pet cat drinks the milk ***from*** <u>milk pot.</u>
- →   I placed the cheque book ***before*** <u>him.</u>
- →   She must read ***by*** then. (It is an adverbial phrase

   Note: Of first three sentences the underlined are the **Prepositional Objects**, when of the last one '***by then'*** is an adverbial phrase, denoting time.

2)   When an object to a preposition preceding a Relative Pronoun (***who, whom, that***, etc. *and they may be understood too),* the preposition is ***<u>used at the end of the sentence</u>***; as,
- →   Here is <u>the book</u> **that** he asked ***for***.
- →   This is the <u>stolen watch</u> **that** the police were searching ***for***.
- →   That is <u>the man</u> **whom** I spoke ***of***.
- →   That is <u>the boy</u> **(whom)** I was speaking ***of***.
- →   Here is <u>the watch</u> **that** you asked ***for***.

3)   When an object to a preposition is a part of Interrogative Pronoun (what for, where from, etc.), the preposition is ***<u>placed at the end of the sentence</u>***; as,
- →   <u>What</u> are you searching ***for***?
- →   <u>Where</u> the traveler does come ***from***?
- →   <u>Who (whom)</u> do you want to speak ***to***?
- →   <u>What</u> are you looking ***at***?
- →   <u>What</u> are you thinking ***of***?
- →   <u>Which of these chairs</u> did you sit ***on***?

4) Sometimes to give emphasis on an object (or as part of an emotion to express), the preposition is ***placed at the end*** *& the object is placed before it or is placed first in the sentence*; as,
   → The young novelist is known all the <u>world</u> **over**. (Known all over the world).
   → <u>This</u> I was talking ***about***.
   → <u>This</u> I insist ***on***.
   → He is known the entire <u>world</u> **over**. (known over the entire world)

5) In a passive structure, when the verb is emphasized, the preposition may be used ***at the end of the sentence***; as,
   → The bed has not been **slept in**. (No one has slept in the bed.)
   → I hate being **laughed at**. (They are laughing at me, I hate it.)
   → When an object of the verb is emphasized, the object set or comes before the main verb which becomes an infinitive verb& with the infinitive the preposition is ***placed at the end***; as,
   → It is a <u>nice place</u> **to live in**. (We live in this nice place.)
   → He needs <u>other boys</u> **to play with**. (He plays with other boys.)

☐ *Summary of, When Prepositions used at the end:*

1) When relative Pronoun is used:
   → That is **what** I am afraid **of**.
   → This is the house **that** she lived **in**.
   → Tom was the person **whom** he talked **to**.

2) When interrogative Pronoun is used:
   → **What** are you looking **at**?
   → **Where** did you buy it **from**?
   → **What** did you say that **for**?

3) In passive structures:
   → The bed has not been **slept in**.
   → I hate being **laughed at**.
   → It was not that to be **aimed at**.
   → I am not that beauty to get being **stared at**.

4) Often in infinitive structures:
   → It is a nice place **to live in**.
   → He needs other boys **to play with**.
   → It was not such a matter **to deal in**.
   → He was not that man **to deal with**.

5) When prepositional objects are emphasized:
   → <u>This</u> you were looking ***for***.
   → <u>This</u> I was talking ***about***.
   → He is known all the <u>world</u> **over**.

Prepositional Object or Complement

☐ A preposition does not stand alone but needs a word or words to move on or to complete its sense, which is usually a **<u>noun</u>** or a **pronoun,** a **phrase of adverbial accusative** or a **clausal structure** [like '–ing' clause or 'wh-' clause, etc.]; as,
   o I listened **to <u>you</u>** attentively. (Here, preposition 'to' shows relation between 'you', a pronoun with a verb, 'listened'. 'You' is <u>the object of the preposition 'to'</u>, getting the answer with the question 'to whom/whom?' In other case, the answers to the questions— 'what for', 'to what', 'where', 'at what time' are also other examples of prepositional objects. Some prepositional objects are also

termed as Indirect objects, though not all. Study the chapter of object or Transitive and Intransitive verbs). Read here the rest of Prepositional Objects.

- He gave the pen *to* <u>Rakesh</u>. (Whom did he give the pen = to Rakesh. The underlined is the prepositional object.)
- We moved on ***towards*** <u>the final peak *of* mountain</u>. (Towards what?)
- I saw a girl *in* <u>the garden</u>. (Where?)
- ***Until*** <u>now</u> nothing happens. (until when?)
- ***By*** <u>then</u> I was merely twenty-one; when I was seduced *by* <u>a woman</u>.

In the above, the underlined are the complements of their preceding prepositions. 'Then' is an adverb, 'by then' an adverbial phrase; when 'a woman' is a noun phrase; here an agent of an action.

- Know the **objects** or **complements** of Prepositions in the following sentences:
-
1) Consider **Noun or Pronouns as Objects** to a Preposition: The preposition may take single or double objects; as,
    - I place my book *on* <u>the table</u>. Don't insist *on* <u>me</u>.
    - I saw a girl *in* <u>the garden</u> watering the plants.
    - The dry leaves fall *from* <u>the trees</u>.
    - The calf runs *over* <u>fields</u> & <u>gardens</u>.
    - The road *run* over <u>hill & plain</u>.

2) While, **Adverbs** are suggested to consider as **Complements to the preposition** when a preposition governs on them; as,
    - She must be tired *by* <u>then</u>. (By that time)
    - She must have reached there *by* <u>now</u>. (By this time)
    - Come away *from* <u>there</u>. (From that place).
    - How far is it *from* <u>here</u> (this place)?
    - ***Until*** <u>now</u> it as not ceased raining.
    - Strange things happen *between* <u>now & then</u>.
    - The brook says, 'I go on *for*<u>ever</u>.' It cannot last *for*<u>ever</u>.

3) **Phrase as Objects or Complements:** 'to whom', 'to what' are questions to have Prepositional Objects, when other 'wh' words helps to find out complements to the Prepositions.
    - ✖ A Noun Phrase may be an object or a complement to the preposition, but an <u>Adverbial phrase is mostly a complement</u> to a Preposition; as,
    - I bought the article *for* <u>under half its value</u>.
    - The old bottle is sold *at* <u>over one rupee each</u>.
    - Mr. Basu was not promoted to the post of Accounts Officer *till* <u>within a few months of his retirement</u>.
    - I did not see her *till* <u>a few months ago</u>.
    - The smoke was coming *from* <u>across the field</u>.
    - I was thinking *about* <u>how to circumvent him</u>.

4) **Clause as Objects:** A Noun Clause like a Noun or Pronoun may be the object or a complement to a Preposition, like a phrase does; as,
    - Pay careful attention *to* <u>what I am doing</u>. (As object to preposition)
    - There is no sense *in* <u>what he says</u>. (As object to preposition)

Omission of Object to a Preposition

- The Object to a Preposition is omitted when the object is a-
    a) Relative Pronoun:
        - The boy (whom) we were looking for has come.
        - These are the good rules (which) to live by.

    b) Demonstrative Pronoun:
        - Here is a chair to sit on (it/the chair).
        - There was a river to drink from. (That river)

    c) Where sense is evident without object, one preposition is also omitted with the object:

- Get up (from bed). Get out (from here.)
- Sit down (on the chair/ on the bench/ on bed), etc.

When preposition itself is omitted

o The Prepositions—*for, from, in, on* —are often <u>omitted from the adverbial phrase of</u> **Place**, **Distance** & **Time**; as,

    o We did it *(in)* last week.
    o I can't walk *(for)* a yard.
    o Wait *(for)* a minute.

❑ If after such verbs as **come, go, arrive, get, send, take, bring**— the word <u>**home** is used as an adverb</u>, we do not need any preposition.

❑ Study the table of 'use of prepositions' & 'without use of prepositions':

Without prepositions	With prepositions
1) He **comes home** at 5 o'clock.	1) He **comes to me** at 5 o'clock.
2) The boy **goes home** at 4 p.m.	2) He **goes to market** at 4 o'clock.
3) We hope to **arrive home** at night.	3) The boss **arrives at office** in time.
4) They **got home** a kitten.	4) I **got to fly a kite**.
5) **Send him his home**.	5) **Send this parcel to Mr. Biswas**.
6) Kindly **take me your home**.	6) Kindly **take this application to** consider.
7) **Bring home** a CD player and enjoy music.	7) **Bring a CD player to enjoy** music.

❑ After verbs like discuss, enter, and time expressing words like next, last, this, one, every, each, some, any—we do not use any prepositions; as,

    o We **discussed** the matter.
    o The dacoits **entered** the house.
    o **Next Tuesday** you will go there.
    o **Last month** we visited Taj Mahal.
    o **This morning** I went the temple.
    o Only **one hour** I read.
    o **Every Sunday** we go to temple.
    o **Each moment** is valuable.
    o **Some time** I enjoyed the music.
    o **Any evening** you visit there.

❑ Study again another table of 'use of prepositions' & 'without use of prepositions':

Without prepositions	With prepositions
1) We **discussed** the matter.	1) We **talked about** the matter.
2) The dacoits **entered** the house.	2) The dacoits **went into** the house.
3) **Next Tuesday** you will go there.	3) You will go there **on Tuesday** after.
4) **Last month** we visited Taj Mahal.	4) We visited Taj Mahal **the month before**.
5) **This morning** I went the temple.	5) I went the temple **in the morning**.
6) Only **one hour** I read.	6) I have read only **for an hour**.
7) **Every Sunday** we go to temple.	7) We go to temple **on Sundays**.
8) Each moment is valuable.	8) I am not sorry **for the moment**.
9) **Some time** I enjoyed music.	9) I enjoyed it **for some reason**.
10) **Any evening** you may visit there.	10) You may visit there **in the evening**.

o Same words may be used as both **Adverbs** & **Prepositions.** We said already a part of speech may be used as other part of speech in a sentence and that (their functions or use) defines their name or identity. Study the followings:

When they are adverbs	When they are prepositions
1) Go & run *about*.	1) Don't loiter *about* in the corridor.
2) Let us move *on*.	2) The book lies *on* the table.
3) Come *down*.	3) We went *down* the slopes of the hills.
4) The bullock cart moves *on*.	4) The cat sat *on* the wall outside.
5) Three men passed *by*.	5) She sat *by* the cottage door.
6) The rain falls *without*.	6) Man cannot live *without* bread.
7) They left the weak man *behind*.	7) The black cat hid *behind* the door.

8) I could not come **before**.	8) I came the day **before** yesterday.
9) Has she come **in**?	9) Is he **in** his room?
10) The wheel came **off**.	10) The driver jumped **off** the car?
11) His father arrived soon **after**.	11) **After** a month he returned.
12) Take this parcel **over** to the post office.	12) He rules **over** a vast empire.
13) I have not seen him **since**.	13) I have not slept **since** yesterday.
Note: adverbs when it merely modifies.	**Note:** Prepositions when it governs nouns or pronouns besides modify or form adv. Ph.

- o **Important Notes- The characteristics what we might note:**

  (1) Prepositions are generally used before Nouns or Pronouns, but remember, prepositions are also used with adjective, or participles or verbs, like in sentence 2 & 3 of the followings. They are used with 'fond', an adjective; and 'jumped', a verb. (However, we have already discussed).
      1. There is a cow **in** the field.
      2. He is fond **of** tea.
      3. The cat jumped **off** the chair.

    - *In sentence 1,* the word 'in' is placed before '*the field*' (mainly 'field'; 'the' is an article to define 'field') & *shows relation between two words,* **'cow'** & **'field' (both are Nouns).**
    - *In sentence 2,* the word 'of' is placed before '*tea*' & *shows relation between two words,* **fond'** & '*tea*' **(Adj.& Noun).**

    - *In sentence 3,* the word 'off' is placed before '*the chair*' (mainly 'chair') & thus *shows relation between the two words,* **'jumped'** & **'chair' (Verb & Noun).**

    - **Note:** Thus, Prepositions generally used before Nouns and they show relation with other words that may be another Noun, or an Adjective or a Verb, like the above.
        - Here, the words— **in, of, off** —are the examples of Prepositions.

  (2) The Nouns or Pronouns which are used after the prepositions, are called its Object, (the Object of the Preposition); and they are always in the Accusative Case.
      Note: Where Normal Objects (objects of Transitive Verbs, Direct & Indirect), Object of Gerund, Infinitive, Participle—can be used in the Nominative Case when they are used as subjects; however, Prepositional Objects are always in the Accusative Case. Study the examples carefully.

  (3) Prepositions along with other words, are often used to form different phrases as **Noun phrase, adjective phrase, phrasal Verbs, adverbial phrase & phrase of preposition**, etc.

  (4) Certain Nouns, Adjectives, Participles & Verbs are always followed by particular Prepositions.

    ➢ Now, we will go through the last feature in details.

Conjugation of Preposition with Other Parts of Speech

- o Certain Nouns, Adjectives, Participles & Verbs are always followed by particular Prepositions.

    A. Certain **Nouns** which are followed by '**for**' Preposition:

1) She had **affection for** none. Don't' cherish **anxiety for** others.
2) In young hood I had **ambition for** becoming a writer, alas! I could become none.
3) I seek **apology for** my fault; yet, she hardly forgives me. She says, it is too frequent.
4) I had no **appetite for** your love, yet you pushed me thousand times.
5) The public have insatiable **appetite for** scandal.
6) You have no **aptitude for** this job. I am sorry.
7) Why do you **blame for**? The tank has no **capacity for** thousand liters.
8) We urgently **need** candidates **for** the recruitment. Make fast the process, C.M.'s order.

9) She was such a noble and kind woman had **compassion** even *for* a dead rat.
10) They sought **compensation for** their loss, we had hardly anything.
11) Your **contempt for** women will make you soon hateful among netizens.
12) There is still no **cure for** the common cold.
13) Little Jack proved quite a **match for** the giant.

❑ And thus, *craving, desire, esteem, fitness, fondness, guarantee, leisure, liking, match, motive, need, opportunity, partiality, passion, pity, prediction, pretext, relish, remorse, reputation, surety*— all the nouns take *'for'* preposition after them.

B. Certain **Nouns** which are mainly followed by '**with**':

14) I have no **acquaintance with** this man, believe me.
15) Regarding this, the country has an **alliance with** Japan.
16) I hate **bargain with** beggars. Have any **comparison with** the two?
17) If had this **conformity with** the declaration by the Government, but alas, we are left for none.
18) What have you **enmity with** him? Resolve that soon.
19) She had **intercourse with** her boyfriend, she proudly admitted.
20) Why is this **intimacy with** him and all these behind your husband?
21) I have no **relation with** her any longer. We are departed since last year.
22) He made **complaint with** the Principal ma'am against her room-mates in drunk.

C. Certain **Nouns** which are mainly followed by '**of**'

23) The celebrated grammarian Patanjali was a **contemporary of** Pushyamitra Sunga.
24) I give **assurance of** surety, no problem. He was **in charge of** the police station.
25) **Distrust of** humanity is a wrong idea for your own existence.
26) They have **doubt of** our projects and schemes. What's next?
27) Sorry sir, I have no **experience of** teachings, see other.
28) **Failure of** goal jumps to give lecture!
29) Keep **observance of** her progress and inform us in time.
30) Have you any **proof of** my guilt? If no, think next time thousand before jump.
31) We were eagerly **waiting for** our result, and the **result of** MBA was declared postponed.
32) They may have **want of** money, but they are not scoundrel.
33) The President **called for** an immediate **cessation of** hostilities among the communities in West India.

D. Certain **Nouns** which are mainly followed by '**to**'

34) We have no **access to** the basement.
35) The then people celebrated Charles I's **accession to** the throne.
36) He affirmed his **allegiance to** the President.
37) It is **alternative to** that medicine.
38) Have you **antidote to** that disease?
39) The citizens grow **antipathy to** (also: towards) the new Act of Government.
40) We shouldn't **approach to** this proposal. It seems **risky for** us.
41) The director has given her **assent to** the proposal.
42) Mother has always special **attachment to** her elder child.
43) Please, give your **attention to** me.
44) You'll get 5% **concession to** the total price of this item.
45) It was **disgrace to** his dignity and he showed his power over us.
46) Pitila has **dislike to** tea. We had no **enmity to** anyone.
47) Give **encouragement to** your child to submit projects on time.
48) It was **exception to** his nature, or he is very fine, cool & temperate.

❑ And thus, *incentive, indifference, invitation, key, leniency, likeness, limit, menace, obedience, objection, obstruction, opposition, postscript, preface, reference, repugnance, resemblance, sequel, submission, succession, supplement, temptation, traitor*— all the nouns take *'to'* preposition after them.

E. Certain **Nouns** which are mainly followed by '**from**'

49) Buddhism teaches that **freedom from** desires will lead to **escape from** suffering.

50) You need total ***abstinence from*** drink, if you want to live.
51) He sighed long after ***deliverance from*** sure death.
52) His ***digression from*** main point is too disgusting to run the conversation.
53) She was given ***exemption from*** the final examination.
54) The President is given ***exemption from*** paying tax to the Govt.
55) Her ***inference from*** ignorance to knowledge is sufficient reason to give her appointment.
56) I need some ***respite from*** this tiresome job.
57) He traces his line of ***descent from*** the Maurya kings.

      ❑ **Note:** *when it means '<u>ancestry or family origin</u>' it takes '**from**'; but when it means '<u>a slope going downward</u>', it takes '**to**'; when it means '<u>coming or going down</u>' it takes '**into**' after it; as,*

58) There is a gradual ***descent to*** the sea.
59) The country's swift ***descent into*** anarchy was bad luck for the countrymen.

o **Conjugation of Preposition with Participle or Adjectives:**

    A. Certain ***Adjectives or Participles*** which are followed by Preposition '*to*'

60) These computers are cheap enough to be ***accessible to*** most people.
61) It was ***adequate to*** meet our needs, but we are undone even with it.
62) The house was ***adjacent to*** the post office.
63) The true gentleman is courteous and ***affable to*** his neighbors.
64) Be ***affectionate to*** your younger brother.
65) Neither was ***akin to*** us. Everything was ***alien to*** our knowledge.
66) Still, he is ***alive to*** his citizens. Why are you ***callous to*** everything?
67) It is ***common to*** every mortal man.
68) He I ***contrary to*** his younger brother.
69) Few things are ***impossible to*** diligence and skill.
70) His duties were of a kind ***ill-suited to*** his ardent and daring character.
71) Newly acquired freedom is sometimes ***liable to*** abuse.
72) He (Dr. Johnson) was somewhat ***susceptible to*** flattery.

    B. Certain ***Adjectives or Participles*** which are followed by Preposition '*to*'

73) It was formerly supposed that malaria was ***due to poisonous*** exhalations.
74) The students are ***obedient to*** their teachers. It was relevant to the treaty.
75) People who are ***averse to*** hard work, generally do not <u>succeed in</u> life. (1st one adjective, 2nd one verb),
76) She is determined to marry that rascal, what can we do her poor parents?

❑ And thus, abhorrent, acceptable, agreeable, amendable, analogous, applicable, appropriate, beneficial, comparable, condemned, conducive, conformable, comfortable, consistent, congenial, consecrated, contrary, creditable, deaf, derogatory, detrimental, devoted, disastrous, entitles, equal, essential, exposed, faithful, fatal, foreign, hostile, impertinent, incidental, inclined, indebted, indifferent, indispensable, indulgent, inimical, insensible, injured, irrelevant, favorable, hurtful, immaterial, hurtful, impervious, indigenous, limited, lost, loyal, material, natural, necessary, obliged, offensive, opposite, painful, partial, peculiar, pertinent, pledged, preferable, prejudicial, prior, profitable, prone, reduced, related, relevant, repugnant, responsible, restricted, sacred, sensitive, serviceable, subject, suitable, suited, supplementary, tantamount, true, etc., — all the adjectives or participles take '*to*' preposition after them.

    C. Certain ***Adjectives or Participles*** which are followed by Preposition '*in*'

77) He is ***absorbed in*** her thoughts. He is in love.
78) You were ***accurate in*** calculation. They stuck ***surprised by*** your talent.
79) I am from ***backward in*** class as per your class division.
80) Peter was ***correct in*** his assumption.
81) The car was ***defective in*** engine.
82) He was ***deficient in*** management.
83) We are not ***experienced in*** this field.
84) He is ***honest in*** his words; we should believe him.
85) I am not ***interested in*** cycling, but it is ***good for*** health.
86) How did you come ***involved in*** this thing?

87) Be ***temperate in*** thoughts and action, success is at your feet.

❑ And thus, abstemious, accomplished, assiduous, bigoted, diligent, enveloped, fertile, foiled, implicated, lax, proficient, remiss, versed, etc.— all the adjectives take **'in'** preposition after them.

D. Certain *Adjectives or Participles* which are followed by Preposition **'with'**

88) I am ***acquainted with*** the President, let me go in, sir, or inform him about my presence. Tell him Peter has come.
89) He was ***afflicted with*** sorrow and told us, 'No'.
90) Let's get ***busy with*** clearing up.
91) I'll be ***busy to*** come to the meeting. She was ***busy to*** listen news on TV.
92) The Dr. is ***busy at*** the moment. Gomez was ***busy at*** her work.
93) He was contemporary with the dramatist Congreve.
94) The guests were ***contented with*** the service.
95) Emily was ***delighted with*** her success or achievement.
96) The text color is ***contrasted with*** its background color.
97) Jayden was ***gifted with*** his remarkable I.Q.
98) It was ***infected with*** poison. We are ***inspired with*** his advice.
99) He was very ***popular with*** his fans and followers.
100) Was she ***satiated with*** her desires? I am ***satisfied with*** my achievement.
101) India is a noble, gorgeous land, ***teeming with*** natural wealth.

❑ And thus, beset, compatible, compliant, conversant, convulsed, deluged, disgusted, drenched, endowed, fatigued, fired, infatuated, infested, intimate, invested, overcome, replete, touched, etc. — all the adjectives take **'with'** preposition after them.

E. Certain *Adjectives or Participles* which are followed by Preposition **'of'**

102) Annikesh was ***accused of*** illegal love ***affair with*** his ex-student, Priya.
103) However, he was ***acquitted of*** all charges, and sent to an asylum considering his mental health.
104) Of course, I am not ***afraid of*** you or anybody you call.
105) I was little ***apprehensive of*** the effects.
106) Being ***apprised of*** our approach, the whole neighborhood came out to meet their minister.
107) We were ***assured of*** the best service. Do you ***aware of*** this?
108) They were not ***cautious of*** the coming danger. He should not be ***deprived of*** his right. It was ***destitute of*** his fate that he did not pass.
109) Naples was then destitute ***of*** what are now, perhaps, its chief attractions.
110) Why do you envious of them?
111) Jawaharlal Nehru was ***fond of*** children.
112) He is a man of deep learning, but totally ***ignorant of*** life and manners.
113) Ashoka, although ***tolerant of*** competing creeds, was personally an ardent Buddhist.

❑ And thus, bereft, bought, certain, characteristic, composed, confident, conscious, convicted, convinced, covetous, defrauded, desirous, devoid, diffident, distrustful, dull, easy, fearful, greedy, guilty, heedless, informed, innocent, irrespective, lame, lavish, negligent, productive, proud, regardless, sanguine, sensible, sick, slow, subversive, sure, suspicious, vain, void, weary, worthy, etc.— all the adjectives take **'of** preposition after them.

F. Certain *Adjectives or Participles* which are followed by Preposition **'from' & 'for'**

114) Man is entirely different ***from*** other animals in the utter hopelessness of his babyhood.
115) Every mother is ***anxious for*** her child. He is ***celebrated for*** his last song.
116) It is ***designed for*** gentlemen. I am not ***eager for*** it or any like that.
117) He was ***destined for*** death for his continuous criminal acts.
118) We were not ***eligible for*** the recruitment, they made it clear upon our face.
119) Mumbai ***is famous for*** its textiles. Do you think you are ***fit for*** this thing?
120) The Moors were ***famous for*** their learning and their skill in all kinds of industries.
121) The gang was ***notorious for*** dacoity in that area since few decades.
122) Coleridge's poetry is ***remarkable for*** the perfection of its execution.

❑ And thus, conspicuous, customary, eminent, good, grateful, penitent, prepared, proper, qualified, ready, sorry, sufficient, useful, jealous, etc. — all the above adjectives take *'for'* preposition after them.

o **Conjugation of Preposition with Verbs:**

A. The Certain **Verbs** which are in most cases followed by Preposition *'to'*

123) The boarders are ***accustomed to*** rise early.
124) Camels are peculiarly ***adapted to*** life in the desert.
125) Ivory readily ***adapts itself to*** the carver's art.
126) The ancient Greeks, though born in warm climate, seem to have been much ***addicted to*** the bottle.
127) Ambition does not always ***conduce to*** ultimate happiness.
128) The African elephant is now ***confined to*** Central Asia.
129) I am ***indebted to*** you ***for*** your help.
130) A residence of eight years in Sri Lanka had ***inured*** his system ***to*** the tropical climate.

❑ And thus, accede, adhere, allot, allude, apologize, appoint, ascribe, aspire, assent, attain, attend, attribute, belong, conform, consent, contribute, lead, listen, object, occur, prefer, pretend, refer, revert, stoop, succumb, surrender, testify, yield, etc.— all the verbs take *'to' preposition* after them.

B. The Certain **Verbs** which are in most cases followed by Preposition *'from'*

131) ***Abstain from*** drink & smoking. They are injurious to health.
132) Suddenly it ***emerged from*** the cave & howled to startle all of us.
133) He ***escaped from*** jail, but within hours he was sent back.
134) It is ***excluded from*** the list. ***Preserve*** it ***from*** rotting.
135) The income ***derived from*** the ownership of land is commonly called rent.
136) The noise from downstairs ***prevented*** me ***from*** sleeping.
137) Please ***protect*** us ***from*** their attack.
138) She ***recoiled*** herself ***from*** their touch and ran very fast leaving them behind far.
139) He has been ***recovering from*** fever after five days.
140) Learn to ***refrain*** yourself from the bad company.

❑ And thus, accede, adhere, allot, allude, apologize, appoint, ascribe, aspire, assent, attain, attend, attribute, belong, conform, consent, contribute, lead, listen, object, occur, prefer, pretend, refer, revert, stoop, succumb, surrender, testify, yield, etc. — all the verbs take *'from'* preposition after them.

C. The Certain **Verbs** which are in most cases followed by Preposition *'with'*

141) I am already ***acquainted with*** the latest developments of the situation.
142) John was an ***associate*** professor ***with*** the Harvard University.
143) I always ***associate*** the smell of baking ***with*** my childhood.
144) He is closely ***associated*** in the public mind ***with*** his horror movies.
145) I ***associate*** myself ***with*** his remarks. (Agree with)
146) The holy tree is ***associated with*** scenes of goodwill & rejoicing.
147) Her later work does not bear ***comparison with*** her earlier novels.
148) The supporters of two leading political parties ***clashed with*** each other.
149) The leaders ***clashed with*** the party members on the issue.
150) The strike was ***coincided with*** the party conference.
151) Her story ***coincided*** exactly ***with*** her brother's.
152) They refused to ***comply with*** the new resolution.
153) He was ***endowed with*** gifts fitted to win eminence in any field of human activity. She ***persevered with*** her violin lesson.
❑ And thus, condole, cope, correspond, credit, deluge, disagree, dispense, expostulate, fill, grapple, intrigue, meddle, part, quarrel, remonstrate, side, sympathize, trifle, vie, etc.— all the above verbs take *'with'* preposition after them.

D. The Certain **Verbs** which are in most cases followed by Preposition *'of'*

154) The convict is finally ***acquitted of*** all charges against him.

155) **_Beware of_** coming danger and take steps accordingly.
156) She **_boasts of_** her beauty and she doesn't know it never live long.
157) You are **_complaining of_** what doesn't exist at all!
158) A man who always **_connives at_** the faults **_of_** his children is their worst enemy.
159) He **_died of_** a superman. The officer **_disapproved of_** all.
160) The writer is evidently **_enamored of_** the subject.
161) He **_healed of_** injury and enlisted his name for participant.
162) Everyone must **_repent of_** his or her ill doings one day.
❑ And thus, despair, dispose, divest, dream, judge, taste, etc.— all the above verbs take **_'of'_** *preposition* after them.

E. The Certain **_Verbs_** which are in most cases followed by Preposition **_'for'_**

163) Should you not **_atone for_** your crime?
164) He spent the whole months **_canvassing for_** votes.
165) People began to **_clamor for_** his resignation.
166) He **_hopes for_** none to come forward to her help in her distress.
167) The lady **_mourned for_** her husband's death and while alive she only quarreled.
168) She **_pined for_** months after he'd gone. I feel **_sorry for_** him.
169) We **_started for_** Kolkata and reached after ten hours only.
170) We **_stipulated_** everything for the execution before long.
171) Ravi **_sued_** Rakesh **_for_** the breach of contract made between them.
172) It is natural in every man to **_wish for_** distinction.
173) He **_yearns for_** nothing.
174) The President **_called for_** an immediate **_cessation of_** hostilities among the communities in West India.

F. The following **verbs** take the preposition **_'in'_**, after them:

175) Isabella **_excelled in_** her unique performance on the stage.
176) She has never been one to **_indulge in_** gossip.
177) She was free to **_indulge in_** a little romantic day dreaming.
178) She was **_involved in_** the publication of the book.
179) How many vehicles were **_involved in_** the crash?
180) You have **_involved_** me **_in_** a great deal of extra work.
181) The cat appears to have **_originated in_** Egypt, or in the East.
182) She **_persisted in_** her search for the truth.
183) Why do you **_persist in_** blaming yourself for what happened?
184) He **_persisted with_** his questioning.
185) His name was **_enlisted in_** the panel for recruitment.
186) In the classical age the ideal life of Hindu was **_divided into_** four stages of ashrams.

G. The following **verbs** take the preposition **_'on', 'into' 'from'_** or **_'by'_** after them:

187) Don't **_comment on_** others, look to yourself.
188) Who **_depends on_** you at home?
189) So, you made a mistake, but there is no need to **_dwell on_** it.
190) She didn't want to **_impose_** her values **_on_** her family.
191) A new tax was **_imposed on_** fuel.
192) He **_insisted on_** his innocence. (He insisted that he was innocent)
193) We had **_resolved on_** making an early start.
194) The government is **_trampling on_** the views of ordinary people.
195) Don't **_trample on_** the flowers.
196) She wouldn't let him **_trample over_** her any longer.
197) The goat **_subsists on_** the coarsest of food.
198) Old people often **_subsist on_** very small income.
199) The sound of his telephone **_intruded into_** his dream.
200) Alexander **_profited by_** the dissensions of the Punjab Rajas.
201) **_Jugged by_** its results the policy of Hastings was eminently successful.

o Exercise-3: **Pick out Prepositions & also their objects**:

a) A black cat sat in the corner of a room.
b) Mrs. Persome asked Mary about the silver candlesticks.
c) There's no going home till morning if this weather lasts.
d) Humpty Dumpty sat on a wall.
e) The boy runs across the road.
f) The traveler slept in the woods beneath a large tree.
g) The dog overturned the burning candle onto the table.
h) You must discuss with me regarding this matter.
i) Owing to acute hunger the man began to eat the leaves of the trees.
j) On went her old brown jacket; on went her brown locks of hair.
k) They rise with the morning lark, and labor till dark.
l) My grandmother sat by the window, looked out & told us ghost tales.

Answers to Exercise-3: **Pick out Prepositions & also their objects**

a) A black cat sat **in** _the corner_ of a room.
b) Mrs. Persome asked Mary **about** _the silver_ _candlesticks_.
c) There's no going home **till** _morning_ if this weather lasts.
d) Humpty Dumpty sat **on** _a wall_.
e) The boy runs **across** _the road_.
f) The traveler slept in the woods **beneath** _a large tree_.
g) The dog overturned the burning candle **onto** _the table_.
h) You must discuss with me **regarding** _this matter_.
i) Owing to acute hunger the man began to eat the leaves **of** _the trees_.
j) On went her old brown jacket; on went her brown locks **of** _hair_.
k) They rise with the morning lark, and labor **till** _dark_.
l) My grandmother sat **by** _the window_, looked out & told us ghost tales.

(The bold lettered words are the prepositions, when the underlined are their objects, objects to the prepositions)

o Exercise-4: **Fill in the blanks with appropriate Prepositions**:

a) He was born _____ a small town _____ the district of Dakshin Dinajpur.
b) We started _____ 5 o'clock _____ the morning.
c) Distribute this _____ Om & Nicky.
d) He refused to take less _____ fifteen rupees for the soap.
e) Here is the book that you asked _____.
f) Who is the person you are speaking _____?
g) Distribute the mangoes _____ the boys.
h) She wants to start _____ seven o'clock in the morning.
i) She has been there _____ three o'clock _____ the afternoon.
j) It has been raining _____ two days.
k) The girl has been suffering _____ 12th instant.
l) She began to write poems _____ his boyhood.
m) He will be in the office _____ tomorrow.
n) I didn't see Mr. Lahiri _____ three days.
o) Here is a chair to sit _____.
p) The man has a reputation _____ honesty. He has the reputation _____ being a good policeman.
q) She fell victim _____ cholera. The victims _____ cholera were immediately sent to a hospital.
r) He supplied cloths _____ the poor. The poor were supplied _____ the cloths
s) We talk _____ literature. They talk _____ something else. I shall talk _____ my daughter _____ her attendance in college.
t) The boy is negligent _____ whatever he does. He is also negligent _____ his duties.

Answer to Exercise-4: **Fill in the blanks with appropriate Prepositions**:

a) He was born _____ a small town _____ the district of Dakshin Dinajpur. (at, in)
b) We started _____ 5 o'clock _____ the morning. (at, in)
c) Distribute this _____ Om & Nicky. (between)
d) He refused to take less _____ fifteen rupees for the soap. (than)

302

e) Here is the book that you asked _____. (for)
f) Who is the person you are speaking _____? (to)
g) Distribute the mangoes _____the boys. (among)
h) She wants to start _____seven o'clock in the morning. (at)
i) She has been there _____ three o'clock _____ the afternoon. (by, in)
j) It has been raining _____ two days. (for)
k) The girl has been suffering _____ 12th instant. (from)
l) She began to write poems _____his boyhood. (in)
m) He will be in the office _____tomorrow. (by)
n) I didn't see Mr. Lahiri _____three days. (for)
o) Here is a chair to sit _____. (on)
p) The man has a reputation _____honesty. He has the reputation _____being a good policeman. (For, of)
q) She fell victim _____ cholera. The victims _____cholera were immediately sent to a hospital. (of, to)
r) He supplied cloths _____the poor. The poor were supplied _____the cloths (to, with)
s) We talk _____literature. They talk _____something else. I shall talk _____my daughter _____her attendance in college. (about, of, to, about)
t) The boy is negligent _____whatever he does. He is also negligent _____his duties. (of, in)

o **Exercise-5**: **Distinguish the prepositions from adverbs in the following sentences**:

1) Come down. (as adverb)
2) We sailed down the river. (as preposition)
3) The man walked round the house. (as preposition)
4) He sat on a stool. (as preposition)
5) The carriage moved on. (as adverb)
6) The soldiers passed by. (as adverb)
7) The man turned round. (as adverb)
8) We all went in. (as adverb)
9) He is in the room. (as preposition)
10) He hid behind the door. (as preposition)
11) I left him behind. (as adverb)
12) She sat by the cottage door. (as preposition)
13) The path leads through the woods. (as preposition)
14) I have read the book through. (as adverb)
15) The storm is raging without. (as adverb)
16) We cannot live without water. (as preposition)

25. Conjunctions, Classification & Functions

o The Chapter includes two main ways of Classification of Conjunctions which are based on **Forms** and **Functions** of the conjunctions; and then their sub-divisions. Firstly, Conjunctions may be divided in this following two ways; as into:
   A. Simple, Correlative & Compound (based on forms or construction of the conjunctions); and as,
   B. Coordinating & Subordinating Conjunctions (based on their functions).

   Again, the second group of classification includes further sub-division of conjunctions, based on **meanings**; as, the **Coordinate Conjunctions are further sub-divided into**:
      a) Cumulative,
      b) Alternative,
      c) Adversative &
      d) Illative

And the **Subordinate Conjunctions** which generally join subordinate clauses, do the following functions, and their sub-divisions based upon. They may join a clause that—
a) Forms a subject or object, as a noun does, to the main verb,
b) Qualifies a noun or a pronoun preceding, popularly known as antecedent,
c) Modify or add meaning to verb, adjective or to another adverb. Doing so, sub-ordinate conjunctions may refer again- time, purpose, cause, condition, result, comparison, and contrast (to form sub-ordinate adverbial clauses in the sentence.)

<u>**Now, read through details**</u>.

Definition: The word or the part of speech that join two words, or phrases or clauses of equal or unequal rank, is called a conjunction. Read below the first group of Classification of Conjunctions.

Simple, Correlative & Compound Conjunctions

- Based on formation or structure, the Conjunctions may be of the following kinds:
    - A) Simple Conjunctions,
    - B) Correlative Conjunctions, &
    - C) Compound or Phrase Conjunctions.

A. Simple Conjunctions: The simple conjunctions are **single word conjunctions**; as, *and, but, or, therefore, still, yet, only,* etc.

The following sentences include the examples of **Simple Conjunctions** (conjunctions of single word) used in them:

- We carved not a line, **and** we raised not a stone.
- Is that story true **or** false?
- The man is poor, **but** honest.
- I was annoyed, **still** I kept quiet.
- Something certainly fell in; **for** I heard a splash.
- We arrived **after** you had gone.
- I would die **before** I lied.
- She must weep, **lest** she die.
- **As** he was not there, I spoke to his brother.
- You will be late **unless** you hurry.
- He is slow **but,** he is sure.
- He is richer **than** I am.
- He was sorry **after** he had done it.

B. Correlative Conjunctions: Some conjunctions are **used in pair** or double in the sentence with the both parts or clauses of the sentence; as,

1. both—and,
2. not only—but also,
3. whether—or,
4. either—or,
5. neither—nor,
6. though — yet, etc.

The use of **Correlative Conjunctions**:

- We do **both** love **and** honor him.
- **Not only** is he foolish, **but also** obstinate.
- **Either** take it **or** leave the place.
- It is **neither** useful **nor** pleasing.
- **Whether** he'll go **or** I have to.
- I do not care **whether** you go **or** stay.
- **Though** he is suffering much pain, **yet** he does not complain.
- **Though** he worked hard, **yet** he failed in the test.

C. Compound or Phrase Conjunctions: The conjunctions which **consist of two** or **more words**, when a phrase is used as a conjunction in the sentence, is known as the **Compound or Phrase Conjunctions**; as, *as well as, inasmuch as, as soon as, in order that, even if, as if,* etc. (They are used with a single part or clause in the sentence. Study the examples.)

The following sentences consist the examples of **Compound Conjunctions**, used in them:

- The notice was published **in order that** all might know the facts.
- I will forgive you **on condition that** you do not repeat the offence.
- Such an act would not be kind **even if** it were just.
- He saved some bread **so that** he should not go hungry on the morrow.

- ○ You can borrow the book **provided that** you return it soon.
- ○ He walks **as though** he is slightly lame.
- ○ I must refuse your request, **inasmuch as** I believe it unreasonable.
- ○ He took off his coat **as soon as** he entered the house.
- ○ He looks **as if** he were weary.

   - ✗ All the above are examples of **compound conjunctions (written in bold)**. **And at the same time, they are** the **sub-ordinate conjunctions**, if we consider the second group of classification, as they join dependent clause with the main.

  - ✗ There are many *compound conjunctions* which are also the *coordinating conjunctions* in function or use.

  - ✗ So, a conjunction (**Simple, Correlative** or **Compound**) in form or structure of one group may be either of the **Co-ordinate** or **Sub-ordinate** too. Regarding this, there is no any contradiction to use. [Like, a man may be a doctor, a father and a husband.]

- ○ The following Correlative & Compound Conjunctions are the **Co-ordinating Conjunctions** too. And thus, you may also find out the rest.
    - ○ **Both** Prakash **and** Pravat were absent from the school.
    - ○ Prakash **as well as** Pravat were absent from school.

Coordinating & Subordinating Conjunctions

Classification of Conjunctions, based on Functions

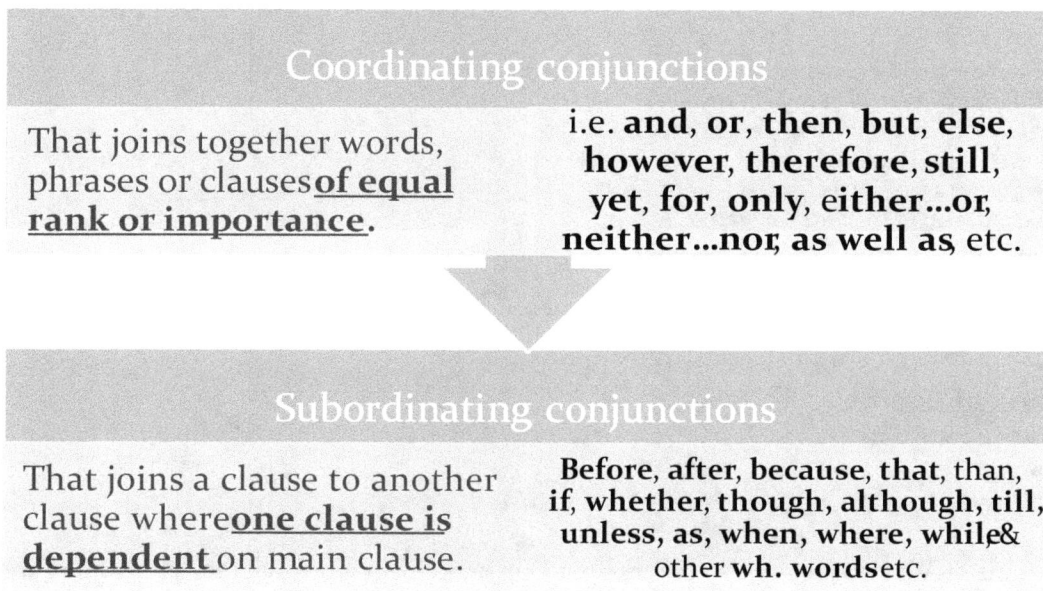

Coordinating conjunctions

That joins together words, phrases or clauses **of equal rank or importance**.

i.e. **and, or, then, but, else, however, therefore, still, yet, for, only, either...or, neither...nor, as well as**, etc.

Subordinating conjunctions

That joins a clause to another clause where **one clause is dependent** on main clause.

Before, after, because, that, than, **if, whether, though, although, till, unless, as, when, where, while** & other **wh. words** etc.

According to function or use, the conjunctions are again of mainly two kinds:
   - **A.** Coordinating Conjunctions, &
   - **B.** Subordinating Conjunctions.

- ○ The following are the main four Functions or divisions of Coordinating conjuncts, according to their meanings. These are as,
- A. **Cumulative or Copulative**

- ▪ That simply joins two words, phrases, clauses of equal rank of action or names.
  - ➢ And, also, too, as well as, both—and, not only—but also, etc.

Of the above, some of Cumulative are also the **Simple Conjunctions** regarding their form out of single word; as, **'and'**, **'also'**, **'too'**, etc.

While, **'both—and, not only—but also**—are the examples of **Corelative Conjunctions** (regarding form), and

'as well as'—an example of **Phrase Conjunction.**

Examples of Cumulative conjunctions in the sentences:
  - o We carved not a line, **and** we raised not a stone.
  - o God made the country **and** man, made town.
  - o Two **and** two make four. Four **and** four make eight.
  - o Bread **and** milk is a wholesome food.
  - o Bed **and** bedsheet I bought.
  - o Vishal **and** Virat are good bowlers. (Vishal is a good bowler and Virat is a good bowler.)
  - o I like tea, **also** I like coffee. I like **both** tea **and** coffee.
  - o You like her, I **too**.
  - o He is a teacher **as well as** a writer.
  - o Sam is **not only** a good player **but also** an excellent singer.

B. Alternative or Disjunctive
  - ▪ That joins two parts or clauses referring a selection or a choice between two alternatives or two different things.
  - ➢ Either...or, neither...nor, whether—or, or, neither, else, etc.

Like the above, here too, some of Alternative Conjunctions are also the **Simple Conjunctions** regarding their form out of single word; as, **'whether'**, **'or'**, neither, **'else'**, etc.
While, 'either—or, neither—nor, whether—or — are the examples of **Corelative Conjunctions**.

Examples of Alternative conjunctions in the Sentences:
  - o She must weep, **or** she will die.
  - o **Either** he is mad **or** he feigns madness.
  - o Is that story true **or** false?
  - o **Neither** a borrower **nor** a lender be.
  - o We can travel by land **or** water.
  - o They toil not, **neither** do they spin.
  - o **Either** you are mistaken **or** I am.
  - o Walk quickly, **else** you will not overtake him.
  - o I must go **whether** he go **or** not go.

C. Adversative or Contrast
  - ▪ The conjunctions that join sentences or clauses that is opposed to or the opposite of what has been said.
  - ➢ Still, yet, only, but, however, nevertheless, though—yet, etc.

Of the above, some of Adversative are also the **Simple Conjunctions** regarding their form out of single word; as, **'still'**, **'yet'**, **'only'**, **'but'**, **'however'**, **'nevertheless'**, etc.

While, **'though—yet** —is an example of **Corelative Conjunction.**

Examples of Adversative Conjunctions in the sentences:
  - o Our hoard is little, **but** our hearts are great.
  - o The man is poor, **but** honest. (The man is poor, but he is honest.)
  - o He is slow **but,** he is sure.
  - o I was annoyed, **still** I kept quiet.

- o I would come; *only* that I am engaged.
- o He was all right; *only* he was fatigued.
- o He is a rogue, *yet* he is my brother.
- o He is a poor; *however*, he manages his family well.
- o *Nevertheless*, the boy was poor; the strength of his mind was amendable.
- o *Though* she suffered a lot, *yet* she uttered no words.

D. Illative (the conjunctions of inference)

- ▪ That denotes or express an inference (the conjunction that joins a clause or sentence that forms an opinion, based on what you already know.)
- ➢ Therefore, for, so, then, so then etc.

Of the above, some of Illative are also the **Simple Conjunctions** regarding their form out of single word; as, 'therefore', 'for', 'so', 'then', etc., and 'so then'—is an example of **Compound Conjunction**.

The use of Illative conjunctions in the sentences:
- o He had been suffering from fever; *therefore*, he was absent in the meeting.
- o Something certainly fell in; *for* I heard a splash.
- o All precautions must have been neglected; *for* the plague spread rapidly.
- o He worked very hard; *so*, he gained his reward.
- o He finished his task; *then* he returned home.
- o All performed their roles; *so, then* it was her turn to act in accordance.

Functions of Subordinating Conjunctions

- o Sub-ordinate conjunctions **join the sub-ordinate clauses**, which may be **Noun Clause**, **Relative** or **Adjective Clause**, or **Adverbial Clause.** Read the following sentences.
  1) *When he will come* is uncertain.
  2) *Why my friend failed* is known to all.
  3) I know *where he lives*.
  4) I know *that he is ill*.
  5) I know the **boy** who did it.
  6) He was a brilliant **player** who did a hat trick taking wickets in the last series.
  7) This is the **place** where I was born.
  8) Do you know the **reason** why he failed in the Exam?

To be noted: In the above, with the first four sentences (from 1 to 4), certain clauses are joined by some certain pronouns or linkers, certain 'wh-'words or by 'that', and we have Sub-ordinate Noun clauses.

In the next four sentences (5 to 8), the clauses are again joined by some relative pronouns or adverbs, so called 'wh adjunctive pronouns or adverbs', and we have Sub-ordinate Relative or Adjective clauses.

Like the above, there are certain conjunctions, do almost the same functions, do join clauses; especially, sub-ordinate adverbial clauses in the sentence.

Relating adverbial clause, a sub-ordinate conjunction does the following functions, besides join the clauses:
Read the chart.

Adverbial Functions of Sub-ordinate Conjunctions

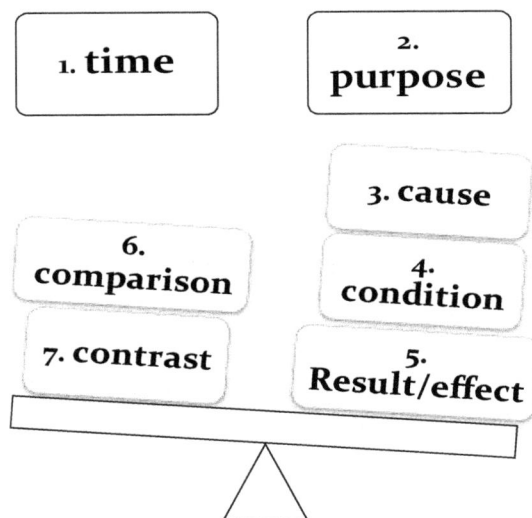

| 1. **time** | 2. **purpose** |

| 3. **cause** |

| 6. **comparison** | 4. **condition** |

| 7. **contrast** | 5. **Result/effect** |

Conjunctions which do the adverbial functions

Adverbial function of conjunction	Examples of conjunction
Time	**after, before, since, as soon as, while, until, as, so long as, till..**
Purpose	**in order that, lest, so that, that..**
Cause	**because, since, as..**
Condition	**provided, supposing, unless, as, if, whether..**
Result/Effect	**so...that**
Comparison	**Than, that, as...as**
Contrast	**though, although, however, even if.**

o   Let's study them now application in the sentences; **how do they do their functions in the sentences:**

❑   <u>Sub-ordinate Conjunctions, denoting-</u>

1) Time:

o   We arrived *after* you had gone.
o   I waited *till* the train arrived.
o   *When* you are called, you must come in at once.
o   Do not go *before* I come.
o   We got into the port *before* the storm came on.
o   My grandfather died *before* I was born.

- o I will stay **until** you return.
- o I would die **before** I lied.
- o Many things have happened **since** I saw you.
- o He returned home **after** he had gone.
- o She returned **as soon as** her husband reached there.
- o **While** I was reading a book, she was cooking for us all.
- o **As** (when) you called, I came to you every time.
- o She continued her act with the villain **as long as** she could and the police reached in time.

2) Purpose:

- o She must weep, **lest** she die. Let her sorrow flow, thereby.
- o We tried hard **in order that** it spin.
- o He is intelligent, **so** he feigned madness.
- o She feigned madness, **so that** she saved herself from that danger.
- o We travel by land or water **so that** we can reach another place.
- o We eat **so that** we may live. We eat **that** we can live.
- o He held my hand **lest** I should fall.

3) Cause or Reason:

- o I cannot give you any money, **because** I have none.
- o **Since** you wish it, it shall be done.
- o I shall be vexed **if** you do that. He may enter **as** he is a friend.
- o **As** he was not there, I spoke to his brother.
- o I did not come **because** you did not call me.
- o He deserved to succeed, **as** he had worked very hard.

4) Condition:

- o You will not succeed **unless** you work harder.
- o You will get the prize **if** you deserve it.
- o He fled **lest** he should be killed.
- o Grievance cannot be redressed **unless** they are known.
- o You will be late **unless** you hurry.
- o He asked **whether** he might have a holiday.
- o Give me to drink; **else** I shall die of thirst.
- o **If** I feel any doubt, I ask.
- o I shall go, **whether** you come or not.
- o **Unless** you tell me the truth, I shall punish you.
- o He will sure to come **if** you invite him.

5) Result/effect/Consequence:
- o He was sorry **after** he had done it.
- o He was so tired **that** he could scarcely stand.

6) Comparison:
- o He is richer **than** I am.
- o Tom runs faster **than** Harry.
- o The earth is larger **than** the moon.

7) Contrast / Concession:
- o Our hoard is little, **but** our hearts are great.
- o The man is poor, **but** honest. (The man is poor, but he is honest.)
- o He is slow, **but** he is sure. I was annoyed, still I kept quiet.
- o I would come; **only** that I am engaged.
- o He was all right; **only** he was fatigued.
- o I hear **that** your brother is in London.

Conjunctions, how distinguished from Relative Pronouns, Relative Adverbs, & Prepositions:

 o *Study them carefully:*
1. This is the house **that** Jack built. (**Relative Pronoun**)
2. This is the place **where** he was murdered. (**Relative Adverb**)
3. Take this **and** give that. (**Conjunction**)
4. He may enter **as** he is a friend. *(Conjunction)*

- **In sentence 1, 'that'** is a relative pronoun, as it is used in place of noun '**house**' and it is relative, as it *introduces a relative or adjective clause* 'that jack built'. Besides, it joins the two clauses.
- **In sentence 2, 'where'** is an adverb, denoting 'a place' and it is relative adverb, as it has *introduced a relative or adjective clause* 'where he was murdered. Besides, it joins the two clauses.
- **In sentence 3, 'and'** is a coordinate cumulative conjunction, that joins two independent parts of a sentence. It is a Co-ordinate conjunction as it joins two clauses of equal rank or independent.
- **In sentence 4, 'as'** is a sub-ordinate conjunction, being closely attached to a sub-ordinate or dependent clause, joins two clauses of a sentence.

Certain Words, used both as Prepositions & Conjunctions:

Preposition	Conjunction
1. Stay **till** Monday.	1. We shall stay here **till** you return.
2. I have not met him **since** Monday.	2. We shall go **since** you desire it.
3. He died **for** his country.	3. I must stay here, **for** such is my duty.
4. The dog ran **after** the cat.	4. We came **after** they had left.
5. Everybody **but** Govind was present.	5. He tried, **but** did not succeed.
6. He stood **before** the painting.	6. Look **before** you leap.

Exercise-1: Distinguish as *Adverb*, *Preposition*, or *Conjunction*, out of the italicized words in the following sentences:

→ He came **before** me.
→ He came two hours **before**.
→ He came **before** I left.
→ Have you ever seen him **since** Monday?
→ I have not seen him **since** he was a child.
→ Man wants **but** little here below.
→ He yearns for nothing **but** money.
→ We shall go, **but** you will remain.
→ He arrived **after** the meeting was adjourned.
→ He arrived soon **after**.

Special attention to the use of Some Conjunctions

 o Actually, every word and every part of speech has special uses which are unique and different from others. However, we use the term '*special attention*' for some. It is due to, to draw our extra attention to them. You will read some words which may seem to be a pronoun, preposition, or an adverb, when actually they are doing the work of a conjunction in the sentences. Here, out of conjunctions, they are:

(1) **Since:** *it means 'since and after the time'; it also means 'as, for' referring reason or cause; as,*
  · Many things have happened **since** I left school.
  · I have not seen him **since** that unfortunate event happened.
  · **Since** you wish it, it shall be done.
  · **Since** you will not work, you shall not eat.

(2) **Or:** *is used to mean 'alternate between two', 'otherwise', 'nearly equivalent to'; as,*
  · You must work **or** starve.
  · Your purse **or** your life.
  · You may take this book **or** that one.
  · The violin or fiddle has become the leading instrument of the modern **or**chestra.
  · You must hasten **or** night will overtake us.

· The troops were not wanting in strength *or* courage, but they were badly fed.

(3) **If:** *is used to mean 'on the condition or supposition that', 'admitting that', 'whether', 'whenever' & also to express 'wish or surprise'; as,*
   · *If* he is there, I'll meet him.
   · *If* that is so, I am content.
   · *If* I am blunt, I am at least honest.
   · *Though* I am poor, *yet* I am honest.
   · I asked him *if* he would help me.
   · I wonder *if* he will come.
   · *If* I feel any doubt I inquire.
   · *If* I only knew!

(4) **Than:** *as a conjunction follows adjectives & adverbs in the comparative degree; as,*
   · Wisdom is better *than* rubies.
   · I am better acquainted with the country *than* you are.
   · I would rather suffer *than* that you should want.

(5) **That:** *is used to express 'a reason or cause', 'purpose or in order that', 'consequence, result or effect'; as,*
   · Not *that* I loved Caesar less, but *that* I loved Rome more.
   · He was annoyed *that* he was contradicted.
   · We sow, *that* we may reap.
   · He kept quiet *that* the dispute might cease.
   · I am so tired *that* I cannot go.
   · He bled so profusely *that* he died.
   · He was so tired *that* he could scarcely stand.

(6) **Lest:** *as sub-ordinate conjunction it expresses negative purpose and means 'in order that...not', 'for fear that', as,*
   · Love not sleep, *lest* thou come to poverty.
   · Do not be idle, *lest* you come to want.
   · He fled *lest* he should be killed.
   · I was alarmed *lest* we should be wrecked.

(7) **While:** *to mean 'during the time that' 'as long as', 'at the same time that', 'whereas'; as,*
   · *While* he was sleeping, a thief entered his house.
   · *While* there is life, there is hope.
   · The girls sang *while* the boys played football.
   · *While* he found fault, he also praised.
   · *While* I have no money to spend, you have nothing to spend on.
   · *While* this is true of some, it is not true of all.

(8) **Only:** *as a conjunction, means 'except that'; as,*
   · A very pretty woman, *only* she squints a little.
   · The day is pleasant, *only* rather cold.
   · He does well, *only* that he is nervous at the start.
   · I would go with you, *only* I have no money.

(9) **Except / without:** *means 'unless',*
   · *Except* you repent (unless), you'll not feel peace at mind.
   · *Except* a man is reasonable, he is not a man of modern world.
   · I shall not go *without* you do.

(10) **Because, for, since:** *of these three conjunctions, 'because' denotes 'the closest cause' 'for' denotes 'weakest reason', while 'since' denotes the cause between because & for; as,*
   · He couldn't attend the meeting, *because* he was ill. (Strong reason)
   · *Since* you say so, I must believe it. (Reason is enough but not strong as denotes by 'because')
   · He gives lecture, *for* he is a teacher. (Weakest reason; anyone can give lecture)

Exercise-2: Join each pair of sentences with a suitable conjunction:
   · My brother is well. My sister is ill.

- He sells mangoes. He sells oranges.
- He did not succeed. He worked hard.
- Ruma reads for pleasures. Ritwika reads for profit.
- He is poor. He is contented.
- The sheep are grazing. The oxen are grazing.
- I lost the prize. I tried my best.
- I like him. He is dangerous.
- I ran fast. I missed the train.
- He remained cheerful. He has been wounded.
- I have a cricket bat. I have a set of stumps.

26. Interjections & Examples

INTERJECTION

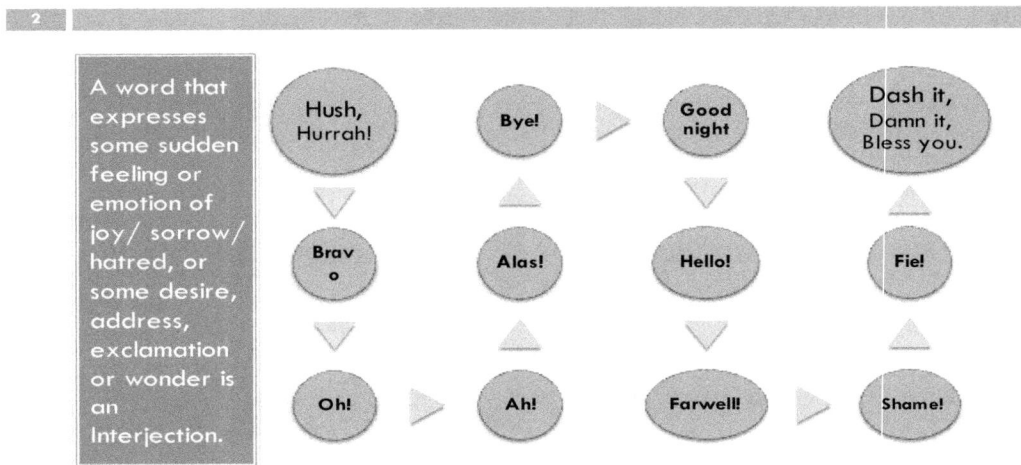

□ A word that expresses some sudden feeling or emotion of joy/ sorrow/ hatred, or some desire, address, exclamation or wonder is an Interjection.

o **The Uses of Interjections:**

- **Alas!** He has lost his watch.
- **Hurrah!** We have won the trophy.
- **Hallow!** How are you?
- **Hush!** (silence/be quiet/shut up) there is someone.
- **Bravo!** You have done it.
- **Oh!** I forget it.
- **Ah!** It's very tasty.
- **Bye!** Bye, O great soul, forever.
- **Good night**, see you tomorrow morning.
- **Farwell!** My pleasure with thy departure.
- **Shame!** You have done so mean.
- **Fie!** You have done this.
- **Dash it**! Who has done these! (To show that you are annoyed about something)
- **Damn**! If I'll apologize. / **Damn**! Who the rascal is? (To refuse to do something; to show you are surprised)
- **Bless you**, you would be a great man.

Note: An interjection that expresses wish, desire, calling or address, may also be used with full stop (.) in the sentence. The use of exclamation (!) is not bound to be used always with the interjection, though generally that may be used.

o **An Interjection may express—**

(1) **Joy & amusement; as,**
- **Hurrah!** We all have passed.
- **Huzzah!** Finally, it is done.
- **Ha!** Today is a great day.

(2) **Grief or sorrow; as,**
- **Oh!** What a great loss that would be.
- **Ah!** She has departed without meeting me.
- **Alas!** My maternal uncle is dead. Alas! I am undone.
- **Alas & alack!** We had missed our bus.

(3) **Surprise or wonder; as,**
- **Ha!** (Also: **hah**) It serves you right! / **Ha!** I knew he was hiding something. So, he is the Peter! (Used to express when one is surprised or pleased)
- **What!** He is Peter! The writer of the book.
- **Ah,** there you are! **Ah,** this coffee is good. **Ah well**, better luck next time. **Ah,** but that may not be true. (Used to express surprise, pleasure, admiration, sympathy)

(4) **Applaud or Approval; as,**
- **Bravo!** You have scored the winning goal.
- **Well done**, John. Here's a biscuit for you.
- **Good Gracious**: I hope you didn't mind my phoning you. Good gracious, no, of course not! (used as to say something by name of God)

(5) **Hatred or abhorrence; Disgust or Ridicule; as,**
- **Fie** upon you, you devilish fool! (to express distaste, disgust, outrage)
- **Shame!** She is so cute & wounded! (to express sympathy, but also 'disgust'); **For shame!** Stop please.
- **Stuff!** Do not do that. (Disapproving); Stuff! Sure, I do not agree with you.
- **Pooh!** = It stinks! Pooh! (express disgust to a bad smell)
- **Tush!** It is suitable for you. The slap of God! (contempt or rebuke)
- **Tut-tut,** I expected better of you! (to express disapproval off something)

(6) **Wish, desire or address (call someone); as,**
- **Welcome home!** Welcome to Oxford! Welcome to central jail! (As a greeting to tell, you are happy or pleased of)
- **Ho!** Who is there? (For calling, but also express disgust); **Ho,** it is suitable for him!
- **Hello!** Who are you ask me that?
- **Hi**= hello: Hi guys! Hi there! How're you doing?

(7) **Attention; as,**
- **Hark!** I hear a step on the stairs! (Used to tell somebody to listen)
- **Hush!** The teacher is coming.
- **Lo!** Something wrong is going on there. (Drawing attention to a surprised thing)
- **Hist!** Someone is talking to the woman. (To draw attention to something)

(8) **Expressing doubt; as,**
- **Hum! / Hmm! / Humph! Hem!** = **Humph**, is that true? (Express doubt or disapproval)
- **Bosh,** is it be!

Interjections are used to express some sudden feeling or emotion. It will be noticed that that they are not grammatically related to other words in a sentence.

(9) **As idiom 'lo and behold':**
- **As** soon as we out, _lo and behold_, it began to rain.

❑ **Certain Phrases are used as Interjections:**
There are certain phrases which are used as the interjections in the sentences. Carefully study the sentences:

- **Ah me!** You hate your life long.
- **Well done friend!** You have done excellent.
- **Good bye!** We don't know will we meet again?
- **O dear me!** What you have done.
- **Bad luck to it!** He tried his best yet.
- **Good gracious!** How one can do this alone.
- **Good heavens!** Who can do it?
- **Well, to be sure!** It is he has done this job.
- **For shame!** Leave me alone.

❑ **Certain Verbs or other Parts of Speech, used as Interjections:**
There are _certain moods of verbs_ or _parts of speech_ that are used as the interjections in the sentences:
a) Imperative:
- **Hear!** What a song she sings.
- **Hear! Hear!** What a sound it is. (_applause_)
- **See!** What a beautiful sight, ripple of light in thee.

b) Subjunctive:
- _Would that I had_ the wings of a dove!
- _If I would have_ billions in my little purse!
- _If she the young Kajol would be,_ my eternal love! Perhaps, perhaps then, I would be the happiest in the world.

(Thus, a whole sentence may be used to express the wish of the speaker and is expressed by the subjunctive mood of the verb.)

c) By infinitive:
- **To think** that I should have played the match!
- **To say** that I fell in love, first or last, is the worth least words!

d) Adjective:
- **Strange!** She went there.
- **Shocking!** How she can say so.

e) Adjective+ Noun:
- **Dreadful sight!** I can't explain.
- **Foolish fellow!** Or how one can behave before sure death.
- **What a mess!** Who can say here live a ward?

f) Adverb:
- **How** vary kind of you! If you didn't do, I fell in indomitable trouble. **How** wonderful!
- **How** beautiful!
- **How** awful is her love for my purse!

g) A full sentence with a pronoun: What a sad thing **it** is!
h) A full sentence with a conjunction: **If** I could see her once more!

❑ **Certain 'Wh' word with the main verb, used as Interjections:**
Sometimes while expressing strong emotion in rush, Auxiliary verb with Subject is left out, and only main verb is used, and sometimes with a 'wh' word; as,

· **Why cry!** And for the man who has already forgotten you?
· **Why wait and spoil life!** Waiting for nothing come readymade.
· **Why go there!** You didn't tell it before.
· **What said!** I can't remember like that anything.
· **How reached!** And alone!
· **Wow!** But where it happened. /**Where happened!**

➤ **Note:** thus, we can express interjections in various ways than till mentioned, for interjections are not only words but it includes sounds various to count, i.e., unending.

❑ **Exercise: <u>Study the examples and note what they express: write so in brackets.</u>**
a. *Alas* for the evil day!
b. *Shame* upon you!
c. *Oh!* What fine things these are.
d. *Oh!* I forgot.
e. *Oh,* that he were present!
f. *Nonsense!* Just get lost from here.
g. *Hush!* Someone is coming towards us.
h. *What noise* is this?
i. *Fie* upon the traitor!
j. *Foolish fellow!* How could they do that!

Answer

a. *Alas* for the evil day! (Sorrow or grief)
b. *Shame* upon you! (contempt)
c. *Oh!* What fine things these are. (praise)
d. *Oh!* I forgot. (Express sorry, feel sorry)
e. *Oh,* that he were present! (wonder)
f. *Nonsense!* Just get lost from here. (abhorrence)
g. *Hush!* Someone is coming towards us. (Drawing attention)
h. *What* noise is this? (Expressing surprise)
i. *Fie* upon the traitor! (contempt/hatred)
j. *Foolish fellow!* How could they do that! (contempt & wonder)

27. The Conversion of Words

Introduction: The term 'Conversion of Words' means, *'one word', i.e., one part of speech, can be used as another.* Some examples we have already come through in the previous chapters. Here, we will discuss and study some more examples, and see setting them side by side, to understand them better.

415. Study the use of 'same' or **similar word in different Parts of Speech** in the following charts:

About	Adverb Preposition	• The tourist wandered **about** in great joy upon the hills. • There is something pleasing **about** him.
Above	Adverb Preposition Adjective Noun	• The heavens are **above**. • The moral law is **above** the civil. • Analyze the **above** sentence. • Blessings come from **above**. (Above place)
After	Adverb Preposition	• They arrived soon **after**. • He takes **after** his father.

	Adjective	•	**After** ages shall sing his glory.
	Conjunction	•	We went away **after** they had left.
All	Adjective	•	**All** men are mortal. It was **all** profit and no loss.
	Adverb	•	He was **all** alone when I saw him.
	Pronoun	•	**All** spoke in his favor.
	Noun	•	He lost his **all**-in speculation.
Any	Adjective	•	Are there **any** witnesses present?
	Pronoun	•	Do **any** of you know anything about it?
	Adverb	•	Is that **any** better?
As	Adverb	•	We walked **as** fast as we could.
	Conjunction	•	**As** he was poor, I helped him.
	Relat. Pron.	•	She likes the same color **as** I do.
Before	Adverb	•	I have seen you **before.**
	Preposition	•	He came **before** the appointed time.
	Conjunction	•	He went away **before** I came.
Better	Adjective	•	I think yours is a **better** plan.
	Adverb	•	I know **better**.
	Noun	•	Give place to your **betters**. (Near ones)
	Verb	•	The boxes **bettered** the sample of his drug addiction.
Both	Adjective	•	You cannot have it **both** ways.
	Pronoun	•	**Both** of them are dead.
	Conjunction	•	**Both** the cashier and the accountant are Hindus.
But	Adverb	•	It is **but** (only) right to admit our faults.
	Preposition	•	None **but** (except) the brave deserves the fair.
	Conjunction	•	We tried hard, **but** did not succeed.
	Relat. Pron.	•	There is no one **but** likes him. (Who does not like him)
Confuse	Verb	•	You **confused** me, which is right & which is wrong.
	Participle	•	You made me **confused** which is right & which is wrong.
	Noun	•	You only raised my **confusion** regarding this.
Down	Adverb	•	**Down** went the 'Royal George'.
	Preposition	•	The fire engine came rushing **down** the hill.
	Adjective	•	The porter was killed by the **down** train.
	Noun	•	He has seen the ups and **down** of life.
	Verb	•	**Down** with the tyrant!
Drown	Verb	•	He **drowned** the kittens in the tub.
	Participle	•	He made the kittens **drowned** in the tub.
	Infinitive	•	I saw the kittens **drowning** in the tub.
		•	I saw him **to drown** the kittens in the tub.
Either	Adjective	•	**Either** bat is good enough.
	Pronoun	•	Ask **either** of them.
	Conjunction	•	He must **either** work or starve.
Else	Adjective	•	I have something else for you.
	Adverb	•	Shall we look anywhere **else**?
	Conjunction	•	Make haste, **else** you will miss the train.

Enough	Adjective Adverb Noun	• There is time **enough** and to spare. • You know well **enough** what I mean. • I have had **enough** of this.
Even	Adjective Verb Adverb	• The chances are **even**. • Let us **even** the ground. • Does he **even** suspect the danger?
Except	Verb Preposition Conjunction	• If we **except** Ravi, all are to be blamed. • All succeeded in the examination **except** Rabin. • I will not let thee go **except** (unless) thou bless me.
For	Preposition Conjunction	• I can shift **for** myself. • Give thanks unto the lord; **for** He is good.
Less	Adjective Adverb Noun	• You are paying **less** attention to your studies than you used to do. • The population of West Bengal is **less** than that of UP, but density is the highest in West Bengal. • He wants Rs 100 for his Tiffin. He won't be satisfied with **less.**
Like	Noun Adjective Preposition Verb Adverb	• We shall not see his **like** again. (Things what he liked) • Arjun & Karna are heroes of **like** skill & vigor. • Do not talk **like** that. It is sold **like** hot cakes. • Children **like** sweets. • **Like** as a father pitied his own children.
Little	Adjective Noun Adverb	• There is **little** danger in going there. • Man wants but **little** here below. • He eats very **little.**
More	Adjective Pronoun Adverb	• We want **more** men like him. • **More** of us die in bed than out of it. • You should talk less and work **more.**
Much	Adjective Pronoun Adverb	• There is **much** sense in what he says. • **Much** of it is true. • He boasts of too **much.**
Near	Adverb Preposition Adjective Verb	• Draw **near** and listen. • His house is **near** the temple. • He is a **near** relation. • The time **nears.**
Needs	Noun Verb Adjective	• My **needs** are few. • It **needs** to be done with care. He **needs** must come. • He is a **needy** child. It is **needful** to us.
Neither	Conjunction Adjective Pronoun	• Give me **neither** poverty nor riches, bless me with wisdom & knowledge. He **neither** says 'yes' nor 'no' whole the time. • **Neither** accusation is true. • It is difficult to negotiate where **neither** will trust.
Next	Adjective Adverb Preposition Noun	• I shall see you **next** Monday. • What **next**? • He was sitting **next** to her.

- I shall tell you more about it in my **next**. (Next visit/ next meeting/next conference, etc.)

No	Adjective Adverb Noun	• It is **no** joke. • He is **no** more. • I will not take a '**no**'. (Refusal of anything)
Once	Adverb Conjunction Noun	• I was young **once**. • **Once** he hesitates, we have him. (When we have him) • Please help me for **once**.
One	Adjective Pronoun Noun	• **One** day I met him on the street. • The little **ones** cried in joy. • **One** should obey his teacher.
Only	Adjective Adverb Conjunction	• It was his **only** chance. • He was **only** foolish. • Take what I have, **only** (but) let me go.
Over	Adverb Noun Preposition	• Read it **over** carefully. • In one **over** he took three wickets. • At thirty a change came **over** him.
Right	Verb Adjective Noun Adverb	• That is a fault that will **right** itself. • He is the **right** man for the position. • I ask it as a **right**. • Serves him **right**! He stood **right** in my way.
Round	Adjective Noun Adverb Preposition Verb	• A square peg in a **round** hole. • The evening was a **round** of pleasures. • He came **round** to their belief. • The earth revolves **round** the sun. • We shall **round** the cape in safety.
Since	Preposition Conjunction Adverb	• **Since** that I have not seen him. • **Since** there's no help, come, let us kiss & part. • I have not seen him **since** (from a particular time)
Sprained	Participle/adj. Verb	• My legs got **sprained**. • You **sprained** his legs.
So	Adverb Conjunction	• I am **so** sorry. • He was poor, **so** they helped him.
Some	Adjective Pronoun Adverb	• We must find **some** way out of it. • **Some** say one thing and others another. • **Some** thirty chiefs were present there.
Still	Verb Adjective Noun Adverb	• With his name the mothers **still** their babes. • **Still** waters run deep. • Her sobs could be heard in the **still** of night. • He is **still** in business.

Such	Adjective Pronoun	• Don't be in **such** a hurry. • **Such** was not my intention.
That	Demon Adj. Demon Pro. Adverb Relat. Pron. Conjunction	• What is **that** noise? • **That** is what I want. • I have done **that** much only. • The evil **that** men do lives after them. • We eat so **that** we may live.
The	Def. article Adverb	• **The** cat loves comfort. • **The** wiser he is, **the** better.
Till	Preposition Conjunction	• Never put off **till** tomorrow what you can do to-day. • Do not start **till** I give the word.
Up	Adverb Preposition Adjective Noun	• Prices are **up**. • Let us go **up** the hill. • The next **up** train will leave here at 12.30. • They had their **ups** and downs of fortune.
Well	Noun Adjective Adverb Interjection	• Let **well** alone. • I hope you are now **well**. • **Well** begun is half done. • **Well,** who would have thought it?
What	Inter Pron. Inter Adj. Interjection Relat. Pron. Adverb	• **What** does he want? • **What** evidence have you got against him? • **What!** You don't mean to say so? • Give me **what** you can. **What** happened then, I don't know. • **What** by fire and what by sword, the whole country was laid waste.
While	Noun Verb Conjunction	• Sit down and rest a **while**. • They **while** away their evenings with books and games. • **While** a great poet, he is a greater novelist.
Why	Inter adverb Relat. Adv. Interjection Noun	• **Why** did you do it? • I know the reason **why** he did it. • **Why,** it's surely Nanak! • This is not the time to go into the **why** and the wherefore of it.
Yet	Adverb Conjunction	• There's more evidence **yet** to be offered. • He is willing, **yet** unable.

416. Exercise: *What part of speech is each of the words in italics?*

1) He kept the *fast* for a week.
2) Don't boast too *much*.
3) *Little* learning is a dangerous thing.
4) Is that *any* better?
5) Please call me *early.*
6) He told us all *about* the battle.
7) We went *after* I came.
8) The minstrels follow *after.*
9) *All* is not lost.
10) He is *all* for amusement.
11) A thing you don't want is dear at *any* price.

12) He is my **best** friend.
13) He is **but** a child.
14) **Enough** of this!
15) His answer was a decided **no**.
16) **Since** you say so I believe it.

Conversion of Words by Prefix or Suffix

417. Words of one Part of Speech (mainly **Verbs**, **Nouns** & **Adjectives**) change to other Parts of Speech, often by adding a prefix or a suffix in the sentences. Here, the conversion of words mainly is grouped into three following patterns; as,

- **Verbs** and their corresponding forms in other Parts of Speech:
- **Nouns** and their corresponding forms in other Parts of Speech:
- **Adjectives** and their corresponding forms in other Parts of Speech:

Study them in the following charts:

418. **(A) Verbs** and their corresponding forms in other Parts of Speech:

Verb	Noun	Adjective	Adverb
Add	Addition	Additional	Additionally,
Advise	Advice	Advisable	Advisably
Agree	Agreement	Agreeable	Agreeably
Admit	Admittance, admission	Admissible	admittedly
Admire	Admiration	Admiring, admirable	Admirably
Act	Act, action, acting	Active, acting	Actively
Verb	**Noun**	**Adjective**	**Adverb**
Acquire	Acquirement	Acquired	--
Acquit	Acquaintance, Acquittal	Acquitted	
Allow	Allowance	Allowable	Allowably
Attract	Attraction	Attractive	Attractively
Accept	Acceptance	Acceptable	Acceptably
Accumulate	Accumulation	Accumulative	--
Account	Accountancy, Accountant	Accountable	Accountably
Apply	Application, Applicant	Applicable	Applicably
Bury	Burial	--	--
Begin	Beginning	--	--
Choose	Choice, Choosiness	Chosen, Choosy	--
Collect	Collection, Collector	Collected, Collective	Collectedly, collectively
Close	Closure	Closed	Closely
Verb	**Noun**	**Adjective**	**Adverb**
Clean	Cleanness	Clean	Cleanly

Complain	Complaint	Complaining	--
Commit	Commitment, committal	Committed	--
Combine	Combination	Combining	--
Compel	Compulsion	Compelling	Compellingly
Comprehend	Comprehension	Comprehensive	Comprehensively
Conclude	Conclusion	Conclusive, concluding	Conclusively
Construct	Construction	Constructive	Constructively
Connect	Connection	Connective	Connectively
Consider	Consideration	Considerable	Considerably
Continue	Continuity, continuation	Continuous	Continuously
Consult	Consultation, consultancy, consultant	Consultative	--
Consume	Consumption, consumer	Consumptive, consumable	--
Verb	**Noun**	**Adjective**	**Adverb**
Co-operate	Co-operation	Co-operative	Co-operatively
Congratulate	Congratulation	Congratulatory	--
Decide	Decision	Decisive, decided	Decisively
Define	Definition	Defined, definable	Definably
Describe	Description	Descriptive	Descriptively
Destroy	Destruction	Destructive	Destructively
Determine	Determination	Determined	Determinedly
Distribute	Distribution, distributor	Distributive	--
Divide	Division, divisor	Divisible, divisive	Divisibly, dividedly
Differ	Difference	Different	Differently
Digest	Digestion	Digestive	Digestively
Detect	Detection, detective	Detectable	--
Deposit	Deposit	Deposited	--
Verb	**Noun**	**Adjective**	**Adverb**
Dominate	Domination	Dominant	Dominantly
Devote	Devotion	Devoted, devotional	Devotionally
Develop	Development	Developing, developed	--
Edit	Edition, editor	Editorial	--
Elect	Election	Elective, electoral	Electively
Educate	Education	Educated, educational	Educationally
Employ	Employment	Employed	--

Engage	Engagement	Engaged	Engagingly
Extend	Extension	Extensive, extendable	Extensively
Exist	Existence	Existent	--
Fail	Failure	--	--
Forget	Forgetfulness	Forgetful	Forgetfully
Govern			
Verb	**Noun**	**Adjective**	**Adverb**
Guide	Guidance	Guided	--
Help	Help, helper	Helpful	Helpfully
Hope	Hope	Hopeful	Hopefully
Honor	Honor	Honorable	Honorably
Ignore	Ignorance	Ignorant	Ignorantly
Illustrate	Illustration	Illustrated, illustrative	Illustratively
Include	Inclusion	Inclusive	Inclusively
Inform	Information	Informative	--
Instruct	Instruction	Instructive	Instructively
Invent	Invention	Inventive	Inventively
Imitate	Imitation	Imitable, imitative	Imitatively
Join	Joint	Joint	Jointly
Know	Knowledge	Knowledgeable	Knowingly
Verb	**Noun**	**Adjective**	**Adverb**
Laugh	Laughter	Laughing, laughable	Laughably
Labor	Labor	Labored	--
Love	Love	Lovable, loving	Lovingly
Manage	Management	Manageable	Manageably
Marry	Marriage	Marriageable	--
Make	Making, maker	Made	--
Mix	Mixture	Mixed	--
Move	Movement	Movable	--
Measure	Measure	Measure	--
Need	Need	Needful, needy	--
Neglect	Negligence, neglect	Neglected, negligent, negligible	Negligently, negligibly
Nominate	Nomination, nominee, nominator	Nominated	--
Note	Notice	Noted	Notably

Verb	Noun	Adjective	Adverb
Notify	Notification	Notified	--
Obey	Obedience	Obedient	obediently
Oblige	Obligation	Obliged, obligatory, obliging	obligingly
Observe	Observation, observance	Observant, observable	observably
Occupy	Occupation, occupant	Occupational	--
Organize	Organization	organizational	organizationally
Operate	Operation	Operational	Operationally
Oppose	Opposition	Opposite	Oppositely
Offend	Offence	Offensive	Offensively
Permit	Permission	Permissible, permissive	Permissibly
Practise	Practice	--	--
Prefer	Preference	Preferable	Preferably
Prescribe	Prescription	Prescriptive	Prescriptively
Verb	Noun	Adjective	Adverb
Prevent	Prevention	Preventive	Preventively
Present	Presence, presentation	Presentational, presentable	Presently, presentably
Preserve	Preservation	Preservative	--
Persuade	Persuasion	Persuasive	Persuasively
Please	Pleasure	Pleasant, pleasing	Pleasantly
Produce	Production, product	Producible, productive	Productively
Provide	Provision	Provisional	Provisionally
Qualify	Qualification	Qualified	--
Quote	Quotation	Quotable, quoted	--
Receive	Receipt, reception	Receivable, receptive	--
Refer	Reference	Referable	--
Reflect	Reflection	Reflective	Reflectively
Reduce	Reduction	Reducible	--
Verb	Noun	Adjective	Adverb
Recover	Recovery	Recoverable	--
Relate	Relation	Relative, related	Relatively
Rely	Reliance	Reliable, reliant	Reliably
Resent	Resentment	Resentful	Resentfully
Remember	Remembrance	--	--
Rotate	Rotation	Rotational	Rotationally

Select	Selection	Selective	Selectively
Separate	Separation	Separable	Separately
Settle	Settlement	Settled	--
Solve	Solution	Solved	--
Suggest	Suggestion	Suggestive	Suggestively
Succeed	Success	Successful	Successfully
Tolerate	Toleration, tolerance	Tolerant, tolerable	Tolerantly, tolerably
Verb	*Noun*	*Adjective*	*Adverb*
Translate	Translation	Translatable	--
Value, Valuate	Value, Valuation	Valuable	Valuably
Vary	Variance, variation	Variant, various	Varyingly, variably
Verify	Verification	Verifiable	Verifiably

419. **(B) Nouns** and their corresponding forms in other Parts of Speech:

Noun	*Verb*	*Adjective*	*Adverb*
Act	Act	Active	Actively
Art; Artist	--	Artful; Artistic	Artfully; Artistically
Awe	Awe	Awful	Awfully
Bag	Bag	--	--
Base	Base	Basic	Basically
Beauty	Beautify	Beautiful	Beautifully
Belief	Believe	Believable	Believably
Book	Book	Bookish	--
Blame	Blame	Blameful, blameless	Blamefully
Blanket	Blanket	Blanket	--
Blast	Blast	Blasted	--
Blot	Blot	Blotting	--
Care	Care	Careful, careless	Carefully, carelessly
Noun	*Verb*	*Adjective*	*Adverb*
Centre	Centre	Central	Centrally
Cement	Cement	Cemented	--
Certificate	Certify	Certified, certificated	Certifiably
Ceremony	--	Ceremonial, ceremonious	Ceremonially, ceremoniously
Character	Characterize	Characteristic	Characteristically
Charge	Charge	Chargeable	--

Noun	Verb	Adjective	Adverb
Charm	Charm	Charmed, charming	Charmingly
Chart	Chart	Chartered	--
Cheer	Cheer	Cheerful, cheerless, cherry	Cheerfully, cheerily
Circle	Circle	Circular, circled	--
Claim	Claim	Claimable	--
Charity	--	Charitable	Charitably
Color	Color	Colorful, colored	Colorfully, colorlessly
Noun	Verb	Adjective	Adverb
Comfort	Comfort	Comfortable	Comfortably
Convenience	--	Convenient	Conveniently
Cage	Cage, encage	Caged, encaged	--
Chain	Chain, enchain	Chained, enchained	--
Colony	Colonize	Colonial	--
Cash	Cash, encase	Cashed, enchased	--
Condition	Condition	Conditional	Conditionally
Consequence	--	Consequent	Consequently
Courage	--	Courageous	Courageously
Credit	Credit	Creditable	Creditably
Crime	Crime	Criminal	Criminally
Curiosity	--	Curious	Curiously
Critic	Criticize	Critical	Critically
Noun	**Verb**	**Adjective**	**Adverb**
Danger	--	Dangerous	Dangerously
Dawn	Dawn	Dawning	--
Deceit	--	Deceitful	Deceitfully
Defect	Defect	Defective	Defectively
Drama	Dramatize	Dramatic	Dramatically
Department	--	Departmental	--
Dimple	Dimple	Dimply	--
Dirt	Dirt	dirty	Dirtily
Disgust	Disgust	Disgusting, disgustful	Disgustingly, disgustfully
Disgrace	Disgrace	Disgracing, disgraceful	Disgracefully
Earth	Earth	Earthy, earthly, earthen	--
Ease	Ease	Easeful, easy	Easefully, easily
Echo	Echo	--	--

Noun	Verb	Adjective	Adverb
Eclipse	Eclipse	Ecliptic	--
Effect	Effect	Effective	Effectively
Electricity	Electrify	Electrified	Electrically
Energy	Energize	Energetic	Energetically
Event	--	Eventful, eventual	Eventfully, eventually
Fable	Fable	Fabled, fabulous	Fabulously
Fact	--	Factual	Factually
Farce	--	Farcical	Farcically
Fire	Fire	Firry	--
Fault	--	Faulty, faultless	Faultlessly
Favor	Favor	Favorable	Favorably
Fear	Fear	Fearful, fearless	Fearfully, fearlessly
Finance	Finance	Financial	Financially
Noun	**Verb**	**Adjective**	**Adverb**
Flash	Flash	Flash, flashy	Flashily
Flavor	Flavor	Flavorless	--
Flaw	Flaw	Flawless	Flawlessly
Fold	Fold	Folding	--
Force	Force	Forced, forcible, forceful	Forcedly, forcibly, forcefully
Form	Form	Formal	Formally
Fright	Frighten	Frightful	Frightfully
Fruit	--	Fruitful, fruitless	Fruitfully, fruitlessly
Glory	Glorify	Glorious	Gloriously
Glare	Glare	Glaring	Glaringly
Grammar	--	Grammatical	Grammatically
Grace	Grace	Graceful	Gracefully
Habit	Habituate	Habitual	Habitually
Noun	**Verb**	**Adjective**	**Adverb**
Hand	Hand	Handy	--
Harmony	Harmonize	Harmonious	Harmoniously
Health	--	Healthy, healthful	Healthily
Help	Help	Helping, helpful, helpless	Helpfully
Honor	Honor	Honorable	Honorably
Human	Humanize	Humane	Humanly

Noun	Verb	Adjective	Adverb
Humor	Humor	Humor	Humor
Hypnotism	Hypnotize	Hypnotic	--
Hypothesis	Hypothesize	Hypothetic, hypothetical	Hypothetically
Idea	--	Ideal	Ideally
Idiocy	--	Idiotic	Idiotically
Idol	Idolize	Idolatrous	--
Impasse	--	Impassable	Impassably
Noun	**Verb**	**Adjective**	**Adverb**
Impatience	--	Impatient	Impatiently
Incident	--	Incidental	Incidentally
Independence	--	Independent	Independently
Industry	--	Industrial, industrious	Industrially, industriously
Innocence	--	Innocent	Innocently
Insignificance	--	Insignificant	Insignificantly
Interest	Interest	Interested, interesting	Interestingly
Intention	Intend	Intentional	Intentionally
Joke	Joke	Joking	Jokingly
Joy	Joy	Joyful	Joyfully
Judge	Judge	Judicial, judicious	Judicially
Justice, Justification	Justify	Just, justifiable	Justly, just, justifiably
King	--	Kingly	--
Noun	**Verb**	**Adjective**	**Adverb**
Labor	Labor	Laborious, labored	Laboriously
Lard	Lard	Lardy	--
Law	--	Lawful	Lawfully
Length	Lengthen	Lengthy	Lengthily
Lethargy	--	Lethargic	Lethargically
List	List, enlist	Listed, enlisted	--
Luck	--	Lucky	Luckily
Lyre	--	Lyric, lyrical	Lyrically
Mark	Mark	Marked	Markedly
Measure, measurement	Measure	Measurable, measured	Measurably

Machine, mechanism	Mechanize	mechanical	mechanically
Medicine	Medicate	Medicinal, medical	Medically
Memory	Memorize	Memorial, memorable	Memorably
Noun	**Verb**	**Adjective**	**Adverb**
Mind	Mind	Mindful, mental	Mindfully, mentally
Metaphor	--	Metaphoric, metaphorical	Metaphorically
Method	Methodize	Methodical	Methodically
Mischief	--	Mischievous	Mischievously
Misery	--	Miserable	Miserably
Mist	Mist	Misty	Mistily
Mistake	Mistake	Mistakable, mistaken	Mistakenly
Mystery	--	Mysterious	Mysteriously
Nation, nationality	Nationalize	National	Nationally
Nature	Naturalize	Natural	Naturally
Neighbor	--	Neighboring, neighborly	--
Nerve	Nerve	Nervous, nervy	Nervously
Number	Number	Numeral, numerical	numerically
Noun	**Verb**	**Adjective**	**Adverb**
Offence	Offend	Offensive	Offensively
Occasion	Occasion	Occasional	Occasionally
Office	Officiate	Official	Officially
Ogre	--	Ogrish	Ogrishly
Omen	--	Ominous	Ominously
Option	--	Optional	Optionally
Order	Order	Orderly	--
Orient	Orientalize	Oriental	--
Origin	Originate	Original	Originally
Pain	Pain	Painful	Painfully, painlessly
Parallel	Parallel	Parallel	Parallelly
Paralysis	Paralyze	Paralytic	--

Passion	--	Passionate	Passionately
Noun	***Verb***	***Adjective***	***Adverb***
Patron	Patronize	Patronal, patronizing	Patronizingly
Person	Personate, personify	Personal	Personally
Power	Power, empower	Powerful, powerless	Powerfully, powerlessly
Satire	Satirize	Satiric, satirical	Satirically
Strength	Strengthen	Strong	Strongly
Sympathy	Sympathize	Sympathetic	Sympathetically
Syntheses	Synthesize	Synthetic	Synthetically
Theory	Theorize	Theoretical	Theoretically
Trust	Trust	Trustful	Trustfully
Vacancy	Vacate	Vacant	Vacantly
Value	Value	Valued, valuable	Valuably
Voice	Voice	Vocal	Vocally

420.   **(C) Adjectives** and their corresponding forms in other Parts of Speech:

Adjective	***Noun***	***Verb***	***Adverb***
Absolute	Absoluteness	--	Absolutely
Able	Ability	Enable	Ably
Abstract	Abstraction	Abstract	Abstractedly
Actual	Actuation	Actuate	Actually
Active	Activity	Activate	Actively
Angry	Anger	Anger	Angrily
Blind	Blindness	Blind	Blindly
Bright	Brightness	Brighten	Brightly
Broad	Breadth	Broaden	Broadly
Central	Centre	Centre	Centrally
Close	Closure	Close	Closely
Complete	Completeness	Complete	Completely
Damp	Dampness	Dampen	Damply
Adjective	***Noun***	***Verb***	***Adverb***
Dead	Death	Deaden	Deadly
Deep	Depth	Deepen	Deeply
Equal	Equality	Equalize	Equally

Adjective	Noun	Verb	Adverb
False	Falsehood	Falsify	Falsely
Fresh	Freshness	Freshen	Freshly
Glad	Gladness	Gladden	Gladly
Hard	Hardness	Harden	Hardly
Idle	Idleness	Idle	Idly
Live	Life, lively	live	lively
Mad	Madness	Madden	Madly
Material	Materialism	Materialize	Materially
Original	Origin, originality	Originate	Originally
Reliable	Reliance, reliability	Rely	Reliably
Adjective	**Noun**	**Verb**	**Adverb**
Respectable	Respect	Respect	Respectably
Soft	Softness	Soften	Softly
Strong	Strength	Strengthen	Strongly
Sure	Surety	Ensure	Surely
Tight	Tightness	Tighten	Tightly
Valid	Validity	Validate	Validly
Vital	Vitality	Vitalize	Vitally
Warm	Warmth	Warm	Warmly
Weak	Weakness	Weaken	Weakly
Wide	Width	Widen	Widely
Wise	Wise, wisdom	--	Wisely
Worse	Worse	Worsen	Worse
Zealous	Zeal	--	Zealously

28. Words-Building (Compounds & Derivatives)

Introduction: The chapter includes- how words are formed from the base words or roots. How Compound Words are formed by Primary (by change of spelling within) & Secondary Derivatives (i.e., adding Prefix or Suffix) or simply by joining two or more words side by side or using a hyphen (-).

421. The simplest forms of words which cannot be reduced to a simpler form than that is, is known as the **Simple** or **Primary Words**, or **Base Words**, or **Roots**.
   - New words can be formed *by adding* some Prefixes or Suffixes to these Base Words, *or by making change* in their forms.

422. **From the base words new words are formed in three ways—**

A. By joining two words so as to make one, which is called a **Compound Word**; as, rail-way, type-writer, white-wash, laughing-gas, etc.

B. By making some change in the body of the Primary Words, are called **Primary Derivatives**; as, 'wrong' from 'wring', 'wit' from 'wise', 'breach' from 'break', etc.

- • **Note:** The change in the Finite Verbs due to tense does not come under this category.

C. By adding some Prefix & suffix or both to the base words or roots, are known as **Secondary Derivatives**; as, 'unhappy' (un-happy), 'goodness' (good-ness), 'lawyer' (law—y-er), etc.

Note: An addition of the particles to the beginning of a base word or root is called **Prefix**; an addition of such particles to the end of the base words is called **Suffix**.

(A) Compound Words

423. The **Compound Words** are mainly Adjectives, Verbs & Nouns (Nominal Compounds).

1. **The Compound Adjectives** are formed from:
   a) **Noun + Adjective or Participle**; as —air-tight, snow-white, milk-white, skin-deep, heel-deep, world-wide, home-sick, heart-broken, hand-made, machine-made, life-long, bed-ridden, etc.
   b) **Adjective + adjective**; as— blue-black, red-hot, dull-grey, dark-brown, etc.
   c) **Adverb + Participle**; as— never-ending, ever-lasting, in-born, well-deserved, well-dressed, etc.

2. **The Compound Verbs** are formed from:
   a) **Noun + Verb**; as —hood-wink, ear-mark, back-bite, etc.
   b) **Adjective + Verb**; as— white-wash, fulfil, dumb-found, safe-guard, etc.
   c) **Adverb + Verb**; as— over-take, under-take, ill-use, ill-behave, over-throw, fore-tell, etc.

3. And for **Nominal Compounds** read the following chart:

Sl. no	Combination of-	Compound Nouns
1	Noun+Noun	Motor-cycle, steam engine, moon light, color TV, blood pressure, book binder, language teacher, founder member, fighter plane; sportsman, batsman; Children's game, lion's paw, rat's tail, etc.
2	Noun+ Verb	Bus-stop, rain fall, earth quake, etc.
3	Noun+ Gerund	Sightseeing, boat racing,
4	Noun+Preposition	Lock up, passerby,
5	noun+noun+noun	Word formation exercise,
6	Noun+Adj.+Noun	Fire-resistant chemicals, scratch resistant glass/fiber;
7	N +Participle +N	Tea producing areas, power driven engine, etc.
8	Pronoun+ Noun	He-goat, she-goat, self-respect, self-confidence, etc.
9	Pronoun+ '-self' & Pronoun+ '-selves'	Myself, yourself, herself, himself, itself, ourselves, yourselves, themselves = (*These are called Compound Pronouns, used as Reflexive & Emphatic Pronouns.*)
10	Adjective+Noun	Black board, postal service, high school, etc.
11	Adj+Adj+Noun	Blue-black ink/color
12	Participle+Noun	Washing machine, dining table, flying fish, etc.

13	Adjective+Verb	Short-cut (an easy way)
14	Adjective+Adverb	Left over (cancelled things)
15	Verb+ Verb	Hearsay (a saying that is heard)
16	Verb+Adjective	Hold-all (a kind of bag)
17	Verb+Adverb	Break down, know-how (vocational knowledge);
18	Verb+Preposition	Make-up, lay out (map/design), lay-off, etc.
19	Adverb+Noun	Over load, after thought,
20	Adverb+Verb	Output, Outlet, etc.

(B) New Words by Primary Derivatives

424. It means *formation of new words by a change in the body of the base words*. Like Compound Words, the new words are also mainly '**Nouns**', '**Adjectives**', & '**Verbs**'. They are formed like in the following:

1. **The formation of Nouns** from Adjective & Verbs:
2. **The formation of Adjectives** from Nouns & Verbs:
3. **The formation of Verbs** from Nouns, Adjectives & other Verbs:

1. **The formation of Nouns** from Adjective & Verbs:

Formation of Nouns	From Adjectives	Formation of Nouns	From Adjectives	Formation of Nouns	From Verbs
Dolt	Dull	Grief	Grave	Seat	Sit
Pride	Proud	Wheat	White	Advice	Advise
Heat	Hot	**Formation of Nouns**	**From Verbs**	Bond	Bind
Loss	Loose	Bit	Bite	Life	Live
Blotch	Black	Dole	Deal	Proof	Prove
String	Strong	Flea	Fly	ditch	Dig

2. **The formation of Adjectives** from Nouns & Verbs:

Formation of Adjectives	From Nouns	Formation of Verbs	From other Verbs	Formation of Nouns	From Verbs
Milch	Milk	Bend	Bind	Fleet	Float
Wise	Wit	Lurch	Lurk	Loss	Lose
Formation of Adjectives	**From Verbs**	Creak, crash	Crack	Song	Sing
Fleet	Float	Slash	Slit	Speech	Speak
Low	Lie	Smash	Smack	Stroke	Strike

Wrong	Wring	Snip	Snap	Bliss	Bless
Blank	Blink			Web	Weave

3. **The formation of Verbs** from Nouns, Adjectives & other Verbs:

Formation of Verbs	From Nouns	Formation of Verbs	From Nouns	Formation of Verbs	From Nouns
Feed	Food	Sell	Sale	Soothe	Sooth
Knit	Knot	Tell	Tale	Bathe	Bath
Gild	Gold	Drip	Drop	Breathe	Breath
Bleed	Blood	Graze	Grass	Use	Use
Calve	Calf	Glaze	Glass	**Formation of Verbs**	**From Adjectives**
Believe	Belief	Clothe	Cloth	Chill	Cool
Halve	Half	Dodge	Dog	Frisk	Fresh
Thieve	Thief	Wreathe	Wreath	Fill	Full
Breed	Brood	Prize	Price	heal	Hale

(C) New Words by Secondary Derivatives

425. It means formation of words by adding Prefixes or Suffixes or both to roots or base words. There are three main sources from which most of the Prefixes & Suffixes have come. The sources are —
1. Teutonic or English,
2. Romanic (i.e., Latin & French) &
3. Greek.

Let's study the charts, first 'prefixes', then by add 'suffixes':

By adding Prefixes

1. Teutonic or English Prefixes:

Prefixes	Meaning of Prefixes	Prefixes + Roots	New Words formed
a-	On, in	A+bed A+sleep A+shore	Abed =on bed Asleep = in sleep Ashore= on the shore
a-	Off, from	A+rise	Arise, awake, amaze, amuse, ashamed
al-	All	Al+one	Alone, Almost, already
be-	By		Become, becalm, befit, befool, betake, beget, beseech, beneath, besides, before
by-	On the side		Bypath, bypass, by-election, etc.
for-	Through, thorough		Forget, forbid, forsake, forgive, etc.

fore-	Before		Forecast, foretell, foresee, forehead, foreman, etc.
forth-	In advance		Forthcoming, forthright, etc.
gain-	Against		Gainsay (say against)
Prefixes	*Meaning of Prefixes*	*Prefixes + Roots*	*New Words formed*
a-	On, in	A+bed A+sleep A+shore	Abed =on bed Asleep = in sleep Ashore= on the shore
a-	Off, from	A+rise	Arise, awake, amaze, amuse, ashamed
al-	All	Al+one	Alone, Almost, already
be-	By		Become, becalm, befit, befool, betake, beget, beseech, beneath, besides, before
by-	On the side		Bypath, bypass, by-election, etc.
for-	Through, thorough		Forget, forbid, forsake, forgive, etc.
fore-	Before		Forecast, foretell, foresee, forehead, foreman, etc.
forth-	In advance		Forthcoming, forthright, etc.
gain-	Against		Gainsay (say against)

2.   Romanic (i.e., Latin & French) Prefixes:

Prefixes	*Meaning of Prefixes*	*New Words formed*
A- Ab- Abs-	Away from	Avoid, Abnormal, abuse, absurd, Absent, abstract, etc.
Ad-	to	Adjoin, adore, advice, etc.
Ac-	--	Accept, acquire, accent,
Af-	--	Afford, affect, affection,
Ag-	--	Aggrieve, aggravate, etc.
Al-	--	Allege, allot, allow, etc.
An-	--	Announce, annex,
Ap-	--	Appoint, appear, appeal, etc.
Ar-	--	Arrive, arrest, arrange, etc.
As-	--	Assign, assume, assert, etc.
At-	--	Attend, attract, attack, attempt, etc.
Prefixes	*Meaning of Prefixes*	*New Words formed*
Ambi- Amb- Am-	On both sides Around	Ambiguous, ambition, amputate, etc.

Ante Anti	Before	Ante-chamber, antecedent Anticipate, etc.
Bene	Well	Benefit, benediction, benefaction, benevolent, etc.
Bis Bi Bin	twice, two	Biscuit, bisect, binocular, etc.
Circum Circu-	around	Circumference, circumstance Circuit, etc.
Com Con Co-	With, together	Compete, command, commence, etc. Contend, conflict, etc. Coexist, cooperation, etc.
Prefixes	**Meaning of Prefixes**	**New Words formed**
Col	--	College, collect (col+lege) (col+lect)
Cor-	--	Correct, correspond (cor+rect)
Cog-	--	Cognate, cognition, etc.
Contra /Contro-	against	Contradiction, controversy
Counter-	against	Counteract, counterpart, countersign, etc.
De-	Down	Depart, descend, deform, etc.
Dis- Di- Dif-	Apart, asunder, not	Disjoin, dishonor, displease, dislike, Diverse, diminish, Differ, difficult, etc.
Dis-	Reversal	Disclose, disappear, discontent, discontinue
Ex-; Ef-; E-	Out of, from	Expel, extract; effort; educate, elect, etc.
Prefixes	**Meaning of Prefixes**	**New Words formed**
Extra- Stra-	Beyond, Outside of	Extraordinary, extravagant, etc. Stranger,
In-, im-, em-, en-, il-, ir-,	In, into, on	Intrude, invade, impress, impose, embrace, employ, enclose, illustrate, irrigate, etc.
Il-, im-, in-, ir-	not	Illegal, illegible, impure, infirm, incorrect, Irregular, irresponsible, etc.
Inter- Intro- Enter-	Within	Interpreter, interaction, Introduce, Entertain, enterprise, etc.
male-/ mal- Mis-	Ill, badly; Less or wrongly	Malevolent, mal-treatment; misuse, Mischief, misfortune, misdeed, misconduct,
Ne- /Neg-	Ill, not	Nefarious, negative, neglect, etc.
Non	not	Nonsense, non-existent, etc.
Prefixes	**Meaning of Prefixes**	**New Words formed**
Ob-, oc-, of-, op- ,	In front of, against	Object, occupy, occasion, offer, Offend, oppose, etc.

Post-	After	Post-date, post-script, etc.
Pre-	before	Predict, preface, prevent, etc.
Pro-, por-, pol-, pur-,	forth	Pronoun, propose, promise; portray, etc. Pollute, purpose, pursue, etc.
Quasi	Half, pretence,	Quasi-permanent, Quasi-judge (a pretended judge)
Re-	Back, again	React, regain, renew, return, etc.
Retro-	Backward,	Retrospect, retrograde, etc.
Se-, sed-	Apart,	Seclude, separate, secure; sedition (sed+ition)
Semi-, demi-	Half,	Semicircle, semicolon; demi-official, demi-god,
Prefixes	**Meaning of Prefixes**	**New Words formed**
Sub-, suc-, suf-, sug-, sup-, sur-, sus-	under	Subordinate, sub-committee; success, suffer, suggest, support, surmount, sustain, suspend, etc.
Super-, sur-	Above, beyond	Superficial, superfluous; Survive, surface, surpass, etc.
Trans-, tra-	across	Transport, transform, traverse, tradition, etc.
Tri-	Three	Tri-color, triangle, etc.
Ultra-	beyond	Ultra-violet, ultra-modern, etc.
Vice-	In the place of, instead of	Vice-president, vice-chairman, viceroy, etc.

3.   Greek Prefixes.

Prefixes	**Meaning of Prefixes**	**New Words formed**
a/an-	Without, not,	Apathy, anarchy, etc.
Amphi-	On both sides	Amphibious
Ana-	Up to, again	Analogy, analyses,
Anti/ant-	Against	Antipathy, antagonist,
Apo	From	apology,
Arch-/ archi-	Chief, head	archbishop, architect,
Auto-	Self	Autobiography, automatic, etc.
Cata-	Down	Cataract, catastrophe, etc.
Dia-	Through	Dialogue, diameter, etc.
Di-	In two	Di-syllable
Dys-	Ill	dysentery
Ec-	Out, from,	Eccentric

Prefixes	Meaning of Prefixes	New Words formed
En-, em-	In	Enthusiasm, encyclopedia,
Eu-	Well	Euphony, eulogy,
Epi-	Upon	Epigram, epitaph,
Endo-	Within	Endogamy,
Exo-	Without	Exogamy
Hemi	Half	Hemisphere,
Homo-	Like	Homogenous,
Hetero-	Different	Heterogeneous
Hyper	Over	Hyperbole, hypertension
Hypo-	Under	Hypocrite, hypothesis, hypotension, etc.
Meta- Meth-	After, substitution	Metaphor, metaphysics, Method, etc.
Prefixes	**Meaning of Prefixes**	**New Words formed**
Mono-, mon-	single, alone	Monologue, monopoly, monarchy, etc.
Pan-	All	Panorama, Pan-American, etc.
Para-, par-	Besides, by the side of	Paragraph, parasite, parable, parallel, etc.
Penta-	Five	Pentameter,
Peri-	Around	Period, periscope,
Poly-	Many	Poly-syllable, polygamy,
Pro-	Before, for	Prologue, program, pronoun,
Pseudo-	False	Pseudo-critic, pseudo-classic,
Syn-sym-, syl-, sy-,	With	Syntax, syntheses, sympathy, Syllable, system, etc.
Tele-	Afar	Telegraph, telephone, television, etc.
Tri-	three	Tri-syllabic, trisect

By adding Suffixes

426.   *The particles added to the end of the base words or roots to form new words* (*may be from nouns to adjectives, verb & adverb; or vice-versa*)— *are called* **Suffixes**.

Like Prefixes, Suffixes have also three main sources. They are-

    1. Teutonic or English,
    2. Romanic (i.e., Latin & French) &
    3. Greek.

    ✱ A lot of, we have already used in the previous chapter of the 'Conversion of Words', i.e., one word can be used in different Parts of Speech. Here we only give focus on the particles and to know their sources, which are generally used to transform the form of Words from one to others.

✖ **Study the following charts carefully:**

1. Teutonic or English Suffixes:

Suffixes	*Roots + Suffixes*	*New Words formed*
-er, -ar, -or, -r	Law-y+er, bank+er Tail+or, beg-g+ar, love+r	Lawyer, banker, doer, worker, tailor, beggar, lover, etc.
-ster	(i) The above and these are mainly to denote agent or doers. **(NOUNS)**	Songster, youngster
-en		(feminine) **vixen** (female fox, also to refer jealous women)
-ard		Drunkard, coward,
-nd		Friend, wind,
-ter, -ther, -der		Daughter, father, mother, Spider,
-dom, -hood	(ii) Denote state or condition, action, quality, i.e., **Abstract Nouns**	Kingdom, wisdom, freedom, childhood, manhood, etc.
-ledge, -lock		Knowledge, wedlock, etc.
-ness, -ing		Goodness, darkness, learning, walking, writing,
-ter, -red, -ship, -scape		Laughter, hatred, friendship, authorship, landscape
-th, -t		Health, depth, truth, wealth, height

Suffixes	*Roots + Suffixes/meanings*	*New Words formed*
-ie, -en,	(iii) Denotes diminutives	Birdie (small bird), maiden, kitten, chicken
-kin, -ling		Lambkin, duckling, gosling, etc.
-let, -ock, -y		Booklet, leaflet, hillock, baby, etc.
-ed,	**ADJ:** 'like', or 'having'	Learned, talented, wretched
-en,	To mean 'Made of'	Wooden, golden, earthen,
-ful	Full of	Hopeful, truthful, truthful,
-ish	Somewhat like	Childish, selfish, blackish,
-less	Without	Fearless, careless, hopeless, senseless,
-ly	Like	Godly, manly, friendly, lovely, kindly, etc.
-some	Full of, inclined to	Gruesome, troublesome, handsome, etc.
-teen, -ty	To mean 'ten'	Seventeen, seventy,
-th	'order' or 'serial no'	seventh, sixth,
-fold	repeated	Tenfold, manifold,

Suffixes	*Roots + Suffixes/meanings*	*New Words formed*
-ern	Direction to	Eastern, western,
-y	With the quality of	Healthy, wealthy, thirsty, needy, mighty
-ward	Turning to	Homeward, upward, downward, forward, backward.

-k	**VERBS**— tal+k (tell) Har+k (hear)	Talk, hark
-le	--	Dibble, sparkle, startle, dazzle, crackle
-er	--	Linger, flutter, falter, glitter, etc.
-om, -m -on,	--	Blossom, gleam, reckon,
-se	(to make) clean+se	cleanse
-en	To cause	Lengthen, shorten, blacken, gladden, strengthen, weaken,
Suffixes	**Roots + Suffixes/meanings**	**New Words formed**
-ly	**ADVERB:** (like)	Boldly, beautifully, slowly, seriously, sincerely, clearly, wisely, etc.
-long	ways	Headlong
-wards	Turning to	Upwards, backwards, downwards, etc.
-way/-ways	Manner	Straightway, anyway, always
-wise	Manner	Clockwise, lengthwise, otherwise,
-s, -se, -ce	El+se	Needs, besides, else, once, twice,
-re	He+re, the+re	Here, there,

2.   Romanic (i.e., Latin & French) Suffixes:

Suffixes	**meanings**	**New Words formed**
-ain, -en, -an	**NOUNS:** (i) denote doer or agent of a thing	Captain, librarian, citizen,
-ary, -ar, -aire		Secretary, scholar, millionaire,
-ee, -y		Employee, absentee, refugee,
-eer, -ier,		Engineer, volunteer, soldier
-our,-eur, -or, -er		Savior, amateur, emperor, doctor, robber,
-ive, -iff		Native, captive, plaintiff, etc.
-ate, -ite		Candidate, advocate, Israelite, etc.
-ant, -ent, -ess	-ess (feminine)	Servant, student, merchant, poetess, lioness
-age	(ii) Denote state, action result of an action, **ABSTRACT NOUNS**	Bondage, courage, postage, breakage, message
-ance, -ence		Disturbance, endurance, innocence, absence, dependence,
-ancy, -ency		Brilliancy, Excellency, urgency, emergency,
-ice, -ise		Justice, service, cowardice, exercise, etc.
Suffixes	**Roots + Suffixes/meanings**	**New Words formed**
-al	**Abstract Nouns:**	Refusal, proposal, trial,
-acy		Intimacy, accuracy, privacy,

-ment		Judgment, improvement, enchantment, punishment
-mony		Ceremony, matrimony, parsimony,
-our, or		Color, honor, error,
-ry, -ery		Chivalry, poetry, treachery,
-eur, -lence		grandeur, pestilence, violence,
-sion		Compulsion, occasion, conversion, illusion, confusion
-som, -son		Ransom, benison, poison,
-tion,		Benediction, tradition, portion,
-ure, -tude		Creature, agriculture, attitude, aptitude, multitude,
-ity, -ty		Reality, unity, cruelty,
-y,		Misery, study, envy, harmony, victory.

Suffixes	**Roots + Suffixes/meanings**	**New Words formed**
-ary		Dispensary, library, glossary, dictionary,
-arium		Sanitarium, aquarium,
-ery, -ry	(iii) Forming **Collective Nouns** of place:	Nursery, cavalry, infantry, jewelry,
-ory		Factory, dormitory, territory,
-age,		Village, cottage,
-ade		Crusade, brigade,
-el, -le		Damsel, parcel, model, castle,
-icle		Article, particle, cuticle,
-ule	(iv) **Forming Diminutives**	Globule, capsule
-et, -let		Locket, pocket, ticket, leaflet, rivulet,
-ot,		Parrot, chariot, ballot, etc.
-ette		Cigarette, etiquette, etc.

Suffixes	**Roots + Suffixes/meanings**	**New Words formed**
-al		National, loyal, legal, mortal, royal, etc.
-an, -ane, -ain		Human, roman, humane
-ar		Solar, lunar, regular, singular, familiar, etc.
-ant, -ent		Vacant, indignant, patient, current, confident,
-ary,	**Adjectives:**	Contrary, ordinary, necessary, temporary,
-arious, -arian		Nefarious, gregarious, humanitarian,
-ate		Fortunate, separate, private,
-able, -ble, -ible		Movable, laughable, lovable, serviceable, etc. Feeble, terrible, sensible, etc.

-ese, -ile,		Chinese, fragile, juvenile,
-ian, -ine		Indian, Australian, feminine, divine, canine
-ive		Captive, active, native, positive
-id		Vivid, lucid, morbid, rigid,
Suffixes	**Roots + Suffixes/meanings**	**New Words formed**
-ous, -ory,		Dangerous, glorious, compulsory,
-lent, -fic		Violent, turbulent, terrific,
-ite, -ete,	**Adjectives:**	Opposite, favorite, complete, obsolete,
-ble, -ple,		Double, triple, simple,
-bond		vagabond
-ate,		Agitate, create,
-esce		effervesce
-ish,	**Verbs:**	Finish, nourish, publish,
-ite, -it		Expedite, credit, merit, inhabit, etc.
-fy		magnify, simplify,

3.   Greek Suffixes:

Suffixes	**types**	**New Words formed**
-ic, -ot	**NOUNS:**	Critic, cynic, cleric, patriot, idiot,
-ist, -ast		Extremist, optimist, enthusiast, etc.
-ic		Logic, magic, music, etc.
-ism, -asm		Criticism, barbarism, patriotism, enthusiasm, sarcasm,
-sis, -sy		Crisis, analyses, paralysis, basis, poesy
-y		Monarchy, democracy, energy, philosophy
-isk	**Diminutives:**	Asterisk (aster+isk)
-ic	**Adjectives:**	Dramatic, comic, tragic,
-istic, -astic		eulogistic, sarcastic,
-ise/ize	**Verbs:**	Civilize, criticize, realize, scrutinize,

29. Compare: Phrase, Clause & Sentence

427.   **What is a Sentence?**

   A group of words with a, or more units of finite verbs that makes a complete sense or expresses a complete thought, is called a Sentence; as,

°   Little Tom sways on the river.

- ○ He hardly could control his boat in the current of the river.
- ○ Sourabh turned to me.
- ○ What can we do to help you?
- ○ He is an aashiq.

Note: a unit of finite verb includes the main verb along with its all helping verbs in the sentence; as,

- • Peter *has been working* on this project since last year. (The three verbs together is considered to be one unit of finite verbs.)
- • Peter *is working* on a project which *took* more than eleven months. (*'is working'*—is considered as one unit of finite verb, whereas *'took'* is considered to be another.)

428. **How to identify a sentence:**
A sentence generally begins with **a Capital Letter** & ends with a **Full Stop (.) or** a **Question (?) or** an **Exclamation Mark (!)**.
- ○ <u>Y</u>ou don't know what you are talking about!
- ○ <u>H</u>ow many days will you take to say this?
- ○ <u>Y</u>ou are a good girl.

429. **If the parts of a sentence** (i.e., the units of a language) **are arranged, according to their size, in ascending order, they are as—**

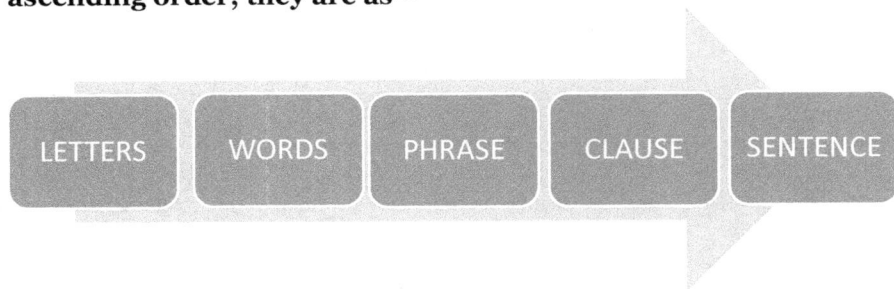

LETTERS   WORDS   PHRASE   CLAUSE   SENTENCE

Letter → Word → Phrase → Clause, and → Sentence

Of the above, whereas, *a word is the smallest unit of language,* (conveys a meaning); *a sentence is the standard unit of a language* that conveys a complete thought of the speaker.

430. **Let's compare them...**

Letter (or, Alphabet)
- ○ ***Letters are the special signs or symbols that build a word;***
- ○ 26 letters (A to Z) in English are called together English alphabet.
- ○ A letter neither forms a meaning nor a thought or a sense of the speaker.

Word
- ○ A word is the smallest unit of language, forms a meaning;
- ○ *A group of letters or simply a letter while conveying a meaning is called a word.*

Phrase
- ○ Two or more words together build a phrase or a clause or a sentence.
- ○ Like a word, a *phrase is also a unit of language*, being a part of a sentence, but *larger than a word* and <u>conveys an extended meaning</u>.
- ○ A phrase consists of a group of words, like a clause or a sentence.

431. **Read the Sentences:**
- ○ The sun rises *in the east*.
- ○ Humpty Dumpty sat *on a wall*.
- ○ There came a giant *to my door*.
- ○ It was a sunset *of great beauty*.
- ○ The tops *of the mountains* were covered with snow.

    o   Show me *how to do it*.

Note: *Examine the group of words, written in italics & bold.* What functions are they doing? Each group conveys a meaning of— *direction, position, movement, quality, possession* and <u>*an action acted upon*</u> (object) or *manner of action*.

All these are the examples of phrases in the sentences.

Let's discuss a bit more with explanation-
- o   The sun rises **in the east**. (*in the east—refers to direction. It is made of a group of words and builds a meaning, broader one merely than 'east'. But it has no finite verb and does not form a complete thought. So, it is a phrase as a part of the sentence. As, it does the function of an Adverb, referring 'direction' only; so, it is an adverbial phrase. In the chapter of Adverb and of phrase, you will get more such examples.*)
- o   Humpty Dumpty sat **on a wall**. (*on the wall—refers to position. It is an adverbial phrase of place.*)
- o   There came a giant **to my door**. (*to my door— it is a phrase & adverb of movement.*)
- o   It was a sunset **of great beauty**. (*of great beauty—meaning 'very beautiful'—describing the scenic beauty of sunset. It is a phrase of Adjective.*)
- o   The tops **of the mountains** were covered **with snow**. (*of the mountains—refers part or possession. The genitive case of Noun. So, it is the noun phrase. The other, with snow forms an object of a preposition. So, it is also a Noun Phrase.*)
- o   Show me **how to do it**. (*Show me, what? How to do it— forms the object of the verb, 'show'. It is doing the function of a noun. So, it is a noun phrase, though begins with a relative or adjunctive adverb. For identity depends on function rather than merely based on forms.*)

    432. Comparison—Phrase Vs Clause:

<u>Phrase</u>
- ➤ A phrase consists of a group of words.
- ➤ <u>It has an extended meaning</u>.
- ➤ <u>It does not contain a subject & a finite verb</u>.

<u>Clause</u>
- ➤ A clause, like a phrase, also consists of a group of words.
- ➤ It <u>has a sense or a thought</u>, complete or incomplete.
- ➤ It <u>contains a subject & a finite verb</u>.

433. <u>Now, Read the following sentences:</u>

- • He has *a chain of gold*.
- • He has a chain *which is made of gold*.

Note: <u>Examine carefully the group of words, in italic & colour.</u>
- • We recognise <u>the first group of words</u> as **a phrase**.
- • The <u>second group of words</u>, unlike the phrase, <u>has something more than a phrase, like it **has a subject**, **'which'** (a relative pronoun) and also a **finite verb** (i.e., predicate) 'is **made** of gold'</u>.
- • The second group of words is called '**a clause**'.

    434. Comparison—Clause Vs Sentence

Clause
- ➤ It is a part of a sentence, conveys a thought, complete or incomplete.
- ➤ A clause also is a unit of language.
- ➤ A clause, like a sentence, has a subject & a finite verb;
- ➤ <u>In a clause there may have more phrases.</u>

Sentence
- ➤ A sentence must have a complete sense or a thought of a person.
- ➤ A sentence is the largest & the standard grammatical or structural unit of language;
- ➤ A sentence must have a subject & a predicate.
- ➤ <u>In a sentence there may have more phrases and clauses.</u>

435. Remember:

Both a clause and a sentence have a subject and a predicate (i.e., finite verb). You have already read their differences too in the above.

In the following sentences, underline the clauses and circle the phrases & recall their differences:

1) People who pay their debts are trusted.
2) Banks trust the non-defaulter customers.
3) We cannot start while it is raining.
4) We can't start in the raining.
5) I think (that) you have made a history.
6) I am sure about your success.

436. **Let's check your answer with the followings**. Did they match all? If 'yes', congratulation! If you score 4 or less out of 6, you need further study them.

1) People ***who pay their debts*** are trusted.
2) Banks trust *the non-defaulter customers*.
3) We cannot start ***while it is raining***.
4) We can't start *in the raining*.
5) I think (that) ***you have made a history***.
6) I am sure *about your success*.

From 1 to 6—all are the sentences, for each one conveys a complete thought or idea of the speaker.
In 1), 3) & 5)—there is more than one finite verb in each sentence. Thus, each one has two clauses. **The bold italic are the sub-ordinate clauses,** while the italic-colored words are the example of phrases.

437. **Kinds of Sentences:**

Sentences are of five kinds, according to the functions or their mode of expression, and these are:

(1) **Assertive Sentence** or Statement:
(2) **Interrogative Sentence** or Question:
(3) **Imperative Sentence** or the Sentence of Order, Request or Advice:
(4) **Optative Sentence** or the Sentence of Suggest, Prayer or Wish:
(5) **Exclamatory Sentence** or the Sentence of feelings or emotion:

Note: Remember, there is another division of sentences, and that is based on their formation or structure. Details are in the chapter of Sentence.

438. **Definitions of Sentences, based on functions & their examples:**

(1) **Assertive Sentence** or **Statement**: An Assertive sentence is also called a Declarative Sentence. They make a statement or declare something; as,
   ▪ Humpty Dumpty sat on a wall.
   ▪ Maa looked at me.

(2) **Interrogative Sentence** or **Question**: A sentence that asks questions; as,
   ▪ Where do you live? What do you like?
   ▪ Do you want it? What's your name?

(3) **Imperative Sentence** or the **Sentence of Order, Request or Advice**: A sentence which expresses commands, requests, entreaties; as,
   ▪ Get out from here. Get lost from my life.
   ▪ You should do it. Please give me a glass of water.

(4) **Optative Sentence** or the **Sentence of Suggest, Prayer or Wish**: A sentence that express wish, prayer or suggest; as,
   • May God bless you, my child.
   • If I were a bird. Let's play football.

(5) **Exclamatory Sentence** or the **Sentence of feelings or emotion**: A sentence that expresses strong feelings; as,
   ▪ What a shame! the dean of the college?
   ▪ Look, how lovely the hill!

30. Detail study: Phrase & its Kinds

439. A phrase is a unit of language, smaller than a clause and a sentence, and larger than a word. A phrase may be a part of a clause as well as of a sentence, but not the reverse. **Like a sentence and a clause**, a phrase also <u>consists of a group of words</u>, but it does not have any finite verb like the clause or a sentence. A phrase builds a meaning block, like a word, but not a sense or thought like a sentence.

7 kinds of Phrases

The classification of phrase depends on the nature of different words and their functions. Or in other words, it can be said, **a phrase does function like words (seven parts of speech, except 'pronoun')**, and are named accordingly; like,

1) <u>Noun or Nominal Phrase</u>,
2) <u>Adjective or Relative Phrase</u>,
3) <u>Phrasal Verbs</u>,
4) <u>Adverbial Phrase</u>,
5) <u>Prepositional Phrase</u>,
6) <u>Conjunctive phrase</u>, and the
7) <u>Phrase of Interjection</u>.

❑ And, we have not any Pronoun Phrase.

440. The Definition of a Phrase: When a group of words, without a subject & a finite verb, **form a meaning**, like a word, in the sentence, is called a Phrase.

441. The Noun or Nominal Phrase: That does the work of a Noun. Study the following sentences:

- <u>It</u> is uncertain.
- **My going home** is uncertain.
- The boy wants <u>something</u>.
- The boy wants **to go home**.

In sentence 1, the word **'it'** is a pronoun and it is the subject of the verb. Similarly, the group of words **'my going home'** in sentence 2 is the subject of the verb 'is'.

In sentence 3, the word **'something'** is the object of the verb 'wants. And similarly, the group of words in sentence 4 **'to go home'** is the object of the verb 'wants.

Thus, in each case, <u>the word</u> or <u>the group of words</u> do the function of a Noun. So, the group of words, which is a phrase, is known as **'Noun Phrase'**, <u>doing the function of a Noun.</u>

✘ **For more examples, read the following sentences:**

1) He likes <u>to play football</u>
2) He enjoys <u>walking by the river side.</u>
3) He enjoys <u>walking in the morning.</u>
4) Akbar, <u>the Mughal emperor</u>, conquered.
5) We made him <u>the captain of the class.</u>
6) <u>Early to bed</u> is a good maxim.
7) We enjoy <u>playing cricket</u>.
8) Did you enjoy <u>reading this book</u>?
9) <u>To win a prize</u> is my ambition.
10) He hopes <u>to win the first prize</u>.
11) He loves <u>to issue harsh orders</u>.
12) I tried <u>to get the sum right</u>.
13) <u>Standing about in a cold wet wind</u> did me no good.

In above, all the underlined have done the work of a Noun, so they are the **Noun Phrases** in the sentences.

442. Exercise-1: Pick out Noun Phrases from the following sentences:

1) His father wished to speak to the Head master.
2) He dislikes having to punish his servants.
3) Horses prefer living in dark stables.

4) Is should hate to do such a thing.
5) Have you ever tried climbing a coconut palm?
6) Thinking good thoughts precedes good actions.
7) He refuses to answer the questions.
8) Promise to come again.
9) Why do you like visiting such a man?
10) Travelling in a hot dusty train gives me no pleasure.
11) He denies stealing the money.
12) You're doing such a thing (that) surprises me.

You may check your answers with the followings.

1) His father wished to speak to the Head master.
2) He dislikes having to punish his servants.
3) Horses prefer living in dark stables.
4) I should hate to do such a thing.
5) Have you ever tried climbing a coconut palm?
6) Thinking good thoughts precedes good actions.
7) He refuses to answer the questions.
8) Promise to come again.
9) Why do you like visiting such a man?
10) Travelling in a hot dusty train gives me no pleasure.
11) He denies stealing the money.
12) You're doing such a thing (that) surprises me.

443. **The Adjective or Relative Phrase:** That does the work of an Adjective. Study the following sentences:
1) He gave me a chain *of gold*. (= a **gold** chain)
2) My friend is *without fear*. (=**fearless**)
3) I am *free from blame*. (=**blameless**)
4) It is a deed *of a hero*. (a **heroic** deed)
5) He is a man *of fame*. (=**famous** man)
6) This is a cycle *made in England*. (**English** cycle/ *English made* cycle)

❏ Within bracket the bold word is the single form of Adjective phrase written in italic. In each case, the phrase does a work of an Adjective; they each have described certain Nouns.

❏ **Now study the following pair of sentences carefully:**

1) Tata was a <u>wealthy</u> man.
   o Tata was a man ***of great wealth***.
2) The magistrate was a <u>kind</u> man.
   o The magistrate was a man ***of kindly nature***.
3) The chief lived in a <u>stone</u> house.
   o The chief lived in a house ***built of stone***.
4) I like to see a <u>smiling</u> face.
   o I like to see a face ***with a smile on it***.
5) The coolies belonged to a <u>hill</u> tribe.
   o The coolies belonged to a tribe ***dwelling in the hills***.
6) The king wears a <u>golden</u> crown.
   o The kings wear a crown ***made of gold***.

✖ Study the table relating **Adjectives & their corresponding Adjective Phrases:**

Adjective	Adjective Phrase
1) A <u>purple</u> clock	1) A cloak <u>of purple color</u>.
2) A <u>white</u> elephant	2) An elephant <u>with white skin</u>.
3) A <u>jungle</u> tracks	3) A track <u>through the jungle</u>.
4) A <u>blue-eyed</u> boy	4) A boy <u>with blue eyes</u>.
5) A <u>deserted</u> village	5) A village <u>without any inhabitants</u>.
6) A <u>blank</u> page	6) A page <u>with no writing on it</u>.
7) The <u>longest</u> day	7) The day <u>of greatest length</u>.

8) The <u>Spanish</u> flag	8) The flag <u>of Spain</u>.
9) A <u>heavy</u> load	9) A load <u>of great weight</u>.
10) He is **well**.	10) He is **fit & fine/healthy & sound**.
11) A **valuable** ring was found yesterday.	11) A ring **of worthy** was found yesterday.
12) **Heroic** deeds deserve our admiration.	12) **Deeds of a hero** deserve our admiration.
13) Much has been said about the **Swiss** scenery.	
14) The Rajputs were passionately fond of **martial** glory.	13) Much has been said about the scenery **of Switzerland.**
15) **Numerical** superiority is a great advantage.	14) The Rajputs were passionately fond of glory **of war**.
16) I have passed two **sleepless** nights.	15) The superiority **of numbers** is a great advantage.
17) He is a **professional** cricketer.	16) I have passed two nights **of sleepless**.
18) This book contains many **biblical** quotations.	17) He is a cricketer **by profession**.
19) She wants **medical** advice.	18) This book contains many quotations **of Bible**.
20) A **tall** soldier stepped forth.	
21) He is a <u>friendless</u> man.	19) She wants advice **of medical expert**.
22) They came to a **muddy** path.	20) A soldier **of high length** stepped forth.
23) He carried a **blood-stained** sword.	21) He is a man *without a friend*.
24) I met a little **cottage** girl.	22) They came to a path *covered with mud*.
25) Balu was a highly **impudent** person.	23) He carried a sword *stained with blood*.
26) From this **mountain**-village came the army chief at present.	24) I met a little girl *from a cottage*.
27) The Rajput leader was a **hopeful fearless** soldier.	25) Balu was a man *with plenty of impudence*.
28) Nelson was a **fearless** boy.	26) From this village *in the mountains* came the army chief at present.
29) Nobody likes a **bad-tempered** person.	27) The Rajput leader was a soldier *full of hope and free from fear*.
30) I admit that he is a **sensible** man.	28) Nelson was a boy *without a fear*.
31) The **mountain** tops were covered with snow.	29) Nobody likes a person *with a bad temper*.
32) He is a **versatile** author.	30) I admit that he is a man *of sense*.
33) It is **useless**.	31) The tops *of the mountains* were covered with snow.
	32) He is an author *of great versatility*.
	33) It is *of no use*.

✱ **To be noted:** Though we may replace many adjectives with the adjective or relative phrases, all <u>adjective phrases</u> cannot be replaced by single Adjectives & vice-versa or that may not suit to the sense of the sentence always; as the followings:

1) The man **in the street** knows it. (**We can't write:** 'The street man knows it', because that may refer or denote a different meaning from the actual sense.)
2) The tree **in front of my house** has been cut down. (Similarly, **we can't write:** 'The front tree'. And the same thing happens for the following phrases too.)
3) A boy **desirous of winning the prize** must work hard.
4) He never felt the witchery **of the soft blue sky**.
5) In a low voice he told the tale **of his cruel wrongs**.
6) The police arrested a man **of one of the criminal tribes**.
7) A man **in great difficulties** came to me for help.
8) Wild beasts **in small cages** are a sorry sight.
9) A man **without an enemy** is a man with few friends.

444. **The Comparative study of Noun & Adjective phrases side by side.** Remember, the phrase, Adjective or Noun, depends on the work they do in the sentence & extension of meaning. **Study the** table.

As a Noun Phrase	As an Adj. or Relative Phrase
1) He enjoys <u>walking by the river-side</u>.	1) The boy **walking by the river-side** is my brother.
2) I gave the book to the <u>desirous of winning the prize</u>.	2) A boy **desirous of winning the prize** must work hard.
3) A turban <u>made of silk</u> is worthy for him.	3) He wore a turban **made of silk**.
4) He has done <u>a shameful deed</u>.	4) He has done a deed **of shame.**
5) He led <u>a blameless life</u>.	5) He led a life **devoid of blame**.

445. Exercise-1: **Italicize Adjective Phrases in the following sentences:**

a) A man in great difficulties came to me for help.
b) He is a person of very considerable renown.
c) Wild beasts in small cages are a sorry sight.
d) A man without an enemy is a man with few friends.
e) He tells a tale with the ring of truth in it.
f) A friend in need is a friend indeed.
g) A stitch in time saves nine.
h) A bird in hand is worth two in the bush.
i) Gardens with cool shady trees surround the village.
j) Only a man with plenty of money buys a car of such luxuries in it.
k) In a low voice he told the tale of his cruel wrongs.
l) Do you know the story of the noble Padmini?
m) He was a lad of great promise.
n) He bore a banner with strange device.

Answer of Exercise-1

a) A man ***in great difficulties*** came to me for help.
b) He is a person ***of very considerable renown***.
c) Wild beasts ***in small cages*** are a sorry sight.
d) A man ***without an enemy*** is a man with few friends.
e) He tells a tale ***with the ring of truth*** in it.
f) A friend ***in need*** is a friend indeed.
g) A stitch ***in time*** saves nine.
h) A bird ***in hand*** is worth two ***in the bush***.
i) Gardens ***with cool shady trees*** surround the village.
j) Only a man ***with plenty of money*** buys a car ***of such luxuries*** in it.
k) In a low voice he told the tale ***of his cruel wrongs***.
l) Do you know the story ***of the noble Padmini***?
m) He was a lad ***of great promise***.
n) He bore a banner ***with strange device***.

446. Exercise-2: <u>Replace the Adjectives in bold by an Adjective Phrase</u> of the same meaning:
a) A **grey** cloud spread over the sky.
b) He dwelt in a **wooden** hut.
c) He had a **bald** head.
d) She wore a **diamond** necklace.
e) It was a **horrible** night.
f) They went by **Siberian** railway.
g) A **grassy** meadow stretched before us.
h) An **earthen** pitcher stood on a **three-legged** table.
i) The **French** flag flew at the top of the **highest** mast.
j) That was a **cowardly** act.

answers

a) A cloud **grey in color** spread over the sky.
b) He dwelt in a hut **made of wood**.
c) He had headed **with bald**.
d) She wore a necklace **made of diamond.**
e) It was a night **full of horrible sight**.
f) They went by railway **that runs through Siberia**. (It is a clause)
g) A meadow **full of grass** stretched before us.
h) A pitcher **made of earth** stood on a table **of three legs**.
i) The flag **of France** flew at the top of the mast **of highest height**.
j) That was an act **of a coward**.

Compare Phrasal Verbs & Idioms

447.   **The Phrasal Verbs or Group Verbs:** A main verb often takes helping or auxiliary verbs in tenses and voice change. This is a normal structure of finite verbs to build a meaning; and in this case, the main verb always dominates the auxiliary or helping verbs to form meaning of the sentence, and even with different auxiliary verbs, the main meaning remains intact, except 'time of an action or state'; as,

- He **is going** to Kolkata.
- He **has been reading** the novel for two hours.
- I **shall have been** there by the time.
- The mango **is eaten** by me.
- He **does not eat** fruits.

The above is the normal usage of verbs along with their helping or auxiliary verbs, as per tense in active or passive voice. They are each a unit of finite verb to form tense or voice change.

But sometimes, the main verb is used with other parts of speech, mainly preposition or an adverb and often with both *forms a special or unique meaning, which is different from the* individual words (they are formed or built of), are called the **Phrasal** or **Group verbs**.

Definition: When *a verb with a preposition* or *an adverb* or *both* builds a completely new meaning is called a Phrasal or Group Verb.

The group verbs are called Phrasal Verbs because they are in the form of a phrase and have a particular meaning from the words they are built of.

Study the following for better understand:

- **Get:** to receive something (verb)
- **By:** the method of doing something (preposition)
- **Get by:** live with difficulty

Did you notice how the words *'get'* and *'by'* have different meanings when they are used individually than when they are used together? When the two words are used together, they form a phrasal verb *'get by'*.

Read another example:

- He *gives* me all that I need.
- *Give up* your bad habit.

In the first sentence, the verb has its general meaning, here to mean 'providing something'. Even we add helping verb with it; like, **'He will give me all that I need'** the main meaning 'providing something' remains intact, only the tense (time of action) is changed. But:

In the second sentence, the verb **'give'** with the preposition **'up'** builds a different meaning from the words *'give'* and *'up'* ('up' to mean above position). Here the group verb **'give up'** *has unique meaning* to mean **'abandon'**.

Thus, a particular verb with different prepositions and adverbial particles *expresses different meanings* and also different, in general, from the words they are built of.

Study, how the phrasal verbs different in meanings from words they are made of:

Verb	Meaning	Phrasal Verbs	Meaning
Bring	Come carrying something	Bring up	Rear somebody
Call	Ask someone to come	Call on	Visit somewhere
Get	Receive	Get up	Awake
Look	See	Look into	Investigate
Make	Prepare	Make out	Comprehend
Put	Keep something	Put on	Wear
Take	Carry something	Take after	Resemble /look like

- I shall *call on* him tomorrow. (I shall *visit* him tomorrow)
- She *brought up* her child to be a kind man, a term full of confusion.

- I **get up** early every day.
- Please sir, **look into** the matter. He made us homeless.
- Do you **make out** the difference between a verb and a phrasal verb?
- **Put on** your uniform, it is time to move on.
- The girl **takes after** her mother.

Some of Phrasal Verbs for their universal use & significance in expressions are also termed as **Idioms**.

However, the term '*idioms* 'refer to all kinds of phrases that includes *prepositional*, *nominal*, *relative*, certain *phrasal verbs* & also *adverbial* which are **significant and very popular** in meaning since long past to be **used by people**.

However, please study the chapters of '**Idioms**' for more details & examples.
And for more **Phrasal Verbs** to know in details and examples, please go through the next chapters of '**List of Phrasal Verbs**'.

448. **The Adverbial Phrase:** That does the work of an Adverb.
   1) He was **at that place** (there). The arrow fell **on this spot** (here).
   2) Goutam babu does his work **with care**. (Carefully).
   3) The thief fled/ran away **at a great speed**. (fast/quickly).
   4) Come **before long/ at an early date** (soon).
   5) The coins from the bag scattered **in all places** (everywhere).
   6) He answered **in a rude manner** (rudely).
   7) He fell **to the ground** (down).
   8) He does his work **without any care** (carelessly).
   9) I have no money **at this moment** (now).
   10) No such diseases were known **in those days** (then).

❑ More about Adverbial Phrases:

   11) He came to *see me*. (purpose/reason)
   12) He fell *from the tree*. (direction)
   13) Come *into the garden*. (adv. of place)
   14) This must be done at *any cost*. (manner)
   15) He lives *on a small income*. (manner)
   16) Quinine is good *for malaria*. (purpose/ causes)
   17) I have done well *on the whole*. (manner)
   18) He swims *in the pond*. (where-place)
   19) She lived *in the middle of a great wood*. (place)
   20) I stood *on the bridge at midnight*. (place & time)
   21) I took him *on the strength of your recommendation*. (Why-reason)

❑ Some more adverbial phrases, try them to use in your sentences:

Adverbial Phrases	*Adverbial Phrases*
1) In a loud voice	11) On either side of the street.
2) Without further delay	12) In a shady nook
3) With one voice	13) To the last man
4) For certain	14) With a smile
5) Just in time	15) At sixes and sevens
6) Up in arms	16) At the eleventh hour
7) Of no consequence	17) On the top of the hill
8) Out of fashion	18) In future
9) With great satisfaction	19) At nine o'clock
10) In the twinkling of an eye.	20) With great promptitude.

❑ Like relative phrases many can be replaced by single adverb or word, but not all. **However, see the chart, which can be replaced like in the following:**

Adverbs	Adverbial Phrases
1) Bravely	1) In a brave manner/ with bravery
2) Unwisely	2) In an unwise manner/ without wisdom
3) Swiftly	3) In a swift manner/ with swiftness
4) Beautifully	4) In a beautiful style
5) Formerly	5) In former times / once upon a time
6) Recently	6) Just now / at a recent date
7) Soon	7) Before very long/ at an early date.
8) Here	8) At this place
9) There	9) At that place
10) Away	10) To another place
11) Abroad	11) To or in a foreign country
12) Now	12) At this moment
13) Then	13) In those days, etc.

❑ Besides, there are many phrases which can be used as *both as Adjective and* as *Adverb*. Study the chart.

As an Adjective Phrase	*As an Adverbial Phrase*
1) The man in the room rushed out.	1) He is in the room.
2) The work at night I don't like.	2) Knock me at night.
3) The man sleeps at noon, doesn't mean idle.	3) They went there at noon.
4) The crowd in the bazaar was very noisy.	4) The crowd halted in the bazaar.
5) Have you heard of the man in the moon?	5) How could be a man in the moon?
6) A house on an island was washed away.	6) They live on an island.
7) Awful is the gloom beneath her.	7) Then why did she look beneath her?
8) Is this the train to Peshawar?	8) It usually goes to Peshawar, Sir.

449. Exercise-1: Replace the Adverb Phrases by an Adverb of same meaning:

1) The bodies were mangled **in a terrible manner.**
2) Let us cease work **from this very moment**.
3) It was just **on this spot** that he died.
4) The child replied **with perfect truthfulness.**
5) He arrived at that moment.
6) I hope that he will come **at a very early date.**
7) He seems to have acted **with great promptitude.**
8) No one would dare to answer him **in an impudent way.**
9) I accept your statement **without reserve.**
10) I thank you with **all my heart**.
11) He succeeded **in the long run**.
12) He is ignorant **to a proverb**.
13) The post-boy drove **with fierce career.**
14) He has been painted **in his proper colors.**
15) The wind blew **with great violence.**
16) He has proved his case **to my satisfaction.**

450. Exercise-2: Replace the Adverb in italics by an Adverb phrase of same meaning:

1) The pigeon flies **swiftly**.
2) Did Rama behave **well**?
3) Go **away**.
4) The dying man replied **feebly**.
5) **Gently** fell the rain.
6) We will pitch the tents just **here**.
7) He expects to get promotion **soon**.
8) He builds his house **there**.
9) They have only **recently** arrived.
10) Al though hungry, the soldiers worked **cheerfully**.
11) He spoke **eloquently**.
12) **Soon** the sun will set.
13) Do you work **thoroughly**?
14) They were hurrying **homeward**.
15) The door was **suspiciously** open.
16) **Formerly** he worked at the School of Economics.
17) He tried **hard**.

451. The Prepositional Phrase:

In the chapter of Preposition, we have discussed 6 kinds of Prepositions. Of them the number 4 is about the Prepositional Phrase. Read the definition and study the examples.
- He stood *in front of* me.
- I was *at the point of* death.
- *In the teeth of* strong opposition, the bill was passed.
- *On account of* his illness, he failed in the Exam.

➢ In most cases the prepositions do the function of an Adverb, i.e., they are adverbial in nature; as in 'in front of' denotes the position of verb, 'where did he stand?'

❑ The Prepositions which are formed by two or more words, with the force of a single preposition at the end, is called the **Prepositional Phrase** or **Complex Preposition**; as, *according to, because of, as for owing to, due to,* etc.

❑ Here is a list of Prepositional Phrase which is actually drawn from the chapter of Prepositions. Study them, if done already, here as a revision:
1) Act **according to** my instructions. Why don't you come **along with** us?
2) **Agreeably to** the terms of the settlement, I herewith enclose my cheque for Rs 20000.
3) He could not attend the classes **because of** his illness.
4) **By reason of** his perverse attitude, he estranged his best friends.
5) **In consequence of** his illness, he could not finish the work in time.
6) **In event of** his dying heirless, his nephew would inherit the whole property.
7) There is an open field **in front of** our house. He got the flat **in lieu of** all his sundry.
8) I took Arts **in place of** science. **In spite of** hard labor, he could not succeed.
9) Mrs. Gosh joined the meeting **instead of** her husband. He went there **instead of** me.
10) **Owing to** excessive rain, the flood occurs this year.
11) Rs 75,000 **in full settlement of** all your claims up-to-date.
12) Whatever he does, he does **with an eye to** the main chance.
   ❑ **Exception:** Some phrases do not take any simple preposition at end; as, 'on this side', 'on board', etc.
13) **On this side** you can see the stretched green land.
14) **On board**, she recalled her boyfriend & rushed towards the door.

❑ **Check the list of Complex Preposition or Prepositional Phrase:**

Prepositional Phrases	Meaning...	Examples
At home in	Familiar with/skilled in	He is quite at home in Mathematics.
At the top of	Highest point	The man began to cry at the top of his cry.
Because of	Due to reason	She could not sing because of cough & cold.
By dint of	With help	By dint of hard work, he succeeded.
By force of	By power of	Even a difficult thing is made easy by force of habit.
By means of	Way of/virtue of	He won the honor by means of selfless service.
By the side of	Beside	A small river flows by the side of the small village.
By virtue of	With help	She stood first by virtue of hard labor.
For the sake of	For/cause	Netaji sacrificed his life for the sake of his country.
For want of	Due to lack of	The drought occurs for want of rain.
In accordance with	accordingly,	Your action is not in accordance with your word.
In connection with	Relating	In connection with your query, I am writing this letter.
In case of	If happen (something)	In case of his death his son will get the benefit.
Prepositional Phrases	*Meaning...*	*Examples*
In common with	Agree with	You should also be favored with the others.

In course of	During the time	In course of conversation, he also mentioned it.
In consideration of	Considering	In consideration of his hard work, he may succeed.
In defense of	In support of	The pleader made a good proceeding in defense of his client.
In favor of	In support of	The students spoke in support of their teacher.
In front of	Before/at front	They saw a hut in front of the palace.
In keeping with	Accordance with	His interest in religion is in keeping with his age.
In lieu of	Instead of/in place of	Please take my subscription in lieu of her.
In opposition to	On contrary of	Your view is in opposition to mine.
In order to	For/ due to	In order to get a good result, he studied very hard.
In quest of	For seek of	He went to the town in quest of any job.
In regard to	Regarding/about	I have nothing to say in regard to this matter.
In reply/response to	Giving reply	In response to your advertisement, I am writing this.
Prepositional Phrases	***Meaning...***	***Examples***
In respect of	Regarding	In respect of service, he is senior to me.
In spite of	Even of	In spite of his poverty, he refused help.
In support of	In support of	The students spoke in support of their teacher.
In the teeth of	Against	In the teeth of strong opposition, the bill was passed.
In view of	On considering	In view of the importance, I'll take prime carefulness.
On account of	Because of/due to	On account of his illness, he failed in the Exam.
On behalf of	For (somebody)	On behalf of me kindly give it to my wife.
On the brink of	At the point of	Bengal was on the brink of a terrible famine in 1942.
On the eve of	At the moment	He made a great confusion on the eve of the occasion.
On the point of	At the moment of	She was on the point of bursting into tears.
With a view to	For purpose of	He went to Delhi with a view to taking part...
With reference to	Referring/mentioning	With reference to your letter, I have the honor to inform you.

452. **The Conjunctional** or **Conjunctive Phrase:** The conjunctions that consist of two or more words, they are called the **conjunctional phrases**; as, *as well as, inasmuch as, as soon as, in order that, even if, as if,* etc.
The Correlative (that are used in pair; as, *either—or, neither—nor, though—yet,* etc.) & **Compound Conjunctions** (that are used with two or more words, i.e., *as well as, inasmuch as, as soon as, in order that, even if, as if,* etc.) –are the examples of **Conjunctional Phrases**; as, [for more details about the classification of Conjunctions, please read the chapter of Conjunctions.]
   1) He walks ***as though*** he is slightly lame.
   2) I must refuse your request, ***inasmuch as*** I believe it unreasonable.
   3) He took off his coat ***as soon as*** he entered the house.
   4) He looks ***as if*** he were weary.

❑ **Study them some more in details:**

The Correlative Conjunctions are again classified into — *Cumulative*, *Alternative* & *Adversative* in nature. They are like the followings:

A. **Cumulative Correlative**: (both—and, not only—but also)
   o   We **both** love **and** honor him.
   o   **Not only** is he foolish, **but also** obstinate.

B. **Alternative Correlative**: (Either...or, neither...nor, whether—or)
   o   **Either** take it **or** leave it.
   o   It is **neither** useful **nor** ornamental.
   o   **Whether** he'll go **or** I have to.
   o   I do not care **whether** you go **or** stay.

C. **Adversative Correlative**: (though—yet,)
   o   **Though** he is suffering much pain, **yet** he does not complain.
   o   **Though** he worked hard, **yet** he failed in the test.

   ❏   **And, more examples of Compound Conjunctions** which also belong to the Conjunctional Phrase (a phrase which consists of two or more words). Remember, the Compound Conjunctions in form or structure may also be either of both, Sub-ordinate Conjunction or Co-ordinate Conjunction regarding the function.
o   The notice was published **in order that** all might know the facts.
o   I will forgive you **on condition that** you do not repeat the offence.
o   Such an act would not be kind **even if** it were just.
o   He saved some bread **so that** he should not go hungry on the morrow.
o   You can borrow the book **provided that** you return it soon.
o   I must refuse your request, **inasmuch as** I believe it unreasonable.
o   He took off his coat **as soon as** he entered the house.
o   He looks **as if** he were weary.

   ❏   All the above are also the **Sub-Ordinate Conjunctions**; besides they are the examples of **Compound Conjunctions**.
❏   But, as we said, a **Compound Conjunction** may also be a **Co-Ordinate Conjunction** like the following, and they all belong to the **conjunctive phrase**:
o   Prakash **as well as** Pravat were absent from school.
o   **Both** Prakash **and** Pravat were absent from the school.

453. **The Interjectional Phrase:**
Like Pronoun, Interjection has almost no* Phrases, or have few to mention. Many grammarians wish to exclude even, the interjection to be a part of the 'Parts of Speech'. However, as they have not given any different name (substitute term for interjection), we like continue to honor it as one of the 'Parts of Speech' as the other seven.

   Note-1: * = The word of negation 'no' (an adjective) can be used with both singular & plural following it. 'Interjection has **almost no** Phrases'; it means it has 'few' or 'some phrases though'. It does not hint 'zero'.

To realize the **Phrase of Interjection**, please study the following pages (copied from the chapter of Interjections.) They are like the following:
✓   **What a pity!** he drowned!
✓   **By Jove!** we have got it.
✓   **Good heavens!** Protect us from this danger to grab.

   ❏   *Definition:* When two or more words together express an emotion is called a **Phrase of Interjection.**

Certain Phrases used as Interjections
There are certain phrases which are also used as the interjections in the sentences. Carefully study the sentences:
   1)   **Ah me!** You hate your life long.
   2)   **Well done friend!** You have done excellent.
   3)   **Good bye!** We don't know will we meet again?
   4)   **O dear me!** What you have done.

5) **Bad luck to it!** He tried his best yet.
6) **Good gracious!** How one can do this alone.
7) **Good heavens!** Who can do it?
8) **Well, to be sure!** It is he has done this job.
9) **For shame!** Leave me alone.
10) **Alas & alack!** We had missed our bus.

Certain Verbs or other Parts of Speech, used as Interjections too

There are <u>certain moods of verbs</u> or <u>parts of speech</u> that are used as the interjections in the sentences:

a. <u>Imperative:</u>

→ **Hear!** What a song she sings.
→ **Hear! Hear!** What a sound it is. (*applause*)
→ **See!** What the sight is.

b. <u>Subjunctive:</u>

→ *Would that I had* the wings of a dove!
→ *Would that I had* billions of dollars!
→ *Would that I had* that great soul of Jesus!
　　　　　　(Thus, the whole sentence in subjunctive mood used in expressing wish of the speaker)

c. <u>By infinitive:</u>

→ **To think** that I should have played the match!
→ **To say** that I should go there! Why you not then?

d. <u>Adjective or Adverb:</u>

→ **Strange!** She went there.
→ **Shocking!** How she can say so.

> **Note:** *Think:* strange or shocking—what? Or who? Is it 'she' or 'her going there' or 'saying that'? Are the words adjectives or adverbs? However, here in the above sentences the words are used as **Interjections that expresses emotion of the speaker.**

e. <u>Adjective+ Noun:</u>

→ **Dreadful sight!** I can't explain.
→ **Foolish fellow!** Or how one can behave before sure death.
→ **What a mess!** Who did all these!

f. <u>Adverb:</u>

→ **How** vary kind of you! If you didn't do, I fell in ...
→ **How** wonderful! **How** beautiful! How awful it is.

g. <u>A full sentence with a pronoun:</u>

→ What a sad thing **it** is! She died in shock of her husband's death.

h. <u>A full sentence with a conjunction:</u>

→ **If** I could see her once more! But I know it is now an improbable word to hope for her any longer.

'*Wh' word sometimes with main verb, used also as Interjections*
Sometimes while expressing strong emotion in hasty, Auxiliary verb with Subject is left out, and <u>only main verb is used, with a 'wh' word</u>; as,

1) **Why cry!** And for the man who has already forgotten you?
2) **Why wait and spoil life!** Waiting for nothing come readymade.
3) **Why go there!** You didn't tell it before.
4) **What said!** I can't remember like that anything.
5) **How reached!** And alone!
6) **Wow!** But where it happened. /**Where happened!**

Note: Thus, we can express interjections in various ways than till mentioned, for interjections are not only words but it includes sounds various to count, i.e., unending, I meant to say.

31. The list of Phrasal Verbs

o We said, Group or Phrasal Verbs are formed by combining **Verbs** and **Adverbs** or **Prepositions** or **both**. Let's check in the following:

A. Verb + Adverb = Phrasal Verbs

Verb	Adverb	Phrasal Verbs	Meanings
Bear	Down	Bear down	He was determined to bear down all obstacles. (to defeat)
Break	Away	Break away	The prisoner broke away from captivity. (escaped suddenly)
Bring	Out	Bring out	My first novel was brought out in 2020 during lockdown. (published)
Call	Out	Call out	He was called out for an urgent task. (summoned)
Go	Up	Go up	The price of essential commodities is going up. (increasing)
Set	Down	Set down	The police set down the complaint. (recorded)
Run	Over	Run over	A poor dog was run over by the car.
Turn	Aside	Turn aside	We should not turn aside from the path of honesty.

B. Verb + Prepositions = Phrasal Verbs

Verb	Preposition	Phrasal Verbs	Meanings
Bring	On	Bring on	The damp weather has brought on his illness. (led to)
Call	At	Call at	We called him at his house. (met)
Carry	On	Carry on	I am carrying on the project of publishing my academic books since 2021. (continuing)
Laugh	At	Laugh at	Your friends may laugh at you. Still, you move on. (mock at/show negligence)
Look	After	Look after	Parents look after their children to their utmost end. (take care of)
Put	On	Put on	You don't need put on you are an honest man. (take disguise)
Run	At	Run at	The tiger ran at the deer. (chased)
Set	Up	Set up	I set up my White Home by June, 2020. (founded)

C. Verb + Adverb + Prepositions = Phrasal Verbs

Verb	Adverb	Prepositions	Phrasal Verbs	Meanings
Look	Down	Upon	Look down upon	We should not look down upon the poor. (hate)
Set	Out + for	-	Set out for	They set out for the picnic spot early in the morning. (started)
Do	Away	With	Do away with	The young actress tried to do away with herself. (kill/try to commit suicide)
Fall	--	In + with	Fall in with	The Principal fell in with the decision of the guardian committee. (agree/give consent)

o **Study the following Phrasal Verbs used in sentences, arranged alphabetically: It begins with 'A':**

A for 'Act', 'Aim at'

Group Verbs	Examples	Meanings
Act against	We should not act against other's opinion in general.	Do anything against
Act for	He is acting for his client.	Working on behalf of
Act on	He acted on my advice. So, his failure is my responsibility.	Worked according to
Act upon (1)	The medicine acts upon the heart.	affects
Act upon (2)	They acted upon our instructions.	Did as per
Act upon (3)	Acting upon the news, I went there.	Based upon/ depending on
Act up to	The machine does not act up to my expectation.	Work according to

Aim at	Riya aims at nothing.	(Wish target or goal)

B *for* 'Bear', 'Blow' 'Break', 'Bring', 'Burst'

Group Verbs	Examples	Meanings
Back up	He **backed up** his friend's claim.	(supported)
Bear away	Preston bore away the prize for his talent.	Won
Bear down	He is determined to bear down all obstacles.	To defeat/ overcome
Bear on	These are the issues that bear on the welfare of the society.	Relate to
Bear out	The report bears out the accusation to be true. Dr. Roy will bear me out what I'll say.	Supports/ confirms
Bear up	The soldiers bore up their courage against all odds.	Kept up/ sustained
Bear with	I have to bear with her patiently during this difficult period.	tolerate
Blow		
Blow away	The wind blew away all dry leaves.	Drove away
Blow in/into	The door opened and the school boys blew into the class rooms.	Arrive noisily, cheerfully
Blow off	The chimneys blow off thick smoke.	Emit
Blow out	Don't blow out the fire. We need it later.	Extinguish /put out
Blow over	• The storm soon will blow over and weather would be fine and pleasant. • The present disturbances will soon **blow over**.	(Pass off)
Blow up (1)	Opponent soldiers **blew up** the buildings.	(exploded)
Blow up (2)	A storm is blowing up.	Blowing fiercely
Blow up (3)	You don't need to blow up your credits.	Exaggerate
Break		
Break away	The prisoner broke away from captivity. The accused broke away from the lock-up	Escaped suddenly/ freed himself
Break down (1)	His health broke down under the pressure of work.	Grew worse
Break down (2)	He **broke down** in the middle of his speech.	(failed) collapsed
Break forth	The sun broke forth from the clouds, and Arjuna killed Joydrowth.	Suddenly came out/ appeared
Break in /into (1)	The robbers broke in at night and took away all with them.	Forced their way in
Break in (2)	The horses are being broken in.	Trained
Break in (3)	He **broke in** our serious discussion and asked for a glass of water.	(interrupted)
Break into	Dacoits broke into the building last night.	Entered by force
Break in upon	The mob broke in upon the meeting and submitted their petition.	Made their way in by force
Break off (1)	He broke off in the middle of his speech.	Stopped speaking
Break off (2)	Sophia broke off her engagement with Fellix.	separated
Break out (1)	A devastating fire broke out due to short circuit.	Started suddenly
Break out (2)	Several prisoners broke out from jail.	Escaped by breaking.
Break through (1)	Scientists have broken through new and important inventions in the fight against cancer.	Invented or made something new.
Break through (2)	Luis Suarez broke through the defense of his rival team.	Found way/ forced a passage
Break up (1)	Our school will break up from next Saturday. The meeting broke up at 5 p.m.	close
Break up (2)	They **broke up** their relation and entered another soon.	(Ended relationship)
Break up into (3)	The ship was broken up into parts in the clash against the rock under water.	Separated or ruin
Break with	Everyone should break with the superstition about religion. There should be only one of Humanity. It means coexist, cooperation, tolerance, peace and prosperity for all living beings.	Give up
Bring		
Bring about	Following blind ego, falsity, pretention and blind love for fantasy	cause

	will bring about only our own ruin before time.	
Bring back (1)	I shall bring back the book tomorrow.	Return
Bring back (2)	The sight of the village brought back old memories.	Restored
Bring back to	The change of place brought him back to his health.	Restored to
Bring down	The price of essential commodities has been brought down a bit since last week.	reduced
Bring down	The enemy aircraft was brought down.	Force sth. down by firing
Bring forth/in	All trees bring forth new tender leaves during rainy season.	Produce /beget
Bring forward	All these matters were brought forward in the meeting for discussion.	Raised or presented
Bring in	My business brings in good income.	Yields/profits
Brings in (2)	They tried to bring new fashion in the publication.	introduce
Bring off	Our football team brought off a grand victory.	won
Bring on (1)	The damp weather has brought on his illness.	Led to.
Bring on (2)	He has brought on this disgrace to himself.	caused
Bring out	My first book brought out in 2013. It was a book of poems.	published
Bring out (2)	Proper training will bring out the best in him.	Reveal, nurture
Bring round (1)	The patient was brought round by careful nursing.	Made restored to
Bring round (2)	After proper counseling he was brought round.	Made cure to /overcome
Bring to	The girl fainted but was soon brought to.	bring her to conscious
Bring under	Her indomitable spirit can't be brought under.	subdued
Bring up	After the death of his father, he was brought up by his mother.	reared
Burst		
Burst in	My friend burst in my house and informed of my father's accident.	Enter a room or building suddenly
Burst in sb	We were talking, then a beggar burst in us seeking help.	interrupted
Burst on	We were tensed of, when he burst on the scene.	Appeared suddenly
Burst forth	A tiger burst forth from the jungle	Came out suddenly
Burst into	The woman burst into tears at the news of her husband's death.	Fell in cry terribly
Burst open	The door burst open with a gust of wind and we could see only lightings around.	Open suddenly and violently
Burst out	He burst out weeping like a child.	

C *for* 'Call' 'Carry', 'Cast', 'Catch', 'Cheered', 'Clear', 'Come', 'Cry', 'Cut'

Group Verbs	Examples	Meanings
Call at... (of a train)	The train calls at Didcot & Reading.	To stop at a place for a short time
Call at (2)	We called him at his house.	met
Call away	She was called away from the meeting to receive an urgent phone call.	To ask sb to stop what they are doing and to go somewhere else
Call back	• She said she'd call back. • I'm waiting for Uday to call me back. • Call her back; she said it was urgent. • Do you call me back?	To telephone sb again; to telephone sb who telephoned you earlier
Call for (sth)	His mater called for an explanation of his conduct.	needed/ required sth
Call for (sb)	I'll call for you at 7 O'clock.	To collect sb to go somewhere
Call forth	Your speech called forth an angry response from him.	Elicited /produce a particular reaction
Call in (1)	He called in a doctor.	Sent for/ called for help or service
Call in (2)	The National Library has called in all overdue books.	Ordered the return of
Call off	The boss called off the meeting with us to attend the another.	(cancelled)
Call on/upon	I now call upon the chairman to address the meeting.	Invite or ask sb to

	I feel call upon to warn you about gambling.	speak/ feel that I ought
Call out	The fire brigade was called out by the authorities before it was too late.	Summoned /to ask sb to come in emergency
Call over	The students are called over by their roll numbers.	To give attendance
Call to	I called to my friend from the roof.	Addressed loudly
Call up (1)	Call up Rahim to save you from this crisis.	To make a telephone call to sb
Call up	She could not call up the verse and got zero marks.	Remember /to bring sth back to your mind
Call upon (2)	He was called upon to explain his conduct.	ordered
Carry		
Carry about	He carries about a folding chair wherever he goes.	To take sth with
Carry away /off	He was carried away by his enthusiasm. The little dog was carried away by the current.	driven
Carry away (2)	Don't get carried away. Wait, there are more waiting…	Extremely excited
Carry back	The incident carried him back to his childhood days.	Returned to the past
Carry off (2)	Covid 19 has carried off many of our brother and sisters.	taken the lives of
Carry off	He carried off all the prizes. Nick carried off the best prize.	won
Carry on	I am carrying on the work while he is away.	continuing
Carry out (1)	I shall carry out what I have promised. However, I know I always forget.	fulfill
Carry out (2)	He agreed to carry out my orders.	(execute)
Carry through	Only courage carried him through this crisis.	Helped him to overcome …
Carry through	He carried through the work successfully.	completed
Cast		
Cast about for	He is casting about for an opportunity to escape.	Looking for
Cast aside	He has cast aside his family for a foolish reason!	forsaken
Cast away (1)	He cast away his old clothes and entered the washroom.	Thrown away.
Cast away (2)	The ship was cast away on the coast of Africa.	(wrecked)
Cast down	He is easily cast down. However, you can't say, he has tendency to commit suicide.	depressed
Cast off (sth)	I am trying to cast off my poor image, so that they think it twice.	Shun/ abandon
Cast out	If you come to me, I shall not cast you out.	reject
Catch		
Catch at	A drowning man catches at a straw.	Try to seize
Catch on	She is very quick on to catch on to things. She is intelligent.	To grasp or understand sth
Catch out	Many investors were caught out by the fall in share price.	To surprise and put them in difficult situation
Catch up on	I have a lot of things to catch up on.	To spend extra time doing new things.
Catch up in	Innocent passers-by got caught up in the riots.	To become involved accidently
Catch up with	• Go on ahead; I'll catch up with you. • Don't wait for me. You guys go on. I will go on my bike & catch up with you soon.	To reach sb who is ahead by going faster than him.
Catch up with	Will India catch up with the developed countries?	To be in same level improving faster than others
Cheer		
Cheer on	The audiences cheered the players on in the stadium.	To give shouts in encouragement in sports

Cheer up	• Oh, come on—cheer up! • Give Mary a call; she needs cheering up. • Bright curtains can cheer up a dull room.	To make sb or sth cheerful

Clear		
Clear away/out	Ask the servant to **clear away** the table. The sweeper **cleared out** the drain.	To clean
Clear away (2)	The mist has cleared away after the sunrise.	dispersed
Clear off	Jack worked overtime to clear off arrears of work.	To finish or complete
Clear off (2)	Clear off from here.	Get out
Clear out (2)	Please, clear out my room.	Leave
Clear up	The sky is clearing up.	Gets rid of clouds/ becomes clear

Come		
Come about	When did the accident come about? Can you tell me how it came about?	Happen/ take place
Come across (1)	He spoke for a long time; but his meaning didn't really come across.	To be understood /come over
Come across (1)	Kinsley came across his ex-girlfriend. He stepped forward and kissed her forehead to make surprise all there.	Met by chance
Come across (2)	Father came across the thing what he had lost before five months.	Found a thing by chance
Come across (3)	I hoped she'd come across with some more information.	To provide or supply sth what you need
Come after	The night guard came after the thief; however, the thief escaped.	chased
Come along (1)	Come along, it is getting late.	hurry
Come along (2)	When the right opportunity comes along, she'll take it.	To arrive /appear
Come apart	The book just came apart in my hands.	To break into pieces
Come around	Your mother has not yet come round from the anesthetic.	Come to/to become conscious again
Come around (2)	Do come around and see us some time.	To visit a place a place for short time
Come around (3)	He'll never come around to our way of thinking.	Change one's mood or opinion
Come at (1)	She came at me with a knife. The rioters came at us last night with swords and others.	attacked
Come at (2)	We're getting nowhere—let's come at it from another angle.	To think about a problem or situation from different angle
Come away from	The plaster has started come away from the wall.	To become separated from
Come away with	We came away with the impression that all was not well with their marriage.	To leave a place with a particular feeling or impression
Come back	You came back very late last night.	Returned
Come back	Long hair for men seems to be coming back in.	To become popular again
Come before	The case comes before the court next week.	To be presented
Come between	I hate anything come between us.	Sth to damage a relationship
Come by (1)	She came by the house.	Made a short visit
Come by (2)	How did you come by his purse? Jobs are hard to come by these days.	(get)/obtain
Come down (1)	The new bridge came down after its inauguration in Kolkata. Minister says, "We look into the matters."	collapsed
Come down (2)	The rain came down in torrents.	fell
Come down from	She came down from Oxford.	To leave a university

Come down from	He has come down from North Bengal. He has come down from China.	From one place to another, generally from north to south.
Come down on	Don't come down so hard on her.	Criticize sb severely/ punish
Come down to	The name has come down from last century.	Sth that comes from long past
Come down with	I think I'm coming down with flu.	To get an illness that is not very serious.
Come forward	He came forward and offered his help.	(Voluntarily give help or information)
Come from	Where do you come from?	The place where sb lives
Come of	B. R. Ambedkar came of a poor family.	Was born in
Come off (1)	When will the festival come off?	Take place
Come off (2)	When I tried to lift the jug, the handle came off.	Became separated from
Come on (1)	The project is coming on nicely.	Growing
Come on (2)	Come on, we will be late for the function.	Hurry on
Come on (3)	The rainy season is coming on in the coastal areas.	Beginning
Come out (1)	The rain stopped and the sun came out.	appeared
Come out (2)	When is your next book coming out?	Publishing
Come over (1)	He will never come over to our side.	Change side
Come over (2)	Why did you come over here?	travelled
Come round	Father came round his sufferings soon, and began mix with us.	(recovered/cured)
Come through (1)	A message has come through here that are going to resign?	reached
Come through (2)	May your father come through soon.	Recover/ come round
Come upon	We came upon some boys playing in the field. We sought help from them.	Found by chance

Cry		
Cry down	Don't cry down his achievements. Think, what labor he gave we can't.	Underestimate /decry
Cry off	We said we would go but we had to cry off at the last moment.	abandon
Cry to	The helpless man cried to the rioters for his life.	begged
Cry up	A trader cries up his own goods.	Extols/ exaggerates
Cry out	Peter cried out for help, none heard, none came.	Shouted loudly
Cry out against	People of one community often cry out against what they should not. None love patience is our destination!!	Protest sth

Cut		
Cut away	They trimmed the plants, cutting away the uneven branches.	clipping
Cut down (1)	Please cut down your story. It is almost a novel in length.	Shorten
Cut down (2)	The physician advised him to cut down his consumption of animal protein.	reduce
Cut in	She kept on cutting in our conversation.	Interrupting
Cut off (1)	The baby is cut off from its mother.	Separated
Cut off (2)	He was cut off at an early age.	Died
Cut out (1)	One of the aircraft's engines cut out.	Stopped functioning
Cut out (2)	Maizie was cut out for this job.	Suitable
Cut out (3)	Sonny cut Sophia out in the competition.	defeated
Cut up (1)	The mother was terribly cut up at the death of her own son.	Upset
Cut up (2)	He cut up the bread.	Cut into pieces

D *for* deal, do, draw

Group Verbs	Examples	Meanings
Deal in (1)	He deals in rice.	Trades in
Deal in (2)	The book deals in detail about Phrase, Clause & sentences.	discusses
Deal out	The profits will be dealt out among the investors.	distributed

Deal with (1)	They try to deal politely with the customers.	Behave with
Deal with (2)	He dealt with the difficult problem easily.	Solved.
Do		
Do away with (1)	'Why to do away with death penalty?' he said.	abolish
Do away with (2)	The woman tried to do away with herself.	Kill (also 'do in'
Do for (1)	The mutual disbelief does for any relation.	ruins
Do for (2)	This piece of stick will do for a scale.	Serve or used as
Doff (contraction of 'do off')	Doff your coat.	Take off
Don (contraction of 'Do on')	Don your coat.	Put on
Do in (1)	The young actress was so depressed that she felt like doing in herself.	killing
Do in (2)	He looked very done it.	exhausted
Do over (1)	He was done over by a gang of anti-socials.	Attacked and injured severely.
Do over (2)	We are doing over the drawing room.	Having decorated
Do up (1)	Who is to do up your room every day?	arrange
Do up (2)	We are having the kitchen done up.	Repaired.
Do with (1)	We can no longer do with his insolvency. (Inability to pay due)	tolerate
Do with (2)	What will you do with these match sticks?	What use make of
Do with (3)	A politician has to do with all sorts of men.	Deal with
Do with (4)	Please return the book when done with.	Finished
Do without	He can hardly do without his private secretary.	Manage without

Draw		
Draw away	His attention was drawn away by the loud noise.	Diverted.
Draw back	The chairman drew back declaring the time-table of the innings.	Receded/retreated
Draw in	The Rajdhani express is drawing in.	Entering the station
Draw on	Evening was drawing on.	Approaching
Draw out (1)	The girl is very shy and needs to be drawn out to talk.	Encouraged
Draw out (2)	The professor drew out the interview with MR. Rahaman intentionally to test his patience for the job.	prolonged
Draw to	I drew to Priya from the first day.	Felt attracted by
Draw up	He drew out the contract.	Wrote out

Drop		
Drop away	His friends dropped away with his name growing.	Became fewer/drop off
Drop by	Some friends dropped by to see me.	Made short visits
Drop by	On his long journey, he **dropped by** at every metropolitan.	(Stopped for a visit)
Drop in	On my way back, I shall drop in at her house.	Pay a casual visit
Drop off	My friends dropped off one by one after we got marriage everyone.	Reduce in number/ became fewer
Drop off (2)	I always dropped off during the long prayer on each Sunday.	Fell asleep
Drop out		

Fall

Group Verbs	Examples	Meanings
Fall apart (1)	The glass **fell apart**.	(Broke into pieces)
Fall apart (1)	Their marriage finally fell apart.	broke
Fall away (1)	The film-star's fans fell away with the decline of his popularity.	Deserted /left him
Fall away (2)	The black spots are yet to fall away from your face.	Disappear
Fall away (3)	He has much fallen away since I saw him last.	Become lean
Fall back	The enemy fell back with the advance of our troops.	Retreated
Fall back upon	The army fell back upon a new line of defense.	Had recourse to
Fall behind	France fell behind Germany in coal production.	Failed to keep level

		with
Fall for	Mr. P falls for every pretty face he sees only to see hardly any heart in them.	Yields to charm of
Fall in (1)	The game teacher asked his students to fall in.	Get into a line.
Fall in (2)	The new building fell in within a year.	Collapsed
Fall in with (1)	Subba fell in with his best friend Kanak in the fest after a decade.	Met by chance
Fall in with (2)	Finally, he fell in with our decision.	Agree/give consent
Fall off (1)	Attendance in classes has fallen off after the exams in schools.	Decreased
Fall off (2)	False friends fall off in misfortune.	Drop off
Fall on/upon (1)	Miscreants fell on/upon them.	Attacked fiercely
Fall on/upon (2)	The full cost of the ceremony fell on the students.	Incurred
Fall out	The boys fell out with each other with the issue of goal.	Quarreled
Fall through	Our holiday plans suddenly fell through.	Failed
Fall to	He fell to eating with greater gusto.	began

G *for* Get, Give, Go

Group Verbs	Examples	Meanings
Get about /around (1)	The news of our President's death gets about sooner than we hoped.	spread
Get about /around (2)	• The scandal of his affair with a widow got about in a day. • News soon got around that he had resigned.	Spread (as a rumor)
Get about /around (3)	She gets about/around with the help of a stick.	
Get across	Your meaning didn't really get across.	To be communicated /understood
Get ahead	• She wants to get ahead in her career. • Who doesn't want to get ahead? • She wanted so and she got ahead.	To make progress (further than others)
Get along with (1)	It is the right time to **get along with** your enemies all, and set up peace with them.	(To be friendly with someone)
Get along (2)	It's time we are getting along.	Leaving the place
Get at sb (1)	She's always getting at me.	Criticizing sb
Get at sth (2)	• The fox could not get at the grapes. • The files are locked up and I can't get at them.	Reach
Get at sth (2)	• In this situation, truth is hard to get at. • The truth is sometimes difficult to get at.	Find out
Get away (1)	We're hoping to get away for a few days at Easter.	To have a holiday or vacation
Get away (2)	• The prisoner got away last night. • Thieves got away with computer equipment worth three lacs.	Escaped
Get away (3)	• The culprit can't get away. • He can't get away with only imprisonment of three months! • No body can't get away insulting me like that.	Go unpunished /receive relatively light punishment
Get back (1)	• When did you get back last night? • When will you get back from there?	Return
Get back (2)	• She's got back her old job. • She got back her lost iPhone after six months from riverbed.	To obtain sth again after having lost it
Get back at sb	• Finally, the rabbit **got back at** the rat and drove it away. • I'll find a way of getting back at him!	(To get revenge on somebody)
Get back in	• Jadavas finally got back in power in Bihar. • Will communist ever return in West Bengal.	To win election after having lost the prev. ones
Get back to sb	• I'll find out and get back to you.	To speak or write again later as a reply

	• She said she would get back to me within few days.	
Get behind with	• I'm getting behind with my work.	Failing to make enough progress
	• He got behind with his profession.	
Get by	Most of salary men here got by on a small salary.	Managed to live.
Get down (1)	Did you get down his address?	Write down
Get sb down	Saying that you only got him down.	Felt him depressed
Get sth down	I got the medicine down!	Swallow sth usually with great difficulty
Get down to (2)	Let's get down to our work.	Begin
Get in /into	• What time is the flight expected to get into Bagdogra from Chennai? • The train got in late.	Arrive
Get into (1)	• Father got me into the school.	Admitted
Get into (2)	• Don't get into a running train.	Enter
Get into (3)	• He got into trouble with police when he was still a student. • I got into conversation with a Italian student.	To become involved in/ to reach a condition
Get off (1)	Get off me, that hurts!	Tell sb to stop touching
Get off/ get sb off	• We got off straight after breakfast. • She got her child off to his school every day. • We got off in mid of the meeting.	To leave
Get off to	I had great difficulty getting off to sleep.	To fall asleep
Get off with sb	• Steve got off with Tracey at the party. • Do the youths go there to go off with somebody?	To have sexual or romantic relation with sb
Get off (2)	We were lucky to get off.	Escape
Get on	I am getting on in my studies.	Making a good progress.
Get out (1)	His secret got out to all.	Became known
Get out (2)	Few passengers were lucky to get off from the burning train.	escape
Get over	The old man could not get over the shock of his son's death.	Overcome
Get round (1)	He knows well how to get round his first customers to his views.	Influence
Get round (2)	Do you find any way of getting round the problem?	Solving
Get through (1)	Many failed the test and few got through.	Passed
Get through (2)	Please join us as soon as you get through your personal task.	Complete
Get up (1)	What time does he get up?	Wake up
Get up (2)	The old lady slowly got up, went through the gate and disappeared.	Stood up
Give		
Give away (1)	The chief guest along with others gave away the prizes on school sports day.	Distributed
Give away (2)	The soldier didn't give away any secret to our enemy.	Reveal
Give back	Could you give back my book?	return
Give forth	The engine gave forth a lot of smoke.	emitted
Give in	The powerful soldiers, somehow, **gave in**, and the citizens were saved from the inevitable deaths by their hand.	(surrendered)
Give off	The fire **gave off** dense smoke.	(emitted)/give out
Give out (1)	After few days, our stock of rice will give out.	Exhaust
Give out (2)	The blst furnace is giving out a lot of heat.	Emitting
Give out (3)	The chairman gave out the new interest on HBL and FDs.	declared
Give over (1)	Before exams, most of students give over to their studies what they don't through the year.	Devoted himself
Give over (2)	The accused were given over to the police. The working PM gave over the charge to the new PM of the state.	Handed over
Give up (1)	You should give up smoking.	Stop
Give up (2)	Don't give up hope in difficult times. Give up bad habit if you want to improve your life.	abandon

Go		
Go about	I hate this going about for the promotion of my book.	Moving about
Go about	A strong rumor is going about that he will leave us shortly.	Is in circulation
Go abroad	I never went abroad in my life time, and yet I am a refugee! Mr. Das often goes abroad to attend his business meeting.	Away from home, especially visit to a foreign country
Go after	The soldiers went after the enemy	Chased
Go against	The police will go against the public interest.	Oppose
Go along	As you go along, soon it will be found interesting.	Continue accepting
Go ahead	All arrangements are going ahead to celebrate the occasion.	Making progress
Go aside	Don't go aside from the path of virtue.	Deviate
Go at (1)	The two brothers go at each other at the slightest provocation.	attack
Go at (2)	They are going at it to complete the road in due time.	Making the best possible effort.
Go away	The beggar has gone away with all his belongings.	Left the place
Go back upon/from	I cannot go back upon or from my word.	Fail to keep
Go beyond	You should not go beyond your limits.	Cross limit/exceed
Go by (1)	You cannot always **go by** appearances.	judge from /according to
Go by (2)	They talked of days gone by.	Past
Go by (3)	I shall go by what my teachers says. It is a good rule to go by.	To be guided by/follow order
Go down	The sun has gone down.	Sunset
Go down (2)	The price of butter has gone down.	Reduced
Go down (3)	Netaji is gone down as a great patriot.	Regarded as
Go down (4)	He has gone down with fever.	Suffered from
Go for	He goes for a scholar here, since he was a gold medalist in his graduation.	Regarded as
Go for (2)	Shall I go for a doctor?	Fetch/bring
Go in for	We shall go in for next B. Sc's exam.	Sit for
Go in for (2)	Public will go in for abolition of this custom.	Favor/support
Go off (1)	The bomb went off and many people were injured.	Exploded
Go off (2)	The party went off well.	Passed
Go off (3)	The pistol went off suddenly.	Was discharged
Go on	The meeting went on for ten minutes, and we left the place.	Continued
Go out (1 & 2)	Go out in the sun. The lamp has gone out after twelve minutes.	Go outside/ extinguished
Go over	He went over to opposition party.	Changed side
Go over (2)	Please go over the accounts.	Examine
Go through	I shall go through the papers.	Examine fully
Go through (2)	My father went through great suffering those twenty minutes, and he died.	Experienced
Go through (3)	I heard the proposal went through without any opposition.	Was accepted
Go up	The price of essential commodities is going up.	increasing
Go upon	He does not go upon any fixed principles.	Follow
Go with	I'll go with you in this matter.	Agree with
Go without	He has been going without food for five days.	Passed time except

Grow		
Grow apart	The happiest couple grew apart from last year.	Stopped having a close relationship
Grow away from sb	They have grown away from each other; now they live at different places.	Become less close or depended
Grow back	The plant grew back in the rainy season.	
Grow up	Grow up man, why cry over love and love, a meaningless game on thy earth!	(To stop acting like a child)

H *for* **Hand, Hang, Hold**

Group Verbs	Examples	Meanings
Hand down	The custom has been handed down to the present generation.	Passed on to next generation
Hand in	The minister has handed in his resignation to the Governor.	Tendered/given/offered
Hand on	Hand on the book to your friend.	Pass on
Hand over	The accused was handed over to the police by the villagers.	Delivered

Hang		
Hang about/around	The little child hangs about/around his father.	Remain close to
Hang about/around	Why do you hang about the examination hall?	Move suspiciously close to sth/sb
Hang back	I am not here to hang back from my place.	Go back
Hang down	He hung down his head with shame; but I was shameless! I kept my head up.	Bowed down one's head
Hang on (1)	I do not like to hang on others for my bread.	Depend on
Hang on (2)	Through these years I hanged on in the project.	Stuck to someone/something
Hang on (3)	Would you hang on a minute, please?	Wait
Hang on (4)	He hung on until we put him down.	Hanging from sth
Hang out (1)	People hung out flags to welcome the Prime Minister.	displayed
Hang out (2)	We **hanged out** in the boat whole night and passed a pleasant night with thousand stars over our heads.	(To spend a lot of time with someone in a place)
Hang over (1)	Do not hang over the open balcony.	To bend down
Hang over (2)	The meeting has been hung over.	postponed
Hang together	You should all hang together and achieve success.	Support one another
Hang up (1)	A notice was hung up on the wall.	Put up/suspend
Hang up (2)	I cut short the telephone conversation and hung up.	Replaced the receiver
Hang upon	The crowd hung upon the leader's words.	Listened attentively to

Hold		
Hold back (1)	**Hold back** your wrath! It is improper to **pass over** us like that!	(To stop yourself from doing something)
Hold back (2)	• **Hold back** your weakness from your dear ones, and you are safe. • Truth can never be held back.	(hide/conceal)
Hold by	• Only friends held by in your difficult time.	Adhered to
Hold in	Hold in your temper. None here to bear with.	Check
Hold off (1)	Milo should hold off from such agitation.	Keep aloof/ maintain distance from
Hold on (1)	Please hold on for a minute.	Wait
Hold on (2)	The rain held on for two hours.	Continued
Hold on (3)	We should hold on the course through all opposition.	Stick to
Hold out (1)	She always held out her helping hands to known and unknown.	Extended
Hold out (2)	The doctor held out little hope of his recovery.	Promised/assured/gave
Hold up	He **held up** long hours and we were about to lose our patience.	(delayed)
Hold with	They hold with us in this matter.	agree

K *for* **Keep, Knock**

Group Verbs	Examples	Meanings
Keep at	We need to keep at our principles.	Stick to
Keep away/off	Keep away from bad company. Fire keeps off wild animals.	Keep aloof
Keep back	I never kept back anything from my lover.	Concealed
Keep down	You must keep down your anger.	Control/ suppress

Keep from	Keep from bad habits.	Refrain
Keep in (1)	It is wise to keep in while it is lighting.	Stay indoors
Keep in (2)	The fire will keep in till tomorrow.	Continue burning
Keep in (3)	Are they able to keep in with us anymore after the incident?	Agree with us
Keep off	Alertness keeps off many dangers.	Wards off
Keep on	Keep on. You must reach your goal.	Continue
Keep out	I was kept out of the business.	Put me outside
Keep to	You should always keep to your principles.	Adhere to
Keep under	Please keep your temper under control.	Keep in check
Keep up	Skipper Cook always kept up pressure on the Indian team.	Maintained
Keep up with	You must keep up with the changing world.	Keep pace with

Knock		
Knock about	Employees of Central Govt. have no fixed place to live in, they knock about at different places.	Leads an unsettled life
Knock down	He was knocked down by taxi.	Hit by
Knock down	The building was knocked down.	Broken down
Knock off	The workers usually knock off at five o'clock.	Stop work
Knock off	The shopkeeper will knock off thousand rupees if you want to buy the Peter's book.	Deduct
Knock out	Mary Kom knocked out her opponent in the next two rounds.	Defeated
Knock out	I was knocked out by the news.	Overwhelmed
Knock sb up	Please knock me up at five O'clock.	Make wake up
Knock up sth	Mother knocked up a meal for us.	Prepared hurriedly
Knock up	He was knocked up after work of five hours.	Tired/ exhausted

L for **lay**, **Let**, **look** & *miscellaneous*

Group Verbs	Examples	Meanings
Lap sth up	It's a terrible movie but audiences everywhere are lapping it up.	Accept or recive sth with great enjoyment
Lap sth up	The calf lapped up the bucket of milk.	Drink all of sth with great enjoyment
Lapse into	• She lapsed into silence again. • The patient lapsed into Coma soon after the accident.	Gradually pass into a worse or less active state or condition
Lark about /around	They larked about the last few months and now making complaints of their poor result.	Enjoyed themselves behaving in silly ways
Lash out at	Maizie suddenly lashed out at the boy without any provocation.	To suddenly try to hit sth or sb
Lash out at	In an article Peter lashed out at his all critics.	To criticize in an angry way
Laugh at sb	The experts laugh at my accent; but my don't care attitude ignores them always. / Don't laugh at me.	Making jokes of sb/ridicule
Laugh off	• I laughed off his suggestion of my resign from the post. • When something is likely to be beyond your patience, learn to laugh off them.	Didn't take sth serious and laugh them away

Lay		
Lay about	He began to lay about him in anger.	Deal blows
Lay aside	We need to lay aside something for our bad days.	Keep apart/ cast aside
Lay by/in	Lay by something for the future.	Store up for future use
Lay down	Our freedom fighters laid down their lives to the cause of the country's liberation.	Sacrificed
Lay down (2)	No such rules are laid down in the book of Constitution.	Written
Lay in/by/up	Hoarders laid in food for the future. He laid up enough for the future.	Stored
Lay off	Some workers were laid off for their agitation.	suspended
Lay on (1)	The mother laid her hand on her son's head.	Put

Lay on (2)	Taxes at highest rate were laid on liquid.	imposed
Lay out	He laid out his all in the business.	Expended
Lay out (2)	The garden is well laid out.	Arranged/ decorated
Lay up	I am laid up with fever.	Confined to bed

Let		
Let sb down (1)	The machine won't let it down.	Fail to help or support
Let sb/sth down (2)	Edith speaks French very fluently, but her pronunciation lets her down, like Peter to his English.	Make sb/sth less successful than they or it should be
Let sb in	What let her in this situation?	Make sb involved in
Let in	<u>Let</u> him <u>in</u>.	(allow sb to enter)
Let sb off	Let her off all these. This is our business. Whatever let me face.	Allow sb not to do
Let sb off	She was let off with a warning. They were our cousins. They let us off lightly.	Not punish sb/ give them only light punishment
Let sb out	• Being her friends, it is our business to let her out of this situation. • Counselling is very important to let her out from this worse condition.	To make sb not to feel alone/ help someone to come out depression
Let out	Suddenly she let out a scream of terror. There was a long snake facing towards her eyes.	To give a cry out of excitement of joy or sorrow
Let up	The pain finally let up.	To become less strong
Let up (2)	We mustn't let up now.	To make less effort

Look		
Look about for	Charlotte is looking about for a house in the new town.	Searching for/look for
Lok after	Parents look after their children out of love.	Take care of
Look at	Look at the birds sitting on the tower.	Gaze at/ask to see
Look down upon/at	• He **looks down at** them as they were his eternal slaves, and he is the Lord, equal of God. • Don't look down upon the poor.	Humiliate /deride
Look for	We looked for better treatment from your son-in-law	Expected
Look for (2)	I am looking for the file which has yellow cover.	Searching for
Look forward to	We looked forward to our uncle's visit during that time. He brought gifts and blessings for us all.	Expecting with pleasure
Look in	I shall look in his house when I pass by his.	Pay a short visit
Look into	Don't worry. I'll look into the matter soon.	Enquire into
Look on/ upon (1)	We looked upon you only as our well-wishers, but we were wrong.	regarded
Look on (2)	The house looked on to the river. The balcony looks on the river.	Faced/overlooks
Look out for	The police were looking out for the criminal. The eagle is looking out for a prey.	Watch/search for
Look over	The authority looked over his application and finally sanctioned his leave for two months.	examined
Look through	Please look through the letter and say, where are mistakes.	Examine carefully
Look to (1)	Look to your own affairs.	Attend
Look to (2)	I look to you for help.	Rely on
Look up (1)	Pamela **looked up** and asked nothing.	Saw up
Look up (2)	Prices of all things including essential commodities are looking up since few months, and there is no extra income or DA.	Increasing /rising
Look up (3)	Please look us up while returning from London.	Visit
Look up (4)	Look up a nearest meaning of the word in dictionary.	Find out

| Look up (5) | After a dull period, Peter's business is looking up. | improving |
| Look up to | I look up to him as my elder brother. | respect |

Make

Group Verbs	Examples	Meanings
Make after	The Royal Bengal tiger made after the deer was a terrible sight in our last trip in Sundarbans.	chased
Make away with	Farah made away with her own life.	destroyed
Make for	I made for Delhi, then I had to call off , and I got down at Kanpur Station to return.	Started a journey
Make of	What do you make of the word?	Understand
Make off	The new bride made off with all ornaments in the house.	Escaped
Make out	I could not make out what he said.	Understand
Make out	Make out a list of your books.	Prepare
Make over	The going principal made over charge me.	Delivered /hand over
Make up (1)	Who make up this loss?	Compensate
Make up (2)	More two boys will make up the team.	Complete
Make up (3)	We made up our quarrel.	Made understanding
Make up (4)	They made up (their minds) to return.	decided

P *for* Pass, Pick, Pull, Put & others

Group Verbs	Examples	Meanings
Pass away (1)	The clouds have passed away.	dispersed
Pass away (2)	My old grandfather died last week.	Died
Pass by (1)	We pass by her house every day.	Go by
Pass by (2)	We should not pass by our younger's faults.	Overlook /ignore
Pass for	He is passed for a great scholar.	Regarded
Pass off (1)	The train has passed off.	Ceased gradually
Pass off (2)	He should be punished for trying to pass off false coins.	Deceive with
Pass off well	The ceremony passed off well.	Was a success
Pass of worse	The ceremony passed off worse.	Was unsuccessful
Pass on	Let us pass on another subject.	Proceed
Pass over	My claim was passed over.	Neglected/ turn down
Pass through (1)	Crude oil passes through the pipe.	Goes through
Pass through (2)	The crew of the boat **passed through** terrible sufferings.	(underwent)/ experienced

	Pick	
Pick at/on	Why do you always pick at/on me?	Find fault with
Pick out (1)	• Can you pick out the adverbs in the following sentences? • Can you pick out the culprits in the gathering? • **Pick out** the correct word from the options, and fill in the blanks.	Identify /choose
Pick out (2)	He picked up Italian tune in the piano.	Played
Pick up (1)	Where did you pick up your English?	Learn
Pick up (2)	The smugglers were picked up by the police.	Arrested
Pick up (2)	Do you pick the bags from my aunt while returning?	Collect
Pick up (3)	I asked her to pick me up on her way to home.	To give a lift
Pick up (4)	Share price has forgotten to pick up long days.	Improve in business
Pick up (5)	Where did you pick up malaria?	Effected by
Pick up (6)	Suddenly the car picked up speed and disappeared.	Gathered
Pick up (7)	Our TV cannot pick up all these channels. We don't have cables.	Receive
Pick up (8)	I fell ill during COVID-19, but soon picked up.	Recovered

	Others	
Point out	He **pointed out** the audiences with his views and secured his victory in the coming election.	drew attention to

	Pull	
Pull at	The workers are pulling at the heavy machine.	Trying to remove
Pull apart	Failing to yield me, they started pulling me apart.	Criticize unfavorably
Pull down (1)	The municipal authority decided to pull down the old buildings in the locality to avoid further loss of lives.	Demolish
Pull down (2)	He looks much pulled down.	Lowered in health or spirits
Pull in (1)	He is pulling in a lot of money publishing books new every day.	Earning
Pull in (2)	He was pulled in by SEBI for questioning.	Detained/arrested
Pull in (3)	The train pulled in on time.	Entered the platform
Pull off (1)	Pull off the cover and see what's in.	Remove
Pull off (2)	Our team pulled off a brilliant victory.	achieved
Pull out of (1)	The train pulled out of the station.	Left
Pull out of (2)	He was pulled out of difficult situations.	Come out from
Pulled out from	The lorry pulled out from behind the car.	Over crossed
Pull over	The driver **pulled over** the bus in the last second and saved us all.	(Moved the vehicle to one side of a road and stopped)
Pull through (1)	He is in great difficulties; but he will pull through if we offer him a little help.	overcome
Pull through (2)	He was critically ill, but has pulled through.	Recovered
Pull together	It will be done in a week, if we do it pulling together.	Working in harmony
Pull up (1)	I pulled up, as I saw a traffic police showed his hands.	Stopped
Pull up (2)	He was pulled up for his misbehavior.	Reprimanded /scolded
Pull up with	Initially he was trailing but soon he pulled up with others.	Improved relatively

	Put	
Put about	I hear many stories that are being put about.	Spreading rumors
Put across	Jacob failed to put across his views to the commission.	Communicate successfully
Put aside (1)	We all need to put aside some amount of money for future use.	Save
Put aside (2)	Put aside your work and listen to me.	Stop sth for a time
Put away (1)	Put away enough money for your son's education.	Lay aside/ put aside/ save
Put away (2)	I tried much but had to put away the idea of buying a car of my own.	Give up/ abandon
Put away (3)	The patient was suffering much and finally he had to be put away with a legal permission.	Put death
Put back	Put back the book in its proper place.	Restore
Put by	Ants put by some food for the winter. Why shouldn't we?	Preserve/accumulate
Put down (1)	The rebeliion can't be put down by the govt.	Suppressed
Put down (2)	Put down only the names of the first and second according to group event.	Write
Put forth (1)	I put forth all my energy in this task, and could modify it in seven days.	Exerted
Put forth (2)	Trees put forth new leaves in the rainy season.	Generates
Put forward	One member of the house put forward the proposal to be considered.	Introduced
Put forward (2)	Dr. R.D. put forward a new theory on solar energy it may bring a revolution.	Advanced
Put in (1)	I have put in my claim before the commission.	Submitted
Put in (2)	Mr. Dutta has put in twenty years' service in teaching.	completed
Put in (3)	I could not put in a word among them.	Utter a word/ say sth.

Put in (4)	Please, put in a good word for me.	Plead on my behalf
Put off (1)	The meeting was put off.	Postponed
Put off (2)	Getting back home we put off our clothes.	Removed
Put on (1)	Put on your dress, we'll go out a long drive.	wear
Put on (2)	You needn't put on a gentle man.	disguise
Put on (3)	The blame was put on me.	Charged upon
Put on (4)	He has put on a lot of weight. Peter and Om put on ninety runs.	added
Put out (1)	The fire brigade team successfully put out the fire.	Extinguished
Put out (2)	The death of the General put out the soldiers.	Dishearten
Put out (3)	He is a good man. He always puts out his hand for others.	Offers help
Put out (4)	He put out his hand to take the book from table.	Stretched out
Put out (5)	Eyes of Pithwiraj Chowhan were put out in the camp of enemies.	Taken out /drawn out
Put through (1)	The task was put through twelve months.	Carried out
Put through (2)	After many attempts, the Internet connection was put through.	Established /run through
Put through (3)	The trainers in Military Academy had to put through rigorous schedule.	Had to undergo
Put up (1)	Rahul Dravid was a depending player who could put up a stiff resistance against rough bowlers in Test matches.	offer
Put up (2)	A notice is to put up soon regarding this.	Hung up
Put up (3)	Put up a fence round the garden.	raise
Put up (4)	I am putting up with my friend.	Staying for sometime
Put up with	None can put up with such kind of behavior.	tolerate

Run

Group Verbs	Examples	Meanings
Run about	The children started to run about in great panic.	Hurry from one place to another
Run across	I ran across my old friend in the ceremony after a decade about.	Met by chance
Run after	The police ran after the thief; they caught and carried him by neck and shoulder.	Pursued
Run after (2)	Do not run after money; but who listens to the words?	Pursuit/hunt for
Run against	Peter is running against odd situations with the shop keepers.	Fighting against
Run along	Now, children, run along!	Be off/run
Run at	The tiger runs at the deer.	Chased
Run away	Leo ran away and joined the army.	Left home
Run away with	The dog ran away with a piece of meat.	Fled with /stole
Run away with	The business proposal will run away with a lot of money.	Lead to expense
Run-away	They had a run-away victory in the match. (run-away victory= an idiom)	Easy/an easy task
Run down (1)	The tiger ran down the fox and punished it with death.	Catch by chase
Run down (2)	• Mother looks much run down through works for three hours. • The battery has exhausted.	Exhausted /run out
Run down (3)	The man was run down by a reckless lorry on the rajpath.	Run over down
Run into (1)	He ran into debt.	Fell in debt.
Run into (2)	The bus ran into the railing.	Collide with
Run into (3)	The publication has run into ten editions.	Continued
Run into (4)	I met an old friend in the journey.	Met unexpectedly
Run off	The thief saw a policeman and ran off.	fled
Run on (1)	Our discussion ran on for hours together.	continued
Run on (2)	The engine runs on CNG.	Work on
Run out	• The stock of food ran out. • Water ran out of the tank. • The garrison didn't surrender until provisions ran out.	Exhausted
Run over (1)	An old man was run over by a lorry.	Knocked down
Run over (2)	In rainy season, the water of the river runs over its banks every	overflows

	year.	
Run over (3)	She ran over the pages before entering the examination hall.	Glanced over hastily
Run through	Bullets ran through the body of the escaping terrorist.	Pierced
Run through (2)	I ran through the book and bought one for me.	Examine quickly
Run through (3)	Most of us, we run through our fortune for a chance of a Govt. appointment.	Use up /waste
Run to	The money required for the promotion run to a few lacs of rupees.	amount
Run up (1)	The boys ran up a flag on the pole.	Hoisted
Run up (2)	Our long stay at the Daman Diu Hotel ran up a big bill.	Caused to grow quickly
Run up (3)	Price of petrol ran up to Rs- 112. This is the third time within a month.	increased
Run upon (1)	The cyclist ran upon the lamp post and broke his thin helmet.	Collided with
Run upon (2)	I ran upon a new idea to publish many booklets upon English Grammar to make them handy.	Be engrossed with

S *for* See, Send, Set, Stand & Others

Group Verbs	Examples	Meanings
See about	I must see about lunch. I will see about your proposal.	Prepare/consider
See about	He says he won't help, does he? Well, we'll soon see about that.	To deal with sth/ Will secure that he will...
See in	• I don't know what she finds in him. • What did you see in that black spot?	Find sb/sth attractive or interesting
See off	I'll go to the station to see off my friend.	To bid farewell going up to station airport etc. who is starting a journey.
See off (2)	The home team saw off the challengers by 68 runs.	Defeat sb in a gme or fight
See out	I've had this coat for y, and I'm sure it will see me out. The car has enough fuel to see our destination out.	Run till end of life or term/ to last longer than
See over	We need to see over the house again before we can give you the offer.	To visit a place to judge it carefully, valuation, worth, etc
See through	Her courage and humor saw her through	Let her considered or allowed/ to give help or support
See to	Will you see to the arrangements for our next meeting?	To deal with sth.
Send		
Send away/off	I'm sending the files off to my boss tomorrow.	To send sth to a place by post or mail
Send down/up	We should send him down for his misbehavior.	Send sb to prison
Send for	Please send for a doctor.	Call for/summon
Send forth sth	He opened his mouth and send for a stream of noise.	To produce a sound or signal, so that other can hear
Send off	The data I sent off to my H.M. has not reached to him.	To send sth by post or mail
Send on	We sent our furniture on a ship. They sent theirs on an airship, but it couldn't reach ever for it struck accident in the mid of air.	To send sth to a place so that it arrives before you get there.
Send out	Have the invitations been sent out yet?	To send sth to a lot of people or place
Send up	Fifty boys have been sent up for higher studies in Canada.	Send sb to a place for higher study or to prison

Set		
Set about	Paul set about packing since morning.	Began
Set aside (1)	The High Court set aside the judgement of the lower court.	Cancelled
Set aside (2)	Mother sets aside some money to spend in need.	Save for a time being
Set by	The beggar set by a huge amount of money by begging.	Saved
Set down (1)	The car set me down on the way.	Left me descend
Set down (2)	The police set down the complaint of the woman.	Recorded
Set forth (1)	Leon sets forth his views in his books.	exhibits
Set forth/off /out	• Sophia set forth her journey in last November. • Nicole set off for Japan. • Dean set out for England last week.	Started/leave for
Set off (2)	The frame set off the picture.	Increase beauty
Set off (3)	The gains were set off against losses.	balanced
Set in	The rainy season has set in.	Started/begun
Set on/upon	The dogs were immorally set upon the convict.	Let attack
Set out (1)	They set out for the picnic spot early in the morning.	Started/ leave for
Set out (2)	He set out his goods for display.	disperse
Set to/in	Let us set to work at once.	begin
Set up (1)	They set up a new school.	founded
Set up (2)	The local people set Ramesh up as their candidate in the Panchayat election.	Present/produce
Set up (3)	They set up hue and cry.	Raised
Set up (4)	He set up as a lawyer.	Began a profession

Stand		
Stand against	All the members of the staff committee stood against the decision of the principal.	Opposed
Stand aside	Please stand aside to let the chairman pass.	Give place
Stand aside	He stood aside from the contest.	Took off/withdrew his name
Stand at	The total contribution so far stands at Rs ten thousand.	Is equal to
Stand by (1)	He will always stand by me.	Support
Stand by (2)	I merely stood by when they fought.	Was a silent onlooker/ stand off
Stand by (3)	In this tumultuous situation, the army is standing by to support the civil authorities.	Being ready
Stand for	White stands for purity. The letter 'L' stands for 'Learning.'	Symbolizes
Stand in (1)	The hero is absent; you are asked to stand in for him.	To be substitute
Stand in (2)	This is a pretty big amount; let me stand in with you.	Share expenditure
Stand off from	I stood off from the debate.	Didn't participate in
Stand out	Her performance stood out from the rest.	Was prominent/ conspiciuous
Stand over	The question will stand over for the present.	Left for later settlement
Stand to	We should stand to our principles.	Stick to
Stand up for	They are determined to **stand up for** their rights.	(vindicate)/support
Stare at	The little boy is **staring at** us.	(Looking fixedly)

T *for* Take, Tell, Turn

Group Verbs	Examples	Meanings
Take aback	I was taken aback at the news of his insult in public.	surprised
Take after	The child takes after its mother.	Looks after/resembles
Take away	Do not take away books from the shelf.	remove

Take back	I will not take back my words.	Withdraw/take off
Take by	The dog took the cat by its neck.	Caught by
Take down (1)	Take down the names of the students	Register/write down/record
Take down (2)	Take down the book from the shelf.	Take a thing from up
Take (sb) for	Everyone took him for an honest man.	Consider/regard as
Take from	This will take from your reputation as a teacher.	lower
Take in (1)	He has taken in this plot of land for a garden.	enclosed
Take in (2)	I was taken in by the grocer.	cheated
Take in (3)	I cannot take in the meaning of the passage.	understand
Take in (4)	We shall take in 100 boys this year.	admit
Take into	Before selecting him, his health has to be taken into consideration.	To be considered
Take off (1)	The boy took off his shoes after return from his school.	Put off
Take off (2)	Do not take off a lame man.	mimic
Take off (3)	The plane will take off at 7 a.m.	Start flying
Take off (4)	Take your hands off my shoulders.	Remove/move off
Take off (5)	The morning bus service will be taken off the route from next week.	withdrawn
Take on	I decided to take on extra job for a better livelihood.	Undertake
Take (sb) on	I shall take you on at table tennis, though at other time we are two best friends.	Accept as an opponent
Take out	Take out the aching tooth.	remove
Take over	The new President will take over the charge of the government on next month of November.	Accept
Take to (1)	The young boy has taken to drinking recently.	(been) addicted to
Take to (2)	I took to the boy from the first.	Became fond of
Take up (1)	He took up my case.	Adopted/accepted
Take up (2)	Mr. Peter took up the problem to solve it.	Undertook
Take up (3)	The car takes up too much place. We will replace it with a mini one.	occupies
Take up (4)	He takes up a pen and began to write.	Takes
Take up (5)	I shall take the matter up with the principal and let's see what can be done.	Present /produce
Take up with	I was taken up with a book.	Absorbed in
Take upon	He took upon himself the burden of the family.	Took responsibility

Tell		
Tell against	The evidence told against the accused.	Did harm to
Tell off (1)	The superintendent told off six policemen to guard his own quarter after the threat of death.	Selected and appointed to a special duty.
Tell off (2)	The teacher told him off for quarreling with his class-mates.	Spoke angrily/rebuke
Tell on/upon	Smoking started to take upon his health.	Affect

Turn		
Turn about	The boys turned about and hurried for home.	Cancelled the programme
Turn against	I do not know why he turned against me.	Became hostile to
Turn away (1)	The sight pained me and I turned away.	Turned my face
Turn away (2)	Turn away the idea from your mind.	dismiss
Turn aside	We should not turn aside from the path of honesty.	Deviate
Turn back	Don't turn back a beggar from your door.	Send back/reject to give anything
Turn down	The principal has turned down our proposal.	Reject
Turn in (1)	I turned in early last night.	Went to bed

Turn in (2)	We saw a hut and turned in for shelter.	Entered in passing
Turn off	Turn off the switch.	Shut
Turn on (1)	Turn on the switch.	open
Turn on (2)	The case turns on his report.	Depends on
Turn out (1)	The man must be turned out from here. He is continuously making nuisance.	Driven out
Turn out (2)	His story turned out to be the best in the competition.	Proved
Turn out (3)	The people turned out in large numbers to see the sight.	assembled
Turn out (4)	The mill turns out 100 pair of clothes every day.	produces
Turn to	Turn to God and He will save you.	Pray/surrender
Turn up	A huge crowd turned up for the match.	appeared

Use, Work, Write

Group Verbs	Examples	Meanings
Use up	**Use up** your nails and pail to reach your goal.	(To use completely)
Work at	The carpenter is working at the chair.	Engaged in making
Work in (1)	The water has worked in all round the packing box.	Penetrated
Work in (2)	Please try to work in a few more illustrations on the subject.	Introduce
Work off (1)	You must work off the accumulated work.	Dispose of/reduce
Work off (2)	Unless you work off your excess fat, you will fall ill.	Get rid of
Work on (1)	The engine works on diesel.	Runs by burning
Work on	The workers worked on day and night and the road was made complete in record time indeed.	Continued working on
Work out (1)	Yes, finally it **works out**. He agreed with us.	exercises/proves successful
Work out (2)	I still cannot work out the sum.	solve
Work out (3)	I have worked out your share of Rs 10 lac.	Calculate
Work out (4)	The scientists have worked a medicine to cure cancer completely.	Discover/find out
Work out (5)	The players are working out in the field before the match begins.	Undergoing exercise
Work up	The mob were worked up by his fiery speech.	excited
Write		
Write down	Write down your name and address on a piece of paper.	Record
Write (sb) down	You can write him down as a useless fellow.	Take him to be
Write off (1)	Write off a short account of your performance in last one year in the previous company.	Prepare quickly
Write off (2)	The loss was written off.	Cancelled in writing/taken as recovery not possible.
Write out	Please, write out your name and address.	Write in full
Write up	He needs to write up some lines for my published books.	Write with praise

32. The Idioms

454.   We have already studied, there are different kinds of phrases- from Noun to adjective and verb to Adverb. Some of these phrases, as Nominal, Relative, Adverbial, Prepositional and many of Phrasal verbs have their special uses in the English language since long past, they are called '**Idioms**'.

❑   So, idioms are not only from phrasal verbs but may be prepositional, nominal, relative or adverbial (as '**by hook or by crook**', '**off & on**', etc.). They sometimes may form an object to the verb, a complement, or other. Carefully study the examples and their roles in the sentences. For this, you may analyze a sentence too, for your better understanding.

❑   **Study the Idioms & their meanings, begins with 'A':**

1. On the question of dowry-system we are **at one** (*of the same opinion—[complement]*).
2. It is **all one** (*just the same*) to me whether I stay at Balurghat or go to Delhi.
3. The matter is now **above board** (*open or openly-[relative phrase]*), and anybody can see and comment on it.
4. The storm broke out **all of (on) a sudden** (*suddenly-[adv phrase]*).
5. I was quite **at sea** (*perplexed*) in this matter.
6. It was **all but** (*very nearly, almost*) impossible.
7. The man thinks himself to be, **as it were** (*like, as if*), the lord of the earth.
8. He is **at his wit's end** (*completely puzzled*) in the face of trouble.
9. He is **all in all** (*the supreme man*) in hi locality.
10. The sale of the book is **at a low ebb** (*diminishing*).
11. He is not **at all** (*in any degree*) a scholar.
12. She comes to my house **at times** (*occasionally*).

13. Do not waste time, as your examination is **at hand** (*close by, about to happen*).
14. "I immediately felt **at home** (*feeling at ease*)."
15. The rebels surrendered **at discretion** (*unconditionally*).
16. Keep bad companions **at arm's length** (*at a distance*).
17. They are **at dagger's drawn** (*highly enraged at, in open enmity with*) with each other.
18. The cat is **at bay** (*in a dangerous position, in a tight corner*) in the room and so turns back to attack.
19. He can teach Grammar 36 hours **at a stretch** (*continue without break*).
20. I am **at a loss** (*puzzled*) and find no way to escape from this situation.
21. His eldest son is **a thorn in his side** (*a constant source of annoyance*).
22. All the problems of Mathematics are **at his fingers' ends** (*ready knowledge*).
23. This savings will do **at a pinch** (*in case of emergency*).
24. The articles in the room were **at sixes and sevens** (*in disheveled condition*).

25. We reached the station **at the eleventh hour** (*at the last hour*).
26. The beggar on road side is **as good as** (*similar to, practically no more than*) dead.
27. The life of the discoverer of an unknown land was **at stake** (*in a dangerous position*).
28. He seems to be a worthless person **at the first blush** (*at first sight*).
29. I am afraid you two friends are **at cross-purposes** (*misunderstand each other*).
30. He works **against time** (*with utmost speed*).
31. He wanted that everybody would be **at his beck and call** (*under one's absolute control*).
32. I can sing many Bollywood songs **after a fashion** (*to a certain degree, not much*).
33. The woman is **an ugly customer** (*a difficult person to deal with*).
34. This book would not be **a drug in the market** (*unsalable for lack of demand*).
35. Throughout the lectures of Peter, the students are **all ears** (*deeply attentive*) in the seminar hall.
36. I was **all eyes** (*eagerly watching*) to see our C.M. but her speech only disheartened.

37. This land is **a bone of contention** (*a subject of dispute*) between two brothers in the family.
38. This act is **a dead letter** (*no longer in force*), let us know new one.
39. It is **a far cry** (*long way of*) from Balurghat to London.
40. It is **a far cry** (*no easy transition*) from Capitalism to Communism.
41. The bank would not accept **a man of straw** (*a man of no substance, poor*) as a guarantor.
42. Unemployment is **a hard nut to crack** (*a difficult problem to solve*) eternal.
43. watching short-clips videos were **all the rage** (*very popular*) in certain times.
44. The police are on **a wild goose chase** (*a fruitless search*) to catch the thief.
45. You can rely on him; a he is **a man of his words** (*a trustworthy person*).
46. Only a few years ago he entered the firm and he is now **at the top of the tree** (*at the head of profession*).
47. This is the point **at issue** (*in dispute*).
48. The death of his wife was **a bolt from the blue** (*a sudden unexpected event*) to him.

❏ Study the Idioms & their meanings, begins with 'B':

49. I know he will do the job **by hook or by crook** (*by any means*).
50. There is **bad blood** (*ill feeling*) between the two families.
51. The secret of the case has been **brought to light** (*disclosed*) by the police.
52. **Birds of a feather** (*of the same nature or kind*) flock together.
53. One should know that the life is not a **bed of roses** (*a very comfortable situation*).
54. He **bids fair** (*seems likely*) to rival his brother as a doctor.

55. He only **beats about the bush** (*talk irrelevantly*) in telling the story.
56. I saw him to be **beside himself** (*out of one's minds*) with grief.
57. He visits the place **by fits and starts** (*irregularly*).
58. The price of essential commodities is increasing **by leaps and bounds** (*very swiftly*).
59. Mr. P was **behind the scenes** (*in the off side of the event*) of the successful drama.
60. **By the bye (way)** (*incidentally*) he asked me about the nature of my job.
61. Seeing the accident his **blood ran cold** (*to be horrified*).

62. The people of the village are **by and large** (*generally speaking, on the whole*) peasants.
63. He is **by far** (*in every respect*) an honest man.
64. He is **by long odds** (*most decidedly*) the best poet of the country.
65. Mr. G is one of the **big guns** (*a leading personality*) of the locality.
66. The miscreants **beat** the traveler **black and blue** (*beat severely*).
67. The chief minister took a **bird's eye view** (*a superficial conception*) of the flood-stricken area from a helicopter.
68. She is a **book worm** (*who only reads book*), and does nothing except reading.
69. He was **brought to book** (*gave punishment*) by the Head master for his offence.
70. The General of the enemy soldiers agreed to **bury the hatchet** (*cease fighting*).
71. A modest man never **blows his own trumpet** (*praising oneself*).
72. He wants to leave the place **bag and baggage** (*with all belongings*).
73. She wastes her time by **building castles in the air** (*indulge in doing fictitious things*).

74. His observations on the subject were **beside the mark** (*irrelevant*).
75. Corruption as well as unemployment is a **burning question** (*matter of great importance*) today.
76. There are **black sheep** (*men of bad character*) in every community.
77. He **burnt his fingers** (*get oneself into trouble*) by helping anti-socials providing them shelter in his house.
78. He was **born with a silver spoon in his mouth** (*born in wealth and luxury*).

Study the Idioms & their meanings, begins with 'C':

79. His honesty cannot be **called in question** (*dispute the truth of a statement*).
80. Do not **call a person by names** (*abuse someone*).
81. His conduct should be **called to account** (*ask one to answer for one's misconduct*).
82. Now Prabir is simply **coining money** (*earning large sum of money*).
83. Everybody should **call a spade a spade** (*to speak frankly, plainly*).
84. The secret behind the matter has at last **come to light** (*publish*).
85. Mr. Dey is **coming to the front** (*attain prominence*) in politics.

86. The boy has **cut a sorry figure** (*make a poor result in any action or in exam*) in the final examination.
87. He **changed color** (*become shocked and turned pale*) when I asked him about his result in the examination.
88. Shiba joined the contest and **carried the day** (*succeed in a contest*).
89. I can't **call to mind** (*recollect*) the girl's name.
90. It is raining **cats and dogs** (*pouring heavily*) for two days.
91. His words **cut her to the quick** (*hurt one's feeling*).
92. Tenida, one of Narayan Gangapadhyay's characters, used to tell **cock and bull stories** (*nonsense and absurd stories*).
93. She came to me shed **crocodile tears** (*show of insincere sorrow through tears*) at my father's death.
94. Della was **carried off her feet** (*be wild with excitement*) when she discovered a proper gift for Jim.
95. His thesis contained **chapter and verse** (*full and precise reference to authority*) for the new theories he discussed therein.
96. By his skill in arguing he **carried his point** (*defeat the opponent in debate*).
97. Employment is the **crying need** (*the essential*) of our youths to-day.

98. My scheme **came to grief** (*failed*) for want of fund.
99. You will **come to grief** (*be ruined*) if you follow that rogue.
100. The accountant of the company was charged with **cooking the accounts** (*prepare false accounts*).
101. The prince became king when he **came of age** (*be adult*).
102. Whatever he takes he **carries all before him** (*be completely successful*).
103. Doing so, you only **cutting your own throat** (*ruin oneself*).
104. He met me in the street and **cut me dead** (*make deliberate insult by ignoring*).
105. The journalist **cut him short** (*to interrupt one*) in the middle of his confession.

106. The labor dispute in the company **came to a head** (*reached a crisis*) this week.
107. The police **caught a Tarter** (*encounter a person who prove to be stronger than the first*) in the man whom they arrested first.
108. In the contest he **came off second-best** (*is defeated*).
109. He **curries favor** (*adopt mean ways to ingratiate oneself*) with his rich relatives.

Study the Idioms & their meanings, begins with 'D' & 'E':

110. Sanskrit is **dead language** (*a language out of use*) today when it should not be.
111. The soldier **died game** (*die fighting bravely*) against the enemy soldiers.
112. His father **died in harness** (*die while working*) and he was appointed in his place.
113. In the **dead of night** (*mid-hours of night*) Mr. Prime Minister declared the country is in emergency.
114. While telling you should **draw the line** (*fix the limit*) where to end.
115. The two statements **do not hang together** (*are not consistent with each other*).
116. He is **every inch** (*entirely*) a miser fellow.
117. His every attempt to be a rich man **ended in smoke** (*failed*).

Study the Idioms & their meanings, begins with 'F':

118. How a man of **flesh and blood** (*human nature*) can endure much than that.
119. His projects fell flat on the readers. His speech **fell flat** (*fail or have no effect*) on his hearers.
120. Many people in this vast world live **from hand to mouth** (*live without making any savings for future*). If you have nothing to do, think about them.
121. He helped me many times in my need, I am thinking how to **foot the bill** (*to pay for it*).
122. He left the service for good and engaged himself in writing novels.
123. Mr. Gupta **falls foul of** (*quarrel with*) everybody.
124. As he is a humbug, everybody **fights shy of** (*avoid from dislikes*) him.
125. This year the crop has **fallen short of the expectations** (*can't meet expectation*) of the farmer.
126. She was **far and away** (*very much*) the best of the singers who sang in the function.
127. His fame soon spread **far and wide** (**also:** far & near) (*everywhere*)

Study the Idioms & their meanings, begins with 'G':

128. The use of credit cards is **gaining ground** (*become more general and popular*) among the middle class.
129. Of late he is **giving himself airs** (*behave arrogantly*) with everybody.
130. He has **got rid of** (*be free of*) his unwelcome visitor.
131. He **got the better of me** (*overcome one*) at last.
132. He was guilty but **got off easy** (*get a light sentence or punishment*).
133. He should not **go back on** (*fail to keep*) his word.
134. Boys **give ears to** (*listen to*) the lectures of the teacher attentively.
135. It will **go hard with him** (*prove a serious thing for one*) if he does not shun his evil company.
136. It **went hard with us** (*proved a serious thing for one*) to continue our studies when our father was dead.
137. She **went out of her way** (*take special effort and trouble*) to help the distressed.

138. Her simplicity **goes to my heart** (*touch one deeply*) then, and then her cruelty causes bloodshed.
139. This subject is **Greek (or Hebrew)** (*which could not be understood*) to me.
140. In need friends **give you a cold shoulder** (*treat one in cold manner*) is not a friend indeed.
141. Now-a-days, they are mostly biased **giving a false coloring to** (*misrepresent*) incidents; so, why to read them at all; and even read, why to believe them blindly.
142. She is **great a hand at** (*expert at*) organizing cultural programs.
143. He behavior **give a handle to** (*give a scope to*) suspicion.
144. A political leader should have the **gift of the gab** (*ability to talk fluently*).

Study the Idioms & their meanings, begins with 'H':

145. Both of your arguments should not **hang together** (*be consistent*).
146. Your argument will **hold water** (*unsound thing; unfit for scrutiny*) in the seminar.
147. You should try **heart and soul** (*with sincerity*) to solve the problem.
148. Anil is **hand and glove** (*very intimate*) with his friends.
149. A wife always **hopes against hope** (*hope for something in a critical moment, when it is difficult to manage*) is an eternal problem to some poor husbands to maintain their livelihood within limited income.

150. The women raised a **hue and cry** (*outcry or noise*) seeing the dacoits coming towards them.
151. He has **hit the nail on the head** (*say or do the right thing*) on this topic.
152. There is no **hard and fast** (*fixed*) rule in this matter.
153. This point will not **hold good** (*be applied*) in this discussion.

154. I believe that he **has a hand in** (*is concerned*) this matter.
155. I am tiring of hearing her **harp on the same string** (*dwell tediously on the same subject*).
156. Becoming **hard of hearing** (*somewhat deaf*) in danger of others is one of the common social diseases.
157. People generally become **hard of hearing** (*somewhat deaf*) in old age.
158. As a politician he was **head and shoulders** (*very much*) above his contemporaries.
159. When he delivers lectures the listeners **hang on their lips** (*listened eagerly*).
160. The dishonest businessmen should be dealt with severely, but the Govt. **hangs fire** (*hesitate*) to do so.
161. Our fate **hung in the balance** (*not decided*).
162. He may be a handicapped boy, but his **heart is in the right place** (*faithful & true-hearted*).

Study the Idioms & their meanings, begins with 'I':

163. The minister carried out the project **in the teeth of** (*in defiance of*) opposition.
164. She took my advice **in good part** (*without offence*).
165. I am **in a fix** (*in a trouble situation*) and unable to take a decision.
166. **In fine** (*in the conclusion*) he uttered the key point of his discussion.
167. Diligence is sure to be rewarded **in the long run** (*ultimately*).
168. He jumped out of the running bus **in the nick of time** (*just at the right moment*).
169. The Police Inspector investigate the **ins and outs** (*full details of anything*) of the case.
170. He spent much time to probe into the matter and lost a pretty sum of money **into the bargain** (*in addition*).
171. She told me that her son had got **into hot water** (*into trouble*).
172. He described the event **in a nutshell** (*in brief*).
173. He tried **in vain** (*fruitless*) to pass the examination.
174. He did the work **in high spirits** (*joyful*).
175. The color of the screen of TVs are **in character** (*similar*) with that of Windows.
176. The boy is **in the good books of** (*favorite with*) the class-teacher.

177. That girl is **in the bad books of** (*not favorite with*) her teachers in the college.
178. The patients should not keep the doctor **in the dark** (*in ignorance*) of his or her illness.
179. The game will again start at 6p.m., and the players **in the meantime** (*between the time*) practice a little.
180. The police officer informed that the troubled situation is **in hand** (*under control*).
181. A spirit of unrest is **in the air** (*found everywhere*) of the house.
182. The rogue murdered the man **in cold blood** (*deliberately and without a passion*).
183. The police requested him to register his complaint **in black and white** (*in writing*).
184. Everybody says that his business is **in the running** (*good prospect in a competition*).
185. The preparation for election is going **in full swing** (*in full energy*).
186. Since marriage you are **in bad odor** (*in bad repute*) with my relatives.
187. She seems to be **ill at ease** (*uneasy*) now and then.
188. I repaid his insult **in kind** (*in the same way*).
189. Every man remains **in a state of nature** (*nakedly*) at the time of birth.

Study the Idioms & their meanings, begins with 'K':

190. He always keeps in touch with his **kith and kin** (*friends and relatives*).
191. You cannot **keep pace** (*progress at equal rate*) with me though you may try very hard. It is called 'intelligence'.
192. He reads science journals regular and **keep in touch with** (*possess the intimate knowledge of*) the latest development.
193. The quarrelsome woman **kicked up a row** (*make great noise*) again and hit her son violently this time to knock him down.
194. I find you **know a thing or two** (*be wise or cunning*).
195. Every time I go, she **keeps a good table** (*provide food luxuriously*). Yet I don't know is it her love or other.
196. My poor father **kept up appearances** (*keep up an upward show, but condition is opposite*), though earned nothing ocean, and he died a king.
197. I was unable to **keep the wolf from the door** (*keep off starvation*) and I took fasting every time during the Shibaratri.

198.   You can trust him; he **knows what's what** (*know the ways of life, experienced*).

Study the Idioms & their meanings, begins with 'L':

199.   The new accountant of the office **leaves no stone unturned** (*use all available ways*) to satisfy his superiors.

200.   The leader of the thieves took the **lion's share** (*the major portion*) of the booty.

201.   Ram, a poet, felt **like a fish out of water** (*in a strange situation*) when he was to assist a businessman.

202.   It is heard that some ruffians **laid hands on** (*attack and insult*) Peter when he was returning from the seminar.

203.   In India under the British rule some people always tried to satisfy the British rulers for **loaves and fishes** (*material benefits*).

204.   Relatives **left** the young boy and his mother **in the lurch** (*leave into difficulties*) when his father died.

Study the Idioms & their meanings, begins with 'M':

205.   People gathered in large number to hear his **maiden speech** (*first lecture*).

206.   Rabindranath Tagore **made his mark** (*make oneself distinguished*) at an early age.

207.   He **made up his mind** (*decided*) to enter into business leaving his job with bank.

208.   He **makes a clean breast of** (*confess frankly*) the unfair matter he was connected with.

209.   The whole plan proved to be a **mare's nest** (*a false belief, a worthless thing*).

210.   The boy **made light of** (*treat lightly*) the teacher's warning.

211. The businessman **makes the most of** (*make the best advantage of*) the opportunity to expand his business.

212.   I am sure the boy **means business** (*is eager*).

213.   The horror film **makes the girl's blood creep** (*make one horrified*).

214.   He **moves heaven and earth** (*makes every possible effort*) to have a good job.

215. During war or such like emergency there are always some people **make a pile** (*make a fortune*) taking advantage of the situation.

Study the Idioms & their meanings, begins with 'N':

216.   He will prove himself to be **not worth his salt** (*quite worthless*) if he fails in the examination this year also.

217. He is **not worth his salt** (*quite worthless*) if he fails at this juncture.

218.   He visits my house now and then.

219.   The singer is **not in voice** (*not able to sing*) because of cough.

220.   The law of capital punishment has now become **null and void** (*of no validity*) in most of the advanced countries.

221.   All their efforts were **nipped in the bud** (*destroy at the root*) owing to lack of fund.

222.   I could understand **neither head nor tail** (*nothing*) of the subject.

223.   This type of job is **not in my line** (*out of my knowledge or sphere of action*).

Study the Idioms & their meanings, begins with 'O':

224.   His present action is not **of a piece with** (*pouring heavily*) his past actions.

225.   This is **of a piece with** (*in keeping with*) the rest of his conduct.

226.   She has been working **on and off** (*at intervals*) five years with this project.

227.   She comes here **off and on** (*now and then*).

228.   The guards were **on the alert** (*on vigilant*).

229.   This custom is now **out of date** (*gone out of use*).

230.   A political leader often delivers his speech **out of hand** (*extempore*). The boy has become **out of hand** (*out of control*) of his father.

231.   The boys are **out of spirits** (*sad*) having no job.

232.   I see, his behavior is really **out of the way** (*strange or abnormal*). She went **out of the way** (*took special effort difficult for her*) to help me.

233.   He says he feels **out of sorts** (*ailing, sick*).

234.   Chandan, my friend, has poetry **on the brain** (*rest constantly in one's thoughts*).

235.   Democracy soon to be **on its last legs** (*reaching the verge of ruin*) everywhere in the world due to the extreme corruption from its head to tail.

236.   There was a time I was, Peter was **over head and ears** (*entirely*) in debt.

237.   His popularity is **on the wane** (*decreasing*).

238. He is **out and out** (completely) a rogue.
239. **On the whole** (after all) the book is well-written.
240. The deal left him thousands of rupees **out of pocket** (being a loser).
241. The meal we took in an inn in the last summer was **of a kind** (of a bad kind).
242. It is unwise to do anything **on the spur of the moments** (without deliberation).
243. The growing mistrust and hatred among the nations show that another great war is **on the cards** (not unlikely).
244. She is **on the wrong side** (more than) of thirty.
245. The unsettled case of land-dispute keeps the man **on tenterhooks** (in a state of anxiety).

Study the Idioms & their meanings, begins with 'P':

246. Do not trust a man who **plays fast and loose** (say one and do another thing).
247. The police examined the **pros and cons** (in details) of the murder case.
248. Discipline is **part and parcel** (an essential portion) of a student's life.
249. I know Anil's nature is to **put a spoke in other's wheel** (hinder one in the execution of one's plan).
250. This unexpected new difficulty **put me on my mettle** (roused me to do my best).
251. When it is a case of cheating, I **put my foot down** (take a determined step), for it is now a growing habit in men.
252. You did right **put me in mind** (remind) once again to send him a mail.
253. All the members of the municipality **put their heads together** (consult one another) to discuss the problem of their locality is the good sign of democracy, which is now **on the wane** (decreasing) is the danger for democracy, extreme decrying and less co-operation.
254. I **pay him back in his own coin** (treat one in the same way as he treats) paying him not for the recharge one.
255. In return of my trust, he **played me false** (deceived).
256. He **puts** his newly composed grammar book **on the market** (put for sale).
257. Kumar **put a good face on** (bear up with courage) his defeat in the war.
258. He **pins his faith to** (give full reliance upon) women's right to education.
259. The major often do this mistake, they **play with fire** (trifle with serious matters unknowingly) and hurt the sentiments of the minority.
260. We love to speak benevolence, but hardly to **put our hands in our pockets** (give money in charity).
261. He is a straightforward man who can **put two and two together** (make a correct inference).
262. Please don't **put the screw on** (give pressure to do something) me, let me decide what I should do in this situation.
263. You will **put your foot in it** (to make serious mistake) if you do not appear in the examination.

Study the Idioms & their meanings, begins with 'R':

264. Finally, he **rose to the occasion** (make oneself ready for an important situation) in conducting publication of his own book for that goal.
265. The people **rose in arms** (rise against) against the tyrannical ruler every time.
266. My appeal for correction of name has been put in **red-tape** (hindrance to disposal of any matter due to bureaucratic method), only they didn't need any while their type-writer input wrong.
267. The 26th January is a **red-letter day** (memorable day, holiday) for all Indians.
268. The dacoits were caught in **red-handed** (be caught in the time of committing crime).
269. The drivers of the distant-plying buses **rest on their oars** (stop and have rest in the time of working).
270. The ministers of the country do not pay attention to the **rank and file** (common undistinguished people), who send them to the cabinet.
271. He is the **right-hand man** (most close and efficient assistant) of his chief.
272. Try to **read between the lines** (realize the significance of the writing) of the passage for précis writing.
273. During his tour to the village, he **rubbed shoulder** (come into close contact) with the common people of the country.
274. The workers work **round the clock** (the whole day) and we have our buildings, shopping malls, etc.

Study the Idioms & their meanings, begins with 'S':

275. He is a **slow coach** (a lazy person) and so he cannot prosper in life.
276. As a social reformer, he **set his face against** (sternly opposed) the leading parties.
277. The manager **sent him about his business** (dismiss authoritatively) as he was lazy and disobedient.

278. He, being poor, has but one **square meal** (*full meal*) a day.
279. Be cautious during typing to avoid **slip of the pen** (*a slight careless mistake in writing*).
280. Forgive her, **slip of the tongue** (*a slight careless mistake in speaking*) is her normal habit or disease. By heart, she is a great one.
281. Should he not be punished for his **sharp practice** (*dishonest dealings*)?
282. I **shook the dust off my feet** (*depart indignantly*) from the meeting as it seemed merely disgusting and intriguing against the head master.
283. A renowned novelist lives at a **stone's throw** (*a short distance*) of my house.
284. The people in the locality **shook in their shoes** (*tremble with apprehension*) seeing the army entering the village.
285. This **speaks volume for** (*be abundant evidence of*) his honesty and sincere attitude to his work.
286. Though in distress, **stick to your colors** (*remain steady and faithful to one's principle*), my boys.
287. Vidyasagar **stuck his chin out** (*show firmness*) in the introduction of widow-marriage in Bengal.
288. Vidyasagar was bold enough to **stick his neck out** (*expose oneself to harsh criticism by acting or speaking boldly*) in working for widow-marriage in the country.
289. Vidyasagar **stuck to his guns** (*maintain one's position under attack* to make the society free from age-old illiteracy and superstitions.
290. Every student should **steer clear of** (*take care to avoid*) bad company and any sort of intoxication.
291. At this hour of crisis, it is no good **splitting hairs** (*quarreling over trifling points*).
292. He has nothing to boast of, yet he is **swollen-headed** (*conceited*).
293. He **serves his time** (*go through an apprenticeship*) in Kolkata Medical College and expects to be a complete doctor soon.
294. I **showed my hand** (*to disclose one's plan of action*) to him expecting his co-operation or at least encouragement but it happened other.
295. Don't trust one who doesn't **stick at nothing** (*unsteady or undetermined*).
296. This occupation has **stood me in good stead** (*proved to be useful*).
297. It **stands to reason** (*an undoubted fact*) that a rich person can seldom be a man of outstanding creative genius.
298. Now that I have lost all my power and money, he is **showing his teeth** (*in a threatening mood*).
299. I **smell a rat** (*have reason to suspect*) in his uncalled-for beneficence.
300. On the approach of the villagers in groups the dacoits **showed a clean pair of heels** (*ran away*).
301. She **stood her ground** (*remain undisturbed*) against all adverse situations.
302. His **stars are in the ascendant** (*fortune favors*).
303. The news of death of popular leader **spread like wild fire** (*spread rapidly*).
304. She **strained every nerve** (*make utmost effort*) to nourish her fatherless child.
305. **Sitting on the fence** (*be in between two opinions and hesitate which side to join*) is now a general trend of the politicians.
306. He dreams of **setting the Ganges on fire** (*do or hope a surprising thing*).

Study the Idioms & their meanings, begins with 'T':

307. In spite of all his brag he had **to eat humble pie** (*to apologize humbly, to yield under humiliating circumstances*).
308. Take care what you say! You will have **to eat your words** (*to retract your statements, to take back what you have said*).
309. I am prepared **to meet you half-way** (*come to a compromise with you.*)
310. It is silly **to meet trouble half-way** (*i.e., to anticipate it; to worry about it before it comes*).
311. The cost of living has increased so much that he finds it difficult **to make both ends meet** (*to live within his income*).
312. He **took exception to** (*object to*) my remark the other day.
313. He wants **to pay off old scores** (*to take revenge*) and be satisfied.
314. A sentimental person **takes** everything) **to heart** (*be deeply affected*).
315. At the leader's encouraging words, his followers **took heart** (*to take courage*).
316. Seeing the police coming the thief **took to his heels** (*ran away*).
317. The student was **taken to task** (*rebuke, scold*) for his misconduct to junior teachers.
318. Why do people **turn a deaf ear to** (*do not hear to*) a person in danger, just look to yourself you'll get your answer.
319. He has **turned over a new leaf** (*change the course for better life*) by publishing his own book.
320. He who stays by **through thick and thin** (*under all conditions*) is a real friend.
321. My colleagues **throw cold water** (*discourage showing indifference*) on my new plan publishing a new book on composition after the book on grammar.

322. You can **turn your hand to** (*undertake a new job*) any work that suit you better.
323. He **turns** his new deal **to account** (*make profit*).
324. He was pacing **to and from** (*here and there*) in the room.
325. Unemployment, corruption is **the order of the day** (*the present state of thing*).
326. He translated the Bengali passage into English **to the letter** (*to every detail*).
327. We must fight **tooth and nail** (*with one's utmost power*) to eradicate illiteracy from our country.
328. The villagers voted in his favor **to a man** (*everybody without exception*).
329. He **turns up his nose** (*show disdain*) at your property earned by unfair means.
330. He has **too many irons in the fire** (*engaged in many jobs at the same time*), yet he proceeds steadily.
331. We need guards who are **true to their salt** (*faithful to the employer*).
332. This dress suits her **to a T** (*correctly*).
333. **The long and the short of** (*the whole subject in a few words*) what I want to say is that I shall not join you in your new business.
334. The new officer wants **to take stock of** (*to look at carefully*) the whole matter before starts the investigation.
335. The explorers **took life in their hands** (*face great risk*) at every step of their journey in the unknown region.
336. His friend **took the wind out of his sails** (*make one's action ineffective by anticipation*) in his work of publishing an English Grammar book.
337. The man, being unable to work, wants **to rest on his laurels** (*to retire*).
338. He has **made good the loss** (*to compensate the loss*).
339. I know **the ins and outs** (*full details*) of his present deplorable condition.
340. He has become rich and now **takes thing easy** (*do not labor*).
341. Peter profited in the business **taking a leaf out of his friend's book** (*imitate one or profit by one's example*).
342. While giving him punishment, you should **take into account** (*consider*) also his noble deeds.
343. This is **the thing** (*the proper thing*) you should attempt.
344. I **tried my hand** (*make an effort*) to write science fiction at late hours and I failed entire.
345. It is difficult for a poor man like Peter **to keep his hand above water** (*to keep out of debt*).
346. Her manager was a wicked man **to the backbone** (*to the core*).
347. He **took away my breath** (*to surprise one very much*) when he gave me news of his becoming gold medalist in doctorate.
348. Try your best **to crow over** (*to win over*) your opponent.
349. You should not expect me **to see eye to eye** (*in complete harmony*) with you in this work.
350. She is a habitual liar, so everybody **takes** her words **with a grain of salt** (*doubt*).
351. This shoe fits you, madam, **to a nicety** (*exactly*).
352. Don't **thrust your nose into** (*interfere unnecessarily*) anybody's affair.
353. He has **two strings to his bow** (*two sources of income to live on*) as he is working in a Govt. office and privately practicing in Homeopathy.
354. The patent has **turned the corner** (*pass over the crisis*).
355. A he **talks sharp** (*talk about business only*), nobody likes him.

Study the Idioms & their meanings, begins with 'U' & 'W':
356. A business has its **ups and down** (*rise and fall*).
357. I asked the shop-keeper to give me a dictionary book with meanings **up-to-date** (*to the present time*).
358. Your performance was not **up to the mark** (*equal to the standard*).
359. The book which he requires is **under his nose** (*at very close to one's presence*), but being absentminded he cannot see it.
360. The lecture hall is filled **up to the eyes** (*fully*).

361. Consult with him; he is a person of **well-balanced** (*reasonable*) opinions.
362. My proposal was accepted **with one voice** (*unanimously*).
363. A wearer knows **where the shoe pinches** (*where the trouble lies*).
364. The king ruled his subjects **with a high hand** (*with oppression*).
365. He did the job **with might and main** (*with the utmost strength*).
366. He **washes his hands of** (*refuse to do anything more*) the whole matter.
367. I can accept your statement **without reserve** (*full*) if you add this point to it.
368. Gandhiji received Louis Fischer in his Ashram **with open arms** (*with an open heart, warm welcome*).
369. Sachin **won his laurels** (*acquire a distinction or glory*) in cricket.
370. She **won her spurs** (*acquire one's reputation*) as a pop singer.

371. The Indian Railway soon to become a ***white elephant*** *(a costly unprofitable object)* to the Govt. after the Indian Airlines.

372. At the battle of Marengo, Napoleon was ***within an ace of*** *(on the point of)* defeat. (i.e., he was very nearly defeated.)

33. Detail study: Clause & its Kinds

455. Like a phrase, a clause is also named after its roles or functions in a sentence. Based upon clauses, the classification of sentences (according to structure) also depends.

456. **What is a clause?**
   ➢ A group of words, with a finite verb and subject that forms a part of a sentence is called a **phrase**. Unlike a phrase, a clause conveys a thought or an idea of the speaker. Study the chart:

A Phrase	A Clause
1) A phrase consists of a group of words.	1) A clause also consists of a group of words.
2) A phrase <u>does not have a subject & a predicate;</u>	2) A clause must <u>have a subject & a predicate (i.e., a finite verb);</u>
3) A phrase forms a meaning, like a single word, may be some broad;	3) A clause conveys a sense or a thought, complete or incomplete;
4) It is <u>a smaller unit of language,</u> comparatively smaller than a clause.	4) It is also a <u>unit of language, comparatively larger</u> than a phrase.

457. **For example:**
   - ▪ *As he is ill*, he cannot come.
   - ▪ This is the boy *who did it*.
   - ▪ If we count finite verbs, we have two in each of them that means, here, each sentence consists of two clauses.
   - ▪ The clauses in sentence-1, are— '*he cannot come*', '*As he is ill*' &
   - ▪ In sentence-2, the clauses are— 'This is the boy', 'who did it.'

How to find <u>clauses</u> in a sentence

458. As said, by count of finite verb number (two or more together, like main verb with its auxiliaries must to be considered only as one unit, as are found in different tenses). Then point out its subjects, objects, others, etc. to mark the entire clause. For illustration, read the followings:
   • Nicky is not a stupid boy.
   • You are a boy and I am a girl.
   • Madhuri Dixit who is an actress won the prize.

➢ If we count the number of finite verbs in the sentences they have:
   • The sentence 1 has only one finite verb is equal to (=) It has one clause. The sentence is **Simple Sentence**.
   • The sentence 2 and 3, both have two finite verbs each = they have two clauses each;
   • When a co-ordinate conjunction **'and'** is used in the 2ⁿᵈ sentence, we have used the sub-ordinate conjunction **'who'** in sentence no- 3.
   • Thus, the 2ⁿᵈ sentence is a **Compound Sentence** while <u>the third sentence</u> is a **Complex Sentence**, based on the nature of clauses used (i.e., defined by what kind of conjunctions have been used in them, in the clauses and how do they role in the sentence.)
   • So, often we see one thing is influenced by some other, by certain other things used in or used as.
      • ***So, to define number of clauses:***

   • **Points to be remembered:** Finite verb is the main indication of a clause; either it is of a Principal, Sub-ordinate or Co-ordinate clause. **Every clause must have a finite verb** or a finite verb group (i.e., helping + main verb to be considered only as one unit of finite verb) i.e.,
      • **one finite verb / one-unit finite verb = one clause.**

Kinds of Clauses

459. According to function or use, clauses are of the following three kinds. They are:
   A. **Principal** or **Independent Clause**,
   B. **Co-ordinate** Clause (where the clauses are of equal rank, linked by a Co-ordinate Conjunction)
   C. **Subordinate** or **Dependent Clause** (where the clauses are depended on a principal, and linked by a Sub-ordinate Conjunction)

✖ Based on Clauses, Sentences are also of three kinds: (This division of sentences, we call, is 'According to Structure'.)
   A) **Simple** Sentence (with only one principal clause),
   B) **Compound** Sentence (principal + co-ordinate clause)
   C) **Complex** Sentence (principal + at least 1 sub-ordinate clause)

A. Principal Clause

460. The clause which can stand by itself as a complete & separate sentence without depend on any other part but other may depend on it, is called the **Principal Clause**.
   A Principal Clause by itself also can form independent sentences. Study the examples:
   1) I shook my head.
   2) I won't let you down.
   3) I'll do something.
   4) I came to the living room at midnight.
   5) I will the Allahabad University and repeat from there.
   6) I wished (that) he would figure out (that) I wanted to cry.
   7) Baba looked like (as if) I had stabbed him.

All the underlined are the example of Principal Clauses or Simple Sentences.

B. Co-ordinate Clause

461. Read the sentences & find out Co-Ordinate Clause:
   1) I went to Kolkata *and then left for Delhi*.
   2) He does not know me *but I seek help from him*.
✖ In the first sentence the **verbs— 'went'** & **'left'** have a common subject— 'I'.
   So, there are two clauses respectively— "I went to Kolkata" & *"then I left for Delhi"*—& they can stand by themselves as two complete sentences, as:
   a) I went to Kolkata.
   b) Then, I left for Delhi.
Both are independent & of equal rank. Thus, they both are the Principal Clauses. However, the later (2nd main or principal) when connected with **'and'**, the clause become a co-ordinate clause. In the sentence, the conjunction, **'and'** is an example of **Cumulative Co-ordinate Conjunction** that joins two clauses of equal rank.

✖ In the 2nd sentence the **verbs— 'know'** & **'seek'** have two different subjects— **'He'** & **'I'**. And here the two clauses are— "He does not know me" & *"I seek help from him"*. They are both independent, as they can stand by themselves as two different sentences; as,
   a) He does not know me.
   b) I seek help from him.
Here too, the two Principal Clauses are connected by a co-ordinate conjunction **'but'** which is Adversative or express a contrast idea (another kind of Co-ordinate Conjunction) and thus, here too the sentence is a **Compound Sentence.**

Definition

The principal clause which is directly linked with a co-ordinate conjunction is named after it, as **Co-ordinate clause,** when the other is left to call as the **Principal Clause** in the sentence.
If we again read the above sentences in this way-
→ I went to Kolkata

...and then left for Delhi.

&

→ He does not know me

...but I seek help from him.

The italic and bold clauses— '*and then left for Delhi*', '*but I seek help from him*'—are two examples of **Co-Ordinate Clauses.**

Note: To understand 'Co-ordinate clause better, study well the chapter of Conjunctions and its classification.

462.Some examples of **Co-Ordinate Conjunctions are:** *and, but, yet, or, not only...but also, either...or, neither...nor, therefore,* etc. Study them in the sentences and note their roles.

Kinds of Co-ordinate Clauses

463.The division of Co-ordinate Clause depends on the kinds of Co-ordinate Conjunctions. In other words, we can say, the division depends on the functions of Co-ordinate Conjuncts which are as the followings:

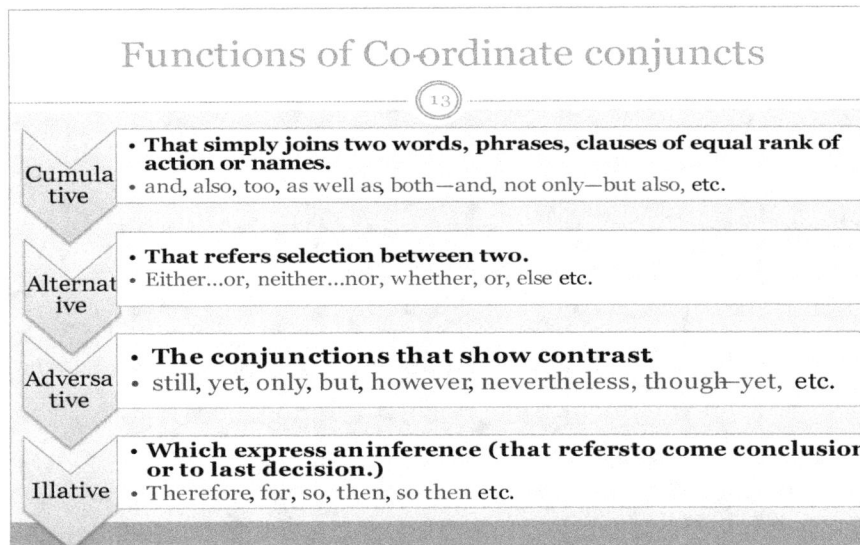

Functions of Co-ordinate conjuncts
(13)

Cumulative	• **That simply joins two words, phrases, clauses of equal rank of action or names.** • and, also, too, as well as, both—and, not only—but also, etc.
Alternative	• **That refers selection between two.** • Either...or, neither...nor, whether, or, else etc.
Adversative	• **The conjunctions that show contrast** • still, yet, only, but, however, nevertheless, though–yet, etc.
Illative	• **Which express an inference (that refers to come conclusion or to last decision.)** • Therefore, for, so, then, so then etc.

> **Cumulative Co-ordinate Clause:**
- We carved not a line, ***and*** we raised not a stone.
- God made the country ***and*** man, made the town.
- Vishal & Virat are good bowlers. (Vishal is a good bowler & Virat is a good bowler.)
- **Note:** If such conjunctions are used to refer a single object or a subject; i.e., a single thing, it is better to treat as a simple sentence, but not as a compound; as the following:
- Two ***and*** two make four. (***Here:*** the two and two make only one number that is four; which is not possible without the other.)
- Bread ***and*** milk is a wholesome food. (It is also an example of simple sentence. The food is made of the two 'bread and milk', but not possible without the other.)

> **Alternative Co-ordinate Clause:**
- She must weep, ***or*** she will die.
- ***Either*** he is mad, ***or*** he feigns madness.
- Is that story true ***or*** false? (Is that story true or is that story false?)
- ***Neither*** a borrower, ***nor*** a lender be.
- We can travel by land ***or*** water. (We can travel by land, or we can travel by water.)
- They toil not, ***neither*** do they spin.
- ***Either*** you are mistaken, ***or*** I am.
- Walk quickly, ***else*** you will not overtake him.

> **Adversative Co-ordinate Clause:**
- Our hoard is little, ***but*** our hearts are great.

- The man is poor, **but** honest. (The man is poor, but he is honest.)
- He is slow, **but** he is sure.
- I was annoyed, **still** I kept quiet.
- I would come; **only** that I am engaged.
- He was all right; **only** he was fatigued.

> **Illative Co-ordinate Clause:**
- Something certainly fell in; **for** I heard a splash.
- All precautions must have been neglected, **for** the plague spread rapidly.

464.   **Study more Co-ordinate Clauses. Try to find out their types:**
- Loaf about less on Sundays **and** you will be without a headache on Monday.
- He put it in an envelope **and** (he) sealed it.
- Father snatched the letter away from Swami **and** (he [the father]) tore it up.
- It required no vehicle except his own body **and** (it) cost him nothing but his energy.
- We just had to make the most of each other **and** we did.
- We started out, **and** up went the kite like a bird.
- I tripped **and** fell over the rocks.

C. Sub-ordinate Clause

465. Read the following sentence and find out Sub-ordinate Clause:
   *As he **is** ill,* he cannot **come.**

> **'is' & 'come'**—both are the Finite verbs. **'is'** is a primary auxiliary used as main verb in the sentence.
>
>   So, the sentence has two clauses.
>   **The clauses are:** As he is ill, &…he cannot come.

> Now the question is what kind they are? (According to the completion of sense)
>   o   **As he is ill …**

- The part, obviously, not telling us a complete sense; as it depends on something, other part of the statement; and the clause is linked by a Sub-ordinate Conjunction **'as'**;
- As **"As he is ill"** can't stand by itself; can't make the sense complete; so, it is a "Sub-ordinate Clause", while **'he cannot come'** is a **Principal** or **Main Clause.**

Definition

The clause that can't stand by itself, and which for completion of sense, **depends on the main clause**, is called the **Sub-ordinate Clause.** A sub-ordinate clause is essentially connected with sub-ordinate conjunctions. Some of sub-ordinate conjunctions are as the followings:
   • *Before, after, because, that, than, if, whether, though, although, till, unless, as, when, where, while, why, how,* etc.

> **A Sub-ordinate** clause is also known as **'Dependent', 'Nonessential'** or **'Nonrestrictive'** clause by different grammarians.

466.   Let's have a glance of Sub-ordinate Conjunctions **which form Sub-ordinate Clauses. Study the conjunctions that do function like an adverb:**

Adverbial function of conjunction	Sub-ordinate conjunctions
TIME	after, before, since, as soon as, while, until, as, so long as, till.
PURPOSE	in order that, lest, so that, that.
CAUSE	because, since, as.

CONDITION	provided, supposing, unless, as, if, whether.
RESULT/EFFECT	so...that
COMPARISON	that, as...as
CONTRAST	though, although, however, even if.

Their examples you will study through the following three kinds of sub-ordinate clauses.

Kinds of Sub-ordinate Clauses

467. Examine the following sentences. First, underline the finite verbs:
   a) I expect **that** I shall get a prize.
   b) The umbrella **which** has a yellow handle is mine.
   c) **When** I was younger I used to fly kites.
   d) I remember the house **where** I was born.

   ○ If we count Finite Verbs, we will get two in each of them in the above sentences (which are underlined), that means, each sentence has two clauses, which are joined by – *'that', 'which', 'when', & 'where'.* The words are the **sub-ordinate conjunctions**, while the clauses in italic, are the examples of 'Sub-ordinate Clauses to form each **Complex Sentence** in a, b, c, d serial number.

   ○ Now the question is, 'what kind of sub-ordinate clauses they are?' **Please study the definitions in the following chart:**

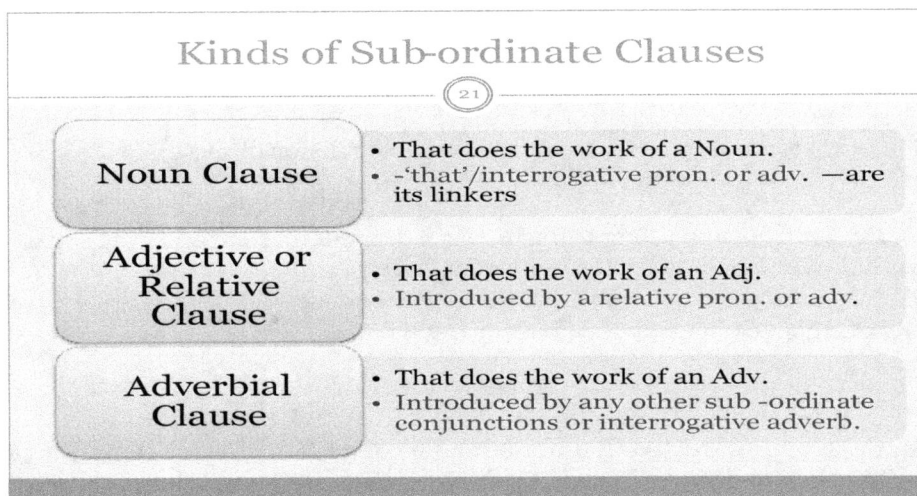

Kinds of Sub-ordinate Clauses

(21)

Noun Clause	• That does the work of a Noun. • –'that'/interrogative pron. or adv. —are its linkers
Adjective or Relative Clause	• That does the work of an Adj. • Introduced by a relative pron. or adv.
Adverbial Clause	• That does the work of an Adv. • Introduced by any other sub-ordinate conjunctions or interrogative adverb.

   1. Noun Clause

▪ I expect **that I shall get a prize**.

I expect... (**What** do you expect?)

Ans.: ...that I shall get a prize. = object to the verb 'expect'.
   Subject+ verb + object
The complete sentence is consisted of **Subject+ verb + object**; of which the object ... **'that I shall get a prize'** itself is a clause & has done the function of a Noun. So, it is a **'Noun Clause'**.

• To know which are the Noun Clauses, study the functions of a Noun, first.

The Functions of Noun:

Nouns do the following functions. It is used-
   1. As subject to the verb,
   2. As object to the verb,
   3. As object to a preposition,
   4. As complement to the subject or object,

5.   As phrase-in-apposition.

Function of Noun clause/As used	Examples
a) The subject of a verb	• *When he will come* is uncertain. • *Why my friend failed* is known to all.
b) The object of a verb	• I know *where he lives*. • She said *that she did not love me or anybody*.
c) The object of a preposition	• I know nothing of *what he will do*. • It depends on *how he behaves*.
d) The complement to a verb	• **That is** *what we expected*. • **The truth is** *he is ill.*
e) as noun in apposition [to give more information to either subject, object or complement]	• It *that he has come*, is true. • There is a rumor *that he is a dead*. • The news, *that he is dead*, is fake.

How to find a clause to be a **Noun**, or an **Adjective** or an **Adverb** is the best way to know the function or role of the clause in the sentence rather than knowing about different conjunctions (sub-ordinate), relative or interrogative pronoun or adverb, though that helps a far.
Study the examples carefully, wherein all the sub-ordinate clauses are only the Noun Clauses. Study their functions:

1.   I know *that he is ill*. [what do you know? = that he is ill. object to the verb]

2.   They say *(that) he is ill*. [what do they say? = object to the verb. 'that' is understood.]

3.   The truth is *he is ill*. [complement to the verb]

4.   It, *that he is ill,* is true. [as noun in apposition]

5.   *That he is ill* is known to all. [as subject of the verb]

6.   I know *how ill he is*. /I know *how he is*. [what do you know? = the answer is 'object' to the verb 'know'. Though, 'how'-a relative adv., the clause is a Noun Clause]

7.   I know *why he is ill*. ['why'- a relative adv., but the clause is again a Noun Clause. a answer to the question, 'what do you know? Answer is an object to the verb 'know']

8.   I shall enquire *is he ill*. [without a connecting word but simply as a question. The clause is again a Noun Clause. what will you enquire?]

9.   I shall enquire *if he is ill*. [this if clause is also a noun clause]

10. I shall enquire *who is ill*. ['who'-a relative pronoun, and the clause is again a noun clause.]

11. I ask him *if he is ill*. [the clause is a direct object; so, it is a a noun clause.]

12. I ask *if/whether he is ill*. [example of noun clause]

468.   **More Examples of Noun Clauses:**
   1)   Swami knew how strict his father could be.
   2)   They said that even the headmaster is afraid of him.
   3)   This is what I want to tell you about.
   4)   He said it was all his fault.
   5)   Claude & I didn't understand what he meant.

6) Do you want to know <u>what became of your kite?</u>
7) <u>When he will come,</u> is uncertain.
8) <u>Why my friend failed</u> is known to all.
9) I know <u>where he lives</u>. That is <u>what we expected</u>.
10) She said <u>that she did not love me or anybody</u>.
11) I know nothing of <u>what he will do</u>.
12) It depends on <u>how he behaves</u>.

→ All the underlined are the examples of Noun Clauses.

2. *Adjective or Relative Clause*

▪ The umbrella **_which has a yellow handle,_** is mine.

<u>Which umbrella</u> is yours? = '*which has a yellow handle*'.

The clause describes its antecedent **Noun, 'umbrella'**, which is the subject of the main clause. So, the answer of the question (i.e., the sub-ordinate clause) does the function of an Adjective. So, it is an **Adjective or relative Clause.**

▪ I remember the house **_where I was born_**.

Here again, the underlined sub-ordinate clause, **_where I was born_**', describes its antecedent noun, 'the house'. So, here, the clause, again is an example of **Adjective** or **Relative Clause**.

Study the Functions of Adjectives to know an adjective clause better:

✘ An Adjective describes a noun or a pronoun. It describes:
    a) To say of good or bad qualities;
    b) To say of number (quantity);
    c) To say of measurement, if any, etc. of a Noun or Noun Equivalent word or words in the sentences.

➤ Find out similarities of functions of **Adjectives Clauses (with functions of adjectives) in the sentences**:
1) I know the **boy** <u>who did it</u>.
2) He was a brilliant **player** <u>who did a hat trick taking wickets in the last series</u>.
3) This is the **place** <u>where I was born</u>.
4) Do you know the **reason** <u>why he failed in the Exam</u>?
5) I have lost the **book** <u>(which) you gave me</u>.
6) That is the **man** <u>(whom) I saw</u>.
7) The **book** <u>(which) he bought</u> has been lost.
8) I have forgotten **the story** <u>(that) he told me</u>.
9) You can see **the cat** <u>as he really is</u>.

In all the above sentences, the **underlined sub-ordinate clauses describe their antecedent nouns in bold**. And thus, all the sub-ordinate clauses here, are the examples of **adjective** or **relative clause.**

• **Comparative study of Noun clause & Adj. clause**

➤ Noun Clauses	➤ Adjective Clause
a) Tell me <u>who did it</u>.	a) Tell me about the **person** <u>who did it</u>.
b) Tell me <u>when he will come</u>.	b) Tell me the **time** <u>when he will come</u>.
c) Tell me <u>why you have done this</u>.	c) Tell me the **reason** <u>why you have done this</u>.
d) I know <u>how he did it</u>.	d) I know the **way** <u>how he did it</u>.

3. *Adverbial Clause*

▪ <u>When I was younger,</u> I used to fly kites.

'When I was younger', the clause denotes <u>a time</u> of 'when I used to fly kites.

When did you use to fly kites? **Ans.:** 'When I was younge_r_'. The answer to the question denotes the time of an action, so it is an **Adverbial Clause.**

The above-mentioned clause depends on main for its sense to complete, so, the clause is also termed as the Dependent or Sub-ordinate Adverbial Clause, and
    'I used to fly kites'—is the **Principal Clause** in the sentence.

For better understand an adverbial clause, we need to study the **Functions of Adverbs**:

✖ An Adverb do the following functions, **add meaning** <u>to a **verb**</u>, **an adjective** or **an adverb**, etc.
  ➢ It mentions a **time**;
  ➢ Tells about **place** where something happens;
  ➢ Referring a cause or **reason**;
  ➢ Telling about result or **effect** of an action;
  ➢ Referring **condition**, **purpose** or **manner**;
  ➢ Tells of **concession**, **compare** or **contrast**;
  ➢ States a **frequency** of an action, etc.

469. **Study the following chart how the adverbial clauses are:**

Function as:	Examples
a) Indicate time	1. Wait _until I come_, 2. He came _when I was there_. 3. Strike _while the iron is hot_. 4. He came _after I had left_. 5. I went out _before he arrives_. 6. Go on your task _till it is finished_. 7. _As_ he entered the school gate, an idea occurred to him.
b) Indicate place	1. Stay _where you are_. 2. Return _whence you come_. 3. I am able to find out _wherever you go_. 4. Go _wherever you like_ to. 5. She went out _you know the place_. 6. Start from _where you finished last day_.
c) Indicate cause or reason	• I could not come _because I was ill_. • _As I was ill,_ I could not come. • _Since I am ill,_ you'll lead the party. • I am sorry _that you said this_.
d) Indicate result	• What have I done _that you desert me_? • I am so tired _that I cannot walk_. • He is such a fool _that I cannot depend on him_.
e) Indicate manner	• Travel _as you like_. • It happened _as I expected_. • I'm not sure _how it happened_.
f) Indicate purpose	• We read _that we may learn_. • He works hard _in order that/so that he may succeed._ • Walk slowly _lest you should fall_.
g) Indicate condition or supposition (if clause)	• _If I succeed,_ I shall help you. • I shall not go _unless you come_. • I may come _in case I have time_.

h) Indicate concession or contrast	1. _Though he is poor_, he is honest. 2. _Even if I fail_, I shall not give up hope. 3. _Although they were present_, they said nothing. 4. _However, you strong may be_, I am not afraid of you. 5. _Whatever you may say_, I do not believe you. 6. _Whoever he may be_, he cannot be allowed.
i) Indicate comparison or degree	• He is not so tall _as his brother is._ • He is as wise _as you are._ • She is taller _than you are._
j) Indicate frequency	• I visit to the cinema hall _whenever a good film is shown._ • She comes always _when I visit the town._

470. **Compare clauses as Noun & Adverb; table-1:**

As Noun Clause	_As Adverbial Clause_
• I am sure of you will succeed. (Object of preposition)	• I am sure you will succeed, as you are a brilliant. (Refers to cause]
• He is satisfied of that you are right. (Object of preposition)	• He is satisfied that you are right. (Refers a cause of his being satisfied.)
• Be careful of what you say. (Object of preposition)	• Be careful what you say as you are a direct speaker. (refers cause of his being 'careful'.)

471. **Compare Clauses as Adjective & Adverb; table-2:**

➢ _As Adjective Clause_	➢ _As Adverbial Clause_
• My **brother** _who is ill_ cannot come. • The **picture** _which was spoiled_ has been thrown away. • I shall send my **brother** _who will do the work._ ➢ Each one describes its antecedent nouns, in bold.	• My brother cannot come, _because he is ill_. • The picture has been thrown away _because it was spoiled_. • I shall send my brother _that he may do the work_. ➢ First two refers 'cause', while the 3rd refers to 'purpose'.

472. **We can convert a clause to another in most cases:**

✖ The **type of a clause (sub-ordinate) depends upon the work done by it**, but **not on linking words solely**.

✖ Based on its work, role or function, a clause may be **a Noun, Adjective or Adverbial**. Study the chart:

A sentence in different clauses:

The **type of a clause depends upon the work done by it**, but not on linking words.

That's why a clause may be **a Noun/Adjective/Adverbial** clause.

I know *where he lives*.	**Noun clause,** (object of 'know' by question —what do you know?)
I know the place *where he lives*.	**Adjective clause,** (qualifying or describing the 'place' by question—which place?)
I shall go *where he lives*.	**Adverbial clause,** (add meaning to the verb 'shall go'-by question —where? Where will you go?)

Conditionals (if clause) -Meaning & Explanation

473. The term **'conditional'** literally means **'*depending on something*'**; as, 'Payment is conditional upon delivery of the goods.'

> ➤ *What does the above sentence mean?*

= If the goods are not delivered, the money will not be paid.

✖ The same thing happens to a conditional clause or sentence, where **the impact of the main clause is conditioned on the dependent clause**, i.e., 'one action (the action of main clause) will not happen unless the other (the action of the dependent or 'if' clause) i.e., it also means the main clause of such sentence is not entirely independent, it is a but a bit different from other principal or main clauses with their Sub-Ordinate Adverbials.

✖ *The Conditionals generally begin with* **'if',** *but also sometimes with* **'unless', 'when'** *or any other word with the verb form that* **express the condition** *of* **'possibilities** *or* **'certainty'** *of an action or state (i.e., something must happen or be true, if another thing is to happen or be true.'); as,*
  → If I were a bird, I had two wings.
  → If I had wife, she should cook me delicious food.
  → If it rains, the picnic will be cancelled.
  → If you heat ice, it melts.

474. **Read the chart of four Conditionals:**

Conditionals

(45)

	If Clause	Main Clause
Zero Conditional: (facts, habits & scientific truths) ✓(present+present/ past+past)	oIf I wake up late, oWhen I woke up late, * Express certainty	I miss the bus. I missed the bus.
First Conditional: [likely future result of an present action] (present+future)	oIf I wakeup late, * Express possibility , real or unreal	I will miss the bus.
Second Conditional: [imaginary situations in the past about future; thinking of future standing in the past] (simple past+pastof future)	oIf I woke up late, * But I did not wake up late, & I did not miss the bus(unreal fact)	I would miss the bus.
Third Conditional: (imaginary situation in the past; same situation as of 2nd, using only in perfect tenses) (past perfect+ past of future perfect)	oIf I had wokeup late yesterday, * But I hadn't woke up late, and I didn't miss the bus. (unreal fact)	I would have miss the bus.

⚓ There are **four kinds of Conditional Sentences** in English. They are as the above shown in the chart and in the following read their illustrations and examples more in sentences:

A. **Zero Conditional:** While other three conditional sentences express 'possibility', real or unreal, Zero Conditional is used to express '**certainty**', i.e., _talk about facts, habits & scientific truths_ that is _**always true, or was true**_ in the past; as,
  → If you **mix** blue and red, you **get** purple.
  → If you **heat** ice, it **melts**.
  → If I **asked** her to come with us, she always **said,** 'No'.
  → If you **heat** water, it **boils**.
  → Water **boils if** you **heat** it.
  → **When** you **heat** ice, it **melts.**
  → Ice **melts when** you **heat** it.
  → If it **snows**, the grass **gets** white.
  → The grass **gets** white **if** it **snows**.
  → **When** it **rains**, the grass **gets** wet.
  → The grass **gets** wet **when** it **rains**.

  Form: _Both the clauses (if clause & the main clause) are always in the same tense:_ **_present + present_** _or **past + past**)_

B. **First Conditional:** <u>express a possible situation in the future standing in the present.</u> It predicts a likely result in the future of a present situation or action by 'if' clause; as,
  → **If** I **finish** my task this afternoon, I **will have** time to go the party tonight. (It is still morning and I can do it, because still I have enough time.)
  → **If** it **rains**, we **will stay** at home.
  → He **will arrive** late **unless** he **hurries** up.
  → Sophia **will buy** a new car, **if** she **increases** her savings.
  → **If** he **finishes** on time, we **will go** to the movies.
  → We **will go** to the movies **if** he **finishes** his work on time.

  (_If_ or _the conditional clause_ is in present tense, while the _main clause_ is in future tense.)

C. **Second Conditional:** used to talk about the consequences of a hypothetical action (**hypothetical**—which are <u>less likely to happen </u>at present or in the future, _as time is left a little to complete the task_ (if you

394

were a superman or others helped you, you probably could; but you are not a superman & not others helped you); as,

→ If I **finished** my task this afternoon, I **would have** time to go the party tonight. (In the current situation, it is now noon or early afternoon, a little chance to complete the task by the time.)

→ If I **were** a rich woman, I **would travel** around the world. (But I am a poor woman; it is the reality, and so, there is little probability to travel around the world.)

→ If I **weren't watching** TV, I **would be playing** tennis. (But time for both actions is now over.)

→ We **would go** to Paris this summer **if** we **passed** in all subjects. (As already we failed there is no chance to go to Paris.)

→ If I **were** an alien, I **would be** able to travel around the universe. (But am I? No, so I can't travel like an alien.)

(**If clause** simple past, while the **main clause** is in conditional past, i.e., past of future, e.g., verb with **'would'** or **'should'** as past form of will or shall & the base verb)

D. **Third Conditional:** used to talk about **an imaginary situation in the past** that had not happened, so its consequences are also impossible to happen or did not happen; as,

→ If you **had studied**, you **would have passed** the examination.

→ If I **hadn't been** sick, I **would have gone** to your party.

→ If I **had finished** my task this afternoon, I **would have had** time to go to the party tonight. (Now impossible)

→ If I **had travelled** to Italy, I **would have visited** Luca. (But I had not travelled to Italy and, therefore, I did not visit Luca.)

→ If you **had got** a good mark, **would you have complained** to the teacher? (But your mark was bad, so we don't know for sure what you would have done.)

→ What **would you have done** if it **had snowed** last weekend? (But it didn't snow.)

(**If clause** past perfect, while the **main clause** is in conditional past perfect, i.e., past of future perfect, e.g., verb with **'would have'** or **'should have'** as past form of will have or shall have)

475. **The Conditional Tense of Modals:**

✱ With the help of **'shall'** & **'will'**, we form Future Tense. When a future tense is used for reporting, they often changed into past of future, 'will' & 'shall' are turned to **'would'** or **'should'** (and thus some other modals too, like 'can' to 'could', 'may' to 'might', 'must'/ 'have to' to 'had to', etc.)

✱ This change of form from Future to Past Future of the Modal Verbs is known as **Conditional Tense** of shall or will or **Conditional Tense** of **Modals**. Thus, we have four conditional forms of shall or will. They are:

(A) **Simple Conditional:** (would/should + base verb); as,

→ He **said** that he **would go** there soon.

→ I **told** her that I **would write** for her.

→ Peter **said** that he **would write** a book on composition soon.

(B) **Progressive Conditional:** (would/should + be+ -ing form of base verb)

→ I told him that I **would/should be writing**.

→ She said that she **would be waiting** for me forever.

→ They said that they **would be waiting** for us there.

(C) **Perfect Conditional** &: (would/should + have+ 3rd form of base verb)

→ He said that the train **would have left** before they arrived the station.

→ Priya said that I **would have gone** before she reached there at the bus-stop.

→ Jubinal assured us that the train **would have left** the station before the blast occurred.

(D) **Perfect Progressive Conditional:** (would/should + have been + -ing form of base verb)

→ He said that he **would have been dancing** after it began.

→ Kanchan said that he **would have been performing** even after he reached nineteen.

→ She **would have been singing** till it was declared over.

➢ **Note:** Generally, **'if', 'unless', 'when' clauses** are known as **Conditional Clause** & the above are known as **Conditional past of Modals**.

476. Sometimes, introducing conjunctions **'if', 'unless'** or **'when'** which determine or denote Conditionals, are sometimes left understood or omitted in the sentences; as,
   - **Had I been** *(If I had been)* rich, I would help you.
   - **Were I** *(If I were)* present, I would oppose you?
   - ***I succeed*** *(If I succeed),* I shall help you.
   - You have not come, I shall not go, = (I shall not go **unless** you come.)
   - I have time, I may come in. = I may come in; **in case** I have time.
   - He gets leave, sure he will come. = He will come **provided** he gets leave.
   - I succeed or not, I shall try. = I shall try, **whether** I succeed or not.

477. **Exercise (identify what kind of conditional, used):**
   1) If you do not win scholarship, your father will be very sad.
   2) If I have enough strawberries, I will bake a strawberry cake for you.
   3) If you don't brush your teeth regularly, your teeth decays.
   4) If she had found his phone number, she might have called him for the party.
   5) If I could have spoken English very well, I would have talked to the tourists from London.
   6) I wouldn't have called if I had known that she wasn't at home.
   7) If I won the lottery, I would travel a lot.
   8) If they sold the land, they would be rich.
   9) If it rains, we will cancel the trip.
   10) If you study, you'll pass the exam.
   11) If you throw salt to the water, it boils later.
   12) If I were you, I wouldn't drink anymore?
   13) If I understood what the teacher said, I could tell you.
   14) If she had gone on a picnic, she would have had a lot of fun.

Wish Clause

478. The **Wish Clauses—are often <u>Noun clauses</u> (with or without 'that',** & **<u>Adverbial clauses</u> (with the linker 'if').**

In sentence, 'wish clause' appear to be another principal clause (**when they are noun clause actually**) as sub-ordinate conjunction 'that' remains omitted here and sometimes the principal clause too; <u>& with **'if'** they are often Adverbial clauses.</u>

A 'wish clause' can be used in three sets or forms or in tense; as,

(A)   **Wish + Past Tense of the verbs** (here, the wish is about 'Now' of Present time); as,
   1)   I wish I could see it.
   2)   I wish she weren't here.
   3)   I wish Rossie knew the answer.
   4)   I wish you had more money to lend.
   5)   I wish you had a heart to know me better.
   6)   If I were a bird! **(The principal clause is omitted here; if she were a bird, she would do something; what? The listener knows well.)**
   7)   We wish she could see it.
   8)   We wish Martin weren't there.
   9)   Paul wishes he weren't here among us.
   10) Poulomi wishes if she had wings.
   11) Poulomi wishes if they had a car.
   12) They wish if they had jobs.

(B)   **Wish + Past Perfect Tense of the verbs** (here, the wish is about 'then' of Past time):
1)   I wish I had been there.
2)   She wishes she hadn't come here ever.
3)   They wish they hadn't come this dusty place.
4)   I wish if I had been there. (adv.cl)
5)   If only I hadn't seen him. **(Principal Clause is omitted)**
6)   If only you had been mine, O selfish heart!
7)   If only you had been my husband.

(C)   **Wish + would/should + Action Words** (We are not happy about the situation now & we wish it would change in the future):

1)   I wish he would come one day.
2)   He wishes he would go from my life; O tragedy to bear thereafter!
3)   He wishes he would go; I like to give him 'welcome'.
4)   Jane wishes my dear friends would learn English from this page as well.
5)   I wish to be a lesbian; male hearts are too cruel!!
6)   If only he wouldn't do that.

479. Sometimes, particularly in language & literature, conjunctions are often omitted or understood. Here, such examples are:
1)   <u>I wished</u> he would figure out I wanted to cry.
→   <u>I wished</u>**(that)** he would figure out **(that)** I wanted to cry.
2)   <u>Baba looked</u>; I had stabbed him.
→   <u>Baba looked</u> **like/as** I had stabbed him.
3)   I am sure, I had had a rank, he would have stood up, shook hands with me.
→   I am sure if I had had a rank, **(that)** he would have stood up, **and** shook hands with me.

34. The Mood (or the manner of expression)

480.   **Mood:** Mood that <u>denotes the state of verbs</u> (how it is used in the sentence) and this defines the manner of expression of the speaker. It tells us about the state of a verb cum sentence in which state it is, what it expresses. It tells us thus, which is *a statement* or *a question*, or *an order* or *command, prayer, wish* or *hope,* made or represented by the form of verb. Thus, <u>a Verb may be in the following three main states</u> which defines different functions of verbs. The three main states of a verb are:
  ➢   Indicative,
  ➢   Imperative &
  ➢   Subjunctive

Note: Where a **case** defines the state of a Noun, a **mood** defines the states of a verb which again defines the function of a sentence. Where there is no verb, expressed or implied, there is no life in a sentence.
        The secondary auxiliary verbs are called modals, for they define the mood of a verb in a sentence.
(A) Indicative: The **Mood** denotes a <u>statement</u>, <u>question</u>, or a <u>supposition,</u> taken as a fact to happen—is called **Indicative Mood.** It is used-
  1)   To **state a fact** (the function of assertive sentence)
  2)   To **ask question** (interrogative)
  3)   To **express supposition which is taken as a fact**. (**may** or **must** happen)

(B) Imperative: The **mood** denotes <u>order</u> or <u>command</u>, <u>threats</u> or <u>warn</u>, <u>request</u>, <u>advice</u> or express <u>prayer</u>—is called **Imperative Mood.** It is used-
  1)   To **give order or command,**
  2)   To **threaten or to warn,**
  3)   To **make request or implore,**
  4)   To **give advice or exhort** (*try hard to persuade*),
  5)   To **express entreaty or prayer.**

(C) Subjunctive: The Mood of the verb that expresses a <u>wish</u> or <u>hope</u>, <u>desire</u>, <u>intention</u>, or the <u>resolution</u>, <u>purpose</u>, <u>condition</u> or <u>supposition (unreal to happen or hardly to be a fact)</u> is called the **Subjunctive Mood**. Thus, it is used to express-

1) In certain traditional phrases, **to express a wish or hope**, (with exclamation at the end.) (**subject+be/v1**)
2) **To express desire, intention, or resolution**. (**be+v3**)
3) After the verb 'wish' to **indicate supposition which is unreal or contrary to fact**.
4) After 'if', 'as if', 'as though', '**had+subject+ been**' to indicate unreality and improbability.
5) After '**It is time+subject+v2**, to imply that 'it is already late.
6) After **would rather+subject+v2**, to indicate preference.

The state of verbs in conditional clauses fall to the subjunctive mood. If already studied conditional & wish clauses, the subjunctive mood is easy realized.

Verb forms in Indicative Mood

481. **Study the examples of verb in Indicative Mood in the sentences:**
1) He goes. He does not go.
2) Rama goes to school daily.
3) Is she ill? Do you like tea?
4) Have you discovered it?
5) If he goes there, he will be punished. (The supposition is 'he will be punished' & that is taken as a fact to happen in relation to the condition, 'if he goes there')
6) If it rains, you must not come. (The fact is 'you must not come' & it's based on the condition 'if it rains'.)
7) When my parents were away, my grandmother would take care of me.
8) He'd always be the first to offer his help.
9) He is a would-be actor.

- **Supposed to be fact or true— fall to Indicative Mood,** but if such ones are not supposed to be a fact or to be true or which are improbable, they fall to the Subjunctive mood of the verb or sentence.

- **'would-be'** is an adjective, always used before a noun, meaning '*who is learning*, *under training* or *struggling to be; as,***)**
10) Thapa is a would-be doctor. (He is under training)
11) Shilpa is a would-be nurse. (She would be a nurse, if she completes her course; the supposition which is taken as a fact)
12) Taniya is a would-be sister. (Related medical or church)
13) Rana is a would-be collector.
14) Rohan is a would-be banker.
15) An advice for would-be parents. (Who hope to become father or mother soon)

- **'Would be'** is also used as the conditional past of 'will be':
16) He said he would be here at eight o'clock.
17) She asked if I would help her.
18) They told me that they probably wouldn't come.
19) She burned the letter, so that her husband would never read them.
20) She rings the bell, so that her pet dogs would hear & come for her help.
21) She would not change it, even though she knew it was wrong.
22) It would not work, even though we poured petrol into it.

- Used to say also what we like, love, hate, etc.:
23) I'd love coffee. I'd not like tea.
24) I'd not like tea in every half an hour.
25) I'd be only too glad to help.
26) I'd hate you to think you were criticizing me.
27) I'd rather come with you.
28) I'd you rather come with me.

- Imagine, say, think which are to be fact, not only imagination:
29) I'd imagine the job will take two days.
30) I'd say he was about fifty.

31) She doesn't think she'll get a job.

32) She should worry with all her qualifications. (ironical)
33) She doesn't need to worry.
34) Should anyone call (if anyone call), please tell them I'm busy.
35) He asked what time he should come.
36) I said that I should be glad to help.
37) Does he read? Are you a student?
38) Have you bought a camera?

- ▪ Exception
- ▪ If 'would' is used for talking about the result of an action or event that you merely imagine, hope or desire, but not to come as fact, as it is too late, or the condition is not going to happen, as the following, it is said to be in the 'Subjunctive Mood'; as,

- ✕ She'd look better with shorter hair. (Hardly possible she would trim her hair.)
- ✕ If you went to see him, he would be delighted. (The condition didn't happen or took place, so his becoming 'delighted' is not now possible, at least for that reason.)
- ✕ Get up! It would be a shame to miss the train. (It is taken, already the train is missed by them.)
- ✕ She'd be a fool to accept it. (If she accepted, but that didn't happen)
- ✖ If I had seen the advertisement in time, I would have applied for the job.
- ✖ They would never have met if she had not gone to Emma's party.

Verb forms in Imperative Mood

Read examples of Mood- Imperative in the following sentences:
As it is used-

- • To give order or command,
- • To threaten or warn,
- • To make request or implore,
- • To give advice or exhort (try hard to persuade),
- • To express entreaty or prayer.

✖ The sentences are:

1) **Come** here. **March** on. **Let** him **go**.
2) **Move**, or you die. (Unless you move, you'll die: Indicative)
3) **May I come** in, sir? **Please give** me the book, I need it very urgent.
4) You **should not tell** lies. **Read**, and you **learn** (If you read, you'll learn: Indicative.).
5) **Have mercy** upon us. Give us our daily bread.
6) You **should not drink** and **drive**.
7) We **should be** more careful.
8) A present for me? You **should not have**! (Used to express 'thanks' to somebody politely)
9) You **should stop worrying** about it.
10) **Should I call** him & apologize? (Asking for advice)

✖ **Note-1:** The Imperative Mood can strictly be used in the second person, '**spoken to**'. But in the **first & third person, a like sense** is expressed by the use of the auxiliary verb, '**Let**'.

✖ **Note-2: The subject of a verb** in the imperative mood **(you) is usually omitted**. Read through the examples.

11) **Let** me **go**. (I want to go.)
12) **Let** him **do**. (He is willing to do.)
13) **Let** her **sing** and dance. (She is willing...)
14) **Open** your book at page no 379.
15) **Take care** of your health.
16) **Try** to do better.
17) We **should arrive** before dark.
18) I **should have finished** the book by Friday.
19) In order that training should be effective it **must be planned** systemically.
20) She recommended that I **should take** some time off.
21) I wish you'd be quiet **shut up** for a minute.

22) Let's me think what the next we **should do**.
23) **Would** you **mind** leaving us alone for a few minutes?
24) **Would** you **open** the door for me, please?
25) **Would** you **like** a sandwich?
26) **Would** you **have dinner** with us on Friday?
27) In case you **should need** any help, here is my number.
28) **Should** I **go**? What **should** they **do** in that situation?
29) **Should** we **help** her, she misbehaved in the last time.
30) Save me. **Help**! **Have pity** on us!

Verb forms in Subjunctive Mood

482.   **The Mood- Subjunctive** which express-a <u>wish</u> or <u>hope</u>, <u>desire</u>, <u>intention</u>, or the <u>resolution</u>, <u>purpose</u>, <u>condition</u> or <u>supposition (not a fact)</u> **has two forms in its credit**:
   A) <u>Present Subjunctive</u>, &
   B) <u>Past Subjunctive.</u>

Note-1: Kindly follow the table:

Present Subjunctive		Past Subjunctive	
'Be' Verb	**Other Verbs**	**'Be' Verb**	**Other Verbs**
I be	I speak	I were	I spoke
We be	We speak	We were	We spoke
You be	You speak	You were	You spoke
(S)he be	She speak (not 'speaks')	(S)he were	(S)he spoke
They be	They speak	They were	They spoke
Arrangement of words in Present Subjunctive		**Arrangement of words in Past Subjunctive**	
Subject+be	Subject+base form of verb (V1)	Subject+were	Subject+past form of verb (V2)
(No Passive)	Be+3rd form of Verb (in Passive)	Had+subject+been (in passive form)	(No Passive)

483.   **Arrangement of Words in Present Subjunctive:**
1) **May/if + Subject + be** (<u>to express a wish or hope</u>, without exclamation at the end.)
   - **May she be** happy.
   - **If it be** (**not**: is) sin to work hard, I am a sinner.

2) **to express wish, hope or desire (as in Optative Sentence) with 'should be' + '-ing' or 3rd form of verb; as**
   - The roads **should be less crowded** today. (We hope so, though hardly to happen)
   - It **should be raining** now, according to the weather forecasting. (It was expecting, but not happened really)
3) **Subject + base form of verb (V1)[other than 'be' verb] / V1+subject** (<u>to express a wish or hope</u>, with exclamation at the end.)
   - **God bless** you!
   - **Heaven help** us!
   - Long **live the king!**

4) **Be+3rd form of Verb (in Passive)** (<u>to express desire, intention or resolution of the speaker.</u>)

○ I move that Mr. Gupta **be appointed** the Chairman.
○ We recommend that the subscription **be increased** to ten rupees.
○ It is suggested that an over pool **be built** to relieve the jam of the city.

484. **More Examples of Present Subjunctive**

1) Long **live** our struggle! Long **live** the king!
2) **May** they **be** happy. **May** she **have** a better groom.
3) If he **wants, I'll do** for him. If you **want, I'll do** never.
4) The train **should have arrived** 30 minutes ago.
5) What **would** you **do**, if something else **happened** to you then? (The thing did not happen; past subjunctive)
6) If you **should change** of mind, do **let me know**. (I already know she would not change her mind.)
7) We **work** that we **may live**. (To mean purpose)
8) She **works hard** that she **may succeed**. (purpose)
9) Work and you **will succeed**. Touch it, and you die.
10) I **warn** you **lest** you **should** fail.
11) **Follow** me, or you'll **be punished**.
12) If he **be** there, he **will help** you.

Note: A lot of subjunctive similar statements that tend to be fact fall to Indicative Mood; so why, presently Subjunctive tends to be merged with Indicative Mood. However, as still exist, carry on with its features and examples to be used separately.

485. <u>Arrangement of Words in Past Subjunctive:</u>

1) **Subject+wish+subject+were/v2**
   ○ **I wish I knew** his name. **I wish this were** possible.
   ○ **I wish I were** a millionaire. **I wish I were** an eagle.
   ○ **She wishes the car belonged** to me.
   ○ I **wish I had** the virtues.

2) **If+subject+were/v2**
   ○ **If I, were** you (i.e., but I am not you), I should do it.
   ○ I would go there, **if I were** you (but I was not)
   ○ **If he were** (not was), he would have come.
   ○ **<u>If we started</u>** now, we would be in time. (But we didn't start yet)

3) **As if+subject+were/v2**
   ○ He orders me about **<u>as if I were</u>** his wife. (But I am not).
   ○ She pretends as if she were dead.
   ○ She acted her role as if she was the bandit.

4) **As though+subject+were/v2**
   ○ He walks **<u>as though he were</u>** drunk. (But he is not).
   ○ He sang as though his mother were in hospital. (But not really)
   ○ He failed as though he were not in the classes for long. (he was present in the classes)
   ○

5) After **would rather**, use **'you' or 'he'** as **subject& v2**, to indicate preference.
   ○ I **<u>would rather</u> <u>you went</u>** by air (I should prefer you to go by air).
   ○ They **would rather you paid** (should prefer you to pay) them by cheque.
   ○ I would rather she took divorced from the cruel man.

6) **Had+subject+been+participle/adj/adv/noun complement**
   ○ **Had he been** present (i.e., but he was not), he would oppose you.
   ○ **<u>Had I been</u>** there (but I was not), I would save her from them.
   ○ **Had she been** my wife, what the fuck she would do?

7) **It is time+subject+v2/progressive form** with **'were'** with all persons and number; as,
   ○ **<u>It is time</u>** we started. (Implying, we are already late)

- o **It is time** we <u>were</u> eating.
- o **It is time** she <u>were giving</u> lecture in the classes.

486.   **More Examples of Past Subjunctive**

1) ***Were he here*** *(if he was present here, but he was not)*, I ***would*** tell him this. I ***wish*** that he ***would*** pass.
2) *I **wish I were** a millionaire.* ***Wish*** that ***he were*** here.
3) *I **wish I were** a bird.* I ***wish*** the ***thief were*** punished.
4) She ***wishes the house belonged*** to you.

- ▪ (wish + subject + past form of verb/were)
- ▪ Indirectly, subjunctive mood can also be used to give advice; as,

5) I ***would*** not drink, ***if I were*** you. *(The mood is subjunctive, as it is not true, you would not be me & I would never be you.)*
6) I ***should*** wait a little longer, ***if I were*** you.
7) ***Would*** that he ***had lived*** to see it. *(Expressing strong wish, but it would never be happened, because he is already dead)*
8) ***If I were*** asked to work on Sundays, I ***should*** resign.
9) ***If I were*** a bird, I ***would*** fly in the sky.
10) ***If he should*** come, I ***should*** go. (a mere or unreal supposition that didn't happen)
11) He ***went*** there so that he ***might see*** the sight. (purpose)

Note: The difference of Indicative & Subjunctive in case of supposition or condition is, one is fact, and another is in imaginary merely.

35. Classification of Sentence, based on Functions

487. **What is a Sentence:** A group of words, with at least one subject & one finite verb that makes a complete sense.

<u>**We can define it another way. The term 'sentence'-**</u>

- ➤ consists of a group of words;
- ➤ It contains <u>a subject</u> & <u>at least a finite verb</u>;
- ➤ May consist of one or more Phrases;
- ➤ It may consist of one or more Clauses;
- ➤ Have a complete sense.
- ➤ Begins with a capital letter & ends with- . /? /! marks.
- ➤ It is the largest structural unit of a language, while a word is the smallest.

Classification

488. A sentence does different functions to express sense of the speaker. It may be used to give information, to ask questions, to give order, request, advice, or command as well as it may express a wish, hope, desire, blessing or prayer. On account of these multi functions of a sentence, sentences are divided or grouped into the following five kinds. Have a quick look at the PowerPoint slide:

CLASSIFICATION OF SENTENCE—1

ACCORDING	**F**UNCTIONS	**Assertive** • **That states a fact** or makes an assertion or a statement.
		Interrogative • **That asks a question**, begins with a helping verb or wh. word & ends with a question mark.
		Imperative • **That expresses order, request, advice** where the subject (you) is left out or understood.
		Optative • **That expresses a desire, wish, prayer or blessing.**
		Exclamatory • **That expresses a sudden feeling or emotion** like wonder or fear, usually ends with an exclamation.

489. **Assertive Sentence:** **That states a fact** or **makes an assertion** or **a statement**, usually begins with a subject & ends with a full stop (.), is called an Assertive Sentence or Statement. Sometimes, examples are more effective to understand than mere illustrations. So, study the following examples and guess their functions:

1) Humpty Dumpty sat on a wall.
2) The cow is a useful animal.
3) It is worshipped in Hindu religion.
4) He is my best friend.
5) Hope (I hope), you will pass the examination.
6) Rabindra Nath was a Bengali Poet.
7) He was also a novelist, short-story writer and an excellent composer of songs, besides a singer.
8) The boys are not reading at any school.
9) Yes, I can do the job. No, I cannot do the job.

What did you notice in them? What functions did they do in the sentences? Are they as the followings?

Functions	Sentences
1) To describe a situation or an event, or to give introduction:	1) There is a small river, Atreyee, which pass through the town, Balurghat. Peter lives here from long past when he wore half pant.
2) To narrate a thing:	2) Teacher said that Darjeeling is the queen of hill. Mr. Peter is a teacher.
3) To give information or reporting:	3) India won the last World Cup.
4) Asserting a fact:	4) Yes, I can do the job.
5) Denying a fact:	5) No, I can't do the job.
6) Illustrating:	6) Some of the best poets of our time are A, B & C.
7) Describing a process:	7) The preparation of teas goes through a number of stages.
8) Stating a cause, result, purpose, etc.:	8) She cannot attend the school because of her illness. He worked hard, so he passed. He had worked hard, so that he could pass.

490. **Interrogative Sentence:** **A sentence that asks a question**, *begins with a helping verb or wh. word & ends with a question mark(?), is called an* Interrogative Sentence or Question; as,

1) Does she like tea or coffee? What is today's menu?
2) Where do you live? Who is our best friend?
3) What is in your mind? Can't we live alone?

4) Did he write any novel? What is his name?
5) Is he really a writer? Have you read his any novel?
6) What are you reading? Why is the woman shouting?
7) Can he swim? Will they come today?
8) Does she not read at any school?
9) Why do wives quarrel with their husbands?
10) Why do we fall in love with women or beautiful girls thousand times?

An Interrogative sentence do the following functions:

Functions	Sentences
1) To ask questions, enquiring or asking for information: 2) Asserting: 3) Ask for help, requesting, or seeking permission: 4) Ask for opinion or advice: 5) Expressing doubt, etc.:	1) What is your name? Why were you absent from school? 2) Who doesn't want money? (To get reply 'everyone wants') Who is not scared of devil? ('everyone is scared of') 3) Would you please help me to come out of this worse situation? Will you please call a doctor? I need an immediate treatment. May I come in, sir? 4) What should we do, will you suggest for anything? 5) Who knows when rain will stop? (uncertain). Are you a man? (No, a devil.)

491. **Imperative Sentence:** <u>**That expresses a command (order), an entreaty (request), or an advice and similar things;**</u> where the subject (you) is left out or understood, is called an Imperative Sentence. An imperative <u>may end with</u> ***full stop*** or ***question mark*** at the end. Study the examples:
1) Be quiet. Have mercy upon us.
2) Will you pass the tray, please?
3) Please give me the pen.
4) Sit and study your lesson.
5) Write this essay within five hundred words.
6) I wish you write it for me. (Request; or an order, politely asked)
7) Lend me your bicycle. Finish it within ten minutes.
8) Do not sit on the desk. You should not be there alone.

Study the functions of Imperative sentence in the chart, given below:

Functions	Sentences
1) Order, commanding, or instructing: 2) appealing, or entreating: 3) Permitting: 4) Prohibiting: 5) Advising: 6) Suggesting or seek for suggestions: 7) Reminding:	1) Stop talking. Soldiers, march ahead; we can't stay here long. Do the job as I say. 2) Please give me a piece of bread. Please, don't accept my love; I am a devil in heart. 3) You may smoke, but your lunch is at your own risk. Yes, you may come in; but here is none. 4) Do not smoke here. You can't go there. Don't make a noise. 5) Do not idle away your invaluable time, or you will have no time even to repent. 6) Let me explain the matter. Let's go for a picnic. We should celebrate the occasion. 7) Kindly remember the date of wedding.

492. **Optative Sentence: A sentence that expresses a desire, wish, prayer or blessing**, is called an Optative Sentence. An Optative may end with a **full stop** or **exclamation** (!) an exclamation is used with the desire or wish that is not real (Study subjunctive mood). The modals – **may, should**, & the verb **wish, were** – are vastly used in this kind of sentences; as,
1) May you live long. May God bless you.
2) I wish you soon be cured. I wish you to be cured.
3) I wish you should be cured soon.
4) May you not win the race.

5) If I were a bird! If I had been a millionaire!
6) May the girl sing well. May the old man have peace.
7) I wish you must grow up soon. (Wish or prayer: 'I want you to grow up soon.')

Study the functions of Optative that do in the sentence:

Functions	Sentences
1) To express **Wish** or **Desire:**	1) I wish you a long life. If I were a bird! If I had been a billionaire! If I had two wings! I wish I were taller than my love!
2) Expressing **Prayer:**	2) Long live the king. May you live long. May God bless you. May everyone's son
3) Giving **Curse:**	flourish in life. **May she be** happy.
	3) May she live long, and feel the pain of old age by firsthand experience.
4) To express **Blessing:**	4) May God protect you from all dangers. **God bless** you! **May Heaven help** you in all!

493. **Exclamatory Sentence:** <u>**A sentence that expresses a sudden feeling or emotion**</u> due to *wonder, fear, approval, or compliment*, etc., <u>usually ends with an exclamation after interjection, and a full stop (.) at end of the sentence,</u> is called an Exclamatory Sentence (that expresses exclamation; strong feelings). The words of Interjection like, – bravo, hurrah, well-done & other parts of speech like, hear, how, what, shocking, strange– are often used in the exclamatory sentences. Study the examples:
   a. **Well done friend!** You have done excellent.
   b. **Good bye!** We don't know will we meet again?
   c. **O dear me!** What you have done.
   d. **Bad luck to it!** He had tried his best yet.
   e. **Hear!** What a song she sings.
   f. **Strange!** She went there.
   g. **How** vary kind of you!
   h. **How** beautiful!
   i. **Shocking!** How she can say so.

   ✷   The words which are generally used in an exclamatory sentence to express strong emotion or feelings are called the Interjections. For more such words, study the chapter of **Interjections.**
   j. **How cold** the night is!
   k. **What a shame!**
   l. **Hush!** The teacher is coming.
   m. **Oh!** What a beautiful scene.
   n. **How beautiful** the bird is!
   o. **What!** He can't swim.
   p. **Wow!** He read excellent. It sounds like a song.
   q. **Shame!** She doesn't leave even her boss!

Study the functions, Exclamatory do in the sentence:

Functions	Sentences
1) Expressing wonder	1) What a grand hotel is this!
2) Expressing joy	2) Hurrah! I have completed the project.
3) Expressing grief	3) Alas! I am undone in life.
4) Expressing pity	4) Oh! You have failed. I am sorry.
5) Expressing disgust	5) Phi! She did a devilish job. How untidy the room is!
6) Greeting	6) Hello! My friend, we are meeting after long days.
7) Encouragin	7) Bravo! Well done! What a shot he did. Carry on.
8) Wish &	8) Good morning. Good evening. Good night.
9) Bid good-bye or farewell	9) Good-bye! We shall not meet again. / Bye! See you soon.
10) Make a taunt	10) Yea! You are a Shakespeare of our time.

494. One more functional category of sentence (rhetorical).

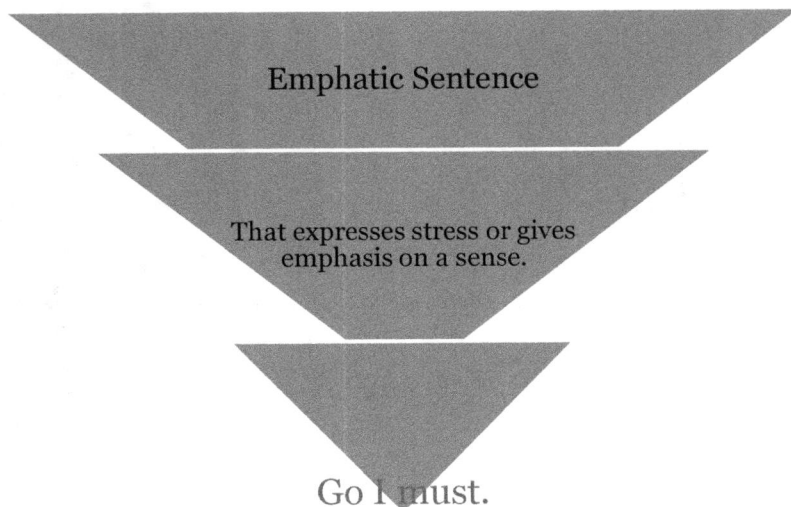

Emphatic Sentence

That expresses stress or gives emphasis on a sense.

Go I must.

- ✖ **Explanation:** 'Go I must.' It means, 'I must go.' A simple Assertive sentence to express the certainty of his going or to give more emphasis on the sense, shifting the main verb 'go' or modal 'must' before the subject **'Must I go'** (and often using 'do' before main verb; **'I do go there in time.'**)— is termed as the 'rhetorical use of exclamatory sentence'.

- ✖ An Emphatic sentence, actually, is a variation of Assertive or Exclamatory Sentence, made often by shifting the main verb before subject or use 'do or did' before the main verb (in assertive). Some more examples of such sentences are:
  a. **Go,** you must there in time. Don't worry.
  b. You **do** believe me I was not that man.
  c. **Must** you be a rascal (You must be a rascal.)
  d. **Killing him** you are a criminal! (You are a criminal by killing him.)
  e. **Go,** you must go there. (Using double times, the main verb 'go'; first 'go' to give emphasis)
  f. **Attend** you must be there. (You must attend there.)
  g. **Dance** he did well on the stage.
  h. **Hit** he the ball, excellent, like Sachin Tendulkar!
  i. I **myself** did it. She **herself** went there. (Using a reflexive pronoun)
  j. You yourself correct **first.** (Giving emphasis on the adverb 'first', using it at last; while it should be, **'First, you correct yourself'** in the assertive sentence.)
  k. She **herself** loves. ('She merely loves herself.')

Formation of Affirmative & Negative Sentences

495. All the five or six (including emphatic, if we take it as a different kind, though I don't think so except to be a variation)—can be expressed in negative sense side by side as the affirmative sense of the sentence. Study the chart:

Sentence in Affirmative way	Sentence in Negative sense
1. I know you. (*Assertive*)	1. I don't know the person. (*Assertive*)
2. Will you go? (*Interrogative*)	2. Have you not finished this? (*interrogative*)
3. Come at once. (*Imperative*)	3. Don't run in the sun. (*Imperative*)
4. God might save him. (*Optative*)	4. May God not forgive his sin. (*Optative*)
5. How foolish! (*Exclamatory*)	5. Is he not a fool, doing like this! (*Exclamatory*)
6. Must I go. (*Emphatic*)	6. Must you not do it. (*Emphatic*)

- ▪ **'Affirmative'** means that affirms something; & **'negative of the sense'** means that denies something. Thus, each kind of sentence can be expressed either in affirmative or negative sense.
- ▪ In the above, the sentences (in the affirmative column & in the negative column) are different in meaning & expression from each other; as the followings:
  → You went there. = You didn't go there.

406

→ Will you like tea? = Wil you not like tea?
→ Do it. = Don't do it.
→ God bless you. = God might not forget your sin. (God may not bless you.).
→ How you can do it! = How can't you do it (such an easy task)!
→ Go I must there. = Must not I go there.

- In all the above cases the sentences are converted from affirmative to negative, and their sense have also been changed. For this conversion of sense and sentence, study the following chart of <u>adverbs (mainly) to form</u>

The Words of Negation & Affirmation
(adverbs or compounds)

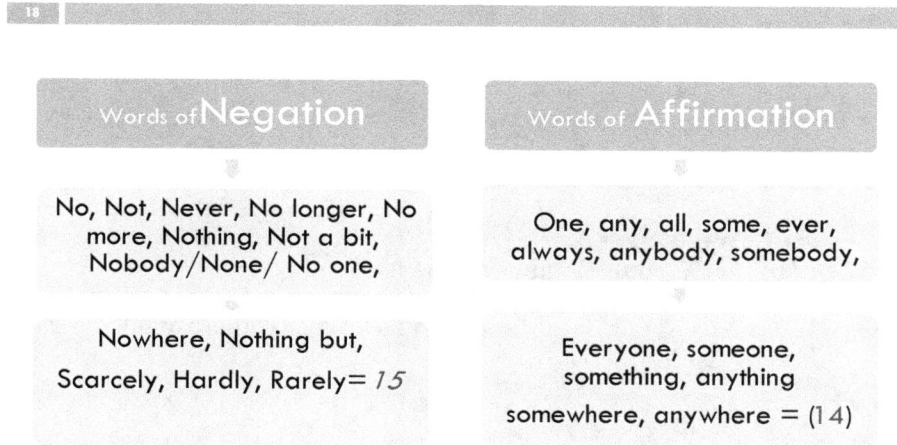

Words of **Negation**	Words of **Affirmation**
No, Not, Never, No longer, No more, Nothing, Not a bit, Nobody/None/ No one,	One, any, all, some, ever, always, anybody, somebody,
Nowhere, Nothing but, Scarcely, Hardly, Rarely= *15*	Everyone, someone, something, anything somewhere, anywhere = (14)

<u>Negation and Affirmation.</u>

- How to form negative sentences with the help of words of Negation, study the following chart. However, more details in the allotted chapter: **How to form negative sentences-**

1) By 'Do' helping verb (do/does/did + not)	· He reads a book. = He **does not** read a book. · They run a race. = They **do not** run.
2) By other auxiliaries— ('Be', 'Have' & Modal verb+ no/not)	· We are going. = We **are not** going. · They were sailors. = They **were not** sailors. · I have a bi-cycle. = I **have no** bi-cycle. · You can do it now. = You **cannot** do it now. · We shall visit there. = We **shall not** visit the place.

3) By some Adverbs, besides no, not: —
 	
 (Nobody, none, no one, never, nothing, nowhere, scarcely, hardly
 	
 and to keep sense, retained, use of antonyms of main words, along with negation.)
	· I <u>always remember</u> you.
	     = I **never** <u>forget</u> you.
	 · There were <u>so many people</u>.
	     = There were **none**.
	 · It will be distributed <u>to everyone</u>.
	     = It will be distributed <u>to **none**</u>. /**no one**
	 · I <u>want everything</u>.
	     = I want/<u>decline</u> **nothing**.
	 · God is e<u>verywhere</u>.
	     = **No one** can say God is <u>**nowhere**</u>.
	 · I <u>liked</u> my friend very much.
	     = I **hardly** <u>disliked</u> my friend.

<u>How to form affirmative sentences from negative-</u>

1) By omitting 'do/does/did not' & 'no' or 'not' Adverb from the sentence	I do not like it. > I like it. You have no car. > You have a car.
2) By use of (adverbs)— (Ever, always, anybody, all, every one, anyone, anywhere, everywhere etc.)	I **never** forget you. >I **always** remember you. I hate **none**. >I love **everyone**.
3) By antonym	She **loves** me **not**. > She **hates** me.

How to form interrogative sentences-

1) **By use of 'Do' verb:** (Do/Does/Did+ Sub.+ Main Verb+ Obj.+ Others)	Rita sang a sweet song. = **Did** Rita sing a song? He reads a novel. = **Does** he read any? I apology to you. = **Do** you apology me?
2) By use of other Helping or Modal Auxiliaries: (H.V./M.V.+ Sub.+ Main Verb+ Obj.+ Others)	I am reading a book. = **Are** you reading? She has done her task. =**Has** she done her task? You will be there? = **Will** you be? You may come in.= May I come in, sir?
3) In case of "Wh' words: ('Wh'+ H.V./ M.V.+Sub.+ Main Verb+ Obj.+ Others)	I went to Kolkata. = **Where did** you go? I am eating rice. = **What are** you eating? I have a car. = **What do** you have? He had gone there to meet her. = **Why had** he gone there?

36. Classification of Sentence, based on Structure

496. Here is the 2nd way of Classification of Sentences. This time it is based on Structure / Construction / Clauses.

Based on Clauses, Sentences are of three kinds:
A. **Simple Sentence,**
B. **Compound Sentence** &
C. **Complex Sentence**.

✘ Read the slide:

CLASSIFICATION OF SENTENCE—2

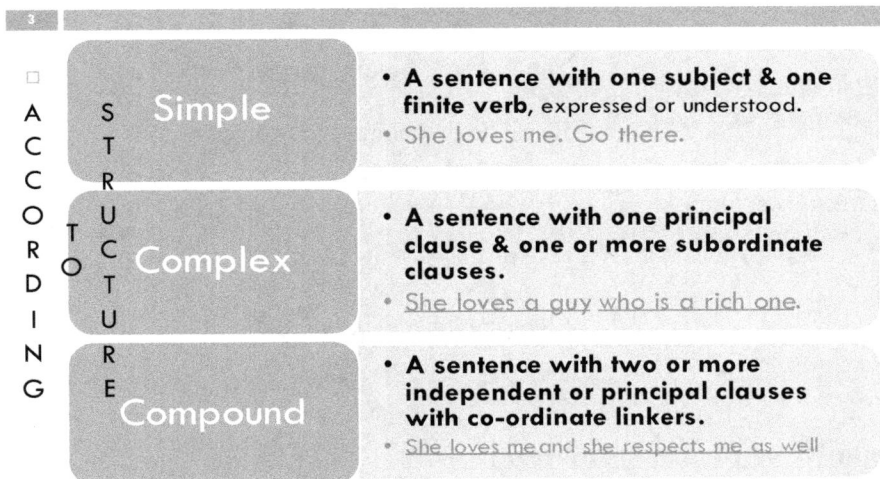

ACCORDING to STRUCTURE

Simple
- **A sentence with one subject & one finite verb,** expressed or understood.
- She loves me. Go there.

Complex
- **A sentence with one principal clause & one or more subordinate clauses.**
- She loves a guy who is a rich one.

Compound
- **A sentence with two or more independent or principal clauses with co-ordinate linkers.**
- She loves me and she respects me as well

✷ Explanation:

A. **Simple Sentence**: A sentence in which there is only one principal clause **(i.e., one subject & one finite Verb)**. Read the examples:
   1) His courage won him honor.
   2) She turned to me.
   3) I decided to stick to the agenda.
   4) Your husband might have killed Zara Lone.
   5) He had a clear motive.
   6) Two whistles are enough for the signal.
   7) She fought with me for a year.
   8) She loved you a lot too, Keshav.
   9) Why women's love is invisible to us?
   10) Seven people raised their glasses high in the air.

B. **Compound Sentence**: A compound sentence is formed of <u>at least one principal & one co-ordinate clause.</u> Sometimes, it is said a compound sentence is composed of two or more principal clauses; whereas, a principal clause is connected with a co-ordinate conjunction. <u>Read the definition</u>:

✷ <u>A sentence with two or more</u> independent or <u>principal clauses with or without any sub-ordinate clause</u> joined together by co-ordinate conjunctions, is called the **Compound Sentence**.

✷ The following Co-ordinate Conjunctions are generally used to form Co-ordinate clauses and Compound Sentences:

(1) And, also, too, as well as, both—and, not only—but also, **etc.** (meaning cumulative or addition of word, phrase, clause of equal rank);
   1) We carved not a line, **and** we raised not a stone.
   2) God made the country **and** man-made the town.
   3) Vishal & Virat are good bowlers. (Vishal is a good bowler & Virat is a good bowler.)

(2) Either...or, neither...nor, or, else etc. (that refer selection or alternation between two);
   4) She must weep, **or** she will die. **Either** he is mad, **or** he feigns madness.
   5) Is that story true **or** false? **Neither** a borrower, **nor** a lender be.
   6) We can travel by land **or** water. They toil not, **neither** do they spin.
   7) **Either** you are mistaken, **or** I am. Walk quickly, **else** you will not overtake him.

(3) Still, yet, only, but, however, nevertheless, whereas, though —yet, etc. (meaning adversative or contrast between two or more);
   8) Our hoard is little, ***but*** our hearts are great.
   9) The man is poor, ***but*** honest. (The man is poor, but he is honest.)
   10) He is slow, ***but*** he is sure. I was annoyed, ***still*** I kept quiet.
   11) I would come; ***only*** that I am engaged. He was all right; ***only*** he was fatigued.

(4) Therefore, for, so, then, so then etc. (meaning Illative or Inference; coming to conclusion).
   12) Something certainly fell in; ***for*** I heard a splash.
   13) All precautions must have been neglected, ***for*** the plague spread rapidly.

Above all the examples are the examples of using **Co-ordinate Conjunctions** to form **Co-ordinate Clauses**; and thus, they are (the sentences) are also the examples of **Compound Sentences**.

However, point to remember: Co-ordinate Conjunctions are used not always to make Compound Sentences, but bare Simple sentences too.

497. When two or more subjects <u>joined by 'and'</u> & they are **inseparable** <u>denoting a single fact</u>, one is incomplete without the other, or the thing will not be made at all, the sentence is not a Compound but a Simple Sentence.

The following are not Compound sentences, though used Co-ordinates; as,
1. She **and** I are great friends.

2. The PM **and** MPs agreed to pass the bill.
3. Meera **and** Anjali are walking together.
4. Curry **and** rice is my favorite dish.
5. The sum **and** substance of this story is poor.
6. Two **and** two make four.
7. Bread **and** milk is a wholesome food.

The above look like compound, but they are not, as subjects are inseparable. The subject formed by co-ordinate cannot be broken up. The two here make a single fact. Without one, other is invalid to mean. They are examples of Simple Sentences.

498. How to find a Compound Sentence

A Compound sentence must have **at least one Principal and one Co-ordinate Clause** (Co-ordinate clause means = Principal Clause with Co-ordinate Conjunction) & may have any number of sub-ordinate clauses or not at all; as,

1) The moon was bright **and** we could see our way.
2) Night came on **and** rain fell heavily **and** we got very wet.
3) Anil called at 5.30 **and** I told him that you had gone out.
4) I shall do it now **or** I shall not do it at all.
5) He gave them no money **nor** he did help them anyway.
6) He threw the stone **but** it missed the target.
7) He **neither** obtains success **nor** deserves it.
8) He is **either** a mad **or** has the mentality of a criminal.
9) I both thanked him **and** rewarded him.
10) They love & torture, they love torture & love. −Peter.
11) I am ill, **but** I shall go.
12) I went there **and** (I) found that my brother was ill.
13) The book which you gave me was a good one, **but** I have lost it.
14) Man is guided by reason, **and** beast by instinct.
15) The horse reared **and** the rider was thrown.
16) I called him, **but** he gave me no answer.
17) **Either** he is drowned **or** some passing ship has saved him.
18) He rushed into the field, **and** foremost fighting fell.
19) Man proposes, **but** God disposes.
20) Listen carefully **and** take notes.

499. Compound Sentence is used to avoid needless repetition of same words **by contraction** or **giving shortened form**, or **letting them understood** in the following way-
   a) <u>With two or more predicates are for one subject</u>:
      o **He** came and (**he**) delivered a lecture.
      o **I** was pleased but (**I**) could not do anything.

   b) <u>For two or more subjects there is one predicate</u>:
      o They (**are wrong**) as well as you **are wrong**.
      o Either he (**must go**) or his brother **must go**.
      o He **is** poor but (he **is**) honest.

500.   Relative Pronouns or Adverbs may also form Compound Sentences, besides Sub-ordinate Relative clause and complex sentence. Study the following:

Generally Relative Pronouns and Relative Adverbs do function of Sub-ordinate Conjunctions and they form Complex Sentences, but with the following they do form co-ordinate meanings, and thereby they have formed Compound Sentences:
1) He helped me, **which** (=and this/it) was very kind of him.
2) I went to Kolkata, **where** (=and there) I stayed for one month.
3) I went to the Principal, **who** (=and he) spoke kindly to me.
4) At last, I found him, **which** (=and this) relieved me of my anxiety.
5) They arranged for a priest, **who** (=and he) offered a ten-thousand – rupee package for the cremation.

When **relative pronouns or adverbs are used as co-ordinate conjunctions, they should be separated by comma from the principal clauses,** unless they are taken to be sub-ordinate conjunctions and the sentences are the complex sentences, in place of compound; as,

→ I went to Kolkata where I stayed for a month. ('the place where I stayed')

→ I went to Kolkata which is the capital of West Bengal.

The last two sentences are the examples of Complex Sentence.

Complex Sentence

C. **Complex Sentence:** A complex sentence is formed of <u>one principal & at least one sub-ordinate clause.</u>
Definition:

❑ The sentence with at least one Sub-ordinate clause and at least one Principal Clause, is called the Complex Sentence.

❑ A clause with Sub-ordinate conjunctions is called sub-ordinate clause, and the clause may be **a Noun Clause, Relative** or **Adjective Clause,** or an **Adverbial Clause.** A Sub-ordinate clause in collaboration with a Principal Clause builds a Complex Sentence; as the following:
  ○ I thought of Raghab who was at that moment was attending a party.
  ○ She gave me the same feeling (that) she gave me last.

501. Whether a sentence is complex or compound—how to find out?

It is determined by the combination of Principal clause with at least one Sub-ordinate or Co-ordinate Clause in the sentence.

❖ A Complex sentence must have **at least one Principal and one Sub-ordinate Clause** (Sub-ordinate clause means = Principal Clause with Sub-ordinate Conjunction or Relative Pronoun or Relative Adverb, etc.). A complex sentence may have more than one sub-ordinate clauses which may also be joined by co-ordinate conjunctions; as,

➢ **The boy** <u>who came here yesterday</u> and <u>whom you must have seen</u> **is my brother.** (In the sentence, there is one Principal clause 'The boy is my brother' & two Sub-ordinate clauses which are joined by a co-ordinate conjunction 'and'. The sentence is Complex Sentence.)

➢ <u>As he is ill</u>, and <u>(as) the doctor has advised him for rest,</u> **he cannot come to welcome you.** (Here also the two sub-ordinate clauses are joined by a co-ordinate conjunction 'and', but the sentence is the Complex sentence. It has one Principal & two sub-ordinate clauses.)

502. More examples of Complex Sentences:
  1) They rested **when** evening came.
  2) **As** the boxers advanced into the ring, the people said they would not allow them to fight.
  3) **If** the news made you uncomfortable, the proof will make you even more so.
  4) After my uncle arrived, they took over the cremation.
  5) Even though he had died, I felt the fire must hurt him.
  6) I remembered how he would dress me up for school when I was a child.

❑ Let's have a revision of some pages from the chapter of Sub-ordinate Conjunctions to understand better the Sub-ordinate Clauses as well as the Complex Sentences.

503. Know the Functions of Sub-ordinate Conjunctions that join clauses (adverbial) which express:

Functions of Sub-ordinate Conjunctions

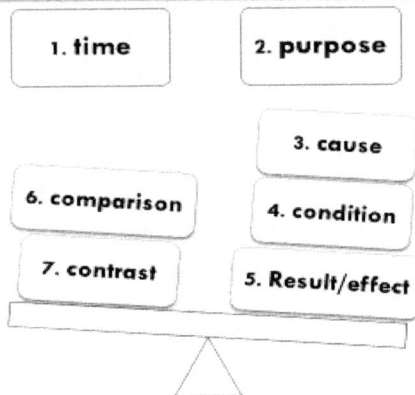

Let's see now the Conjunctions & their Functions they do in the sentences:

Adverbial function of conjunction	Examples of conjunction
Time	After, before, since, as soon as, while, until, as, as long as, till...
Purpose	In order that, lest, so that, that...
Cause	because, since, as, for,
Condition	provided, supposing, unless, as, if, whether,
Result/Effect	so...that, that,
Comparison	than, as...as
Contrast	Though, although, however, even if.

❏ Sub-ordinate Conjunctions cum Sub-ordinate Clauses do the following functions in Complex sentences. Study the examples:

(1) Conjunctions that refer 'Time':
1) We arrived **after** you had gone.
2) I waited **till** the train arrived.
3) **When** you are called, you must come in at once.
4) Do not go **before** I come.
5) We got into the port **before** the storm came on.
6) I would die **before** I lied.
7) My grandfather died **before** I was born.
8) I will stay **until** you return.
9) Many things have happened **since** I saw you.
10) He returned home **after** I had gone.

(2) Purpose:
11) She must weep, **lest** she die.
12) We tried hard **in order that** it spin.
13) He is intelligent, **so** he feigned madness.
14) We eat **so that** we may live.
15) He held my hand **lest** I should fall.
16) She feigned madness, **so that** she saved herself from imminent danger.
17) We travel by land or water **so that** we can reach another place.

(3) Cause or Reason:

18) I cannot give you any money, **for** I have none.
19) **Since** you wish it, it shall be done.
20) He may enter **as** he is a friend.
21) **As** he was not there, I spoke to his brother.
22) I did not come **because** you did not call me.
23) He deserved to succeed, **for** he worked hard.

(4) Condition:

24) You will not succeed **unless** you work harder.
25) He fled **lest** he should be killed.
26) He asked **whether** he might have a holiday.
27) You will get the prize **if** you deserve it.
28) You will be late **unless** you hurry.
29) I shall be vexed **if** you do that.
30) Grievance cannot be redressed u**nless** they are known.
31) Give me to drink, **else** I shall die of thirst.
32) **If** I feel any doubt, I'll ask.
33) I shall go, **whether** you come or not.
34) He will sure to come **if** you invite him.
35) **Unless** you tell me the truth, I shall punish you.

(5) Result/effect/Consequence:

36) He worked very hard, **so that** he might pass.
37) He was so tired **that** he could scarcely stand.

(6) Comparison:

38) He is richer **than** I am.
39) He is **as** intelligent **as** Biram.
40) Tom runs faster **than** Harry.
41) The earth is larger **than** the moon.

(7) Contrast / Concession:

42) Our hoard is little, **but** our hearts are great.
43) The man is poor, **but** honest. (The man is poor, but he is honest.)
44) He is slow, **but** he is sure.
45) I was annoyed, **still** I kept quiet.
46) I would come; **only** that I am engaged.
47) He was all right; **only** he was fatigued.
48) I hear **that** your brother is in London.

504. The Interrogative Pronouns or Adjectives, Relative Pronouns or Adverbs (wh.& that)—they also join subordinate clauses (mainly Noun or Relative clauses) to form Complex Sentences; as the following:

1) He could trace his umbrella **which** was blue. (Relative Adj.; adj. or relative Clause).
2) He was surprised to see the man **that** was his own brother.
3) I do not know **why** she did not join us. (Reason—adv. clause)
4) I do not know **why** she had gone.
5) I do not know **where** she had gone. (Place—adv. clause)
6) He could trace his umbrella **where** he had left it.
7) She was the girl **whom** I loved immense. (Relative clause)
8) You are talking to the man **who** was my brother. (Relative clause)
9) I didn't know **that** she had gone. (Concession conj.)
10) Make hay **while** the sun shines.

505. Besides, Simple, Compound & Complex, there are <u>two more structural categories of sentences. Read their</u> <u>definitions:</u>

Complex Compound

✶ A sentence with one principal & two or more sub-ordinate clauses and **_where the sub-ordinate clauses_ or _complex sentences are joined by a co-ordinate linker_**. [Peter choices a term 'variation or a kind' of Complex, but not a separate kind of sentence, however]. You may read the examples:

1) **She loves her master** who is soft hearted **and** who has bright personality.
   (The sentence has 1 principal, 2 sub-ordinates. However, the two sub-ordinates are joined by 'and' a conjunction. It is an example of **Complex Compound** Sentence.)

2) **I shall go there** when you come, **but (I shall) return** as soon as you leave the place.
   (The sentence has 2 principals, 2 sub-ordinates. However, the two complex sentences are connected by 'but', a co-ordinate Conjunctions. It is an example of **Complex Compound** Sentence. The two complex sentences are joined by conjunction 'but'.)

3) As he is ill, **he cannot move out, but we expect** that he will come round before the ceremony ends.
   (The sentence has 2 principals, 3 sub-ordinates. The two complex sentences are added by conjunction 'but'. It is also an example of Complex Compound Sentence)

4) **I am a professor** who teaches students in a college **and you are a high school teacher** who teaches his students at a school.

5) **Either he is an engineer** who works in the corporate **or he is the boss** who provides recruitments to the people like us.

Compound Complex

✶ A sentence with two or more principal clauses; when one is independent, the other is in the complex sentence and both (simple & complex) are joined by a co-ordinate conjunction, is called Compound Complex. [Peter choices a term 'variation or a kind' of Compound, but not a separate kind of sentence]. **Read the** examples:
   1) **She loves me _but_** as I am unattainable, **she loves you**.
   2) **I am a teacher _and_ you are a doctor** who treats patients at the hospital.

   ▪ In the above both sentences, there is one principal clause which is independent and it is joined by a complex sentence by a co-ordinate conjunction 'and'. So, it is compound and complex, Compound Complex.

37. Analysis of Simple Sentence, as Subject & Predicate

506. **Read the Sentences:**
   a. The flower bloomed.
   b. Bob painted.
   c. The girls of the team were all good students.
   d. Bill told everyone about the wreck.
   e. Mary sobbed.
   f. Tom plays the piano well.

507. **Subject & Predicate:** Every complete sentence has two main parts: a subject and a predicate.
Simply, 'subject' is the **doer of an action, who or what does something**; or the person or a thing **of whom or which something is said**; as,
   ° _The flower_ bloomed.
   ° _Bob_ painted.
   ° _The girls of the team_ were all good students.
   ° _Bill_ told everyone about the wreck.
   ° _Mary_ sobbed.

° *Tom* plays the piano well.

Basically, the **term 'predicate' refers to the finite verb or the unit**. However, in broad sense, it includes the entire part of the verb along with its object or objects, adverbials and complement in the sentence. Though, briefly to say, **'what is said about the subject', is called predicate**; as,

- ° The flower *bloomed.*
- ° Bob *painted.*
- ° The girls of the team *were all good students.*
- ° Bill *told everyone about the wreck.*
- ° Mary *sobbed.*
- ° Tom *plays the piano well.*

508. Simple Subject & Complete Subject:

Every subject is built around one noun or a pronoun (or a noun equivalent word).
The **simple subject** (*what we told as 'root subject' in the heading*) is only the *main word* in a complete subject about whom or what something is said; as the following:

° The four new **students** arrived early.

✓ In the sentence, the underlined is the complete subject, while the word in bold, is the Simple or Root Subject. So, the simple subject in the sentence is- **students.**

The **complete subject** is the main noun word or noun equivalent word along with its all qualifiers or adjuncts (adjective or adjective equivalent words, are popularly known as adjuncts to a subject). In the above sentence, the underlined is an example of complete subject.

509. Simple Predicate & Complete Predicate:

A **simple predicate** (or the root predicate word) is always the verb or verbs (that link up with the subject) that expresses an action or state about the person or thing; as,

- ° Sara's sister *took us bowling yesterday.*
- ° The four new students *arrived early.*

✓ Here, in the above, while the underlined are the examples of Complete Predicate, the simple or root predicates are only the unit of finite verbs. Thus, the Root or Simple predicate words are respectively— **'took'** & **'arrived'**, written in bold in the lines.

The **Complete Predicate** is the verb and all its modifiers (adverb or adverbials), objects & complement, which are popularly known as the **extension to predicate**. In the above sentences, the underlined, which are respectively — 'took us bowling yesterday' & 'arrived early'—are the examples of Complete Predicates.

510. Practice, find out 'simple subject' & 'complete subject' from the followings:
- ° **I** am a teacher.
- ° **Arindam Dutta** is a doctor.
- ° **Chetan** is a student of class X.
- ° **'Chetan'** reads in class X?
- ° **Burza Khalifa** is a large building.

➤ Who is a teacher? Who is a doctor? Who is a student? Who reads in class X? Which is a large building? (Always, ask question to the verb. About who or what are the sentences? —are the simple or complete subject in the sentences.)

511. More examples, try yourself:
- ° She lifted the cake to take it to Raghav.

- ○ That is the real reason.
- ○ I don't need anyone.
- ○ I thought you might be hungry.
- ○ My phone rang.
- ○ Old friends are old friends.
- ○ Bob, Peter & Shyam visit there.
- ○ You are crazy.
- ○ What are you doing here?
- ○ Please, don't pressurize me.

512. **Now, find out 'simple predicate' & 'complete predicate' from the same sentences, taken earlier:**
- ○ I **am** *a teacher*.
- ○ Arindam Dutta **is** *a doctor*.
- ○ Chetan **is** *a student of class X*.
- ○ 'Chetan' **reads** *in class X*.
- ○ Burza Khalifa **is** *a large building*.

- • What's telling about 'I' in the first sentence?
- • What's telling about 'Arindam Dutta' in the 2nd sentence?
- • What's telling about 'Chetan' in 3rd & 4th sentences?
- • What is told of Burza Khalifa?

✓ When the underlined words are examples of **complete predicates**; the words, written in bold—are the examples of **simple predicates**. Thus, the simple predicate words are— **'am' 'is', is, reads, & 'is'** respectively.

513. **Ways to find out 'predicate'?**
- ➢ Ask question to the subjects; as, "what is he" or "what are they doing" / what does he or it do? etc.?
  - ✓ 'He **is a doctor**. (What is he?)
  - ✓ He **is running**. (What is he doing?)
  - ✓ She **is studying**, etc. (What is she doing?)

514. Let's check, read the followings and find out **subject** & **complete subject**, **predicate** & **complete predicate** from them:

a. Rony and his dog run on the beach every morning.
   - → About whom is the sentence?
   - → Who run on the beach every morning?

b. We spilled popcorn on the floor.
   - → About whom is the sentence?
   - → Who spilled popcorn on the floor?

c. My little brother broke his finger.
   - → About whom is the sentence?
   - → Who broke his finger?

d. His Uncle Bob asked for directions.
   - → About whom is the sentence?
   - → Who asked for directions?

e. Those soldiers carried guns.
   - → About whom is the sentence?
   - → Who carried guns?

f. Our honorable guests arrived in time.
   - → About whom is the sentence?
   - → Who arrived in time?

✓ *Your answer, in each case, is the 'subject' of the respective sentence.*

Now find out 'predicate' & 'complete predicate' from them:

→ What's telling about 'him' or 'them' in the sentences?
→ What do they do? / What are they doing? Or what are they in their profession? /What is stating about a thing? /What do they have or possess or be?

- *Here, your answer, in each case, is the 'predicate' of the sentence respectively, simple & complete.*

515. **Compound Subject:** A Compound Subject is made up of 'more than one noun or pronoun'; as,
   ○ *Team pennants*, *rock posters* and *family photographs* covered the boy's bedroom walls.
   ○ *Her uncle* and *she* walked slowly through the art gallery and admired the beautiful pictures exhibited there.
   ○ *My little brother* and *my cousin* broke their fingers.
   ○ *His Uncle Bob* and *Aunt Betty* asked for directions.
   ○ *Those soldiers* and *agents* carried guns.

516. **Compound Predicate:** A Compound Predicate is made up of more than one verb relating to the same subject in the sentence.

   ○ Mother ***mopped*** and ***scrubbed*** the kitchen floor.
   ○ My little brother ***bruised*** and ***broke*** his finger.
   ○ His Uncle Bob ***looked*** and ***asked for*** directions.
   ○ Those soldiers ***carried*** and ***used*** guns.

38. Further Analysis: Study of Subject Adjuncts, & Extension to Predicate

517.   In the first stage of analysis of a sentence, we have studied, a sentence has two main parts— **the Subject** & **the Predicate**; as,

SUBJECT	PREDICATE (Chart-1)
1) Dogs	bark.
2) The sun	gives light.
3) The child	is dead.
4) The boys	made Rama captain.
5) My father	gave me a watch.
6) The flames	spread everywhere.
7) The flames	spread in every direction.
8) The hour to prepare lessons	has arrived.

Each Sentence has a **Subject** & a **Predicate** (they are essential to a sentence).

We may also call these **two main parts** of a Simple Sentence as *'subject-group'* & *'predicate-group'*, or 'complete subject' & 'complete predicate'; and they consist of:

Subject Group	Predicate Group

1. Simple subject or root subject-word, and 2. Adjuncts to the subject, if any (the qualifiers or attributes),	1. The unit of finite verb cum simple predicate, 2. Object (Direct & Indirect), 3. Attributes to the object (qualifiers), 4. Complement, (subjective & objective), 5. Adverb or adverbials, which are also known as Adverbial Qualification or Extension to the Predicate.

518. **Simple & Complete Subject:** The main noun or noun equivalent word with its qualifiers that denotes a person or thing who or which does anything, or about whom or which something is said.

The point is a **subject may consist of one word** or **more words**.

Read the sentences: -

1) **Dogs** /bark.
2) **India** /is our motherland.
3) The **sun** /gives light.
4) The **child**/ is dead.
5) The **boys** / made Rama captain.
6) My **father**/ gave me a watch.
7) The **flames**/ spread everywhere.
8) The **flames**/ spread in every direction.
9) **Swimming** in the pond / is now not a good habit.
10) The **hour** to prepare lessons/ has arrived.

In sentence-1 & 2, the subject consists of one word, i.e., 'dogs' & 'India' respectively.
In the sentences from 3 to 8, the subjects consist of two words;
In sentence 9, it consists of four words; while
In sentence -10, the subject consists of five words only.

In case of subjects that consist of several words, there is always one word which is most important than the others. The chief word in the complete subject is known as **Root** or **Main Subject-word**' or the so-called **Simple Subject**'. Thus, the **bold word** in each is the example of **simple subject** in the sentences, while the underlined are the examples of Complete subjects.

❑ **A complete subject consists of the simple subject word along with its modifiers or the adjuncts.** The adjuncts to the subject may vary from adjective to participle, possessive noun or pronoun to case in apposition, and the most common thing is an article. Now, read them in details.

- o '*Little child* wants to play.'
- o *Stone walls do* not make a prison.
- o A barking sound the *shepherd* hears.

→The main subject words are 'child', 'walls', & 'shepherd', **which are also called simple subjects**, when 'little' is an adjective; 'stone' is a noun used as adjective to form the compound noun 'stone walls', and 'the' before shepherd is an article.

519. **Simple & Complete Predicate:** It denotes the unit of finite verb (main with helping) along with its objects, complement and adverbials.

A word or a group of words that **is said about the subject** (said about the person or thing).
Like a complete subject, **a complete predicate too may consist of one or more words;** as,

1. Peter / **runs**.
2. Peter / **runs** fast.
3. Peter / **runs** very fast.
4. India / **is** our motherland.
5. My father/ **gave** me a watch.
6. The boys / **made** Rama captain.
7. The flames/ **spread** everywhere.
8. Swimming in the pond / **is** now not a good habit.

In sentence 1, the Predicate consists of one word. In sentences 2 & 7, the predicate consists of two words; while,

In sentences 3 to 6, the complete predicate consists of three words, and
In sentence 8, the complete predicate consists of six words. Thus, a predicate may consist of any number of words.

The most essential word in a Predicate is always the finite verb (i.e., the unit of finite verb, the main with its helping) **which is termed as 'simple predicate'; then comes others.**

If the Predicate consists of one word, that is definitely the finite verb. If that consist of several words, the chief or essential word of all others is also the finite verb. Thus, the most important word in the predicate is always the finite verb. So why, the verb is also called the **Main Predicate Word'**.

Thus, in sentences from 1 to 8, the bold words are the example of **main predicate words,** and the underlined are the example of complete predicate.

A complete predicate includes simple predicate, object to the verb, adjuncts or attributes to object, complements (subjective or objective) and adverbials (which is popularly known as Extension to Predicate).

520.   Exercise-1: In the following sentences separate **the Subject & the Predicate Group** & then underline the **main subject word** & the **predicate-word**:
1.   The cackling of geese saved Rome.
2.   All matter I indestructible.
3.   No man can serve two masters.
4.   A sick room should be well aired.
5.   I shot arrow in the air.
6.   Up went the balloon.
7.   The naked everyday he clads.
8.   Into the street the piper stepped.
9.   Sweet are the uses of adversity.
10. Dear, gentle, patient, noble Nell was dead.

Check your Answer:

If we separate the **Subject** & the **Predicate Group** & then underline the **main subject word** & **predicate-word in the following way**:

Subject Group/complete subject	Predicate Group/ complete predicate
1. The **cackling** of geese	1. **saved** Rome.
2. All **matter**	2. **is** indestructible.
3. No **man**	3. can **serve** two masters.
4. A sick **room**	4. should be well **aired**.
5. **I**	5. **shot** arrow in the air.
6. The **balloon**.	6. **went** Up.
7. The naked **he**	7. **Clads** every day.
8. the **piper**	8. **Stepped** into the street.
9. the **uses** of adversity.	9. **are** Sweet.
10. Dear, gentle, patient, noble **Nell**	10. **Was** dead.

521.   **What shaped the Subject**
(Generally a Noun or a Noun Equivalent word)

The main Subject Word, or Simple Subject is always a Noun or a Pronoun, or a Noun Equivalent word. However, it is often used with its qualifiers, we say 'adjuncts' to the subjects, form 'complete subject'.
A 'Noun Equivalent' is a word or words other than Nouns or Pronouns that does the work of a Noun in the sentence, that may be *an adjective*, *a gerund*, *participle*, *infinitive verb* or a *phrase* & even *a clause*; as,
1.   ***He*** / tried his best.
2.   The ***rich*** / are not always happy.
3.   ***Talking*** overmuch / is the sign of vanity.
4.   ***To err*** / is human.

5. ***To find fault*** / is easy.
6. ***That you loved her*** / was known to all.

The bold italic words are the <u>simple subjects</u> in the above sentences.

Note: Sometimes, the main or simple subject can't form expected meaning with a single word and we need the complete subject, i.e., sentences 3 to 6.

How is a Subject Shaped (by noun or noun equivalent along with its attributes or adjuncts):

Subjects & Adjuncts to Subject variant

1.	A Noun:	1.	**India** is our motherland.
2.	A Pronoun:	2.	**He** reads a story.
3.	An Adjective:	3.	**The virtuous** are happy.
4.	An Infinitive:	4.	**To error** is human.
5.	<u>An Infinitive Phrase:</u>	5.	**To have done that** is risky.
6.	A Gerund:	6.	**Swimming** is a good exercise.
7.	<u>A Verbal Noun:</u>	7.	<u>The writing of letters</u> is now a lost art.
8.	A Phrase:	8.	**Success at any cost** was his aim.
9.	A Clause:	9.	<u>That you stand first</u> is known.
10.	A Quotation:	10.	**"All the world is a stage"** occurs in Shakespeare.

522. **Adjuncts to the subject** (so called Enlargement or Attributes)—are mainly the Adjectives or Qualifiers. They are known as **Enlargement** or **Attribute to the Subject,** we already read some. Read here some more examples:

1. ***New*** <u>brooms</u> / sweep clean.
2. ***Barking*** <u>dogs</u> / seldom bite.
3. ***Peter's*** <u>father</u> / was a teacher.
4. ***My*** <u>views</u> / are same as hers.
5. <u>Akbar</u>, ***the emperor***, / invaded Kashmir.
6. <u>An Akbar</u>, ***my friend***, is an Insurance Agent of Balurghat.
7. <u>A desire ***to excel***</u> / is commendable.
8. <u>A stitch ***in time***</u> / saves nine.

The bold italic words are the attributes or adjuncts to the subjects in the above sentences, whereas the underlined are the complete subjects in the sentences.

The attributes or adjuncts may vary from one to other. They may be **Adjective, Participle, Possessive Noun** or **Pronoun, Noun in apposition, Gerundial Infinitive,** even **Adverbials** that do work like an adjective in the sentences.

Study the Sentences (chart-2)

Sent No	Subject			Predicate
	Subject word	**Attribute**	**Type of attribute**	
1	brooms	New	Adjective	sweep clean.
2	dog	Barking	Participle	seldom bite.
3	father	Peter's	Possessive Noun	is a teacher.
4	views	My	Possessive Adjective	are same as hers.
5	Akbar	the emperor	Noun in Apposition	invaded Kashmir.
	Akbar	my friend	Noun in Apposition	is an Insurance Agent of Balurghat.
6	desire	A, to excel	Article & Gerundial Infinitive	is commendable.

| 7 | stitch | A, in time | Article; Adverbial but do the work of an adjective | saves nine. |

Study the Adjuncts to subject-variants

1.	An adjective:	1.	A good boy is loved by all.
2.	A Participle:	2.	Flying clouds are seen in the sky.
3.	A Participial Phrase:	3.	The boy playing on the lawn is my brother.
4.	Noun/Gerund, used as Adjective:	4.	The street boy is laughing. Drinking water should be pure.
5.	A Gerundial Infinitive:	5.	Water to drink should be pure.
6.	A Noun or Pronoun in Possessive case:	6.	My brother is ill. / His father's watch is stolen.
7.	A Noun or an Emphatic Pronoun in apposition:	7.	Rama, my brother, is ill. He himself did it.
8.	A Preposition with an Object:	8.	A man of principle is liked by all.
9.	An Adv. Used as an Adj.	9.	The then king did it. The down train is coming.
10.	An Adj. Clause:	10.	Boys who work hard succeed.

523.   Exercise-2

In the following sentences, pick out the complete subjects, then separate simple subjects from their Attributes:

1. The boy, anxious to learn, worked hard.
2. A burnt cow dreads the fire.
3. Birds of feather flock together.
4. The attempt to scale the fort was an utter failure.
5. The days of our youth are the days of our glory.
6. Ill habits gather by unseen degrees.
7. The dog, seizing the man by the collar, dragged him out.
8. The streets of some of our cities are noted for their crookedness.
9. A house divided against it cannot stand.
10. Deceived by his friends, he lost all hope.
11. The man carrying a hoe is a gardener.
12. One man's meat is another man's poison.
13. My days among the dead are past.
14. With his white hair un-bonneted, the stout old sheriff comes.

Study the Analysis of the sentences in chart-3:

Sent. No	Subject			Predicate
	Subject word	**Attribute**	**Type of attribute**	
1	boy,	The, anxious to learn,	Article, Adjective with object	worked hard.
2	cow	A burnt	Article with Participle	dreads the fire.
3	Birds	of feather	Preposition with Noun as qualifying words or Adj. Equiv.	flock together.
4	attempt	The, to scale the fort	Article, Gerundial Infinitive	was an utter failure.
5	days	The, of our youth	Article, prepositional phrase denoting time.	are the days of our glory.
6	habits	Ill	Adjective	gather by unseen degrees.
7	dog,	The, seizing the man by the collar,	Article; qualifying words or adj. equivalent	dragged him out.

8	streets	The, of some of our cities	Article, words show part of something	are noted for their crookedness.
9	house	A, divided against itself	Article, adj. phrase	cannot stand.
10	he	Deceived by his friends,	Adj. phrase	lost all hope.
11	man	The, carrying a hoe	Article, Noun in Apposition	is a gardener.
12	meat	One man's	Adj. with noun's possession	is another man's poison.
13	days	My, among the dead	Possessive adj., Noun with preposition as qualifying words	are past.
14	sheriff	With his white hair un-bonneted, the stout old	Both adj. equivalent	comes.

Extension or Adverbial Adjuncts

524.   <u>If</u> we divide a complete predicate, we have

Helping verb+ the predicate word + object + complement + adverbials

The adverb, adverb-equivalent or adverbials is sometimes called as **Extension** or **Adverbial Qualification.**

A complete predicate, often, includes a complement. The complement may be Subjective or Objective (if the verb is Intransitive, the complement is Subjective, if the Verb is Transitive, the complement is always Objective. Study in details).

Study the following sentences in the next chart, and try understand their parts or components.

1.   He went home.
2.   He rose to go.
3.   The flames spread in every direction.
4.   Spring advancing, the swallows appear.

Sl. No	Subject			Predicate		
	Subject-word	Attribute	Type of attribute	Predicate word/Verb	Adverbial Qualification	Type of Extension
1	He			went	home.	Noun used as Adverb
2	He			rose	to go.	Infinitive used as adverb
3	flames	The	article	spread	in every direction.	Adv. phrase
4	swallows	The	article	appear	Spring advancing.	Absolute phrase, denoting time.

525.   **Adverbial Adjuncts to Predicate:** The adverb or adverb equivalent words are also known as **Predicate Modifiers, Extension** or **Adverbial Qualification.** Read the chart:

1.	An Adverb:	1.	He acted **wisely.**
2.	Adj. used as an Adv.	2.	He died **happy.** (happily)
3.	An Adverbial Phrase:	3.	They walk **side by side.** (How?)
4.	A Participle:	4.	He went away **disappointed** (or weeping.)
5.	A Gerundial Infinitive:	5.	He came **to see me.** (Why?)
6.	An Adverbial Object:	6.	He walked **all day**/five miles. (How long? / How far?)
7.	A Preposition with Object:	7.	He arrived **in time.** (When?)
8.	An Absolute Phrase:	8.	**The sun having set,** we left the place. (Referring time)

9.	An Adverbial Clause:	9.	He went away *after I had left*.

526. Transitive Verbs & Objects (Direct & Indirect)

If the verb is transitive, it must have at least one object, and the single object must be Direct Object, either it is animate or inanimate object, [like having Principal & helping verb. If a sentence has single verb, that must be the principal verb, if two, another may be helping verb. For, a compound or complex sentence must have two or more principal verbs in them] A Transitive Verb may have two or more objects. If have two, one is Direct, and another is Indirect. [Generally, the inanimate object is the Direct and the animate Object is the Indirect Object, though that may differ]. Read the examples:

1) Birds builds <u>nest</u>.
2) I know <u>him</u>.
3) Peter gave <u>Rakesh a pencil</u>.
4) Naughty children love <u>fighting</u>.
5) The foolish crow tried <u>to sing</u>.
6) Our soldiers tried <u>to scale the cliff</u>.
7) All good children pity <u>the poor</u>.
8) I promised <u>him a present</u>.
9) He teaches <u>us Geometry</u>.
10) Father bought <u>Mini a doll</u>.

The Analysis of the above Sentences:

Sl. No	Subject		Predicate		
	Subject-word	**Attribute**	**Verb**	**Object**	**Types of Objects**
1	Birds		builds	nest.	the Object is a Noun
2	I		know	him.	A Pronoun
3	Peter		gave	Rakesh a pencil.	Indirect & Direct Object
4	children	Naughty	love	fighting.	A gerund or verbal Noun
5	crow	The foolish	tried	to sing.	An infinitive
6	soldiers	Our	tried	to scale the cliff.	'to scale'— an infinitive; 'the cliff'—the object of infinitive verb
7	children	All good	pity	the poor.	An Adjective used as a Noun
8	I		promised	him (i.o.)	a present. (d.o.)
9	He		teaches	us (i.o.)	geometry. (d.o.)
10	Father		bought	Mini (I.O.)	a doll (d.o.)

How an object shaped

527. <u>Study</u>, 'how is an Object shaped?'

| 1. | A Noun: | 1. | I <u>like the **boy**</u>. |
| 2. | A Pronoun: | 2. | We <u>did **it**</u>. |

3.	An Adjective:	3.	Everybody <u>loves the</u> **good**.
4.	An Infinitive:	4.	He <u>likes</u> **to swim**.
5.	A Gerund:	5.	He <u>likes</u> **swimming**.
6.	A Phrase:	6.	I <u>know</u> **how to do it**.
7.	A Clause:	7.	I <u>know</u> **that he did it**.
8.	A Quotation:	8.	He <u>said,</u> **"Do it at once."**

To identify objects properly in the analysis of a sentence, we need to know of them (here briefly; for details go to the chapter of 'Glossary of Objects' & 'Transitive Verbs'.

Study the Objects glossary: including 2 mains

Objects	About them & Examples
Direct Object	The thing or person an action is directly acted upon is called Direct Object. If there are two objects, generally, the inanimate thing tends to be the Direct Object. (However, it may differ.) If there is only one object in the sentence, it is always the Direct Object, irrespective of animal or thing. • I gave him ***a book***.
Indirect Object	An action for whom or to who, or to what is acted, is called the Indirect Object. When there are two objects, the object that refers to man or animal tends to be an Indirect Object. (However, it may also differ.) • I gave ***him*** a book.
Factitive object	When an object of Transitive Verb requires a complement, the verb is called Factitive, and its object is termed as Factitive Object. **A Factitive Object always requires a complement.** • I made ***him*** a fool. (F. O. + complement) • We made ***him*** captain. **'fool'** & **'captain'**—are complements in the sentences.
Cognate object	In case of intransitive verbs **when an object generates from the verb itself.** ('cognate' means originates 'what is similar in meaning') • He runs ***a race***. • She sings ***a song***.
Retained object	It means the object which is left or retained in Passive voice. We learnt a verb may have two or more objects in a sentence. If there are both Direct & Indirect objects, either one takes the place of the subject in Passive, whereas another is retained or left as it was; the left one or retained one object is termed accordingly its meaning. • A book was given **me** by my father. • I was given **a book** by my father.
Reflexive Object	When an object reflects the pronoun in the subject, is called the reflexive object. Read the examples. • They hurt ***themselves.*** • I taught ***myself.***
Infinitive Object	When an infinitive verb forms an object of a verb. • He likes ***to go***. • She loves ***to sing***.
Object of an Infinitive Verb	When an infinitive verb takes an object itself; as, • He likes <u>to go</u> ***to school***. • She loves <u>to sing</u> ***Rabindra Sangeet***.

528. The Points *to be Noted*:

❑ **If a sentence has only one object** (i.e., if a finite verb has only one object) **that must be the Direct Object** (irrespective of animate or inanimate).

❑ *Considering this,* all the above-mentioned objects as, <u>Infinitive Objects</u> (to go, to sing), <u>Reflexive Objects</u> (myself, themselves), <u>Cognate Objects</u> (a race, a song), <u>Factitive Object</u> (him)—are also the **Direct Objects** in the sentences.

❑ In case of the Retained object, either Direct or Indirect object may take the place of a subject, and the other is retained. So, a retained object may be a direct or an indirect.

❑ **Read again**, if there is one, that must be the Direct object, irrespective of animate or inanimate; but, if there are two, Direct object be termed with the most important one, upon whom or which the action is acted upon directly; as,

1. He shot his gun to the castle. (Targeting the castle).
    - ❏ Here, 'gun' is Direct Object, 'castle'—is the Indirect.

2. The police shot him to death. (here 'him' is the direct object. The action is directly acted upon him.)

3. He hit him with a stick.
    - ❏ Here again, 'him' is the Direct Object, while 'a stick' is an Indirect.

4. Teacher gave us some tasks to do at home.
    - ❏ And here, 'tasks' is Direct Object, while 'us' is the Indirect Object.

- ❏ **So, we need must consider the importance of the word, not based upon animate or inanimate to be Direct or Indirect Object in the sentence.**

Attributes or Adjuncts to Object

529.   **Attributes** or **Adjuncts to the Object:** As some words, like adjectives, participles or articles—adds meaning or qualifies the noun or pronouns in the subjects, so as they do also to the objects. **Like subjects,** objects may have the same kinds of **adjuncts or attributes to qualify or add meaning to them**.
Read the followings sentences, and study the adjuncts to the objects:
1. He shot _a big_ **panther**.
2. The world knows **nothing** _more of its greatest men_.
3. The Eskimos make **houses** _of snow & ice_.
4. _Her_ **arms** across her breast she laid. (She laid her arms across her breast.)
5. The architect drew _a_ **plan** for the house.
6. Serpents cast _their_ **skin** once a year.
7. Rock _the_ **baby** to sleep.
8. He enjoys _his master's_ **confidence**.
9. I recognize _his_ **voice** at once.
10. Cut _your_ **coat** according to your cloth.

In the above sentences, the bold words are the examples of **Objects**, when the underlined and italic words are their **adjuncts** or **attributes**.

Study the following charts of Analysis showing the attributes of Objects:

Sl. No	Subject		Predicate			
	Subject-word	_Attribute_	_Verb_	_Object_	_Object attribute/ Complement_	_Adverbial Qualification Or others_
1	He		shot	panther.	_a big_	
2	world	The	knows	nothing	_of its greatest men._	_more_
3	Eskimos	The	make	houses	_of snow & ice._	
4	she		laid.	arms	_Her_	across her breast
5	architect	The	drew	plan	_a_	for the house.
6	Serpents		cast	skin	_their_	once a year.
7			Rock	baby	_the_	to sleep
8	He		enjoys	confidence.	_his master's_	
9	I		recognize	voice	_his_	at once.

10			Cut	coat	_your_	according to your cloth

Complement (Subjective or Objective)

530.   A complement is **a word** or **a phrase** or **a clausal structure** that completes the meaning of a **noun or noun equivalent that are used either as a subject or an object**. Thus, complements are subjective or objective.
In case of Intransitive (or Linking) verb, when verbs require more words other than the simple predicate and adverbials, the words are termed as subjective complement which generally complete the sense of the subject; as,
He is a student. (Here, student is a complement to the intransitive verb. And as it refers back to the subject, it is called subjective complement.)

A complement itself is usually a noun or an adjective, a verb form like to be a or a participle or a gerund, an infinitive verb, or an adverb, used as an adjective or a clausal structure like –ing clause **or** 'wh' clause.

Study the chart:

Complement may be used as both - subjective & objective.

36	
1. Adjective	• We are ready. (subjective) • We made him happy. (objective)
2. Participle	• It looks charming. • I found him tired.
3. Noun	• He was appointed chairman. • He called me a traitor.
4. Possessive	• The book is mine, not Ram's. • He made my cause his own.
5. Infinite	• The water seems to boil. We saw him to go • I heard him say this. We saw him go / going.
6. Noun Clause	• The report is that he is ill. • We make ourselves what we are.

531.   **Study the following sentences, and identify complements after separate the complete predicates.**
   1.   Black clouds are gathering. The sky grew **dark**.
   2.   The boys have been reading. They are dancing.
   3.   She spoke distinctly. The boy ran a mile. He is **worried**.
   4.   He is a **student**. I was a **teacher**. He **is professional**.
   5.   Venus is a **planet**. It is **me**. The workman seems **tired**.
   6.   The book is there. The house is **to let**. Shyamali is **he, not she**.
   7.   The building is **in a dilapidated condition**. John became a **soldier**.
   8.   Roses smell **sweet**. The child appears **pleased**.

The Underlines are the complete Predicates, whereas the words in bold are Complements to the Subject. The complements are generally a noun, or pronoun, an Adjective, infinite or others. (Study in details in the respective chapter of verb & complement.)

532. **Exercise-3**

Underline the complete Predicate first & then pick out the complement in each of the following sentences, and say whether it is a Noun, an Adjective, or others.:

1) The earth is round. He looks happy. Sugar taste sweet.
2) The old woman is dead. The weather is cold. The child is there.
3) He became unconscious. He is a good type of the modern athlete.
4) The old gentle man is of a gentle disposition.
5) The children look healthy. To-day she seems sad.
6) The cup is full to the brim. His grammar is hocking.
7) Ugly rumors are about him and his girl-friend.
8) Peter and his quarrelsome spouse were never a pride of their village, and there were more two such couples.
9) This morning he seems in a good spirit. Giving to the poor is lending to the Lord.
10) The matter appears of considerable importance. Every man is the architect of his own fortune.

533. **Transitive Verbs of Incomplete Predication & Objective Complement:**

We said, a transitive verb has object or objects. But, sometimes, Transitive verb too requires a complement. In spite have its object the verb cannot complete its sense. It requires then extra words beside the object. The extra word or words are known as Complement. As it actually completes the sense of the object, the complement is known as **Objective Complement**. Read the examples:

1) The boys made Rama Captain.
2) The jury found him guilty.
3) His parents named him Peter.
4) He kept us waiting.
5) Nothing will make him repent.
6) His words filled them with terror.
7) Shyam called his cousin a genius.
8) Exercise has made his muscles strong.
9) He kept us in suspense.
10) The court appointed him the guardian of the orphan child.

Study the following chart relating Object & Objective Complement:

Sl. No	Subject		Predicate		
	Subject-word	Attribute	Verb	Object	Complement
1	boys	The	made	Rama	Captain.
2	jury	The	found	him	guilty.
3	parents	His	named	him	Peter.
4	He		kept us		waiting.
5	Nothing		will make	him	repent.
6	words	His	filled	them	with terror.
7	Shyam		called	his cousin	a genius.
8	Exercise		has made	his muscles	strong.
9	He		kept us		in suspense.
10	court	The	appointed	him	The guardian of the orphan child.

534. **Adjuncts to Subject or Object & Adv. Adjuncts:** Adverbial adjuncts are often confounded with complements. It is well to remember that words, phrases or clauses which show — *how*, *when*, *why* or *where* an action is performed, are adverbial adjuncts. <u>The adverbial adjuncts directly modify the verbs,</u> whereas, the <u>complements are related to Subjects or Objects</u> in the sentences. However, here we will compare **the adjuncts to subjects** and **the adverbial adjuncts** in the sentences. Read the chart:

As adjuncts to subject	As adverbial adjuncts to predicate
1. The **defeated** team also got a cup. (adj. equivalent)	1. She went away **laughing**. (adv. equivalent)
2. The **crying** woman arrived there.	2. I saw a tiger **roaring**.
3. The **bereaved** mother came to Lord Buddha.	3. The woman disappeared **weeping**.
4. The **laughing** girls are students.	4. The cow is seen **wounded**.

Infinitive & Gerundial Infinitive

535. Know the use of **'gerundial infinitive'**. When an infinitive is used with a Noun or a Pronoun to form subject or object is called so. <u>A Gerundial Infinitive can be used both in the subject & in the predicate group.</u> Study the chart, how do they form & work:

In subject group	In predicate group

❏ Examination <u>to pass</u> is not so hard. (adj. equivalent)
   ○ Noun with infinitive verb
❏ Women <u>to consider</u> mother was a great teaching of Lord Ramakrishna.
❏ To love her was a good experience.
	❏ He went to market to buy medicine. (adv. equivalent)
	   ○ Noun with infinitive verb
	❏ His teachings were to develop inner possibilities.
	❏ My friend came to see me.

See the difference between: **Infinitive** & **Gerundial Infinitive**

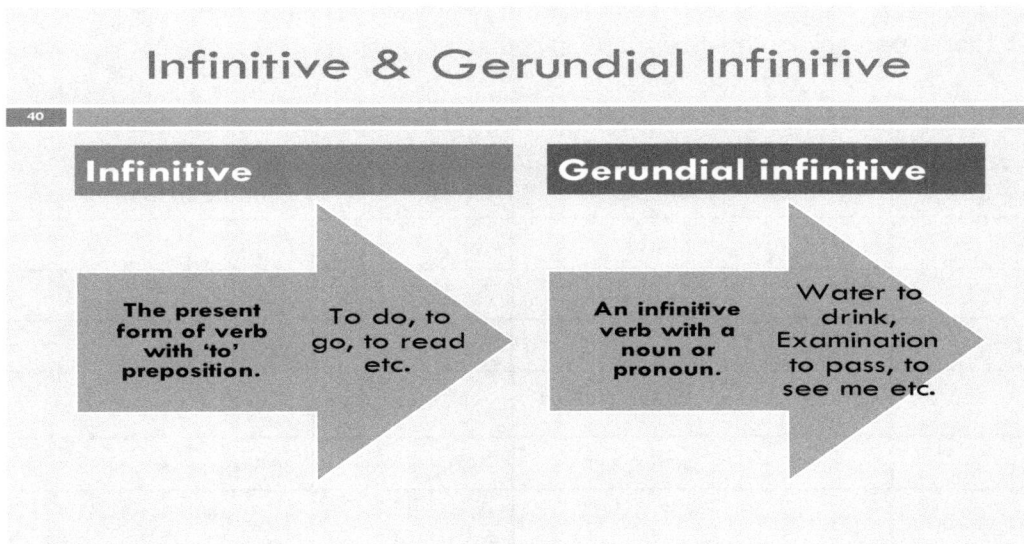

536. A Preposition generally precedes before a Noun or a Pronoun, we learnt it in the chapter of Preposition. The noun after a preposition is sometimes known as the 'object of a preposition.' Here we will see through chart how a **Preposition is used with a Noun** both in subject & object group.

In Subject	In Predicate

1.	A man **of principle** is respected by all.	1.	All respect a man **of principle**.
2.	Arriving in time is our habit.	2.	We arrived **in time**.
3.	A girl **in the garden** is seen watering plants by all.	3.	I saw a girl **in the garden** watering the plants
4.	Dry leaves **falling from trees,** is a natural sight.	4.	The dry leaves fall *from* **the trees.**
5.	The book **on the table** is mine.	5.	I place my book **on the table**
➤	In subject they are adjective equivalent: mostly a preposition with noun as a qualifying part or adj.	➤	In predicate they are, besides an adjective equivalent, also they sometimes **do function of an adverbial**, used as modifiers to the verbs, to an adjective or to another adverb.

537.   The role of a Part of Speech may alternatively be changed according to uses and needs. Study the alternative use of adverb & adjective:

Use of adv. as adj. in sub. group	Use of adj. as adv. in pred. group
1. The **fast** train derailed this morning.	1. He breathed **ice/dead**.
2. **The then** Prime Minister had signed the treaty.	2. She sang **happy**.

538.   Drawing Conclusion to the **Analysis of a Simple Sentence.** Read the Sentences and analyze them into Subject & Predicate Group and show their adjuncts or adverbial qualification:

1.   Dushshashan, quite pale with fright, rushed from the battle field.
2.   Determination to do one's duty is laudable.
3.   Around the fire, one wintry night, the farmer's rosy children sat.
4.   Home they brought the warrior dead.
5.   His friends elected him secretary of the club.
6.   This circumstance certainly makes the matter very serious.
7.   My uncle has been teaching me mathematics.
8.   Who are you?

Study the Analysis of the (Simple) Sentences

Sl. No	Subject		Predicate			
	Subject-word	*Attribute*	*Verb*	*Object*	*Complement*	*Adverbial Qualification*
1	Dushshashan	quite pale with fright	rushed			from the battlefield
2	Determination	to do one's duty	is		laudable	
3	children	the farmer', rosy	sat			Around the fire, one wintry nigh,
4	they		brought	the warrior	dead	Home
5	friends	His	elected	him	secretary of the club.	
6	circumstances	This	makes	the matter	very serious	certainly
7	uncle	My	has been teaching	mathematics, me		
8	you		are		Who	

Read some more examples:

1.   The other day my younger brother saw two men fighting each other.

429

2. The Judge, accepting the verdict of the jury, found the prisoner tremendously guilty.
3. On hearing of my misfortune, all my friends ran to my help.
4. An intelligent boy, the son of a very poor man, badly needs your help to be able to continue his studies.

Study another phase of Analysis of Simple Sentences

Adjunct to Subject	Subject Proper	Finite Verb	Object with Adjectives	Complement	Adverbial Adjunct
my younger	brother	saw	two men	fighting with each other	The other day
The, accepting the verdict of the jury	Judge	found	the prisoner	guilty	tremendously
all my, On hearing my misfortune	friends	ran	----	----	to my help
An, Intelligent, the son of a very poor man	boy	needs	your help	to be able to continue his studies	badly

39. Analysis of Compound & Complex Sentence

539.   The Analysis of a Sentence (Compound & Complex) refers to the 'breakdown the sentence (compound or complex) primarily into – Principal, Co-ordinate & Sub-ordinate Clauses, and then, if necessary, to breakdown each clause further as Subject and Predicate and according to their adjuncts or extensions (as we have done with a Simple Sentence in the previous chapter).

Analysis of a compound sentence

540. **Read the Sentences:**
  1. All good children pity the poor, and poor the poorest.
  2. Naughty children love fighting, do you?
  3. Our soldiers tried to scale the cliff and they did succeed.
  4. He came to see me when I was in trouble; but when I asked him for pecuniary help, he pleaded inability.
  5. On my return from school, I went to my mother to ask for food; but I found that she was lying ill of fever and my younger sister was nursing her.

541.   **In analyzing a Compound Sentence,**
a) First, <u>break up the sentence into as many clauses as there are units of Finite Verbs,</u> expressed or understood (each unit finite verb takes the main and helping verbs together);
b) Identify Principal & Co-ordinate Clauses;
c) Identify any Sub-Ordinate Clause, if any there is, and show their relation with the Principal or the Co-ordinate;
d) Next, <u>analyze each clause separately,</u> if necessary or asked by your teacher; otherwise, for exams, generally, mere clause analysis is enough.

You may check the analysis of the above five sentences in the following way, as given in the chart. Study thoroughly:

a)	b)	c)	d)

	Principal Clause	*Sub-ordinate with Principal*	*Co-ordinate Clause*	*Sub-ordinate with Co-ordinate*
1.	All good children pity the poor,		and poor the poorest.	
2.	Naughty children love fighting,		(and) do you?	
3.	Our soldiers tried to scale the cliff		and they did succeed.	
4.	He came to see me	when I was in trouble;	But... he pleaded inability.	when I asked him for pecuniary help,
5.	On my return from school, I went to my mother to ask for food;		i) but I found ... ii) and my younger sister was nursing her.	that she was lying ill of fever

542. **Read again for more examples:**
1. Though I was ill, I tried my best; but, as ill luck would have it, all my exertion ended in smoke.
2. Long ago, when I was yet a student, I once went to Darjeeling, where I was charmed by the beautiful mountain scenery that greeted me on all sides.

If we analyze the sentences accordingly the above, follow the chart:

	a) *Principal Clause*	b) *Sub-ordinate with Principal*	c) *Co-ordinate Clause*	d) *Sub-ordinate with Co-ordinate*
1.	I tried my best;	Though I was ill,	but, all my exertion ended in smoke.	as ill luck would have it,
2.	Long ago, I once went to Darjeeling,	when I was yet a student,	Where (and there) I was charmed by the beautiful mountain scenery	that greeted me on all sides.

As per clauses, the above two sentences have been analyzed. Now, if we want further analysis of the above clauses as **subject**, **predicate**, **adjuncts to subjects** and **extension to the predicate**, then, we should follow the next step (what we have done with simple sentences).

Sl. No	Clauses	Kind of Clause	Subject			Predicate			
			Connective	Subject Proper	Adjuncts to Subject	Predicate Verb	Object with adjuncts	Complement	Adv. Adjuncts
1-a)	I tried my best	Principal		I		tried	my best.		
b)	Though I was ill	Adv Clause	though	I		was		ill.	
c)	but... all my exertion ended in smoke	Co-ordinate	but	exertion	all my	ended			in smoke.
d)	as ill luck have it	Adv Clause	as	luck	ill	have	it		

2-a)	Long ago, I once went to Darjeeling	Principal		I		went			Long ago, once, To Darjeeling
b)	When I was yet a student	Adv Clause	when	I		Was		A student	yet
c)	Where I was charmed by the beautiful mountain scenery	Co-ordinate	Where (=and there)	I		Was charmed	By the … scenery		
d)	that greeted me on all sides.	Adjective Clause	that (understood)	that (=the scenery)		greeted	me		On all sides.

543.   **Exercise-1**

Analyze the following compound sentences:

1. I am sorry that you have disobeyed my orders; however, as this is my first offence, I let you off this time with a simple warning, and hope you will not give me any trouble in future.
2. We should all love India, where we were born and which is one of oldest countries in the world, and should never do anything that may bring discredit upon her in any way.
3. Just as the destruction was completed Newton opened the chamber door, and perceived that the labors of twenty years were reduced to a heap of ashes.
4. I was in the same school with the person you speak of; but as he was senior to me by a few years we did not mix much with each other.

To do so, use the following table, or make such ones, after the first step:

Complete Analysis of a Compound

SI. No	Clauses	Kind of Clause	Subject			Predicate			
			Connective	Subject Proper	Adjuncts to Subject	Predicate Verb	Object with adjuncts	Complement	Adv. Adjuncts
1									
2									
3									
4									
5									

Analysis of a complex sentence

544.   In analyzing a Complex Sentence, we have to do almost same thing, we did for a Compound.

First, to divide a complex sentence into clauses, based on number of the unit of Finite Verbs. Identify their types, as Principal, Sub-ordinate or Co-ordinate clauses. If need further analysis, have to follow the next step what is done with a simple sentence.

Study the sentences:

1.   When I was a student, I was one day taken to task by the Principal of my college for having played on behalf of an outside club, though he had ordered us not to do so.
2.   Having been informed that my brother who had gone to Delhi to attend the Legislative Assembly was lying seriously ill of fever there, I applied for one week's leave of absence in order that I might go to him to arrange for proper treatment.

Study the analysis (**first step into clauses**):

Clauses	Kind of Clause	Connectives
(a) I was one day...of an outside club (b) When I was a student (c) though he ...not to do so	Principal clause Sub. Adv. Clause, qualifying '**was taken** in (a)' Sub. Adv. Clause, qualifying '**having played** in (a)'	when though
2. (a) Having been **informed**, I **applied for** one week's leave of absence (b) That **my brother** was lying seriously ill of fever there (c) Who had gone to Delhi to attend the Legislative Assembly (d) In order that I might go to him to arrange for proper treatment.	Principal clause Sub- Noun Clause, object to verb '**informed**' in (a) in participle form Sub. Adj. Clause, describing '**my brother**' in (b)' Sub. Adv. Clause, describing '**applied for**' in (a)'	that who In order that

Now further analysis of the above clauses as '**subject**', '**predicate**', '**adjuncts to subject**' and '**extension to the predicate**' (The 2nd step of analysis).

Adjunct to Subject	Subject Proper	Finite Verb	Object with Adj.	Complement	Adverbial Adjunct
	I	was taken	by the Principal of my college	to task	one day, for having played on behalf of an outside club,
	I	was		a student	when
	He	had ordered	us		not to do so
Having been informed	I	applied			for one week's leave of absence
my	Brother	was lying			seriously ill of fever there
	who	had gone			to Delhi to attend the L. Assembly

I	might go		to him to arrange for proper treatment.

545. A Few Difficulties in Analysis

1. In case "Quoted sentences": -

❖ **He said**, "I cannot come to you today. My brother is ill and I have to attend on him. You may, however, expect me tomorrow."

→ **The quotation consists of three sentences**, which cannot be taken separately in their relation to the principal verb '**said**', three sentences together act as the **object** to the verb, '**said**'.

→ The quotation has been taken in this case **as a long compound word**, a **noun equivalent**, and object to some transitive verb. Here, it is 'said'; as, — I said, "**I am ill**". What did I say? = that I am ill = an object to the verb 'said'.

→ I was surprised by his '**I don't care**' attitude (a **compound adjective** describing the noun 'attitude')

→ However, if we treat each sentence separately, analysis is same, as we did of earlier simple sentences.

2. 'Parenthetic' expressions or phrases:

1) He is, **I am sure**, something of a poet.
2) His conduct, **I believe**, is good.
3) Why do you, my friend, **I don't know**, hate me?
4) Why do you, **it is not clear**, not talk to me now-a-days?
5) But you should, **I am likely agreed**, do so.

→ All the above are simple sentences while the **bold written words are parenthetic expressions**; almost like the 'Phrase or Noun in apposition'.

→ As phrase in apposition, the parenthetic expressions **are thrown into the sentence, to provide more information to the main** and they easily can be taken out without injuring the sense of the main.

→ 'Parenthetic expressions or Phrases' can be analyzed separately, as an independent sentence.

❑ **'Parenthetic'** expressions in compound

1) He is, **I am sure**, something of a poet & his poetry are too good to read by others.
2) His conduct, **I believe**, is good & too good to converse with.
3) Why do you, my friend, **I don't know**, give me light and snatch it away?
4) Why do you, it **is not clear**, begin to talk and stop forever?

→ All the above are compound sentences with two principals while the **bold written words are parenthetic expressions**; and they can be analyzed separately, as told already. In the sentences they **are thrown to provide more information to the main sentence, subject or verb**; and they may be taken out without injuring the sense of the main.

❑ **'Parenthetic'** expressions in complex

1) He is, **I am sure**, something of a poet who reads alone his poetry.
2) His conduct, **I believe**, is what is not suitable for his own age.
3) He is the man who, **I believe**, did it.
4) This is the boy who, **I think**, came the other day.

→ All the above are complex sentences with only one principal & one sub-ordinate clauses while the **bold written words are parenthetic expressions**; and they can be analyzed separately as independent sentence.

→ **Like Parenthetic Expressions,** there are also the '**Parenthetic Phrases**'.

❑ Some more Parenthetic Phrases

1) He is, **to tell the truth**, not quite frank.
2) I was, **to be frank**, much surprised.
3) I am, **of me**, ok.

→ In above all cases, the '**phrases within commas before & after**', can be analyzed separately and similarly can be taken out without injuring the main sense.

3. In case introductory- 'There' & 'It'

1) <u>There</u> is a man here. (A man is here/Here is a man.)
2) <u>There</u> was once a king in India, named Dasaratha.

= (Once a king, named Dasaratha lived in India.)

→ 'There' in the above cases have <u>lost its force of meaning as an adverb of place</u>, and are used only to introduce the sentence.
→ As custom '<u>**There**</u>' will fall in the group as an **Adv. adjunct** but <u>it is better to treat it</u> as '<u>**Introductory Subject**</u>' as— '<u>**It**</u> is raining.'

546. Exercise-2, **Analyze the following Complex Sentences:**
  a) I know that he was absent at that time.
  b) There is no knowing when he will come.
  c) Tell me where she lives.
  d) Had I been present there, sure I opposed this.
  e) It is a misfortune that you could not do anything.
  f) You can never expect that, because you are talented, others will willingly make way for you in order that you may go ahead of them.
  g) As I was absent at the time the incident took place, I had to depend for information about it on my friend who had seen everything with his own eyes from his house that stood close by.
  h) The two men, who were following a few yards behind me, came to a halt when they saw me stop.

40. Synthesis, or Joining of Simple Sentences

547. Literally, '**Synthesis**' is nearly the <u>opposite term of</u> '**Analysis**', <u>and yet to be different</u>; whereas, it is ***nearest the opposite*** of the word '**split-up**'.

The term '**Synthesis**' means '**Joining of Simple Sentences**' to make a larger Simple Sentence, or a Compound or Complex Sentence; So, we will discuss this chapter under three main heads:

  A. Synthesis of Simple Sentences to make <u>a Simple Sentence</u> (other than they were),
  B. Synthesis of Simple Sentences to make <u>a Compound Sentence,</u>
  C. Synthesis of Simple Sentences to make <u>a Complex Sentence.</u>

On the other hand, '**Split-up**' means **to break up a sentence to make as far possible independent sentences** (**not like:** what actually 'Analysis' does). In split-up, we try to give independent form of the essential or important parts of a sentence to make as far possible smaller independent simple sentences. Read more about it in the next chapter.

  A. Synthesis of Simple Sentences to make <u>a Simple Sentence</u> (other than they were),
The following are the chief ways of combining two or more Simple sentences into one or single Simple Sentence:
  a) By using a Participle,

b) By using an Infinitive,
c) By using a Preposition with a Noun or Gerund,
d) By using a Noun or a Phrase in Apposition,
e) By using the Nominative Absolute Construction,
f) By using an Adverb or Adverbial Phrase.

To make Single Simple Sentence

a) **By using a Participle:**
- He jumped up. He ran away.
  = *Jumping up*, he ran away.
- He was tired of play. He sat down to rest.
  = *Tired* (or, *being tired*) of play, he sat down to rest.

b) **By using an Infinitive:**
- I have some duties. I must perform them.
  = I have some duties *to perform*.
- He wanted to educate his son. He sent him to Nalanda.
  = He sent his son to Nalanda *to educate* him.
- He is very fat. He cannot run. = He is too fat *to run*.

c) **By using a Preposition with a Noun or a Gerund:**
- He has failed many times. He still hopes to succeed.
  = *In spite of failures* many times he hopes to succeed.
- Her husband died. She heard the news. She fainted.
  = *On hearing* the news of her husband's death, she fainted.

d) **By using a Noun or Phrase in Apposition:**
- Mr. Pranab Mukherjee was elected the President of India. He was the Finance Minister of India before that.
  = Mr. Pranab Mukherjee, *the former Finance Minister of India*, was elected the President of India.
- Geoffrey Chaucer was born in 1340. He is the first great English Poet.
  = Geoffrey Chaucer, *the first great English poet*, was born in 1340.

e) **By using the Nominative Absolute Construction:**
- The soldiers arrived. The mob dispersed.
  = *The soldiers having arrived*, the mob dispersed.
- The town was enclosed by a strong wall. The enemy was unable to capture it.
  = *The town having been enclosed by a strong wall*; the enemy was unable to capture it.

f) **By using an Adverb or Adverbial Phrase:**
- The sun set. The boy had not finished the game.
  = The boys had not finished the game *by sunset*.
- The Moon rose. The journey was not ended.
  = The Moon rose *before the end of the journey*.

Now, read in details

548. Joining by use of a **Participle**: (for more practice) (1)

1. The magician took pity on the mouse. He turned it into a cat.
   = ***Taking** pity on the mouse*, the magician turned it into a cat.
2. We started early. We arrived at noon.
   = ***Starting** early*, we arrived at noon.
3. We met a man. He was carrying a log of wood.
   = We met *a man **carrying** a log of wood.
4. He seized his stick. He rushed to the door.
   = ***Seizing** his stick*, he rushed to the door.
5. The hunter took up his gun. He went out to shoot the lion.

436

= ***Taking*** *up his gun,* the hunter went out to shoot the lion.

6. A crow stole a piece of cheese. She flew to her nest to enjoy the tasty meal.
   = ***Stealing*** *a piece of cheese,* the female crow flew to her nest to enjoy the tasty meal.
7. The wolf wished to pick a quarrel with the lamb. He said, "How dare you make the water muddy?"
   = ***Wishing*** *to pick a quarrel with the lamb,* the wolf said, "How dare you make the water muddy?"
8. A passenger alighted from the train. He fell over a bag on the platform.
   = ***Alighting*** *from the train,* the passenger fell over a bag on the platform.

9. Nanak met his brother in the street. He asked him where he was going.
   = ***Meeting*** *his brother in the street,* Nanak asked him where he was going?
10. My sister was charmed with the silk. She bought ten yards.
    = ***Being charmed*** *with the silk,* my sister bought ten yards.
11. The steamer was delayed by a storm. She came into port a day late.
    = ***Being delayed*** *by a storm* the steamer came into port a day late.
12. He had resolved on a certain course. He acted with vigor.
    = ***Having resolved*** *on a certain course,* he acted with vigor.
13. He staggered back. He sank to the ground.
    = ***Staggering*** *back,* he sank to the ground.
14. They had no fodder. They could give the cow nothing to eat.
    = ***Having*** *no fodder,* they could give the cow nothing to eat.
15. A hungry fox saw some bunches of grapes. They were hanging from a vine.
    = A hungry fox saw some bunches of *grapes* ***hanging*** from a vine.
16. Cinderella hurried away with much haste. She dropped one of her little glass slippers.
    = ***Hurrying*** *away with much hasty,* Cinderella dropped one of her little glass slippers.

549. Joining by use of an **Infinitive** (for practice) (2)

1) Napoleon was one of the greatest of Generals. He is universally acknowledged so.
   = Napoleon is universally acknowledged ***to be*** one of the greatest Generals.
2) He did not have even a rupee with him. He could not buy a loaf of bread.
   = He did not have even a rupee with him ***to buy*** a loaf of bread.
3) Every cricket team has a captain. He directs the other players.
   = Every cricket team has a captain ***to direct*** the other players.
4) You must part with your purse. On this condition only you can save your life.
   = You must part with your purse ***to save*** your life.
5) He went to Amritsar. He wanted to visit the Golden Temple.
   = He went to Amritsar ***to visit*** the Golden Temple.
6) The robber took out a knife. He intended to frighten the old man.
   = The robber took out a knife ***to frighten*** the old man.
7) He wants to earn his livelihood. He works hard for that reason.
   = He works hard ***to earn*** his livelihood.
8) The strikers held a meeting. They wished to discuss the terms of the employers.
   = The strikers held a meeting ***to discuss*** the terms of the employers.
9) He has five children. He must provide for them.
   = He has five children ***to provide*** for them.
10) I speak the truth. I am not afraid of it.
    = I am not afraid ***to speak*** the truth.
11) The old man has now little energy left. He cannot take his morning constitutional exercises.
    = The old man has now little energy left even ***to take*** his morning constitutional exercises.
12) The Rajah allowed no cows to be slaughtered in his territory. It was his custom.
    = It was the Rajah's custom not ***to allow*** cows to be slaughtered in his territory.
13) He formed a resolution. It was to the effect that he would not speculate any more.
    = He formed a resolution to the effect ***not to speculate*** any more.
14) Everyone should do his duty. India expects this of every man.
    = India expects every man ***to do*** his duty.
15) She visits the poor. She is anxious to relieve them of their sufferings.
    = She visits the poor ***to relieve*** them of their sufferings.
16) He collects old stamps even at great expense. This is his hobby.
    = This is his hobby ***to collect*** old stamps even at great expense.

17) He must apologize for his misconduct. It is the only way to escape punishment.

= He must apologize for his misconduct **to escape** punishment.

18) I have no aptitude for business. I must speak it out frankly.

= **To speak it out frankly**, I have no aptitude for business.

19) He was desirous of impressing his host. So, he was on his best behavior in his presence.

= He was on his best behavior in the presence of his host **to impress** him.

20) He has risen to eminence from poverty and obscurity. It is highly creditable.

= It is highly creditable of him **to rise** to eminence from poverty and obscurity.

550.   Synthesis by use of '**Prepositions with Nouns** or **Gerunds**' (for more Practice) (3)

1) He was ill during the last term. He was unable to attend the school.

= **Due to ill** during the last term, he was unable to attend the school.

2) I forgave her faults. That has not prevented her from repeating it.

= **In spite of forgiving** her faults that has not prevented her from repeating it.

3) The word of command will be given. You will then fire.

= You will fire **on having** the word of command.

4) He set traps every night. He cleared his house of rats.

= **By setting** traps every night, he cleared his house of rats.

5) The judge gave his decision. The court listened silently.

= **On silence** of the court, the judge gave his decision.

6) He has a good record. It is impossible to suspect such a man.

= **Due to good record**, it is impossible to suspect such a man.

7) You helped me. Otherwise, I should have been drowned.

= **On having** your help, I am saved from drowning.

8) I have examined the statement. I find many errors in them.

= **On examining** the statement, I find many errors in them.

9) It rained hard. The streets were flooded.

= **On raining** hard, the streets were flooded.

10) He amused us very much. He sang a funny song.

= **By singing** a funny song, he amused us very much.

551.   Synthesis by use of '**Nouns** or **Phrase in Apposition**' (for more practice) (4)

1) There goes my brother. He is called Rama.

= There goes my brother, **Rama**.

2) The cow provides milk. Milk is a valuable food.

= The cow provides milk, **a valuable food**.

3) Coal is a very important mineral. It is hard, bright, black & brittle.

= Coal, **a hard, bright, black & brittle substance**, is a very important mineral.

4) We saw the picture. It is a very fine piece of work.

= We saw the picture, **a very fine piece of work**.

5) Tagore's one of the most famous works is Gitanjali. Gitanjali is a collection of short poems.

= Tagore's one of the most famous works is Gitanjali, **a collection of short poems.**

6) Nicky's mom was a millionaire. She sent him to Australia for his higher education.

= Nicky's mom, **a millionaire**, sent him to Australia for his higher education.

7) Bagha was my faithful dog. After his death I never took another as my pet.

= After death of my Bagha, **a faithful dog**, I never took another as my pet.

8) Jawaharlal Nehru died in 1964. He was the first Prime Minister of India.

= Jawaharlal Nehru, **the first Prime Minister of India**, died in 1964.

9) He is selected as our captain. He is the first boy of our class.

= He, **the first boy of our class**, is selected as our captain.

10) His only son died before him. He was a lad of great promise.

= His only son, **a lad of great promise**, died before him.

552.   Synthesis by use of '**Nominative Absolute Phrase**' (for practice) (5):

When subjects are different, Nominative Absolute is popularly used for the Synthesis; as,

1) His friend arrived. He was very pleased.

= *His friend having arrived*; he was very pleased. (**On arrival of his friend**, he was very pleased: **By Preposition with a Noun**)

2) The rain fell. The crops revived.

= *The rain having fallen*, the crops revived.

3) The storm ceased. The sun came out.
   = *The storm having ceased*; the sun came out.
4) The holidays are at an end. Boys are returning to school.
   = *The holidays being at an end*, boys are returning to school.
5) It was a very hot day. I could not do my work satisfactorily.
   = *The day being very hot*, I could not do my work satisfactorily.
6) The king died. His fitting son came to the throne.
   = *The king having dead*, his fitting son came to the throne.
7) His father was dead. He had to support his widowed mother.
   = *Father being dead*, the son had to support his widowed mother.
8) Rain was plentiful this year. Rice is cheap everywhere.
   = *Rain being plentiful this year*, rice is cheap everywhere.
9) The prisoner was questioned. No witness came forward. The judge dismissed the case.
   = *The prisoner being questioned and no witness came forward*, the judge dismissed the case.
10) The letter was badly written. I had great difficulty in making out its contents.
    = *The letter being badly written*, I had great difficulty in making out its contents.
11) The sun rose. The fog cleared away. The light house was less than a mile away.
    = *The sun having risen*, the fog cleared away to see the light house less than a mile away.
12) The train was ready to leave the station. The passengers had taken their seats.
    = *The passengers having taken their seats*; the train was ready to leave.
13) The porter opened the gate. We entered.
    = *The gate being opened by the porter*, we entered.
14) The stable door was open. The horse was stolen.
    = *The stable door being open*, the horse was stolen.

553. Synthesis by use of **an Adverb** or **Adverbial Phrase** (6):
   1) He answered me. His answer was correct.
      = He answered me *correctly*.
   2) He forgot his umbrella. That was careless.
      = He forgot his umbrella *carelessly*.
   3) The man is dead. It is certain.
      = *Certainly,* the man is dead.
   4) The train is very late. That was usual.
      = *Usually,* the train is very late.
   5) I shall come back. I shall not be long.
      = I shall come back *for a short duration*.
   6) He kicked the goal-keeper. It was his intension to do so.
      = He kicked the goal-keeper *intentionally*.
   7) She was obstinate. She refused to listen to any advice.
      = She *obstinately* refused to listen any advice.
   8) He spent his all money. This was foolish.
      = He *foolishly* spent his all money.
   9) He appealed for leave. It was not granted.
      = *Vainly* he appealed for leave.
   10) It must be done. The cost does not count.
       = It must be done *at any cost*. (Adverb of Manner; also, can say: Preposition with a Noun)

554. **Exercise-1:** Combine the following set of sentences into Single Simple Sentences (Miscellaneous):
a) He was a leader. He did not follow other men. Such was his nature.
b) I bought this hat two years ago. It is still good. It is fit to wear.
c) He devoted himself to public affairs. He never took a holiday. This continued for thirty years.
d) The man was innocent. He could defend himself. He refused to speak. He was afraid of convincing his friend.
e) He stuck his foot against a stone. He fell to the ground. He made his clothes very dirty.
f) He goes to school. She wishes to learn. He wants to grow up honest, healthy and clever.
g) There was a man hiding in my garden. He was armed with a gun. He was a Pathan. My notice was drawn to it.
h) The soldiers were starving. Their ammunition was expended. Their clothes were in rags. Their leaders were dead. The enemy easily defeated them.

Check your Answer, Exercise-1:

Combine the following set of sentences into Single Simple Sentences (Miscellaneous):
- He was a leader. He did not follow other men. Such was his nature.
a) Being a leader, not to follow other men, was his nature.
- I bought this hat two years ago. It is still good. It is fit to wear.
b) This hat, bought two years ago, is still good and fit to wear.
- He devoted himself to public affairs. He never took a holiday. This continued for thirty years.
c) Devoting himself to public affairs, he never took a holiday for thirty years.
- The man was innocent. He could defend himself. He refused to speak. He was afraid of convincing his friend.
d) Being afraid of convincing his friend and yet having ability to defend himself, the innocent he refused to speak.
- He stuck his foot against a stone. He fell to the ground. He made his clothes very dirty.
e) Sticking his foot against a stone, he fell to the ground, making his clothes dirty.
- He goes to school. She wishes to learn. He wants to grow up honest, healthy and clever.
f) In order to learn, grow up honest, healthy and clever he goes to school.
- There was a man hiding in my garden. He was armed with a gun. He was a Pathan. My notice was drawn to it.
g) My notice was drawn to an armed Pathan hiding in my garden.
- The soldiers were starving. Their ammunition was expended. Their clothes were in rags. Their leaders were dead. The enemy easily defeated them.
h) Being starved, ammunition expended, clothes in rug & leaderless, easily they were defeated by the enemy.

To make a Compound Sentence

B. Synthesis of Simple Sentences (two or more) to make <u>a Compound Sentence:</u>

Simple Sentences may be combined to form a Compound Sentence <u>by the use of</u> **Co-ordinate Conjunctions**. There are <u>four kinds of Co-ordinate Conjunctions</u>; all can be used to form Compound Sentences; as,

A) *Joining by* **Cumulative Conjunctions**, when the sentences express ideas of equal rank. Such conjunctions are— and, also, too, as well as, both—and, not only—but also, etc.
   1) We carved not a line, **and** we raised not a stone.
   2) God made the country **and** man, made the town.
   3) Vishal & Virat are good bowlers. (Vishal is a good bowler & Virat is a good bowler.)

B) *Joining by* **Adversative Conjunctions**, when expressing ideas contrast each other. Such conjunctions are — still, yet, only, but, however, nevertheless, though—yet, etc.
   4) Our hoard is little, **but** our hearts are great.
   5) The man is poor, **but** honest. (The man is poor, but he is honest.)
   6) He is slow, **but** he is sure. I was annoyed, **still** I kept quiet.
   7) I would come; **only** that I am engaged. He was all right; **only** he was fatigued.

C) *Joining by* **Alternative Conjunctions**, when two or more sentences express alternation or selection between two or more. The conjunctions are— either...or, neither...nor, whether, or, etc.:
   8) She must weep, **or** she will die. **Either** he is mad, **or** he feigns madness.
   9) Is that story true **or** false? **Neither** a borrower, **nor** a lender be.
   10) We can travel by land **or** water. They toil not, **neither** do they spin.
   11) **Either** you are mistaken, **or** I am. Walk quickly, **else** you will not overtake him.

D) *Joining by* **Illative Conjunctions**, for the sentences which express inference, or conclusion type ideas. The conjunctions are— therefore, for, so, then, so then, etc.:
   12) Something certainly fell in; **for** I heard a splash.
   13) All precautions must have been neglected, **for** the plague spread rapidly.

555.   More Examples of Compound Sentences. Hope, you understand <u>which simple sentences there are</u>:
   1) The moon was bright **and** we could see our way.
   2) Night came on **and** rain fell heavily **and** we got very wet.
   3) I shall do it now **or** I shall not do it at all.
   4) He gave them no money **nor** he did he help them anyway.
   5) He threw the stone **but** it missed the target.

440

6) He **neither** obtains success **nor** deserves it.
7) He is **either** mad **or** he has become a criminal.
8) He helped me, **which** (=and this/it) was very kind of him.
9) I went to Kolkata, **where** (=and there) I stayed for one month.
10) I went to the Principal, **who** (=and he) spoke kindly to me.

556. **Exercise:** Combine each set of Simple Sentences to make a Single Compound Sentence:
1) He does well. He is nervous at the start.
2) The way was long. The wind was cold.
3) It is raining heavily. I will take an umbrella with me.
4) It was stormy night. We ventured out.
5) I am in the right. You are in the wrong.
6) We can travel by land. We can travel by water.
7) The train was wrecked. No one was hurt.
8) The paper is good. The binding is very bad.
9) The river is deep and swift. I am afraid to dive into it.
10) Bruce was lying on his bed. He looked up to the roof. He saw a spider.
11) Most of the rebels were slain. A few escaped. They hid in the woods and marshes. The rebellion was quickly suppressed.
12) Make haste. You will be late. There is no other train till midnight. That train is a slow one.

You may tally your answers with the following: (don't worry, variation may happen)

o He does well. He is nervous at the start.
1) He is nervous at the start, but he does well. (In spite of being nervous at the start, he does well.: **Simple Sentence**)

o The way was long. The wind was cold.
2) The way was long and the wind was cold.

o It is raining heavily. I will take an umbrella with me.
3) It is raining heavily, so I will take an umbrella with me.

o It was stormy night. We ventured out.
4) It was a stormy night, yet we ventured out.

o I am in the right. You are in the wrong.
5) I am in the right, but you are in the wrong.

o We can travel by land. We can travel by water.
6) We can travel by land and by water.

o The train was wrecked. No one was hurt.
7) Though the train was wrecked, yet no one hurt. /The train was wrecked, still no one was hurt.

o The paper is good. The binding is very bad.
8) Though the paper is good, its binding is very bad.

o The river is deep and swift. I am afraid to dive into it.
9) The river is deep and swift; therefore, I am afraid to dive into it.

o Bruce was lying on his bed. He looked up to the roof. He saw a spider.
10) Lying on his bed Bruce looked to the roof and he saw a spider.

o Most of the rebels were slain. A few escaped. They hid in the woods and marshes. The rebellion was quickly suppressed.
11) Killing most of the rebels, though few escaped hiding in the woods and marshes, the rebellion was quickly suppressed.

o Make haste. You will be late. There is no other train till midnight. That train is a slow one.
12) Make haste, or you will be late, and the next train is not before till midnight and it is a slow one.

To make a Complex Sentence

C. Synthesis of Simple Sentences to make a Complex Sentence.

557. For joining two or more sentences to make single Complex, we generally do turn one or more simple sentences into Sub-ordinate Clause or Clauses (i.e., into **Noun Clause**, **Relative Clause** or to **an Adverbial Clause**), while the other is turned into the **Principal Clause**. For this goal, we need also to study or take a revision of Relative Pronouns, or Adverbs as well as go through the Sub-ordinate

Conjunctions which are used to form Sub-ordinate Clauses. Study the examples carefully and see how the <u>conjunctions (sub-ordinate), relative pronouns</u> or <u>adverb</u> do join the sentences.

a. Joining of simple sentences <u>by turning one</u> into a Noun Clause: In the following examples the Sub-ordinate Clause is a Noun Clause:
1) He will be late. That is certain.
→ = It is certain that he will be late.
2) She is drunk. That aggravates her offence.
→ = That she is drunk aggravates her offence.
3) He may be innocent. I do not know.
→ = I do not know whether he is innocent.
4) He is short-sighted. Otherwise, he is fit for the post.
→ = Except that he is short-sighted he is fit for the post.
5) The clouds would disperse. That was our hope. Our hope was cheering.
→ = Our hope that the clouds would disperse, was cheering.
6) The game was lost. It was the consequences of his carelessness.
→ = The consequence of his carelessness was that the game was lost.

b. Joining <u>by turning one simple sentence</u> into Adjective or Relative Clause: In the following examples the Sub-ordinate Clause is made a Relative or Adjective Clause:
7) A fox once met a lion. The fox had never seen a lion before.
→ = A fox who had never seen a lion before, met him (a lion)
8) She keeps her ornaments in a safe. This is a safe place.
→ = She keeps her ornaments in a safe which is a safe place.
9) A cottager and his wife had a hen. The hen laid an egg every day. The egg was golden.
→ = A cottager and his wife had a hen which laid a golden egg every day.
10) The theft was committed last night. The man has been caught.
→ = The theft was committed last night by the man who has been caught.
11) The time was six o' clock. The accident happened then.
→ = The time was six o' clock when the accident happened.
12) He has many plans for earning money quickly. All of them have failed.
→ = He has many plans all of them which have failed for earning money quickly.

c. Joining <u>by turning one simple sentence</u> into Adverbial Clause: In the following examples the Sub-ordinate Clause is made an Adverbial Clause:
13) I waited for my friend. I waited till his arrival.
→ = I waited for my friend until he came.
14) He fled somewhere. His pursuers could not follow him.
→ = He fled where his pursuers couldn't follow him.
15) Let men sow anything. They will reap its fruit.
→ = As men sow, as they reap.
16) He was not there. I spoke to his brother for that reason.
→ = As he was not there, I spoke to his brother.
17) We eat. We wish to live.
→ = We eat so that we may live.
18) Don't eat too much. You will be ill.
→ = If you eat too much you will be ill.

558. **Exercise-3: Combine each set of Simple Sentence into one Complex sentence:**
1) I wrote the letter. It contained the truth. He praised me for it.
2) Honesty is the best policy. Have you never heard it?
3) He came to see me. He wanted to tell something. His father was dead. He had been ill for a long time.
4) He took the medicine. He then felt better. It cured his headache.
5) He gave an order. He is obeyed. They fear to offend him.
6) Your conduct is very peculiar. I am unable to understand it.
7) He is sure to receive his pay. It is due to him. Why then does he worry?
8) His servants disliked him. They flattered him. He was very harsh to them.
9) The speed of the boat was remarkable. It was going against the current. it was going against the wind. These facts should be kept in mind.

10) The man talks most. The man does least. This very often happens.

Match your answers (of exercise-3)

1) I wrote the letter. It contained the truth. He praised me for it.
   1) He praised me for the letter I wrote _which_ contained the truth.
2) Honesty is the best policy. Have you never heard it?
   2) Have you never heard _that_ honesty is the best policy?
3) He came to see me. He wanted to tell something. His father was dead. He had been ill for a long time.
   3) He _who_ came to see me, wanted to tell something _that_ his father _who_ had been ill for a long time, was dead.
4) He took the medicine. He then felt better. It cured his headache.
   4) _After_ he took the medicine, he felt better _which_ cured his headache.
5) He gave an order. He is obeyed. They fear to offend him.
   5) _As_ they fear to offend him, his order is always obeyed.
6) Your conduct is very peculiar. I am unable to understand it.
   6) I am unable to understand your conduct _which_ is very peculiar.
7) He is sure to receive his pay. It is due to him. Why then does he worry?
   7) Why does he worry to receive his pay _which_ is sure and due to him?
8) His servants disliked him. They flattered him. He was very harsh to them.
   8) _As_ he was very harsh to his servants, they disliked him and they flattered.
9) The speed of the boat was remarkable. It was going against the current. It was going against the wind. These facts should be kept in mind.
   9) _Though_ the boat was going against the current and wind, the speed of the boat was remarkable to keep in mind.
10) The man talks most. The man does least. This very often happens.
   10) The man _who_ talks most does least, happens very often.

41. Split-up of a Sentence

559.   The term '**Split-up**' _is just the opposite of_ '**Synthesis**' or joining of sentences. In split-up, we do split, i.e., separate or **break up a sentence to make as far possible independent sentences** (not like: what actually 'Analysis' does). In split-up, we try to give independent form to some essential or important parts of a sentence (i.e., **clauses, phrases, participle, adjective or adverb**, sometimes also the **infinitive, phrase in apposition, & Nominative Absolute, etc.**) are turned to be smaller independent simple sentences.

560.   There are **three main ways to split up** a long sentence into various small simple sentences:
   A. First, break up the sentence into Clauses as per Principal & Co-ordinate (in case of Compound Sentence);

or

   B. Break up the sentence into Clauses as per Principal & Sub-ordinate (if the sentence is a Complex one). Try each of them to give independent sentence forms, removing the linkers, & borrowing some required words, like finite verbs (as giving non-finite verbs the finite forms), &

   C. Find out, if any, (in case of Simple Sentence or Principal Clause)
   1) Participle or Adjective,
   2) Infinitive,
   3) Preposition with a Noun or Gerund,
   4) Noun or Phrase-in-Apposition,
   5) Nominative Absolute, or
   6) Adverb or Adverbial Phrase— try to use them in different independent simple sentences in the following ways:

561.   **For an example, study the following:**

(1) Everybody _knows_ that the boy who _came_ to me for help _is_ a liar _and_ a cheat.

In the above sentence, there are <u>three finite verbs expressed</u>—**knows, came & is**. They easily can be used in independent sentences. The underlined words are the linkers which are to remove (or not to use) in the new sentences.

If you notice carefully, you will find two adjectives— *'liar'* & *'cheat'*, connected by 'and'. We may also try to use two Adjectives in two different sentences; as,

→ A boy came to me for help.

→ He is a liar.

→ He is a cheat.

→ Everybody knows this.

Remember: Arrange the sequence of incidents properly & don't lose the sense of the whole.

Study more examples:

(2) Napoleon, <u>the greatest of French soldiers</u>; Wellington, <u>the greatest of English Generals</u>; and Nelson, the <u>greatest of English Admirals</u>, all <u>heroes of their respective countries</u>, were contemporaries.

After split up, the independent short simple sentences are-

→ Napoleon was the greatest of French soldiers.

→ Wellington was the greatest of English Generals.

→ Nelson was the greatest of English Admirals.

→ They were all heroes of their respective countries.

→ They were contemporaries.

In the above long sentence, we had four Phrases in Appositions (underlined), with one finite verb. The long sentence itself is a Simple sentence, is split up into five short simple sentences.

(3) Bassanio **told** Antonio <u>that he **wished** to repair his fortune by marrying a lady whom he dearly **loved**</u> and whose father, <u>who has lately **dead**</u>, had **left** her sole heiress to a large estate.

After split up, the independent short simple sentences are-

→ Bassanio wished to repair his fortune by marrying a lady.

→ He loved her dearly.

→ Her father was lately dead.

→ He had left his heiress to a large estate.

→ Bassanio said all this to Antonio.

In the above long sentence, there are five clauses in total with five finite verbs, in bold. They are used in five independent sentences after the split up. The long sentence was a Complex one.

To be Noted: So, for split up, we have to hunt for **finite verbs** cum **clauses** as well as look for <u>Participles or Adjectives</u>, <u>Adverb or Adverbial Phrase</u>, <u>Noun or Phrase in Apposition</u>, <u>Infinitive</u>, use of Gerund, <u>Nominative Absolute</u>, etc. to form independent Sentences; as read more examples.

(4) Everybody admires the man who passed all the University examinations <u>as a private student</u> <u>while working as a humble railway points man</u> <u>at a lonely station</u>.

After split up:

1) Everybody admires the man.
2) He passed all the University examinations.
3) This he did as a private student.
4) He was working as a humble railway points man all this time.
5) His posting was at a lonely station.

In the above long sentence, the underlined are the adverbials- <u>adv of manner</u>, <u>time</u> & <u>place</u>. The three adverbials are used as three different sentences, (iii), (iv), & (v), while sentence (i) comes from principal clause and (ii) from the sub-ordinate clause.

(5) When Newton was fourteen years old, <u>his mother's second husband being now dead</u>, she wished her son to leave school and assist her in managing <u>the farm **at Woolsthrope**</u>.

After split up:

1) The second husband of Newton's mother was now dead.
2) Newton was fourteen years' old at that time.

444

3) She wished her son to leave the school.
4) She had a farm at Woolsthrope.
5) She wished him to help her in managing it.

In the above long sentence, the underlined is the use of **Absolute Phrase**, and the words **in bold is an example of adverbials, denoting place**. Both they have turned into sentences, (i) & (iv); while others have come from three clauses—Sub-ordinate, Principal & one Co-ordinate.

(6) I seem to myself like a child, playing on the sea-shore, and picking up here and there a curious shell or a pretty pebble, while the boundless ocean of Truth lies undiscovered before me.

After split up:

  ·   A child often plays on the sea-shore.

  ·   He picks up here and there a curious shell.

  ·   Or he picks up a pretty pebble.

  ·   I seem to myself like such a child.

  ·   The ocean of Truth lies before me.

  ·   It is boundless.

  ·   It lies undiscovered.

The above long sentence is a Complex Sentence with one Principal & One Sub-ordinate clause only. But in the sentence, there are **participle phrases used as phrase in apposition**—'playing on the sea-shore', 'picking up here & there', two adjectives or participle words—boundless & undiscovered, two objects—'a curious shell' & 'a pretty pebble', and one adverbial 'before me'. All they are used in separate sentences.

Split up through Analysis

❑   We said, '**split-up' is the opposite term of 'Synthesis'**, but not of '**Analysis'**. We can 'split-up' a sentence well, if we have first-hand knowledge of analysis. Let's see. Read the following sentences.

1. The other day my younger brother saw two men fighting each other.
2. The Judge, accepting the verdict of the jury, found the prisoner tremendously guilty.
3. On hearing of my misfortune, all my friends ran to my help.
4. An intelligent boy, the son of a very poor man, badly needs your help to be able to continue his studies.

In the Analysis, they are like:

Adjunct to Subject	Subject Proper	Finite Verb	Object with Adjectives	Participle/ Complement	Adverbial expansion
my younger	brother	saw	two men	fighting with each other	The other day
1) The 2) accepting the verdict of the jury	Judge	found	the prisoner	guilty	tremendously
1) all my 2) On hearing my misfortune	friends	ran	----	----	to my help
1) An 2) intelligent 3) the son of a very poor man	boy	needs	your help	----	badly, to be able to continue his studies

Note

If you carefully study, you will find your necessary elements for split-up the sentences, mainly input (are) in the columns of Adjuncts to Subjects, attributes to object, complement/participle, & Adverbials.

You will find there— **Participle or Adjectives, Phrase-in-Apposition, Absolute Phrase, Complement & Adverbials** which are necessary for split-up or break up a sentence to make many independent short simple sentences.

Infinitive & Gerund are also important guides for split-up a sentence that we generally find in the columns of **Subjects, Objects**, or in the **adverbial expansion.**

For example, in sentence 1, *the complement* & *adverbials*— both can be converted into independent simple sentences, *along with separate one for the main verb.*

In sentence 2, the ***phrase in apposition*** is in the Adjuncts to the Subject; that can be turned into independent simple sentence <u>along with the *complement*, *adverbials*, & *main verb*.</u>

In sentence 3, *the **preposition with gerund***, *'On hearing'*, noted in the adjuncts to the subject, & *the object of the gerund 'my misfortune'* as well as others, like adjectives, adverbials—can separately be given simple sentence forms.

In sentence 4, the adjective, possessive, adverbials—can be broken down to form separate sentences borrowing suitable verbs and introductory subjects, **there, it** etc.

Thus, after split-up into Small Sentences:

1.
   - It was another day.
   - My younger brother saw two men.
   - They were fighting with each other.
2.
   - The jury passed a verdict. (**The jury decided something on it.**)
   - The Judge accepted the verdict of the jury.
   - He found the prisoner guilty.
   - His guilt was tremendous.

3.
   - I was in misfortune.
   - My friends heard this.
   - They all ran to me.
   - They all wanted to help me.
4.
   562.   There is a boy. **Split up of Complex Sentences: More examples:**

   -
   - He is intelligent. (**The boy is intelligent.**)
   - But his father is <u>very</u> poor.
   - The boy wants to continue his studies.
   - He badly needs your help.

1) When I was a student, I was one day taken to task by the Principal of my college for having played on behalf of an outside club, though he had ordered us not to do so.

2) Having been informed that my brother who had gone to Delhi to attend the Legislative Assembly was lying seriously ill of fever there, I applied for one week's leave of absence in order that I might go to him to arrange for proper treatment.

After Analysis into Clauses:

Clauses	Kind of Clause	Connectives
1/(a) I was one day...of an outside club	Principal clause	when
(b) When I was a student		though
(c) though he ...not to do so	Sub. Adv. Clause, qualifying **'was taken in (a)'**	

	Sub. Adv. Clause, qualifying '**having played** in (a)'

2. (a) Having been **informed**, I **applied for** one week's leave of absence	Principal clause	that who In order that
(b) That **my brother** was lying seriously ill of fever there	Sub- Noun Clause, object to verb '**informed** in (a)' in participle form	
(c) Who had gone to Delhi to attend the Legislative Assembly	Sub. Adj. Clause, describing '**my brother**' in (b)'	
(d) In order that I might go to him to arrange for proper treatment.	Sub. Adv. Clause, describing '**applied for**' in (a)'	

We have now seven clauses in total after analyzing the above two complex sentences. What, if we now analyze further as Subject, predicate and to their adjuncts:

Adjunct to Subject	Subject Proper	Finite Verb	Object with Adj.	Complement	Adverbial Adjunct
	I	was taken	by the Principal of my college	to task	one day, for having played on behalf of an outside club,
	I	was		a student	when
	He	had ordered	us		not to do so
having been informed	I	applied			for one week's leave of absence
my	Brother	was lying			seriously ill of fever there
	who	had gone			to Delhi to attend the L. Assembly
	I	might go			to him to arrange for proper treatment.

The Analysis is only to help you better understand about Split-up. Beyond that, it does not have connection with 'Split-up'. However, after split-up, the smaller simple sentences are, as the followings:
1. I was a student of a college.
2. The Principal had ordered us not to play for an outside club.
3. But I played on behalf of an outside club.
4. One day, the Principal sir took me before the task (commission).

1. My brother had gone to Delhi.
2. He went/was there to attend the Legislative Assembly.
3. He was lying ill of fever there.
4. It was serious.
5. I was informed of that.
6. I might go to him there.
7. I had to arrange for him proper treatment.
8. So, I applied for one week's leave of absence.

Split up of Complex Compound

563.   **Split up of Complex Compound Sentences** (where at least two complex sentences (or two subordinate clauses) are joined by a Co-ordinate Conjunction.)
1.   Though I was ill I tried my best; **but** as ill luck would have it all my exertion ended in smoke.

2. Long ago, when I was yet a student I once went to Darjeeling, **where** (and there) I was charmed by the beautiful mountain scenery that greeted me on all sides.

If they are analyzed:

Clauses	Kind of Clause	Connectives
a) I tried my best	Principal clause	Though but as
b) Though I was ill	Sub. Adv. Clause, qualifying '**tried**' in '(a)'.	
c) But all my exertion ended in smoke	Principal Clause, Co-ordinate to '(a)'	
d) As ill luck would have it	Sub. Adv. Clause, qualifying '**ended**' in '(c)'	
a) Long ago, I once went to Darjeeling	Principal clause	When Where (and there)
b) When I was yet a student	Sub- Adv. Clause, describing 'went' in (a)'	
c) Where I was charmed by...scenery	Principal Clause, Co-ordinate to '(a)'	
d) That greeted me on all sides	Sub. Adj. Clause, qualifying '**scenery**' in (c)'	

The New Simple Sentences will be like the followings:
1. I was ill.
2. Yet, I tried my best.
3. But it was my ill luck.
4. All my exertion ended in smoke.

1. It was long ago.
2. I was yet a student.
3. I went to Darjeeling.
4. The mountain was full of beautiful scenery.
5. It was on all sides.
6. I was charmed.

564. A Few Difficulties may arise in *Analysis,* but not in *Split-up.* Study them attentively:

Split-up of 'Quoted Sentence', 'Parenthetic Phrase & Clause'

In case **"Quoted sentences": -**
   He said, "I cannot come to you today. My brother is ill and I have to attend on him. You may, however, expect me tomorrow."
➤ **The quotation <u>consists of three sentences</u>**, which cannot be taken separately in their relation to the principal verb '**said**', but have to be <u>treated as a single part of speech</u>, **object** to the verb, '**said**'.
➤ The quotation has been taken in this case **as a long compound word**, a **noun equivalent**, object to the transitive verb 'said'; as, I said, "**I am ill**".
➤ I was surprised by his '**I don't care**' attitude (a **compound adjective** describing the noun, 'attitude').

In analysis, the above expressions, may arise difficulties. However, we can split -up them easily. Study the sentences, after split-up of the 'quotations':

a. **He said**, "I cannot come to you today. My brother is ill and I have to attend on him. You may, however, expect me tomorrow."
   1) I cannot come to you today.
   2) My brother is ill.
   3) I have to attend on him.
   4) You may, however, expect me tomorrow.
   5) He said all these to me.

b. I said, "**I am ill**".
> 1) I was ill.
> 2) I said that to him.

c. I was surprised by his "**I don't care**' attitude".
> 1) He had 'I don't care attitude'.
> 2) I was surprised by that.

565.   **Parenthetic Phrases:**
> a. He is, **to tell the truth**, not quite frank.
> b. I was, **to be frank**, much surprised.
> c. I am, **of me**, ok.

➤In all the above cases, the '**phrases within commas before & after**', are called '**Parenthetic Phrases**' and they can be analyzed separately and similarly can be taken out without injuring the sense. In the above sentences, they are used in Simple Sentences. Their split-ups are as the followings:

> a. He is, **to tell the truth**, not quite frank. = He is not quite frank. It is true.
> b. I was, **to be frank**, much surprised. = I was surprised. Frankly I like to say that.
> c. I am, **of me**, ok. = Are you asking about me? I am ok.

566.   More 'Parenthetic Expressions' for Split-up:
> a. He is, **I am sure**, something like a poet.
> b. His conduct, **I believe**, is good.
> c. Why do you, my friend, **I don't know**, hate me?
> d. Why do you, **it is not clear**, not talk to me now-a-days?
> e. But you should, **I am likely agreed**, do so.

➤   All the above are simple sentences while the bold written words are **parenthetic expressions**, they are thrown into the main sentence, like a phrase in apposition or an Absolute Phrase. They can be analyzed separately. In the sentences they **are thrown in as independent elements**; and they may be taken out without injuring the sense.

Study, how we can split up them:

a. He is, **I am sure**, something like a poet.
> o   He is something like a poet. I am sure about that.

b. His conduct, **I believe**, is good.
> o   His conduct is good. I believe so.

c. Why do you, my friend, **I don't know**, hate me?
> o   I like address you as my friend. Why do you hate me? I don't know the reason.

d. Why do you, **it is not clear**, not talk to me now-a-days?
> o   You are not talking with me now-a-days. What is the reason? /Why are you doing so? It is not clear to me.

e. But you should, **I am likely agreed**, do so.
> o   But you should do. I am likely agreed to that.

f. I was surprised by his '**I don't care**' attitude.
> o   He had 'I don't care' attitude. I was surprised by that.

When 'Parenthetic' expressions used in Compound

a. He is, **I am sure**, something of a poet & his poetry are too good to read by others.
b. His conduct, **I believe**, is good & too good to converse with.
c. Why do you, my friend, **I don't know**, give me light and snatch it away?
d. Why do you, it **is not clear**, begin to talk and stop forever?

➢ All the above are compound sentences with two principals <u>while the bold written words are</u> **parenthetic expressions**; they can be analyzed separately. In the sentences they **are thrown in as independent elements**; and they may be taken out without injuring the sense.

❏ Study their Split-up

a. He is, **I am sure**, something of a poet & his poetry are too good to read by others.
   o   He is something of a poet. His poetry are too good to read by others. I am sure about that.
b. His conduct, **I believe**, is good & too good to converse with.
   o   His conduct is good. But it is too good to converse with. I believe so.
c. Why do you, my friend, **I don't know**, give me light and snatch it away?
   o   You give me light. And you snatch it away too. Why do you do all these with me? I don't know the reason of it.
d. Why do you, it **is not clear**, begin to talk and stop forever?
   o   You begin to talk. And you stop it forever. Why do you do this? It is not clear.

When 'Parenthetic' expressions used in Complex

a. He is, **I am sure**, something of a poet who reads alone his poetry.
b. His conduct, **I believe**, is what is not suitable for his own age.
c. He is the man who, **I believe**, did it.
d. This is the boy who, **I think**, came the other day.

All the above are complex sentences with only one principal & one sub-ordinate clauses <u>while the **bold written words are parenthetic expressions**</u>; they can be analyzed separately.

❏ Split-up of Parenthetic expressions in Complex

a. He is, **I am sure**, something of a poet who reads alone his poetry.
   o   He is something of a poet. He reads his poetry alone. I am sure about that.

b. His conduct, **I believe**, is what is not suitable for his own age.
   o   He is of old age (i.e., old enough by age). His conduct does not suit to his age. I believe that.

c. He is the man who, **I believe**, did it.
   o   Someone has done it. He is the man. I believe this.

d. This is the boy who, **I think**, came the other day.
   o   A boy came the other day. This is the boy. I think that.

Use of 'It' & 'There' in Split-up

567.   In split-up, **'there'**, **'it'** as introductory subjects are often required to introduce separate & simple sentences (besides other words & suitable finite verbs as necessary); as,
a. They went out in the raining. = **It** was raining. They went out **then** (during that time).
b. A man in the school was collapsed in heart attack. = **There** was a man in the school. He collapsed **there** in heart attack.
c. A king, named Ashoka ruled over Magadh in India. = **There** was a king. His name was Ashoka. **Once** he ruled over Magadha.

   ✳   As custom '**There**' is to fall in the group of an '**Adv. Adjunct**'; <u>but when they are used as **introductory subjects**, they lose the force to call anymore as Adverbial adjuncts.</u>
      ✳   '**It**', *as impersonal pronoun* **refers to any animal, child,** <u>it also, often, mean any preceding or succeeding statement, a phrase, a clause, and even a sentence.</u> (Study in details in the chapter of Pronouns).

d. It is easy ***to say so.***
→ You may say anything. It is easy.

e. **It is hard _to believe him._**
→ I can't believe him. It is very hard.
f. **It is time _to go now._**
→ The time has arrived. We should go now.
g. Two people were fighting in the field.
→ **There** were two peoples in the field. They were fighting.
h. Ashoka ruled India.
→ **There** was a king. His name was Ashoka. He ruled India.

568. If we have got mastery over analysis of sentences, and know its parts well, to identify and understand, we are always free to do Split-up of Sentences directly (without any analysis, as shown in the above through few pages.)

So, we can jump or return to the split-up in the direct mode or manner, as did earlier. Practice with some more examples:

1) When Newton was fifty years old and had been hard at work more than twenty years studying the theory of light, he one day went out of his chamber leaving his little dog asleep before the fire.
   a. Newton was now fifty years old.
   b. He had been hard at work more than twenty years.
   c. He had been studying the theory of light.
   d. One day he went out of his chamber.
   e. He left his little dog before the fire.
   f. It was asleep.

2) A right-minded man will have the courage to live honestly within his means; for he who incurs debts is in spirit a dishonest as the man who openly picks your pocket.
   a. A man may incur debts.
   b. Another man may openly pick your pocket.
   c. The former is dishonest in spirit like the latter.
   d. So, a right-minded man will live within his means.
   e. He has the courage to do so.

3) Everybody should learn how to swim because swimming is a fine exercise and is often the means of saving one's own life.
   a. Swimming is a fine exercise.
   b. It is often the means of saving one's own life.
   c. So, everybody should learn how to swim.

4) One morning when the giant was lying awake in bed, he heard some music, which sounded so sweet to his ears that he thought it to be the king's musicians passing by.
   a. One morning the giant was lying awake in bed.
   b. At that time, he heard some music.
   c. It sounded very sweet to his ear.
   d. He thought it to be the kings' musicians.
   e. They were supposed passing by.

569. **Exercise: Split up the followings into Simple sentences:**

   a. On a dark night Subhas Chandra Bose set out from home in disguise to escape into Germany where he wanted to organize a strong army to fight against the British.
   b. As we reached the heritage building with the desire of visiting the interior, we found the building closed it being a scheduled weekly holiday and we felt much disheartened.
   c. Hearing a girl crying for help, a youth plunged into the water and managed with great difficulty to bring her to shore.
   d. Seeing that his end is near, Hamlet suddenly stabbed his uncle with the poisoned sword, and avenged at last the murder of his father.
   e. A Metro Railway employee, Biswajit Biswas, pulled back a woman attempting to jump to her death at the Tallygunj station but fell off the edge of the platform himself and was killed.

You may check your answers of the above 'Exercise', here:

a. It was a dark night. Subhas Chandra Bose set out for home. He was in disguise. He was to escape into Germany. He wanted to organize a strong army there. The army was to fight against the British.
b. We reached the heritage building. We had a desire of visiting the interior. We found the building closed. It was a scheduled weekly holiday. We felt much disheartened.
c. A girl cried for help. A youth heard it. He plunged into the water. He managed to bring her to shore. He did it with great difficulty.
d. His end was near. Hamlet saw this. He stabbed his uncle suddenly with a sword. The sword was poisonous. He at last avenged the murder of his father.
e. It was at the Tallygunj station. A woman attempted to jump to her death. Biswajit Biswas was a Metro Railway employee. He pulled back the woman. He fell off the edge of the platform himself. He was killed.

42. Direct & Indirect Speech (Change of Narration)

570. **Narration:** The French derivative word, '**narration**' means '**the act of recounting**', which 'relates some action or occurrence' (i.e., 'to *tell somebody about something that you have experienced or already happened.*)

Speech: The English word, 'Speech', on the other hand, means '**a session of speaking**'; 'a long oral message given publicly, usually by one person'. It also means for '**talk**'.

So, let's see, both the terms mean for same thing, '**delivering an oral message**' to a second or third person other than the speaker himself, while the speaker is in the first person. But who conveys the message or the message is speaking to, may be of any person.

Direct Speech & Indirect Speech

A speech can be delivered in two ways, **directly**, by quoting 'the exact words of the speaker' or **indirectly**, by 'delivering the message without using exact words of the speaker'.
Thus, we have –

    i. **Direct Speech** (when we quote actual words of the speaker)
ii. **Indirect speech** (reporting or delivering the message without quoting exact words of the speaker.)

571. **General Features of 'Direct Speech'**

1. The Direct Speech is generally **put within inverted commas, single** or double (**'...' /"..."**) and sometimes using colons (:).
2. The verb, generally placed before the quoted words is called the **reporting verb**. [However, the reporting verb can also be used after a quotation.]
3. We **use comma (,)** before the quoted speech.
4. The quoted speech **must begin with the capital** letter.
5. Sometimes, the subject & the reporting verb are placed after the quoted speech. In this case, verb comes first and then the subject.

Direct Speech looks like...

The student said, "I shall go to school."

Or

"I am very sorry to wake you up, sir," said the stranger.

Note the differences

➢ Rama said, 'I **am** very busy **now**.' (Direct speech)
➢ Rama said **that** he **was** very busy **then**. (Indirect speech)

❑ What to be noted?

Let's Discuss...

- We use **inverted commas** in direct speech, of course to mark off the exact words of the speaker. In the indirect speech that is replaced with a linking word, **'that'**.
- The proper noun **'I'** is changed into **'he'**.
- The verb **'am'** in direct speech is changed to **'was'**.
- The adverb **'now'** is changed to **'then'**.

5 Major Rules of Narration Change

572.   Study the **five major rules** of Narration Change that follows 'Narration Change of different kinds of sentences' along with some extra guidelines for each kind.

1) **Use of Linkers-** that, if/whether, wh- words or infinitive verb. See the chart:

	Linker or Conjunction	used, in case of the sentence is-
1	that	Assertive sentence
2	If/whether or wh- words	Interrogative
3	Infinitive/that	Imperative
4	That	Optative (Sentence of wish or prayer)
5	That	Exclamatory

Note: **'that'** linker is often omitted in Spoken English; as,

He said to me, 'I don't believe you.'
He said he didn't believe me.

2) **Change of Tense** or **verb forms**: When reporting verb is in past tense, all present tenses of Direct Speech are generally changed into corresponding Past Tenses (with some exceptions); as see the table:

	Tense in D. Speech	Becomes/ change into	Tense in Ind. Speech
1.	Simple present	Change into	Simple past
2.	Present Continuous	,,	Past Continuous
3.	Present Perfect	,,	Past Perfect
4.	Present Perfect Continuous	,,	Past Perfect Continuous
5.	'Shall' of future	,,	Should
6.	'Will' of future	,,	Would or should
7.	Simple past	,,	Past perfect
8.	Past continuous	,,	Past perfect continuous

Exception (1): tenses may not be changed, if the statement is one universal truth or a habitual fact;
Or
If reporting verb is in present or future tense.

3) **Change in Person, Number, Case, Gender of Pronouns & Possessive Adjectives:** This change occurs in accordance to relation with the reporter and hearer. Carefully study the charts:

Note: '1st person in quoted speech changes to subject of reporting verb in the Indirect Speech;

2nd person changes to person spoken to; &, there is no change in 3rd person.

Person in D.S.	Changes to	Person of Ind. Speech
1st person (I, we, me, us, my, our) of Direct Speech	Changes to	Person, Number, Gender, case of Subject of Reporting Verb

Prabir says to his uncle, 'I am going to Kolkata tomorrow.'
> **Prabir** tells his uncle that **he (Prabir)** is going to Kolkata next day.

2nd person (You, your) of Direct Speech	Changes to	Person, Number, Gender, case of the person spoken to in the Direct Speech

Father said to **me**, '**You** should obey your teachers.'
> Father told **me** that **I** should obey our teachers.

There is no change in the third person.

You said, '**he** is a coward.' > You said that **he** was a coward. >You told him a coward.

4) Change in **Demonstrative Pronouns, & adverbs of time and place**: (Words expressing nearness in time, place or pronouns changes to words expressing distance.)

	Demonstrative Pronouns	Changes to	In Indirect Speech
1.	This	Change into	That
2.	these	,,	those
3.	That	Remain unchanged	That
4.	those	,,	those
5.	It (impersonal pronoun)	,,	it

Note-1: Study the below chart about '**the Adverbs of Time**'.

	Adverbs of Time in (Direct Speech)	Changes to	In Indirect Speech
1.	Now	Changes into	Then
2.	Today		That day
3.	Yesterday	,,	The day before/ the previous day
4.	Tomorrow	,,	The next day/ the following day
5.	Next day (week, month) etc.	,,	The following day (week, month, etc.)
6.	This day/night	,,	That day/night
7.	Last night	,,	The previous night/ the night before
8.	Ago	,,	before
9.	Hence (for this reason/from now)	,,	thence
10	Thence (for that reason/ from then/starting from that time)	Remained unchanged	thence

11.	thus	,,	In that way; /so
12.	The day before yesterday	,,	Two days before
13.	The day after tomorrow	,,	Two days after
14.	A year ago,	,,	A year before; the previous year

Note-2: Now, study the chart about **the Adverbs of Place**.

	Adverbs of Place in (Direct Speech)	Changes to	In Indirect Speech
1.	Here	Change into	There
2.	Hither (to this place)	,,	Thither (to/towards that place)
3.	There	Remain unchanged	there
4.	Thither	,,	thither
5.	Thence (from that place)	,,	thence

Note-3: 'Come' & 'go' may be interchanged with the narration change.
Note-4: These changes rely upon situation, time & place when or where the speaker speaks this, and thus they also may not change.

5) **Other Important Changes in Indirect Speech from Direct:**

Note: Vocatives are popular in imperative sentence.

	Other Changes from Direct Speech	Changes to	In Indirect Speech
1.	Says to/said to	Changes to	tells/told

The old man said to his son, "My son, you must not spoil your time."
>The old man **told his son affectionately** that he must not spoil his time.

2.	In interrogative, linker	If/whether	is used.

He said, 'Will you listen to such a man?'
> He **asked** them **whether** they would listen to such a man.

3.	In interrogative, linker	'wh' word	is used.

He said to me, 'What are you doing?'
> He **asked** me **what** I was doing.

4.	In Imperative, urged,	request, advice, order	etc. is used.

He said, "Be quiet and listen to my words."
> He **urged** them to be quiet and listen to his words.

5.	Exclaim in joy/sorrow	is used in	exclamatory

Alice said, "How clever I am!"
> Alice **exclaimed** that he is very clever.

Narration Change: Assertive Sentence

1) She says to me, "You told me, so I have done the work for you."
→ She tells me that as I told her, so she has done the work for me.
2) Mrs. Bose said, "I take coffee daily in the afternoon."
→ Mrs. Bose said that she takes coffee daily in the afternoon.
3) Rama said to me, "I drive very fast."
→ Rama told me that he drives very fast.
4) "The weather is fine today," the reporter said.
→ The reporter said that weather was fine that day.
5) "My mother cooks best," Ratna said to her friend.
→ Ratna told her friend that her mother cooks best.
6) He said, "My master is writing letters."
→ He said that his master was writing letters.
7) Sophia said, "I have passed the examinations."
→ Sophia said that she had passed the examinations.
8) "I know her address", said Gopi.
→ Gopi said he knows her address.
9) Father said, "Moon revolves round the earth."
→ Father said Moon revolves round the earth.
10) "English is easy to learn", said our teacher one day in the classroom.
→ One day in the classroom our teacher said that English is easy to learn.
11) He said, "I may go there."
→ He said that he might go there.
12) "My son leaves for Delhi tomorrow", father said.
→ Father said that his son would leave for Delhi the next day.
13) "You are very wicked; so, I shall not play with you", my friend said.
→ My friend told me that I am very wicked; so, she would not play with me.
14) I said to him, "The sky is blue."
→ I told him that the sky is blue.
15) "Father, if you put me into a good school, I shall be very glad.", said the little girl.
→ The little girl told her father that she would be glad if he would put her into a good school.

Narration Change: Interrogative

1) "Are you ill?" my father said to me.
→ My father asked If I was ill.
2) Shilpa said to her friend, "What are you doing?"
→ Shilpa wanted to know from her friend **what** she was doing.
3) My friend said to me, "When will you go home?"
→ My friend enquired of me when I should go home.

a. We replace reporting verbs of direct Speech with **'enquire'**, 'ask', 'want to', etc.
b. Linker—**if/whether** or 'Wh' word 'is used.
c. In case of Yes/No type question, linker- **'if/whether'**, is used.
d. When a choice has to made or there is an alternate possibility, **'whether'** is preferred to use as linker.
e. **'Wh-'** word is used as linker when the reported speech is a 'Wh'- question.
f. **Question of direct speech changes to statement** or assertive sentence, and **we use full stop (.)** in place of question mark (?).
g. Other Rules are same as of Assertive Sentences.

4) She said to me, "Will you take tea or coffee?"
→ She asked me **whether** I would take tea or coffee.
5) "Are you coming with us?" my friend said to me.
→ My friend enquired of me **whether** I was going with them.
6) Robert said, "John is a good boy, is not he?"
→ Robert said that he assumed/thought John was a good boy.
→ Robert assumed John to be a good boy.

7) I said to Indira, "You can speak Hindi, can't you?"
   → I said to Indira that I thought she could speak Hindi.
   → I hoped Indira could speak Hindi.

h. In *case Narration Change of question tags*, the words—**assume, think, doubt, hope** or **believe**—may be used <u>following an</u> **infinitive** or as a separate verb <u>after linker</u> **'that'**.
i. **In such cases, <u>if/whether are not used.</u>**
j. *Such question tags are often said to be tentative statements, for speaker is not sure about the result or answer.* The <u>speaker asks these questions for some assurance</u>.

Narration changes of Question Tags:

8) The father said to his child, "You will do the task, won't you?"
   → The father told his child that he hoped he would do the task.
   → The father hoped his child to do the work.
9) "The officer did not agree to do that, did he?"
   → He said that he didn't believe that the officer had agreed to do that.
10) Ramesh said, "They will never return, will they?"
   → Ramesh said that he believed that they would not return.

Narration Change: Imperative

1. He said to me, "Please help me with a grammar book."
2. The father said to his son, "My boy, be brave and active."
3. "Samar, come in due time in the meeting," my boss said to me.
4. "Let's walk fast," said my friend.

➤**What did you notice in the sentences?**

They expressing...
1. He said to me, "Please help me with a grammar book." (...request)
2. The father said to his son, "My boy, be brave and active." (...advice)
3. "Samar, come in due time in the meeting at White Home," my boss said to me. (...order)
4. "Let's walk fast," said my friend. (...suggestion)

Notes
✓ The direct speeches expressing either *order,* or *request,* or *advice,* or a *suggestion.* They are called **imperative sentences.**

✓ The change of Imperative sentences from direct to indirect speech are almost same as we did in assertive sentences, except the followings:

We may use different reporting verbs to express the imperative mood:

Rules of Narration Change: Imperative Sentences
Rule No-1:
The reporting verbs are changed into—**order, request, advice,** or **suggest/propose** & others.
To express request, order or advice, **'tell'** or **'ask'**—may also be used sometimes when imperative mood is uncertain (when you are confused about 'order' or 'suggest', etc.).

Note: See the matrix of words, expressing Imperative Mood:

imperative mood expressing words/verbs	Meanings
Order	Tell somebody to do something
Request	Ask for something politely
Advise	To tell somebody what you think they should do

Command	Give instruction to do something, generally in force or military
Beg/implore	Ask for something anxiously, for you need it very much
Entreat	Asking for something to do or to have in a serious & often in emotional way/ earnestly request someone
Urge/encourage	Advise or to try hard to persuade somebody to do something
Bid	To offer to do work/ provide a service/offer to pay, /attempt
Forbid	Order somebody not to do something
Warn	Strongly advise somebody to do or not to do something
Remind	Help somebody to remember something

Rule No-2:

To express the imperative mood, i.e., <u>verbs of reported speech often changed into</u> **infinitive.**

1) My friend said to me, "Go home at once."
→ My friend **advised** me to go home at once.
2) Tina said to me, "Please help me with a grammar book."
→ Tina **requested** me to help her with a grammar book.
3) The teacher said, "Silence."
→ The teacher **ordered** us to be silent.
4) I said to him, "Excuse me sir."
→ I **begged** him to excuse me.
5) "March on," said the general.
→ The General **commanded** his soldiers to march on.
6) "Don't forget to bring the medicine," he said to me.
→ He **reminded** me to bring the medicine.
7) "Please, please don't go on election duty," said my wife.
→ My wife **begged/implored** me not to go on election duty.
8) "Don't go near the fire, boys," said the officer.
→ The officer warned the boys not to go near the fire.
9) "Come in," she said to me.
→ She invited me to go in.
10) "Go on, try once again," said Parimal.
→ Parimal urged/encouraged me to try once again.
11) The old man said to the officer, "Please sir, pass my file."
→ The old man entreated the officer to pass his file.

Some Questions or Exclamation in form, express also Imperative mood, like **command** or **request**, and they follow imperative structure to change the narration.

12) "Will you keep quiet!" the teacher said to the students.
→ The teacher bade/told/ordered the students to keep quiet.
13) "Would you lend me your book, please?"
→ He requested me to lend him my book.
14) "Would you show me your ticket please?"
→ The ticket checker asked the passenger to show his ticket.

Important Notes:

✓ Sometimes, the **subject** & the **reporting verb** are placed after the quoted speech. In this case, <u>generally the verb comes first and then the noun subject</u>. But if it is pronoun subject or the reporting verb has an object and others, it follows normal syntax. (subject +verb +object +others)

✓ Question (?), exclamation (!), or Comma (,) are used as necessary before end of quotation and & use Full stop (.) at the end of the statement.

✓ **First letter of the quotation or first letter of the sentence must be in capital** but first letter after quotation is not bound to be capital.

Imperative mood may also exit in the form of Question tags, like Question and exclamation:

15) "Close the door, won't you?" he said to me.
→ He asked/requested me to close the door. (The question tag— 'won't you'—has been left out.)

16) "You should go home, don't you?"
→ He advised me to go home. (The question tag— 'don't you'—has been left out.)

Question Tags in Direct Speech of imperative sentence, where unnecessary to change, are generally left out in the Indirect Speech.

Read also the following:

Note: In interrogative sentences, in case of question tags, we have used the verbs—'doubt', think, hope, assume, believe, etc. The verbs are not necessary in the imperative mood in question tags. Normal imperative verbs should be used; **a request, order, advice**, etc.

Use of Vocatives in Imperative:

For Changing Direct Speech into Indirect:

a) **Read the table:**

Other Changes from Direct Speech	Changes to	In Indirect Speech
1. My boy/ My son/My dear	Changes into	Affectionately/ with affection

The old man said to his son, "My son, you must not spoil your time."
>The old man **told his son affectionately** that he must not spoil his time.
>The old man **affectionately advised** his son **not to spoil** his time.
The Old man **forbade his son with affection to waste** his time.

| 2. Sir, please | Are replaced with | Kindly, Politely/Respectfully/ with respect |

The clerk said to his boss, "Please excuse my fault, sir, for this time."
>The clerk **respectfully requested** his boss to excuse his fault for that time.

| 3. If 'Proper nouns' are used in address, in the Direct speech | They become | Objects of the verbs in Indirect Speech |

He said, "Samir, do the work for me please."
>He requested **Samir** to do the work for **him**.

| 4. Some words like 'friends, 'gentlemen', 'countrymen' | Changes to | Addressing them as... |

The leader said, "**My brothers and sisters**, give me your votes."
>**Addressing them as** brothers and sisters, the leader appealed to people for their votes.
>The leader, **addressing people as his brothers and sisters,** appealed for vote.
> **Addressing them as his brothers and sisters**, the leader requested to people to give their votes.

b) In Some cases, **Vocatives should be avoided,** where it is not necessary:

c) **Use of Not**: In the Indirect Speech of the negative imperative sentence, **'not' is placed just before the infinitive verb, or use 'forbid'**

When 'forbid' is used, 'not' is not used.

5.	If 'vocatives' are casual in use, avoid them in Indirect speech.

- I said to him, "Excuse me sir."
✓ I begged him to excuse me.
- The father said to his boy, "Do not run in the sun."
✓ The father advised his boy not to run in the sun.

✓ The father forbade his boy to run in the sun.

Use of 'Let' in the Narration Change

1) He said to me, "Let us go home."
→ He **suggested** to me that we **should** go home.
2) I said to my friend, "Let us have some music."
→ I **proposed** to my friend that we **should** have some music.

Note-1:
   a. In the Direct Speech, when '**Let**' expresses a proposal or suggestion, use '**propose**', or '**suggest**' as the reporting verb.
   b. Use '**should**' for 'Let' after subject of reported speech.
   c. Use linker, '**that**'

3) "Let her do whatever she likes," her father said.
→ Her father said that she **might do** whatever she liked.
4)
5) He said, "Let me come in."
→ He **requested** that he **might be allowed** to come in.
6) He said, "Let me have some milk."
→ He wished that she **might have** some milk.

Note-2:
   a. But when 'Let' in the Direct Speech does not express a proposal it should be changed into '**might**' or '**might be allowed**' or into some other form according to the sense.
   b. 'Might be allowed' is followed by an '**infinitive verb**' in the indirect speech.
   c. However, 'might' follow only simple tense of the verb in the indirect speech.
                                                                    d. Use linker, '**that**'

Narration Change: Optative

Rule No-1: As an Optative Sentence express **wish** or **prayer,** the reporting verbs will be changed into
                              (**Wish, Pray, desire, Hope, bless**, or **yearn**)
Know their meanings:

The verbs to be used in Indirect speech	Their meanings
Wish	Want something to happen; Want something to be true, even though it is unlikely or impossible.
Pray	Ask for help; Hope very much that something will happen.
Desire	Wish for something; Want something
Hope	Want something to happen & think it is possible.
Bless	Ask God to protect somebody;
Yearn	Long; want something very much, especially when it is very difficult to get.

Rule No-2: The conjunction '**that**' is used.

Rule-3: The optative sentence changed into assertive in the Indirect Speech.

Note: The person spoken to in the Direct Speech is omitted in the Indirect Speech.

1) The old man said to me, "May God bless you."
→ The old man prayed that God might bless me.
2) The old woman said to me, "May you live long."
→ The old woman wished that I might live long.
3) The holy man said, "May holy spirit rest upon you."
→ The holy man wished (or prayed) that holy spirit might rest upon me.
4) The old priest said to me, "May you succeed."
→ The old priest wished that I might succeed.

Narration Change: Exclamatory

Rule No-1: As the Direct Speech expresses an outburst of **'grief', 'joy', 'shame',** etc. the reporting verbs must be changed into...

See the matrix with their meanings:

The verbs to be used in Indirect speech	Their meanings
Exclaim/ cry out	**Say something suddenly and loudly**, especially because of strong emotion or pain.
Applaud	**To show your approval of somebody or** something by clapping hands or making any sound.
Swear	**Make a serious promise** to do something; Use rude or offensive language, when you are angry of something.
Welcome/Bid	**Wish someone tenderly** by wishing good morning, good afternoon, /Good bye, etc.
Bless	**Ask God to protect somebody;**
Congratulate	**Tell somebody that you are pleased about her success and achievement.**
Confess /repent	**Admits own faults**

Rule No-2: The interjections or exclamations will be changed into words as shown in the matrix and they are used with the preceding reporting verbs:

See the matrix with their meanings:

The Interjections, used in the D.S.	As they will be changed into:
Alas!	Expressing sorrow or grief **(Exclaim with grief / sorrow; exclaim sadly)**
Hurrah!	Expressing delight or joy **(Cry out/exclaim in joy/ with delight)**
Bravo!	Applauding or praising somebody **(applaud +object +saying that +...)**
By Jove	Swearing...due to any cause

	(Swear by Jove)
What a / How...	Used in sorrow, grief, or in praise of something. (What or how will change to **'great' or 'very'**) & reporting verb would be as: **(Exclaimed in wonder/ exclaimed in pain**, etc.)
Fie!	Expressing disgust ((Exclaim in disgust) (Expressed his disgust and said that.../ Exclaimed that it was shameful & said)
Poor fellow!	Feel pity for someone (Pitied the man and exclaimed that...)
So, help me Heaven!	Pray to God (Prayed to Heaven to help him and resolved not to /to do something)
Who knew...!	(He said that none knew...)
Good gracious! **Good Heavens!**	Expressing joy (Exclaim with wonder) (Exclaim with delight)
Good Morning /Good bye	Wishing someone tenderly (welcome / bid)

Note: Normally **'great'** is placed before a **noun**; and **'very'** is placed before an **adjective.**

1) He said, "What a fool I am!"
→ He **cried out with grief** that he was a great fool.
2) The Giant said, "How selfish I have been!"
→ The Giant **confessed with regret** that he had been very selfish.
→ The Giant **repented** that he had been very selfish.
3) The children said to each other, "How happy we are here!"
→ The children **cried out with joy** saying to each other that they were very happy then.
4) The children said to each other, "How happy we were there!"
→ The children **felt sorrow** saying to each other that they had been very happy there.

Rule No-3: The conjunction **'that'** is used.

Rule-4: the exclamatory sentence changed into assertive in the Indirect Speech.

Note: The person spoken to in the Direct Speech may be used or omitted in the Indirect Speech, as it suits to.

The reporting verbs- **'welcome'**, **'wish'**, **'bid'** & **'congratulate'**—may also be used in the exclamatory sentence.
5) The host said to me, "Good Morning!"
→ The host **welcomed me wishing** good morning.
→ The host **wished** me good morning.
6) They said to the departing friends, "Good Bye, Our friends!"
→ They **bade** good bye to their friends.
7) They said to the invitees, "Welcome!"
→ They **bade** welcome to the invitees.
8) He said, "Congratulation, my friend!"
→ He congratulated his friend.

Note: The verb, **'Wish'** also comes with an optative sentence.

Reporting of 'One-word Replies' & 'Multiple Sentences'

<u>One-word replies</u>— **'yes'**, **'no'**, **'yesterday'**, **'tomorrow'**, **'today'**, **'surely'**, etc.—are <u>found in dialogues or conversations.</u>

1) She said to me, "Do you know the boy who recites so nicely?" I replied, "**No.**"
   → She asked me if I knew the boy who recited so nicely. <u>I replied that *I did not know him*</u>. (Or *I did not*.)

2) She asked me, "Will you take a cup of coffee?" I said, "**Yes.**"
   → She asked me whether I would take a cup of coffee. <u>I replied that *I would take*</u>. (Or *I would*.)

When one-word replies are converted into Indirect Speech, they **must be in complete sentences** (in terms of the preceding statements or questions) as shown in the examples:

More Examples

3) "When will you go to Burdwan?" I said to him. "**Tomorrow**", he replied.
   → I asked him when he would go to Burdwan. He replied that *he would go (there) next day*.
4) "When did you come?" She asked me. "**Yesterday**", I said in reply.
   → She asked me when I had gone (there). I replied that *I had gone yesterday.*
5) "Will you join us in the picnic?" They asked. (Question) "**Surely**", I said.
   → They asked me if I would join then in the picnic. I said that *sure I would join them. (**Surely, I would**)*
   → They invited me to join in the picnic. **I assured them of my joining.**

Reporting Multiple Type of Sentences in one frame:

6) I said to the boy, "Who are you? Whom do you want?"
   → I asked the boy who he was and whom he wanted.

7) Sanchita said to Kusum, "I don't feel well. I think you will not mind if I do not go to school today. Perhaps you will submit the project for me."
   → Sanchita **informed** Kusum that she *felt unwell* (*didn't feel well*), and **hoped** that she would not mind if she *did not go to (remained absent from)* school that day. She **also said** that **perhaps** she (Kusum) would submit the project for her (Sanchita).

What to do:

Rule No-1: if the sentences are of same kind, <u>one reporting verb can be used & other Reported Speeches may be added</u> to each other <u>by Conjunctions</u>, like: **'and'**, **'or'**, **'but'**, as the case may be:

8) Sergeant (to man): Stop! Didn't I tell you to stop? You can't go there.

Note: *Look, the speech of the Sergeant is the combination of <u>Exclamatory</u>, <u>Interrogative</u> & <u>Assertive sentences</u>. So, to turn this speech into Indirect, one Reporting verb is not sufficient, at least three reporting verbs are needed to convey three moods of the speaker.*
   → The sergeant **ordered** the man to stop. He, then, **angrily asked** the man if he (the sergeant) had not told him (the man) to stop. The sergeant **also told** him that he (the man) could not go there.

What to do:

Rule No-2: if the sentences are of different kinds, <u>separate reporting verbs are used in the Indirect Speech for them.</u>

43. The Conversion or Transformation of Sentences

573.   This Chapter includes the Conversion or Transformation of Sentences from **One** kind to **another** <u>(what we have already learnt or discussed in the previous chapters)</u> **& vice-versa.** So, in the sense, it is just like compilation of that knowledge, and apply to for practice as through revision of the earlier ones. From practical sense, here is nothing new to discover.

A learner (when we are here, we might consider, he) **has already learnt** —

a. <u>That a word can be used in different Parts of Speech</u>, by derivative or without derivative;

b. That a phrase can be extended into a clause & a clause can be contracted into a phrase (simple to complex & compound, and vice-versa);

c. That a sentence can be written in different tenses;

d. That a sentence can be made with or without comparison;

e. That a sentence can be expressed in different voice (Active or Passive), moods or in manner of expression as well as in a different narration; (from Direct to Indirect & vice-versa) and thus, like many others.

Let's begin this 'chapter of conversion' with an adverb 'too', when 'too' can be expressed in other means or approach.

Conversion of Adverb 'too'

574.   Conversion of Adverb 'too'

Generally, we can replace the word 'too', with others like 'very', 'so', along with other changes in the sentence or inclusion of words, as shown below (Sl. No-1):

1) The news is **too** good. = The news is **very** good.
2) The news is **too** good to be true.
→   The news is **so** good *that it can't be* true.
3) These mangoes are **too** cheap to be good.
→   These mangoes are **so** cheap *that they can't be* good.
4) He drove **too** fast for the police to catch.
→   He drove **so** fast *that the police couldn't catch* him.
5) It is never **too** late to mend.
→   It is not **so** late *that it can't be* mended.
6) He is **too** ignorant for a postman.
→   He is **so** ignorant *that he is not suitable candidate* for a postman.
7) You are **too** late to hear the first speech.
→   You are **so** late *that you couldn't hear* the first speech.
8) My heart is **too** full for words.
→   My heart is **so** full *that I am eager to say* many words.
9) She was sobbing **too deeply** to make any answer.
→   She was sobbing **so much** *that she can't make* any answer.
10) She is **too** proud to beg pardon.
→   She is **so** proud *that she can't beg* pardon.
11) He is **far too** stupid for such a difficult post.
→   He is **so much** stupid *that he is not suitable* for such a difficult post.
12) He speaks **too fast** to be understood.
→   He speaks **so fast** *that he cannot be understood* by others.
13) This tree is **too high** to climb.
→   The tree is **so high** *that you can't* climb.
14) The bag was **too heavy** for me to carry.
→   The bag was **so heavy** *that I couldn't* carry.
15) The shirt is **too small** for him.
→   The shirt is **so small** *that he can't* wear.
16) The work is **too much** for any man to do single-handed.
→   The work is **so much** *that no a single man can do* it.
17) The fact is **too evident** to require any proof.
→   The fact is **so much evident** *that it doesn't need* or require any proof.

Conversion of Degrees (adj. & adv.)

575.   'Degrees' or 'Forms of Comparison occur to Adjective and Adverb, and one form of comparison can be change to other. Study the examples:

(From positive to comparative, superlative & vice versa. (Sl. No-2))

1) I am as strong as him.

- He is not stronger than me.
- None of us is the strongest. Who is the strongest here? (Answer will be 'None' = No one)

2) This razor is not as sharp as that one.
- That razor is sharper than this one. Or, 'This razor is less sharp than that one.'
- That razor is one of the sharpest.

3) Few historians write as interestingly as Joshi.
- Joshi writes more interestingly than most historians.
- Joshi is one of the few historians who write most interestingly.

4) No other metal is as useful as iron.
- Iron is more useful than any other metal.
- Iron is the most useful of all metals.

5) India is the largest democracy in the world.
- No other democracy in the world is as large as India.
- India is larger than any other democracy in the world.

6) Mumbai is one of the richest cities in India.
- Mumbai is richer than most other cities in India.
- Very few cities in India are as rich as Mumbai.

7) Burza Khalifa is not only the tallest building in the world. (superlative)
- Burza Khalifa is one of the tallest buildings in the world. (superlative)
- Burza Khalifa is not taller than few other buildings in the world. (comparative)
- Few other buildings in the world may be taller than Burza Khalifa. (comparative)
- Few other buildings in the world are at least as tall as Burza Khalifa. (positive)
- Burza Khalifa is perhaps not as tall as few other buildings in the world. (positive)

8) Peter is not one of the cleverest boys in the class.
- Some boys in the class are cleverer than Peter.
- Peter is less clever than some other boys in the class.
- Peter is not so clever as some other boys in the class.

9) No other grammar book is as popular as of Peter's 'Complete English Grammar'.
- Peter's 'Complete English Grammar' is more popular than any other grammar book.
- Peter's 'Complete English Grammar' is the most popular of all grammar books.

10) It is better to starve than beg.
- Begging is not as good as Starvation.
- Starvation may be the best of all things like begging. (Begging is one of the worst things.)

11) He loves all his sons equally well.
- No son he loves better than all others.
- There is no son he loves the best / most.

12) Some beans are at least as nutritious as meat.
- Meat is not more nutritious than some beans.
- Meat is not the most nutritious comparing to some beans.

13) The airplane flies faster than birds.
- No bird can fly as fast as an airplane.
- An airplane flies the fastest among all birds.

14) Helen of Troy was more beautiful than any other woman.
- No woman was as beautiful as Helen of Troy.
- Helen of Troy was the most beautiful woman.

15) This newspaper has a bigger circulation than any other morning paper.
- No any other morning paper has as circulation as this newspaper.
- This newspaper has the biggest circulation among all morning papers.

Conversion of Active & Passive

576. A sentence in the Active form can be changed into the Passive form, and vice-versa (Sl. No-3):

1) Brutus stabbed Caesar.
- Caesar was stabbed by Brutus.

2) The people made Gopal their king.
- Gopal was made king by the people.

3) Who taught you grammar?

- By whom was you taught grammar?

4) The Principal gave him a reward.

- He was rewarded by the Principal.

5) The Romans expected to conquer Carthage.

- Carthage was expected to be conquered by the Romans. / It was expected Carthage would be won (conquered) by the Romans.

6) One should keep one's promise.

- One's promise should be kept.

7) I know her. = *She is known to me.*
8) I know the girl, Rossie by her name.

- The girl, Rossie by her name, is known to me.

9) The police were taking me to prison.

- I was being taken to prison by the police.

10) Her behavior vexes me often.

- I am often vexed by her behavior.

11) It is time to shut up the shop.

- It is time for the shop to be shut up.

12) The mayor's speech was loudly cheered.

- The audience loudly cheered the mayor's speech.

13) Someone has picked my pocket.

- My pocket has been picked.

14) Our army has been defeated.

- The enemy has defeated our army.

15) I shall be obliged to go. = Duty will oblige me to go.
16) People admire the brave and honest.

- The brave and honest are admired by people.

17) Who taught you such tricks all this?

- By whom were you taught such tricks that all?

18) Brutus accused Caesar of ambition.

- Caesar was accused of ambition by his friend Brutus.

19) One expects better behavior from a college student.

- It is expected better behavior from a college student.

20) They showed a video of 'Titanic'. = A video of Titanic was showed.
21) You must endure what you cannot cure.

- What cannot be cured must be endured.

22) He made me do the work. = I was forced to do the work.
23) Nature teaches beasts to know their friends.

- Beasts are taught to know their friends by nature.

24) We expect good news from her. (We are expecting...)

- Good news is being expected from her.

25) He showed me the greatest respect.

- I was showed the greatest respect (by him).

26) Alas! We shall hear his voice no more.

- Alas! His voice will not be heard any more.

27) Shall I ever forget those happy days?

- Should those happy days be forgotten ever?

28) Do you not understand my meaning?

- Isn't my meaning understood? /Is my meaning not understood?

29) We must listen to his word. = *His words must be listened to.*
30) He pretended to be a Baron. (He was pretending...)

- He had been pretending to be a Baron.

31) You never hear of a happy millionaire. = It is never be heard of a happy millionaire.
32) The public will learn with astonishment that war is imminent.

- It will be learnt with astonishment that war is imminent.

33) Did you never hear that name? = Was it not heard that name (by you)?
34) Without effort nothing can be gained. = If you don't effort, you will gain nothing.
35) He was a chosen leader. = We chose him our leader.
36) By whom was this jug broken? = Who broke this jug?

37) I was offered a chair. = He (/They) offered me a chair.
38) This question will be discussed at the meeting tomorrow.
- • I will discuss this question at the meeting tomorrow.
39) He will be greatly surprised if he is chosen.
- • If we choose him, it will surprise him greatly.
40) He was arrested on a charge of theft, but for lack of evidence he was released.
- • Police arrested him on a charge of theft, but for lack of evidence they released him.

Conversion from Affirmative to Negative

577. Study the following examples for the conversion of Affirmative sentence to Negative, and vice-versa (Sl. No-4):

1) As soon as he came, he made objections.
→ No sooner had he come, he made objections.
2) These fishing nets are all the wealth I own.
→ I own wealth nothing except these fishing nets.
3) I always love my motherland as a child loves her mother.
→ I always love my motherland no less than as a child to her mother. / There is hardly any difference of my love to my motherland and a child's to her mother.
4) Brutus loved Caesar.
→ Brutus had nothing but love for Caesar.
5) I was doubtful whether it was you.
→ I was not sure that it was you.
6) Old fools surpass all other fools in folly.
→ There is no fool like an old fool.
7) He is greater than me.
→ I am not so great as him.
8) Alfred was the best king that ever reigned in England.
→ No other king as good as Alfred ever reigned in England.
9) Everest is the highest mountain in the world.
→ No any other mountain is as high as the Everest.
10) He is sometimes foolish. = *He is not always wise.*
11) He failed to notice me when he came in.
→ He didn't notice me when he came in.
12) He was more rapacious than a griffin.
→ A griffin was not more rapacious than him.
13) He was as rapacious as a griffin. = He was not less griffin than rapacious.
14) Ashoka was the greatest king of the Maurya.
→ No other king of the Maurya was as great as king Ashoka.
15) Ashoka was greater than Chandra Gupta Maurya.
→ Chandra Gupta Maurya was not greater than king Ashoka.
16) The rose by any other name would smell as sweet.
→ No any other name of rose would lessen its smell as sweet.
17) Everybody will admit that he did his best. = Nobody will deny that he did the best.
18) Only a millionaire can afford such extravagance. = None but a millionaire can afford such extravagance.
19) Every man makes mistake sometimes and that defines his life.
→ There is none who does not make mistake and that doesn't define his or her life.
20) I care little what he says about me. = I do not care much what he says about me.
21) As soon as he saw me, he came up and spoke to me.
→ No sooner had he seen me he came up and spoke to me.
22) He must have seen the Taj Mahal when he went to Agra.
→ It is hardly possible that he has not seen the Taj Mahal when he went to Agra.
23) Nobody was absent. = Everybody was present.
24) None lives immortal. = Everybody is mortal.
25) No one can deny that she is pretty.
→ Everybody admits that she is pretty.
26) God will not never forget the cry of humble.
→ God will always remember the cry of humble.

27) I am not a little tired. *= I am tired very much.*
28) There was no one present who did not cheer.

→ Everybody was present there cheered.

29) I never in my life laid a plan and failed to carry it out.

→ I always in my life laid a plan and succeeded to carry it out.

30) Not many men would be cruel and unjust to a cripple.

→ Few men would be cruel and unjust to a cripple.

31) No man could have done it better.

→ Hardly a man could have done it better.

32) The two brothers are not unlike each other.

→ The two brothers are like each other.

33) The two brothers are not like each other.

→ The two brothers are unlike each other.

34) He has promised never to touch wine again.

→ He has promised to keep off ever from wine.

35) We did not find the road very bad.

→ We found the road on average condition.

36) There is no smoke without fire.

→ There is hardly any smoke without fire.

37) It is not likely that he will ever see his home again.

→ It is unlikely that he will ever see his home again.

Conversion of Interrogative to Assertive

578. The following are about the conversion of sentences, Interrogative to Assertive and vice-versa (Sl. No-5):

1) What though we happen to be late?

✓ It does not matter much though we happen to be late.

2) Why waste time in reading trash?

✓ It is foolish to waste time in reading trash.

3) Were we sent into the world simply to make money?

✓ We were not sent into the world simply to make money.

4) How can man die better than facing fearful odds?

✓ Man cannot die better than facing fearful odds.

5) When can their glory fade?

✓ Their glory can never fade.

6) Was he not a villain to do such a deed?

✓ He was a villain to do such a deed.

7) No one can be expected to submit for ever to injustice.

✓ Who expects to submit for ever to injustice?

8) There is nothing better than a busy life.

✓ Is there anything better than a busy life?

9) Nowhere in the world will you find a fairer building than the Taj Mahal.

✓ Where will you find a fairer building than the Taj Mahal?

10) It is useless to offer bread to a man who is dying of thirst.

✓ Is not it useless to offer bread to a man who is dying of thirst?

11) We could have done nothing without your help.

✓ What could we have done without your help?

12) That was not an example to be followed.

✓ Was that an example to be followed?

13) What though the field be lost?

✓ Nothing would be even if the field be lost.

14) Is that the way a gentleman should behave?

✓ That is not the way a gentleman should behave.

15) Who does not know the owl?

✓ Everyone knows the owl.

16) Shall I ever forget those happy days?

✓ I shall not ever forget those happy days.

17) Who is so wicked as to amuse himself with the infirmities of extreme old age?

18) Why waste time in this fruitless occupation?

    ✓ There is no one so wicked to amuse himself with the infirmities of extreme old age.

19) Is this the kind of dress to wear in public?

    ✓ We should not waste time in this fruitless occupation.

20) Can you gather grape from thorns or figs from thistles?

    ✓ This is not the kind of dress to wear in public.

    ✓ You cannot gather grape from thorns or figs from thistles.

Conversion of Exclamatory to Assertive

579. The following are about the conversion of sentences, from Exclamatory to Assertive and think vice-versa (Sl. No-6):

1) How sweet the moonlight sleeps upon this bank!

    ✓ The moonlight very sweetly sleeps upon this bank.

2) If only I were young again!

    ✓ I wish I were young again.

3) Alas! That youth should pass away!

    ✓ It is sad to think that youth should pass away.

4) How beautiful is night!

    ✓ Night is very beautiful.

5) To think of our meeting here!

    ✓ It is strange that we should meet here.

6) O what a fall was there, in my nature and sense!

    ✓ There was a great fall in my nature and sense.

7) How cold you are!

    ✓ You are very cold.

Transform the followings into Exclamatory:

8) It is very horrible night.

    ✓ How horrible night is it!

9) It was extremely base of him to desert you in your time of need.

    ✓ What a base of him to desert you in your need of time!

10) It is hard to believe that he did such a deed.

    ✓ Unbelievable! he did such a thing!

11) I wish I had met you ten years ago.

    ✓ If I had met you ten years ago!

12) It is very stupid of me to forget your name.

    ✓ How stupid I am to forget your name!

13) He leads a most unhappy life.

    ✓ What an unhappy life he leads!

14) I wish I had come one hour ago.

    ✓ If only I had come one hour earlier!

15) Ah, what a sight was there! = There was very beautiful sight.
16) What a piece of work is man! = A man is a wonderful piece of work.
17) What a wonderful creature an elephant is!

    ✓ An elephant is a very wonderful creature.

18) How awkwardly he manages his sword!

    ✓ He manages his sword very awkwardly.

19) O that we two were infants playing!

    ✓ I wish we were two infants playing.
    ✓ I wish we were two infants again and play together.

20) If only I had the wings of a dove! = I wish I had the wings of a dove.
21) If only I knew more of this! = I wish I knew more of this.

Conversion of Parts of Speech

580. Study the following examples of conversion of parts of speech used in the sentences (Sl. No-7):

1) That kind of joke does not **amuse** me. (verb)
✓ That kind of joke does not give me any **amusement.** (noun)
2) It **costs** twelve rupees. (verb) = The **cost** is twelve rupees. (noun)
3) He has **disgraced** his family. (verb)
✓ He is a **disgrace** to his family. (noun)
4) He **fought bravely**. (verb, adv)
✓ He put up a **brave fight.** (Adj, noun)
5) The treaty of Salbai should be **remembered** as one of the landmarks in the history of India. (verb)
✓ The treaty of Salbai is worthy of **remembrance** as one of the landmarks in the history of India. (noun)
6) I cannot **consent** to your going. (verb)
✓ I cannot give my **consent** to your going. (noun)
7) He gave a **curt reply.** (adj. noun) = He **replied curtly**. (verb, adv)
8) He showed **generosity** even to his enemies. (noun)
✓ He was **generous** even to his enemies. (adjective)
9) There is **slight difference** between the two shades. (adj. & noun)
✓ The two shades are **slightly different.** (adv., adj.)
10) The act made them **free**. (adjective)
✓ The act gave them **freedom**. (noun)
11) He examined the document **carefully**. (adverb)
✓ He examined the document with **care**. (Noun with preposition)
12) We passed an **anxious** hour. (adjective)
✓ We passed an hour **anxiously.** (adverb)
13) Few write in a more **interesting** manner than him. (adjective)
✓ Few write more **interestingly** than him. (adverb)
14) He **presumptuously** ignored my advice. (adverb)
✓ He **presumed** to ignore my advice. (verb)

Replace the underlined Nouns by Verbs:

15) He rejected all our _proposals_.
✓ We **proposed** him all the times only to be rejected.
16) Steel gains _strength_ from the addition of nickel.
✓ Steel **strengthens** by addition of nickel.
17) He made an _agreement_ to supply me with firewood.
✓ He **agreed** to supply me firewood.
18) His _purpose_ is not clear from his letter.
✓ He **intends** what is not clear from his letter.
19) You cannot gain _admission_ without a ticket.
✓ You cannot be **admitted** without a ticket.
✓ We cannot a**dmit** you without a ticket.
20) He has no _intention_ of leaving the city. = He does not **intend** to leave the city.
21) I have a _disinclination_ for work today. = I **don't intend** to work today.
22) He made a _success_ of all his undertakings.
✓ He **succeeded** in all his undertakings.
23) These mangoes have a sweet _smell_ but a sour taste.
✓ These mangoes **smell** sweet but have sour taste.

Replace the underlined Adverbs by Verbs:

24) The defenders _successfully_ repelled every attack on the city.
✓ The defenders **succeeded** to repel every attack on the city.
25) This scene is _surpassingly_ beautiful.
✓ This scene **surpasses** all in beauty.
26) He is _admittedly_ the greatest general of the country.
✓ They **admit** him to be the greatest general of the country.
27) They welcomed the good news most _joyfully_.
✓ They **enjoyed** very much to welcome the good news.

Replace the underlined Nouns & Adverbs by corresponding Adjectives:

28) In all <u>probability</u> the day will be fine.
✓ It is all **probable** that the day will be fine.
29) The rats gave us a great deal of <u>trouble</u>.
✓ The rats were very **troublesome**.
30) He was dismissed for <u>negligence</u> rather than <u>competence</u>.
✓ The office dismissed the **negligent** him rather than being less **competent**. / He was **negligent,** for this he was dismissed, but not for being less **competent**.
31) He was <u>admittedly</u> clever, but he <u>evidently</u> lacked industry.
✓ He was **admitted** (participle adj.) as clever, but it is **evident** he lacked industry.
32) The merchant had great <u>success</u> in all his dealings, and was <u>naturally</u> esteemed by his fellow citizens.
✓ The merchant was great **successful** in all his dealings, and it was **natural** his fellow citizens esteemed him.

Replace the underlined Verbs & Adjectives by corresponding Nouns:

33) Though the ant is small it is as <u>intelligent</u> as the elephant.
✓ Though the ant is small, its **intelligence** is equal to an elephant.
34) He said he <u>regretted</u> that he had <u>acted</u> so hastily.
✓ He said that he is **sorry** for his **act** in hastiness.
35) He was so <u>active</u> in his old age that everybody <u>admired</u> him.
✓ The old man got **admiration** from everybody for his superb **activeness**.
36) Before I <u>pay</u> you, what is <u>due</u> you must <u>sign</u> this receipt.
✓ I need your **signature** before the **payment** of the **due**.
37) The best way to be <u>healthy</u> is to be <u>temperate</u> in all things.
✓ No one can gain **health** without **temperament** in all things.

Replace the underlined Nouns & Adjectives by corresponding Adverbs:

38) Her dress was <u>poor</u> and <u>mean</u>.
✓ She wore her dress **poorly** and **meanly**.
39) He broke the rules without any intention of doing so, but it does not follow that his punishment is <u>wrong</u>.
✓ He broke the rules without any intention of doing so, but it does not follow that he is punished **wrongly**.
40) His mistake was <u>evident</u>, but his sincerity was also <u>obvious</u>.
✓ **Evidently,** he did mistake, but **obviously** he was sincere too.
41) By a <u>careful</u> analysis of these substances, you will see that they differ in <u>essence</u>.
✓ If you **carefully** analyze these substances **essentially** you will see the difference in them.

Conversion of Simple, Compound & Complex

581.   In conversion, sl. No- 8. When we do transform **Simple Sentences to Compound or Complex**, simply we do change or enlarge —
- A participle or an adjective,
- A preposition with Noun or Gerund,
- An Infinitive verb,
- A Noun or the Phrase in apposition,
- The Absolute Phrase,
- Double Objects or A complement,
- The Adverb or Adverbial Phrases

— into Clauses (co-ordinate & sub-ordinate) accordingly; as,

1) <u>**Having done** his lesson</u>, he went out to play cricket. (simple)
✓ <u>*After he had done* his lesson</u>, he went out to play cricket. (complex)
✓ <u>*He had done* his lesson</u> and then went out to play cricket. (compound)

Note: You may take a revision of the chapters— 'Classification of Sentences, based on structure', 'Analysis' & 'Synthesis' for better understand the parts, and do better conversion.

By convert the present participial into a clause; as they generally imply:

- Time,
- Cause,
- Concession,
- Condition, etc.

In the above sentence, it denotes an action happened earlier than the other.

2) **_Walking_** *along the street* one day I saw a dead cobra.
   - ✓ *While I was walking* along the street one day I saw a dead cobra.

3) **_Being_** overpowered, he surrendered.
   - ✓ *Because he was* overpowered, he surrendered.

4) **_Running_** *at top speed*, he got out of breath.
   - ✓ *Because he ran* at top speed, he got out of breath.

5) **_Possessing_** *all the advantages of education and wealth*, he never made a name.
   - ✓ *Although he possessed* all the advantages of education and wealth, he never made a name.

6) **_Following_** *my advice*, you will gain your object.
   - ✓ *If you follow* my advice, you will gain your object.

7) Seven were killed, **_including the guard_**.
   - ✓ Seven were killed, *if the guard is included*.

And by Change others:

8) To his eternal disgrace, he betrayed his country.
   - ✓ He betrayed his country, and this was to his eternal disgrace. *(The relative phrase has turned into a clause)*

9) Besides robbing the pilgrims, he also murdered them.
   - ✓ He not only robbed the pilgrims but also murdered them. *(The prepositional phrase has turned into a clause and that is linked with a co-ordinate conjunction with the main)*

10) He must work very hard to win the first prize.
   - ✓ He must work very hard, or he will not win the first prize. *(The infinitive has turned into a clause)*

11) Notwithstanding his hard work, he didn't get the expected outcome.
   - ✓ He worked hard, yet he did not get the expected outcome. *(The preposition with noun has turned into an independent clause)*

12) The teacher punished the boy for disobedience.
   - ✓ The boy was disobedient, so the teacher punished him. *(The adverbial phrase has turned into a sub-ordinate adverbial clause)*

13) He finished his exercise and put away his books.
   - ✓ Having finished his exercise, he put away his books.
   - ✓ After he had finished his exercise, he put away his books.

14) Not only did his father give him money, but his mother did too.
   - ✓ Besides his father giving him money, his mother also did the same.
   - ✓ It is not that his father only gave him money but his mother too.

15) He was a mere boy but he offered to fight the giant.
   - ✓ In spite of his being a mere boy, he offered to fight the giant.
   - ✓ Though he was a mere boy, he offered to fight the giant.

16) He must not be late, or he will be punished.
   - ✓ In the event of his being late, he will be punished.
   - ✓ If he is late, he will be punished.

17) You must either pay the bill at once or return the goods.
   - ✓ Falling prompt payment, the goods must be returned by you.
   - ✓ If you not pay the bill at once, you must return the goods.

18) We must eat, or we cannot live.
   - ✓ We eat to live. If we do not eat, we cannot live.

19) He confessed his crime.
   - ✓ He confessed that he was guilty.
   - ✓ He was guilty and he confessed it.

20) He bought his uncle's library.
   - ✓ He bought the library which belonged to his uncle.
   - ✓ He bought a library and it belonged to his uncle.

21) On the arrival of the mails the ship will leave.
   - ✓ The ship will leave as soon as the mails arrive.

22) He owed his success to his father.

    ✓   The ship will leave after the mails arrive.

    ✓   It was owing to his father that he succeeded.

    ✓   He succeeded and this he owed to his father.

23) He worked hard to pass the examination.

    ✓   He worked hard so that he might pass the examination.

    ✓   He wanted to pass the examination and he worked hard for that reason.

24) Only Indians are admitted.

    ✓   If you are not an Indian you cannot be admitted.

    ✓   You are an Indian and you can be admitted.

25) He succeeded unexpectedly.

    ✓   He succeeded although his success was not expected.

    ✓   He succeeded and it was unexpected.

26) The management was thoroughly bad.

    ✓   The management was as bad as it could be.

    ✓   The management was bad and it was profoundly.

27) A man's modesty is in inverse proportion to his ignorance.

    ✓   The more ignorant a man is, the less modest he is.

    ✓   If the man is ignorant, he is less modest, is the correct proportion.

(From Complex to Simple)

How Noun Clauses turn to be Nouns or Noun phrase in the Simple Sentences:

28) He said <u>that he was innocent</u>. (Noun Clause)

    ✓   He declared **his innocence**. (Noun)

    ✓   He declared **to be innocent**. (adjective)

29) <u>That you are drunk</u> aggravates your offence.

    ✓   **Your drunkenness** aggravates your offence.

30) Tell me <u>where you live</u>.

    ✓   Tell me **your address**.

31) It is a pity <u>that we should have to undergo this disgrace</u>.

    ✓   <u>*Our having to undergo this disgrace*</u> is a pity.

32) ***It is proclaimed*** that all men found with arms will be shot.

    ✓   ***According to the proclamation*** all men found with arms will be shot. (by preposition with a noun)

33) He remarked <u>how impudent the boy was</u>.

    ✓   He remarked on the ***boy's impudence***. (by preposition with a noun)

34) <u>How long I shall stay</u> is doubtful.

    ✓   ***The duration of my stay*** is doubtful.

35) Except **that he hurt his hand**, he was lucky.

    ✓   Except ***for the hurt to his hand***, he was lucky.

By use of single adjective or adjective phrase for the Adjective Clauses:

36) He died in the village <u>where he was born</u>.

    ✓   He died in his **native** village.

37) The moment <u>which is lost</u> is lost forever.

    ✓   A lost moment is ***lost*** forever.

38) Men <u>who have risen by their own exertions</u> are always respected.

    ✓   ***Self-made*** men are always respected.

39) They <u>that are whole</u> have no need of the physician.

    ✓   ***Healthy persons*** have no need of the physician.

40) We came upon a hut <u>where a peasant lived</u>.

    ✓   We came upon a ***peasant's hut***.

41) Youth is the time <u>when the seeds of character are sown</u>.

    ✓   Youth is the ***time for the formation of character***.

42) The exact time <u>when this occurred</u> has not been ascertained.

    ✓   The exact time ***of the occurrence*** has not been ascertained.

43) The son <u>who was his chief pride in his old age</u> is dead.

44) I have no advice <u>that I can offer you</u>.

✓ His son, **_the pride of his old age_**, is dead.

✓ I have no advice **_to offer_** you.

Study how the Adverb Clauses turn to adverbs or adverbial phrases mostly and also to others sometimes (turns to noun, adjective, infinitive; thus to any, a per sense and requirement), and the sentences become Simple Sentences:

45) The captain was annoyed <u>that we had not carried out his orders</u>.

✓ The captain was annoyed **at our not having carried out his orders.** (why was the captain annoyed at?)

46) You can talk <u>as much as you like</u>.

✓ You can talk **to your heart's content.** (how much can I talk?)

47) Success & everything come <u>if a man will only work & wait</u>.

✓ Only work and waiting **diligently** bring success and everything to a man. (how?)

48) I am pushing my business <u>wherever I can find an opening</u>.

✓ I am pushing my business **in every possible direction.** (where?)

49) He will not pay <u>unless he is compelled</u>.

✓ He will pay **only under compulsion.** (in what condition?)

50) You have succeeded <u>better than you hoped</u>.

✓ You have succeeded **beyond your hopes.**

51) <u>When the cat is away</u> the mice will play.

✓ **In the absence of the cat** the mice will play.

52) He does not always speak <u>as he thinks</u>.

✓ He does not always speak **his thoughts.**

53) He was so tired <u>that he could not stand</u>.

✓ He was **too tired to** stand.

54) A soldier will always do as he is commanded by his superiors.

✓ A soldier will always carry out (or execute) the **commands of his superiors.** (noun phrase)

55) I was surprised when I heard him talk so.

✓ I was **surprised to hear** him talk so.

56) If I make a promise, I keep it.

✓ I make promise **only to keep** it.

57) As the war ended, the soldiers returned.

✓ The war **being ended**, the soldiers returned. (turns to present participle)

58) While there is life there is hope.

✓ Life and hope are **inseparable.** (use of an adjective, in place of adverb of condition)

59) As you sow, so you will reap.

✓ You will but reap the fruits of your sowing. (turns to a gerund)

Conversion of Compound to Complex

60) Search his pockets and you will find the watch.

✓ If you search his pockets, you will find the watch.

61) Do as I tell you, or you will regret it.

✓ Unless you do as I tell you, you will regret it.

62) Waste not, want not.

✓ If you do not waste, you will not want.

63) He wishes to become learned; therefore, he is studying hard.

✓ He is studying hard so that he may become learned.

64) I am glad that he has recovered from illness.

✓ He has recovered from illness and I am glad at it.

65) We can prove that the earth is round.

✓ The earth is round, and we can prove it.

66) I have found the book that I had lost.

✓ I had lost a book, but I have found it.

67) If he is at home, I shall see him.

✓ He may be at home, and in that case, I shall see him.

68) We sow so that we may reap.

✓ We desire to reap; therefore, we sow.

Conversion of Narration

582. Conversion of Narration (Indirect to Direct & vice-versa; Sl. No-9): For more, go through the chapter of Narration Change, i.e., only to the previous chapter. Here is provided a space not more than a little much:

1) He enquired whether my name was Peter.
   ✓ He said to me, "Is not your name, Peter?"

2) As the stranger entered the town, he met by a policeman who asked him if he was a traveler. He replied carelessly that it would appear so.
   ✓ As the stranger entered the town, a policeman met him who asked, "Are you a traveler?" "So, it would appear", he answered carelessly.

3) The prince said that it gave him great pleasure to be there that evening.
   ✓ The prince said, "It gives me great pleasure to be here this evening."

4) He said, "Let us wait for the award."
   ✓ He proposed that they should wait for the award.

5) The teacher often says to me, "If you don't work hard, you will fail."
   ✓ The teacher often says if I don't work hard, I shall fail.

Conversion: From <u>One</u> to <u>Thirty-Two</u>

583. For conversion one sentence to thirty-two, we choose **here** 'a simple sentence' which is also an <u>Assertive Affirmative</u>, in the <u>Active Voice</u>; it is also in the <u>Present Indefinite Tense</u> and of <u>Direct Speech</u>, besides being a Simple sentence. We can convert the simple sentence to as many. Read the sentence:

'You do the work.'

Type of Sentences	Examples
1. Assertive & Affirmative	You do the work.
1. Assertive & Negative	You don't do the work.
2. Interrogative	Do you do the work?
3. Imperative	Do the work. / I let you to do the work. You are ordered/ advised to do the work. You are asked to do the work.
4. Optative	Let you do the work. / I wish you to do the work. /May God give you power to do the work.
5. Exclamatory	What! you have not yet done the work.
6. Complex	What you do is a work.
7. Compound	Someone will do the work and it is you.
8. Passive	The work is done by you.
9. Indirect speech	He asks me to do the work.
10. Present Continuous	You are doing the work.
11. Present Perfect	You have done the work.
12. Present Perfect Continuous	You have been doing the work since Friday.

13. Past Indefinite	You did the work.
14. Past Continuous	You were doing the work
15. Past Perfect	You had done the work.
16. Past Perfect Continuous	You had been doing the work for three hours.
17. Future Indefinite	You will do the work
18. Future Continuous	You will be doing the work.
19. Future Perfect	You will have done the work.
20. Future Perfect Continuous	You will have been doing the work before we reach there.

Type of Sentences: now by modals	Examples
21. By use of 'can'	You can do the work. — express ability
22. By use of 'may'	You may do the work. — giving permission
23. By use of 'must'	You must do the work. — strong necessity
24. By use of 'will'	You will do the work. — futurity
25. By use of 'could'	You could do the work. — past ability
26. By use of 'might'	You might do the work. — past possibility
27. By use of 'should'	You should the work. — morality
28. By use of 'would'	You would do the work. — futurity in past
29. By use of 'ought to'	You ought to do the work. — obligatory
30. By use of 'used to'	You used to do the work. — past habit
31. By use of 'need'	You need to do the work. — necessity
32. By use of 'dare'	How dare you to do the work! — wonder at courage

44. The Use of Punctuations (includes 16)

584. **What is Punctuation?** = Punctuation is an art of giving the expression a pause <u>by some marks</u> or <u>points (not dividing a sentence)</u>, so as to make the meaning clearer.

Let's see the punctuations at a glance:

Sl. No	Punctuations	Signs	Representing or Meanings (main)
(1)	Capital Letters	A, B, C ... Z	To begin a sentence or fresh line of poetry
(2)	Full Stop	(.)	Greatest pause, or end of an Assert. or Imperative Sentence
(3)	Question Mark	(?)	Is used after each Direct Question.
(4)	Exclamation	(!)	Used after Interjections or after Exclaim. Sentence
(5)	Comma	(,)	Shortest pause, after Nominative Absolute, etc.
(6)	Semicolon	(;)	A pause of greater importance than comma

(7)	Colon	(:)	Introducing a quotation
(8)	Dash	(—)	To indicate an abrupt stop, or change of thought.
(9)	Hyphen	(-)	used to connect the parts of a Compound word
(10)	Apostrophe	(...')	Show omission of letter(s), genitive case
(11)	Inverted Commas	('...'/ "...")	To enclose words of the speaker
(12)	Use of Brackets	(...),{...}, [...]	_To enclose a parenthesis_
(13)	Asterisk (*),		To point out something is missing
(14)	Dot-dot-dot ...,		To show incomplete statement:
(15)	Oblique (/)		To mean 'either'/ 'or'
(16)	Parenthesis	point out by (...)/ ,...,	an inserted extra statement by a word, phrase or a clause, used separately in the sentence.

Read them again with examples. Let's begin with the use of Capital Letter.

Use of Capital Letters

1. Use of Capital Letters

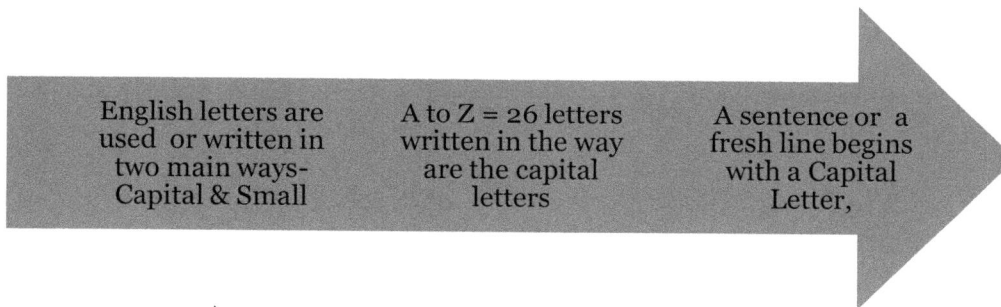

English letters are used or written in two main ways- Capital & Small

A to Z = 26 letters written in the way are the capital letters

A sentence or a fresh line begins with a Capital Letter,

Sl. No	Illustration	Examples
1.	First letter of a sentence must be in capital letter.	• _He_ was a great ruler of _Maura_ dynasty in _India_.
2.	First letter of Proper Noun or Proper adjective must be in capital.	• _Gautama Buddha_ never met with _Asoka_. You must love an _Indian_.
3.	The title of an Honorable person must be in capital.	• _The Minister_ met with the _Principal_ of the college.
4.	First letter of a poetic line (each) must be in capital.	• _Twinkle Twinkle_ little star,
		• _How_ I wonder what you are.
5.	'I' to mean first person and 'God' to mean almighty, & all Nouns & Pronouns which indicate the Deity, always be in Capital Letter.	• With due respect, _I_ like to draw your attention. He prayed to _God_ whole night. The _Lord_, He is the _God_.
6.	'O' of interjection must be in capital.	• _Oh_ my _God_! he is no more.
7.	First letter of a quotation must be in capital.	• He said, "_Will_ you lend me your book, please?"
8.	Abbreviation is written in capital after use of full stop.	• _L.L.B., M.A., B.A., B.Sc., M.K. Gandhi was_ the father of nation.

2. **Full Stop,**
3. **Question &**
4. **Exclamation**

2. Full Stop (.)	Examples
a) After each complete sentence	• A farmer had three sons. Come here.
b) After short forms or abbreviations	5 a.m., M.Phil., Mr. P.N. Sarkar, Saidpur B.M.A. High School.

3. Question Mark (?)	Examples
a) After a direct question	• What's your name? • How old are you?
But not after an indirect question	• He asked me what my name was.

4. Exclamation Mark (!)	Examples
a) After any expression of emotion as, wonder, fear, excitement, joy etc.	• What a beautiful sight! / How strange! • Hurrah! We have won the match.
b) After interjections or any part of speech used so:	• Milton! Thou shouldst be living at this hour. Gone! Dead! Accident! • Oh! Hurrah! Alas! Oh dear! etc.

5. Comma (,)

The comma represents the shortest pause and is the most frequently used sign of all marks.

Study the uses of Comma (,) in the following chart:

5. Comma (,)	Examples
a) <u>Between words of same parts of speech</u> or <u>repeated words</u>, if used in a sequence.	• Pompi, Pieu, & Jhumpa are her friends. • He went, found, chose, & bought the things. • She is long, fair, laughing, & kind-hearted. • I will never, never go there. • You must, must do it.
b) Between phrases, clauses of same character, often to avoid the repetition of subject.	• <u>I went to Kolkata, met my aunt, & came back.</u> • <u>He entered the room, wrote a letter, and then left the place.</u>
Exceptions: <u>But when</u> only <u>two words or phrases</u> of the same character are <u>joined by</u> <u>'and'</u>, the comma is not required.	• <u>Ram and Shyam</u> went there. • <u>Swimming in the river</u> and <u>swimming in the pond</u> are good for health.
c) But <u>when words go in pairs,</u> the comma is placed between each pair.	• Rifles and bayonets, spades and axes, drums and trumpets littered the ground.
d) Between co-ordinate clauses. (We may not use too.)	• He is ill, and his father too is away. • He is away now, but will return shortly.

e) To mark off noun or noun clauses from adjective clauses, if there is more than one.	• I do not know where he is, when he will come, or what his present state is. • I know the girl who is beautiful, who is fair, who is soft-hearted, and who is proud.
Exceptions: i) When there is only one adjective clause, it does not need to separate from its noun.	• The dog I bought has died. • I saw your brother who told me this. • I saw your brother, who told me this. (exception)
ii) But if that is lengthy, comma can be used.	• The man, who promised to help me if I would approach him, has gone away.
iii) It is applicable even to a long complex noun clause, used as a subject.	• That his brother who has done so much for the club will be elected its secretary, is known to all.
f) To mark off adverbial clauses or phrases in apposition or the Absolute Phrases, & also participial phrases that might be expanded into clauses or sentences.	• In order that you may succeed, I shall help you with money. • Saral, after he had left the place, went direct to the Magistrate. • Ram, having returned home, went to see her. • Disappointed of the prize, he left the place.
g) Comma is used even to mark off a single adverb in a sentence.	• This, then, is my story. • I shall, however, help you.
Exception: But when the Adverbial clause or the phrase follows the principal clause, the comma is omitted.	• I was glad when I saw you. • He came after I had left.
h) Before or after the Vocative Case or the Nominative of Address.	• Tarun, come here. / Stop, boys. • Sir, be seated, please. • Hello, who is speaking?
i) Before & after the phrase in apposition. *If ends with it, use full stop.*	• Ashoka, the emperor of India, took Buddhism. He came, to the surprise of all. • A tiger, two meters long, was shot dead.
j) After an absolute construction:	• The sun having set, we left the place. • Dinner over, the guests departed. • To tell you the truth, I consider him fool.
k) After words like 'yes', 'no':	• Has he come? No, he hasn't. • Will you go to school? Yes, I'll.
l) To separate the name of a town, a state, a country in the same sentence (to indicate the omission of a preposition)	• He is from Kolkata, West Bengal, India. • (He is from Kolkata of West Bengal in India.)
m) To separate the day of a month from its year. (Here also to indicate the omission of a preposition)	• She was born on 8th May, 2002. • (She was born on 8th May of the year 2002.)
n) To indicate the omission of a verb	• Virtue leads to happiness; vice, to misery. (Vice leads to misery.)
o) To mark off a quotation.	• He said, "I love you."

6. **Semicolon (;) &**
7. **Colon (:)**

> The semicolon (;) denotes a longer pause than the comma. In other words, it represents a pause of greater importance than that of comma.

> The colon (:) introduces a quotation or examples, often followed by a dash.

The Use of Semicolon (;)

Semicolon (;)	Examples
a) Between co-ordinate clauses when are not joined by conjunctions.	○ To err is human; to forgive, divine. ○ I have heard his statement; it is improbable story.
b) When they are joined by conjunctions that express contrast or inference like—therefore, yet, then, however, so, otherwise – they follow semicolon, and after them, we use generally a comma (,), except 'yet' & 'then' (they are not followed by comma.)	○ He is ill; *therefore,* he will not come. ○ He helped me to his best; *yet* I failed in my attempt. ○ You don't believe me; *then* I am leaving the job. ○ She was weak student; *however,* she passed. ○ He did not work hard; *so,* he could not succeed. ○ You must do it for him; *otherwise,* he will be angry with us.
c) When commas are used in smaller division, the semicolon can be used there in some larger division, even before a conjunction.	○ The boy, who had stood first in the examination, was given a very good prize; and it was expected, this would encourage him to exert himself still more to keep up his position. ○ He was a brave, large-hearted man; and we all honored him.

The Use of Colon (:)

Colon (:)	Examples
a) After a statement, <u>complete in itself;</u> when followed by another or a series, <u>connected without a conjunction, or a</u> <u>dash or a full stop;</u> <u>may refer</u> cause, result <u>or contrast.</u>	○ He is from Kolkata, West Bengal, India: he worked his best and won the silver cup. ○ He stood first: I stood last. ○ They were without provision: they suffered a good deal.
b) Before giving some examples	○ Examples of common gender are: parent, sovereign, child, etc. ○ Send me the following goods: a good pen, some paper, one knife.
Can be replaced by a dash (—)	○ She wanted— a good pen, some paper, one knife, etc.
c) To introduce a quotation:	○ She said: Of all my friends, you are the best.
Can be replaced by a dash (—), or *comma + inverted commas*	○ She said— Of all my friends, you are the best. ○ She said, "Of all my friends, you are the best."

8. Use of Dash (—)

Dash (—)	Examples
a) To mark <u>an abrupt break or stop or</u> <u>change of thought, in the sentence</u>	1) We were all guilty of this, I, he and —. 2) Here is a great—scholar all of us.
b) To <u>mark 'words in apposition'</u> as explanation or examples; or 'to resume a scattered subject:	1) I have lost my all—health, wealth & reputation. 2) Raima, Kabita, Sabita—all were present there. 3) Friends, companies, relatives—all deserted him.
c) To <u>give examples:</u>	Verbs are two kinds—Finite & Non-finite.
d) To insert a <u>parenthesis</u> (a comment made aside or as addition) as b)	1) He told us—and he wept as he did so—how he had lost his all. 2) At the age of five—such is the power of genius—he could read English quite well.
e) To <u>introduce quotation,</u>	She said— Of all my friends, you are the best.
f) <u>To indicate hesitation.</u>	I am un—able. / I have fai—led.

9. Use of Hyphen (-) &

10. Apostrophe (')

Hyphen (-)	Examples

a) to <u>form compound words</u>,	Father-in-law / son-in-law; passer-by, man-of-war, jack-of-all-trades, etc.
a) to <u>form compound words</u>,	Father-in-law / son-in-law; passer-by, man-of-war, jack-of-all-trades, etc.
b) to <u>carry out words from one line to another.</u>	He has no abi- -lity.

Apostrophe (-')	Examples
a) **In contracted forms** as showed in verbs: to indicate some letter or letters have been left out & to show time)	I'm, you're, (s)he's, they're, e'en (for even), hon'ble (for honorable), etc. I get up early at 4 o'clock in the morning.
b) To indicate **the genitive case** of nouns & certain pronouns. (See noun's chapter for details of Genitive case)	It is Rahim's book. The table's legs are broken. God's mercy etc.
c) To *form the plural of letters & figures*	Underline your i's, and cross your t's. Add two 5's & four 2's.

11. Inverted Commas

Double Inverted Comma ("-")	Examples
a) To quote somebody's speech	"Where are you going?", asked his mother.
b) To mention 'a title of a work' or 'a book'; & also to point out some <u>particular word</u>, <u>phrase</u> or a <u>clause</u>.	o He wrote **"Pather Panchali"**, **"Apur Sansar"** etc. o Here **"me"** refers to the poet. o The word **"right"** is an adjective here.

Single Inverted Comma ('-')	Examples
a) To introduce a quotation within another quotation.	The teacher says to the boys, "Never say, **'I can't'**."
b) Do all the functions of the Double Inverted Comma:	He wrote 'Pather Panchali', 'Apur Sansar' etc. Here 'me' refers to the poet. The word 'right' is a verb here.

Brackets, Asterisk, Dot-dot-dot & Oblique

12. Use of Brackets (...), {...}, [...];
13. Asterisk (*);
14. Dot-dot-dot (...), &
15. Oblique (/)

Brackets ( )/ { }/ [ ]	Examples
a) *To enclose a parenthesis* like a <u>pair of dashes</u> or <u>commas.</u> **Note:** When we need more than a pair of brackets, generally we use the others for almost same purpose or meanings.	• He learnt (such is the power of genius) the alphabet in one day. • He learnt— such is the power of genius— the alphabet in one day. • He learnt, such is the power of genius, the alphabet in one day.
b) To introduce an explanation (as done by dash)	• I have lost all I had in the bag (five rupees). • I have lost all I had in the bag— five rupees.

Asterisk(s) (*)	Examples
a) To point out something is missing or intentionally left out (words or clauses)	My brother * * at last succeeded in getting the post. (* *who had tried so long)

b) To show importance or note of something.	* It was very praiseworthy. / ** it is a verb.
Dot-dot-dot (...)	**Examples**
a) To show incomplete statement:	He did, because ...
Oblique (/)	**Examples**
a) To mean 'either'/ 'or'	He / She is responsible. (He **or** She is responsible)

Parenthesis

What is Parenthesis?
- **A word**, **phrase**, **clause** or a **sentence** when inserted as an extra explanation or idea into a large sentence or passage & which would be complete without it & generally which is marked off or <u>separated from the rest mainly by brackets</u> or <u>dashes</u> or <u>commas</u>, before & after of a parenthesis.
  - A parenthetic phrase or clause ***do function*** as the ***'case in apposition'*** in a sentence. But <u>*when a parenthesis gives explanation*</u> a <u>*'phrase in apposition' adds information*</u>.

Examples of Parenthesis (Phrase, Clause or Sentence):

1) He is, ***to tell the truth***, not quite frank.
2) I was, ***to be frank***, much surprised of her come.
3) I am, ***of me***, ok.
4) The sun is, ***so to speak***, the lamp of the universe.
5) This is, ***I think***, a bare truth.
6) The sun is, ***so to speak***, the source of all energy on earth.
7) If you are in the wrong (***and I am sure you are, whatever you may say***) why don't you admit it?

➢ In above all cases the '**phrases within commas before & after**', can be analyzed separately and similarly can be taken out without injuring the sense.

1) He is, **I am sure**, something like a poet.
2) His conduct, **I believe**, is good.
3) Why do you, my friend, **I don't know**, hate me?
4) Why do you, **it is not clear**, not talk to me now-a-days?
5) But you should, **I am likely agreed**, do so.

➢ All the above are simple sentences <u>while the **bold written words are parenthetic expressions**, they are thrown into the main sentence, like a phrase in apposition or an Absolute Phrase.</u> They can be analyzed separately. In the sentences they **are thrown in as independent elements**; and they may be taken out without injuring the sentences.

'**Parenthetic**' expressions in compound

1) He is, **I am sure**, something of a poet & his poetry are too good to read by others.
2) His conduct, **I believe**, is good & too good to converse with.
3) Why do you, my friend, **I don't know**, give me light and snatch it away?
4) Why do you, it **is not clear**, begin to talk and stop forever?

➢ All the above are compound sentences with two principals <u>while the **bold written words are parenthetic expressions**</u>; they can be analyzed separately. In the sentences they **are thrown in as independent elements**; and they may be taken out without injuring the sense of the sentences.

'**Parenthetic**' expressions in complex

1) He is, **I am sure**, something of a poet who reads alone his poetry.
2) His conduct, **I believe**, is what is not suitable for his own age.
3) He is the man who, **I believe**, did it.
4) This is the boy who, **I think**, came the other day.

482

➤ All the above are complex sentences with only one principal & one sub-ordinate clauses <u>while the **bold written words are parenthetic expressions**</u>; they can be analyzed separately.

Note: The *double commas*, *dashes* or *brackets* are generally used for such Parenthetic Expressions.

45. Subject & Verb Agreement

585. Actually, there should not be at all such a chapter to call, '**subject-verb agreement**'; for such thing does not refer to any new thing, or any essence to discuss separately from others. However, looking at the importance and need for different competitive examinations, here it is made a sum up or summary of all, related verb and subject relation, or so called the conjugation of subjects and verbs; (i.e., different verb forms relating person, number (of the subjects), change of verb forms as per tense, voice change, narration change, assertive, interrogative, affirmative, negative, use of different moods, and words, and whatever it can include thus. However, who already gets mastery over English Grammar can go through the chapter considering it as a revision of their lesion they have already learnt.

Sometimes to brief the discussion, as it tends to be long, we have freely chosen multi charts to give focus on the forms of verbs according to subjects, and somewhere with examples. A learner's task is to go all through them giving equal importance to each point, and discussion.

Let's begin—

586. **Read the sentences: Underline the subject and the verb in each sentence:**

India's ambassador to United Nations, <u>**TS Tirumurti**</u> on Sunday (local time) <u>**expressed**</u> grief over the sudden death of India's Representative at Ramallah, Mukul Arya.
   <u>**Mukul Arya**</u> <u>**was found**</u> dead inside the Indian embassy in Palestine on Sunday. "<u>**This is**</u> truly shocking. A wonderful <u>**colleague snatched**</u> away so young. My deepest condolences to his family," <u>**Tirumurti tweeted**</u>.

(Have you noticed in the sentence the verbs always have agree in number, person and tense of the sentence. This is called the subject & verb agreement.)

Study each chart with equal importance:

1. 'Be' Verbs:			
Tenses	**Persons**	**Singular**	**Plural**
Present Tense >am, is, are 1/1/4	1st Person	<u>I am</u>	We are
	2nd Person	You are	You are
	3rd Person	S/he **is**	They are
Past Tense >was, were 2/4	1st Person	<u>I was</u>	We were
	2nd Person	You were	You were
	3rd Person	S/he **was**	They were
Future Tense >shall be, will be 2/4	1st Person	I **shall be**	We **shall be**
	2nd Person	You will be	You will be
	3rd Person	S/he will be	They will be

2. 'Have' Verbs:			
Tenses	**Persons**	**Singular**	**Plural**
Present Tense >**has, have** 1/5	1st Person	I have	We have
	2nd Person	You have	You have
	3rd Person	<u>S/he **has**</u>	They have
Past Tense >**had** 6 of 6	1st Person	I had	We had
	2nd Person	You had	You had
	3rd Person	S/he had	They had
Future Tense >**shall have, will have** 2/4	1st Person	<u>I **shall have**</u>	<u>We **shall have**</u>
	2nd Person	You will have	You will have
	3rd Person	S/he will have	They will have

3. 'Do' Verbs & Others in Simple Tenses			
Tenses	**Persons**	**Singular**	**Plural**
Present Simple > **do, does** 1/5	1st Person	I do	We do
	2nd Person	You do	You do
	3rd Person	<u>S/he **does**</u>	They do
Past Simple >**did** 6 of 6	1st Person	I did	We did
	2nd Person	You did	You did
	3rd Person	S/he did	They did
Future Simple >**shall do, will do** 2/4	1st Person	<u>I **shall do**</u>	<u>We **shall do**</u>
	2nd Person	You will do	You will do
	3rd Person	S/he will do	They will do

4. 'Do' Verbs & Others in Continuous Tenses			
Tenses	**Persons**	**Singular**	**Plural**
Present Continuous with **'be'** helping verb	1st Person	<u>I **am doing**</u>	We are doing
	2nd Person	You are doing	You are doing

>am/is/are **doing** 1/1/4	3rd Person	<u>S/he **is doing**</u>	They are doing
Past Continuous >**was/were doing** 2/4	1st Person	I was doing	We were doing
	2nd Person	You were doing	You were doing
	3rd Person	S/he was doing	They were doing
Future Continuous >**shall/will be doing** 2/4	1st Person	<u>I **shall be doing**</u>	<u>We **shall be doing**</u>
	2nd Person	You will be doing	You will be doing
	3rd Person	S/he will be doing	They will be doing

5. 'Do' Verbs & Others in Perfect Tenses

Tenses	Persons	Singular	Plural
Present Perfect: >has/have +p.p. of base verb (done) 1/5	1st Person	I have done	We have done
	2nd Person	You have done	You have done
	3rd Person	<u>S/he **has done**</u>	They have done
Past Perfect >**had done** 6 of 6	1st Person	I had done	We had done
	2nd Person	You had done	You had done
	3rd Person	S/he had done	They had done
Future Perfect >**shall/will have done** 2/4	1st Person	<u>I **shall have done**</u>	<u>We **shall have done**</u>
	2nd Person	You will have done	You will have done
	3rd Person	She will have done	They will have done

6. 'Do' Verbs & Others in Perfect Continuous Tenses

Tenses	Persons	Singular	Plural
Present Perfect Continuous with 'have' + 'been' & **continuous form of verb** >has/have been **doing** -1/5	1st Person	I have been doing	We have been doing
	2nd Person	You have been doing	You have been doing
	3rd Person	<u>S/he **has been doing**</u>	They have been doing
Past Perfect Continuous >**had been doing** 6 of 6	1st Person	I had been doing	We had been doing
	2nd Person	You had been doing	You had been doing

	3rd Person	S/he had been doing	They had been doing
Future Perfect Continuous >shall/will have been doing 2/4	1st Person	<u>I shall have been doing</u>	<u>We shall have been doing</u>
	2nd Person	You will have been doing	You will have been doing
	3rd Person	She will have been doing	They will have been doing

587.   The following subjects in bold letters are followed by Singular Verbs:
(1)   An **Uncountable Noun** always follows a verb of Third Person Singular Number.
   o   **Water** is essential for us.
   o   **The grass** was getting long.
   o   **The boy's hair** will be cut etc.

(2) **'Much', 'little', 'a little', and 'the little' are used with uncountable nouns, and they take** always the singular verb in a sentence; as,
   o   **Much** <u>money</u> has been spent trying to repair the fan.
   o   **Only a little** <u>of the food</u> has been eaten.
   o   **The little food** we had was eaten up by a cat.
   o   **Little sugar** is left with us.

(3) A word or phrase of **measurement** takes a singular verb of 3rd person.
   o   **Five miles** is too far to walk.
   o   **One hundred rupees** is to cover.
   o   **Two hours** is a long time to wait.
   o   **Two hundred rupees** seems reasonable for the article.

(4) When the subject phrase begins with **'The number of/A large amount of'/ 'One of'**, the verb is singular.
   o   **The number of months** in a year is twelve.
   o   **The number of problems** we face is increasing.
   o   **The number of messages** I got was increasing from her.
   o   **A large amount of money** was collected by Sarada.
   o   **A large amount of people** gathers in a fair.
   o   **One of** you is responsible for the sin/crime/murder.
   o   **The number of students** in the class is fifty.

(5) **'Someone/*No one/None/ Nothing'** or **None of/ Neither of/ Either of/Any of + plural noun'** follows singular verb.
   o   **Someone/No one/None** comes here.
   o   **Nothing** comes out of nothing.
   o   <u>**None of** these pens</u> works.
   o   <u>**Neither of** my friends</u> speaks French.
   o   <u>**Either of** these watches</u> is stolen.
   o   If <u>any of your friends</u> is interested, let me know.

(6) When the two words or phrases **express a single thing** or **a unit**, the verb must be singular.
   o   **Rice and fish** is main food of Bengali people.
   o   **Law and order** was under control.
   o   **Time and tides** waits for none

(7) <u>**Titles** and **names** of a country, book, organization or a state, may look plural in form, but they always take a singular verb</u>; as they refer to one thing; as,
   o   **The Beijing Olympics** was held in 2008.
   o   **The United States of America** is a country to the north-west of India.
   o   **The United Nations** is the name of an organization.
   o   **'Love and Reason'** is a collection of poems.
   o   **'The Three Musketeers'** is a classic creation of the author.

(8) When two singular nouns are joined by '**and**', they make plural number, but if the both names or nouns refer to **single person**, singular verb is to be used or followed; as,
- o **The Headmaster** and **Goutam Das** is one person.
- o **Peter** & **Mr. Peter** is only one person.
- o **The secretary** and **chairman** of the school comes to the institution this morning.

But, if they refer two different persons, joined by '**and**', they are always followed by plural verb; as,
- o **The Secretary** and **Goutam Das** are present there in the meeting hall.
- o **Saint Peter** & **Mr. Peter** were two different men.
- o **The secretary** and the **chairman** of the school were there in the meeting hall.

588.   In the following case the verb agrees either Singular or Plural, it depends on sense.
(9) A verb, agrees singular or plural, according to the sense, with the words— '**Who** or **What**', **What/Which** + **Noun**' etc.
- o **Who** knows the man? /**Who** are the people behind the main door?
- o **What** has happened? /**What** numbers is **he** talking about? /**What** numbers are **you** talking about?
- o **What/Which** <u>day</u> is suitable?
- o **What/Which** <u>days</u> are suitable?
- o **What numbers** are shown in the result board?

(10) **If two** or **more singular subjects** <u>are preceded by</u> **Each/Every/No** and even joined by 'and' the verb is singular.
- o **Each boy** and **each girl** was given a sweet.
- o **Every teacher** and **every student** has to have an identity card.
- o **Every man**, **woman** and **child** was going to fair.
- o **No boarder** and **no caretaker** was found in the hostel.

(11) But if '**each**'/**every** <u>follows a plural subject</u>, the verb is plural.
- o <u>The pupils **each**</u> have to give the test.
- o <u>The customers **each**</u> have to pass through the gate.
- o <u>People **every one**</u> there were involved in the riot.

(12) Adjective '**No**' is generally followed by a singular subject or noun, and thus, a singular verb is used. But, it is followed by plural Nouns, the plural verb form is used.
- o **No pupil** has failed in the examination.
- o **No pupils** have passed the examination.

(13) After '**There**' <u>the verb agrees with its complements</u>.
- o <u>There</u> was **a loud bang**.
- o <u>There</u> were **some books** on the table.

(14) Some **nouns with plural look**, take singular verb.
- o **The news** is very good. **Mumps** is a dangerous disease. **Gymnastics** is a physical exercise. **Physics** is a subject. **The innings** is well played.

(15) Some **nouns, always in plural form**, also take plural verb.
- o <u>My few **belongings**</u> have been packed. <u>The paper **goods**</u> are cheap. <u>My **savings**</u> have been gone to buy a car.
- o <u>The **earnings** of the family</u> are poor. (however, it means the earnings come from different sources or from more than one member of the family.)

(16) **After a fraction** the <u>verb agrees with the **following noun**</u>.
- o **Three quarters** of a **potato** is water.
- o **Almost half** the **plants** were dead.

(17) <u>When the subject denotes **amount**,</u> the verbs agree with the subject in number and person.
- o **A large amount of money** was collected by Sarada.
- o **Large amounts of money** were collected (for different schemes.)

(18) If a phrase comes after the noun, the verb agrees according to first noun.

- o **The house** between the two gardens is empty.
- o **The houses** between the two roads have been burnt.
- o **The price** of books has gone up.
- o **The price** of daily commodities is going up.
- o **The cover pages** of his creation are not bad.
- o **The condition** of the patients was not out of danger.
- o **The color** of those flowers is attractive.
- o **The colors** you chose were excellent.

(19) A phrase in apposition does not make the subject plural; here too, the verb follows the first noun.
- o Mr. Das, **the headmaster**, is an honorable person.
- o My colleagues, **the teachers of B.M.A. High School**, are honest.

(20)   A phrase with '**as well as**', '**along with**', **together with**, **accompanied with**, **with**', '**of**' does not make the subject plural; verb here simply follow the 1st noun/pronoun
- o Mr. Sarkar **as well as** his brothers was in the train.
- o The headmaster **along with** all his teachers was honored.
- o The students, **together with** their English teacher, have performed the drama.
- o Mr. Sarkar **accompanied by** his family members is attending the ceremony.
- o The tigress **with** its cubs is playing.
- o This pair **of** trousers needs cleaning.

(21) After '**not only...but also**', the verb agrees with the nearest phrase
- o **Not only** Ashok **but also** his friends are purchasing the book.
- o **Not only** the players **but also** the coach was given warm welcome.

(22)   When two phrases are joined by '**Either...or**', '**or**', '**Neither...nor**', the verb usually agrees with the nearest
- o **Either** Saturday **or** Sunday is OK.
- o **Either** my brother **or** my sisters are looking after the pet.
- o **Ajanta** or **you** are to blame.
- o **Neither** you **nor** he is reliable.
- o **Neither** Raju **nor** his sisters have come.

(23)   '**Some**' refers to **both singular** and **plural**.
- o **Some people** were there till then.
- o **Some** hears the voice and runs towards the spot.

(24)   Two or more words or phrases when connected by '**and**' or such conjunctions, the verb will be plural; but when they refer to **same person/idea** the verb will be singular.
- • **You, he and I** are very sorry. / **I, he and you** were guilty.
- • **Swapan** and **Goutam** go travelling at weekends.
- • **Rice and wheat** are imported. (Separately they are meant)
- • **Rice and wheat** is my food of the evening. (Referring a 'meal')
- • **The H.M. of the school** and **Goutam babu** is the same person.
- • **The Headmaster** and **Secretary of the Institution** is one.
- • **The Headmaster** and the **Secretary of the Institution** are against this proposal.
- •

(25)   When a subject follows '**Most of**', '**A number of**', '**The majority of**', '**A lot of**' – a plural verb is generally used.
- o **Most of patients** were released.
- o **A number of people** have applied for the post.
- o **A majority of members** were opposed to the policy.
- o **A lot of people** are facing the problem.

(26)   But the subject begins with '**The number of**' always follow a singular verb and '**The numbers**' follow a plural verb.
- o **The number of people** has increased suddenly.
- o **The numbers** you have mentioned were fake.

(27)   '**Many a/many an**' agrees singular verb

- o **Many a** man has been invited in the meeting.
- o **Many an** admirer has praised his paintings.

(28) '**a great many/too many**' agrees plural verb
- o **A great many** children are making much noise.
- o **Too many** mistakes have been made in this writing.

589. When Noun Agrees Plural Verb:
(29) '**many**', '**a few**' –are used with countable nouns, and they take the plural verb in a sentence; as,
- o Many of my friends are waiting for their results.
- o A few of my colleagues are rich ones.

(30) A **pair noun** is plural in form and takes a plural verb.
- o His new **glasses** are very fine.
- o My **trousers** are grey in color.
- o **Scissors** are used for cutting papers.

(31) But if such noun is used with a phrase preceding it, the verb follows the first noun.
- o This pair of **trousers** needs cleaning.
- o Two pairs of **trousers** are needed.

(32) **Group or collective nouns** (when they are meant individually or different opinions are hint) often follow plural verbs
- o My **family** have not come to decisive position to move to Siliguri.
- o The **crowd** were in a happy mood. They were shouting, dancing, etc.
- o The **team** are not playing well this season.
- o **The group members** have been debating which song to sing.
- o **The jury members** were different in opinions.

(33) But **when it refers to impersonal unit**, **same thought**, or **express single idea**, the verb is singular.
- o The **family** owns a car. The **team** is full of energy.
- o The **govt.** is considering the tax problem.
- o The **whole class** was told to stand up.
- o The **committee** needs more time.
- o The **group** sings really well.
- o The **jury** takes the right decision.

(34) **When we talk about whole group**, we use singular verb. But **when we talk of people's thoughts, it agrees plural verb.**
- o **The committee** consists of ten members.
- o **The committee** don't understand what the expert is saying.

(35) '**More than one**' agrees with singular verb but '**more than two**' take a plural verb.
- o **More than one bridge** has been damaged.
- o **More than two bridges** have been damaged.

(36) The nouns e.g., **police, people, livestock, cattle, poultry, dozen** etc. have a plural meaning agree with plural verbs.
- o **The police** arrest a man for questioning.
- o **People** have to follow the rules of the country.
- o **Cattle** are kept in a farm for their milk and meat.
- o **A dozen of pencils** cost of rupees fifteen.

(37) **Certain adjectives preceded by the definite article** are used as nouns, they talk of groups of people and they take plural verb.
- o **The blind** are not neglected nowadays.
- o **The rich** are not always happy.
- o **All the sick** were hospitalized.
- o **The old** are greatly respected.

- **The unemployed** are losing hope.
- **The beauty** are always charming.

590.   Study, how verbs change its forms according to Tense and Nouns as its subjects in the sentence:

Tense	Types	Function/Definition	Examples
Present Tense	Indefinite	Habit and general action	I write. He writes
	Continuous	Action going on	I am writing. He is writing.
	Perfect	Just completed action (whose time is not given)	I have written. He has written.
	Perfect Continuous	Started in the past and still going on	I have been writing. He has been writing.

Tense	Types	Function/Definition	Examples
Past Tense	Indefinite	Action completed in the past	I wrote. He wrote.
	Continuous	Action continuing in the past	I was writing. He was writing.
	Perfect	Action done earlier than another action in past	I had written. He had written.
	Perfect Continuous	Action continued for some time in the past	I had been writing. He had been writing.

Tense	Types	Function/ Definition	Examples
Future Tense	Indefinite	Action to happen in the future	I shall write. He will write.
	Continuous	Action to continue in the future	I shall be writing. He will be writing
	Perfect	Action will be complete before a particular time in the future	I shall have written. He will have written.
	Perfect Continuous	Action to continue for some time in the future and also end in the future.	I shall have been writing. He will have been writing.

591.   **Sequence of Tense:**

Sequence of tense occurs in sentences with clauses in Narration Change. It tells about the rules that the tense in the main clause should govern the tense in the sub-clauses.
- 1) If the main clause is in the present or future tense the verb in the sub-clause may be in any tense.
- But if the main clause is in the past tense, the verb in the sub-clause must be in the past tense.

Study the examples of Sequence of Tense in the following chart:

Main clause	Sub-clause

He says /will say	that he went to school. (Past Tense) that he goes to school. (Present Tense) that he will go to school. (Future Tense)
He said	that he was ill. that he had gone. that he was going. /that he went.
Note:	For details, please study the chapter of Narration Change

About Peter

Mr. Peter is a penname of the writer, an Indian and a teacher in West Bengal. Most of his academic works are the products of his professional career what he held over twenty years and continuing… Mr. Peter loves to publish his books in the self-publishing platforms, like Amazon (for worldwide) and notionpress.com (for India). For this, Peter heartily pays his gratitude to Amazon, notionpress.com and for marketing to Flipkart, Amazon & social media. The Peter's books are now **available for purchase and read on Amazon** in 3 formats—eBook, Paperback, Hardcover. The books (paperback) which are published at Notion Press Pvt. Ltd., Chennai, are only for the Indian Market and available to buy on **notionpress.com, Flipkart, Amazon**, and **google play store**, etc.

One may order on notionpress.com, (type **Mr. Peter** in the search box), and may apply the following coupons:

Coupon Codes	Book Name	Buy for	Discount %	Rebate Prices
unique00 / bulk00	**A Book of Advanced Writing Skill, the Complete Version (incl. Part-1, 2 & 3)**	1 & more	15 & 23	~~780~~ 663 & 601
PujaDeal10 / Deal11	Development of Writing Skill, Part-3	1 & more	18 & 24	~~365~~ 300 & 278
PujaDeal9 / Deal10	Development of Writing Skill, Part-2	1 & more	18 & 24	~~365~~ 300 & 278
PujaDeal8 / Deal9	Steps to Composition (Development of Writing Skill, from Primary to Secondary Level, Part-1)	1 & more	20 & 26	~~300~~ 240 & 222
PujaDeal7 / Deal8	**Rhetoric & Prosody**	1 & more	20 & 26	~~240~~ 192 & 178
PujaDeal6 / Deal7	**Question Bank of English Grammar & Composition**	1 & more	20 & 28	~~559~~ 448 & 403
PujaDeal5 / Deal5	Study of Subject-Verb Agreement, Narration Change, Use of Punctuation; including Analysis, Synthesis & Split-up	1 & more	20 & 26	~~301~~ 241 & 223
PujaDeal4 / Deal4	Detail Study of Phrases, Clauses & Sentences, including Idioms & Phrasal Verbs	1 & more	20 & 26	~~290~~ 232 & 215
PujaDeal3 / Deal3	Study of Adverbs, Prepositions, Conjunctions & Interjections	1 & more	20 & 26	~~260~~ 208 & 193
PujaDeal2 / Deal2	All about Verbs (Forms, Functions, Conjugation, Tense, Voice Change, Forming Questions & Negation)	1 & more	18 & 26	~~420~~ 345 & 311
PujaDeal1 / Deal1	Study of Nouns, Pronouns, Adjectives & Articles (detail study)	1 & more	20 & 26	~~280~~ 224 & 208
unique01 / bulk01	**Peter's 'English Grammar' (Complete Version of English Grammar)**	1 & more	23 & 30	~~1201~~ 925 & 841

FOR COPIES MORE THAN ONE, SELECT THE 2ND COUPON, GIVEN IN EACH ROW IN THE FIRST COLUMN

Author page URL's:

https://www.amazon.com/author/mr.peter
https://www.amazon.in/~/e/B09QW2P4TY (For Indians, this and next)
https://notionpress.com/store/s?NP_Books%5Bquery%5D=Mr.+Peter

https://www.amazon.co.uk/~/e/B09QW2P4TY
https://www.amazon.de/~/e/B09QW2P4TY
https://www.amazon.fr/~/e/B09QW2P4TY
https://www.amazon.co.jp/~/e/B09QW2P4TY
https://www.amazon.es/~/e/B09QW2P4TY
https://www.amazon.it/~/e/B09QW2P4TY
https://www.amazon.com.br/kindle-dbs/entity/author?asin=B09QW2P4TY

If the above coupons do not work, contact to https://www.facebook.com/profile.php?id=100081822070172
or   https://www.facebook.com/groups/mr.peter

Printed in the USA
CPSIA information can be obtained
at www.ICGtesting.com
LVHW080859280524
781044LV00018B/178